XAVIER RYNNE

VATICAN COUNCIL II

ORBIS BOOKS

Maryknoll, New York 10545

The Catholic Foreign Mission Society of America (Maryknoll) recruits and trains people for overseas missionary service. Through Orbis Books, Maryknoll aims to foster the international dialogue that is essential to mission. The books published, however, reflect the opinions of their authors and are not meant to represent the official position of the society.

To obtain more information about Maryknoll and Orbis Books, please visit our website at www.maryknoll.org.

Introduction © 1999 by Francis X. Murphy.

This edition published in 1999 by Orbis Books, Maryknoll, NY 10545-0308.

Some of the material in this book appeared originally in different form in *The New Yorker.*

Manufactured in the United States of America

ISBN 1-57075-293-1

THE AUTHORS DEDICATE THESE PAGES WITH APOLOGIES
TO THOSE "LEARNED AND PIOUS" READERS WHO HAVE
BEEN LED ASTRAY,* AND WITH BEST WISHES TO ALL
LOVERS OF OPEN WINDOWS AND FRESH AIR.

* The efforts of "Xavier Rynne," I'm afraid, must be
condemned, derided and dismissed by any well-informed reader. Besides, the books . . . are a positive
danger to the soul. *I have seen very many learned
and pious Christians led into mortal sin by them.*
—Anonymous reviewer, *Triumph,* Jan. 1967.

Contents

Introduction to the 1999 Edition

Anyone with the good fortune to be standing in the piazza fronting St. Peter's Basilica in Rome at eight a.m. on October 11, 1962, was treated to a pageant of dazzling splendor. Suddenly the bronze doors of the papal palace were thrown open. Out poured a torrent of light. Then, led by a phalanx of papal guards, row upon row of bishops in pontifical garb marched across the sun-bathed piazza, wheeled right, and disappeared into the vast basilica.

Bringing up the rear of this august procession was a brace of ermine-caped courtiers and red-soutaned clerics, then the oriental patriarchs in their festooned finery, and finally the cardinals. Climaxing this splendor was Pope John XXIII, seated on the *sedia gestatoria* and looking small, uncomfortable, almost scared, until he suddenly reacted to the hurrahs of the immense crowd—perhaps fifty to sixty thousand people who filled the piazza and trailed down the Via Conciliazione. As Pope John wheeled to the right and was carried up the steps leading into the great basilica of St. Peter's tears trickled down his face. He had lived to fulfill his dream. Vatican Council II had begun.

•

In the years since that resounding event, the Catholic church has been turned upside down. Pope John had summoned the world's 2,500 Catholic bishops to Rome to modernize the church. Updating—*aggiornamento*—was the innocuous-sounding word he used to camouflage the fact that he was calling for a revolution. In his great opening discourse, he set out a vast vision of ecclesial renewal that was meant not merely to restore the church to a form more consistent with the spirit of Christ, its founder. It was intended to be a challenge to the world that would invade the consciousness, and thence the consciences, of all humankind.

With the concurrence of the shrewd, aged German cardinal, Agostino Bea,

John had invited observers from the other Christian churches to attend this assembly in order to emphasize the fact that Christian unity was a primary objective of the Council. John extended the command, "You shall love your neighbor as yourself," to include all of humanity, believer and unbeliever, friend and enemy alike.

The ground rules of Catholicism for centuries before the Council had called for total loyalty not only to God in the person of Jesus Christ, but to the Church in the person of the pope. There were of course educated Catholics who were unhappy over papal policies; within the Vatican there were prelates who condemned the pope's attitudes and decisions. Many criticized his personal foibles. But for the vast majority of clergy and faithful the pope represented, unquestionably, a Holy Father. He was to be loved and venerated as the visible representative of Jesus Christ Himself.

The mystique that accomplished this almost universal admiration within the church had developed over a longer history. In recent times, it had been greatly encouraged by the political fortunes of the popes of the nineteenth century who had been deprived of their possession of the Papal States and had made themselves "prisoners" of the Vatican. This circumstance, along with the fact that in almost every part of the world Catholics felt themselves under attack, made the faithful look to Rome for a heroic figure under whose protective auspices they could rally.

With the election of John XXIII, however, this ecclesial image-making suddenly disintegrated. This pope was an extraordinary human being whose personality would tolerate no subterfuge. Quickly, the centuries-old panoply of Vatican pageantry began to come apart. In the context of John's spontaneous expansiveness, the cortege of brocaded nobles surrounding the papal presence at audiences and public ceremonies were recognized as faded if not comic hangovers from the Middle Ages. The ermine and the vermilion costumes were shabby; the antiquated swords and maces were useless; and the display of semi-oriental splendor was theatrical rather than religious. It certainly had nothing to do with the spiritual values which the papacy was intended to serve.

Strangely enough Pope John actually liked this pageantry. Despite the fact that he seemed fearful each time he was raised on the *sedia gestatoria,* he rather enjoyed the extravagance represented by the papal cortege. Consequently he did nothing to abolish it. But he recognized it for exactly what it was; and knew that it had outlived its usefulness.

Journalists and historians question whether John knew that an ecumenical council held at a time of great social change would result in the chaotic situation that continues to face the Catholic church and the papacy today. If he did not, he was certainly told in graphic terms by his shrewd, almost omniscient, secretary of state, Cardinal Domenico Tardini.

In the course of his dramatic discourse opening the Council, John referred to the cardinals and other counselors who besieged him with dire warnings as "prophets of doom." "They pay no attention to history, the great teacher of mankind," was the way he finally dismissed them. But he also laid down a crucial principle that in the Council the debate would be totally open and free. "There will be no condemnations," was his order. And despite the fact that many of the men serving him in the administrative offices of the Vatican openly opposed his policies and teamed up against him with conservative cardinals and bishops from outside, he pushed on with his plans for a thorough reformation of the Church "in head and members."

Insisting that history is the greatest teacher, John had opened Vatican Council II with the observation that the church "no longer needs to confront the world with severity." Without repudiating the past, he said that the time had come for a reevaluation of the church's inner structure and a consequent updating in its dealings with the world. This attitude of honest analysis prevailed during the subsequent four years of the conciliar discussions, despite the opposition of most of the Vatican officials attempting to curb the debates and dilute the Council's achievements.

•

I happened to be in Rome teaching at the Redemptorist Academie Alfonsiana, on the Faculty of Moral Theology, during the preparations for Vatican II as well as throughout the Council. Never one to shrink from politics at any level, I began compiling notes about the intrigues and secretive manipulations by a number of prominent prelates as the agenda for the Council was being formulated. I pulled these notes together into an article and submitted them to John Chapin, a literary agent. He in turn put me in touch with Robert Giroux, vice president and senior editor of Farrar, Strauss & Cudahy. He liked my piece and thought it worthy of publication. When he asked me where I'd like to have it placed, I replied, without the slightest hesitation, "In *The New Yorker*." Somewhat taken aback, Bob said, "Oh Father, I think there's too much religion for *The New Yorker*." I stuck to my guns and after some discussion Bob agreed to send it to Bill Shawn, the editor of *The New Yorker*.

Two days later Bob called me with the good news that my piece had been accepted. Going over the manuscript in preparation for its final submission, Bob suddenly said, "And what name are you going to use for the author? Since you are involved with the papal curia, it might be dangerous." Although the article contained nothing heretical or unorthodox, its revelations of the gossip and activities of the curia might infuriate members of that group. "They might report you to the Holy Office and have you relieved of your professorship," he said. All of a sudden the name Xavier Rynne (my middle name and my mother's maiden name) popped into my mind. "Excellent," Bob said. And that was the name I used.

The article, a "Letter from Vatican City," was published in *The New Yorker* at the very start of the first session of the Council. A long and apparently authentic account of names and activities, guesswork and facts about the preparations for the Council, it sent shock waves through the assemblage of cardinals, bishops, and priests. Many were outraged, and some frankly appalled. A surprising number became hell-bent on pursuing the whereabouts of Xavier Rynne, an effort which fortunately, except for a few close calls, was unsuccessful for the duration of the Council. "Who the hell is Xavier Rynne?" became a persistent question throughout the Council and for many years after the deliberations ended.

Although the conciliar debate resulting in the Church's historic self-critique was supposed to be conducted under the rule of secrecy, the fanfare with which the Council opened and the gravity of the matters under consideration proved too great a burden for the traditional Vatican organs of information.

Meanwhile, thanks to Xavier Rynne, a rare spotlight had been focused on the Vatican's entrenched inner circle. The prelates and clerics of the Roman Curia who determine church policies from the top were thus exposed to conciliar criticism, much to the chagrin of their supposititious leader, Cardinal Alfredo Ottaviani of the *ancien* Holy Office (formerly known as the Inquisition), who considered himself the paragon of orthodoxy.

From its inauguration, the Council had proven a startling event, providing journalists, TV and radio commentators by the hundreds with hard news: Pope John referring to some of his counselors as "prophets of doom"; Cardinals Liénart and Frings upsetting the first meeting by demanding a free election of the commissions that would produce the Council's documents; the frequent skirmishes between curial cardinals and their opponents; the gracious confrontations of adversary prelates and *periti* in the *Bar Jonah* and the *Bar Rabbas,* the coffee, snack, and toilet facilities provided by Pope John in the sacristy and interior vestibule. ("If we do not let them smoke somewhere," he is reported to have advised, "they'll be hiding their cigarettes under their mitres.")

Over the course of the next three years the Council's annual two-month sessions were reported in extraordinary detail through twelve subsequent *New Yorker* articles by the stealthy Xavier Rynne. (Eventually these were assembled into four volumes—one for each year—with the currrent one-volume compendium issued in 1968.) Each article created a firestorm of controversy within the assemblage. But, for all the hue and cry, the speculation and interrogations, no one seemed capable of identifying the author of the missives.

(It was only at a clerical gathering in Baltimore some twenty years later that I admitted authorship to the departing Apostolic Nuncio, Pio Laghi. Asked why, after all these years of pseudonymity I was coming up out of the catacombs, I replied, "If I died tomorrow the Jesuits would claim him [Rynne] and the Redemptorists would be delighted to be rid of him.")

Nonetheless, as I had been writing articles for *America, Catholic World, The New York Times, Boston Globe, Los Angeles Times, Baltimore Sun,* and other journals, suspicion soon fell on me. In particular, the professors at the Jesuit-run Biblicum questioned me strenuously and often. However, by the assiduous use of casuistry, I managed to preserve my anonymity although some of my closer friends and an occasional sharp critic were certain that I was their man.

I had been appointed a *peritus* through the good graces of the Redemptorist bishop of Monterey-Fresno, Aloysius Willinger, a close friend of Cardinal Cicognani, the Vatican Secretary of State. Shortly after the arrival of the first *New Yorker* article in Rome, he questioned me as to the authorship, concluding with the observation that there were many expressions that sounded like mine. That evening he had Archbishop Egidio Vagnozzi and a few younger bishops to dinner and, finding them ignorant of the Rynne article, took great glee in disabusing them of their ignorance.

With the Superior General of the Redemptorists, Father William Gaudreau, an American from Massachusetts, things worked out somewhat differently. Meeting him in the monastery corridor one morning, he asked me if there was such a thing as *The New Yorker.* On my acknowledgment that there was, he asked whether there was an article on the Council. With my assurance that there was, he wanted to know why I had not given him a copy. I promptly complied. A few days later he returned the journal to me in a brown bag with the request that I walk along with him.

"Murph," he said, "there are a number of expressions that sound like you."

I bowed my head in acquiescence.

"It would be dangerous to be Xavier Rynne," he said.

"Yes, Father, it would be dangerous," I replied.

"You are not Xavier Rynne?"

"No, Father, I am not Xavier Rynne," I answered precisely. "I am Francis Murphy."

Thereafter, despite the fact that Gaudreau was the victim of innumerable inquiries by bishops, superiors general at the Council, and the media, he never again questioned me about the matter.

One morning at the Council I ran into Cardinal Spellman of New York, surrounded by a group of junior bishops.

"Good morning, Xavier," said his Eminence.

"Oh," I replied, "I wish you had not said that."

"What do you mean?"

"This means that you do not participate in the episcopal infallibility that the Council has been arguing about."

"I never said I was infallible," said the cardinal in mock alarm.

"No, and now you've proven it," I retorted with a laugh.

At this point the cardinal called me to his side. "Are you in any difficulty?" he inquired.

"No, not so far," I replied.

"Well, if you are do not hesitate to come to me."

About a month later I learned that I was going to be called to the Holy Office to be put under an extremely rare oath of secrecy under pain of excommunication. When I inquired as to the subject matter for the oath, I was told I would be informed after I arrived at the Holy Office. I replied that I simply refused to take a blind oath. The next morning I sought out both Cardinal Spellman and the English Cardinal John Heenan, suggesting that if I were not back in the conciliar hall by noon they should send somebody after me.

I arrived at the Holy Office and awaited the arrival of Archbishop Pietro Parente, Assessor of the Congregation, who entered promptly at ten o'clock. He was accompanied by two monsignori, one of whom was Henry Cosgrove, an acquaintance of mine from Brooklyn.

"Kneel down," said the archbishop in Italian, "and we will take the oath of secrecy."

"Not until I know why," was my caustic response.

"I will tell you after the oath."

"No, Monsignor. I am not taking an oath about something of which I do not know the substance."

"You will be told . . . "

"No, Monsignor," I interrupted. "And what are these two gentlemen doing here?"

"One is my secretary, the other a translator."

"It is obvious that I need no translator. Henry," I said, turning to the American monsignor, "you can be my secretary."

With the archbishop's temper rapidly rising, I asked if he wanted to interrogate me regarding the magazine with little pieces of paper he had tucked under his arm. On his acquiescence I took an oath about what I might know regarding that particular magazine. He began reading me a series of quotations, and for each I agreed that they were written by one Xavier Rynne, but carefully added that I was Fr. Francis Murphy. Then he came to a defamatory passage about himself, describing his expulsion from Rome some twenty years earlier by Pope Pius XI. *"Listen,"* he said, *"you understand that Pius XI was a little sick in the head."*

"Henry," I shouted to my newly-acquired secretary, "write that down!"

Suddenly realizing the significance of what he had just said, the archbishop bolted out of the room. The three of us stood silently, not knowing exactly what to do. Finally, I whispered the closing prayer of the oath, dismissed the monsignori, and walked quickly back to my quarters. I never heard from the archbishop again.

•

At the close of Vatican Council II, the pope and bishops promulgated sixteen documents under the rubric, "It seemed good to the Holy Spirit and to us." Nevertheless, one of the prelates who signed those documents along with the pope and 2,500 bishops was heard to exclaim, "They will never bind us." It was the cardinal of Genoa, Giuseppe Siri, one of the leaders of the so-called *coetus patrum* or coalition of prelates in opposition to the mind of the majority. They were led by Cardinals Ottaviani and Brown of the Holy Office and some 400 other bishops, mainly old world and Latin American die-hards. Together with the majority of the Roman curia, they succeeded in holding back the implementation of the Council's decrees, thus occasioning confusion and rebellion on the part of the priests, nuns, clerics, and lay people who had followed the debates, read the documents, and demanded their implementation.

Despite that slowdown, in the years since the Council's close, much has been accomplished in implementing its decrees and constitutions. Liturgical reform embracing the laity as a "royal people, a chosen race" into the intimacies of the church's sacramental life has been greatly enhanced, so much so indeed as to awaken warning signals in Rome.

While the collegial nature of the church's rule has been implemented in part through the Roman Synod of Bishops meeting every two or three years, the curia has managed to deprive that structure of the exercise of real power by manipulating the list of attendants and by insisting that the Synod's function is consultative rather than deliberative. Thus instead of the Synod dictating church policies, that function remains in the hands of the curial offices or congregations which claim to act in the pope's name.

This fact greatly limits the objectives of the Council to confront the "signs of the times." It also militates against ecumenical endeavors looking to a reunion of the Orthodox and Protestant churches with Rome. Thus among the first challenges facing the church in the twenty-first century will be a restructuring of the Roman curia—an immense, Herculean task. Papal rule must be reorganized to allow true collegiality of the bishops with and under the pope, who will then decide church policy by consensus, thus giving the Roman Synod of Bishops deliberative functions. This structure will better prepare the Catholic church for reunion with the Orthodox churches where this type of rule prevails. Such a reform will also facilitate a federation with the Protestant and Anglican churches, giving each proper representation in the Roman Synods without destroying their current internal structures.

Somehow, the Christian churches with an authentic appreciation of the Trinity and, thus, the Incarnation of Jesus Christ in this world, will have to draw together in a federation, if not a truly substantial unity of faith and practice. Under the aegis of the pope as Peter's successor, the heads of the various Christian denominations, truly representative of their respective faithful, will have to guide the universal church in its encounters with the oriental and non-Christian religions—Islam, Buddhism, Hinduism, Confucianism, and various strains of animistic cult.

Just how this is to be accomplished is a mystery. Yet a recent agreement of some sixty-six religious groups in Great Britain could serve as a preliminary step in this direction. Without mentioning the word God, the signers, both theists and non-theists, agreed to the formula of a "Reality that infinitely transcends all that we can see, touch, feel, smell, taste, and chew." All faiths, the statement continues, share the ideals of compassion, service, justice, peace and concern for the environment. While serving as the least common denominator, this agreement currently centers on the peace needed to initiate the preliminary step toward the unity that must prevail if the world is to continue in being.

•

In reissuing this book in 1999 the intention is not to break new historic ground or to comment on the philosophical underpinnings of the Catholic church. Rather, it is simply to recount a remarkable tale, one that is in danger of disappearing with the generation that witnessed it. Some have claimed that these insider articles published by Xavier Rynne changed the course of Vatican II at its outset; others charge that they destroyed the ability of the council to guard some of the church's most cherished traditions. I believe such claims, whether for good or ill, are exaggerated. These articles did, to be sure, have an influence on the rubric of secrecy, making it clear that the work of the church could no longer be conducted entirely behind closed doors. The early exposure of the political machinations of certain curial officials helped to empower those bishops—the majority, as it turned out—who were hoping for more sweeping reform.

This story is recounted for the millions of Catholics today who know only the fruits of the Second Vatican Council's efforts. It is recounted for the millions of older Catholics who were on the periphery of the historic deliberations and had to personally change the way they practiced their religion. It is also recounted for those outside of the Catholic church who will marvel at the human strengths and frailties, the courage, and entrenched convictions that were the fabric of the Second Vatican Council. An understanding of this story remains essential to an understanding of the Catholic church today, and to a positive engagement in the challenges facing all Christians in the years to come.

Francis X. Murphy, CSSR
aka Xavier Rynne

THE FIRST SESSION

"A Council"

According to Pope John, it was towards the end of 1958, shortly after assuming the papacy, that he engaged the late Cardinal Tardini in a troubled conversation regarding the state of the world and the Church's role in it. In a time of agitation and anxiety, amidst apparently hopeless clamorings for peace and justice, he asked his Secretary of State what might be done to give the world an example of peace and concord between men and an occasion for new hope, when suddenly there sprang to his own lips the words, "A Council!" Uncertain of his most intimate aide's reaction to such an idea, and expecting to be deluged with a torrent of objections from this seasoned diplomat, the pope was overwhelmed when Cardinal Tardini responded with an immediate assent: *"Si, si! un Concilio!"*

About a month later, the pope received a strikingly different reaction to his inspiration. This occurred on January 25, 1959 and came from a group of close associates, following the celebration of a mass for Church unity in the Benedictine monastery adjacent to the basilica of St. Paul's Outside the Walls. The pope gathered round him the eighteen cardinals present for the occasion and talked to them intimately of the affairs of the Church. He first told them of his intention to hold a local Synod for the diocese of Rome, to renew the Christian way of life in the center of Christendom. Then turning his attention to world conditions, he painted a brief and vivid picture of the good and evil influences struggling to control the contemporary world. He pointed to the sanctity and the moral confusion that exist side by side in villages, cities, and nations throughout the world, and to the continual temptation facing modern man to make an idol of scientific progress. In order to proclaim the truth, he said, and to reanimate the faith of Christians, and thereby to contribute to the well-being of the world here and now, he had decided to call a Council of the

3

Universal Church. Then he turned to the cardinals, and said simply: "I would like to have your advice." The cardinals to a man sat mute before him. Not a single word of response was uttered.

The pope has candidly recorded his disappointment: "Humanly we could have expected that the cardinals, after hearing our allocution, might have crowded around to express approval and good wishes." He put the kindest and most charitable interpretation on their unanimous failure to show any spontaneous reaction: "Instead there was a devout and impressive silence. Explanations came on following days. . . ."

Cardinal Tardini's original assent to the pope's inspiration regarding the Council was immediate and sincere; we have Pope John's word for it. It is probable that later the cardinal had serious doubts about the feasibility of so vast an undertaking as an Ecumenical Council and, more particularly, about directing it primarily toward the reunion of Christians. It is believed that Tardini was the first to broach the idea of a Roman Synod, perhaps as a delaying tactic, or more likely as a pilot-project to give the pope and the Curia some notion of the complexities involved in organizing a worldwide synod. Little by little, Vatican officials began to confront the pontiff with stiff objections to the idea of a Council, its objectives, and the possibility of holding it within a few years. Some serious-minded counsellors were convinced that ten, even twenty, years of preparation were necessary.

The result of these doubts was a maturing determination on the pontiff's part to hold the Council well within the first years of his pontificate. Being a realist, he had the normal fears of a man of his advanced age that his pontificate might not prove a long one. On the very day of his election as pope, a remark about the choice of his name echoed this feeling: "Nearly all [the previous pontiffs named John] had a brief pontificate."

European clerics were of two minds regarding Pope John. In some Vatican circles it was thought that he would not go down in history as a great pope, although his regime would probably be recorded as having had critical significance for the Church. Yet others pointed to the fact that, for all his simplicity and humility, the pope got important things done—things so far-reaching and profound in their implications that his pontificate might well outrank even those of his most notable predecessors in this century. Thus many Roman officials actually found the Holy Father an enigmatic personality. He made no secret of the fact that he did not consider himself a theologian but rather a pastor of souls. He assured a Protestant minister received in private audience that, although as head of the Church he was infallible when proclaiming matters of faith and morals, it was another matter when it came to abstruse theological questions. Then, said the pope, he had to consult his official theologian.

4

Actually there was a core of deep spiritual wisdom in almost everything Pope John said. Though easy to understand, his words continually reached into the profoundest mysteries of the faith. Pope John lived on a level that was close to the ground, able deftly to put rulers of nations quickly at ease when they visited him amid the splendors of the Vatican court, and at the same time to talk familiarly to a group of fifty couples celebrating their twenty-fifth wedding anniversary, reminding them that while the love they bore each other was like the roses the women were wearing for the occasion, it had not been without the thorns that always accompany roses. Neither as adept at languages as his predecessor nor as indefatigable in granting private and public audiences, he was a bit loquacious where Pius XII was judicious, warm and intimate where Pope Pius was correct. Entering a room filled with priests to whom he was granting a semi-private audience, Pope John immediately searched the group for old friends and acquaintances. *"Ah, i miei amici!"* he exclaimed, or cried *"I miei alunni!"* with unfeigned joy. And after the formalities of listening to and delivering an address, he would descend from his throne to allow visitors to kiss his ring and exchange words of friendly greeting, often to the annoyance of his secretaries who would try gently to disentangle him and move him to his next appointment. In preparation for President Eisenhower's visit to Rome, the pope took English lessons from huge Monsignor Thomas Ryan, the Irish counsellor on the staff of the Vatican Secretariat of State, and the few words of greeting he memorized came out with a bit of a brogue. On the well-known occasion* when America's First Lady arrived, he waited in the library trying to choose one of two alternative greetings suggested by his secretary, "Mrs. Kennedy, Madame; Madame, Mrs. Kennedy," but when the doors opened and he saw her, he extended his arms in greeting and exclaimed: "Jacqueline!" Pope John expressed his philosophy of action in the French epigram: *"Il faut faire quelque chose; il faut faire faire quelque chose; il faut laisser faire quelque chose,"* that is, there are some things one must do oneself, some things one must make others do, and certain things to be left alone.

From the moment when Angelo Roncalli accepted his election to the papacy, a new style and new direction were given to papal affairs. It was characteristic of this Italian countryman from the north—he was born on November 25, 1881, in the little village of Sotto il Monte, outside Bergamo on the Lombard plains—that as the voting in the conclave (of October 1958) began mounting in his favor, he prepared for this eventuality by selecting a name and writing out a short speech of acceptance that would stand in history as both prophetic and programmatic. Asked by the Dean of the Sacred College, Cardinal Eugène

* *Time*, January 4, 1963.

5

Tisserant, by what name he desired to be known, he said simply: "I will be called John." Then he brought out the piece of paper on which he had been writing and began to read:

The name John is dear to me because it is the name of my father. It is dear because it is the title of the humble parish church where we received baptism. It is the solemn name of innumerable cathedrals throughout the world, and first of all the blessed and holy Lateran basilica, our cathedral. It is the name which, in the long series of Roman pontiffs, has been most used. Indeed there have been twenty-two unquestionably legitimate supreme pontiffs named John. Nearly all had a brief pontificate.

We have preferred to shield the smallness of our own name behind this magnificent succession of Roman pontiffs. And was not St. Mark the Evangelist, the glory and protector of our dearest Venice, he whom St. Peter, Prince of the Apostles and first Bishop of the Roman Church, loved as his own son, also called John? But we love the name of John, so dear to us and to all the Church, particularly because it was borne by two men who were closest to Christ the Lord, the divine Redeemer of all the world and Founder of the Church: John the Baptist, the precursor of our Lord. He was not indeed the Light, but the witness to the Light. And he was truly the unconquered witness of truth, of justice and of liberty in his preaching, in the baptism of repentance, in the blood he shed. And the other John, the disciple and Evangelist, preferred by Christ and by His most Holy Mother who, as he ate the Last Supper, leaned on the breast of our Lord, and thereby obtained that charitable love which burned in him with a lively and apostolic flame until great old age.

May God dispose that both these Johns shall plead in all the Church for our most humble pastoral ministry which follows the one so well brought to its end by our lamented predecessor of venerable memory, Pius XII, and those of his predecessors so glorious in the Church. May they proclaim to the clergy and to all the people our work by which we desire to "prepare for the Lord a perfect people, to cut straight the windings of every street, and make rough paths into smooth roads, so that all mankind shall see the saving power of God" (Luke 3:4–6). And may John the Evangelist who, as he himself attests, took with him Mary the Mother of Christ and our Mother, sustain together with her this same exhortation, which concerns the life and the joy of the Catholic Church and also the peace and the prosperity of all peoples.

My children, love one another. Love one another, because this is the greatest commandment of the Lord. Venerable brethren, may God in His mercy grant that, bearing the name of the first of this series of supreme pontiffs, we can, with the help of divine grace, have his sanctity of life and his strength of soul, unto the shedding of our blood if God so wills.

This was a fairly long Latin explanation, but it was an excellent homily. It was a humble, sincere enunciation of his program: he intended to be a pastoral pope, one who would devote himself to spreading the

Word of God and the Church throughout the world. Thus he began his pontificate by reassuring the cardinals who had just elected him that their choice had been a wise one.

At once the new pope's personality began to emerge in a way that astonished his entourage. His first move was to ask the cardinals to remain in conclave until the following morning, because of his dislike of being alone and his desire to be surrounded by those associated with him in the guidance of the Church. This unprecedented act gave rise to an incident that was to have a certain far-reaching effect within the Curia. For immediately after the pope had given his blessing *urbi et orbi* from the balustrade of St. Peter's, the then Monsignor Tardini and a number of Vatican officials who were not cardinals came rushing into the sealed rooms of the conclave to be the first to pay their respects to the new pontiff. They were met by the imposing Cardinal Dean, Eugène Tisserant, who as senior member of the conclave furiously accused them of breaking its inviolability. Turning to Monsignor Tardini in particular, the cardinal informed the officials that they were excommunicated.

The next morning, of course, Pope John with a certain mock serious-ness lifted the penalty thus apparently incurred by these overzealous officials. But the relationship between *Il Francese* (as Cardinal Tisserant was known in Rome) and the man who within two months would be created a cardinal and appointed Secretary of State, suffered an almost fatal shock. Because of this, the subsequent resignation of Cardinal Tisserant from his position as prefect of the Congregation for the Oriental Churches Congregation was attributed to pressure from Tardini. How-ever, the resignation was in reality an act of deference to the wishes of the pope, by way of setting a good example, for Cardinal Tisserant was at that time head of both the Vatican Library and the Oriental Congrega-tion. As a result of the increase in the number of cardinals in the Curia (in four consistories held by Pope John, those of December 1958 and 1959, March 1960 and January 1961), there were not enough important posts to go round. It is said that at this juncture the pope spoke to four or five of the oldest cardinals, asking them to relinquish their positions as heads of Congregations. After the interview, the pope was seen standing in some amazement, shaking his head and saying out loud: "But they refused, they refused! Never in my life did I think anyone would refuse the pope. . . ." It is in the light of this incident that Cardinal Tisserant's withdrawal from one of his posts should be understood.

Pope John worked strenuously at changing the atmosphere of quasi-adoration that surrounded his predecessor, Pius XII. He curtailed the length of ceremonies in St. Peter's and attempted to reduce the fulsome forms and titles used in the columns of *L'Osservatore Romano*. Speaking to Raimondo Manzini, the new editor of this newspaper whom he brought from Bologna, the pope is reported to have answered the question, "What is the new style to be, Your Holiness?" by saying: "When you speak of me in my official capacity, say 'the supreme pontiff' then write simply 'the pope' for everything else." Nor had there ever been question in the pope's mind of giving titles of nobility or extraordinary honors to any members of his family. Speaking on this subject one day and recalling the spartan attitude of his eighteenth-century predecessor, Benedict XIV, who forbade his relatives to come to Rome from Bologna during his pontificate, Pope John said it was sufficient honor for his brothers and family that he was pope. In fact they were his guests in Rome on several occasions, but every effort was made to keep these visits on a quiet and homely level, as much to avoid embarrassment for these unobtrusive countryfolk as out of deference to the pontiff's wishes.

From the day of his election John XXIII showed that he intended to take seriously his claim to be a pastoral pope by giving greater prominence to his role as Bishop of Rome. Although he did not interfere in the actual administration of the diocese—he had a Cardinal Vicar and two auxiliary bishops to attend to this business—he began to make direct contact with his priests and people by personally visiting parishes, colleges and other institutions, and by paying courtesy calls on the sick, the orphaned, and the imprisoned.

Preparing for the Council, Pope John kept an invisible but firm hand on the 800 theologians and experts who were called to Rome to prepare the agenda. In less than three years, they sifted and codified a mountain of facts pertaining to ecclesiastical affairs in the modern world and bearing on everything from the rigid norms of canon law to the price of beeswax in Nigeria. The pope had proclaimed the goal of the Council to be an *aggiornamento* or a "bringing up to date." Vatican ultra-conservatives hopefully interpreted this as a face-saving device whereby, after a great display of rhetoric and ceremonial pageantry, nothing would be changed. On the other hand the term was understood by many, if not the majority, of the bishops as a decision in favor of major improvements in the Church's practices. The pope himself spoke of a renewal that would restore "the simple and pure lines that the face of the Church of Jesus had at its birth." Luther, Calvin and Melanchthon must have started in amazement in their graves to hear such words on the lips of the Pope of Rome. Alfred Loisy's cynical remark, "Jesus founded the Kingdom of God, and what came forth but the Church of Rome," seemed to have lost its bite. Pope John, of course, had no intention of changing any of the basic doctrines of the Church. In Catholic tradition there was no room for any reversal of position with regard to the articles of the creed or the laws of the Ten Commandments. Yet Cardinal Augustin Bea, head of the Secretariat for Christian Unity, stated flatly that while the Church could not reverse dogma, it could clarify it—in other words, reappraisal and reassessment were clearly in order.

For the most part, there were only obscure hints in the world press of the pressures from German, Dutch, French, Eastern and other Catholics for a modernization of the way in which the Church was facing internal problems. Some groups were openly agitating for a reorganization, if not abolition, of the Roman Curia. Others wanted changes in the laws and regulations affecting marriage and education, the mass, the sacraments, liturgical ceremonies, the inquisitorial and condemnatory procedures of the Holy Office, clerical dress and the unseemly pomp of prelatial vestiture, and a redefinition of the rights and duties of bishops and laymen in the Church's structure.

Just as in the third and fourth centuries Clement of Alexandria, Origen, Basil, the Gregories, Jerome and Augustine gave an originally Semitic creed a Greco-Roman dress, and in the twelfth and thirteenth centuries Bernard, Thomas Aquinas, Bonaventure and Duns Scotus succeeded in adapting it to the complicated atmosphere of the medieval world, so it was now time for a rephrasing or restatement of the Christian message in terms intelligible to the educated, cosmopolitan laity of today. A reassessment of responsibilities in the Church, including a proper role for the laity, depended upon recognition by the bishops of their own rightful place in the Church. For while monarchical, the Church was not totalitarian in structure, and while the pope was supreme teacher and lawgiver, as successor of Peter who in turn represented Christ, the head of the Mystical Body, the Holy Father's function after all was defined by Christ in the words, "And thou once strengthened, confirm thy brethren" (Lk. 22:32).

Eastern theology tended to exalt the role of the pope (and all ecclesiastical office) by regarding it as a gift of Christ to the Church. When designating Peter as the Rock upon which he was to build the Church, the Son of God gave his institution a final safeguard against error and perversion, and a guarantee that it would last until the end of time. Modern Roman theologians unfortunately have been tempted to interpret this metaphorically-oriented fact too literally, not only insisting on the idea of the Rock as the foundation or support of the Church's unity, but pushing it to its furthest logical development and considering the pope as thereby endowed with absolute and sole governmental power. This concept (quite apart from the dogma of infallibility) is a far cry from Christ's intention, who founded his Church on the College of Apostles. He gave to each Apostle equally a commission to preach, teach and baptize all men everywhere, and then spoke of Peter's function rather as serving his brethren: "Feed my lambs and my sheep," and "Confirm thy brethren."

History indicates, unfortunately, that the Church in the West frequently succumbed to the temptation that affects all worldly institutions. It assumed features of the political society in which at various times it found itself—in the fourth and fifth centuries adopting the legal structure of the later Roman Empire, and in the Middle Ages becoming a feudal power. In the fourteenth and fifteenth centuries it barely escaped succumbing to the opposite temptation of so exaggerating the collegial approach as to make the general council supreme over the pope. In line with secular governments of succeeding ages, which were strongly opposed to movements favoring democratic tendencies, Roman churchmen reacted against all forms of representative government by so exaggerating the monarchical nature of the papal power that both in the later Middle Ages and in more recent times members of the Roman Curia, the administrative arm of the Vatican, have frequently exercised a kind of tyranny. Acting, theoretically at least, on behalf of the pope, they have not infrequently gone far beyond his wishes on the excuse that they alone were able to cope with dangers to faith and morals presented by the complicated problems of the day, as well as by the intricate administrative demands of a world-wide Church.

This tendency reached its climax in 1870 at Vatican Council I, an event which by a weird series of historical coincidences proved clearly that the Church was both a human and divine institution. The necessity to clarify the pope's position in the Church as supreme teacher and guide (as well as law-giver) was occasioned by the centrifugal tendencies of French and Central-European bishops, allied in good part with secular rulers. These anti-Roman movements (known as Gallicanism and Josephism respectively) were reactions against the absolutist tendencies of Roman curialists. However, the dogma of papal infallibility in matters of faith and morals was one thing; the definition of papal supremacy as implying the *exclusion* of the rest of the episcopacy was another. The bishops who convened for Vatican Council I had no intention of separating the pope from the rest of the Church, particularly from themselves. Yet this almost happened when the constitution on papal infallibility was taken out of its context within the prepared schema dealing with the nature of the Church, and was defined separately. At this point the seizure of Rome and the outbreak of the Franco-Prussian war brought the council to a premature halt. Its work remained unfinished.

The result was a curious misdevelopment of theological thinking about the nature of the Church. The majority of Catholic theologians fell in with the triumphalistic reaction of Roman theologians, who unhesitatingly began to push this onesided view of the papacy to its farthest conclusions. Years later in a famous speech at Vatican Council II (see page 87) the bishop of Bruges, Emile Josef de Smedt, characterized this view as a childish display of "triumphalism, juridicism, and clericalism."

In recent years, despite Pope Pius XII's efforts to bring the Church's teaching abreast of the intellectual and moral problems of the age, the tendency toward one-man rule during his reign was carried so far that, in the interregnum, it was officially acknowledged that something had to be done "to restore the ecclesiastical organism." Exasperated in his later years by the backwardness of so many of his Curial colleagues, Pius XII apparently decided to "go it alone" as regards doctrinal and moral teaching. This unfortunately left the Curia even more in control of administrative processes and encouraged many of the evils connected with careerism, both within the Curia itself and externally on the part of bishops who hesitated to decide anything without first considering its possible effect in Rome.* Meanwhile Pius XII kept up his brilliant critiques of complex problems posed by advances in the fields of genetics, medicine and surgery, psychology and psychiatry, and by socio-economic developments that have affected the areas of civil liberty and personal freedom. While Pius XII's pronouncements were always greeted with outward adulation, it was obvious that little serious attention was being paid to what he was saying by his more intimate administrative collaborators. Hence they were not only unprepared to cope with his successor, who had been reading and absorbing these teachings, but were appalled when Pope John began quietly and firmly reducing theories to practice. It is hardly to be wondered at that, three months after his election, the Roman cardinals were perplexed and stunned by his announcement of a Council.

Since the Catholic Church is an organism, nothing happens within one sector of the body ecclesiastic without having some effect in its other parts. Along with the juridical problems that have dogged it throughout the nineteen hundred years of its history, the Church from its earliest days has been afflicted by outbreaks of heresy and schism. In fact, the difficulties of the later Middle Ages were an immediate consequence of the breakdown in theological thought resulting from nominalist tendencies in philosophy. Outright warfare against various Manichean and other heterodox movements—the Albigensians in France, the Waldensians in Italy, the Cathars in central Europe—plagued the so-called Age of Faith. When combined with the corruptive elements that subsequently arose

---

* To an American bishop whom he consecrated for a missionary diocese, the late Archbishop of Philadelphia, Cardinal Dennis Dougherty, said in reference to a bishop's relations with Rome: "My dear young man, when you face Jesus Christ in eternity as one of His bishops He is not going to ask you how you got along with the Roman Curia, but how many souls you saved."

from papal involvement in political and dynastic struggles, the tragic inevitable result was the great split in European Christendom spear-headed by the Lutheran revolt. As a consequence of this latest protesting deviation from Roman Catholicism, there was a tightening of procedures for thought-control within the Church and a revival of inquisitorial methods during the Counter-Reformation.

By the nineteenth century, the Church found itself on the defensive before the intellectual attacks of the Enlightenment and the rationalist disdain for supernatural phenomena accompanying the early emergence of the modern physical sciences. Some theologians, mainly outside the Roman sphere of influence, attempted to combine Catholic teaching with the idealism of Kant and the evolutionism of Hegel. Thus the German theologian George Hermes and the Bohemian Anton Guenther, despite their genuine piety, were finally condemned. Following their proscription, danger signals were up against every type of liberalism, with the ultimate rejection of the social thought of the Abbé de Lamennais and the suppression of the philosophical theories of Don Antonio Rosmini, although neither of these men seem to have been properly read or fundamentally understood by their Roman-trained critics. This could also be said of the ecumenical thought of the German J. Adam Moehler and the preoccupation with development of doctrine that brought into the Church the great English churchman John Henry Newman.

Two forces gradually took possession of the Roman Curia—a fear-inspired ruthlessness in dealing with every semblance of nonconformity in theological thought, and a determination to explain the traditional doctrines of the Church only within a rigid and static framework. Such tendencies ran counter to the spirit of a new age searching for a dynamic philosophy to explain the great expanse of movements caused by the opening up of so many new avenues in the physical sciences—the theory of evolution in the development of the universe, the new life-prolonging discoveries in medicine, and the vast social and economic changes accelerated by the industrial revolution.

Some astute Catholic theologians endeavored to find a solution for the Church's difficulties through a reapplication of the principles of Thomistic philosophy and a restatement of theology along scholastic lines. But they were disconcerted by developments in the field of biblical criticism which, on the Protestant side, reflected the rationalistic spirit of the century and seemed to empty the Bible of its supernatural content. Friedrich Christian Baur's *Life of Christ*, in German, paralleled in French by the ex-seminarian Ernest Renan's *La Vie de Jésus*, rejected Christ's divinity, thereby ridiculing all supernatural happenings recorded in the New Testament, while Friedrich Schleiermacher and the German critics generally reduced the Old Testament to a series of folkloristic legends.

The Roman reaction was swift and thorough. A *Syllabus of Errors* was drawn up and published with condign condemnations by Pope Pius IX in 1864, five years before the opening of Vatican Council I. This listing of modern errors was complete, including ideas in every field of nineteenth century interest, from political and social theory to scriptural and theological thought. The definition of papal infallibility in 1870 was considered the *riposte juste* to all danger of secular aberration by providing a supernatural safeguard against the demoniacal errors into which the world at large seemed determined to hurl itself.

By the turn of the twentieth century a second wave of Catholic thinkers, who had hoped to face up to the new ways of thought set in motion in all branches of knowledge by modern discoveries, was summarily suppressed by the condemnation in 1907 of the heresy of Modernism (Pope Pius X's decree *Lamentabili* and his encyclical *Pascendi*). This drove a number of Catholic exegetes and apologists such as Alfred Loisy of France, the English convert George Tyrrell, and the Italians Ernesto Buonaiuti and Romulo Murri out of the Church, although the two main instigators of the movement, the lay theologian, Baron Friedrich Von Huegel, and the Abbé Henri Brémond survived in communion with her.

The condemnation of Modernism as such was probably justified, for it was a heresy which in its essential features emasculated Christian doctrine by holding (1) that man's only means of knowing anything about God was by internal, personal religious experience; (2) that there was no objective reality behind such concepts as the Trinity, the divinity of Christ, the Incarnation, and the Resurrection, although within the cultural milieu in which these notions had their origin, they were good and useful for focusing a man's attention on his religious experiences; and (3) that these dogmatic formulas were undergoing a constant, purely natural evolution (for example, the Modernists explained the dimensions and import of the movement launched by Jesus Christ as completely beyond the imaginative perception of that interesting first-century rabbinical genius Himself, whose intention was to stir the people of the time to religious fervor by announcing the nearness of the end of the world).

What attracted some people to Modernism were the half-truths that it embodied. It was true to say, for example, that personal religious experience, whereby man makes contact with God through prayer and meditation, was an essential element in the life of the Church. It was also a fact that doctrinal formulas do not represent adequately the spiritual objectivity that they define, simply because the subject of these dogmas is either God Himself who is infinite, or some aspect of God's dealings with man which by definition is a mystery. Divine revelation was not given to man merely to satisfy his desire for truth or his curiosity about the mystery of God. It was meant as a means whereby man could make contact with his Maker and as a result of this encounter direct the dynamic forces of his entire being toward the fulfilment of his personality in knowing, loving and serving God with his whole heart and soul. Finally, it was certain that the divine message contained in the Bible had been unfolded in the Church gradually, at times in a painful dialectic that reached successive climaxes in the great councils of the Church and in the dogmatic definitions of the Roman pontiffs.

The theologians and thinkers who at first accepted the Modernist theories were aware of these basic truths and considered their elaboration as a true response to the evolutionary doctrines and dynamic drives of the world about them. Unfortunately, such real Modernists as Loisy, Tyrrell and Buonaiuti went much further in accepting as a premise for these considerations the inner core of Kantian idealism and Hegelian evolutional dynamism, denying objective reality to anything beyond the sphere of natural phenomena.

The real misfortune within the Church attendant on the condemnation of Modernism was the creation of a terrifying atmosphere of suspicion and distrust. Every thinker and publicist within the Church who did not conform unhesitatingly to the static formulation of the Church's teaching, as expressed in Roman-controlled manuals, was suspected of heresy. An oath against Modernism was concocted that it still imposed on all newly-elected bishops and each year required of professors and lecturers in theology at pontifical and ordinary seminaries.* A secret society referred to unpopularly as the *Sapinière*† was formed for ferreting out and delating to the Holy Office the writings and teachings of Catholics in every field, but particularly in biblical studies, in history and philosophy, and in theory underlying the physical and political sciences. Thus works of such eminent orthodox historians as Monsignor Louis Duchesne and Monsignor Pierre Batiffol were put on the Index Librorum Prohibitorum, and numerous other prominent ecclesiastics were removed from their teaching posts. However, groups of determined churchmen rode out this tide of suspicion and condemnation. Father F. M. Lagrange, O.P., for example, retired to Jerusalem and founded the (Dominican) Biblical School, while working away at the essential problems of scriptural exegesis and preparing scholars who would be able with confidence to face the intellectual problems of the next generation. In church history, patrology and philosophy, likewise, Catholic scholars prepared by the solid training given at

* Modified in 1967.
† The members of this society, *Sodalitium Pianum*, or "Pian Society," delated books, manuscripts, and even class notes to the Holy Office. Its coordinator seems to have been Monsignor Umberto Benigni (d. 1934), of whom the *Enciclopedia Cattolica* says: "It is premature to give a definite judgment with regard to various facets of his life, and his varied and often obscure activities." *EC*, v. 2 (1949) 1347.

such universities as Louvain in Belgium, Nijmegen in Holland, Freiburg in Switzerland, Innsbruck in Austria, the Catholic faculty of Tübingen, Germany, and the Catholic Institutes in Paris, Lille and Toulouse, continued to do the spade work necessary to keep the Church abreast of modern research.

The two world wars slowed down the pace of these intellectual movements, but immediately upon the close of World War II, in France particularly and in the northern European countries gradually, a new theological ferment was discovered in full motion. Utilizing in particular the great advances made since the turn of the century in the study of scripture and the early Church Fathers, a group of younger Jesuit and Dominican theologians interested themselves in a return to the sources of the Church's doctrine. They sought to renew the vigor and deepen the impact of Catholicism in a world that had largely repudiated the old-fashioned faith of its fathers. These men included the Jesuits Henri de Lubac, Jean Daniélou, and Henri Bouillard; and Yves Congar, M. D. Chenu, and A. M. Dubarle of the Dominican House of Studies at Le Saulchoir. Fathers Congar and de Lubac started a series of studies devoted to the nature of the Church. They spoke of "true and false reform in the Church" and of "soundings for a theology of the laity." Two books that caused a sensation were de Lubac's volume on the supernatural, and Le Chartier's *Essay on the Problem of Theology,* the latter of which was put on the Index on February 1, 1952. They thus provoked a controversy that brought charges of a "new theology" and accusations of a return to the Modernist heresy of relativism against the main exponents of the new movement. They were further suspected of falling into line with the existentialist leanings of the lay Catholic philosophers, Emanuel Mounier and Maurice Blondel. In particular two Roman theologians, Reginald Garrigou-Lagrange, O.P. and Charles Boyer, S.J. attacked the scriptural exegesis and the implications for the development of doctrine of the "new theology." Delations to Rome, frequently consisting of submission for condemnation by the Holy Office of mimeographed classnotes or type-written monographs, alarmed the Holy See as early as 1946. By 1950 rumors spread that Pope Pius XII was about to bring out a scathing condemnation of the new men and their theologizing.

In August 1950 that pontiff published his encyclical *Humani Generis,* which was hailed in conservative circles as a new *Pascendi,* intended to nip in the bud heretical tendencies in scriptural study and every approach to modern positivism in historical and theological research. (A story went around Roman circles that on the day after the encyclical's publication, Father Garrigou-Lagrange was seen stalking through the cloisters of the Angelicum college with a brace of six scalps neatly tucked under his belt.) In actual fact, however, *Humani Generis* was a more or less well-balanced document, condemning outright obvious heretical tendencies and warning theologians and scriptural exegetes to be prudent, but at the same time insisting that the Church's scholars utilize all the latest advances in scientific methods of research to deal with such difficult problems in theology as relativism in the expression of revealed truths, the employment of non-scholastic philosophy in the elaboration of Christian doctrine, the person of Adam and original sin, polygenism, evolution, the significance of the supernatural order, the real presence of Christ in the eucharist, existentialism and mysticism, and the objective value of dogma.

What was immediately noticeable about the document was its paternal spirit. It cited no one for condemnation; nor did ecclesiastical censure occur after the publication of the encyclical, although eventually several professors and two French provincials, a Jesuit and a Dominican, were relieved of their posts by being shifted to other assignments. Although certain tendencies and ideas had been proscribed, the encyclical made no attempt to stifle theological initiative; rather it encouraged a vital and existentialist investigation of modern problems, merely cautioning against bizarre attempts to accommodate Catholic teaching to contemporary philosophical fads and materialistic errors.

Meanwhile, in the practical sphere, a far-reaching movement tending toward ceremonial reform in the interest of spiritual apperception had been started. The movement began as far back as the previous century, with Dom Guéranger's books on the liturgical year. This reassessment of the outward manifestation of the Church's religious life—the celebration of the mass being the principal expression of Catholic worship, together with the seven sacraments from baptism to extreme unction—had been accompanied by attempts to deepen the spiritual life of the laity, by insisting upon their active and intelligent participation in the official liturgy and prayer of the Church. The Benedictines in the great European abbeys of Maria Laach and Beuron in Germany, of Einsiedeln in Switzerland, and of Solesmes in France, for example, had started schools for popularizing the Gregorian chant and enabling the layman to utilize the priestly character given him in baptism by taking an actual part in the ceremonies of the liturgy. This latter movement was strenuously opposed by many older Roman theologians and by a large number of bishops trained in Rome, on the score that it smacked of Protestant ideas whereby the distinction between laymen and priests was all but done away with. Hence the so-called "dialogue mass" and any suggestion that liturgical functions should be carried on in the vernacular languages were frowned upon, if not strictly banned. (The papal master of ceremonies, Monsignor Enrico Dante, for example, had been saying mass regularly for a convent of nuns for the past thirty years. As Secretary of the Congregation of Rites, having full power in these matters, he never once allowed them to have a dialogue mass.)

However, as these movements were accompanied by solid historical research and thorough-going spiritual and theological benefits, they gradually won favor in many parts of the Catholic world, causing Pope Pius X, at the beginning of this century, to acknowledge their existence and Pius XII, at midcentury, to attempt to both stabilize and justify them in his great encyclical on the liturgy known as *Mediator Dei*. As discussion at Vatican Council II would bring out so clearly, the eastern branch of the Church, though treated in good part as a sort of step-daughter by the Roman Curia, had preserved almost intact the most important features of the liturgy in the early Church. Hence the so-called "innovators" in the western half of the Church soon discovered that what they were so painfully trying to achieve through the liturgical movement and by a return to patristic theology was an everyday part of the religious heritage of their eastern brethren. Although these churches were also in the throes of attempting to modernize their liturgical practice, their requirements had more to do with abbreviating ceremonies (that once occupied the whole morning, if not the whole day, for people in an agricultural society) and adapting them to the needs of the industrial age, when men have so many other distractions.

This rediscovery of the Eastern Church's relevance to liturgical and theological thought had been made by numerous theologians and a small group of interested lay intellectuals in various western countries. It had been ignored, for the most part, by the bishops of the West. Hence, at the Council the latter were amazed to find Eastern prelates taking such an active part in the debates and coming out for solutions to problems raised by the schemata on Divine Revelation, Christian Unity, and the Nature of the Church, which western theologians had been years in discovering through hard research and fear (and for which they had had to fight strenuously with the authorities in Rome).

The notion, for example, of the collegial character of the organization of the Church based on the original body of Apostles was everyday doctrine among Melchite, Greek, Syrian, Chaldean and Lebanese Catholics. It was frowned upon by the Roman curialists. Actually this doctrine had been well stated and insisted upon at Vatican Council I, in the preparatory schema concerned with the nature of the Church. It was to have been considered in connection with the definition of papal infallibility, before that doctrine was torn from its context by the maneuverings of a clique of cardinals and bishops, led by Cardinal Manning with the assistance of Pope Pius IX. Yet this doctrine of the collegiality of the bishops was given scant recognition by the Preparatory Theological Commission in its schema on the Church prepared in 1961–62 under the chairmanship of Cardinal Ottaviani.

Similar observations could be made regarding the proposals for dealing with the nature of divine revelation at the new Council. Here, in reaction to Protestant insistence on Scripture as the sole norm of faith, scholastic-minded theologians had gradually slipped into the habit of considering Christ's words and deeds as having been recorded and handed down in the Church through two virtually separate vehicles—the written word of the New Testament and tradition. The latter was then utilized as a deposit by which the magisterium, or teaching authority, of the Church could justify some of the doctrinal definitions that took place in the development of Catholic theology down through the centuries, and which seemed to have only a tenuous (the technical word is *implicit*) expression in the written scriptures. The very title of the Theological Commission's draft betrayed modern Roman-bound thought on this subject, for it was announced as "On the Two Sources of Divine Revelation." This idea was strenuously opposed in the Council by the Eastern bishops, who were joined by a majority of the better informed western prelates. They all insisted that there was only one *source* of divine revelation: God in the person of His Son Jesus Christ. If a distinction were to be made between Scripture and tradition, it should be done only by recognizing both as vehicles, not sources, for the transmission of the originally revealed teachings of Christ, it was maintained. Here again in turning his mind to these problems, Pope John could see no other solution than to call his bishops together for a full-fledged discussion in Council.

In the government of the Catholic Church over the course of the last two hundred years or so—at least since the French Revolution—the Congregations of the Roman Curia achieved a startling supremacy, so much so as evidently to have given many members of these administrative organs the impression that, for all practical purposes, they were the Church. Bishops, priests and faithful were dealt with as a sort of mass appendage to the Vatican. Many of these officials seem to have felt that they were the effective executors of absolutist papal power over the clergy and faithful, and their decisions should not only be law but that their opinions on doctrinal, moral and political matters were manifestations of papal infallibility. In the appointment of bishops all over the world, the creation and apportionment of dioceses, the surveillance of faith and morals, the authorizing and control of religious orders and congregations, the dispensing of Church funds for missionary enterprises, and the safeguarding of tradition and orthodoxy affecting every aspect of Catholic life, they gradually came to have the final say. A network of apostolic nuncios and delegates accredited to national governments or to the episcopates of various countries (as in the United States) provided them with information concerning prelates and religious generally throughout the world. Personal contact with former Roman fellow-students as well as occasional trips to the Americas, to different parts of Europe, and even to Africa and the Far East, accomplished with a certain *éclat,* if not triumph—their local hosts were obviously highly honored to be entertaining a member of the Roman Curia—gave them a feeling that they understood better than anyone else, including the pope, the needs of the Church in the modern world. It is not surprising that they were legalistic-minded in the extreme, for the observance of protocol and regularity of legal procedures, as they well knew, were simple means for exercising control over an institution as vast as the Catholic Church. Likewise a sceptical and suspicious attitude toward innovation of any kind, particularly in areas of doctrine, Scripture and the moral aspects of psychological research and psychiatric practice also provided weapons in the interests of supreme control. Finally, the gentle but continual intimidation of bishops through procrastination in granting them the use of special faculties for the administration of the sacraments, the ordination and government of their priests and people, and the close surveillance of what was said and written (particularly by clerics all over the world) guaranteed the undisputed supremacy of this circle in church matters generally.

No reasonable man can deny, of course, the possibility of error in doctrinal matters and the need for caution and prudence in asserting religious truths. Yet a prudent mind was not a closed one, and caution and care were not identical with rigidity of thought and narrowness of view. The problem came down to the question asked of Christ by Pilate, "What is Truth?" For Catholic theologians generally, religious truth was first a series of propositions that captured the facts of divine revelation regarding the nature of God and His dealings with mankind, as well as those historical happenings that have been preserved in the Christian "deposit of faith" as necessary for an understanding of the divinely revealed truths. And second it was a spiritual experience that came from a confrontation with Jesus Christ, the Son of God, who was present in His Church in the world and who, through the graces of the Spirit, demanded the full ordination of man's powers, intellectual, voluntary, and sensitive, in His service.

Difficulty arose, however, when any group of theologians attempted to force a univocal expression of these truths on the Church, particularly if they wielded directive power. For while the strictly logical, Thomistic approach in theology was not only useful but perhaps necessary for the achievement of clear and precise concepts of religious truth, it was not the *only* way these ideas have been, or could be, expressed. There was the whole tradition of patristic as well as of oriental theology which Aquinas himself sought to incorporate, in part at least, in his thirteenth-century summation of Catholic truth, but which had a technique and manner of expression all its own.

What was even more fundamental to an understanding of this problem was the fact that men of a juridical persuasion seemed to have made the possession of certain religious truths the final end of their religion. There was a saying in Rome that any slip in the moral, social or political fields would eventually be forgiven, but even a minor doctrinal deviation was fatal as far as an ecclesiastical career was concerned. It was precisely this attitude that was being combatted by the theologians from beyond the Alps, who pointed out that Christ announced that He was not only the Truth, but that He was also the Way and the Life (Jn. 14:6). History proves that over-preoccupation with the niceties of theological expression has brought great evils upon the Church in the form of both verbal and sanguinary conflict, and has resulted in a falling away from the Church of the majority of modern intellectuals who have been appalled by the *odium theologicum* that frequently has replaced the not-so-simple Johannine injunction: "Brethren, if you do not love your brother whom you can see, how can you love God, whom you cannot see?" (1 Jn. 4:20).

While early patristic churchmen were struggling to elaborate and protect the essential truths of the Christian faith, they changed the concept of man's final end or purpose from the Platonic contemplation of the Good and the Stoic love of man to eternal beatitude which man must earn here on earth, under divine stimulus, not only by believing certain truths with all his heart and soul, but by conforming his behavior to the way and life of Christ here and now. One of the strangest paradoxes in history was that dyed-in-the-wool Roman theologians whose whole theology was oriented toward combatting the older Protestant shibboleth of "justification by faith alone," had all but succumbed to the temptation of proclaiming a univocal religious orthodoxy as the foremost requirement by which a Catholic participated in the Church. It was as though "justification only by the scholastic definition of religious truth" were the final test.

A factor in this attitude was certainly the fact that these men were born and brought up as Catholics and never really confronted any other religious experiences except by reading about them in the form of strawmen propositions to be demolished in a textbook. What was wrong with the Roman Curia was not so much the personnel as such. Its members were often intelligent, cordial, progressive-minded as regards material values, and pious. The main obstacles were the four groups in charge of the Holy Office, the Congregation of Seminaries and Universities, and to a lesser extent the Congregations of Rites and the Sacraments. Here old-fashioned, restrictive fears both for integrity of doctrine and uniformity of practice saddled the Church with a backward and frequently ominous outlook toward the modern world. The officials here were perfectly characterized by Pope John XXIII himself in his opening discourse at Vatican Council II as "prophets of doom."

In the end what seems to have convinced Pope John of the need to call a Council was not only the parochial outlook of most of the men about him in the Vatican, but the backward attitude of so many bishops in the stabilized areas of the Old and New Worlds. Though good men and hard-working administrators of both the spiritual and corporal works of the Church, they knew nothing about the new spirit fermenting in the minds and hearts of so many of the clergy, young and old, and now being discussed in the writings of the more advanced theologians, lay intellectuals, and church scholars.

So the pope decided to bring the bishops of the whole world together to let them educate each other as to the true role of the Church in a suffering, morally confused world, two-thirds of it poverty-stricken amid unprecedented plenty in the rest, living in fear of thermonuclear warfare and total destruction, and seemingly unable to disentangle itself from the mess. In a century which knew the reality of evil in the horrors of two world wars, in racist persecutions and genocide on a hitherto unimaginable scale, in the widespread successes of totalitarianism (the communist branch in particular), and in the spread of materialistic atheism, why was the Church not accomplishing more effectively the worldwide mission entrusted to it by Christ? In such a world, why was the whole family of Christ so disunited? Were not these internal quarrels and differences unworthy of Christians, and perhaps more emotional than real? It was time, the pope argued, for the Church to go about reclaiming its own lapsed members, converting the modern pagan who hungered after justice, and drawing back into the fold of Christ *all* the flock, more particularly those separated mainly by historical prejudices and misunderstandings, such as the Eastern Orthodox and the more traditionalist Protestant bodies.

Pope John's knowledge of these problems and his interest in their solution was explained by one thing: his whole life. Though born a farmer, with his feet solidly planted on the soil of the Lombard plain, he quickly proved himself a pilgrim in this world, from his teens travelling the length and breadth of the European continent, and gaining considerable knowledge of the Near East. He made his first trip to Rome as a youthful seminarian of twenty, and immediately decided to win himself a scholarship to finish his ecclesiastical training there. While neither his year of national service in the Italian army in 1901 (he achieved the rank of corporal on duty and was promoted to sergeant on returning to civilian life) nor his stint as a chaplain during World War I enlarged his geographical horizons, his career as a young priest, secretary to Giacomo Radini-Tedeschi, bishop of Bergamo, brought him into contact with currents of social thought and economic facts of life that alarmed the whole of Europe before the outbreak of the first world war. He travelled in France and northern Europe frequently with Bishop Radini, and through this extremely able and activist prelate became acquainted with the men who were to rule the Church in the next generation. He had also tasted the bitterness of ecclesiastical intrigue and Roman suspicion, when he took a principal part in the attempt to bring up to date the Church's social and economic thinking in accordance with the prescriptions of Pope Leo XIII's encyclical *Rerum Novarum,* and found himself under the shadow of the taint of radicalism for his troubles. His knowledge of men and their problems had been increased by his military career, as well as by the work he did for the youthful intellectuals of Bergamo, both as a seminary professor and as a university student-counsellor before being summoned to Rome by Pope Benedict XV in 1921. There he took over the Italian presidency of the Society for the Propagation of the Faith (a position similar to that later occupied by Bishop Fulton Sheen in New York). Although he came on the Roman scene as a new man at the age of forty, he was personally instructed by Pope Benedict XV to break with the older ways of doing things and given sufficient authority to remove the center of the Society from France (Lyons) to Rome. He was given the task of revitalizing the financial setup of this organization, after he had personally visited every diocese in the Italian peninsula as well as the more effective centers in France, Germany, Poland, and the former Austro-Hungarian Empire. His success was two-fold: he fortified the financial strength of the Society enormously, and while taking a superficial interest in ecclesiastical affairs on the periphery of Roman Curial society (his reputation as a *conférencier* won him invitations to lecture on the church fathers at the Lateran University), he created an organization which proved substantially effective in giving assistance to Italian foreign mission efforts. In the wake of this success, he was created an archbishop in 1925 and sent to Sofia as apostolic visitor, with the task of patiently investigating the possibility of improving the position of Catholics in an Orthodox-dominated region and achieving some sort of amicable arrangement with governments and people inclined to be anti-Roman. In 1934 he was shifted to Istanbul and made Apostolic Delegate for both Turkish and Greek Catholics. Since throughout his life he was primarily a pastor at heart, he interested himself in the practical problems of everyday Catholic life in all the countries of the Near East, acquiring a facility in the local languages and encouraging people to use their native tongues in many liturgical ceremonies rather than Latin. He also encouraged the publication of spiritual and doctrinal treatises in the native languages.

His post-war diplomatic years in Paris, as apostolic nuncio to de Gaulle's newly created Fourth French Republic, gave him an exceptional knowledge of the Church's needs in a new world whose political and spiritual foundations had to be rebuilt from the ground up. He was involved in the aftermath of the controversy over the "new theology." He was an interested though not a directly involved spectator of the experiment conducted by the worker-priests, and experienced with Cardinal Suhard and the French episcopate the anxiety of not knowing whether the Church in France, or in Europe for that matter, was to continue to decline or achieve a renaissance. Finally, he witnessed the birth of UNESCO and despite the anticlerical tendencies manifested by that institution's earliest organizers, forced the Holy See to take an active interest in its proceedings, having recognized at once the importance of this worldwide educational and cultural movement for Catholics throughout the world. In 1953, having been created a cardinal by Pope Pius XII, he was allowed to fulfill the ambition of his early days as a priest and to serve directly as a pastor of souls by being made patriarch of Venice. In his sermon upon entering the diocese, he assured the Venetians that all his life he had wanted to be nothing other than a parish priest, and he said that he was happy, as old age came upon him, to have his wish fulfilled. He was then 72 years old, but displayed no senile characteristics whatever. He immediately set about visiting the whole of the diocese, quietly but effectively reorganizing it. Instead of condemning the annual Venice Film Festival, he gave it his blessing and acted as host to committees and participants. He arranged for St. Mark's Cathedral to be the setting of the world première of Igor Stravinsky's "Sacred Canticle to Honour the Name of St. Mark." On the very day he left for Rome as a member of the conclave to elect a successor to Pius XII, he was correcting proofs of a diocesan synod.

It was against this background that John XXIII, shortly after his election, was inspired to undertake the difficult and even perilous task of summoning an Ecumenical Council, the first such Council in almost one hundred years, and only the twenty-first in nearly two thousand years, according to traditional Roman Catholic reckoning.

THE COUNCIL'S FOUR STAGES

Pope John referred to the Councils of previous ages as "shining lights" in the Church's annals. The phrase occurred in his opening discourse of

October 11. In the same talk he also described the Church's "prophets of doom" as behaving "as though at the time of the former Councils everything was fully triumphant for the Christian idea and way of life, and for true religious liberty." Together, these remarks constituted another way of saying that the history of the great Councils was mixed. Not one of the Ecumenical Councils—not excluding the latest—was convened without a clash of ideas (even, on occasion, of fists), as a result of which theologians and prelates got hurt, some finding themselves unceremoniously ushered into schism or heresy. None of the earlier Councils was wholly successful on what may be termed the level of polity, though in the end they all managed to clarify theological doctrine. Summoned by the emperors of the Roman Empire, the first seven Councils dealt mainly with the doctrines of the Trinity and the two natures—divine and human—in Christ. But they ended in a state of apparently hopeless tension between East and West, with the Byzantine emperors in virtually full control of the Church in the East and their subjects weaned away from any ecclesiastical loyalty to or communion with Rome. While in the West the papacy managed to preserve a great measure of independence, it got itself involved in political entanglements which hampered its spiritual effectiveness, from the days of Charlemagne and the Holy Roman Empire right down to modern times. (In 1903 the last of the Habsburgs in Austria exercised his so-called "Right of Exclusion" or veto power in the election of the pope himself, and the government of Spain, under a concordat, still has the right to approve or veto new bishops.) The great Councils of the Middle Ages, through their failure to bring about a true reform of the Church, contributed directly to the Protestant revolt and the subsequent fracture of western Christendom. At Trent, in the middle of the sixteenth century, the popes shook off the blandishments of the Renaissance and the mirage of a Crusade and inaugurated a Counter-Reformation. But the new movement never fully got into orbit, owing to the inveterate politicking of many Catholic churchmen. A century ago, Vatican Council I (1869–70) proved in many respects to be a premature effort to face the problems of a revolutionary age. After having proclaimed the doctrine of papal infallibility (not unanimously: two bishops—one of them the bishop of Little Rock, Arkansas—voted against it, and fifty-five out of six hundred prelates abstained), it disbanded when the Italians seized Rome on September 20, 1870. Vatican Council I thus remained unfinished. One of the first things Pope John did, once he had made up his mind to hold Vatican II, was to declare Vatican I definitively closed. In this connection it is said that each time a Vatican official approached John XXIII with a suggestion for postponing his new Council, the pope advanced the target date. His original plan had looked to the autumn of 1963 for the convocation. After their first incredulous reaction, some of his immediate collaborators were appalled by his dismissal of their contention that a great amount of time and complex preparations were needed for such a step.

Despite his advanced age (he celebrated his eighty-first birthday while the Council was in session), despite the hesitations of the preceding pontiff (a man admittedly far more astute than himself), despite his Secretary of State who died in the summer of 1961 without having deflected the pope from his original decision in the slightest degree, despite the precariousness of world conditions, Pope John opened Vatican II in St. Peter's basilica on October 11, 1962. If some advocates of postponement were prompted by the hope that eternity would spare them the ordeal of a Council, they had only themselves to blame for the fact that Vatican II was inaugurated one year earlier than planned.

What had helped to solidify the pope's determination to get on with the Council was the success (or lack of it) he experienced with his Roman Synod, preparations for which had proceeded throughout the first year of his pontificate. In a single year he had hustled his procrastinating pastors and theologians through a mountain of socio-religious facts and legal documents to enact some 755 articles that gave expression to his idea of how the Christian life should be pursued in today's world. As the setting for the Synod, whose sessions were held during the week of January 24–31, 1960, he naturally chose the basilica of St. John Lateran, which was his proper cathedral as Bishop of Rome. Instead of discussions by theologians and parish priests, he was persuaded to schedule a four-day reading of the prospective Synodal Acts prepared by a commission, inviting written proposals and emendations from the priests and religious clerics belonging to the diocese of Rome. (Invidious comment, particularly on the part of foreign clerics stationed in Rome, implied that this "rubber stamp" Synod was serving as an unfortunate precedent for the Ecumenical Council, yet a number of changes were made in the proposed statutes as a result of these readings and suggestions.) Knowing the propensity of his Italian clerics for long-winded oratory, Pope John had decided to do the talking himself. In five talks, three of which were delivered in the synodal sessions, and a fourth and fifth at the church of the Gesù to clerics and nuns living in Rome, he supplied a full commentary on the Synodal Acts which were officially promulgated on June 28, 1960, the vigil of the feast of the Apostles Peter and Paul. The pope's talks ranged over a wide spiritual field, touching on some of the most profound mysteries of the Christian faith: belief in God as a Trinity of love; redemption from sin by the earthly sufferings and death of the Son of God become a man; the resurrection and the hope of seeing God "face to face," in the graphic phrase employed by St. Paul. They also touched on the pitfalls and dangers of life in the modern world that could lead to damnation. But Pope John insisted much more on a positive approach whereby priest, seminarian, nun and layman, putting their shoulders to the wheel of life, could achieve decency, stability, security and a touch of holiness no matter what the physical and social conditions in which they found themselves. This was the spirit permeating the majority of the synodal regulations, though the structure and the wording of the document followed the usual style of canonical legislation.

In actual fact, canon law experts were considerably disturbed by the principles enunciated in this document. "That's not law," more than one canonist commented openly. To which the Holy Father's reply was equally frank and simple: "It's not intended as a strictly legal document." If he had wanted to publish "pure" law, he would merely have reprinted verbatim sections from the current Code of Canon Law by which the Church Universal was governed. Some canonists disliked the fact that the pope had set a precedent that could lead to a new conception of law in the Church. Despite their legal trappings, these regulations were intended in his mind to be a sort of *vade mecum,* or guide for Christian living. Along with an assertion of the rights and obligations that flowed from the free acceptance of the Church as the guardian and guide of one's relations with Almighty God, the Synod exhorted Catholics on such matters as the type of prayers to be said; the courage clerics should exhibit in defending their dignity and honor if attacked in public, without of course descending to unseemly exchanges; the respect they must show the guardians of public order, the attention they must pay to traffic regulations, financial and tax laws, old age pensions for employees, and even annual visits to the cemetery. Penalties for violations of the law were held to a minimum, affecting principally those in clerical orders. Of considerable disappointment to foreign priests in the Eternal City—and especially to Americans and Germans—were the requirements that the cassock must be worn in the streets, and the tonsure observed, the shaving of the back of the head that in Europe generally marks all clerics (not only monks) as men set aside for the service of the Lord. Clerics likewise were forbidden to attend all public spectacles, from operas to races. (As more than one prelate remarked, if the priests in Rome were allowed to go to public concerts and the opera, or even only to the better cinemas, who else would be able to get in? For there were more than five thousand priests alone in the environs of the Vatican.)

One innovation that was certainly due to Pope John's own way of thinking—it is reported that he personally wrote out the ordinance—concerned priests who had fallen away from their calling. Artice 35 of the Synodal Statutes reads: "Priests laboring under censure or other penalty, or who have perhaps unhappily left the Church, should never cease to confide in the mercy of the Lord and the humaneness and decency of ecclesiastical superiors. Other priests, particularly those who were joined to them in friendship, motivated by heavenly charity, should sedulously strive to cultivate this trust in their minds. Towards all these unhappy men who persevere in their defection that norm is to be used which Pius XI found so fruitful: The less we can speak to men about God, the more it behooves us to speak to God about men. In these matters then, which are truly pitiful, no one is to be deprived of the friendliness of his fellow priests, or of consolation in his adversities, or even of temporal assistance should the circumstances call for it." The revolutionary character of this regulation for the treatment of lapsed priests in Rome was fully brought out by the Jesuit Father Domenico Grasso, writing in *Civiltà Cattolica* (November 5, 1960), the most influential Italian ecclesiastical journal. "We should not be surprised to learn," says Father Grasso, "that this article was actually dictated by the Holy Father. For it reflects the full pastoral solicitude with which John XXIII has marked his pontificate. 'Unhappy' is indeed the proper designation for those who were once part of the clergy and are now cut off. Until the present, the Church, for reasons obvious to everyone, has taken a position of great firmness in regard to such persons. Against no others has it perhaps employed equal measures, for while ever ready to receive the penitent, it has been inexorable in its conditions. Frequently, however, this attitude on the part of ecclesiastical authority has caused priests, influenced by considerations of a moral or psychological character, to break off all relations with these unfortunate colleagues, even those who were once their friends. As a result, the *infelices* not infrequently have ended up by losing their faith. The Roman Synod definitely placed such prejudices in their proper perspective. Everyone had a right to God's mercy, hence priests who had an obligation to approach souls in need of divine grace had also the same obligation toward their former colleagues. In fact, there is an even stronger title, for these men are in greater need of understanding and pardon. Many scandals could be avoided if this norm were followed in all cases." It had taken the courage and determination of Pope John to put this change on the books. It is known that Pius XII gave serious consideration to this problem and for a year or so forced the Congregation of the Council and the Sacred Apostolic Penitentiary to grant dispensations allowing unfrocked priests to marry legally; but that once he got absorbed in other problems, the Curial officials returned to their former practices.

With the Synod a *fait accompli*—it went into effect November 1, 1960—John XXIII had demonstrated to his own satisfaction at least that it was possible to organize theologians and experts as a working team. He found out what had to be done to produce in a year's time a document as thorough and well-knit as the regulations of the Synod. He next turned his full attention to plans for the Ecumenical Council.

The scope of this enterprise was staggering, for it meant the questioning of each one of the Church's 2,500 residential bishops and prelates, the heads of all male religious orders, and the faculties of Catholic universities (of which there were some thirty-seven in different parts of the world) to discover what they considered to be the more important problems facing the Church today and how they should be handled. A letter signed by Cardinal Tardini, Vatican Secretary of State and, by the pope's appointment head of the Ante-Preparatory Commission for the Council, was despatched to the Church's prelates on June 18, 1959 by the Secretary General for the Council, Monsignor Pericle Felici, titular Archbishop of Samosata, and Cardinal Tardini's choice for this all-important administrative post, as one of the more intelligent and tougher prelates in the Vatican service.

The bishops were requested to cooperate fully with preparations for the Council. Close to two thousand answers were received and catalogued in a relatively short space of time. What gave particular significance to the replies was the fact that no limitations were placed either on the matters to be considered or the manner of dealing with problems or proposals. The pope made it clear from the start that he wanted to hear the mind of the whole of the Catholic world on the condition of the Church today.* The vast material thus accumulated (the so called *vota* were eventually printed in book form) was examined and arranged in some two thousand files. After an initial analysis, national reports were compiled and synthesized to give, with facts and figures, a bird's-eye view of the situation of the Church in each country, and an overall view of the common problems viewed as important by the majority of the bishops.

It was with this material that the so called Preparatory Commissions, new bodies created by the pope on the feast of Pentecost (June 5, 1960) went to work. These bodies† included a Central Preparatory Commission

---

* It is known that the proposals regarding the relations between Church and State, as well as those having to do with liberty of conscience, prepared by the faculty of the Catholic University of America in Washington, D.C. for submission to the Theological Commission were withheld by the university authorities. This fact was brought to the attention of the Secretary of the Congregation for Universities and Studies during the Council, who expressed considerable annoyance over such arbitrary action. "The Pope," he said, "made it clear that he wanted the faculty consulted, and not merely the authorities."

† The Preparatory Commissions and Secretariats were as follows: (1) CENTRAL COMMISSION—President, Pope John XXIII; Secretary, Archbishop Felici. (2) THEO-LOGICAL COMMISSION (*properly* Com. on Faith and Morals)—Pres., Cardinal Ottaviani; Sec., Fr. S. Tromp, S.J. (3) COMMISSION FOR BISHOPS AND THE GOVT. OF DIOCESES—Pres., Cardinal Mimmi, later Cardinal Marella; Sec., Fr. Berutti, O.P. (4) COMMISSION FOR DISCIPLINE OF THE CLERGY AND FAITHFUL—Pres., Cardinal Ciriaci; Sec., Fr. Berutti, O.P. (5) COMMISSION FOR RELIGIOUS—Pres., Cardinal Valeri; Sec., Fr. Rousseau, O.M.I. (6) COMMISSION FOR THE SACRAMENTS—Pres., Cardinal Masella; Sec., Fr. Bigador, S.J. (7) COMMISSION FOR THE LITURGY—Pres.,

that eventually was to pass on and coordinate the work of the others.

Speaking at a solemn vespers in St. Peter's on that day, the pope summarized what had gone before and was to come after, stating that "an Ecumenical Council takes place in four stages: first there is an introductory, exploratory, ante-preparatory* and general phase, which has lasted till now. This is followed by a preparatory phase, properly speaking, which we have just announced. Thirdly, there is the celebration or general meeting of the Council in all its solemnity. Finally, there is the promulgation of the Acts of the Council, that is, what the Council has agreed to determine, declare, and propose with respect to and for the improvement of thought and life, a deeper increase in spirituality and apostolic fervor, and the glorification of the Gospel of Christ, as applied and lived by His holy Church."

While the pope had appointed the heads of the various Congregations of the Roman Curia as chairmen and secretaries of these Commissions— thus Cardinal Ottaviani and Father Sebastian Tromp, S.J. were, respectively, chairman and secretary of the Theological Commission; Cardinal Amleto Cicognani and Father Athanasius Welykyj, chairman and secretary of the Commission for the Oriental Churches—he made it clear that the Curia and the Council were intended to be kept separate. Speaking on the above occasion, the pontiff said:

The Ecumenical Council has its own structure and organization which cannot be confused with the ordinary functions of the various departments that constitute the Roman Curia. The latter will carry on as usual during the Council. The preparation of the Council, however, will not be the task of the Roman Curia but, together with the illustrious prelates and consultors of the Roman Curia, bishops and scholars from all over the world will offer their contribution. This distinction is therefore precise: the ordinary government of the Church with which the Roman Curia is concerned is one matter, and the Council another.

It was on this occasion likewise that he clarified the aims of the Council. He conceived of it as a demonstration and living proof to the

---

Cardinal G. Cicognani, later Cardinal Larraona, Sec., Fr. Bugnini, C.M. (8) COMMISSION FOR STUDIES AND SEMINARIES—Pres., Cardinal Pizzardo; Sec., Fr. Mayer, O.S.B. (9) COMMISSION FOR ORIENTAL CHURCHES—Pres., Cardinal A. Cicognani; Sec., Fr. Welykyj. (10) COMMISSION FOR MISSIONS—Pres., Cardinal Agagianian; Sec., Msgr. Mathew. (11) COMMISSION FOR APOSTOLATE OF THE LAITY—Pres., Cardinal Cento; Sec., Msgr. Glorieux. (12) COMMISSION FOR CEREMONIAL—Pres., Cardinal Tisserant; Sec., Msgr. Nardone. SECRETARIATS: (1) PRESS AND INFORMATIONAL MEDIA—Pres., Archbishop O'Connor; Sec., Msgr. Deskur. (2) PROMOTING CHRISTIAN UNITY—Pres., Cardinal Bea; Sec., Msgr. Willebrands. (3) ADMINISTRATION—Pres., Cardinal Di Jorio; Sec., Msgr. Guerri.

* Though the term "ante-preparatory" is both a neologism and redundant, it was used (*antipreparatorio,* in Italian) to distinguish clearly between the two preparatory phases.

world of the Church in her perennial vigor of life and truth. He wanted her legislation and practice brought up-to-date so as to reflect modern circumstances; and he desired that her theology be made concrete and dynamic, in line with her divine mission so as to be ready to face the great problems of the contemporary world. "If after this is accomplished, our separated brethren wish to realize a common desire for unity," said the pope, "they will find the way open to a meeting and a return to the Church."

Behind the scenes at the Vatican, the Council was looked upon with mixed feelings, ranging from passive acquiescence to outright alarm. It was perhaps understandable that the pope's frequent talk of unity with the separated brethren in Orthodox and Protestant bodies might have given some officials nightmares. As they saw it, the pope did not understand fully the doctrinal issues involved in these matters; and in their view he was unwittingly encouraging those Catholic theologians and apologists who had been flirting with heterodoxy by minimizing Catholic truth during the last thirty years or so. It was feared likewise that a gathering of the bishops of the whole world in Rome could only result in the forcing of issues that some officials felt they themselves alone were truly competent to deal with. These men acted as if they believed the majority of the bishops throughout the world were not sufficiently informed to know what it was all about. There was also an uneasiness lest efforts be made to suppress certain authority exercised by Curial officials, or more particularly to reorganize their offices and reshuffle their personnel.

They further realized that there was considerable unhappiness among groups of bishops with the whole system of apostolic delegates and muncios, who were frequently considered as little more than Vatican informers and meddlers. Irish and Australian bishops in particular had little use for Italian ecclesiastical diplomats; Cardinal Amleto Cicognani as apostolic delegate in the United States for twenty-three years, by way of exception, managed to enjoy the complete respect and affection of the American bishops and laity.

Members of the Holy Office understandably felt that they alone were competent to deal with all matters of faith and morals and keep a tight hold on the theological traditions of the Church as expressed in the scholastic terminology of Roman textbooks. The liturgical movement, so strong in Germany, France, parts of Canada, the mid-western United States and in many mission territories, was flooding the Congregation of Rites with insistent demands that the use of the vernacular languages in the mass and other Church rites be authorized on a universal scale. Similarly the Holy Office and certain professors at the Roman universities were convinced that the "new" biblical scholars had sold their scriptural birthright for a mess of Germanic rationalism parading under such

30

formidable and dangerous terms as *Formgeschichte, Redaktionsgeschichte* and *Heilsgeschichte,* but by means of admonitions and condemnations these Curialists felt that they could keep the situation in hand. The gathering of the bishops of the whole world in the Eternal City, pessimists feared, might precipitate theological clashes that could endanger the Church's unity and control by Rome.

The pope, of course, was of an entirely different opinion. He hoped that, by assembling the bishops in Council, they would demonstrate the unity of the Church, assert its awareness of the world about it, and thus pave the way for a re-Christianization of modern man. The pope had announced the Council's goal as an *aggiornamento,* or a bringing up-to-date of the Church. The story was often repeated that the pope, asked by a visiting cardinal for a simple explanation of the Council, went to the nearest window, opened it wide, and let in the fresh air. A French bishop, on hearing this story, drily observed: "When the pope indicated that we were to open the windows of the Church, he meant the Curia windows."

Many responsible non-Italian prelates (and not a few Italian ones too) had come to believe that the time was approaching to break the stranglehold on ecclesiastical thought and practices exercised by the self-perpetuating clique in the Curia which dictated Roman Catholic policy and, to a large extent, controlled the pope himself. This tightly-knit group had thus far successfully resisted all but the most innocuous changes dictated by the exigencies of modern life. They had long been conscious not only of dissatisfaction on the part of churchmen outside their circle but of movements in the intellectual and spiritual life of the Church that were opposed to official Curial thought and doctrine. They would have been content to continue on their forceful way, restraining the thinking of the Church within what they considered its ancient and sacred ways. To these men, the announcement of the new Council came as a severe shock. As for the majority of bishops, what they feared most was that the new Council would be a mere pageant, run off by officials in rubberstamp fashion. They felt that if the Council failed to come to grips with the really basic spiritual ills and moral issues of the day, it would destroy the hope that its proclamation had aroused in the hearts of thinking Catholics and non-Catholics alike. It was obvious that when Curialists and bishops met in Council there was bound to be a reverberating clash.

Although the new Council was the last thing in the world the above officials desired, once they were convinced of the pope's determination to go ahead, they proved themselves not without resources. Enjoying the advantage of being on the spot and in control of Vatican activities, they quickly rallied to dominate the commissions that were to organize the Council. They made their trusted friends the presidents and the secretaries, inviting at first only "safe" men from various parts of the world to sit in as experts. Gradually, as complaints mounted that some of the outstanding theologians of the Church in France, Germany, and Belgium had been excluded, they called these people to Rome, but it was then too late for them to have any effect on the proposals to be placed before the bishops in council. Unable to control the important Central Commission, which had the final say on the agenda and was composed chiefly of cardinals, they did the next-best thing and arranged to have the conservative cardinals—Ottaviani, Ruffini, Siri, Pizzardo, Marella—lead the discussions. What was more to the point, they saw to it that the reports of this commission's meetings published in *L'Osservatore Romano,* the Vatican newspaper, reflected their line of thought. The information contained in these generally dull, perfunctory news releases was for the most part merely a rehash of the doctrinal explanations to be found in the old, stereotyped larger *Roman Catechism,* buttressed by an appeal to the current code of canon law. About the only revolutionary proposal that was officially admitted to have been considered was the possibility of the Council's coming out for a stabilized, universal calendar.

It was a poorly kept secret, however, that this Central Commission's meetings were far from harmonious. Several times, resolutions to abolish outright the Congregation of the Holy Office were brought to the floor. In the sessions that took place in June 1962, after Cardinal Ottaviani had ordered that the Italian translation of a pastoral letter on the Council written by the Dutch bishops be withdrawn from circulation, the Indian cardinal—vehemently supported by Cardinals Döpfner of Munich, König of Vienna, and Liénart of Lille—came to the aid of Cardinal Alfrink of Utrecht, by informing the representative of the Holy Office that while ecumenical councils usually ended with someone in schism, this time, for once, it would not be the outsiders, because they happened to represent not merely the majority of the Church but the *sanior pars,* and they expressed their disdain for the "freemasonary" (a nasty word in European ecclesiastical circles) of those Italian prelates who had held the Church in thrall too long. So pointed did the debate become that the pope eventually sent for the leading figures to calm them down. He did not tell them to abandon their positions, however—a healthy sign of the free discussion that was to follow in the Council.

A close look at the *Annuario Pontificio,* the official yearbook of the Vatican, revealed a curious fact that was at the heart of the present difficulties within the Church. The twelve Roman Curial Congregations, though each was headed by a cardinal, were controlled by an interlocking directorate of bishops and monsignors, all Italian. The assessor or administrative director of the Holy Office, for example, was Archbishop Pietro Parente, who was responsible for investigating any matters dealing with faith or morals in the Church. At the same time, Archbishop Parente was a consultor of the Consistorial Congregation, which was entrusted with the creation of new dioceses, the nomination of bishops, and the supervision of their activities. He was a member of the Congregation of the Council, which watched over the discipline of both clergy and laity and had the right to revise the acts of national councils. (It also passed on disputes concerning legacies and bequests.) He was a consultor of the Congregation for the Propagation of the Faith, whose competence extended to the missionary field, and a member of the Congregation of Rites, which dealt with the Church's ceremonies and conducted the processes whereby a person was raised to the altar as a saint. He sat in on the Pontifical Commission for Cinema, Radio, and Television, and had a place in the pope's official Chapel. Finally, he was a member of the Commission for Latin America. (On one occasion, addressing a group of bishops from South America, together with the superiors of various religious orders that had missionaries there, he offended most of his auditors by remarking, "My subject has to do with Paraguay, Uruguay, and all the other *guai*"—the Italian for "troubles.") It was incredible that a man of Archbishop Parente's temperament could be appointed to so sensitive a position as his present post in the Holy Office, for his personal history hardly reflected the stability or civility one expected of Vatican officialdom. Born near Benevento in 1892, he was ordained a priest in 1916 and consecrated archbishop of Perugia in 1955. In the 1930's, as rector of the Propaganda College in Rome, he managed to incur the anger of Pius XI and had to leave the Eternal City. Powerful friends persuaded Pius XII to recall him to grace and promote him to the archbishopric of Perugia, but he disillusioned both the laity and clergy of that Umbrian city so much by his interference in political and social matters that in 1959 he was, as the *Annuario* tersely put it, "translated" to the titular see of Ptolemais, and brought into the Holy Office as assessor. It was Archbishop Parente, along with another conservative, Archbishop Pericle Felici, who had the most to say as to who would, and who would not, be placed on the preparatory commissions for the Council.

Archbishops Parente and Felici were only two of a host of Italian names that appeared on every other page of the part of the *Annuario* devoted to the Roman Curia. (Here and there, of course, one came across such names as Martin O'Connor, Paul Maria Krieg, Romuald Bissonnette, Francis J. Brennan, and Thomas Ryan, but, with the exception of Archbishop O'Connor and Monsignor Brennan, these men did not head offices.) By the peculiar workings of ecclesiastical fate, these same Italian names appeared toward the top of the lists of members of the preparatory commissions charged with responsibility for proposing the agenda of the Council. Though, in all, some eight hundred bishops and theologians from every corner of the world were brought to Rome for

33

consultation regarding this agenda, certain outstanding Catholic figures were curiously excluded, or only invited as consultors toward the very end of the preparatory period. Among those excluded or invited late were the American Jesuits John Courtney Murray and John L. McKenzie; the French theologians Henri de Lubac, M.-D. Chenu, and Jean Daniélou; and Hugo and Karl Rahner, of Innsbruck. These men were apparently considered to hold too wildly liberal views, and therefore were dangerous.

Recently some officials had devised a plan aimed at giving themselves absolute control over the Church's intellectual life. Disturbed no little by the independent thinking of Pius XII, who in later years made it his business to reassess the Church's attitude toward many phases of modern thought, they counted on reasserting their safe theses and doctrines after his death. Pius XII had, for one thing, emancipated the church's scriptural scholars by giving them a mandate to employ legitimate modern discoveries to help the Church understand divine revelation. It was known that he had also worked on a complete reorganization of the Roman Curia, but that when he fell sick in 1954 he had had to abandon the project. Consequently, when he died, in 1958, and the conclave elected the seventy-six-year-old diplomat and Patriarch of Venice who became Pope John XXIII, the men of the Curia must have breathed a sigh of relief. They were no doubt convinced that Divine Providence was on their side. The new pontiff was not an intellectual. He made no pretense of being a theologian. With a little careful maneuvering, they could have their way.

One of the first things they had decided to undertake, according to many observers, was a complete reorganization of ecclesiastical studies, whereby they could directly influence the teaching of theology in all seminaries throughout the world. The fact, for example, that the Jesuits and the Dominicans had the two best schools of scriptural studies—the Biblical Institute in Rome, and the Ecole Biblique in Jerusalem, respectively—was alarming, particularly since the better students turned out by these faculties were imbued with the new approach to the Bible. The curial plan called for a vast agglomeration of all the Catholic universities in Rome—primarily the Gregorian, the Angelicum, and Propaganda—under the leadership of the Lateran University, which would eventually also absorb such schools as the Jesuit-run Biblical Institute, the Capranica, and the Ecclesiastical Academy. The first step in this direction was a move to bring the Lateran itself up to true university status (which Pius XII had always refused). At the time, it was actually little better than a glorified seminary with mediocre graduate schools of law and theology. To justify its right to be called a university, it aggregated to itself the Carmelite school of theology and the Redemptorist institute of moral theology, organized a faculty of pastoral theology, and brought under its aegis two new schools—one for nuns and one for teaching brothers—

whose objective was the issuing of a licentiate, or master's degree, in religion.

It was at this juncture that the thunderbolt of Pope John's announcement of the forthcoming Council struck. This was followed almost immediately by a severe setback to the plan for gathering all the universities under the aegis of the Lateran. The campaign had started with an attack on the Biblical Institute published in the December, 1960, issue of *Divinitas,* the journal of the Lateran University, by Monsignor Antonino Romeo, secretary to Cardinal Pizzardo, head of the Congregation of Seminaries and Universities. Quite clearly, it was intended that this would be followed immediately by action on the part of the Holy Office; the works of several professors of the Biblical Institute, as well as of individual French and German theologians, would be condemned and proscribed. The next move, it may be assumed, would have been to call for control of all the theological faculties in Rome, and eventually throughout the world, by a safe school of theology—the Lateran, for example. As things turned out, the plan overreached itself. Intending to confront Pope John with a *fait accompli,* the officials had seen to it that Monsignor Romeo's article was kept from his eyes, and they refused to print in *Divinitas* the reply of the rector of the Biblical Institute; instead, they sent a free copy of the original article to every bishop in Italy. This proved their undoing, for one of the Italian bishops, on a Vatican visit, unwittingly offered the pope his sympathies on the fell state of theological affairs as revealed by Monsignor Romeo's article. This was the first Pope John had heard of the matter. When he read the article, he gave vent to one of the few angry outbursts of his pontificate. He had his secretary call the rector of the Biblical Institute and assure him of the pope's complete confidence in the school's orthodoxy. Next, he required Cardinal Pizzardo to write a letter to Cardinal Bea, former rector of the Institute, in which Pizzardo disclaimed any responsibility for the article, or knowledge of it before it was printed. This was a double humiliation, for all Rome knew that the article could never have been written without the clearance, and even the encouragement, of Cardinal Pizzardo.

The matter did not end there, however. Returning to the attack at the beginning of the scholastic year 1961, the Holy Office informed the general of the Jesuits that two professors at the Biblical Institute, Stanislas Lyonnet and Maximilian Zerwick, were to be removed from the faculty as being under suspicion of teaching erroneous doctrine. Fortunately for the cause of fair play as well as that of academic freedom, the Jesuit general decided that it was time to take a stand. He informed the secretary of the Holy Office that he had personally examined the teachings of these two professors and could find no fault in them. He asked proof of their errors. As it was against the principles of the Holy Office ever to justify its activities, the matter died there and the two men remained at their posts. In June, however, at the close of the school year, the Holy Office forced the Vatican Secretary of State to intervene and suspend the two professors in question.

Actually, what was happening in Catholic biblical scholarship seemed to be fully in line with the *aggiornamento* proclaimed by Pope John as the aim of his new Council. Using discoveries in the archaeological, literary, and historical fields relating to the time of Christ, the scriptural men hoped to arrive at a closer appreciation of Christ's words and deeds through study of the context and atmosphere in which they occurred. They made a clear distinction between biblical theology—the systematic presentation of the religious truths revealed by Christ as these truths were understood by the Apostles and early disciples, and as they were embodied in the New Testament—and modern theology, which was the result of the elaboration of these truths under the guidance of the Church down through the ages. Since the Catholic Church was a living organism, its thinking about God and about man's relation to his eternal destiny must be something both dynamic and evolving. It began with certain basic truths about the nature of God and His dealings with man, which were revealed in and through the Church and whose principles were unchangeable. Yet the cultural atmosphere in which these truths were appreciated and lived was continually changing. In each age the Church had to be alert to restate or even rephrase them, so that they would be understood by the current generation. On both counts, the Catholic thinker today ran headlong up against a certain type of intransigent thinking.

This position was typified by Cardinal Ruffini of Palermo, who, though specializing in biblical research as a young priest, turned against the modern trend. He felt that the Bible must be interpreted in what could only be termed a fundamentalist sense—that to admit of any change in our appreciation of the words and deeds of Christ was to betray the Church by acknowledging that its teachers had been wrong. In an article published on page one of *L'Osservatore Romano* in June, 1961, he demonstrated the lengths to which some Italian theologians were prepared to go. The subject was Pope Pius XII's emancipating encyclical on the study of the scriptures, called "Divino Afflante Spiritu" and published in 1943. In it Pope Pius had written:

In the words and writings of the ancient Oriental authors, the literal sense does not appear with as much clarity as it does in writers of our times. What they—the authors of the Bible—intended to signify by their words cannot be determined solely by the laws of grammar or of philology. It is absolutely necessary that the exegete go back to the manner of thinking of the Orient in those far centuries, so that, helping himself *with the resources of history, of archaeology, of ethnology, and of the other sciences,* he may discern and recognize what literary genres the authors of that ancient age wished to use or actually did employ. . . . The exegete cannot determine *a priori* what were the forms of speech and expression used by these authors. He can only do this by the attentive study of the ancient literatures of the Orient.

In direct contradiction of this and literally rejecting Pius XII's words, Cardinal Ruffini wrote:

How can one suppose that the Church has during nineteen centuries presented the Divine Book to its children without knowing the literary genre in which it was composed, if this is the key to exact interpretation? Such an assertion becomes all the more absurd when one takes into account that a large number of these superior-minded critics not only call for new applications of the theory of literary genres in regard to the inspired books but remit to the future a definitive explanation; that is to say, to the time when one will come to understand better, *through the study of history, of archaeology, of ethnology, and of the other sciences,* the manner of speaking and writing of the ancients, particularly the Orientals.

What bothers one about this attack, which called the teaching of Pius XII "absurd," was the fact that in Rome, under the pretense of defending an endangered orthodoxy, it was possible publicly to criticize a solemn pontifical document—but only if you happened to be a member of the right team. The experiences of the Jesuit Father Lombardi, who made some mild suggestions for a reform of the papal household and the internationalization of the Curia, provided a case in point. His book was immediately withdrawn from circulation, and he was at once sent back to his Institute for "A Better World" in Marino and told to stay there. On the other hand, an outrageous pamphlet on the biblical question by Monsignor Spadafora was printed several weeks before the Council opened and widely circulated among those bishops known to be favorable to the intransigent position in this matter. The brochure, less articulate and much more confused than the original attack on the Biblical Institute by Monsignor Romeo, contained two articles originally published in Rovigo and a third prepared for (but never printed in) *Divinitas.* Despite its hysterical approach, it may be said to have done some good in that it inspired a clear-cut, precisely worded reply from the Biblical Institute in French, German, Spanish and English, that was sent to the bishops gathered for the Council. As for the author, not a word critical of him was issued by Curial offices.

It has been said that the most important factor in the formation of the rigid or closed ecclesiastical mind was the conviction, explicitly formulated in Italian seminaries, that the function of the theologian was to preserve Catholic doctrine from the least taint of change or error. "No heresy has ever originated in Italy" was the erroneous but persuasive axiom used in inculcating this conviction. A second factor was a method of instruction that was essentially a lecture-memory exercise, the student being trained to absorb attentively the words of the professor, to analyze by a rigidly logical interpretation of the terms the significance of the doctrine being explained, and, finally, to repeat verbatim the text of the lectures or of the manual in use. While the accusation that the medieval scholastic theologians spent their time arguing over the number of angels who could dance on the point of a needle was obviously absurd, since it confused two orders of reality—the spiritual and the material—which those same scholastics, as philosophers, carefully distinguished, it was indicative of the extreme use to which Aristotelian logic had been, and was still being, put by such theologians. They dealt in propositions that must be either true or false. Having reduced the teachings of Christ to logical concepts, they proceeded to draw conclusions—always on a logical plane, of course—that frequently took no account of the logic of facts and events. When they encountered scriptural passages or historical events that embarrassingly failed to accord with their logical conclusions, they blindly forced the issue. Thus, in the matter of the seven sacraments, which was now an uncontroverted doctrine of Catholic belief, these theologians maintained that all seven sacraments were specifically instituted by Christ, and were given to the Church as instruments of grace in the very form and manner in which they were administered today. This thesis, however, was by no means undisputed. One school of thought, for example, was convinced that there was no certain evidence of the existence of the rite of the anointing of a dying person until about the sixth century. As a matter of fact, Pope Leo the Great, in the fifth century, though he twice discussed the way in which a priest was to minister to the dying, said not a word about anointing—and he was a traditionalist, bent on promoting uniformity of practice. There was, indeed, no agreement on the number of the sacraments until the thirteenth century, when the Church set the number at seven. This view of events made no impression on the Roman theologian, who still required his students to memorize texts asserting that Jesus personally instituted all seven sacraments in the way in which they were now administered.

To take some of the starch out of possible recalcitrants, the Curialists insisted upon the use of Latin as the language of the Council. What was being aimed at, again, was a logical exposition or formulation of doctrine that could be nailed down tight and recorded in a dead tongue. But in actual fact Latin was only the language of the Western, Roman, or Latin Church. The Greek, Slavic, Coptic, and other Eastern rites each had their own language. And it became ironically clear as the Council sessions began, that Italian prelates were by no means as good Latinists as was commonly believed, and that the stilted type of purified Renaissance

Latin used for official documents was not really much more than a cultured doggerel. When it came to Ciceronian or patristic Latin, many Northern Europeans made the Italians sound like stuttering chickadees.

One great unknown element in the preparatory stage of the Council was the part that would be played by the North American bishops. They seemed at first, with few exceptions, to show little interest in or understanding of the issues at stake. In Europe they were regarded as a hard-working, ingenuous, but theologically deficient lot. Many of them seemed to feel, for example, that the current liturgical movement, which went to the very heart of the attempt to renew the inner life of the Church, was for the most part merely a fad—a matter of introducing the dialogue mass, abolishing Latin in favor of the vernacular in liturgical rites, and allowing laymen to read the Epistle and the Gospel. A few of them even seemed to think that it was only a question of rubrics. Actually, the liturgical movement meant much more; namely, a return to the great sense of mystery with which the Apostles and Fathers of the early Church announced the good news of the Kingdom of God founded in the world by Jesus Christ. The early Christian apologists stressed the tremendously mysterious nature of a religion that maintained that its founder was both God and man at the same time, that he had submitted to death on the Cross to redeem all mankind from sin, and that he had established an organization in which could be found forgiveness of sins and participation in the life of God through the reception of Christ in the eucharist. To the tough, cynical Greeks and Romans of the ancient world, such ideas were ridiculous, as St. Paul admitted, and they also proved a stumbling block to the adherents of Judaism, from which Christianity sprang. The modern Roman-trained theologian tended to teach these all but incredible truths as if they were everyday facts. He simplified the life and teachings of Jesus so that any Sunday-school teacher could break them down into easily-digested stories for children. Despite a great display of Latin learning, he apparently believed that these truths should be taught to modern man on that level, as if they were so many commonplace happenings.

The leading figure in the group of intransigents—or "prophets of doom," to use the pope's phrase—was Cardinal Alfredo Ottaviani. Born in 1890 in Rome, with the black dirt of Trastevere (as a local saying goes) beneath his feet, he was ordained a priest in 1916. A teaching career followed in Roman seminaries and universities. Learned in canon law, he taught this subject for 20 years at the Lateran University. He was made a domestic prelate while working in the Secretariat of State and became Assessor of the Holy Office in 1935, as a protégé of Cardinal Canali. In 1953 Pius XII elevated him to the rank of cardinal-deacon, and in the same year he became pro-secretary of the Holy Office. In 1959 he was appointed secretary of the Congregation of the Holy Office by John XXIII (who was President of the same body). It was not until 1962, oddly enough, that Cardinal Ottaviani became a bishop—for in that year Pope John elevated all the cardinal-deacons to the episcopate. This brilliant career could be summed up in three words: a Curia man. Cardinal Ottaviani was astute, scholarly, and at times witty. For years he had run a school within the Vatican grounds, as well as a summer *colonia* at Frascati, for poor children from the *borgate* outside the Vatican walls. Like all his fellow-bishops throughout the world, he was a strong opponent of communism. He had published a first-class textbook on the Church and public law, and in 1961 a book of addresses entitled *Il Baluardo* ("The Bulwark").

In 1961 he and his conservative colleague, Cardinal Siri of Genoa, were prevented by the Vatican from publicly interfering in local Italian politics. When the Christian Democratic Party first moved into coalition with the Nenni Socialists (in 1961), the Vatican prepared for the reaction to this event by advising that no Italian bishops were to make public comments on the matter. Cardinal Ottaviani failed to heed this admonition and spoke out against the move. To his considerable surprise, he was told the very next day that, as an Italian prelate, he too was required to show greater forbearance with regard to Italy's political affairs. Apparently Cardinal Siri decided to show his disdain for this Vatican injunction by departing from his usual custom of publishing, during the Lenten season, a long commentary denouncing leftist trends in social and economic affairs in Italy. Instead he put out a pious epistle on "Visits to the Blessed Sacrament," which was so out of keeping with his usual line that its unexpected publication, prominently displayed on page one of *L'Osservatore Romano,* was interpreted as a gentle if not pointed rebuke.

The third member of the group, Cardinal Ruffini, was an excellent Latinist, as well as a caustic and clever prelate. He was the kind of churchman who forgot nothing he was ever taught but, since becoming a teacher himself, resisted learning anything more. He made his studies at the Pontifical Biblical Institute some forty years ago, and taught scripture before his elevation to the hierarchy as archbishop of Palermo in Sicily. One of his pupils, who later became Cardinal Alfrink of Utrecht, disagreed with his former teacher at the Council in the debate on theology (see page 79). Other members of the intransigent group included Archbishop Dino Staffa, secretary of the Congregation for Seminaries and Universities, Archbishop Pietro Parente already mentioned, and Monsignor Antonio Piolanti, Rector Magnificus of the Lateran University.

During the last fifteen years, it was Cardinal Ottaviani who took the lead among these men and their like-minded associates in the role of what might be called a twentieth century "hammerer of heretics." In their view, while preserving the great heritage of the Church it was more important to caution and to condemn than to encourage and to persuade.* In an age in which religion had suffered unprecedented losses and inroads, the wisdom of their position was at least open to question. One fact was clear, however. Their view was not consistent with that of the present Visible Head of the Church, who summoned the Council, as he said, not to condemn, but to proclaim the Church's ecumenical and pastoral role.

As the opening date for the Council neared, from the four corners of the world men of every breed and circumstance began to converge on Rome. They were the sons of peasants and princes, of bankers and laborers, of tribal chiefs and trolley-car conductors. Emanuel Mabathoana, bishop of Maseru, was the grandson of the "Lion of the Mountain," chief of the Basutos in South Africa; Bishop Dlamini of Umzimkulu was a member of the royal family of Natal. Cardinal Gracias saw the light of day in the slums of Karachi, Cardinal Siri's father was a Genoese longshoreman, and Archbishop Kominek of Wroclaw was the son of a Silesian miner. The youthful-looking Philippe Nguyen Kim Dien worked as a street-cleaner and rag-picker before entering the seminary; since becoming bishop of Cantho, Vietnam, he had given up the episcopal palace as too luxurious for a poor country. When a friend saw him driving his tiny 4-horsepower French CV, he remarked: "We do not know what he has sold or pawned to buy that, after all his charities, but you can be sure that in this land of mandarins the image he presents is revolutionary."

Bishop Botero Salazar of Medellín, Colombia, had turned his palace, a gift from his family, into a school for workers, installing himself in a shed in one of the *barrios* on the edge of town, while the auxiliary bishop of Lyons, Monsignor Ancel, lived with a group of priests in a *banlieu* of Lyons and supported himself by part-time work in a basket-factory. In Argentina, a group of prelates had become known as the "bishops with wooden crosses and croziers." In Lima, Peru in 1959, Bishop Dammert Bellido of Cajamarca declared: "One area in which, with the best of

* In a radio interview (December 1962) Cardinal Ottaviani replied to a question regarding his position as leader of a "conservative group of Council fathers" as follows: "My personal position is that of a man who has, from the nature of his office, the duty to keep the deposit of faith intact and who, at the same time, must leave full freedom to the progress which is necessary to better clarify, understand and expose Catholic teaching. Let us never forget: not all that is new is true and good merely because it is new. There are some opinions in theology today which are, if not false, at least debatable. In this situation, it is a completely positive action to defend the basic data of Holy Scripture and of Tradition, to avoid permitting some truths of the faith to be obscured, under the pretext of progress and adaptation."

intentions, we still provoke scandal in some and disgust in others is in the lack of simplicity in the decoration of our churches and the riches with which we surround our ceremonies. In all innocence, we stretch our resources to obtain the costliest ornaments, which are in doubtful taste to begin with, while at the same time children of God are suffering from hunger, sickness, and misery. This is a true cause for scandal in the Church today. Sumptuosity is not in accord with the poverty of our age."

In Chile, Bishop Larrain Errázuriz of Talca handed over 366 acres of his episcopal domain at Los Sillos to eighteen impoverished families. Cardinal Silva Henriquez of Santiago had a similar project in hand for slum-dwellers. Bishop Jobst, vicar apostolic of the Kimberleys in Australia, bought 400,000 acres of semi-desert land for the economic rehabilitation of the nation's aborigines. At Trivandrum in India, Coadjutor-Bishop Pereira visited every fishing village in his diocese on the coast of Kerala, in an attempt to introduce a program of technical, economic and social development. In San Antonio, Texas, Archbishop Lucey became the champion of social justice for the *braceros* or Mexican "wet-backs" who came to the United States seasonally for farm work.

Of the intellectuals among the conciliar Fathers, Cardinals Frings of Cologne, Liénart of Lille, Ruffini of Palermo, Alfrink of Holland and Meyer of Chicago had licentiates or doctorates in scripture. Cardinal Tisserant, who was dean of the Sacred College, had the distinction of having been elected a member of the French Academy. When Cardinal Montini left Rome to become the new archbishop of Milan, it was noted with amazement that he took away with him ninety cases full of books. Bishop Wright of Pittsburgh and Archbishop Hallinan of Atlanta had acquired a reputation for their learning and wide knowledge of the social and political problems of the day. Cardinal König of Vienna was the author of a three-volume work on comparative religion. Bishop Weber of Strasbourg was noted for contributing frequent articles and scholarly reviews to French ecclesiastical journals. Cardinals Bea and Suenens were theologians in their own right, and so were Bishops Dwyer of Leeds and Philbin of Down and Connor.

The flocks of the more than 2,500 bishops who attended the Council ranged from the smallest—that of Bishop Gunnarson, vicar apostolic at Holar, Iceland, where there were 806 Catholics cared for by one diocesan and 8 religious priests, to the largest—that of Cardinal Meyer of Chicago, who had 2,119,000 Catholics, 3 auxiliary bishops, 1,264 diocesan, and 1,549 religious clergy under his care.

Under John XXIII, the more homely but universal aspect of the pope's role as a pastor came to the fore. Pope John said frequently that his first love in the priesthood had always been the pastorate; and it was becoming noticeable that more and more bishops were being appointed who were former pastors of churches, unlike earlier days when the majority came from the ranks of seminary professors and diocesan administrators. In the actual ministry, greater attention was now being paid to what might be called the dynamic sociology of pastoral activity. In Bologna, infested after the war with a militant communist worker movement, Cardinal Lercaro organized his "flying squad" of priests and catechists. Similar efforts were made by Archbishop Morcillo Gonzales in Zaragoza and by Archbishop Modrego y Casáus in the down-trodden suburbs of Barcelona. Bishop Baccino of San José de Mayo, Uruguay, devoted a pastoral letter to the need for "an awareness of modern reality in adapting our pastoral efforts to the necessities of the hour." On this score, bishops all over the world had been stirring themselves to prayerful activity, revolutionizing methods of catechetical instruction, injecting new life into the liturgy, and combining spiritual realism with the use of modern techniques in the lay apostolate.

On the strictly spiritual level, Archbishop Kiwanuka of Rubaga in Africa himself presided and preached at the annual retreats for his clergy; Archbishop Rayappan of Pondicherry and Cuddalore traveled through much of his native India similarly employed. In almost every diocese in the world special attention was being paid to the foundation and guidance of seminaries, and specialists were engaged in soliciting vocations for the priesthood and religious life. Bishop Raymond of Allahabad was an expert catechist and Archbishop Gopu was himself director of the catechetical center at Hyderabad. Bishops Raspanti of Morón and Kémérer of Posadas in Argentina rivalled Cardinal Lercaro and Bishop Himmer of Tournai in publishing up-to-date directories for the celebration of mass and other liturgical functions. Archbishop Angelo Fernandes, coadjutor bishop of New Delhi, himself served as commentator for the Holy Week services being celebrated by his archbishop, Joseph Alexander Fernandes. In West Bengal, Bishop La Ravoire Morrow of Krishnagar assisted at the mass chanted in Bengali, while Bishop Van Bekkum of Ruteng in Indonesia was not only a theoretician of the liturgical renewal, having taken a leading part in the Liturgical Congress at Assisi in 1956, but he adapted the ceremonies of confirmation to local tribal customs, and was greeted by baptized and unbaptized alike with immense joy. (They kissed his episcopal ring with their noses when welcoming him to the "parish councils," which replaced the traditional tribal gatherings and were usually preceded by a chanted mass in the local dialect and two or three hours of religious-inspired dancing.) Archbishop Zoungrana of Ouagadougou made a special study of the manhood initiation rites among the local tribes, with the idea of eventually Christianizing them; and Bishop Chitsulo of Dedza, Nyasaland, completed a translation and adaptation of the Roman ritual into the Cinyanja language. Bishop Van Cauwelaert of Inongo in the Congo was the leader among African bishops determined to adapt the liturgy to local customs, beginning with a consecration of the new-born to the Creator, prayers and supplications for the sick and dying, and a wake and funeral rites. "We are looking for courageous directions from the Council that will assure us of a true and realistic liturgical renewal," he wrote in his last pastoral letter before the Council met.

In the modern political arena, a number of bishops have played an active and dangerous role by insisting upon civil liberty for their people. Archbishop Pérez Serantes and Bishop Boza Masvidal were expelled from Cuba, and Bishops Panal Ramirez and Reilly were caught in the Trujillo reign of terror in the Dominican Republic. Bishop Ferreira Gomes was exiled from Portugal for supporting the right of workers to organize in political associations, as was Bishop Pildáin y Zapiáin of the Canary Islands because he supported resistance to the state-controlled unions in Spain. In the foreground, of course, were the heroic figures of Cardinal Wyszynski and the Polish bishops, as well as the whole Catholic episcopate of the "Church of Silence" not only in Europe but in the Orient. More recently too, in Moslem countries, new waves of persecution had broken out against the Church, requiring heroic courage and astuteness on the part of the bishops.

In the cause of social justice and peace on both a local and worldwide scale, Archbishop Duval of Algiers had taken a particularly bold stand, while Cardinal Döpfner in Berlin, Auxiliary Bishop Gutiérrez Granier in La Paz, and Patriarch Meouchi in Lebanon helped to pacify dangerous national crises. And in the new nations, both native and foreign-born bishops played a part in encouraging and helping to direct the forces striving for independence. In South Africa Archbishops Hurley of Durban and McCann of Capetown; Archbishop Rummel of New Orleans and Archbishop Leonard of Madhurai, took strong stands against governmental pressure and local racially-inspired drives.

Three outstanding bishops represented the Church of the Ukraine in exile—Archbishop Hermaniuk of Canada, Bishop Kornyljak of Germany and Archbishop Senyshyn of the United States, while Bishop Sipovic stood for the scattered Bielorussians and Bishop Brizgys the Baltic peoples. Among the thirteen Armenian bishops of Egypt, Liban, Turkey and Iran, Bishop Zohrabian was the outstanding leader, while Patriarch Meouchi not only represented the Maronites of Lebanon and Patriarch Maximos IV Saigh the Melchites, but they brought to the Council the solid, ancient traditions of the Eastern Church with its liturgy and theology reaching all the way back to apostolic times.

Side by side with the European and American bishops, whose present status, in spite of all the economic, social and political ills plaguing the western world, was both stable and assured, the vast throngs of African, Asian, and Oceanic prelates, both native and missionary, brought with them to the Council an experience and determination rivalling the enthusiasm and drive manifested by the first Apostles and their immediate successors. It was for this reason that Pope John's optimistic and increasingly positive predictions that the Council would renew the face of the Church seemed to be more than justified. As the great day of the solemn assembly's opening approached, he had reason to believe that his Council would indeed restore "the simple and pure lines that the face of the Church of Jesus had at its birth."

THE COUNCIL OPENS

To anyone who had the good fortune to be standing in front of the bronze doors leading into the papal palace, on the north side of St. Peter's Square, at eight o'clock on the morning of Thursday, October 11, 1962, there was suddenly revealed a dazzling spectacle. At that moment, two papal gendarmes, resplendent in parade uniform of white trousers and black topboots, coats, and busbies, slowly swung the great doors open, exposing to a portion of the crowd row upon a row of bishops, clad in flowing white damask copes and mitres, descending Bernini's majestic Scala Regia from the papal apartments. In rows of sixes, an apparently inexhaustible phalanx of prelates filed out of the Vatican palace, swung to their right across St. Peter's Square, then wheeled right again, to mount the ramplike steps leading into the basilica. Every now and then, this white mass was dotted with the black cassock, full beard, and cylindrical headdress of an oriental bishop, and here and there with the bulbous gold crown and crossed pectoral reliquaries of a bishop of the Byzantine rite. Toward the end came the scarlet ranks of the Sacred College of Cardinals. Finally, the pope appeared, carried, in deference to the wishes of his entourage, on the *sedia gestatoria,* and looking rather timid, perhaps even frightened—as he always did when first mounting this oriental contraption—but gradually warming to the mild acclamation of the overawed crowd, and gently smiling and quietly weeping as he was carried undulantly forward, blessing the onlookers. At the entrance to the Council hall in the basilica, the procession halted while the pope dismounted and walked the length of the nave to the Confession of St. Peter.

Before the high altar the pope had ordered the substitution of a simpler, more informal style of throne for the pretentious "doctoral" throne, with a red damask backdrop and canopy, that the organizers of the Council had thought proper. The significance of this was soon made clear by the pope's opening speech, which stressed the Council's pastoral or ministering role over the dogmatic or condemnatory approach. After the traditional hymn *Veni Creator Spiritus,* a solemn mass of the Holy Spirit was celebrated, in which the Epistle and the Gospel were chanted in both Greek and Latin, to signify the unity of both parts of the Church, East and West. The celebrant was the elderly but vigorous Cardinal Tisserant, bearded dean of the College of Cardinals. A touch of Byzantine court ceremonial followed the mass, as the cardinals mounted the steps of the papal throne one by one, with their scarlet mantles trailing behind them, to make their traditional obeisance to the See of Peter. After the bishops' solemn profession of faith in unison, the recitation of the litany of the Saints and more prayers from the Greek rite, Pope John began to deliver his sermon.

In clear resonant tones that could be distinctly heard throughout the basilica, the pope, after a few introductory remarks, said that he was tired of listening to the prophets of doom among his advisers. "Though burning with zeal," he said, these men "are not endowed with very much sense of discretion or measure." They maintained that "our era, in comparison with past eras, is getting worse, and they behaved as though they had learned nothing from history, which is nevertheless the great teacher of life." They were, he said, under the illusion that "at the time of the former Councils, everything was a triumph for the Christian idea and way of life and for true religious liberty," and he added, "We feel that we must disagree with these prophets of doom, who are always forecasting disaster, as though the end of the world were at hand," and continually warning him, "in the course of our pastoral office," that the modern world was "full of prevarication and ruin."

As the listeners heard these words, their attention focussed unconsciously on the face of Cardinal Ottaviani, secretary of the Congregation of the Holy Office, who was seated at the pope's immediate right; on the face of the recently consecrated seventy-eight-year-old Archbishop Enrico Dante, the papal master of ceremonies, at the pope's left and half a step to the rear; on Cardinal Siri, of Genoa, and on Cardinal Ruffini, of Palermo, sitting in the tier reserved for the Sacred College along the main aisle of the basilica; on Pericle Felici, Secretary General of the Council; on Pietro Parente, assessor of the Holy Office; on Dino Staffa, of the Congregation of Seminaries and Universities; on Pietro Palazzini, of the Congregation of the Council; and on the other Roman monsignors who stood on the various rungs of the ladder that constituted the *cursus honorum* of the Curia. These were the faces of some of the prophets of doom of whom the Holy Father was speaking, since they were the advisers he saw regularly on purely pastoral matters. (It was well known that these doomlike sentiments were not shared by the Secretary of State,

Cardinal Cicognani; by the prefect of the Congregation for Propagating the Faith, Cardinal Agagianian; by the secretary of the Congregation for the Oriental Churches, Cardinal Testa; or by the secretary of the Consistorial Congregation, Cardinal Confalonieri.) The pope then proceeded to outline, serenely and optimistically, what he expected of the Council and why he had summoned it. "Divine Providence," he said, "is leading us to a new order of human relations." It was imperative for the Church "to bring herself up to date where required," in order to spread her message "to all men throughout the world." While the Church must "never depart from the sacred patrimony of truth received from the Fathers," she must "ever look to the present, to new conditions and new forms of life, introduced into the modern world, which have opened new avenues to the Catholic apostolate."

Then came the phrases, so pregnant with meaning, that either alarmed or gratified his listeners, depending on their theological outlook. The pope said that he had not called the Council to discuss "one article or another of the fundamental doctrine of the Church . . . which is presumed to be well known and familiar to all; for this, a Council was not necessary." Thus were ruled out the hopes of those who had expected the Council to proclaim some new dogma, isolated from the rest of Christian doctrine, in the manner of the previous Ecumenical Council, in 1869–70, which concentrated on the dogma of papal infallibility. No, said the pope; "the world expects a step forward toward doctrinal penetration and the formation of consciences." This must be "in conformity with authentic doctrine," of course, but it "should be studied and expounded according to the methods of research and literary forms of modern thought." In other words, doctrine was to be made more intelligible to contemporaries in the light of advances in biblical, theological, philosophical, and historical knowledge.

He next touched on a subject that was almost taboo in traditionalist Catholic theological circles, saying, "The substance of the ancient doctrine of the *depositum fidei* is one thing; the way in which it is expressed is another." That is, Catholic doctrine remained the same in substance, but the formulations of it varied and were not to be regarded as unalterable ends in themselves. The task of the Council, he told the assembled prelates, was to find the best formulas for our time, without being too hidebound or showing a too slavish respect for those of a previous age. He further emphasized the pastoral rather than the doctrinal note, by declaring, "Nowadays, the bride of Christ prefers to make use of the medicine of mercy rather than that of severity. She considers that she meets the needs of the present day by demonstrating the validity of her teaching rather than by condemnation." This was an unmistakable disavowal of the inquisitorial and condemnatory approach of the Holy Office.

Finally, the pope turned his attention to the problem of Christian unity. "The entire Christian family has not yet fully attained the visible unity in truth" desired by Christ, he said, and the Catholic Church "therefore considers it her duty to work actively so that there may be fulfilled the great mystery of that unity." He said that the key to "the brotherly unity of all"—embracing not only Christians but "those who follow non-Christian religions"—was "the fullness of charity," or love. Thus Pope John put his seal on the methods and goals of the ecumenical or worldwide movement for reunion and on Catholic participation in it.

This inaugural address to the Council, carefully worded and balanced, and containing a bold message of renewal and reform, marked the end of the closed mentality that had characterized not a few Catholic bishops and theologians since the sixteenth century. Whether this message reached all the prelates to whom it was addressed, or would be heeded by all it did reach, was another matter; one could not cease being a prophet of doom overnight. But the Council as a whole received the pope's message gladly. Whatever changes were to come must be made by the bishops themselves. In calling the Council and in addressing it as he did in his opening speech, the pope made the great essential contribution which no one else could possibly have made. After his address, John XXIII did not enter the Council hall again until the next-to-last day of the session. He watched and heard the daily proceedings on closed-circuit television in his private apartments.

Despite the brilliance of the opening ceremonial, it was felt that there was an incongruity between the outward show, largely reflecting the court etiquette of a by-gone age, and the pastoral purpose of the Council. Some Fathers regretted, in particular, that they were mere passive auditors of a polyphonic symphony, magnificently chanted as this was, instead of being allowed to join the celebrant in a mass that would have given better expression to the corporate feeling of the assembly. As if to compensate for such defects and forestall misapprehensions about a "rubber-stamp" Council that might have been forming, Pope John took great pains on the following days to create the "right atmosphere" by talking to the diplomatic corps and special missions, the press, and the observer-delegates, in a number of intimate gatherings held in the Sistine Chapel and the Hall of the Consistory. Speaking to the journalists (October 13th) before the great mural of Michelangelo's "Last Judgment," Pope John effectively reminded his hearers of their responsibility to report the truth and of the importance of the press in the modern world. Referring to the temptation of journalists to tamper with the truth, he departed from his text momentarily to remind them that he had said "temptation," and was not accusing them of actual fabrication.

The most touching encounter was unquestionably the one which the pope and Cardinal Bea had with the observer-delegates, representing various non-Roman churches and religious bodies, whose presence at the Council was unprecedented in the annals of Roman Catholicism. It was the fruit of months of delicate negotiations and a visible token of the new policy toward ecumenism and the problem of reunion which the pope had adopted. Departing from custom in a precedent-shattering move, the pope received the delegates in the Hall of the Consistory, appropriately, and then sat down with them in a square, in much the same way as he was accustomed to sit with the cardinals in consistory. It was a small but significant detail that he sat on the same kind of chair as the delegates, rather than on his throne. The impression made by this brotherly gesture was immediate and lasting. After a few words by Monsignor Willebrands, secretary of the Secretariat for Promoting Christian Unity, who introduced the delegates as "our brethren in Christ," Pope John began his talk.

Speaking in French, he assured them of his heartfelt welcome and his hope that their presence would hasten the day when Christ's prayer, "That they may be one," might be fully realized. If they could read his heart, he said, they would perhaps have a better idea of what he was thinking than from his words. Charity was the key to progress in the ecumenical sphere, as his past experiences in Sofia, Istanbul and Athens had shown. He said it was pointless to engage in controversy. What was needed was mutual understanding and tolerance: "Though we did not discuss, we loved each other. . . ." As for the ultimate goal of reunion, "the Christian virtue of patience must not be allowed to harm the virtue of prudence, which is equally fundamental." The important thing, he said, was that they had come and were there, for which he could only say, repeating the words of the Psalmist, "May God be blessed every day!"

On the following Monday (October 15th), Cardinal Bea, speaking before the observers at a reception in the Hotel Columbus, addressed them as "my brethren in Christ." This phrase, he said, reminded him of the immeasurable grace of Christian baptism, which had formed bonds that were "stronger than all our divisions." The awareness of these bonds had moved their parent bodies to send them to Rome where Pope John had created the Secretariat for Promoting Christian Unity so that non-Catholic communities could be in a better position to follow the work of the Council. It was to be regretted, of course, that not all were able to come, he said, referring to the absence of the Greek Orthodox Church. But this should be regarded as a mere temporary setback. Then, after explaining that the Secretariat was at their disposition, and would arrange to see that the observers were kept abreast of developments by periodic meetings, Cardinal Bea said that he wanted the delegates to speak their minds freely with regard to the course of the Council, letting the Secretariat know their criticisms, suggestions, or desires. He could not always guarantee a solution, but he assured them that he would do whatever was possible to meet their wishes. Dr. Edmund Schlink, observer-delegate for the Evangelical Churches of Germany, replied to the cardinal in the name of the delegates, stating that he had been particularly impressed, thus far, by two things: the insistence of both the pope and the cardinal that a distinction must be made between revealed truth and its formulation, and the progress already made by the Church of Rome in biblical studies. Bishop Antony, observer-delegate for the European exarchate of the Russian Orthodox Church, associated himself with the remarks of Dr. Schlink.

The observer-delegates were one of the pleasant surprises of the Council. All the important non-Roman communions except the Greek Orthodox, the World Baptist Alliance, and certain fundamentalist churches, were represented. They held the status of honored guests in "the house of their father," to use the pope's expression, being handed the same secret schemata as the Fathers, allotted the best seats in the house, and provided with a translation service that was so sorely missed by some of their hosts. They were admitted to all the daily general congregations, and to as many meetings of the commissions as they wished to attend. Nothing like it had ever happened before in the history of the Catholic Church. Though all this made the observers reluctant to say anything that might embarrass their hosts, they were clearly grateful for the courtesy and attention shown them. Their sentiments were summed up, in part, by the famous Protestant theologian Oscar Cullmann, professor at the Sorbonne and the University of Basel, who disclosed in an interview (November 23rd) that he was especially impressed by the freedom of the debates and the voicing of diametrically opposite concepts of fundamental religious positions. But he also noted the Fathers' absolute agreement on the articles of the creed, and their unanimous loyalty to the Holy See. He said he could see large areas for agreement between Catholic, Protestant, and Orthodox thought on many dogmatic issues.

The appearance, at the last minute on October 12th, and contrary to everyone's expectations, of delegates from Moscow—the Archpriest Vitaly Borovoi and the Archimandrite Vladimir Kotlyarov—in their long black robes and high-crowned hats, created something of a sensation. Their arrival represented the first official connection between the Vatican and the Russian Church in hundreds of years. It was all the more remarkable in view of the fact that until very recently the Russians had been indulging in their usual innuendoes about the "power politics" of the Vatican. According to the Soviet news agency, Novosti, the Russian delegates expressed their pleasure at the "unaffected friendship" of the pope, but not everyone in Rome was pleased by their presence. The

Ukrainian bishops of the Byzantine-Slavic rite outside Russia—active participants in the Council—met to formulate a protest against Soviet persecution of the Church behind the Iron Curtain. The Vatican Secretariat of State persuaded the bishops to shelve the protest, but one of their number leaked it to the Italian press, and as a consequence Monsignor Willebrands had to clarify the position of the Church (in a press interview on November 23rd) by stating that the Russians were most welcome, that there had been no dealings with the Soviet government, and that their presence could not be interpreted as a political maneuver.

Close to a thousand reporters were on hand for the opening days of the Council. All the worldwide news services down to the Italian Communist daily *Unità* arranged for coverage. Little by little, however, the number of journalists dwindled, owing to the nature of the Council and to the manner in which press relations were handled under the rather dictatorial direction of Archbishop Felici, its Secretary General. The pope put at the disposal of the press the whole ground floor of the first building outside the Vatican on the Via della Conciliazione, but reporters were barred from the Council meetings as such and had to make do with distilled news contained in a daily bulletin prepared under the Secretary General's direction. Despite vociferous complaints from the press, this bulletin was often worded in such fashion that it seemed to be written in advance of the news it was reporting and dealt only in generalities, favoring the Curial line. Though the bulletin eventually became more informative,* it consistently disregarded the axiom that names and facts made news. Organized by members of the Curia, the Council was conducted in the strictest possible secrecy, but Italian commentators maintained that this only guaranteed the widest possible circulation for the Council's more intimate doings, and a pasquinade quickly made the rounds: "Why the great conciliar secrecy? Because secrets spread faster."

This challenge to journalistic enterprise was met by Paul Brindel, a free-lance American writer, who turned up in the back row of a choir during the Council mass on November 11th, as official Vatican photographs later revealed. (He had been interviewing some young Californians, protégés of Cardinal Agagianian, who were members of the Armenian choir, and somehow obtained a cassock, joined their ranks, marched past three cordons of Swiss guards and Vatican plainclothes operatives, and entered St. Peter's through the sacristy door.) The London *Tablet,* one of the oldest and best-informed Catholic weeklies, complained that the wording of one Council press release was couched in "English so peculiarly

---

* The Holy Office threatened to excommunicate the Press Office for revealing the name of one of the Fathers who had made a definite proposal—the only time such a lapse occurred—in its bulletin relating to the 29th General Congregation on November 28th. The name in question was that of Cardinal Ottaviani.

outrageous that one hardly knows whether to laugh or cry," and pointed out that in one document the word "condemn" appeared fifteen times in twenty-four pages, despite Pope John's inaugural address. It was not surprising that many applications for press credentials were lost, or that most reporters who obtained a blue leather *Permesso* found it to be next to worthless; it did not even help them buy tax-free Vatican City cigarettes.

Perhaps the most striking moment at each day's Council meeting was the fifteen-minute period before the Fathers came to order in St. Peter's and got down to the day's business. By that time most of the prelates were at or near their places in the two long serrated banks of benches covered in green, as well as in the six galleries between the pillars, of the central nave of the basilica. The episcopal purple contrasted here and there with a dash of the white, grey, brown or black religious habit worn by a Dominican, Franciscan, or Eastern-rite bishop, and with the brilliant scarlet of cardinalatial robes.

Cardinals and bishops could be seen stopping one another in the aisles or on the benches, or being accosted by some eager ecclesiastic. Other prelates used this period for meditation and prayer, and many of them called this and the period which followed their favorite moments of the day. Precisely at nine, as the organ sounded, the Fathers seemed to come to order simultaneously and were all at their places. When the mass, which was said each day in a different rite by different Fathers in turn, was celebrated in Latin, the whole congregation of prelates and bishops answered the prayers in dialogue form. When mass was conducted by one of the Eastern bishops, a lector explained the diverse actions from the pulpit. Usually the Oriental liturgies required the assistance of a choir which was supplied by one of the appropriate colleges in Rome, such as the Russicum, the Maronite, the Greek, or the Armenian. During mass very few breviaries were in evidence, for the Fathers felt that active participation in the official prayer of the Church was an essential part of their conciliar activity. On his return to the United States, Cardinal Ritter of St. Louis referred to the 26 different rites used at these masses. Few bishops, he said, had any detailed knowledge of these different rites, let alone the opportunity to witness them. "And yet," he added, "the various rites have not only been tolerated but encouraged from apostolic times." Cardinal Ritter termed the whole experience "the grace of a lifetime."

The Council got under way at its first business session (1st General Congregation) on Saturday, October 13th, under the presidency of Cardinal Tisserant. The agenda called for the election of members to the various conciliar Commissions, ten in all, the successors to the Preparatory Commissions, which were to present the draft proposals for decrees (schemata) and consider the amendments proposed by the Council in the course of the debates. Sixteen members for each Commission were to be elected by the Council itself, while eight members would be appointed directly by the pope.

As soon as the Secretary General announced that the Council would proceed to the election, Cardinal Liénart of Lille rose and read a prepared statement in which he suggested that instead of voting immediately for the Commissions, the Fathers meet in national or regional caucuses and attempt to agree upon slates of candidates for the different Commissions. He pointed to the fact that there were already some 47 episcopal conferences in existence, most of whose members were then in Rome, so that it would not be difficult to proceed in this way. He added that it would result in a choice of better candidates because the Council would have more time to consider qualifications, than if it acted immediately on the basis of a list of the members of the various Preparatory Commissions, distributed to the Fathers at the beginning of the session.

Cardinal Frings of Cologne immediately seconded the proposal of Cardinal Liénart and said that he was doing so in the names of the other German-speaking cardinals. The vigorous applause that greeted this unexpected move made it perfectly clear what the sentiments of the assembly were, and no vote was deemed necessary. After the Secretary General had consulted for a moment and informed the Council which cardinals could be elected to the ten Commissions, Cardinal Tisserant adjourned the meeting, after it had sat for only a bare fifteen minutes.

The repercussions and implications of this dramatic turn of events were endlessly commented on by the press. The French periodical *Informations Catholiques Internationales* characterized it as one of the three "curtain-raisers" which set the tone of the first session of the Council in that it expressed the Council's "courage to act"; the other two being the pope's opening discourse ("courage to think") and the Council's message to the world ("courage to speak").

Between Saturday and Tuesday, October 16th, when the Council was scheduled to meet again to vote for the Commissions, the Fathers engaged in a feverish round of caucusing in an attempt to agree upon lists of candidates. If the bishops had been slow at first in getting to know each other, this consultation, by breaking down barriers, served to fuse them into a real corporate body. Different national or regional lists were drawn up—Asian, African, Spanish, Italian, French, etc.—but there was nothing exclusively nationalistic about them. A serious effort was made to make them as international as possible in fact, on the model of the Italian list which had been compiled along these lines at the suggestion of Cardinal Montini, seconded by Cardinal Siri. There were frequent consultations between various groups toward this end and in order to avoid giving the appearance that exclusive national blocks were being formed. The combined list known as the "Central and northern European" seems to have been the most influential when the voting actually began on October 16th.

A difficulty arose when it was realized that the two-thirds majority required by the regulations, in accordance with the usual practice in canon law, would be difficult to attain and might prolong the elections unduly.* Accordingly Cardinal Ottaviani moved, on the 16th, that a simple majority suffice for election. Since the Council was bound by the Rules of Procedure, an appeal was made by the Council to the pope, who ruled, before the first announcement of the results of the balloting on Saturday, October 20th, that a simple majority would suffice, in accordance with the wishes of the majority of the Council. This proved to be the first of a number of significant papal interventions designed to speed the work of the Council in the sense desired by the majority.

Because the electronic computer was not capable of handling the ballots, the latter had to be counted by hand. This was done by pressing into service seminarians who were attending the various ecclesiastical colleges and universities in Rome. When the Council reconvened on the 20th to hear the results, only the members of the first seven conciliar Commissions could be announced. The pope at once announced the appointment of the eight members for the Liturgical Commission reserved to him, so that that Commission could present the schema on the Liturgy which the Council was destined to take up on Monday, the 22nd. However, with respect to this and the other Commissions, he derogated from the rules by appointing nine instead of the required eight members, in order to give himself greater flexibility in controlling the composition of the Commissions. On the whole, the feeling at the time was that between the elected and appointed members, the Commissions turned out to be fairly representative of the Church, both as to schools of thought and nationalities, all things taken into consideration. The Council "did not vote for the Curia," although many of the same members served on both the Preparatory and corresponding conciliar Commission. The Italians felt slighted however that they had not won better representation in the voting. The pope used his prerogative to redress this balance, to a certain extent, and also to round out the geographical distribution of the membership. It was noted with some disquietude that the ninth member the pope added to the Commissions in most cases turned out to be the secretary of the corresponding Roman Congregation. The immediate purpose was apparently to provide a certain continuity of experience. But as the course of the Council proved, it was the majority of the Council

* Art. 39 of the Rules of Procedure provided that a two-thirds majority was required for the first and second balloting; only on the third balloting would a simple majority suffice.

itself that largely determined matters, not this or that member of the auxiliary Commissions.

After the results of the voting on the first seven commissions were made known to the Fathers on Saturday, October 20th, at the 3rd General Congregation, a document was distributed to the Fathers for their consideration. It was a "message to mankind" submitted by the Holy Father with the suggestion that it be amended, if necessary, and then proclaimed to the whole world as the first official act of the Council in session. The Fathers spent the whole morning considering amendments that ran all the way from requests to insert a clear and definitive condemnation of communism to an appeal not to say anything until the Council itself had produced its first accomplishment.

Bishop Guerry of Cambrai revealed the true genesis of this message of the conciliar Fathers to the world in an interview he gave soon after the close of the First Session. Early in September 1962, several bishops wrote to the Cardinal Secretary of State suggesting the capital importance of presenting a message to the world at its opening and before the debates on theological issues began. They later learned with considerable satisfaction that this idea had come from two Dominican theologians, Fathers Chenu and Congar, who had drawn up a document with this end in mind and sent it to six cardinals in different countries. The text, based on the principles of natural morality, was extremely interesting and conducive to a dialogue with non-Christians, but it was not suitable for a Council since it made no mention of Christ, the Savior. Hence it had to be abandoned.

Four French bishops were then asked to prepare a more suitable text. They did so from an entirely different angle, namely, the evidence for God's love for mankind. Their message drew attention to the Church's solicitude for the material and spiritual welfare, sufferings and aspirations of all people. But these cares and necessities were presented as proof of man's need of faithfulness to the Gospel of Christ and of Christ's love of man.

It was this message that was presented, at Pope John's insistence, first to the Cardinal Secretary of State, then to the Presidency of the Council, and finally to the Fathers for their discussion and approval. The only change admitted into the original text was a reference to the Blessed Virgin Mary, made at the suggestion of Bishop Ancel, auxiliary bishop of Lyons.

During the remainder of the First Session, the pope went about his daily tasks almost as if nothing extraordinary were taking place in the great basilica below his rooms. He issued a new constitution detailing the procedures to be followed on the death of a pope, apparently to avoid the kind of commercial exploitation that surrounded Pius XII's death and burial. He appointed new bishops, apostolic delegates and nuncios, and occasionally made a quick, unannounced visit to various parts of Rome. Though he made frequent allusions to his advanced age and the possibility of his passing on into eternity soon (it was commonly being said in Rome that he was to have an operation on December 10th), his manner was always cheerful and optimistic. He evidently felt that in summoning the Council, in addressing it as he did on opening day, and in starting the vast educative process which the conciliar dialogue had become, that he had carried out the mandate given him by the Church. The rest was up to the Holy Spirit.

DEBATE ON THE LITURGY

On Monday, October 22nd, in the 4th General Congregation, with Cardinal Gilroy presiding, discussion of the schema on the liturgy was inaugurated by Cardinal Larraona, chairman of the Preparatory Liturgical Commission, who described how the Church must keep abreast of the times by adapting its ceremonies to the necessities of individual nations and peoples. The secretary of the Commission, Father Antonelli, O.F.M., then gave a brief résumé of the eight chapters comprising the schema.

This chore accomplished, the Fathers turned their attention to the schema itself. Its proposals were both praised by the progressive-minded bishops as an important step toward the modernization of the Church, and condemned by the traditionalist bishops as undesirable, with a number of them manifesting a determined opposition to any change in the Church's rites and insisting especially on the retention of Latin in the mass as a guarantee of church unity.

The debate was initiated by Cardinal Frings of Cologne, followed by Cardinals Ruffini of Palermo, Lercaro of Bologna, Montini of Milan, Spellman of New York, Döpfner of Munich, Tatsuo Doi of Tokyo, Silva Henriquez of Santiago, Chile—all men of considerable experience, who in varying degrees had experimented with adapting the Church's liturgy and rites to the requirements of a people whose outlook, preoccupation with social and economic problems, and emotional and intellectual interests, differed immeasurably from those of past ages. The present liturgical practice of the Church was formulated for the most part at a time when an agricultural society was dominated by a monastic spirituality.

It was pointed out by Cardinals Frings, Lercaro, Montini, Döpfner and Doi that the schema generally was in keeping with the necessities of the hour, for it reflected Pope John's admonition that the Council should concern itself with concrete facts, with the pastoral and practical aspects of the Church's mission in the world. It was likewise asserted that it had an ecumenical appeal. The document was essentially "Christo-centric" in character, based on a scripture-centered piety and spirituality. However, it was quickly noted by the two German cardinals that the original document prepared by the Liturgical Commission had been altered; certain important sections dealing with the biblical foundations of the liturgy had been suppressed, while an admonition had been inserted cautioning that the schema laid down only general principles, for the application of which direct recourse must be had to the Holy See. As the speakers pointed out, this latter insertion, "by unknown hands," could strip the conciliar decisions of their effect, leaving the reforms considered so essential by the bishops at the mercy of certain Roman officials, as had been the case up to the present. Hence they asked that the original text be made the basis of the discussion.*

What a large number of bishops desired, and this was in accord with the first chapter of the schema, was that national or regional commissions be constituted that would have power to legislate the liturgical changes needed in different nations; and that at Rome, a central commission made up of experts and representatives of the regional groups should meet periodically to coordinate and supervise the work of these local groups. In the end, of course, the approbation of the Holy See would be required since it was the pope's prerogative and duty to safeguard the doctrine and practices of the Church. In effect, such an arrangement would however greatly reduce the powers of the Sacred Congregation of Rites, which up to now had been the sole legislative body controlling the Church's liturgy.

Involved in this discussion was a much deeper problem, namely that of the extent of the powers of bishops, both as the administrators of their sees and as a collegiate body in succession to the college of apostles. Roman officials had generally shown little liking for the national conferences of bishops that had been multiplying in various countries during the last fifty years. But as the recent constitution of such a body for the South American bishops, encouraged particularly by Archbishop Samorè of the Vatican Secretariat of State, had proved, such an agency could become an essential instrument for coordinating the Church's efforts to safeguard the faith and win back the disaffected in large areas of the world. The debate on the liturgy was thus the occasion for a preliminary skirmish in what would prove to be one of the essential problems before the Council.

A large amount of conciliar interest was aroused by the apparently innocuous question of the use of Latin in the western liturgy generally. Cardinals Ruffini and Spellman were the first to broach this topic, commenting on the schema's preface which laid down the principle that

* These changes were made *after* the text had been approved by the Central Commission and *before* it was circulated to the bishops.

the vernacular languages should be employed more generally in the mass and in the administration of the sacraments. The cardinal of New York expressed his opinion that, for the sake of unity and uniformity, the mass in Latin as it was now celebrated in the Roman rite should be retained intact. But he favored the use of the vernacular in most of the other ceremonies of the Church.

The apostolic delegate to the United States, Archbishop Vagnozzi, condemned the schema as badly constructed and full of loose definitions. He suggested that it be reworked on the basis of Pius XII's encyclical *Mediator Dei* and referred to the Theological Commission presided over by Cardinal Ottaviani.

Archbishop Dante, the papal master of ceremonies and secretary of the Congregation of Rites, rose to condemn the schema as both ill-conceived and too radical. In his opinion it should be reduced to a few simple principles. He stated that while the conferences of bishops in different countries might propose changes to the Holy See, only Rome could decide what should and should not be done. He insisted that the mass must continue to be said in Latin, as well as the breviary by all those bound to recite the divine office daily. He complained, finally, that the schema was incomplete for it said nothing about the veneration of relics. This latter point was seized upon by the Spanish prelate who followed him, Bishop García Martínez, who rose to ask how much longer the Church was to be embarrassed by such "relics" as Our Blessed Lady's milk and veil, St. Joseph's sandals, and the like. He had to be cut off by the President, Cardinal Gilroy, with *"Satis, satis,"* but not before he had managed to suggest that these things "be reverently buried and heard of no more" (*reverenter sepeliantur et deinceps nulla mentio fiat*).

The general discussion on the liturgy was continued on the following day, October 23rd, in the 5th General Congregation presided over by Cardinal Spellman. In his first speech on this theme, Cardinal Ottaviani cautioned the Fathers to be clear and precise in their employment of theological terminology. He questioned the propriety, for example, of the use of such terms as "the Paschal mysteries," and threw cold water on the notion that the liturgy ought to be a principal means of instructing the people, thus revealing his opposition to the whole tenor and purpose of the liturgical movement. He suggested that the schema ought to be referred to his own Theological Commission for an overhauling. Cardinal Ritter of St. Louis then spoke in favor of the schema, contenting himself with general observations about its implementation. He was followed by a succession of prelates (including Fares of Catanzaro, Italy, Argaya Goicoechea of Spain, and D'Avack of Camerino, Italy), who were critical of the schema.

At this point Cardinal Spellman allowed a narrator to speak for him, because the Fathers were having difficulty in understanding him. The Council then turned its attention to Chapter I of the schema, and the discussion was led off by Cardinal Ruffini who felt that the schema as a whole should be reconsidered in the light of the principles enunciated by *Mediator Dei,* in particular by the thought that the Holy Father was to remain judge in these matters and that he alone (through the Curia, of course) was to decide; hence conferences or groups of bishops were to have no competence. Great prudence must be exercised in introducing the use of vernacular languages because of the danger to the Church's unity.

Cardinal Feltin of Paris then spoke on a more practical level. He made it plain that most people today knew little about the Church. If by chance a poorly instructed Catholic or even non-Catholic layman should find himself at mass, it ought to be immediately obvious to him that he was witnessing something tremendously significant, holy and profound. But, as things were at the present time, said the cardinal, with the priest praying at the altar in Latin, accompanied by some of the congregation in a dialogue mass, or more commonly with the latter completely silent, the impression was easily given that the viewer was witnessing some kind of magical rites, good perhaps for those who understood them, but meaningless as far as the ordinary person was concerned. Actually the mass was the Word of God in action, bringing Christ to the hearts of the faithful by the prayers and lessons of the introductory or catechetical part, and then representing both the Last Supper and the sacrificial act of redemption on the Cross in the offertory, consecration and communion. The sanctification thus enacted should be immediately obvious to believer and unbeliever alike; but this could only be accomplished if both were fully aware of what was being said and done. For the actions as well as the words were sacramental signs. If the words had no immediate meaning for the people, they were failing in one of their primary objectives.

Cardinal McIntyre of Los Angeles spoke in favor of the unaltered retention of Latin in the mass and the Church's existing liturgical legislation. Cardinal Godfrey also opted for a conservative approach; as regards the use of Latin, he was for its retention *in toto* in the mass: *"Debemus levare linguam Latinam,"* he said, meaning, elevate it, increase its importance. Because *levare* in Italian means to pick up and throw away, Cardinal Godfrey was horrified to find himself reported next day in the Italian newspaper *Il Tempo* as having said that Latin should be abolished!

Quite apart from its use in the liturgy, Latin as a medium of communication at the Council proved to be less than a success. Experience showed that many of the Fathers did not understand spoken Latin well enough to grasp what was being said. Cardinal Cushing of Boston was said to have informed the pope frankly of his feeling that a more realistic attitude was needed toward the use of Latin as the language of its sessions. (The story went around that at one of the preparatory meetings, when Cardinal Cushing started to speak in English and was admonished by Archbishop Felici, he asked a neighboring prelate to inform the gathering in Latin that he represented "the Church of Silence.") Even in discussions of simple procedural matters, some bishops came alive only when the proposals were translated into Spanish, Italian, French, English, German, or Arabic. Under these circumstances, it was practically impossible for an assembly of nearly three thousand prelates to "deliberate" or to absorb the more intricate speeches. The old saw that "Latin is the official language of the Church" was simply not borne out at the Council. The Secretariat for Promoting Unity, under Cardinal Bea, was farsighted enough to provide a fairly full translation service for the non-Catholic observer-delegates, and many of the bishops probably wished that the same had been done for them. In fact, long before the Council met, a simultaneous-translation system had been proposed. The pope was said to have suggested that the United Nations translation experts in Geneva be consulted, but Secretary General Felici allegedly never got around to it. After the First Session, it was reported that plans were being made for the installation of a simultaneous-translation system before the Second Session in September 1963.

One of the most interesting discourses at the First Session was given by Maximos IV Saigh, Melchite patriarch of Antioch, who in the last speech on October 23rd ignored the Council's language barrier and spoke in French. The Fathers were delighted by this eighty-four year old prelate from the East, who proved to be one of the most colorful figures at the Council. Desiring to focus attention on an old grievance whereby according to Vatican protocol the Eastern patriarchs have been ranked below the cardinals since the fifteenth century at least, whereas in antiquity and in the early Middle Ages they were traditionally regarded as coming immediately after the pope himself (Lateran Council IV under Pope Innocent III, decreed in 1215 that the order of precedence was: Rome, Constantinople, Alexandria, Antioch, and Jerusalem for the major sees), he had ostentatiously absented himself from the inaugural procession on the opening day of the Council.*

The patriarch began by addressing, first, "their Beatitudes" the Patriarchs, and then "their Eminences" the Cardinals, a subtle maneuver that apparently escaped the attention of Cardinal Spellman who was presiding, but was caught by other alert Fathers. Justifying his use of French instead

* The pope later rectified this situation, in part at least, by naming six of the patriarchs as members of the Congregation for the Oriental Churches. Hitherto only cardinals had been members of Curial congregations.

of Latin, he said that the latter was not the language of the Eastern Church, and that as a consequence he felt it only proper to use a more universal tongue in addressing so Catholic a gathering:

I would propose first that some of the rigidity of the initial principle contained in clause No. 24 (lines 10–11), which reads: *linguae latinae usus in liturgia occidentali servetur*, should be softened to: *lingua Latina est lingua originalis et officialis ritus Romani*.

Secondly, I propose that it be left to episcopal councils in each region to decide if, and to what extent, it is convenient or not to adopt the vernacular in the liturgy. The text only leaves the episcopal conferences the responsibility of proposing the adoption to the Holy See—but there is no need to have an episcopal conference to put forward such a proposal. Any of the faithful could. Episcopal conferences should not be called just to propose, but to decide something, subject to the approval of the Holy See.

I propose, therefore, that clause No. 24 should end thus (lines 16–19): *sit vero conferentiae episcopalis in singulis regionibus . . . limites et modum linguae vernaculae in liturgiam admittendae statuere, actis sancta sede recognitis.* (Let the conference of bishops decide for each region what is to be the manner and the limits of the use of vernacular in the liturgy, the acts being approved by the Holy See.)

In the next ten congregations the question of the use of Latin became a sort of shibboleth, separating into two camps those who were determined to bring the vast teaching and experience of the Church to bear on problems raised by the modern world; and those who were equally determined to restrain the Church's thinking and liturgical practice within the narrow confines of a western juridically-oriented tradition. The latter group quickly rallied round Cardinal Ottaviani and the ultra-conservative faction including, not too surprisingly, most of the older Roman cardinals, with the Irish Dominican Cardinal Browne as their professional, scholastic theologian. The majority of these men had had limited pastoral experience, and apparently lacked the breadth of vision that would have enabled them to rally to the papal plea for a renewal of the Church. Yet it was these very men, curiously, who were loudest in their protestations of loyalty toward the Holy See and in their often-expressed concern for safeguarding the rights of the Holy Father. It was unfortunate that this juridical concept was supported by so many Italian and Spanish bishops, men who had shown little sympathy for the need to modernize the apostolate of the Church in their own dioceses, as well as by certain American and Irish bishops, who seemed uninterested in the basic issues or were quite content with things as they were back home. This attitude was reflected, for example, in the remark of the cardinal of Los Angeles to a fellow bishop who questioned his unbending opposition to all liturgical reform: "You must be a reader of *Worship!*" (His reference was to the well edited monthly, published by the Benedictines of Collegeville, Minnesota, which had for a long time been influential in spreading knowledge of the liturgical movement in the United States and was widely read by the younger clergy.)

During the First Session the prelates from the United States held meetings every Monday at the North American College. They were at first dominated by blocs under Cardinal Spellman and McIntyre, but as Cardinals Ritter and Meyer gained in stature owing to their stand in the conciliar discussions, their leadership made itself felt among the bishops, first from the mid-west and then among a considerable group of the younger men from both the east and the west coasts. Those American bishops who had contact with the prelates and theologians of other lands quickly became aware of the immense educative value of the proceedings. Unfortunately a number preferred to sit at home in their hotels or pensions, bemoaning the waste of time and the interminable longwindedness of the oratory. They left Rome, unhappily, at the close of the First Session almost as uninformed as they were upon arrival. As one prelate was heard to remark, "The Holy Spirit came and departed at the Council and some of these people never even dreamed he had been there."

The 6th General Congregation on Wednesday, October 24th, was conducted under the presidency of Cardinal Pla y Deniel. It began with the celebration of mass according to the Byzantine rite by Archbishop Nabaa of the Melchite Patriarchate of Antioch, one of the Under-Secretaries of the Council, with the students of the Greek College supplying the choral parts. It was a moment of sadness, for on entering the basilica that morning the 83 year-old, retired Archbishop Aston Chichester, S.J. (Salisbury, Southern Rhodesia) had suddenly dropped dead.

Cardinal Tisserant, prefect of the Vatican Library, led off the debate by stating that Latin was not the only liturgical language, calling the Fathers' attention to the fact that Hebrew and Greek had been used by the original Christians, as was indicated by the inscription on the cross in Hebrew, Greek and Latin. He said that the Slavic languages as well as Chinese had been recognized by the Congregation of Rites as permissible liturgical languages, noting, incidentally, that a unique copy of the only missal in the Chinese language could be seen in the Vatican Library.

On rising to talk, the tall graceful Indian Cardinal Gracias (Bombay) spoke of himself as a voice crying in the desert and said that since becoming a bishop he had incessantly striven for a readaptation of the liturgy. However, from his own background he recognized the difficulty caused by the great diversity of languages in the same cultural milieu and country. Still the vernacular languages were absolutely necessary for instructing the ordinary people as well as giving them a taste of a true

Christian experience. He felt in the end that the question of languages should be left to the decision of the conferences of bishops.

Cardinal Bea (Curia) said that the development of thought on the liturgy seemed insufficiently mature to allow the Church to proceed with the founding of a totally new rite, but the Fathers should not close their eyes to the possibility of such a change.

Cardinal Bacci (Curia), on the other hand, was categorical in saying that the mass should not be celebrated in any of the vernacular languages. He reminded the Council that in the middle of the last century Father Rosmini had been condemned for asserting that the use of Latin in the church's ceremonies served to erect a barrier between the people and the priest. He could see no difficulty in allowing the people to read their missals in the vernacular while the priest was celebrating in Latin at the altar. For him, Latin was *the* bond of unity. Yet he could see that in the administration of certain of the sacraments its might be necessary to use the popular languages, but this should not be done without Roman authorization for it was inconceivable that such a decision should be left to episcopal conferences. In that case, what would become of our unity?

The archbishop of Chicago, Cardinal Meyer rose to say that he was fully in accord with Art 24 of the schema, which authorized the use of the vernacular languages in the liturgy, but he could see no reason why this matter had to be handed over to episcopal conferences for solution. What was wrong, he wanted to know, with the bishops individually making such decisions under the control of the Holy Father?

Bishop Van Lierde, the pope's sacristan (for Vatican City) spoke on the liturgy as a spiritual pedagogy and expressed himself in favor of a moderate use of popular languages in order that this function of the liturgy might be better emphasized.

Archbishop McQuaid (Dublin) announced that he was not at all against the Latin language. He wanted it retained in the mass as at present, but could see the usefulness of allowing the vernacular in the administration of the sacraments. He said that each bishop now had the power to determine what was proper in this matter for his own diocese and should not have to submit his judgment to national conferences of bishops.

Archbishop Descuffi (Smyrna) said that he could only express his joy at having heard so many speaking out on behalf of the need for having the mass said in the vernacular languages, for the liturgy was for the benefit of men and not men for the liturgy (*liturgia propter homines et non homines propter liturgiam*). Finally it was wrong to say that special arrangements should be made only for missionary countries, for today every country was a missionary country.

Archbishop Gonçalves do Amaral (Brazil) reminded the Fathers that the humanity of Christ was simply an instrumental cause of salvation and that the mystery of salvation, therefore, which was communicated through the liturgy, did not need really be expressed in the vernacular languages. On the other hand, Archbishop Ramanantoanina (Madagascar) took the viewpoint that both liturgical custom and language should be adapted in accordance with the needs of cultures foreign to the Latin milieu, such as one found, for example, in the missionary areas of Africa and the South Pacific.

Archbishop Parente, assessor of the Holy Office, voiced the irritation of the Curia with the implied criticism being levelled against the arch-conservatives. "Many things have been said here," he declared, "which were neither prudent, just, nor consistent. The schema limps in its very preface; hence it ought to be turned over completely to the Theological Commission for reworking." He wound up by complaining about the continual attacks on the Holy Office and the disdain with which it was treated. "At the Holy Office we are all martyrs," he exclaimed. "We have already yielded on many points, yet this is the thanks we get! If any changes are to be sanctioned by the Council, they must be made with the greatest prudence (*maxima cum prudentia*)."

His colleague, Archbishop Dino Staffa, secretary of the Congregation of Seminaries and Universities, took much the same line. The maintenance of Latin in the liturgy was essential to preserving the Church's unity. Only the Holy See had the right to make decisions for the whole Church with regard to rites as well as doctrine. There could be no question of episcopal conferences having anything to do with such matters.

It was noted that, while Archbishop Parente would speak one or two times more, these were the only interventions in the debate by Archbishops Vagnozzi, Staffa, and Dante.

The day's debate was brought to a close by the speeches of Archbishop Gawlina (Poland), whose flow of oratory had to be interrupted by the President, and Archbishop Seper (Zagreb), who suggested that as Christians were so obviously in a minority in the modern world, every assistance should be extended to them to live the faith as well as possible, and this required that the whole treasury of the liturgy be opened to them in a language that they could understand.

Cardinal Siri (Genoa) opened the proceedings on October 26th by again stressing the theme that the schema should be referred to the Theological Commission because it touched on theological matters. It was dangerous to multiply rites. This left the door open to abuses and constituted a threat to unity. Episcopal conferences might *"proponere,"* but they could not *"statuere."* The Holy See must decide everything on its own authority. And the bishops were reminded of the great importance which the Church attached to the maintenance of Latin as evidenced by the publication earlier in the year of the papal constitution *Veterum sapientiae* (of February 22, 1962), an unrealistic attempt to reimpose a more rigorous study of Latin in seminaries and schools whose provisions were largely ignored (said to have been finagled from the pope in an unguarded moment).*

Speaking in the name of the Dutch episcopate, Bishop Bekkers ('s-Hertogenbosch) said that while the schema was not perfect it embodied the substance of what was necessary for a revival, in the hearts of the faithful, of the mystery-laden life of grace in Christ through a meaningful attendance at mass and participation in the sacraments. On the prerogatives of bishops in these matters, it certainly was the Holy Father's right and duty to reserve certain powers to himself in dealing with individual dioceses or the whole Church. But as successors to the Apostles, the bishops possessed sufficient powers in these matters even though at present they were not exercising them out of deference and loyalty to the Holy See.

Bishop Ancel (auxiliary of Lyons) thought that the schema fully corresponded to the pastoral emphasis which the pope desired the decisions of the Council to have. Unity did not mean that there must be uniformity of rites. There was a marvelous variety between the eastern and western liturgies and this very variety was a mark of the beauty of the Church. Two criteria ought to govern those who would adapt the liturgy: they must have a profound knowledge of and feeling for the liturgy; and they must understand the local psychology. No adaptation would be worthwhile unless it took these two things into account.

A large number, perhaps the majority, of western prelates were inclined to agree with the middle of the road position of Bishop Calewaert (Gent, Belgium), who thought that it was best to retain Latin as the language of the principal parts of the mass in the Roman rite, at least in those countries where the Church was long established and people were used to it, reserving the vernacular for the catechetical or dialogue portion at the beginning of the mass, and for all other liturgical functions.

Yet Bishop Rau (Mar del Plata, Argentina) was for jettisoning Latin altogether in public or parish masses, as an obstacle to the prayer-life of the faithful. "The Church as such," he said, "has no proper culture of its own and therefore no proper language. . . . The liturgy is employed *ratione signi,* after the fashion of a sign, actualizing what is signified; hence if its actions are not immediately understood by the participants, it is impeded in its effects. . . . I will be faithful unto death to the Roman Church, but not to the Latin language!" were his final remarks.

* Actually a forewarning of the attempt to keep theology in its hidebound forms was made in 1961 by the then Monsignor Staffa in a talk at Lateran University. He insisted on the maintenance of three things: an undeviating scholastic approach in philosophy and theology; a vigorous pursuit of the dictates of canon law; and an unswerving use of Latin.

Bishop Lokuang of Taiwan called attention to the very serious mistake made by the Roman Curia in the seventeenth and eighteenth centuries when it destroyed the work of the Chinese missions by condemning adaptations of Chinese customs. He maintained that the Communists had made the problem a very live issue today. "If our people do not pray in their own language, they are accused of subservience to a foreign nationalism . . . " The latter theme was stressed on a later occasion by Bishop Spülbeck (Meissen, East Germany), speaking on behalf of the bishops of East Germany. Most of the Polish bishops likewise testified that the introduction of the Polish language in the mass, which had been in effect for the past fifteen years, was the salvation of the faith in their country.

Japanese Bishop Kobayashi, speaking on the following day, October 27th, noted that the question of the use of national languages was most important to the Japanese. His people had an ancient cultural tradition of their own and Latin could only appear to them as something western and alien. It was a mistake to tie Christianity to the Latin, and therefore, western tradition. The salvation of souls should not be sacrificed to a uniformity that was purely secondary. "Is our unity with the Holy See so feeble that it has to be maintained by a rigid uniformity?" he asked. His remarks were greeted with applause.

Later the same day, toward the end of the 7th General Congregation, Bishop Muldoon of Australia voiced the general feeling of the Fathers when he suggested that sufficient discussion had now taken place on the preface and chapter I of the schema and that the matter should be put to a vote. This intervention was received with loud applause. But the President, Cardinal Ruffini, said that while many Fathers had withdrawn their request to speak, it was impossible, under the existing rules, to curtail the right of anyone who wanted to speak. No rule of closure had been devised by the committee responsible for drawing up the Rules of Procedure.

Nevertheless the following Monday, in the 9th General Congregation on October 29, 1962, the cardinal presidents decided to bring the current discussion to an end and pass on to chapter II of the schema, dealing with the mass.

In the first speech on the new matter, Cardinal Spellman agreed with the need for active participation of the laity in the mass, but came out strongly against giving them communion with both bread and wine, as recommended in the schema, in keeping with the words of Christ: "Unless you eat the flesh of the Son of man and drink his blood . . ." (Jn. 6:53) and as had been the custom in the Roman Church down to at least the twelfth century. He was also against the concelebration of mass by a number of priests using one altar and going through the words and

66

actions together. His priests, he remarked, frequently had to say three masses each on Sundays to accommodate all the people coming to church, and even on week days there were times when it was difficult to get a priest to take care of the ordinary parish masses, funerals and weddings. Hence he could see no need for such an innovation. He was on less solid ground in the judgment of competent theologians, however, when he attempted to argue that concelebration involved the Church in a loss of graces. On the cardinal's behalf, it is only fair to add that a certain theologian had told the American bishops that when 100 priests concelebrated, the Church was 99 masses short!

Spellman was seconded by Cardinal Ruffini who cited hygienic reasons against giving wine to the faithful, and the inconveniences for priests and churches in the matter of concelebration. However he insisted it was the right of the Holy See alone to make concessions in such matters.

The last speech of the day fell like a bombshell on the assembly. It was made by Cardinal Léger of Montreal who came out four-square both for concelebration by groups of priests when possible, and for giving both bread and wine to the people in the eucharist. He said that, as was demonstrated in the Eastern rites where both these practices prevailed, it was a sign of true unity and mutual charity to have a number of priests around the same table imitating Christ and the Apostles at the Last Supper. As for the inconveniences, he could visualize none, other than the need for priests, in charity, to synchronize their prayers and actions at the altar. After all, the mass was not a private devotion of the priest; it was always a public function of the Church with the priest as minister and the people as participants. He cited likewise the daily practice of the Eastern rites in giving communion under both bread and wine; hence he could see no hygienic problem. Finally he asked that the original text of the whole liturgical schema as it left the Preparatory Commission be made the basis of the discussions.

On October 30th, in the 10th General Congregation, with Cardinal Alfrink in the chair as President, the cardinal of England, Godfrey, attempted in a general fashion to reply to the assertions of the cardinal of Montreal. He was afraid that the return to the practice of giving communion with both bread and wine in a country such as his would lead people to think that the Catholic Church was giving in to the Anglicans and some of the other Protestant bodies who had retained this practice. But he was even more concerned for hygienic reasons, because women with lipstick would regularly be approaching the altar for communion. Finally, he asked, what about reformed alcoholics and abstentionists and prohibitionists? As for the concelebration of mass, he could conceive of its propriety on Holy Thursday, and in monasteries where a number of monks might say mass together on private altars and for certain other special gatherings of priests. But he felt generally that when offering a stipend for a mass, people would prefer to have it said by one priest alone.

In his talk, Cardinal Gracias (Bombay) made reference to the danger in which India stood at the moment with the Chinese penetrating its northern borders. He felt that much precious time was now being wasted in the Council for lack of a proper order of business. On this matter of liturgical details, for example, it should be left to the conferences of bishops in each land to decide these things. He suggested that an accord be reached, with the Holy Father's permission, giving the bishops proper authority to decide, and that the Council should then move on to the more important business relating to other schemata. He spoke, he said, in the name of 72 Indian bishops, many of whom were seriously considering returning to their country in its hour of need. He requested the prayers of the assembly for his native land and its leader, Mr. Nehru.

Cardinal Bueno y Monreal of Seville discussed the question of the eucharistic fast with particular reference to evening masses. Then Cardinal Alfrink rose to say that in the matter of giving communion to the faithful, he was not bothered by matters of history, or theology, or hygiene. In refusing to give the chalice to the laity, the Church was depriving them of their right to conform to Christ's injunction. Since there were differences of opinion among the Fathers with regard to this matter, he advocated that its solution be left to individual conferences of bishops in each land or area.

It was at this point that the famous speech of Cardinal Ottaviani occurred, after which he absented himself from the Council's public deliberations until November 14th. He rose to reply in particular to Cardinal Alfrink. What made the situation even more dramatic was that Cardinal Alfrink was the President of the day.

Seeing the way the wind had been blowing during the past few days, with determined expressions of opinion by such eminent figures as Cardinals Frings of Cologne, Döpfner of Munich, Tatsuo Doi of Tokyo, Léger of Montreal, Ritter of St. Louis and Meyer of Chicago, as well as the African bishops almost in a body, in favor of changes of all kinds, particularly regarding the use of the vernacular in the mass, the restoration of communion under both kinds on special occasions, and so on, Cardinal Ottaviani asked, "Are these Fathers planning a revolution?" He warned against scandalizing the faithful by introducing too many changes (an old Holy Office saw). He maintained that the proposal to have communion under both kinds had been turned down by a large majority in the Central Preparatory Commission, and it was only a small minority that was pressing for it now. He was against concelebration because it made the mass seem like something happening in a theater (an unintentional slap at the Eastern rites, where concelebration was normal). The liturgy should be regarded as sacred ground and approached with caution; had not God warned Moses to remove his sandals when approaching the burning bush? This last remark about Moses later caused an Austrian prelate to say that if the liturgy could be modernized merely by removing one's shoes, he would like to be the first to do so.

Unfortunately the cardinal ran on longer than his allotted ten minutes, refusing to be interrupted by the President, Cardinal Alfrink, who politely interposed: "Excuse me, Eminence, but you have already spoken more than fifteen minutes." The secretary general, Archbishop Felici, thereupon conferred with Cardinal Alfrink, and Ottaviani was forced to stop, the microphone being turned over to the next speaker. The Council Fathers expressed their displeasure with the tenor of this speech by applauding Cardinal Alfrink's action. It was this unmistakable sign of the general feeling of the assembly, rather than the intervention of Alfrink, which seemed to have caused Ottaviani to feel insulted and to remain away for almost two weeks.

When the applause had died down, Cardinal Bea noted that the mass was not only a "banquet" (*convivium*), but a "sacrifice" (*sacrificium*), and not merely a "sacrifice of praise," but a propitiatory sacrifice. He was in favor of having the sermon not only recommended but made obligatory at all masses, in order to stress the doctrinal import of the whole action and give greater meaning to the first part, or Liturgy of the Word, which the sermon brings to an end. Similarly the last part of the mass needed overhauling, with some kind of common prayer replacing the unsuitable Leonine prayers for the conversion of Russia, which usually followed the mass and were said in the vernacular.

The Irish Dominican, Cardinal Browne, next treated the Fathers to a scholastic exposition of the thought of St. Thomas on these matters, as if that great thirteenth century savant and saint, who had avidly read and answered the Islamic philosophers in his own day and who was condemned at Paris and Oxford as an "innovator," would not have been in the avant-garde today, in adapting the Church's teachings to modern requirements. As the cardinal droned on, many of the Fathers retreated to Bar Jonah. This refuge from oratory was a little coffee shop set up off a corridor leading from a side entrance to St. Peter's. Because coffee shops are often known in Italy as "bars," one witty prelate with a taste for classical puns quickly nicknamed this one "Bar Jonah," because "Bar-Jonah," Hebrew for "son of John," is a reference to St. Peter in Scripture. The Fathers resorted to Bar Jonah in engulfing numbers for a morning coffee break. The pope himself was credited with originating the idea; he is said to have told the cardinal in charge of the arrangements that if a place to smoke was not provided, "the bishops will be puffing under their mitres." One result of Bar Jonah was that in its narrow confines bishops rubbed shoulders with non-Catholic observers from all over the world, and consequently exchanged views. At times, certain bishops had to be routed out to vote on various amendments, like dawdlers in the cloakroom of the U.S. Senate.

The next day (October 31st) Cardinals Lercaro of Bologna and König of Vienna led off the discussion, giving their full support to the innovations proposed in the schema. And Archbishop Hallinan, one of the few American bishops to be heard from throughout the First Session, showed himself in full agreement. He called the liturgical prayer of the Church the proper corrective for the individualism so prevalent in the modern world; and asked that the liturgy be rendered simple and clear so that it could be understood and appreciated by all who had a part in it, priests, prelates and laity alike.

Surprisingly few American bishops spoke at the Council. Bishop Helmsing of Kansas City gave up his turn saying he had handed in his paper to the Secretariat and did not wish to take up the bishops' time. It was known that the majority of younger and mid-western bishops were not always in agreement with the two American cardinals, Spellman and McIntyre, who seemed to speak for them. Hence Archbishop Hallinan's talk was looked upon as a sort of declaration of independence. It was noted that Bishop Wright of Pittsburgh, considered one of the more forthright of the American bishops, took no part in the current debate, nor was the accomplished speaker, Bishop Fulton Sheen, heard from. It was rumored that in the Monday meetings of the American hierarchy a new spirit was gradually manifesting itself. But the majority evidently felt that making an issue of their stand at an early stage in the game would not be either wise or fruitful.

As the discussion continued on October 31st, Bishop Elchinger (auxiliary of Strasbourg, France) reminded the assembly that in his encyclical on the liturgy, *Mediator Dei,* so often quoted by the conservatives, Pope Pius XII had provided ample theological justification for the custom of concelebration, as practiced particularly by the Eastern Church. Elchinger called for a simplification of the order of the mass and a return to the original text of the schema on this question. The Church was in the hands of the youth of today, he said. It was not possible to attract them by useless traditions or narrow conservativism; the mechanical repetition of prayers or ceremonies, no matter what historical importance might be attached to them, only bored the present generation. But they did comprehend us when we spoke of the Mysteries of the Church and the manifesting of Christ's incarnation through the liturgy. They wanted to comprehend the liturgy and have a direct part in it. It was up to the Church to restore the spirit of community in Christ that was the birthright of every Christian through baptism. This talk was loudly applauded. It was followed by similar observations on the part of the Maronite Bishop Khoury, Archbishop Edelby (Edessa), and Archbishop Aramburu (Tucumán, Argentina).

Finally, Bishop Van Cauwelaert of the Congo, speaking in the name of 262 African bishops, welcomed the expression "paschal banquet" (*pascale convivium*) in the schema. This must not be changed. He begged, further, that in the spirit of the early Church, great attention should be paid to the "new churches of the Gentiles." As Saints Paul and Barnabas had not burdened the new Christians with circumcision and the old rites of the Jewish Law, so the new Churches in Africa and elsewhere ought not to be burdened with the unsuitable ceremonies and traditions of the Roman rite. The Fathers again broke out into loud applause at this statement. But the speaker had to be stopped by the President because he had gone beyond his allotted time.

After a three days' recess occasioned by the feast of All Saints and the next day's commemoration of All Souls, on Sunday, November 4th, the whole Council took part in a solemn papal chapel in St. Peter's to commemorate the fourth anniversary of Pope John's coronation. The solemn high mass was celebrated by Cardinal Montini, archbishop of Milan, according to the Ambrosian rite, rarely if ever used in the Roman basilica before. This departure from custom was justified in the Holy Father's illuminating address. The concurrent feast of St. Charles Borromeo (November 4th), famous reforming archbishop of the period immediately following the close of the Council of Trent, whose acts the pope himself had edited while still a cardinal and on whom he was something of an authority, was seized upon by Pope John to impress upon the bishops a number of salient ideas which he wished to stress, midway through their labors.

After a salute to Latin as "the language in which the prelates of the universal Church communicate with the center of Catholicism, that is the Apostolic See, and which is the traditional language of Councils," he then abandoned this tongue and gave the rest of his talk in Italian, which was "better understood by the greater part of this assembly; better understood by the crowds of faithful who have come here to celebrate the anniversary of their Pastor and Father."

The pope concluded by reminding the Fathers:

It is perfectly natural that new times and new circumstances should suggest different forms and methods for transmitting externally the one and same doctrine, and of clothing it in a new dress. Yet the living substance is always the purity of the evangelical and apostolic truth, in perfect conformity with the teaching of holy Church, who often applies to herself the maxim: "Only one art, but a thousand forms."

71

His message was clearly one of hope and optimism, so typical of the man, but it also contained the semblance of a gentle rebuke to those who, as the debates so far had amply disclosed, were intent upon steering the Council in a direction not desired by the pope, and at variance with his declared wishes.

When the Council resumed with its 12th General Congregation on Monday, November 5th, the topic under debate was still Chapter II of the liturgy schema.

The archbishop of Los Angeles, in a commentary on the words *"actuosa participatio"*—active participation, with reference to the part to be played by the faithful at mass—gave utterance to the following remark: "Active participation of the faithful in the mass is nothing but a distraction" (*Actuosa participatio fidelium non est nisi distractio*). These words caused considerable amazement. The theologian who supplied him with this phrase apparently did not know that it came from an article by Jacques Maritain in which that philosopher had said that religion was a kind of contemplation, and not an action. But it was precisely this notion of religion that had been combatted by the early fathers of the Church, in particular by Ambrose and Augustine, who demonstrated that the Platonic notion of contemplation of the good as the final end of man, even when supplemented by the Stoic and Ciceronian modification in favor of participation in the common welfare of one's fellowmen, was not the Christian idea of religion. Maritain later repudiated the article, but evidently the cardinal's theological mentor had never caught up with this fact. In any case, what further dismayed a large number of the bishops was the fact that since the statement was made so late in the debate, it seemed to indicate that the cardinal of Los Angeles had paid little attention to the heart of the discussion which turned around the mysteries of the faith as they were to be made actual in the lives of both priests and faithful through the liturgy. For his intervention had come after the magnificent avowals of the African and Asian bishops, who had amply demonstrated that, as in the early Church, it was now necessary to adapt the liturgy to the social, intellectual and natural milieu of their people, whose culture, though perhaps primitive and pagan, was not therefore necessarily evil or diabolic. It had come, likewise, after the devastating speech of the Melchite patriarch, Maximos IV Saigh, who proved, along with a number of other Eastern prelates, the absurdity of maintaining that the use of Latin in the mass was necessary so far as the Church Universal was concerned. It was reported that the cardinal of Los Angeles arrived in Rome with a number of prejudices on his mind which he did not hesitate to ventilate, wounding the sensibilities of both the German and Dutch episcopates by referring to them as "disobedient" long before the

Council opened, and expressing a horror for what he called the "noisiness" of the German dialogue and sung masses.

Cardinal Spellman appeared also to have been poorly advised. When these two American prelates who, while vigorous in defense of the retention of Latin* in the mass, came out, contrary to all expectations, in favor of the clergy being allowed to read their breviaries in English, an Italian archbishop was compelled to exclaim: *"Ah! Questi Americani!* Now they want the priest to pray in English, and the people to pray in Latin!"

Among the Italian bishops, a number seemed to feel that the honor of the Italian Church and its presumed theological pre-eminence demanded that they take an active part in all the discussions. Hence their return to the microphone three or four times in the course of the earlier debates. Fares (Catanzaro and Squillace), D'Avack (Camerino), Costantini (Sessa Aurunca), Carli (Segni), and Battaglia (Faenza) were among the names occurring most frequently in this group. All took the same line. The inviolability of Latin must be maintained; the Holy See must continue to control all liturgical matters; the introduction of changes posed a threat to the Church's unity and the integrity of the faith. Battaglia, in the role of a sort of *enfant terrible,* gave vent to the extravagant statement that to say that Latin was a dead language was to commit a crime against Holy Mother the Church whose language it was. Bishop D'Agostino (Vallo di Lucania) ended his peroration with the ringing cry: *"Civis Romanus sum, civis Christianus sum, lingua Latina servetur!"* The Italians generally suffered from a distinct rhetorical disadvantage, in that they required ten minutes to warm up to the theme on which they wished to discourse.

On November 6th the Holy Father at length intervened and ruled that when, in the opinion of the Cardinal presidents, a subject had been exhausted in debate, they had the right to propose a vote to close the discussion and order the Council to pass on to consideration of the next item. Those Fathers who were thus prevented from speaking could submit their speeches in writing to the Secretary General. The announcement was made at 10 A.M. Cardinal Tisserant, who was presiding, immediately proposed that the debate on Chapter II of the liturgy schema be ended. All those in favor were asked to rise. Only a solitary Franciscan bishop remained seated! The move was greeted with general applause.

Accordingly, the same day, in its 13th General Congregation, the

---

* It should be noted here, for what it is worth, that Continental bishops generally found it very difficult to understand the American enunciation of Latin, while the American bishops, by and large, found the Continental enunciation equally baffling.

73

Council was able to pass on to Chapter III dealing with the sacraments and the sacramentals. The following day, an announcement was made that after a discussion of Chapter IV on the divine office, which was to begin on November 7th and would be debated separately like the previous chapters, the Council would then discuss the remaining Chapters V-VIII en bloc, in the interests of shortening the time spent on the first schema. The next schema to be taken up would be that on the "Sources of Revelation," one of the schemata submitted to the bishops during the summer before the Council opened.*

As things turned out, it appears to have been a stroke of genius on Pope John's part not to have given the Council a fixed agenda. It was a pure act of prescience on his part. It requires little hindsight now to realize how extremely important this point was if he was to be successful in guiding the Council's destinies. His experience with the various Preparatory Commissions and with the Central Preparatory Commission, in particular, had revealed both how strong the urge for reform in the Church really was, and also to what lengths the arch-conservatives were prepared to go to "put over" their own ideas. Had an agenda been fixed in advance, the conservatives would certainly have tried, and perhaps succeeded, in imposing an order of business that suited their purposes. The debates would have led off with a discussion of some relatively noncontroversial theme like the text on the Virgin Mary or communications media, during which they would have tried to establish their ascendancy. Later if there had been a serious clash on some fundamental subject, such as the nature of the Church or the role of bishops, they would then have tried to appear as the "martyrs" of truth and so win sympathy for their cause. But they were deprived of the opportunity to put these plans to the test. The choice of the liturgy schema as the first item of business (officially announced in the 2nd General Congregation on October 16th) meant that a topic sufficiently important in itself, both from a theological and practical point of view, but not one that would be likely to disrupt the proceedings, was to serve as a kind of catalyst, drawing out both sides but allowing the advocates of reform to set the tone of the assembly, in accordance with the principles enunciated in the pope's opening speech. While at this point victory was not yet assured, as the debate on the liturgy came to a close and the pace of the Council quickened, the hand of a master strategist on the grand scale began to become apparent, slowly guiding the proceedings—and educating public opinion as he went along.

* Seven only of the 70 schemata approved by the Central Commission were submitted to the bishops in July, 1962, for their study: namely, those on the sources of revelation, the moral order, the deposit of faith, the family and chastity, the liturgy, communications media, and unity.

Still another week was consumed on what might be called liturgical details. Chapter IV of the schema on the divine office occupied the Fathers for two and a half sessions, and through most of the 16th General Congregation on Saturday, November 10th. The 17th and 18th General Congregations, November 12th-13th, were sufficient to wind up affairs with a blanket consideration of the liturgical year, sacred ornaments and vestments, church music and church art. No new principles were laid down, the main lines of cleavage already being apparent, but several interesting things were said.

Cardinal Ruffini, who was presiding on Saturday, November 10th, introduced the proceedings by announcing that applause must cease, especially in the far corners of the hall, because this method of expression was being used by some of the Fathers to give vent to their displeasure as well as their approbation. All speakers ought to be treated with equal respect, especially members of the Roman Curia, "men who know much and live holy lives." He was referring in particular to the case of Cardinal Ottaviani who had apparently been mortified by the treatment accorded his remarks and, as we have seen, absented himself from the assembly. This advice was not well received by the Fathers.

Cardinal Spellman next surprised everybody by speaking for only two minutes and coming out in favor of the proposal that the liturgical calendar ought to be synchronized with the civil calendar.

Speaking the same day (November 10th), the aged Bishop Petar Čule (Mostar, Yugoslavia) put in a long plea for the inclusion of the name of St. Joseph in the canon of the mass, but as he talked on, nervously repeating himself, murmurs began to be heard and Cardinal Ruffini was prompted to interject: "Complete your holy and eloquent speech. We all love St. Joseph and we hope there are many saints in Yugoslavia." The next speaker launched into a long and tedious sermon on the Virgin Mary, which also brought forth murmurs. He too had to be cut off by Ruffini, who remarked: "One does not preach to preachers" (*Praedicatoribus non praedicatur*). Winding up the day's proceedings at 12:45 with the customary Angelus and Gloria Patri, the Cardinal President brought down the house with a loud invocation of the name of St. Joseph.

It was this cutting off of Bishop Čule that prompted Pope John to order the insertion of the name of St. Joseph in the canon of the mass on his own authority (decree announced November 13th, effective Dec. 8, 1962), without waiting for any conciliar recommendation in the matter. This caused great astonishment, but few were aware that the pope, following the debates on closed circuit television in his apartments, knew Bishop Čule personally and also knew that his nervous manner of speaking had a tragic source: he had suffered through one of those long trials made famous by the Communists and was sentenced to four years in a concentration camp in Yugoslavia. He and other prisoners were then put on a train which was deliberately wrecked in an attempt to kill all aboard. The bishop survived, but both his hips were broken. In poor health, he had nevertheless made great effort to attend the Council and speak up for St. Joseph. Thus his wish was fulfilled.

DEBATE ON SOURCES OF REVELATION

The Council next embarked on discussion of the crucial schema *De Revelatione* prepared by the Preparatory Theological Commission under Cardinal Ottaviani and personally presented by him as head of the corresponding conciliar Commission. The schema consisted of 5 Chapters, divided into 29 numbered Articles.

From the very first two opposing parties were locked in heated debate, for this was one of the most important issues before the Council—basic, in a sense, to all else. Recent years had witnessed a swing by many Catholic theologians away from the view largely favored since the Council of Trent that the Bible and tradition were two separate, virtually independent, sources of divine revelation. They had returned to the older position wherein Scripture and tradition must not be thought of as completely independent of each other but as constituting a whole—two modes, the written and unwritten, by which the Word of God came down to us within the framework of the Church. As Father Yves Congar, O.P., a spokesman for the new outlook, put it: "There is not a single dogma which the Church holds by Scripture *alone,* not a single dogma which it holds by tradition *alone.* Obviously this view was also much closer to the traditional Protestant thesis of "the Bible and the Bible alone." The new tendency was virtually ignored by the Theological Commission when preparing its draft.

The debate opened on Wednesday, November 14th, with some admonitory remarks by Cardinal Ottaviani. "There are," he said, "a number of schemata in circulation which are opposed to the one I am about to introduce. But this procedure violates the regulations. . . . The presentation of a schema belongs solely to the Holy Father; hence this way of doing things is hardly respectful of his prerogatives." The cardinal was referring to different drafts prepared by committees of French, German and Dutch theologians, of which the last was said to be the most radical.*
These schemata, in circulation for well over two weeks, had evidently dis-

---

* Of the various drafts, one in particular reflecting the views of Father Karl Rahner, S.J., was approved by the bishops of Austria, Belgium, France, Germany and Holland.

pleased the opposing faction. The cardinal continued: "Here in Council we have the right to propose amendments, but only to the schema proposed, not to any other.

"As regards the 'pastoral tone,' " he went on, "might I remind you that the foundation of all pastoral theology is provided by safe doctrine. The fact that this schema deals primarily with doctrine renders it likewise pastoral. These proposals have been prepared for a Council, hence they have nothing in common with an encyclical or a homily or a pastoral letter. Regarding the complaint that it has not been inspired by the so-called New Theology, might I remark that our teaching is traditional and will and must ever remain the same." Appealing to the theologians and scholars among the bishops at the Council, he concluded by stating that all those who had worked in the Theological Commission and in the Central Committee on this material were scholarly and experienced men, and respect was due the work of such people.

His Eminence was then replaced at the microphone by Monsignor Garofalo, who summarized the contents of the official schema for the benefit of the Fathers. Announcing as the primary end of the Council the defense and promulgation of Catholic doctrine in its most exact form, he declared that doctrine did not change although it could and did develop. Repeating the words of his predecessor, he explained that in style and format the schema was meant to be a decree or formulation, hence it had not been elaborated as a literary document. Its objective, he confessed, was to demonstrate once more that, by its condemnation of error, the Church was ever prompt to purify the world of its errors and evils. This presentation, as far as the majority of prelates were concerned, could not have been more unfortunate coming in the wake of Cardinal Ottaviani's complaints. The immediate result was not hard to predict.

Cardinal Liénart rose at once to lead the opposition. "This schema," he said, "does not please me. It is not adequate to the matter it purports to deal with, namely Scripture and tradition. There are not and never have been two *sources* of revelation. There is only one fount of revelation —the Word of God, the good news announced by the prophets and revealed by Christ. The Word of God is the unique *source* of revelation. This schema is a cold and scholastic formulation, while revelation is a supreme gift of God—God speaking directly to us. We should be thinking more along the lines of our separated brothers who have such a love and veneration for the Word of God. Our duty now is to cultivate the faith of our people and cease to condemn. Hence I propose this schema be entirely refashioned."

As at the opening congregation, the French cardinal was replaced by Cardinal Frings of Cologne, like his colleague a scripture scholar. In a milder tone he announced his *Non placet,* and then tackled the Ottaviani proposition head on. "The primary purpose of a Council is to provide for the pastoral needs of the day," he said, "to teach the truth, to propose its doctrine in such wise that it will be received. At the First Vatican Council complaints were raised about the professorial tone of the schemata, particularly those proposed by Cardinal Franzelin.* Here that approach is even further exaggerated. But what is even worse than the manner of presentation is the doctrine itself. Why speak of two sources of revelation? This is not traditional. Neither the Fathers, nor the scholastic theologians, nor St. Thomas himself, nor the previous Councils knew anything about this way of explaining our teaching. It is not traditional and only in recent centuries, as a result of a false historicism, have certain theologians tried to explain the matter thus."

This statement touched a sore spot, for a primary characteristic of the ultra-conservative theologian was his fear of and disdain for a positive, history-oriented approach to theology. The cardinal of Cologne continued inexorably: "What is said here about inspiration and inerrancy is at once offensive to our separated brothers in Christ and harmful to the proper liberty required in any scientific procedure. We are facing a conflict of schools given to diverse procedures, as was realized at Trent four hundred years ago. It is not the business of a Council to enter into discussions between Catholic theologians. Its task is to react against heresy, but not to interfere when there is no danger of such errors."

Hardly had the German cardinal concluded when his presidential colleague, Cardinal Ruffini of Sicily, took the microphone in hand. "We are now faced with a question of extreme importance," he announced. "It is the heart and matter of the Council. I am not of the opinion of the cardinals who preceded me. This schema pleases me completely. It has been prepared by men who are both eminent and wise. It has been reviewed by men no less eminent on the Central Committee. How then can it be rejected in its totality? Furthermore it is the Holy Father who has given us this matter for discussion. With what right then can we dismiss it without discussion? Granted that it is not perfect, I myself have certain reservations and recommendations I would like to make about it. It will at least give us a basis for our work. Should we consider another schema, we will never finish."

In a more conciliatory tone Ruffini was supported by the archbishop of Genoa, Cardinal Siri. He admitted the justice of many of the criticisms levelled at the schema. However, he pointed out the connection between the proposed condemnations and the heresy of Modernism condemned in

* During Vatican Council I the dogmatic schema prepared by the then Professor Franzelin was finally rejected as too obscure, a fact that gave his students at the Gregorian University no little glee, enabling them to announce: "We always maintained that Professor Franzelin's lectures were obscure. Now we have it confirmed by a Council."

78

1907 by Pope Pius X. He felt it still was necessary to justify that condemnatory action, as did a majority of the Italian bishops. "By discussing the interpretation of Scripture," he said, "it is possible to arrive at a clearer understanding of the faith. Hence let us discuss the schema before us." Cardinal Quiroga y Palacios, of Compostela, Spain, gave similar advice.

But the heavy artillery was now brought into action. In quick succession, the cardinals of Montreal, Vienna, Utrecht and Brussels-Malines rose to demolish the Ottaviani thesis. The Canadian cardinal, Paul Emile Léger, not only proposed the scrapping of the document but went on to make a plea for freedom and tolerance within the world of Catholic scholarship, defending biblical scholars in particular who were opening up new paths of investigation. Though he began his career as a Sulpician, under the tutelage of the old-guard French Canadian hierarchy, and served his Roman apprenticeship as Rector of the Canadian College in the Eternal City, Léger had undergone an interior revolution. He was now a staunch advocate of that inner reform of the Church that aimed at getting back to the fundamental roots, and would restore Catholicism today as a mystery-conscious, apostolic-minded, yet tolerant institution, along the lines of the primitive Church.

Cardinal König, the fifty-seven-year-old cardinal of Vienna, spoke next. A theologian in his own right who had taught moral theology and published books on the study of comparative religion, he rejected the schema as having almost nothing to do with the program called for by the Holy Father. This was the theme, likewise, of Cardinal Alfrink, a pupil of Cardinal Ruffini when doing his theological studies in Rome, and now archbishop of Utrecht. He had long outgrown his teacher's ideas. Before leaving Holland for the Council he had warned his people not to expect miracles or sensations from the Council; and because of well-founded rumors in ecclesiastical circles crediting him with being a principal opponent of the Ottaviani thesis, he disclaimed all desire to prove a hero at the council. With a bow of deference to Cardinal Ruffini, he regretted that he had to contradict his venerable teacher, but he found the schema on revelation nothing more than a re-elaboration of a chapter in any good theology text-book. It certainly was not capable of clarifying the mind of the Church now; nor would it promote in the least the aim of the Council, by renewing the face of the Church so that it could invite all Christians to share with it the treasures of divine Truth.

Striking a practical note, the recently created cardinal of Belgium, Leo Suenens, expressed his fears that in view of all the talking, Vatican Council II threatened to outlast the eighteen years of the Council of Trent. He announced that he was against the schema because it was a botched-up job which had no relevance to the problems of the hour. He proposed a new method of procedure, in the hopes of getting the Council to act in a more parliamentary way. His suggestion was interesting in view of subsequent developments and seemed to prove to those benefiting from second-sight that he was perhaps closer to the throne than had formerly been suspected. Trained at Louvain, long a professor of moral theology there, and since 1945 archbishop of Malines-Brussels, he had written a book on conjugal love which had caused a mild sensation in Catholic theological circles. His intervention marked a kind of turning-point in the debate.

Cardinal Ritter, the cheerful, dynamic archbishop of St. Louis, for all the apparent simplicity of his approach, turned out to be the outstanding American prelate at the First Session. He next took the microphone to announce bluntly that the schema must be rejected: *"Rejiciendum est!"* Warming to the effect of this bombshell, he went on to condemn the draft as pessimistic, negative and full of unjust suspicions and fears. "What a tedious and unrealistic attitude it betrays toward the Word of God which we call the Scriptures!" he said, adding that the schema was calculated to inspire not love for the Bible but rather servile fear.

It was Cardinal Bea, eighty-two years old, feeble-looking, but patently rejuvenated in mind and heart who, with beguiling candor, laid the facts straight on the line. He began by graciously praising the work put into the schema, but informed its authors that they had evidently been marching in the wrong direction. Their end result "did not agree with the purpose set down by the Holy Father in summoning the Council." "What then did the pope have in mind?" he asked. If ever there was a moment when someone should have shouted *"Attenzione!"* to the opposition, this was it. The pope, said Cardinal Bea, had in mind "that the faith of the Church should be presented in all its integrity and purity, but in such manner that it will be received today with benevolence. For we are shepherds."

There was no need now for patristic or theological argument, he continued. "What our times demand is a pastoral approach, demonstrating the love and kindness that flow from our religion." This schema was totally lacking in the pastoral spirit. If a schema like this were to be called pastoral, then the same thing could be said of every theological textbook. "It represents the work of a theological school," he said, "not what the better theologians today think." He pointed out the many references in the schema to biblical scholars; yet there was only one favorable mention —all the rest were held suspect. It was not the Council's business, he said, to do the work of exegetes; to solve problems of inspiration, authorship, or inerrancy. "We must do an ecumenical job." The schema must be radically redone, he concluded, to render it shorter, clearer, and more pastoral. The voice was indeed that of Augustin Bea, but the sentiments were those of the Patriarch of the West, Angelo Roncalli, now Pope John XXIII.

The Melchite patriarch of Antioch, Maximos IV Saigh, concluded the arguments by making a fairly long statement in French: "What we expect is a peaceful and positive message, worthy of the attention of our separated brethren. The spirit of this schema is once again the spirit of the Counter-Reformation. . . . Since Vatican Council I only a partial and incomplete picture of the Church has been presented. The prerogatives of the Visible Head have been put in evidence in such an isolated way that the rest of the body of the Church seems dwarfish in comparison. We must reestablish the true proportions between the body and its head and thus give a truer and more complete picture. I ask once again that the schema on the Church and the hierarchy be submitted as soon as possible. Everything depends on that schema, because we can then take up pastoral and social questions. All of us await that moment."

At the conclusion of the patriarch's speech, as if in fulfillment of his wish, an official announcement was made that the very schema he was pleading for, *De Ecclesia,* would be distributed to the Fathers at the end of the week or the beginning of the next (actually distributed on Friday, November 23, 1962).

Shortly before the end, however, the results were announced of the voting on the liturgy schema as a whole, which took place before the discussions began. The ballots had been handed out by the Secretariat General, marked by each Father with an electronic pencil, and then were handed in to be tabulated by the electronic computer specially installed for this purpose. An overwhelming majority was registered in favor of the advocates of reform who were for the schema; 2,162 votes for, 46 votes against, and 7 abstentions. It was also a victory for the liturgical movement itself, which had inspired its authors throughout. The voting was interpreted by many as a clear sign of the way in which the wind was blowing.

That afternoon and evening the "little councils" of theologians, as they were called, were in a ferment of excitement and optimism. Things seemed to be going in the right direction at last. Rumor had it that at one of the last meetings of the Central Preparatory Commission, in May or June, Cardinal Léger had spoken out equally sharply on behalf of biblical scholars, denouncing the attacks on the Biblical Institute and deploring the obscurantist attitude toward biblical studies shown by the Lateran University.* The African bishops had met on Tuesday to coordinate their efforts with a view toward rejection of the schema. What transpired on Thursday (no congregation) in the Ottaviani camp, after the first day's

* See p. 34 ff.

rebuff, was not generally known. However, it soon became evident that they too had been reviewing their resources.

The next or 20th General Congregation was held on Friday, November 16th, and was introduced by a warning from the President, Cardinal Liénart, who called for an amicable settlement and fraternal consideration of opposing viewpoints. The first speaker was Cardinal Tisserant who, in a rapid flow of Latin that proved too much for the majority of the Fathers, reviewed the policy laid down by Pius XII regarding the investigation of scriptural questions, beginning with the letter of Father Vosté to Cardinal Suhard in 1943. He insisted that the Council should leave the field of Scripture open to free discussion by exegetes and theologians.

Cardinal Gonçalves Cerejeira of Lisbon, the primate of Portugal, then took the microphone to begin the defense of the schema. But his main efforts were directed against the leakage of information to the press which he had observed in recent days. How was it possible for the press to know about what was going to be said before it was actually said in the hall of the Council? He pleaded with all present, therefore—Fathers, experts and observers—to observe the secrecy of the Council. Then, in short order, Cardinals de Barros Câmara, McIntyre, and Caggiano launched into a repetition of the plea by Ruffini for a fair examination of the existing schema, while Cardinal Lefebvre, conscious of his debt to the men on the other side, merely cited his objections to it and then handed his paper to the Secretariat.

Cardinal Santos (Manila) was for retention, but suggested that more thought be given to stating precisely what was meant by "pastoral." Referring to the complaint raised by the cardinal-patriarch of Lisbon, Cardinal Urbani of Venice added that not only were the newspapers, journals and conférenciers of Rome and elsewhere freely discussing what was going on in the Council and airing all disputes, but seminarians in various parts of the world were being "spiritually disturbed" by the apparent confusion among those who were supposed to be the teachers of the Church. Hence he was for retaining the schema as a working basis in order not to give substance to these fears.

Speaking for the South American bishops, Cardinal Silva Henriquez of Chile stated that the pastoral aims of the Council should be directed particularly toward the sheep separated from the fold and hence, as the pope indicated, the Council ought to display an ecumenical spirit. As to the schema, not only was it objectionable from the viewpoint of possible reunion with non-Catholics, but it could not even bring about agreement among Catholics, as was evident from the discussions in seminaries and faculties of theology. Its primary error was to set the Church up as a condemning judge. The pope wanted pastors who counseled and demonstrated love for those to whom they were trying to bring the truth. In a theological sense, he insisted that truth was born of the charity of Almighty God, hence, in all charity, the Council should come out with a doctrine that would be clear, amicable, positive, timely and adaptable to modern needs. His conclusion was: re-do the draft in a much briefer form, and omit all questions of a purely exegetical nature. "We are pastors, not theologians. We have no time for the disputes of the schools."

The Irish Dominican Cardinal Browne (Curia) next rose to demonstrate that not all prelates were pastors, as had been asserted. In true scholastic form, he went through eleven points attempting to prove that since the doctrine of "two sources" [Scripture and tradition] formed part of the Church's doctrinal patrimony, it was therefore to be retained regardless of whether the expression was ancient. Thomas Aquinas, Trent, Vatican Council I, the encyclicals of Leo XIII, Pius XII, etc. were all in agreement on this, he maintained.

The following two speakers were at opposite poles. Conservative Archbishop Fares (Catanzaro, Italy) said that he was afraid of a resurgence of Modernism. The Council of Trent had warned against those who "twist the Scriptures" and Vatican Council I had asserted that dangerous innovators must be "coerced" and errors driven out, as Pius X had done when he condemned this heresy. For Archbishop Bengsch (Berlin), on the other hand, the schema was bad and could not be improved even by amendments. It contradicted the wishes of the Holy Father by reflecting a spirit of condemnation rather than of mercy. It was full of anathemas, censures and suspicions. The Church was made to appear not as our *Mater et Magister,* but solely as our *Magistra* (mistress). Some of the errors castigated in it were so obscure as to be hardly known even by theologians. It was a museum-piece, not something alive.

Bishop Reuss, the auxiliary of Mainz, Germany, called for a decision, by the Council or the pope, on certain fundamental questions such as the "two sources," the nature of the Church, the place of the episcopate and the like, otherwise the bishops would merely be floundering about without getting anywhere. Bishop Gargitter (Bressanone, Italy) was in favor of a completely new, positive and more pastoral schema. The Church owed a great debt of gratitude to Catholic exegetes and scholars generally, and should do nothing to put obstacles in their path. Bishop Hoa Nguyen-van-Hien (Dalat, Vietnam) likewise stressed the pastoral theme, but somehow lost himself in a sermon on the Trinity and had to be called to order by the President.

Some spirit was introduced into the debate by the bishop of Faenza, Battaglia, who labelled the arguments against the schema "fallacies and inanities." He attacked the Biblical Institute and the whole development of modern theology. Then in a rapid fire of irony and sarcasm, he acknowledged that the schema would probably be rejected, while proclaiming himself as a new Daniel in a den of lions, retaining his integrity withal.

Archbishop Guerry (Cambrai) next rose to speak in the name of the French episcopate. He desired to remove a certain equivocation that seemed to overshadow the debate. In speaking about a pastoral approach, there was no room for loose or inexact statements about doctrine. The Word of God must be set before the world in its purity and entirety. What was wanted, actually, was a deepening and enlarging of our doctrinal perspective, to include all the advances made by science and research in our world of today. This was not asking for a diminution but an extension of our doctrinal beliefs. But this should be done with charity, which meant choosing the hard way of working selflessly to approach modern man in his needs and anxieties, and not the easy way out by condemning and negating and rejecting.

After a plea for the scholastic approach of the schema from the archbishop of Florence, Ermenegildo Florit, and a contrary one in favor of rejection by the bishop of Tehuantepec in Mexico, Dom Butler, abbot of Downside in England, closed the day's discussion by aligning himself squarely with the rejecters. Although it had been said that the schema could be corrected, he noted that two days of debate had revealed that agreement was virtually impossible of attainment on the present text. There must be unanimity, or virtual unanimity, when decisions were reached by the Church on doctrinal matters. Experience had shown that there would always be some Non placets, even if the present schema were corrected. Therefore, it was better to scrap it and prepare another that would have some prospect of achieving this unanimity.

The debate on Saturday, November 17th (21st General Congregation), further accentuated the differences of opinion in the assembly and proved the justice of Dom Butler's contention; it was also highlighted by a certain number of personal exchanges and insinuations which, while not transgressing the outward decorum and courtesy expected of the conciliar Fathers, nevertheless testified to the increasing tension on both sides and the conviction that a crisis was at hand.

Cardinals de la Torre of Quito and Garibi y Rivera of Guadalajara (Mexico) first took the floor to argue for retention, at least as a basis for discussion. But they were immediately followed by the youthful-looking, intense Cardinal Doepfner of Munich, who had evidently made up his mind to bring matters to a head. He began by challenging the introductory remarks of Cardinal Ottaviani. "The president of the Theological Commission," he said, "has informed us that in the preparation of this schema, which took two years, there was a general accord on the part of the participating theologians and prelates. Cardinals Frings and Léger, however, have indicated just the opposite. Hence there is at least some doubt as to this accord and alleged unanimity. The regulations under which we operate specify that we can either accept, amend, or reject the schema. My impression is that the Theological Commission was too much under the influence of one school, represented by the Lateran University. There was no concern for any other tendencies. As an instance of this intransigence, I cite the fact that a proposal made by the Secretariat for Promoting Unity, with a view to collaborating with the Theological Commission, was turned down. It was therefore easy to foresee that dissensions would arise in the Council, because in the Council one can speak freely and openly. This is no sign of any irreverence toward the Holy Father, for he is the one who has given us permission to discuss, amend, or reject. Our right to judge is complete and we must finally vote. The schema which we would like to propose has been drawn up by theologians of various tendencies and is quite different in spirit from the one before us."*

This speech was greeted with considerable applause, and caused consternation in the opposing camp. In quick succession, Cardinals Concha (Bogotá) and Bacci (Curia) each put in a plea for the schema, the latter saying that it had been given to the Council by the pope and Central Commission to be discussed, not rejected.

Bishop Schmitt (Metz, France), a scriptural scholar in his own right, led off episcopal comment by referring to the question of "two sources" brought up by Cardinal Browne. Trent had deliberately rejected the use of the terms *"partim . . . partim"* with reference to Scripture and tradition, because this would have implied the sanctioning of a school of thought which was not traditional or in accord with the best tradition.

In apparent good humor Cardinal Ottaviani next took the floor. He proposed, he said, to answer the observations made by Cardinal Döpfner which, though obviously not intended maliciously, nevertheless sprang from misinformation. "It is not true that this schema was made in my name," he said. "In the Commission those matters in the schema that were the subject of discussion or disagreement were put to a vote. It was normal for the opinion of the minority then to be excluded. The members of this Commission came from various countries, from different universities. It is not true that only one opinion or one school of thought was represented." After claiming that members of the Biblical Institute had been invited to sit on the Commission, he concluded by repeating that the rules did not provide for the rejection but merely the discussion of the schema.

This last assertion was immediately and successfully challenged from the floor. An appeal was made to the President to read the Regulations; it

* See p. 76.

was thereupon settled once and for all that schemata could be discussed, amended or *rejected*.* Meanwhile, a member of the Theological Commission whose opinions had not been received by the cardinal disagreed with him about the presence of a member of the Biblical Institute on the Commission, and one of the cardinals said openly: "It's hardly worth repeating that His Eminence is not telling the truth. All the world knows it." Especially in the preparatory stages of the Council, it became generally known, opponents were skillfully maneuvered out of their places at Commission meetings, threatened with reprisals, and votes taken when they were absent, and this arbitrariness continued to a certain extent during the Council particularly in Commissions dominated by the "Old Guard," though on a lesser scale, owing to changed circumstances and a more watchful attitude on the part of the pope.

Archbishop Parente (Curia) next made a feeble attempt to defend a document which contained *"sana doctrina,"* as everyone knew, reiterating in particular its main theory about the "two sources" of revelation, but as he spoke beyond the allotted time he had to be cut off by the President. With his customary disregard for the proprieties, he then demanded time to conclude and stressed once again the soundness of the document for the benefit of the Fathers, "worthy of being recommended for your discussion." His successor Bishop Butorac had hardly finished his remarks in the same sense, when Cardinal Frings took the floor.

"One word is all I desire," he said, "to answer Archbishop Parente. No one denies that revelation comes to us through both Scripture and tradition. What we are arguing about is the *source* of revelation, which is one and unique, namely the Word of God."

Bishop Charue (Namur, Belgium) put his finger on the real difficulty with the Ottaviani approach. Calling attention to the fact that all the Belgian and French bishops were against the schema, he attacked the necessity of repeating the condemnation of Modernism. There were other errors, he insisted, that were just as dangerous. "It is not up to the Council to do the work of the Holy Office or of theologians," he said, "but it is up to the Council not to set the stage for another Galileo incident! Our Council should imitate the Council of Jerusalem, and not put unbearable burdens on those outside the Church or the faith. The fact that the Church can house men of diverse opinions and attitudes gives us hope for the future."

After Bishop Temiño Saiz of Spain had voiced once again what may be regarded as the Italian-Spanish view of the matter, an archbishop from Central Africa, Jean Zoa (Yaoundé), speaking in the name of all African

---

* Art. 33.1 of the Rules of Procedure stated specifically: "Each Father may express his opinion with regard to each schema presented and ask either for its adoption, rejection, or amendment." *Motu Proprio Appropinquante Concilio,* Aug. 6, 1962. (The Rules were an appendix to this document.)

bishops, said that they rallied to the opinions expressed by Cardinals Alfrink, Bea, Léger, and Liénart. The schema "was not satisfactory at all" (*omnino non placet*) and ought to be rejected. He also agreed with what Abbot Butler had said the previous day with regard to moral unanimity. This was the sense also of the two following speakers, Bishop Pourchet (France) and Bishop Hakim (Israel).

The hopelessness of being able to arrive at any kind of compromise on the schema was borne in on the Fathers as they assembled for their 22nd General Congregation on Monday morning, November 19th, with Cardinal Spellman in the chair. Most of the speeches touched on the theme that was uppermost in their minds, namely how to find a way of escape out of the present impasse. It was apparent that the majority of the Fathers were not in favor of the schema as it stood, but there was uncertainty about the wisdom of rejecting it outright. Many felt that to remand it to the Commission that had originally submitted it (the Preparatory and Conciliar Theological Commissions were both headed by Cardinal Ottaviani and staffed by many of the same people) would only complicate matters, hardening Ottaviani and his supporters in their advocacy of it.

Various suggestions were put forth. Returning from India (where he had gone when his country was invaded by China) expressly in order to take part in the important debate, Cardinal Gracias revealed that he was wholly in favor of rejection. It was not possible to say that the Holy Father had approved it, as the opposition was maintaining. What he had approved was the submission of it to the Council, as desired by the Theological Commission—quite a different thing. When a house was falling into ruin it was better to demolish it and build another, rather than to attempt repairs. "The Preparatory Commision had no momopoly of the Holy Spirit and wisdom." The Council was assisted by the Holy Ghost in a way that theologians were not. The schema ought to be re-done, but he had no concrete suggestions about method.

Neither had Cardinals de Arriba y Castro or Gilroy, the first speakers of the day, who inclined to making the best of a bad situation. The following two speakers, Cardinals Meyer of Chicago and Landázuri Ricketts of Lima, were congratulated by Cardinals Léger and Ottaviani, respectively, when each had finished, but they too had nothing concrete to offer in the way of an expedient. Both sides, however, still welcomed support. Bishop Griffiths, one of the auxiliaries of New York, was of the opinion that the schema would have to be rejected *"radicaliter"* and a new one prepared, one, that is, that the whole assembly could accept.

The speech of the morning, however, was admittedly that delivered by Bishop de Smedt, of Bruges, Belgium, a member of the Secretariat for Promoting Unity, who rose to say that he was speaking for the Secretariat. As on an earlier occasion when Cardinal Bea spoke, so on this one, the Fathers had the unmistakable impression that they were listening to the words of the pope himself.

He began by remarking that there had been much discussion about ecumenism or the ecumenical spirit with reference to the subject under debate, some arguing that the schema reflected a proper ecumenical concern, others that it did not. What then was an authentic ecumenical outlook? Speaking as a member of the Secretariat for Promoting Christian Unity, which had been created by the Holy Father expressly for the purpose of aiding the Fathers in the ecumenical aspect of their work, he would attempt to define what an ecumenically-oriented document ought to be. It was one, in short, which favored and promoted a conversation (dialogue) between Catholics and non-Catholics.

Bishop de Smedt then went on to note that, although the Secretariat for Promoting Unity had been created to help with the preparations for the Council and had offered to collaborate with the Theological Commission, "for reasons which I do not care to judge," the Theological Commission "never wished to reciprocate." The Secretariat also proposed the creation of a mixed subcommission, but this offer too was turned down.

In the judgment of the Secretariat, the present schema had "grave faults from an ecumenical point of view: It would not encourage a dialogue with non-Catholics, or represent progress, but a retreat. . . . Today a new method has been discovered, thanks to which a precious dialogue has been begun. The fruits of this method are apparent to all from the presence of the observer-delegates in this council hall. The hour is one of pardon, but also one of great seriousness. If the schema prepared by the Theological Commission is not modified, we shall be responsible for causing Vatican Council II to destroy a great, an immense hope. I speak of the hope of those who, like Pope John XXIII, are waiting in prayer and fasting for an important and significant step finally to be made in the direction of fraternal unity, the unity of those for whom Christ Our Lord offered this prayer: *Ut unum sint.*" There was loud and continuous applause when the bishop finished.

The search for some kind of solution now seemed more imperative than ever. Earlier, Cardinal Rugambwa had suggested asking the Holy Father to stop the discussion now, since the Council could reach no agreement, and proposed taking it up again at the next session on the basis of a new document. Bishop Henríquez Jimenez (Venezuela) felt that any new document must reflect the views of the Pontifical Biblical Commission.

It was Archbishop Garrone of Toulouse who made the concrete proposal about setting up a mixed commission to prepare a new draft. Since the schema could not be returned to the commission that had originated it, "it

88

is necessary that the Theological Commission should work in unison with the Secretariat for Unity and with the *periti* (experts)." This would bring about that unanimity which the whole Council desired.

"The original sin of the Council lay in the defective work of the Preparatory Commissions," observed Archbishop Hurley of South Africa. The proper solution in this case was for the schema to be re-done by a new commission which would be careful to put back into the draft all that had been left out by the Theological Commission.

Finally, Bishop Ancel (Lyons) noted that a two-thirds majority being clearly impossible either for or against any proposal, there was no alternative but to appeal to the Holy Father to appoint new experts to prepare a new schema. The last speaker, Bishop Seitz (Vietnam), proposed that the Council vote on one or another of the suggestions put forth.

Accordingly, on the next day, November 20th (23rd General Congregation), at 10:30 in the morning, the debate was dramatically halted by Secretary General Felici, who announced that a proposal by the Council Presidents would be put to a vote.* Those in favor of halting the discussion of the schema were to vote *Placet* (Yes); those favoring a continuation of the discussion *Non placet* (No). The announcement was then repeated in all six languages by the under-secretaries. Cardinal Frings, the President of the day, explained: "Although this proposal does not please us completely, it seems to me the best solution, the most harmonious, and the one that will best serve the common good." After a moment, Secretary General Felici again said: *"Audiant omnes,* there have been queries about the voting. I repeat: *Placet* means interrupting the debate, *Non placet* continuing with the discussion. Those who have made a mistake can ask for new ballots." At 10:55 he was forced to repeat what he had said.

Apparently there was widespread confusion among the Fathers as to what they were being asked to vote on, owing to the illogical way in which the question had been framed.† While they were deliberating what to do or filling out their ballots, Cardinal Ruffini, sitting at the table of Council Presidents, gratuitously announced: "Interrupting the debate means that this schema will be completely overhauled and changed. Therefore if you vote *Placet,* it means the last of this schema." This attempt to influence votes was not at all well received by the Council. There were many

* Although there was no statement to this effect, the pope had of course permitted this move.

† The question arises whether this was done deliberately, a desperate last-minute move on the part of the supporters of the schema in the hope of winning an overwhelming victory by confusing the voters, or was it merely accidental? The words of Cardinal Ruffini would seem to lend weight to the former supposition, but those of Cardinal Frings appear to rule this possibility out.

protests and much talking. Nevertheless Ruffini repeated his remarks two more times until he was finally drowned out.

The debate was then resumed at 11 A.M., but at 11:23 it was again halted by the Secretary General, who announced the results of the voting: "Present: 2,209 Fathers; 1,368 Placets; 19 invalid votes; and 822 Non placets. Since a majority of 1,473 votes is required, we shall therefore now take up Chapter I of the schema."

Thus the supporters had won a technical victory, but the fruits were to be denied them. It was the conviction of many that the total number of protestors would have been greater but for the confusion surrounding the voting—some Fathers on both sides were known to have voted unwittingly against their principles.

The next morning, while Cardinal Ruffini was presiding, another dramatic announcement was made. Despite the vote, the pope had ordered the schema withdrawn. He had decided that the whole matter should be reconsidered by a special commission, on which Cardinals Bea and Ottaviani would serve as joint presidents, with Cardinals Frings, Liénart, and Meyer representing the liberals, Cardinals Browne of Ireland and Ruffini the traditionalists, and Cardinal Lefebvre of Bourges the center. They were to be assisted by the bishops belonging to the Secretariat for Promoting Christian Unity and the bishops elected to the Theological Commission by the Council, as well as by a number of *periti,* or official theologians. The new decree to be drafted in accordance with the aims of the Council was to be short, irenic in tone, and pastoral in approach.

Though there was nothing more to say, this meeting was prolonged until noon, so that an early breakup would not give rise to rumors. Nevertheless, the essential facts were soon in the newspapers. On this occasion, the Vatican newspaper *L'Osservatore Romano,* which consistently reflected the Curial line, departed from its usual terseness. Although it disclosed some of the details about the impasse, it failed to mention the all-important outcome of the vote, thus veiling the discomfiture of the conservative bloc as long as possible.

Later on the 21st, the aula of the Gregorian University was crowded with an unprecedented number of distinguished auditors (12 cardinals, 150 bishops, innumerable council experts, seminarians and visitors as well as the observer delegate Oscar Cullmann, the German ambassador, etc.) to hear Father Lohfink defend his thesis on Deuteronomy. Normally the subject would have drawn a mere handful of interested persons. They were there to express their elation at the new turn of events and to protest the attitude of the Holy Office toward the Biblical Institute.

It was bewildering how a man of Cardinal Ottaviani's intelligence could have miscalculated so badly. It seems strange that he did not anticipate that the majority would be for reforms which had been advocated in respectable circles for many years now, and were looked upon with favor by the pope. One theory was that Ottaviani's closest advisers and informants—Archbishop Parente and the Franciscan Father Ermenegildo Lio (both of the Holy Office), and those at a farther remove such as Monsignor Joseph Fenton (of Catholic University) and Monsignor Rudolph Bandas (of St. Paul, Minnesota) among others—had convinced him that only a handful of extremist German and French prelates really wanted drastic changes in the Church. Apparently, they and the others who assisted with the preparation of the schema (like the Jesuit Fathers Sebastian Tromp and Franz Huerth, the Dominican Luigi Ciappi, and the Franciscan Carl Balič) could conceive of no other way of presenting Catholic truths than by repeating the tried-and-true formulas of the past and condemning all innovation.

Undoubtedly, the most important single disclosure of the First Session was the great strength shown by the advocates of renewal and reform. It had not previously been known just how influential this tendency in the Church really was.* The chief spokesman in the Curia for the new approach was unquestionably Cardinal Bea, whose efforts over the past two years had been and continued to be nothing short of phenomenal. "My whole life has been a preparation for this," he declared.

The new Secretariat for Promoting Christian Unity, over which he presided, was the first Roman office to have achieved the miracle—Bea's own word—of being completely outside the domination of the Holy Office. Since Bea had been directed by papal decree to collaborate with Ottaviani in drafting a new schema on the sources of revelation, this meant that he had now been given the right to be heard on strictly theological matters, which, up to the present, Ottaviani had successfully retained within the exclusive control of the Holy Office. The consequences of this decision were far-reaching. In effect, it warned the Old Guard that they were not the sole guardians of orthodoxy, and that henceforth they must heed the advice of authentic biblical scholarship and display a more ecumenical spirit. A familiar sight in Rome was the BEA on the poster for British European Airways, accordingly Italian wits soon claimed that a new sign had been posted over the door of the Holy Office: "Travel with BEA."

Another fruitful result of the First Session was the interchange of ideas made possible by the concentration of so many learned priests in one place at one time. Most of the bishops rejoiced at this development, and took advantage of free hours between meetings to brush up on issues by inviting *periti* to lecture before their episcopal conferences. The Holy

* Cf. the statement of Cardinal Frings reported in *The Catholic Transcript*, March 21, 1963: "The majority of bishops share a moderate progressive tendency, and it appears that they will have the two-thirds majority against the more conservative minority."

Office, unaccustomed to so much uncontrolled theologizing, found this distasteful and alarming. Toward the middle of November, Cardinal Ottaviani asked the pope to request the Jesuit fathers of the Biblical Institute not to give any more lectures before individual groups of bishops, and to order the famous Innsbruck theologian Father Karl Rahner, S.J., to leave Rome. When the pope inquired who had asked the Jesuit fathers to lecture, and was told that it had been the bishops themselves, he said he could not be expected to interfere with the legitimate right of bishops to inform themselves regarding the issues before the Council. At the same time, he was said to have shown Ottaviani a testimonial, signed by three cardinals, praising Father Rahner as an outstanding theologian. This incident reminded old Roman hands of the disgraceful treatment meted out to Professor Altaner, the famous authority on the early fathers of the Church, in 1950, when he was told to leave Rome because of his opposition to the project for defining the Assumption of the Virgin Mary. They likewise recalled the shabby treatment recently accorded the Dominican theologian Father Raimondo Spiazzi, who, during the preparatory phase of the Council, was bold enough to publish a pamphlet discussing possible changes in the attitude toward clerical celibacy. The mere suggestion of any revision in this regard being frowned on by the Holy Office as a sure sign of heresy, Father Spiazzi was immediately relieved of his job in the papal Chancery, transferred from his teaching post, barred from Rome, and sent to Tuscany as provincial of his Order. Eventually, this came to the attention of Pope John, who at once ended Father Spiazzi's exile and appointed him a member fo the Council's Preparatory Commission on the Laity.

DEBATE ON COMMUNICATIONS MEDIA

The mood of the Council fluctuated considerably during the weeks of November, from one of discouragement and dejection at the slow pace of the deliberations, to relief at the termination of the debate on the liturgy, then from varying shades of determination, excitement, dejection and frustration over the schema *De Revelatione,* to one of final elation and optimism over the success achieved. Pope John himself appears to have been the only person capable of maintaining a serene air throughout in keeping with his habitual optimism. There was some resentment among the Fathers over the way in which the voting had been handled on November 20th. Yet curiously, the following day, when word of the pope's intervention was announced, there was no applause, merely stunned amazement. The number of smiles as the bishops emerged from their Wednesday congregation clearly betokened the change of mood. The euphoria engendered that day continued to sustain the First Session till the end, despite a renewed controversy over the schema *De Ecclesia.*

On Friday, November 23rd, the Council took up the schema on Modern Means of Communication (including the press, radio, motion pictures and television) in its 25th General Congregation presided over by Cardinal Caggiano, archbishop of Buenos Aires. The mass was said by Archbishop Giacinto Tredici of Brescia, who, that very day, was celebrating the sixtieth anniversary of his ordination to the priesthood. For the occasion a number of priests and lay people from Brescia were allowed to attend the opening ceremonies. The Gospel was enthroned by Bishop Alberto Scola of Norcia, Italy.

As soon as the meeting proper came to order, the Secretary General rose to announce that the next subject for discussion would be the schema on the Unity of the Church, prepared by the Commission for the Oriental Churches. This would be followed by that dealing with the Virgin Mary, and finally that on the Church. The latter two schemata were contained in a separate booklet that was distributed during this congregation, causing considerable distraction to a large number of Fathers who had been anxiously awaiting the document on the Church, for it was feared that, as the work of the Theological Commission, it was bound to reflect the scholastic and juridical approach manifested in the schema on Revelation. It was rumored, likewise, that there had been no attempt to co-ordinate the treatment of the nature of the Church in the various schemata prepared by different Commissions. In the event, both these suspicions proved well grounded.

Cardinal Cento, chairman of the Commission for the Apostolate of the Laity and Communications Media, in his preliminary remarks, stated that the project now being presented had been prepared by a special secretariat presided over by Archbishop Martin J. O'Connor, Rector of the American College in Rome, and for the past fourteen years president of the Pontifical Commission for Motion Pictures, Radio and Television. In turning the rostrum over to Archbishop René Stourm of Sens, who was to give the Fathers a general outline of the schema, Cardinal Cento asked for the good will of the audience in dealing with a matter which, though not strictly theological in nature, was still a most important element in the pastoral work of the Church, for "these instruments of communication could prove to be either a great blessing or a terrible curse both for the Church and the faithful." In turn, Bishop Stourm remarked that while the substance of the schema should prove to be theologically less strenuous than its immediate predecessor, it was precisely here that the Church was called upon to function as a Mother, well aware of the needs of her children. He outlined the schema itself, which was divided into a preface and four parts: the first dealt with the doctrine of the Church; the second provided a commentary on the apostolic function of the means of communication; the third dealt with the disciplinary aspects of these means; and the fourth laid down special considerations for the press, radio and television, and motion pictures.

Cardinal Spellman took the floor immediately after the exposition of the schema. While praising its usefulness, he called for a considerable abbreviation of the material, asking that it be reduced to propositional formulas. This was likewise the gist of Cardinal Ruffini's remarks, though he also stressed the pastoral spirit of the document. Archbishop Enrique y Tarancón (Oviedo, Spain) while agreeing wholeheartedly with the importance of the schema, pointed out the necessity of technical training if modern means of communication were to be employed correctly, and asked if priests were really competent to direct work in this field; or if it should not be stated, definitely, that this was an area where the layman's special training and experience were to be utilized to the full.

Bishop Sanschagrin (coadjutor of Amos, Canada) departing somewhat from the theme under discussion, registered a complaint that bishops were frequently among the last to receive authentic information about the decisions and documents of the Holy See. He requested that air-mail and other quick, international means of communication should be employed by the Vatican, and that the bishops should be informed of major moves or decisions before the latter were given to the press. He cited for example, the considerable stir about socialism that followed the publication of *Mater et Magister,* and the confusion that reigned several years earlier when the changes in the regulations governing the eucharistic fast were first announced in the newspapers. He requested the Council to go on record as insisting on the bishops' right to be informed about official acts of the Holy See before these were released to the press.

Bishop Beck (Salford, England) suggested that it was rather useless for so large and important an assembly as the Council to attempt to discuss at length the employment of particular communication media. In order to save time, he felt the schema should be reduced to a series of propositions outlining the principles involved and laying down guidelines for a dynamic utilization of these indispensable instruments of the Gospel in modern times. Bishop Llopis Ivorra (Coria-Cáceres, Spain) was of a similar mind; but Bishop Bednorz (Katowice in Poland) said that it was absolutely essential for all pastors to recognize the fact that today "we are living in a civilization of the image, and no longer in a civilization of abstract thought." As a consequence, churchmen could not adopt a passive and aloof attitude toward the communications revolution going on about them. Incidentally, he stated his annoyance with photographers who were allowed to pursue their trade in the very midst of liturgical functions in church.

Bishop Charrière (Lausanne and Fribourg, Switzerland) stated that as counsellor of UNDA for fourteen years he felt that it was the Council's duty to insist unconditionally on the importance of this subject for the work of the Church today. Agreeing that modern civilization was devoted to the cult of images, he outlined the concomitant danger of a depersonalization of the individual; and the consequent necessity of keeping in mind that from the very beginning the "Word of God" was communicated "by hearing." Hence, he said, these means of communication were much more important for us as preachers than they were for secular moralists and philosophers. Bishop Fernández-Conde (Cordova, Spain) criticized the failure of the schema to condemn more precisely the evils connected with modern entertainment; whereas Bishop D'Avack (Camerino, Italy) congratulated the authors on the generally optimistic tone adopted, then suggested that along with the positive measures for the effective employment of the proper media in preaching the Gospel, stress should be laid particularly on their use in seminaries and religious houses, and on their non-use as works of mortification and self-denial. He likewise called for the establishment, on a worldwide basis, of Legions of Decency similar to those existing in the United States, and wanted a reminder to fathers of families about their duty to control what their children saw and read.

Archbishop d'Souza (Bhopal, India) said that he regretted the insistence on the rights of the Church expressed in the document. He believed that such declarations were easily misunderstood by modern governments. Rather he felt that the emphasis should be placed on the rights and duties of bishops within the Church to utilize these media, and to entrust their employment to competent laymen rather than to priests whose primary tasks were preaching and the administration of the sacraments. Bishop Cantero Cuadrado (Huelva, Spain) complained about the length of the document, but then launched into such an extended consideration of particular points that he had to be stopped by the Cardinal President for going over the allotted time. Bishop de Castro Mayer (Campos, Brazil) condemned the evils accompanying secular use of the media, while Bishop Heuschen called for mention of the use of international press agencies also. Three speakers brought the morning's discussions to a close. In general, they dealt with the conditions of the press in their own countries: the controlled press in Lithuania; the possibilities of an effective apostolate even where the Church was only a small minority as in Indonesia; and the problems that must be faced in a modern nation like France.

The discussion was continued Saturday, November 24th in the 26th General Congregation under the presidency of Cardinal Alfrink, with Cardinal Wyszynski as the first speaker. But first the attention of the conciliar Fathers was directed to a telegram of congratulation sent to the Holy Father, in the name of the Council, on the occasion of his eighty-first birthday on the morrow. The text was read by Secretary General Felici.

Cardinal Wyszynski spoke of the effectiveness of radio and television in reaching those indifferent to religious values—people who though they never entered a church were tempted, out of curiosity at least, to watch something religious on the radio or television. Hence he asked that Vatican radio and other stations under ecclesiastical control give much more time to the reading of the Gospel and the explanation of the faith. Cardinal Godfrey (Westminster) expressed his doubts about the suitability of this schema as an integral part of the Council's acts. He felt it would be better transformed into a pontifical document for the guidance of clergy and laity; and have the Council confine its attention to the elaboration of a number of principles. He praised the value of television and the cinema, but said that churchmen needed to interest themselves in curbing the excesses and evils to which these propaganda and entertainment media gave rise. In praising the diocesan press, however, he called attention to the necessity for encouraging the laity generally to follow the issues of the day in the secular journals, under the guidance of their pastors, in order that the Church might be kept fully abreast of the world's doings and problems.

The question of church rights was stressed by Cardinal Léger of Montreal. He warned against too great an insistence on them, calling rather for a statement that would make clear the Church's maternal solicitude for the rights of all men to have the truth placed before them. "The power of modern means of communication is so great," said the cardinal, "that it is ridiculous to try to insulate people against it; rather we must adopt it fearlessly, putting an end to the negative type of criticism characteristic of so many churchmen in the past." It was Cardinal Suenens (Malines-Brussels) who brought up the important, practical problems presented by modern journalism, with its disregard for a man's right to privacy. He said great injustice was involved in interference with the mails, eavesdropping, wire- and telephone-tapping, and the invasion of a man's home. He proposed that the Council lay down principles for a code of ethics that would be the equivalent of the rules governing legal and medical practice, and that some organizations, similar to the fair-practice commissions of lawyers and doctors, be set up to discipline the communications media. He suggested finally that Catholic reaction to radio and television presentations should be educated and then utilized to influence the producers. In so doing, great effort should be made to avoid the banal and trite when calling for time in the interest of things religious.

Calling attention to the fact that there were some nine hundred million Christians in the world, Cardinal Bea stated that if they were to cooperate with all men of good will in safeguarding human and divine values in a positive fashion, it would not be too difficult to solve most of the problems connected with means of communication. Picking up the suggestion made the previous day in favor of a world-wide press agency run from the Vatican, he said such a project was urgent and should be encouraged by the Fathers of the Council.

The bishop of Meaux, Jacques Ménager, complained that the schema did not put the part to be played by the laity in the Church in proper perspective. Here, certainly, was the field in which the layman was not only competent but required by the very nature of things to give testimony to the world of a Christian and therefore dignified way of life, by making his presence felt in the use of every type of communications media. Archbishop Perraudin (Kabgayi, Ruanda), speaking in the name of the African bishops, thanked the Preparatory Commission for the schema, which they felt was a great encouragement in facing the problems of a land in turmoil and thirsting for the solid truth of the Catholic faith. Then he made an appeal to the conciliar Fathers generally to aid in the establishment of radios for the people of all Africa, saying that the necessity of getting the Word of God to his people was so pressing now, that in five years' time it would be too late.

Concern for the way in which the Catholic journalists reported events in countries which they either did not know well, or whose peculiar traditions and history they were unable to understand, was voiced by Bishop Gonzalez Martin of Astorga, Spain. This statement was of course a reflection of the sensitivity of the Spanish bishops about the widespread criticism of the way in which their government handled religious minorities, in the Catholic press of France, the Netherlands, Germany and the United States, in particular.

The next speaker, Archbishop Castellano of Siena, brought up the subject of the Index of Forbidden Books and suggested that it be abolished. This was something of a surprise, coming from an Italian prelate. Contrary to reports in the press, however, there was little discussion of this topic on the floor of the assembly. The Fathers were wholly concerned with principles, or tried to be; there was a general feeling that all details relating to the practical application of these principles should be left in the hands of experts. Thus, the Index did not become a burning issue.

When Bishop Ruotolo (Ugento, Italy) launched into a tirade against positivism and idealism in modern art, he was asked by the President to return to the text of the schema. Then, while turning his attention to the question of church music, he quickly got off once more on a philosophical tangent and again had to be interrupted by Cardinal Alfrink. The importance of radio sermons was stressed by Bishop Oña de Echave (Lugo, Spain) who suggested that episcopal conferences should lay down norms for training the clergy in the proper techniques. Bishop de Uriarte

Bengoa (Peru) had to be called to order several times for his vigorous denunciations of priests and religious who wasted time going to the moving pictures instead of attending to their duties in the confessional and in church, but the aged prelate who was hard of hearing appeared not to understand.

The timeliness and importance of the material in the schema were praised by Bishop Nezič (Yugoslavia). He suggested, however, that it would perhaps be better to incorporate it in a separate document published with the Council's approval. In its present state it was too unwieldy for a conciliar decree. He proposed, likewise, that since the schema had been sufficiently exhausted, the Council should move on to a new topic.

Resuming discussion of the Communications schema on Monday, November 26th, in its 27th General Congregation, the Council began its labors that day with a reading to the Fathers of the pope's reply to their telegram of congratulation on his birthday. It was then announced that because of the shortness of the remaining time, the Council would meet in congregation every day except Sunday during December, until the 8th, when it was due to adjourn with a solemn ceremony presided over by the pope. After consideration of the schema on the Unity of the Church, which was to come next, the bishops would take up the schema on the Church.

The distribution of this long-awaited document, prepared by the Theological Commission and touching upon some of the most crucial theological problems in which there was widespread interest, had proved to be a distracting influence on the previous Friday, as we have said. Many of the prelates plunged at once into a study of its pages, thus allowing their attention to be diverted from the subject under consideration, and contributing to the belief that the Council was wasting its time discussing Communications.

Hence there was no appreciable opposition when the President proposed, at 11:10, that a standing vote be taken on ending the debate on Communications Media. The following day this schema too was voted on in principle, the proposal specifying that it be sent back to committee to be shortened and reworked with principles being separated from more practical matters, and the latter incorporated in a pastoral instruction prepared by the Pontifical Commission for Radio, Cinema and Television. The results were overwhelmingly in favor: 2,138 to 15, with 7 invalid ballots.

DEBATE ON UNITY

The tragic disunity of Christians of which contemporaries are so acutely aware today is almost as old as Christianity itself.

The schema on the Unity of the Church, appropriately entitled '*Ut unum sint,*' which was taken up during the remaining hour of the 27th General Congregation, on Monday, November 26th, and debated on the following four days, had been prepared by the Preparatory Commission for the Oriental Churches. It was concerned exclusively with the principles, ways and means of achieving reunion with the Eastern Orthodox. Two other schemata had also been prepared dealing with the general theme of unity, one by the Theological Commission, which had in mind particularly the Protestants, and another by the Secretariat for Promoting Christian Unity, which was concerned with general ecumenical principles. The question naturally arose, why, in view of the obvious similarity of these schemata, and particularly when it was remembered that the Secretariat had been created expressly for the purpose of coordinating all activity in this field,* it had not been decided to present a single schema to the Council, or at least three coordinated drafts that could later be fused into one? One factor unquestionably was the total unwillingness of the Theological Commission to cooperate with any other organ out of a desire to monopolize all theological discussion.† Another was the fact that the Commission for the Oriental Churches, dominated like all the commissions by the corresponding Congregation of the Roman Curia, in this case the Congregation for the Oriental Churches, regarded all the Eastern Churches as its particular sphere, although in fact its activities were traditionally confined almost entirely to contacts with the various Oriental Churches in communion with Rome. The separated Orthodox, by and large, would have nothing to do with either Congregation or Commission, looking upon both as mere "tools" designed to undermine their position and Latinize the East. A certain amount of internecine rivalry, therefore, was undoubtedly responsible for the present situation, which the Central Preparatory Commission either would not, or could not, resolve. It must be acknowledged, likewise, that Cardinal Bea's Secretariat did not at first enjoy, within the confines of the Church, the tremendous prestige which it later acquired, and the advantages of having it coordinate *all* aspects of the problem of reunion, theological as well as practical, were not fully seen at first, although presupposed in theory.

At 11:10 Cardinal Cicognani took the microphone to introduce the schema, which dealt only with the prospects for reunion with the Ortho-

---

* When the Unity Secretariat was first formed (1960) it was thought that it would concern itself only with Protestants within the framework of its larger responsibility, but this soon proved to be impractical. Its members were in contact both with Orthodox and Protestant Churches, individuals as well as corporate bodies, without any discrimination whatsoever. The Secretariat was given a status similar to that of the other conciliar Commissions by the pope on October 19, 1962, during the First Session.

† See p. 88.

dox Churches, as we have said. He pointed to the fact that never before in history had such an effort been made to find ways of drawing all Christians back into the true fold of Christ and asked that all prejudice, fear and distrust connected with the historical causes of the separation now be laid aside. The schema itself was then outlined by Father Athanasius Welykyj, of the Order of St. Basil of St. Josaphat, who had served as secretary of the Preparatory Commission. Noting that problems having to do with rites and ceremonies were being covered by other commissions, he said that the purpose of the present schema was to study the best way of achieving reconciliation with the separated Eastern brethren.

Cardinal Liénart (Lille) led off the discussion. While admitting that the schema contained useful principles, he felt that its general tenor was too authoritative; and that by its insistence on the idea of a "return to the true fold" it was placing a hopeless obstacle in the way of reunion. He suggested that a truly pastoral approach should admit that faults on both sides had contributed in the past to the split between the Churches. Besides, he said, attention should be paid to the fact that the Orthodox Churches were many, each with its own traditions; hence they could not be approached en bloc. What should be brought out, however, was that as the Orthodox Christians were marked with the same baptismal character and shared the same faith and sacraments as Catholics, whatever was holding the various groups apart was accidental and could be removed by a vigorous effort at mutual understanding. For this purpose a special commission should be created to follow up the Council's recommendations.

Cardinal Ruffini (Palermo) spoke next, suggesting that the schema should be coordinated with those prepared by the Theological Commission and the Secretariat for Promoting Reunion. He then listed various corrections to be made in the text, but insisted that while Catholics might not have been exempt from fault in occasioning the split, one should not say that both sides were equally to blame. The Catholic Church "has ever remained firm in the midst of the storms" and was "without spot or wrinkle" in its possession of the truth. Hence it was not proper to speak of others as "parts of the Church," but rather as "parts of Christendom."

Cardinal Bacci (Curia) quibbled about the title "On the unity of the Church," remarking that as the Church was already one, the schema should be called De omnium christianorum unitate procuranda, at once satisfying theological precision and a penchant for elegant Latinity. He was against creating a new commission, however, since "one has the Roman Curia" and use should be made of what already existed.*

* It was always one of the complaints of the Eastern Churches in communion with Rome that the Roman Curia was constantly attempting to override their special privileges and subject them to its own regulations, at variance with Eastern tradition

The day's debate was concluded by Cardinal Browne (Curia) who maintained that the schema was excellent. While in a matter of this kind one should always proceed with extreme charity, still equal care must be taken to safeguard the truth, both from a theological and social point of view. Hence before being discussed in earnest, the schema ought to be completed with a clear statement of theological principles.

The 28th General Congregation convened on Tuesday, November 27th, under the presidency of Cardinal Liénart. The secretary general read a statement announcing that in view of the recommendations of so many prelates, the Holy Father had decided to postpone the Second Session from May 12, 1963 to September 8, 1963, in order to give those from great distances more time at home.

He then read a declaration, in the name of the Commission for the Oriental Churches, intended to clear up objections and confusion regarding the purpose of the schema under consideration. It related only to the Orthodox, not Protestants. In the first part, the intention was to outline the actual situation of those Churches separated from the Catholic Church, and not to give a complete theological explanation of the constitution of the Church. The proposals made in the second part regarding the principles to be applied in working for reunion were without prejudice to what the Theological Commission proposed in its schema on the Church. Finally, the schema was designed to help Catholics adopt a right attitude toward the problem of reunion with the Orthodox.

Cardinal de Barros Câmara (Rio de Janeiro) spoke first on Tuesday. He declared himself to be against any false irenicism, but suggested that in the Litany of the Saints where both those in error and infidels were prayed for, the two categories should be separated, for the *errantes* were not outside the faith.

Patriarch Maximos IV Saigh, speaking in French, said that as the schema dealt with the Orthodox it did not concern Eastern Catholics directly. However, as it was of such great importance, he desired to point out that certain sections, particularly in the first part, would only serve to enrage rather than attract those among the Orthodox who were benevolently disposed toward Catholicism, for these passages were inspired by the old Roman absolutism, and gave an unbalanced picture of both the history and responsibility for the earlier split in Christendom. It must be realized, he insisted, that the Oriental Churches were completely distinct from the Latin Church. They owed their origins directly to Christ and the Apostles, and received their traditions and rites from the Greek and Oriental Fathers. Hence, even in their organization, they were not dependent on

---

and reflecting a western or Latin mentality. This was one of the recurrent themes of the Melchite Patriarch Maximos IV Saigh and his co-bishops.

the See of Rome. Since this was the case, he asked, were Fathers such as Basil, the Gregories, Cyril and Chrysostom to be considered as Catholics of a lower rank than the Latin Fathers? The schema should speak a truly Catholic language. First it should mention the collegial character of the Church's pastorate, the bishops being the successors of the college of Apostles, and then only come to the papal primacy as the basis, foundation and center of that collegiality. Next he recommended that the three separate schemata prepared by the Theological and Oriental Commissions and the Secretariat for Unity should be combined. "When many hands prepare the cooking, the meat is sure to be burnt," according to an old Arab proverb.

Bishop Pawlowski (Poland) warned against any precipitate action that might be intereperted as a false irenicism, while Archbishop Nabaa, one of the Under-Secretaries of the Council (Melchite, Beirut), suggested that while the schema laid down various principles for reunion, the actual work would have to be done on a social level by cooperating with the Orthodox in projects for peace and justice, by observing together special feasts and occasions for joint prayer, and finally by abrogating the recent marriage legislation contained in the new (Curially-inspired) Code of Canon Law for the Oriental Church.

Archbishop Parecattil (Ernakulam, India) objected to a number of expressions in the schema and particularly to a reference to Eastern Christians as "the ornaments of the Church." While he was thankful for the honor, he said that he felt it would be better to be considered an integral part of the Church.

Archbishop Senyshyn (Ukrainian metropolitan of Philadelphia, Pa.) asked that the first eight paragraphs of the schema be eliminated, as they dealt with a subject that belonged within the province of the Theological Commission; by the same token, everything relating to the problem of ecumenism should be taken out of the schema on the Church. It was a defect of the present schema that it said nothing about communion *in sacris* with the Orthodox and that it likened them, rather tactlessly, to the Protestants, although there was all the difference in the world between the two, for the Orthodox had the same hierarchy, sacraments, mass and priesthood as Catholics, whereas the Protestants did not.

Archbishop Vuccino (auxiliary bishop of Paris for Eastern-rite Catholics) expressed his astonishment that this "decree" could be considered as a suitable basis for reunion, when its whole attitude was geared rather to repelling those outside Catholic communion. The pope was referred to as a "shepherd of sheep"; this meant a *diakonia* or service, not a power. The primacy was given to Peter so that he might serve the Church, not dominate it. The schema should bring out the fact that charity rules all in the Church, especially our relations with our brethren.

102

Bishop Fernández y Fernandez (coadjutor of Badajoz, Spain) followed with words of praise for the schema and a long diatribe on the importance of distinguishing carefully between theological principles and practice in the matter of reunion. For Archbishop Edelby (auxiliary to Patriarch Maximos IV), on the other hand, the first section misrepresented the history of the separation and ought to be entirely rewritten. There was too much of a theological flavor about it. Whereas the presentation of the facts ought to be inspired by a spirit of truth in charity and clarity, it gave the impression of a certain animosity toward the East. The statement that "the Catholic Church had always used every means possible to bring about reunion" was simply not true. Everyone knew that both the Catholic Church and the other side had at times striven to prevent reunion. Finally, the absence of any reference to the collegiality of the bishops put the primacy in a false light.

Archbishop Zoghby, Melchite patriarchal vicar for Egypt, speaking in French, was the most outspoken in his analysis of the differences between the Eastern and Western attitudes toward theology and in condemning the evils of Latinization.

Whereas the Latin Church, responding to historical circumstances that were peculiar to it, evolved toward an ever greater centralization, the East, by contrast, had evolved toward an ever greater autonomy. Just as in God there was one sole and same nature, yet there were three distinct Persons, so the same thing was true analogously of the Church: there were distinct Churches, but the Church was nevertheless one. The Catholic Church today was unfortunately crushingly Latin, in that the majority of the faithful belonged to the Latin Church or rite. The 130 bishops belonging to the various Eastern-rite Churches present at the Council were drowned in the midst of the more than 2,000 Latin-rite bishops. The patriarchs, who formerly held synods to which the popes sent legates, were accorded an inferior rank in the present assembly, after the array of cardinals. While the latter might be the glory of the modern Church, they did not exist in those days. The East, he concluded, would never deny its nature and accept Latinization. Hence as long as Christendom remained divided, no Council such as the great assembly now meeting could possibly afford to neglect the problem of reunion. Let the East be the East and the West the West, each Church going its own separate way but collaborating in unity, a unity in diversity, not uniformity. Only when the Roman Church was decentralized and began to respect the traditions of its sister Churches, would there be true hope for the Church Universal.

Bishop Méndez Arceo (Cuernavaca, Mexico) next rose to make some interesting observations about the work of the Council. He began by registering a complaint about the lack of collaboration between the

103

various Preparatory Commissions and the lack of the pastoral spirit displayed by many of the schemata which the Council had so far considered. He criticized the fact that when the Rules of Procedure were drawn up, no provision was made for allowing a true dialogue or exchange of views on the floor. *"Proh dolor!"* he said, "we are the victims of an interminable flood of monologues." He then observed that it was necessary to decentralize the functions of the Curia, and finally made the suggestion that the work of the Council could be effectively entrusted or delegated to a special commission of some 250 bishops, who would have the assistance of the *periti,* but would not be encumbered by the prejudices of the Theological Commission. The day's debate was brought to a close by Bishop Romero Menjibar (Jaén, Spain), who pleaded for unity in diversity, and Father Hage, Superior General of the Basilian Order, who summed up the various points made in criticism of the schema.

Discussion of the schema was continued in the 29th General Congregation on November 28th, presided over by Cardinal Tappouni (Jacobite). The morning's mass was probably the most impressive—certainly the strangest to many of the Fathers—of all those inaugurating the day's proceedings and was celebrated in the Ethiopian rite by the tall, bearded Archbishop Yemmeru Asrate of Addis Ababa. The rite itself was extremely ancient, going back in outline at least to the fourth century, but with many later additions and ceremonies of a distinctly African flavor. It was characterized by a constant dialogue between the celebrant and the faithful, and by moving simplicity and solemnity. The language was classical Ethiopian or Gheez. As the book of Gospels was being enthroned, the spirited chanting of the seminarians and priests belonging to the Ethiopian College on Vatican Hill behind St. Peter's—they also chanted the mass—was accompanied by the deep rhythms of African drums, the ringing of bells, and the shaking of tambourines, causing the New York *Journal American* to headline its story: "African drums boom in Vatican rite" (November 28, 1962).

The schema pleased Cardinal Tappouni on the whole and he wished it to be retained. Cardinal Spellman also spoke in favor of retention. He was followed immediately by Cardinal Ottaviani, who was of the same mind. The speech of Ottaviani, however, was interesting from another angle. Evidently without prior consultation with the Council Presidents, he stated that "after this schema (*Ut unum sint*), it has been announced that we are to take up the one on the Church. But in the treatise on the Church there is again question of unity and ecumenicity, and there are still ten months before the next session. Accordingly I propose that we should not take up the schema *De Ecclesia* now, but should take up the one on the Blessed Virgin Mary. I am astonished that after being informed that the latter subject would be dealt with next, we now find that it has been postponed. As a matter of fact, we have many points in common with our separated brethren. We are united in our love for her. After discussing various points of difference, it is well for us to remember that she can serve to unite us. Hence I wish and ask that we start with this schema on Friday. . . ."

The cardinal then launched into a peroration in which he mentioned the glories of Lourdes, Fatima, and other Marian apparitions with a view to winning acceptance for his proposal. He concluded with the axiom: "Those who explain my [Mary's] prerogatives, will have eternal life" (*qui elucidant me vitam aeternam habebunt*)." This attempt to deflect the Council from its course proved unsuccessful.*

Paul II Cheikho, Chaldean Patriarch of Babylon, then spoke. He was satisfied with the schema as such, but said it proved conclusively that reunion with the Orthodox required more than mere human reconciliation. What was needed was the aid of the Holy Spirit. Consequently, he desired the Council to compile a prayer for unity to be recited frequently, so that God would see fit, in our day, to grant the reunion so earnestly desired by all sincere Christians. Meanwhile, he hoped that a spirit of charity, demonstrated by the Fathers, would spread throughout the world.

Archbishop Tawil (patriarchal vicar for the Syrian Melchites) asked that all the human elements in the schema which might give offense should be removed. For example, he said that the schema referred to the Orthodox bodies as *"coetus"* or assemblies, whereas in fact they were true Churches. It would perhaps be better to refer to them simply as the "Orthodox," as was done in common parlance. At no time was the Eastern Church ever considered as a part of the Roman Church or under its immediate jurisdiction, as parts of the West or the West as a whole were. It always had its own leadership. Finally, the schema noted that everything should be preserved in Orthodox ceremonies which was not against faith or morals. But this was also unnecessarily brusque. "I have personally searched through our liturgy, but can find nothing against either faith or morals!" The great difficulty to be overcome before the Orthodox would ever consider reunion was to remove from their minds any fear of being reduced to the status of those Eastern Catholics already in communion with Rome (Uniats). They believed that the latter were kept in an inferior position and that they themselves would suffer the same fate if reunion took place. Unfortunately, the historical record was not good in this respect. Since the schema did nothing to remove this impression, it should be completely rewritten.

Bishop Velasco (Hsiamen, China, expelled), expressed himself in complete agreement with Cardinals Ruffini and Browne and was for the schema as it stood. To say that the Latin Church had been guilty of the

* See p. 108.

same crimes and excesses in bringing about the rupture between the two parts of Christendom was absolutely false. It was all very well to adopt an irenic approach, but truth and principles must come first. Archbishop Olaechea Loizaga (Valencia, Spain) who followed, was of the opposite view. There were many things in the schema, he said, which were not in harmony with the Holy Father's injunction about a pastoral approach. The statement noted above that the Latin Church had always sought to bring about reunion, must be taken with a grain of salt.

The Maronite Bishop Joseph Khoury, on the other hand, took exception to what he regarded as extreme statements made in the course of the debate. He could not associate himself, for example, with the sentiment that "the East is the East and the West is the West" and that it was merely a question of parallel developments. Unity in Peter meant that there was no longer any East or West but a "new creature," as St. Paul said. The Church must be on guard against becoming too enslaved to any one culture or age. It was not *always* Rome that was required to say *mea culpa.*

The theme of charity was again stressed by Bishop Darmancier, vicar apostolic for the Wallis Islands in the South Seas. However, while Mother Church wept over the dissensions in its ranks that led to schism, it should realize also that not infrequently acts by its own priests and prelates had caused, and were still causing, difficulties. A case in point was the current dissatisfaction of orientals in union with Rome with the new Code of Canon Law mentioned above. The excessively Latin spirit of the latter betrayed a lack of comprehension of the problems and different traditions of Eastern Catholics on the part of the officials who compiled it. There were many other instances of the kind that could be cited.

Archbishop Addazi (Trani, Italy) then treated the Council to a scholastic disquisition on the nature of the Church, in which he said that it was improper to suggest that the Roman pontiffs had in any way been responsible for beginning or continuing the schism. The Orthodox must be invited to "return" to the house of their father, along the path laid down for them by Rome, and that was that.

Bishop Ancel (auxiliary of Lyons) took up the matter of the truth of the faith that had been raised in three or four of the recent talks. He said there was need for a true humility on the part of Catholics, who should realize that they were not "the masters, but the servants of truth." Whereas Catholics could rejoice that the truth had always been held in the Church, it should be a matter of sadness that they had not always given a good account of that truth. "It is not our right to condemn those who have gone wrong, particularly when Catholics have frequently, to say the least, occasioned misunderstandings and difficulties. Now is the time to do proper penance for such wrongs. By acknowledging before God and man the fact that our ignorance and faults have helped bring about these divisions—and not merely those of our forebears—we can begin to cope with the continuing misapprehensions and faults that remain as obstacles to reunion today. Just as in St. Paul's day the Apostle had to object to imposing the obligations of circumcision and the use of special foods on his pagan converts, so today, the Catholic Church should not force issues where the truths of faith are not really involved. In any case, we should not judge our brethren, but ourselves."

Archbishop Assaf (Petra, Jordan) spoke in French. He said that the schema was one of the most important to come before the assembly, since it bore directly on the desire of Pope John for the reunion of Christendom. He was willing to accept it in outline, in accordance with the observation of Patriarch Maximos IV. However, he deplored the oblique references to the liturgies of the Orthodox, which said that they could be retained "as long as they contained nothing offensive to faith or morals." This was an insult to the Orthodox. Of all the matters which were causing friction between the Churches, however, the question of rites was the least of their worries. Their main worry, he said, was the fear of Latinization, in view of the instinctive desires of certain Latin prelates.

Bishop Dwyer (Leeds, England) was the last to speak on Wednesday, remarking that the schema as presently drafted could not possibly make any impression on the Orthodox because if failed to enter into their mentality. Then, broadening his perspective, he noted that unless the decrees of the Council reflected a true spirit of charity and truth, the millions outside the Church would be tempted to feel that "these prelates are not truly serious" about their desire to convert the world.

Just before the Angelus, the secretary general asked the Fathers to join in a novena of prayers to the Virgin Mary in preparation for the feast of the Immaculate Conception (December 8th), when the Council's First Session was scheduled to end, for the spiritual welfare of all the Church's bishops, both those at the Council and those prevented from attending for various reasons. The proposal was inspired by Pope John's inaugural address of October 11th, in which he had made special mention of all bishops who could not be present and asked prayers for them. It was greeted with considerable applause.

On Thursday evening, *L'Osservatore Romano* took note in a special editorial of the rumors which had been circulating regarding the pope's health. It stated that, on his doctor's insistence, the pope had cancelled all audiences since last Tuesday. It was further disclosed that the medical and dietetical treatment which he had been undergoing for some time had produced a rather severe anemia. The anxiety caused by this announcement toward the end of the session paralleled to a certain extent the fear of thermonuclear warfare which had weighed heavily on the minds of the Fathers in mid-October.

The 30th General Congregation on Friday, November 30th, presided over by Cardinal Spellman, saw the end of the discussion relative to the unity schema. First, however, the decision of the Council Presidents to turn down the proposal of Cardinal Ottaviani that the Council should next take up the schema on the Virgin Mary was announced in these words: "We are all agreed about the great importance of this devotion. But for special reasons, particularly in order to prepare for the coming session next September, we have decided to observe the announced order and will take up the schema *De Ecclesia* as the next order of business." With this terse communiqué, the hope of the cardinal of being able to avert another defeat like that suffered in connection with the schema on revelation, vanished.

The debate was led off by Cardinal Wyszynski who said that in his opinion the schema was good. It was important at the present time, when the Church was threatened by atheism and materialism, to insist upon the need for unity. Pius XII had stressed this in *Mediator Dei* and the thought constantly recurred in the works of the Church Fathers. It was not necessary to re-do the schema: certain parts needed correction, it should be abbreviated, and too much insistence should not be placed on the means. The episcopate of each country should be free to adopt whatever means seemed best under the circumstances, because conditions differed greatly from one country to another.

The speech of Cardinal Bea, who came next, began with the remark that the schema, prepared by the Commission for the Oriental Churches, was intended above all to be a homage to the Eastern Churches and could be explained, historically, by what had taken place in the 15th and 16th centuries. It was natural that there should be a separate schema in the light of all that had gone before. But today we were living in a new age, with different requirements. Many points touched upon in the schema belonged to the province of the Secretariat for Unity. For a complete presentation of the problem of reunion it would be necessary to bring together the three schemata now touching on various aspects and make them into one. He revealed that his Secretariat had prepared a special prayer for unity, but that it had not yet been printed. He said, moreover, that the inspiration for the Secretariat had come to Pope John XXIII from plans which Pope Leo XIII had for establishing a "Concilium" along this line, but which had to be abandoned when that pope died.

After Archbishop Trindade Salgueiro (Evora, Portugal) expressed his agreement with the sentiments of Cardinal Bacci reported earlier in the debate, Ukrainian Archbishop Hermaniuk (Winnipeg, Canada) noted that the reunion of Christians would amount to the inauguration of a "new era" in world history. Hence it was important for the Council to work out a constitution that would be truly efficacious in bringing about this end. It should be based on an explanation of the collegiality of the bishops under the authority of the pope. He proposed the creation of two mixed commissions: one composed of Catholics and Orthodox, the other of Catholics and Protestants, to work on theological problems connected with reunion. The present schema seemed to imply too close a connection between the Catholic Church and the Roman rite: it almost said that "there was no salvation outside of the Roman rite."

Archbishop Heenan (Liverpool) put his finger on the crux of the matter when he spoke of the problem of authority as the real issue dividing the Churches, not doctrine as such. The difficulties to be overcome were very great. It would be a "miracle" if the Orthodox were to "submit to Rome." But there was no need to be discouraged. Hitler had forced the persecuted Christians of Central and Western Europe to unite; the Communists might bring about the same thing in Eastern Europe. He deplored the absence of representatives of the Ecumenical Patriarch of Constantinople, as well as any reference in the schema to Protestants and to the Anglicans in particular. Had not the latter always been the first to respond to ecumenical appeals? He was pleased, however, that the observer delegates no longer saw the Church as a monolith and that they would take home with them a more accurate view of the Church's diversity. It was a sign, he said, that Christians were drawing closer to each other and to Christ.

The following day the Fathers were requested to vote on "whether this decree should form a single document with the decree on ecumenism prepared by the Secretariat for Promoting Christian Unity, and Chapter XI, also on the same subject, contained in the schema for a dogmatic constitution on the Church." The results were: 2,068 placets; 36 non placets; and 8 invalid votes. In spite of the carefully worded language of the official communiqué drawn up by the Secretariat for Unity and the Commission for the Oriental Churches jointly, with a view to sparing the Secretary of State as President of the latter body possible embarrassment, the schema on unity was in effect rejected.

DEBATE ON 'THE CHURCH'

The schema *De Ecclesia* was taken up in the 31st General Congregation, on Saturday, December 1st. Cardinal Frings of Cologne was in the chair as President. After mass celebrated by Archbishop Grimshaw of Birmingham, the secretary general made an announcement of great interest to all present. He reported that the Holy Father's health had materially improved and that he hoped to give his blessing from the window in his

109

apartment and recite the Angelus with those assembled in St. Peter's Square. This news evoked loud applause.

At 10:45 A.M., as soon as the voting on the schema *Ut unum sint* had been completed, Cardinal Ottaviani (as chairman of the Theological Commission which had prepared the document) took over the microphone to explain the new schema.

In his introductory talk the cardinal again adopted an approach that had proved annoying to the opposition twice previously. In a jovial and ingratiating mood, he called attention to the fact that the schema represented the work of some 70 learned and skilled theologians, and that it had the approbation of the Holy Father. Nevertheless it was submitted for the Council's examination and possible amendment. Asserting that it was both pastoral and biblical in approach, he maintained that great effort had been made to avoid even the appearance of scholastic formulations. But he could not resist the temptation to assert that, as usual, this seemed to be the main objection to all the Theological Commission's projects. Becoming somewhat jocose, he requested forbearance for the *relator,* Bishop Franič (Split, Yugoslavia) who, he said, was bound to be very conscious of the need for brevity since he could undoubtedly feel, even before facing the Fathers, that the lions were breathing down his neck and hear the shouts: *"Tolle, tolle, subicite eum!"* ("Down, down, take him away!") This observation was greeted with laughter and applause, and the cardinal left the microphone beaming.

Bishop Franič briefly outlined the eleven chapters dealing with the nature of the Church, its component parts, bishops, priests and laity, and its teaching power and authority. He stated specifically that the sections dealing with ecumenism, the laity, and the religious were considered solely from a theological point of view.

Hardly had the *relator's* last words echoed though the hall when Cardinal Liénart took the microphone. After a few generous words for the labor involved in the schema, he said he was glad to see that the Church was treated here as the Mystical Body of Christ, which it was, solely and essentially. But he felt that the schema failed to stress the conclusion implicit in this fact—that the Church was therefore a Mystery. As evidence of this failure, he cited article 7, in which the Mystical Body was made to appear co-extensive with the "Roman Church." Actually the Mystical Body and therefore the Church was much greater, and truly included—as every Catholic schoolboy knew—the souls in purgatory as well as the saints in heaven. What was more, could anyone really deny that those separated from the Church, but who possessed the faith, the sacraments, and remained in a state of grace were not actually members of the Mystical Body and therefore of the Church? It was obvious then that a too juridical spirit had presided over the elaboration of this schema. Before demanding that the whole project be reworked, however, the French cardinal observed that his remarks were not made in a contentious spirit, but in an effort toward arriving at the truth. *"Amicus, Plato; sed magis amica, veritas!"*

As in the debate on revelation, Cardinal Ruffini stood up next to defend the schema "in its entirety." He admitted, however, that there were corrections to be made, citing a few of his own, and concluding with a warning regarding the sovereign rights of the supreme pontiff. He was followed by the archbishop of Seville, Cardinal Bueno y Monreal, who insisted that the whole Church was to be identified with Christ's Mystical Body and that, as a consequence, both the social and mystical aspects of this doctrine should be dealth with in chapter VII. Finally he wanted to know whether the Council's approbation of any of these statements was an extraordinary act of the magisterium?

Cardinal König of Vienna called for an abbreviation of the total schema. He then asked that instead of speaking of the Church's rights, more should be said about its duties, its obligation to preach and bring the Gospel to the whole of mankind so that modern man could realize that humanity, and not merely individual men, had been redeemed by Christ and could partake of His divine life. He noted the absence of any mention of freedom of conscience.

In these sentiments, he was echoed by Cardinal Ritter of St. Louis who insisted that the Church, by summoning the Council, was on parade before the world. The American cardinal made three particular points: 1. The holiness of the Church was not sufficiently emphasized in the schema; 2. The guardianship of the deposit of the faith was not the responsibility of the magisterium alone: all ranks in the Church shared in this in varying degrees; 3. As for the relations between Church and state, the schema should contain a clear statement about liberty of conscience. It should reflect the recent accomplishments in the field of ecclesiology and describe the Church in the light of these new, inspiring insights.

Bishop Bernacki (auxiliary of Gniezno, Poland) took exception to the fact that the primacy of the pope was not covered in a separate chapter— this central doctrine ought not to be hidden under a bushel, at the risk of misleading the separated brethren. In fact so important was it, that he suggested changing the Creed to read: "I believe in the Holy, Catholic, and *Petrine* Church. . . ." The President finally had to cut him off for speaking overtime.

The speech by Bishop de Smedt (Bruges, Belgium), a member of the Secretariat for Promoting Christian Unity, caused considerable comment, both within and without the Council, as did his intervention earlier in the debate on the sources of revelation. He said that while progress in theological thought about the nature of the Church in recent years was

111

echoed to a certain extent in the schema, its presentation of the Church was faulty. He outlined three basic criticisms as follows:

(1) All species of "triumphalism" should be avoided in speaking about the Church. By that he meant the pompous and romantic style habitually used in *L'Osservatore Romano* and in the documents emanating from the Roman Curia. The schema employed this style in speaking of the Church Militant, lining up its members as if in battle array. This approach had little if any relation to the sheepfold of which Christ spoke, nor did it reflect actuality, for today the Church was both persecuted and divided.

(2) The "clericalism" of the schema was equally offensive. The Church was not a pyramid of people, priests, and pope. The Church was essentially the People of God, and in them were to be found the rights and obligations of the Mystical Body. The hierarchy was much more a ministry or service, than a governing body. It was a particular continuation of Christ who came "not to be served, but to serve." Its function was to extend Christ by preaching the Word, and by offering His sanctifying grace to all mankind, the very opposite of any *"hierarcholatria."*

(3) Finally, in place of a juridical concept, the Church should be placed before the world as the Mother of mankind, for we were all reborn through her maternal action. Thus all mankind, as her sons, were brothers, both those within the family and those outside. "Reread pages 15 and 16 of this document," he said, "and see to what misconceptions this legalistic spirit can give rise. No mother ever spoke thus."

Bishop Lefebvre (Congo) proposed, as a compromise, that two different schemata be prepared for each treatise, one from a purely doctrinal and the other from a pastoral viewpoint. But this suggestion was answered immediately by Bishop Elchinger (coadjutor of Strasbourg), who pointed out that the pastoral spirit was not something added to the teaching of the faith, but an essential aspect of the Church.

Addressing the Council, once more, in the name of the bishops from the Congo, Bishop Van Cauwelaert stated that he and his colleagues had been disappointed by the schema. Expecting a joyful announcement of the good news that was the Church, they found themselves faced instead with a rather trite, juridical document. The Church was here described as a static entity, whereas it was a living body with an eschatological destiny. It was useless to proclaim the Catholic Church as the true Church of Christ, if it did not immediately present the face and spirit of Christ to the world. What was wanted was a return to the Church of Jerusalem—one heart, one mind in poverty and charity. The people of Africa were searching for a new manner of living together as a community—a new, solid, holy way of life. The Church could actually offer this to them, but certainly not as here represented.

Winding up the day's debate, Bishop Carli (Segni, Italy), considered by many as one of Cardinal Ottaviani's principal spokesmen, complained somewhat bitterly of the critical approach that many Fathers had adopted toward this schema as well as the schema on Revelation. "We are dealing here with an internal matter regarding the Church," he said, "yet so many insist that we say nothing about those doctrines of ours that could possibly offend Protestants. Thus it seems as though we cannot speak of the Blessed Virgin Mary, nor may we talk of the Church Militant. We dare not mention communism. We can hardly mention ecumenism, and we will be outlawed if we bring up justice or chastity. Thus the Council is slowly petering out before a series of taboos." He was stopped by the President, and then hurriedly added his placet in favor of the schema as such. With applause for the presiding officer's intervention, the Council Fathers joyfully departed.

The previous evening an article in *L'Osservatore Romano* took note of the anti-conciliar activities of certain politically (mainly rightist) groups in France and Italy. Recalling the Masonic attempt in 1869 to hold an Anti-Council while Vatican Council I was in session, and the several attempts of European governments to intervene in the debate on papal infallibility, Professor Alessandrini ["F. A."], admitted that the atmosphere today was totally different as regards the Church's reputation and position. While citing the worldwide news coverage and interest in the Council, he still felt that too many journalists were trying to report the Council as if it were some ordinary parliamentary meeting with its intrigues and counter-movements. The author was actually referring to a series of three articles published the previous week by Indro Montanelli in *Il Corriere della Sera* (Milan), in which this ordinarily "serious" journal allowed the writer to suggest that the pope, from his youth, was for all practical purposes a Modernist, and had called the Council in order to renounce papal infallibility. In the second article Cardinal Tardini's truthfulness and loyalty to the pope were called into question. Finally, the third article judged almost all the protagonists of the Council as hopeless and misguided "revisionists."

Alessandrini likewise took note of an illustrated weekly that "alternated theological teaching with pornographic pictures" and accused the conciliar Fathers of desiring to come to terms with communism, sacrificing the persecuted to the persecutors. Finally, he mentioned the distortions of the communist press only to complain of some journals, "even among our friends," who report the Council as "a more or less dramatic dialectic between 'conservatives' and 'liberals' as if in the great hall of St. Peter's, particular positions and persons were under discussion, and not the great truths of the faith." He commiserated with "the poor Curia, which is the practical expression of the central government of the Church," but which was under such continuous assault. "These are episodes that sadden

Christians," the author asserted, "and little by little excite them to disdain."

While there was some truth in these observations of Alessandrini, particularly as regards the disdain or hatred which extreme rightist groups in north Italy felt for Pope John because of his teaching with regard to social and economic justice, the article in *L'Osservatore Romano* failed to put the finger precisely on this group, composed of powerful industrialists and corporation executives. Instead it chased after pseudo-masons, "laicists," and communists, not stopping to ask whether its own obviously ultra-conservative bias was not the occasion, perhaps even the cause, of much of the so-called controversy. Considering the tenor of the conciliar debates, it seemed less than honest to suggest that there were no disagreements.*

The morning's discussion on Monday, December 3rd, in the 32nd General Congregation with Cardinal Ruffini presiding, brought Cardinals Spellman, Siri, McIntyre, Gracias, Léger and Döpfner to the microphone. The first three had no particularly new light to shed on the subject under consideration, being out of touch with the newer theological thought appearing in central and northern Europe. Cardinal McIntyre did mention one obvious oversight, however, the failure to deal with the problem of infants who died without baptism.

Cardinal Gracias, on the other hand, spoke of the schema as offending against the true hospitality that ought to be the mark of the Church, and the bishops who pledge themselves to be "hospitable" in their consecration. He insisted that the missionary activity of the Church, particularly in a land such as his own, needed new orientation which could only come from a fundamental renewal of thinking in accordance with the will of the majority. He pointed out that Christians were prepared "to go so far as to shed their blood" for the faith was true enough, but insisted that it was not necessary to say things offensive or provoking to non-Christians, in the newer nations. Why say this then, when we were now aware that there were various ways of announcing the truth of the Gospel? He likewise suggested that more attention be paid to oriental philosophers, since the pagans were increasing rapidly in the Far East, and it was only by considering their true mentality that the Church could properly be preached to them.

For Cardinal Léger (Montreal) the schema *De Ecclesia* was the *cardo* or hinge of Vatican Council II. The two months of discussion thus far had at least one great benefit, he contended. They proved conclusively

* *L'Osservatore Romano*, Dec. 1, 1962. One of the organs spreading misinformation was the Rome daily *Il Tempo*, often assumed to be a kind of unofficial spokesman for the Holy Office and of distinct rightist tendency.

how correct Pope John had been in calling for a renewal of the Church through the Council.

Cardinal Döpfner of Munich likewise said that the present schema was of paramount importance both to the Council and to the Church. Hence he proposed a radical change in its structure that would bring out better the fundamental notion of the Church as the People of God, with pope, bishops and laity as coordinate members thereof. There was no particular connection between the different chapters. An insufficient, even superficial, use was made of Holy Scripture. Too much emphasis was placed on the juridical aspects of the Church. Whereas the collegiality of the bishops ought to have been stressed, this idea was merely noted; it was absurd to maintain that emphasis on the episcopate amounted to a downgrading of the papal primacy, since the pope or papacy was the crown of the episcopal order. Finally, the chapters on Church and State and the missions needed to be completely rethought. The revisions should be made by the Theological Commission on the basis of suggestions made in the Council, with the collaboration of the Commissions on the Laity, the Religious, and the Secretariat for Unity.

Of the speakers that followed, Archbishop Marty of Rheims gave the clearest exposition of the Church as a Mystery. The bonds which united it were primarily of a spiritual nature, he said. Its nature as an institution, its hierarchy, its social aspects were definable, ultimately, only in terms of this Mystery, the mystery of the Mystical Body of Christ extended in the world for the salvation of mankind. The Church was the direct intervention of God in the affairs of the world, the chosen instrument by which He intended to redeem all mankind. And its principal function—that of both hierarchy and laity—was to bring knowledge of salvation and the means of achieving it to everyone on this earth. Hence to identify the Church too closely with its juridical or administrative aspects was to misrepresent it or lower it to the level of some earthly association.

While Bishops Gargitter (Bressanone, Italy), Huyghe (Arras, France), and Hurley (Durban, South Africa) rallied to the thesis favored by the majority, the Italian prelates Barbetta and Musto kept hammering away at the line laid down by the Theological Commission. The true difficulty with the schema, said Bishop Rupp of Monaco, putting his finger on the real difficulty, was that the authors had not had in view the same purpose or end desired by the pope and the Council. The text was not calculated to bring about the reunion of Christians or an *aggiornamento*. In fact it was rather scandalous to think that a part of the magisterium could have gone so far as to act in accordance with the excessively juridical notion of the Church described by the schema. Bishop Musto, by contrast, almost wept as he pleaded with the Fathers not to destroy the Church by changing anything in it. His oratory made many of his hearers wonder why he thought the pope had summoned the Council. Finally, running overtime, he was stopped by the President.

The debate continued during the 33rd General Congregation on Tuesday, December 4th, under the presidency of Cardinal Caggiano of Buenos Aires. Cardinal Frings, speaking first in the name of all the German-language bishops, said that the present schema did not represent thinking about the nature of the Church as a whole, but merely a certain theology which did not go back more than a hundred years. There was nothing in it about what the Greek Fathers had to say on the subject, and very little about what the Latin Fathers had to say either. It would have to be completely rewritten to reflect the true catholicity of the Church's thought.

A much more cautious line was taken by Cardinal Godfrey (Westminster), whose remarks revealed that he was still influenced by the "siege mentality" which had characterized relations between the communions not so long ago. The situation in England today, he said, was confusing. It was difficult to know what members of the Church of England or the non-conformists believed. It was sometimes said that English Catholics were neither very enthusiastic Catholics nor very sympathetic toward the separated brethren. They were charitable and patient, however. The important thing was not to give the separated brethren any false ideas about concessions with regard to truth. *"Magna est veritas et praevalebit."*

Discarding any such hesitant, fear-laden approach, the archbishop of Malines-Brussels, Cardinal Suenens came out for a redrafting of the schema on an entirely new basis. As Vatican I was the Council of the Primacy, he suggested, so Vatican II should be the council of the Church of Christ, the light of nations. He proposed that in keeping with Pope John's suggestions in his inaugural talk, the doctrine on the Church should be considered in two stages: *ad intra,* or the nature of the Church as the Mystical Body; and *ad extra,* with respect to its missions "to preach the Gospel to all nations." The latter obviously required a dialogue between the Church and the world today which was looking so desperately to the Church for a solution to its problems. Hence the Church must offer itself as the answer to: (1) All those questions having to do with the decency and dignity of the human person. This included the problem of the population-explosion. (2) Everything having to do with social justice. This included the sixth commandment (which, for all the books written about it, still lacked a proper orientation), private property, the poor. (3) The problem of winning the poor for the Church by teaching them to give themselves wholly to Christ in their homes as well as in foreign missions. (4) The problem of internal peace within nations, and the dangers of war. The proper treatment of these subjects, he said, "involves us in a triple dialogue: with the faithful, with our separated brethren, and with the world outside the Church. This analysis will be seen to be nothing other than a reconsideration of the opening discourse of Pope John."

This key discourse of Cardinal Suenens was greeted with long applause by the Fathers, so much so that it had to be choked off by a reminder from the President, Cardinal Caggiano, that such vociferous reactions were forbidden at the Council.

Cardinal Bea spoke in a similar vein, seconding the thoughts of the preceding speakers. Although Cardinals Bacci and Browne attempted to stem the tide by reiterating the scholastic, juridical approach, Archbishop Blanchet (Paris), Bishop Rabbani (Syria), Archbishop Guerry (Cambrai), Bishop Holland (Portsmouth), and Bishop Hengsbach (Essen), in quick succession, spoke out in favor of a radical reworking of the schema. So did the Maronite Bishop Doumith of Lebanon. The last word of the day, however, was spoken by Archbishop Descuffi of Smyrna and it was along a more reactionary line. That evening *L'Osservatore Romano,* for the first time, carried a much fuller account of what had been said in the debate than usual, even admitting that such themes as the collegiality of the bishops and the sacramental nature of the episcopate had been discussed, and that the juridical aspect of the schema had been criticized.

The intervention of Cardinal Suenens proved to be crucial. At the 34th Congregation on December 5th, with Cardinal Alfrink as president, Cardinal Ruffini spoke in a conciliatory tone, reminding the Fathers that, after all, their disagreements were concerned with the manner of presenting the Church's doctrine, and not with the fundamentals of the faith itself. Whatever the purpose of this statement, Cardinal Montini next took the microphone and, to all intents and purposes, confirmed the suspicion that Cardinal Suenens had been speaking for the pope. Montini approved wholeheartedly of the Belgian cardinal's approach. The Church, he said, was nothing by itself. It was not so much a society founded by Christ, but rather Christ himself using us as His instruments to bring salvation to all mankind.

The cardinal of Milan went on to say that it was up to the Fathers in Council, now, to restate the "mind and will of Christ" by defining the collegiality of the episcopate, by giving a truly ecumenical outlook to the Church, and by insisting that each bishop was "the image of the Father and the image of Christ." The less we insisted on the rights of the Church, he said, the more chance we had of being heard, particularly in those parts of the world that were suspicious of the Church as a paternalistic or colonial-minded institution. Hence it was necessary to send this schema back to the Theological Commission and to the Secretariat for Unity so that it might be completely revised.

117

This was only the second time that the cardinal of Milan had spoken since the opening of the Council. What made his intervention all the more significant was the fact that, over the weekend, in a letter to his diocese (which he faithfully published every week), he was openly critical not only of those members of the Council who refused to follow the newer viewpoint, but he actually laid the blame for the Council's failure to make greater progress on those members of the Curia who had prevented cooperation between the various Commissions during the preparatory phase of the Council. They were obviously failing to follow the pope's lead, he said, as stated in his opening address. A discreet and prudent man such as the cardinal of Milan would never have so revealed his true mind in this way, had he not been certain that he was expressing the thoughts of the Holy Father.

Speaking the same day, December 5th, Patriarch Maximos IV Saigh, took a somewhat conciliatory line saying that it was not out of hostility or prejudice that the rejection of the schema was being proposed. Rather it was in the interests of the Church, which must put its best foot forward in the modern world. He pleaded that neither side in the debate should indulge in suspicions about the good faith of the other. He added that there was no need to insist on the primacy of the pope at this Council; it was a doctrine of faith, well appreciated everywhere. What was necessary was relieving the Church of the burden of legalism and a too cumbersome juridic background. Likewise it would be unjust to consider the desire to give an ecumenical turn to their deliberations as an attempt at attenuating the Church's doctrine. Neither Catholics nor Orthodox had any such desires. Citing several passages in a recently edited Italian work on the history of the Church, he remarked on the lack of realism manifested on almost every page, stating that what was not real could not be theology. Then he called for the reworking of the schema with the assistance of a truly representative commission which would give proper weight to oriental theology.

Archbishops Florit of Florence and Plaza of La Plata, and Bishop Pluta of Poland returned to the Ottaviani line, but time was running out.

The question of the pope's health had become crucial during the final two weeks of the Council and rumors were rife, in Vatican circles, that soon after the close of the Council—December 10th, it was said—Pope John would undergo surgery which his physician had been staving off for the past year or so. Word of this was published by a Netherlands newspaper in mid-November, then knowingly bruited about by some bishops and prelates. Finally, on Friday, November 30th, *L'Osservatore Romano* published a notice saying that the Holy Father was suffering from gastric trouble which had resulted in semi-severe anemia. Upon the insistence of his physician, he had cancelled all audiences from the 27th. No mention was

118

made of a possible operation, but rumor again had it that the pope had had several gastric hemorrhages.

However, on Sunday, December 2nd, Pope John appeared at the open window of his private apartments in the Vatican at noon, and recited the Angelus with the immense crowd in the square below as was his custom—only this time they were reinforced by batteries of TV cameras—despite the fact that it was cold outside. Thanking the crowd for their solicitude and prayers for his health, he then rather casually informed them that "the good health, which threatened for a moment to absent itself, is now returning, has actually returned."

On Tuesday evening, the 4th, it was announced that the pontiff would bless the pilgrims from his window at mid-day on Wednesday instead of holding his usual audience for them and, by way of emphasizing his continued improvement, it was stated that he had received the Cardinal Secretary of State on both Monday and Tuesday.

Deciding to take advantage of the occasion, the Fathers of the Council swarmed out of the basilica, on Wednesday, at 11:45, and joined the immense throngs of priests, nuns and laymen patiently waiting for the Holy Father to appear. Precisely at twelve noon, the papal window opened and the pope began to recite the Angelus. As he finished, the crowd broke into a tremendous roar, accompanied by the tooting of horns and the ringing of bells. The pope quickly signaled for silence. Obviously moved by the tribute, he said: "My sons, Divine Providence is with us. As you see, from one day to the next there is progress, not going down, but in coming up slowly—*piano, piano.* Sickness, then convalescence. Now we are convalescing. The satisfaction afforded us by this gathering is a reason for rejoicing. It is an augury of the strength and robustness which are coming back to us."

Gesturing majestically, he then continued: "What a spectacle we see before us today—the Church grouped together here in full representation: *ecco,* its bishops; *ecco,* its priests; *ecco,* its Christian people! A whole family here present, the family of Christ!"

Alluding to the fact that the Council was soon to close for a while, the pope then spoke of the pleasure it had afforded him thus far—not merely because of the obvious unity of clergy and people in the Church to which it attested, but because it represented all the races of the whole world, for all peoples everywhere had been redeemed by the Savior, Jesus Christ.

The 35th Congregation on Thursday, December 6th, had Cardinal Tisserant as its President. The discussion was preceded by a statistical résumé of the Council's activities, presented by Archbishop Felici, indicating that since the opening day some 1,110 Fathers had either spoken or presented their views in writing. Then Cardinal Lercaro of Bologna, initiating the day's debate, quickly put his stamp of approval on the

119

Montini-Suenens thesis, and spoke eloquently of the Mystery of Christ in the Church of the Poor. With an explicit reference to the pope's opening discourse, wherein he had cited the words of St. Peter: "Silver and gold I have none," the cardinal of Bologna exhorted all in the Church to follow Christ truly "who, though rich, became poor for us." His remarks were received with loud applause.

The secretary general then spoke, making a definitive announcement in the name of the Holy Father. The new norms made it finally and unmistakably clear how the pope wanted the Council conducted. In the nine months between the adjournment of this First Session of Vatican Council II and its Second Session, opening on September 8, 1963, all the schemata—particularly those discussed in Council—were to be reworked by mixed commissions and sent to the bishops for their emendations and comment. The Fathers were instructed to return these to the Secretariat as soon as possible. To coordinate the work of the collaborating commissions, the Holy Father had decided to create a new coordinating commission under the presidency of Cardinal Cicognani.*

The rest of the debate was simply dénouement. The full significance of the papal intervention being comprehended, it was obvious that Pope John had remained on the "pastoral" side of the debate—as he had clearly asserted in his inaugural discourse—throughout the meetings of the Council.

This did not prevent several further statements on the opposite side, such as those by Bishop Compagnone (Anagni), Bishop Hervás y Benet (Ciudad Real, Spain), Archbishop Fares (Catanzaro), and Archbishop Stella (Aquila) which reiterated the tried-and-not-so-true juridic themes. But the rest of the speakers, including Bishop Philbin (Down and Connor —one of the three Irish bishops who spoke at the First Session) and Bishop Renard (Versailles), came out clearly for renovation and renewal. Father Joseph Buckley, the recently elected general of the Marist Order, in a good Massachusetts accent, then gave a fine discourse on the nature of obedience as it must be conceived in the context of the liberty enjoyed by the lay members of the Church in the world of today, and Bishop Hakim (Israel) capped the day's discussion by reiterating the oriental approach.

The final general congregation, the 36th, was held on Friday, December

* The names of the other members were not disclosed until over a week later, in the issue of *L'Osservatore Romano* for December 17–18, 1962: namely, Cardinals Liénart, Urbani, Spellman, Confalonieri, Döpfner and Suenens. Significant differences between the official Latin text of the norms and the translations prepared by the Press Office were brought to light. Cf. *La Civiltà Cattolica*, March 2, 1963, and *America*, March 16, 1963. The popular versions glossed over the facts that the revised schemata were to be channeled through episcopal conferences, when "expeditious"; that general principles were to be treated "above all," and that experts should be consulted on a wide scale, when necessary.

7th, presided over by Cardinal Liénart. After the announcement that Pope John would arrive before midday to speak to the Fathers, the President expressed his sentiments of joy and gratitude to all for the work and good spirit demonstrated by the Council. Cardinal König in the first speech took the opportunity to correct a statement made a few days earlier by Bishop Griffiths, auxiliary of New York, who in his discourse had quoted the Gospel phrase, "Lord, we have labored the whole night long, and have taken nothing." Said the cardinal of Vienna: "We have certainly not done everything, but in these two months we have accomplished great things. Within these halls, by our exchange of viewpoints, we have come to a much greater appreciation of the Church as it is in reality. Despite our differences, we have maintained the charity of Christ, and have prepared ourselves for the presentation to the world of the truth and love of Christ that we daily hope to accomplish in the next session."

Earlier, in an account of the Council in the Paris journal *Le Monde,* the auxiliary bishop of New York had been bracketed with the bishops of Salamanca and Trois Rivières (Canada) as among the more outstanding intransigents at the Council, because of his intelligence and extremely juridical outlook.

Cardinal Lefebvre (Bourges) then gave a vivid but kindly discourse on charity as the heart and life of the Church. This was followed by a rambling, semi-hysterical discourse by Bishop Reyes of the Philippines who insisted on the royal character of the Church's rights, due to the kingship of Christ. Bishop Ghattas (Coptic bishop of Thebes) brought the Council back to a balanced consideration of the true union in faith and love that should mark all the Christian Churches, while Bishop Ancel (auxiliary of Lyons), referring again to the collegiality of the bishops with the pope, said there did not need to be any conflict between the juridical and other aspects of the Church, so long as the former were seen as merely an accidental necessity, and not made the principal consideration of ecclesiastical thought and action. Archbishop Silva Santiago (Concepción, Chile) struck a final blow on behalf of Cardinals Ruffini and Browne. The honor of the last word at the First Session went to the Benedictine Abbot Butler.

At 11:15 the Holy Father arrived on foot, mounted the platform erected over the Confession of St. Peter and started reciting the Angelus. The Fathers applauded his arrival, joined with him joyfully in prayer, and listened avidly as he thanked them for the work they had accomplished in their two months in Council. He indicated his pleasure at the unity and charity displayed, despite their divergences. Giving them his blessing, he then descended the platform unassisted, and left the basilica.

On Saturday morning, December 8th (feast of Immaculate Conception), Cardinal Marella, the archpriest of St. Peter's, chanted a solemn high mass that was sung in unison in Gregorian chant by all the bishops and faithful present in the basilica. At 10:15 Pope John arrived on foot, mounted the platform, and sat down. His appearance for the second consecutive day was not only reassuring, in view of the many rumors about his health, but many of the Fathers present were moved to tears of relief and admiration at the sight of this portly figure, somewhat pale but vigorous in his movements, as he fished for his glasses and began to read his closing address.

As he got absorbed in the reading, he became his old self more and more. His voice was strong and he began to emphasize points by quick movements of the paper in his hand, lifting his head and peering over his glasses from time to time, to note the effect of particular phrases. He admitted that the Council had got off to a slow start, but it was necessary for so many bishops from such diverse nations and cultures to come to know and understand one another's points of view. He touched lightly on the dissensions that had arisen during the First Session, indicating that they were both healthy and necessary for the achievement of a holy liberty, in charity. With a humorous allusion that seemed to escape many of his listeners, he referred to the nine months' work ahead for the conciliar commissions, as a grave but important task "that would be accomplished in silence!"

He indicated that there was no time to lose, with the world as it was today. The Church must use all its resources—bishops, priests, religious men and women, as well as the laity—in pursuing its mission to bring Christ to the world. He exhorted the bishops to do their work by going over the schemas that would be sent to them carefully in the light of what they had learned at the Council, even though they would be absorbed in the pastoral cares of their dioceses. Reminding them that they would all be back in September, Pope John suggested that by bringing the Council to an end by Christmas 1963, they would be both satisfying the desires of the peoples who were looking for concrete results from the Council, and at the same time be properly celebrating the four hundredth anniversary of the closing of the Council of Trent.

With the help of God, he concluded, though the Council did not have directives to give to the world at this point, it still had achieved great things which should prove to be the seeding from which—not alone among Christians but among all men of good will—there would appear a reblossoming of the religious sense that was implicit even in the patrimony of secular cultures. He summoned the whole Church, its priests, religious and laity, to prepare to be the instruments for carrying the message of the Council to the world. In this way, he said, a new Pentecost would be effected, wherein the bond of charity would strengthen the reign of Christ on earth.

Obviously greatly moved by the occasion, Pope John imparted his blessing to the prelates and bishops, dismissing them with fond greetings for their flocks. Then as unostentatiously as he had appeared, he walked down from the platform and out through a side door of the basilica.

POPE JOHN'S REVOLUTION

Evaluations of the significance of Vatican Council II were necessarily somewhat tentative at the end of the First Session; however, certain trends seemed to be evident. The man in the best position to judge the Council's accomplishment was Pope John, and he expressed full satisfaction that the two months' work had been both constructive and epoch-making, despite the fact that no decrees could yet be published as an augury of the assembly's impact on the Church or the world.

Despite the pope's optimism, however, there was still considerable concern behind the scenes. His health was a primary worry for the work of the Council was only half done, and without his drive and paternal charity things could easily be brought to a standstill. While Pope John had accomplished something that would affect the course of the Catholic Church's history until the end of time, the spectrum of possibilities ranged from a miraculous renewal of its life and effectiveness in human affairs here and now, to a severe setback such as it received in the Protestant revolt and the age of the enlightenment. Meanwhile the administration of important church offices still appeared to be in the hands of the ultraconservatives and the signs of their continued power and methods were very much in evidence. *L'Osservatore Romano* in a special edition on December 9th, on the second page immediately behind Pope John's quietly triumphal closing talk, ran an article on the "Work of the Council" by Father Ermenegildo Lio, O.F.M., a Defender of the Bond in the Holy Office. In his article, omitting all reference to the sermon with which the Holy Father opened the Council and laid down directions for its pastoral orientation, the author stated that the Council must get around to condemnations—otherwise it would compromise the position taken by Pope John before the whole world (Father Lio said explicitly) in a radio message delivered last September. This article was then repeated verbatim in a regular issue on December 13th. The casual observer might well ask, who was really running the Catholic Church—the pope and the majority of the bishops in Council, or the advisers of the Holy Office?

Measured by the standards of modern public relations, the First Session was a huge success. It got more sustained publicity over a longer period of time than any other single religious event. Over a thousand journalists covered the opening session, and the effort they made to obtain authentic and live information was in the end a tremendous education for them, and

123

through them, for the millions of people whom the Church would perhaps never have reached without their news stories. Ingenuity, a prime factor in the competence of any journalist, was put to a severe test at Vatican Council II. But day by day, in the more enterprising journals at least, the news became more vivid and more accurate. The problems presented by the secrecy imposed on the Council Fathers and accepted most scrupulously by the observer delegates proved a great hurdle. But each nation or language group, after sufficient clamoring on the part of its reporters, finally found a way to solve the difficulty. In the wake of each conciliar congregation, for example, groups of bishops and experts were made available for questioning by the English, German and Spanish speaking journalists, and these experts gave a sufficiently expanded account of the day's happenings to satisfy most newsgatherers. In the course of the fifth week, the French Catholic daily, *La Croix,* feeling the competition offered by the so-called "indiscretions" of the Italian press, began to link the names of the conciliar speakers with the general import of what they said. This move was certainly known to the French episcopate, to the Secretary General of the Council, and to its Commission for Extraordinary Affairs. Yet nothing was done to stop it. Hence Father Antoine Wenger, the editor, concluded that it was a tolerable way of getting around the secrecy imposed on the Council Fathers and theologians by the rules of the Council. Henry Fesquet, reporter for *Le Monde,* summed up the problem in the Christmas issue of *Témoinage Chrétien.* Though in the end he did not solve the dilemma posed by the necessity of secrecy in the debates to guarantee full freedom to the prelates in their observations, particularly on delicate or controversial matters, and the need of journalists to supply their readers with names and facts, he did think that a solution would be forthcoming before the next session.

In the past, particularly in Italy, the Church had generally had a bad press. This had prejudiced responsible Italian churchmen against journalists generally.* In other parts of the world, complaints had been registered against religious reportage, indicating that Church news was not

---

* Christopher Hollis, author, publisher, and former Member of Parliament, present at the opening session of the Council, had this to say: "The press relations (of the Council) were in the hands of Curial officials. It would perhaps be a discourteous exaggeration to say that this is as if one were to ask the prisoner in the dock to report on his own trial, but it is certainly true that what this first session of the Council revealed above all things—whatever may be its eventual outcome—is the existence among bishops of almost every country in the world of a vast mass of dissatisfaction with the lack of knowledge and imagination of the bureaucracy which has had in its hands the management of the administrative affairs of the Church. The strength of this dissatisfaction notoriously came as a total surprise to most of the officials. They cannot understand it, and therefore they are not the best people to interpret what they are the last people to understand. They try to perform their functions fairly enough, but they are not very competent." (*The Critic,* Chicago, February–March, 1963.)

infrequently distorted or biased. On the whole this could not be said of the reporting of the Council. Conservative-minded Catholics were of course disturbed by the airing of differences of opinion between certain prelates and the majority of cardinals and bishops who took the pope's opening address to heart. It was impossible, however, to have the advantage of great publicity without paying the price of honest reportage. As Pope John himself said: "We have nothing to hide."*

In passing it might be noted that, at least for English-speaking prelates, the first article in *The New Yorker* by the anonymous Xavier Rynne seemed in a literal sense to be "news" when it arrived in Rome. Before reading this article, which was mimeographed by some bishops and passed around quickly among American, English, Irish and Australian prelates, many of them had known nothing of the disputes going on in Rome between some Curial officials and the Biblical Institute, for example; nor had they any true notion of the reason for the pope's insistence on an *aggiornamento*.

In his summation of the First Session, Pope John alluded to the remarkably good reception accorded the Council's activities by men of good will in many parts of the world. This was a fact whose appositeness could be appreciated only by comparison with the belligerently anti-Catholic atmosphere that surrounded Vatican Council I less than a hundred years before. The Holy Father and the Church had good reason for continued optimism in this regard. In the secular press of the United States, Germany and Great Britain numerous attempts had been made to summarize the accomplishments of the Council; and while great attention had been focused on the differences and disputes, even the latter had been interpreted for the most part in a favorable light. There was universal acknowledgment of the fact that this was definitely Pope John's Council. The revolution in Catholic activity and thinking associated with the First Session was recognized as being due almost single-handedly to the pope's decision and his way of doing things.

Immediately before the Council opened Pope John remarked that Catholics in this world had no business acting as if the Church were a museum full of ancient artefacts. In his opening discourse he called for a new formulation of Catholic truths in such fashion that they would penetrate into the consciousness of modern man. He said explicitly that he was thinking of men of science, learning, labor, and industry who were

---

* On November 24th a letter was addressed to Pope John by 19 cardinals, expressing their "disquietude over false doctrines" being aired at the Council (ICI, 15 March 1963). Mentioning articles in the *Revue Biblique* and the *Rivista Biblica*, and a book by Father Nierinck, theologian to the bishop of Bruges, the letter was passed on to the Secretary of State and then to Cardinal Bea, whereupon 5 cardinals withdrew their signatures, leaving these 14 on the list: Pizzardo, Bacci, Marella, Traglia, Ruffini, Siri, Agagianian, Ottaviani, Browne, de Barros Camara, Santos, Godfrey, Bueno y Monreal and McIntyre.

responsible for the magnificent progress this world has made in material achievements. Since the announcement of the Council, he insisted repeatedly that he was an optimist who saw in the present age one of the most hopeful periods in human history, because it challenged the Church to show itself truly to be the Kingdom of God by reaching all mankind with its revolutionary message.

As far as the end results of the First Session were concerned, it could be said without hesitation that Pope John turned the Old Guard's ways of doing things upside down. In this he proved himself a supreme master. If thus far no one had really been hurt, it was owing to his great tact and kindness. Certainly under no other modern pontiff would such latitude have been allowed to men in high places whose minds were so obviously set against the Holy Father's wishes. The extremists were neither *vinti* nor *convinti*. As a matter of fact, after the first shock they adopted two distinct lines of defense. The first maintained that the ultra-conservatives had actually been justified by the Council's course, the fact that no decrees were promulgated being proof that the Holy Father had been merely tolerating the show of independence and near rebellion on the part of radically-minded prelates from the north and east. These latter, they complained, received all the favorable publicity. But the tried and true doctrine was protected by the Holy Spirit, whose influence would certainly be much more manifest *on the right side* at the next session. Following another line, the less balanced group among them were somewhat bitter and unsubtle in their reactions. They referred to themselves as the "remnant of Israel," who had alone remained faithful to the traditional teaching of Holy Mother the Church. They compared themselves to the Maccabees being persecuted for the truth. What they could neither comprehend nor explain, however, was the position of Pope John. The more fanatic occasionally referred to him as a simpleton who had been hoodwinked by the scheming northerners. Meanwhile, they believed he was being used by Almighty God as a kind of scourge, requiring them to practice heroic forebearance, which they did for the good of the Church. One prominent U.S. monsignor went about the campus of a Catholic university mumbling: "The damned Council!" His Italian counterparts had a phrase of similar significance though further removed from the blasphemous.*

---

* *Time's* "Man of the Year" article quoted the Holy Office consultor Monsignor Antonio Piolanti, Rector Magnificus of the Lateran University, as having warned his associates during the Council that "there are rationalist theologians going about Rome seducing innocent foreign bishops," and ominously telling one of his classes, "Remember, the pope can be deposed if he falls into heresy." This must have been said jokingly; whatever his ecclesiastical allegiance, the Rector Magnificus was too competent a theologian to have made the latter statement other than in jest (*Time,* January 4, 1963).

What gave these men hope was the fact that in the meetings of the several sectors of the mixed commission—Cardinal Ottaviani's Theological Commission and Cardinal Bea's Secretariat for Unity—which met during and after the First Session with regard to the schema on revelation, the members of the Theological Commission were able thus far to fight tooth and nail for the Ottaviani position. It was known, for example, that the first two or three sessions proved most difficult. Cardinal Bea was practically forced to agree to a vote on a statement of doctrine concerning the sources of revelation that was ambiguous, to say the least. The result of this vote was in the neighborhood of 19 in favor, as against 16 for rejecting the statement. Cardinal Ottaviani immediately claimed victory. But just as quickly it was pointed out that according to the rules of procedure under which the Council was operating, a majority of two-thirds was required. The matter finally had to be referred to the pope, who settled it summarily. The verdict was, stick to the agreed two-thirds rule.

They likewise knew that *L'Osservatore Romano* was still under their control. If news was not to their liking, it was not news. On January 13, 1963, for example, Cardinal Bea gave a revolutionary talk at Pro Deo University in Rome on the occasion of an annual *agape* or fraternal celebration to which the representatives of various religious denominations in the Eternal City were invited. The cardinal spoke of liberty of conscience, stating that it was his intention to prepare a constitution on human freedom for presentation at the next session of the Council, in which the Fathers would be asked to come out flatly with a public recognition of the inviolability of the human conscience as the final right of every man no matter what his religious beliefs or ideological allegiance. He stated further that the axiom "Error has no right to exist," which was used so glibly by certain Catholic apologists, was sheer nonsense, for error was an abstract concept incapable of either rights or obligations. It was persons who had rights, and even when they were in error their right to freedom of conscience was absolute.* Cardinal Bea further condemned the religious wars of the Middle Ages as an obvious evil, despite the fact that many of them were waged by Catholic prelates and even by a few popes.

In the mind of the Holy Office, these last two statements were so close to heresy that no mention of his talk was made in *L'Osservatore Romano*,

---

* Canon law has always proclaimed that "No one is to be forced against his will to embrace the Catholic faith" (Canon 1351 of the CIC). Despite the absoluteness of this statement, which proceeds from a principle of moral theology that in the end each person is responsible before God according to the dictates of his conscience, absolutist-minded ecclesiastics have frequently not been above trying to force men either to profess a religious belief foreign to their thinking, or prevented them from exercising their contrary beliefs openly.

even though it was the discourse of a cardinal close to the Holy Father, and despite the fact that the Rome daily *Il Tempo* vigorously attacked Cardinal Bea's talk on the following Tuesday. Ordinarily, controversy concerning a cardinal that broke out in the secular press was immediately smothered by indignant reaction in the columns of *L'Osservatore Romano* under the rubric *"Ribalta dei fatti"* or *"In margine,"* in which every possible attempt was made to interpret the prince of the church's words or actions in a light most favorable to conservative Roman teaching. A cardinal's position in *L'Osservatore Romano* was to be defended at all costs. That this semiofficial organ of the Vatican could have actually ignored the discourse of a cardinal of the Curia was simply incredible.

The Council and particularly the First Session seemed to indicate that a major turn-over in Catholic thinking had occurred. Beginning with the discussion on the liturgy, slowly but with deliberate intent, a majority of the bishops, by a process resembling that of parliamentary debate, had begun gradually to strip the Roman Church of the juridical accumulations of centuries. In so doing, they demonstrated that the essential fact about the Catholic faith was not a series of set formulas nor the bond of juridical unity; but its dynamic participation in and witness to the living, redeeming and sanctifying presence of Christ in the world. They talked at first about the language and method of celebrating mass and dispensing the sacraments. But what they proved was that each age and clime has a right to clothe these rites, essential to the well-being of the Christian, in a dress that fitted the culture and intellectual pattern of the times. This was accomplished in a climate of free exchange, with an entrenched minority opposing every step of the way. When a rule of closure was finally admitted, it was immediately employed by Cardinal Tisserant, with the rousing approval of the Fathers who had been arguing liturgical reform for over three weeks. The final vote on acceptance of the liturgy schema as a whole was known to have heartened the Holy Father, who had become somewhat apprehensive over the apparent tenacity of the opposition. It shocked the ultra-conservatives, however, for they immediately reacted by a feverish attempt to dominate the discussion of the next, and for them, crucial schema. Its title, "On the Sources of Revelation," at once betrayed its tendentious character. The Theological Commission responsible for the schema was controlled by the thinking of a small handful of theologians, all connected with the Roman universities, who had in common the belief that there was no other way of presenting the truths of the Catholic faith than by repeating the old and tried formulas and condemning all innovation. Hence their work on the draft decree was quickly labeled by various Council Fathers as "excessively professorial and scholastic, not pastoral, incontinently rigid, theologically immature, incomprehensible, offensive to non-Catholics, unsympathetic to scientific research in theology and exegesis, and too evidently reflecting certain schools of thought." The resulting draft was far from what the pope had in mind as stated in his opening talk; nor was it in accordance with what the majority of the bishops felt was now necessary.

Evidently the ecclesiastical Old Guard had neither been heeding the signs of the times nor reading the theological output of their students, who had grown up and become leaders in the Church at large. A good instance of this was the pitiful appeal made by Archbishop Parente to the native African bishops during the third week of the Council. Most of these Negro bishops had been trained at the Propaganda University in Rome. Parente, therefore, accused them of showing gross ingratitude toward their former teachers by siding with the northern European bishops. But the Africans were actually giving a magnificent lesson to the Council and to the Church as a whole. They had come back to Rome to learn what the Holy Father had in mind with respect to progress for their countries. They took their cue from some forty-two episcopal conferences or organized groups of bishops in different countries or regions, who met regularly, with executive committees for ad hoc activities, during the First Session, and attempted to attain local uniformity of ecclesiastical policy and action. These groupings foreshadowed the later emphasis placed by the Council on the role of episcopal conferences. It was truly amazing to witness all through the First Session the cohesion demonstrated by the 292 African bishops,* who organized a secretariat to represent their nine regional groups in Rome on a permanent basis. Of equal significance was the slowly emerging unity of the South American bishops (some 600 all told) who, thanks in particular to the concern of Rome for the fate of Catholicism in that area, the generous assistance of North American bishops, and their own theological centers, particularly in Chile and Buenos Aires, were gradually witnessing a renewal of Catholic thought along social, economic, spiritual and religious lines, which could alone save the continent from the grasp of communism.

From the theological point of view, this episcopal collaboration according to natural human groupings, proved to be one of the most important accomplishments of the Council, for it marked a return to recognition of the collegial pattern of government and the practice of the early Church as reflected in the letters of the second-century bishop and martyr Ignatius of Antioch and the third-century bishop of Carthage, Cyprian. In defining the relations between the bishops and the pope, as the Council would have to do when it dealt with the structure of the Church, most informed observers in Rome believed that this truly hierarchical development would receive canonical sanction. It would likewise automatically

* The bishops from Mozambique and the near-by islands raised the number from 262 to 292.

facilitate the settlement of the disputed question of the power and position of apostolic delegates and nuncios.

The Council's overwhelming acceptance of the first chapter of the schema on liturgy was a truly revolutionary step, though the fact only slowly began to dawn on observers. An article by the noted Benedictine professor of liturgy, Father Cipriano Vagaggini, published in *L'Osservatore Romano* for December 8th, spelled out the significance of the principles established in this conciliar document. The Church's sacramental and prayer life was now acknowledged to be at the very heart of all its activities. It was the substance of the Catholic faith in action. Hence there could be no question of depriving the people of their proper part in the mass and sacraments—and that participation meant an intimate sharing of these ceremonies and sacred actions. In seminaries and schools there would have to be a new reorientation designed to make the students at once both liturgical- and pastoral-minded. In each country, or cultural area, the local episcopate was to determine how much national custom or native tradition could legitimately be utilized in church ceremonies, while preserving of course the basic meaning and structure of the mass and sacraments, and referring to the Holy See for final approval. This implicitly established the principle of the collegiality of the episcopate as a complement to the pope's position as primate, and recognized the responsibility of episcopal conferences or groupings as units in dealing with the center. The question of the use of Latin in the Western Church was thereby reduced to a matter of minor importance; although it was on this point that the Fathers-in-opposition, at the beginning, chose to make their stand.

It became known that when the Secretary General of the Council saw Father Vagaggini's article, he was outraged. For use had been made of material covered by the secrecy of the Council, and it had not been cleared through him. He was informed however that clearance had been obtained through the Cardinal Secretary of State, the article having been "inspired" by an editor of *L'Osservatore Romano,* on word from above.

Meanwhile Protestant and orthodox reaction was on the whole favorable to the Council. Although a group of 150 French, Swiss and Belgian evangelical pastors meeting in Nogent-sur-Marne, two days after the Council's adjournment, were severe in their attitude: "A few liturgical *aménagements,*" said their spokesman, "and even the rediscovery of certain New Testament truths are not sufficient to have us recognize the Roman Church as a sister in the Christian community, and much less a Mother and Teacher," the reaction of most "disjointed"—the new term used by a Council Father to replace the outmoded "separated"—brethren was both pleasant and hopeful.

Two Russian observers called on the cardinal of Poland before departing for Moscow, and on taking leave of His Eminence, kissed his ring. Even if this represented merely one more move in the intricate political program of the Soviets, its effect on Christians behind the Iron Curtain was bound to be hopeful.

The First Session had a decided effect on the collective consciousness of the bishops themselves. The entire episcopate began to realize what was implied by its collegial character. It began to see itself in the mirror of its true catholicity or universality. As Pope John said on December 8th, "Each man must feel in his heart the beat of his brother's heart. [In the Council] there was thus need for a realization of diverse experiences, for an exchange of reflection, and a mutual encouragement in our pastoral apostolate." The bishops began to understand that it was not sufficient to wait passively for a charismatic inspiration or to repeat the formulas of scholastic manuals. They must take cognizance of the fact that they were the free instruments used by the Holy Spirit in the spreading of the Christian faith, and that they had been given an immense task which they must accept with humility and courage. They had no right to think, in coming to the Council, as Bishop Sheen observed in a sermon to journalists, that a Council made up of 3,000 fallible bishops would become infallible without excruciating effort.

One thing became certain. Most of the bishops quickly came to realize the full significance of their responsibility and their liberty. On December 8th Pope John told them: "These providential debates have brought out the truth and have let the whole world see the holy liberty of the children of God such as it is embodied in the Church."

It was also evident that there were no true heresies menacing the Church today other than the fear of speaking the plain truth. Father J. van Kilsdonk, S.J., university chaplain in Amsterdam, on September 30, 1961, delivered an address before the St. Adalbert Society (of Dutch Catholic intellectuals), in which he said that the nature of the Roman Curia was such that it frequently hampered the freedom of the pope and dominated the bishops. His speech was something of a landmark on the road to *aggiornamento*. He maintained that criticizing the Church could be "a holy duty like practising charity," adding that for the most part the Curia was controlled by "aged men who were conservative and incomprehensible to young people." On October 6th, just before departing for the Council, Cardinal Alfrink of Holland gave a talk in which, while he did not mention Father van Kilsdonk by name, he said that public criticism of the Church was often not wise as it tended to stir up unrest without providing improvement. In December, immediately after the Council, Bishop van Dodewaard (Haarlem) was admonished by the Holy Office not to keep this priest in his position as university chaplain. The Catholic daily *De Tijd-De Maasbode* of Amsterdam editorialized: "Any disciplinary measure against Father van Kilsdonk would create a bad impression on Dutch Catholics with their sensitive love of freedom. . . . A sanction against this speaker, whom the Council demonstrated not to have been wholly in the wrong, would give offense to Dutch Catholics . . . who speak with great enthusiasm about their chaplain, and not only because of his outspokenness." Discussions were then inaugurated by Bishop van Dodewaard and Cardinal Alfrink with the Holy Office the results of which were published by the Bishop of Haarlem in an official statement: "The Holy Office maintains its objections against the way in which Father van Kilsdonk criticized the Roman Curia. But, taking into account the steps already taken by the Dutch Church authorities with regard to the address, the Holy Office also leaves eventual measures to the local Ordinary. The Bishop of Haarlem will not dismiss Father van Kilsdonk from his post as chaplain to students." What conscientious Catholics objected to was the fact that, with the Holy Father daily speaking about a fearless approach to the world, and about the "holy liberty" befitting the children of the Church, one of the offices of the Roman Curia still was attempting to stifle even the mildest criticism of its actions, and more particularly of its personnel.

As Père Rouquette pointed out in *Études* (January 1963) the really serious theological opposition to the Council's accomplishment came mainly from men who were devoted to the Church and its traditions, but who had unfortunately come to identify the present Roman Curial system with an arbitrary divine right of the papacy. They believed themselves in some way as sharing in papal infallibility. It was said of one noted Jesuit theologian that he had his first doubts about infallibility the day he discovered that the reigning pontiff disagreed with one of his opinions.

As regards the Council, these men seemed to forget that the episcopate in session in a Council was an instrument of the Holy Spirit. Thus an American ecclesiologist, in a ponderous attempt to defend his good friend Cardinal Ottaviani from the "drum-fire of journalistic attacks" . . . in articles "remarkably alike for inaccuracy of observation and for pure malevolence" to those found in "the Italian communist press, *Time* . . . *Newsweek*," etc.,* failed himself to distinguish between the Cardinal's function as Secretary of the Holy Office and his position in the Council as a bishop and as chairman of the Theological Commission.† In the latter two capacities, the cardinal needed no defense. He was entitled to his opinions and had a right to express them as he pleased in Council or

* *American Ecclesiastical Review*, January 1963, p. 44.

† "In the light of true history it will be seen that the mission of the Cardinal Secretary of the Holy Office at this latest Ecumenical Council of the Catholic Church has been truly providential" (*American Ecclesiastical Review*, January 1963, p. 53).

outside it. In actual fact as chairman of the Theological Commission he even had an obligation to fight for the retention of the schemata prepared by the committees under his control. But what *Time* and *Newsweek* in particular objected to were the methods the cardinal used both before and after the Council to intimidate and even silence sincere and orthodox men who did not hold his opinions. His American defender said nothing about this accusation.

Since at this juncture a theologian considered it necessary to defend the cardinal's right to his opinion, by the same token, he might have thought it necessary to point out that journalists were free to make informed judgments about the figure made by the cardinal as a leader of what quickly came to be the opposition at the Council; and that theologians were likewise free to criticize his theological opinions and preferences. That the cardinal gave the impression that he was functioning at the Council as head of the Holy Office was unfortunate. For Pope John had made it absolutely clear—as did canon law (canon 222)—that the Roman Curia had nothing to do with a Council. That he likewise appeared to be using that same office to intimidate theologians brought to Rome by the bishops to assist them in understanding the work of the Council made it appear that he was hardly playing the game squarely. It was on this score that the main bulk of criticism was levelled against Cardinal Ottaviani in reports about the Council. On this plane he had to run the risk that every prominent man was exposed to in a free society. He was expressing a viewpoint and attempting to act upon it. He could hardly expect those who disagreed with the propriety of his words and actions not to say so. The cardinal was certainly used to this kind of give and take. It was his overzealous supporters who actually gave rise to most of the exaggeration in estimates of his actions, and who thus cast a shadow on his intentions.

Pope John said, "The Council is an act of faith in God, of obedience to His laws, of sincere effort to correspond with the plan of redemption according to which the Word has become flesh." That these men should be upset by an expression of this truth which was not what they had expected, was understandable. But it was also highly desirable that they should use some other means of expressing their opposition. The oblique, hidden maneuvers which they often employed profoundly astonished and even shocked a great part of the bishops on the "periphery," and in particular many North American bishops, who had been badly impressed by the obvious lack of fair play on their part. Americans who had come to the Council as neutrals, departed transformed in good part because of these maneuvers. It was hardly beside the point when a commentator remarked that thus God seemed "to have brought great good out of evil."*

* *Études*, January 1963.

In the encyclical epistle *Mirabilis ille* which Pope John sent to the bishops of the whole world (dated January 6, 1963, published February 7, 1963) concerning their work in the Council, he said: "We, the bishops of the Church of the Savior, must awaken our consciences to the grave responsibilities we have with regard to our participation in the world-wide apostolate. To have remained and to remain faithful to the purity of Catholic doctrine according to the teaching of the Gospel, of tradition, of the fathers and the Roman pontiffs is surely a great grace, a title for merit and honor. But this does not suffice for accomplishing the command of the Savior when he tells us: 'Go and teach all nations!' (Mt. 28:19) or even for that passage from the Old Testament: 'He has confided to each the care of his neighbor' (Eccl. 17:21)."

To journalists, on the feast of St. Francis de Sales (January 27, 1963), he claimed: "The fact of the Council has caused a great echo in the world. You must certainly ask yourselves what such a lively interest, such a widespread attention, really means? First of all, we can eliminate the interest evoked by the external splendor of the ceremonial. . . . It is caused, thanks be to God, by other things. It seems to us proper to say that the fact of the Council itself has been understood. It is recognized as a striking personification of the Christian message in its entirety, adapted to the exigencies of our times. . . ."

The character of John XXIII was so genuinely unpretentious that one hesitated to call him the hero of the Council, yet the ovations that greeted him on every occasion left no doubt that the majority of the Council Fathers considered him so. It was no small achievement to have launched the Catholic Church into a new era. The reform and renewal of the most ancient continuous institution of Western civilization were not simple matters to initiate. No one believed that the *aggiornamento,* or modernization, that Pope John worked for so strenuously from the first months of his pontificate had been accomplished in the First Session—a mere eight weeks—and the repercussions of much that had happened would not be felt for some time. But the process had been started.

THE SECOND SESSION

The Death of Pope John

Pope John died, after an agonizing illness, on June 3, 1963, at 7:49 P.M. The whole world mourned his passing. Few successors of St. Peter had labored as hard as he to achieve Christ's injunction, "May they all be one," and none had succeeded so completely in convincing the world of his sincerity. Besides his own flock, non-Catholics and non-Christians turned to him as to a father. History alone will determine how he is to be ranked among the popes, but his largeness of spirit, his wisdom, his goodness, and his actions changed the history of the Church, and history itself.

Angelo Roncalli did what he said the Council would do: he opened the windows of the Church and let in fresh air. At the time of his death, he was eighty-one; yet he was a man of today in every sense. The word *aggiornamento,* with which his reign would always be associated, admirably expressed this idea. A man of his own times, said Goethe, is of all times.

It was Pope John's human qualities however that most endeared him to people. As he lay suffering in his last illness, he demonstrated many of his true characteristics—humor, kindness, serenity—in a single remark to his physician: "Don't look so worried. My bags are packed, and I'm ready to go." True humility is a rare quality, but everyone recognized it in him. It was no surprise that after his death this entry was found in his diary, under the date of August 12, 1961: "The Vicar of Christ? Ah, I am not worthy of this title—I, the poor son of Battista and Maria Anna Roncalli, two good Christians, to be sure, but so modest and so humble!" And when one thinks how much he accomplished before his death, the following 1929 entry in his diary, on the occasion of his twenty-fifth anniversary as a priest (he was 49 at this time), seems unforgettable:

Countless priests already dead or still living after 25 years of priesthood have accomplished wonders in the apostolate and the sanctification of souls. And I, what have I done? My Jesus, mercy! But while I humble myself for the little or nothing I have achieved up to now, I raise my eyes toward the future. There still remains light in front of me; there still remains the hope of doing some good. Therefore, I take up my staff again, which from now on will be the staff of old age, and I go forward to meet whatever the Lord wishes for me.

His three most considerable claims on history's attention undoubtedly were his convocation of the first Council of the Church to be held in a hundred years, and his authorship of two great encyclicals—*Mater et Magistra,* which brought up to date the social teaching of Leo XIII's *Rerum Novarum;* and *Pacem in Terris,* the first encyclical ever addressed not only to the Catholic clergy and laity but to "all men of good will."

In some respects, Pope John seemed as old-fashioned as his very conservative advisers. For one thing, he preferred an older fashion in papal dress, choosing to wear the *camauro,* or fur-trimmed cap, associated with Renaissance rather than modern popes (the papal medals and coins struck during his reign show him in profile wearing this cap). For another, the chatty homilies he delivered during public audiences at St. Peter's were exactly what he might have said if he had been a small-town pastor in his native diocese of Bergamo. He also said his prayers as if he were on familiar terms with the angels and the saints. These old-fashioned qualities disarmed and confused his critics in the Vatican entourage, who could not understand how a man of such spiritual simplicity could be so daring, and even revolutionary, in his approach to age-old Catholic usages. They missed the point that, as he saw it, the mission of the papacy was twofold. "Our sacred obligation is not only to take care of this precious treasure (the deposit of faith) as if we had only to worry about the past," he said in 1962. "We must also devote ourselves, with joy and without fear, to the work of giving this ancient and eternal doctrine a relevancy corresponding to the conditions of our era." This statement was a paradigm of his greatness. Prelates who feared change ("fear," Pope John said, "comes only from a lack of faith") and resisted it with denunciations and condemnations, subscribed to the first half only; those who saw progress in change alone tended to harp exclusively on the latter half. Pope John believed in both, and acted on both. He was faithful to the past but devoted to the present, and he was wise enough to know that nothing from the past could really be preserved unless it was made meaningful here and now.

The pontificate of John XXIII was brief—four and a half years, the shortest since that of Pius VIII (1829–30)—but no pontificate in our century had vaster implications for the present and the future. Cardinal

138

Suenens, in his extraordinary address at the special ceremony in St. Peter's during the Second Session's period of crisis (see page 213), reminded his hearers of the intense feelings aroused all over the world by the death of Pope John. "The television, the radio and the press brought his death so close to us that it was like a death in the family. Never has the whole world taken part at such close quarters in the poignant stages of a mortal sickness. . . . The death of John XXIII was precious in the sight of the world. The pope transformed it into a final proclamation of faith and hope; he made it something like the celebration of an Easter liturgy. . . .

"John XXIII is present in our midst in a mysterious and profound way. He is with us by reason of the sacrifice of his life, which he offered for the happy outcome of the Council's labors. On this point there comes to mind an incident at Castel Gandolfo in July of last year (1962). John XXIII had spent the day, pen in hand, studying the preparatory schemata. In the course of an audience he read aloud some of the notes he had written in the margin. Then suddenly he stopped and said: 'Oh, I know what my personal part in the preparation of the Council will be.' And after a pause he concluded: 'It will be suffering.' "

THE ELECTION OF POPE PAUL VI

The news that the Roman Catholic Church—and the world—had a new pope broke unexpectedly on the morning of Friday, June 21, 1963, at precisely 11:18 A.M. When the tall glass doors behind the balcony above the portico of St. Peter's were opened and the red-bordered white papal tapestry (still bearing the Roncalli arms of a tower topped by the lion of St. Mark) was draped over the balustrade, the crowd roared in anticipation of a great moment. As the procession of ecclesiastics filed onto the balcony and the stocky figure of Cardinal Ottaviani, dean of the cardinal deacons, was ushered to the microphone, silence possessed the multitude of one hundred thousand people. In a clear and slightly tremulous voice, the nearly blind cardinal chanted, "I announce to you a great joy. We have a Pope! *Eminentissimum ac reverendissimum dominum* (pause)— *dominum Joannem Baptistam* . . . MONTINI!" Only the rising burst of the "MON" was heard, but it was sufficient. The crowd exploded. Ottaviani resumed patiently, ". . . who has taken the name . . . PAULUM SEXTUM!" There was another vocal explosion from below. Surrounded by the red- and purple-clad retinue, the cardinal withdrew, leaving the glass doors ajar. The man who had just become Pope Paul VI then appeared and advanced firmly to the front of the balcony. With just the slightest indication of a smile—or perhaps a tremor—on his lips, he accepted the tremendous acclamation of the crowd. He was flanked by two old practiced masters of ceremonies—Monsignor Salvatore Capoferri and Archbishop Enrico Dante—who had enacted this unusual ritual three or four times in the last forty years, the dark-skinned, gentle, and cavernous-eyed Capoferri going back to the election of Pius XI, in 1922. At a signal from Dante, the new Holy Father began the formula of his blessing to the city of Rome and to the world. "Blessed be the name of the Lord!" The words rang out in the new pope's clear, melodious voice. "Now and forever and ever!" came the response. "Our help is from the Lord," chanted Pope Paul. "Who has made heaven and earth," answered the crowd. Then, as the pope turned slowly and majestically in a three-quarter circle to cover the whole earth before him with three stately signs of the Cross, he sang out, clearly and precisely, "May the blessing of Almighty God, the Father, Son, and Holy Spirit, descend upon you and remain with you forever."

In his first audience with newspapermen and correspondents, Pope Paul referred ironically to some of the stories about the conclave as being "unusual," echoing Pope John's comment on the accounts of his election ("I could not find a word of truth in them"). Pope Paul was apparently referring to an article in the Italian picture magazine, *Epoca,* which claimed that he actually received a majority vote on the first day of the conclave but that, "very pale, almost speechless, (he) begged the cardinals to meditate—and to let him meditate—on their decision overnight." In order to accede to this Hamlet-like request, the cardinals would have had to fake a "black" burning on Thursday afternoon—and that, said the *Epoca* story, was what happened: "The crowd was manifestly deceived." Not only was this account patently absurd—implying an invalid election, and failure to reckon with the formidable presence of the ranking member of the conclave, Cardinal Tisserant, dean of the Sacred College, who would brook no such nonsense—but it was also significant as a repetition of the charge of indecisiveness from which Cardinal Montini has suffered throughout the latter part of his career.

As if to dispel at the very outset of his reign this false interpretation of his character, Paul VI began at once a series of actions that astonished everyone and were designed to show him to be a vigorous man of decision who knew his own mind. After the public blessing from the balcony, it was time for lunch, but instead of eating alone, as formal papal etiquette required, he ate with the cardinals at the big table set up for conclave meals in the Borgia apartments, and he sat not at the head place but in his old seat. At the end of lunch, he indicated that he was reappointing Cardinal Cicognani, Pope John's appointee, as his Secretary of State. Then, instead of waiting the customary few days before moving into the sealed-off private apartments vacated by his predecessor, he insisted on moving in right away. That night, Romans noticed lights behind the third-floor windows that had been dark for eighteen days. Though the formal ceremonies of the conclave were traditionally concluded by a second and third "obedience" of the cardinals, the new pope, after receiving all the conclavists in the Hall of Vestments, said simply, "We will do the rest tomorrow." He seemed anxious to begin receiving his aides and making decisions, and soon was at his desk writing out, in his own hand, a draft of the speech that he would deliver the next day over television—a speech containing a reassurance that an expectant world-wide audience was waiting to hear: he would continue the Ecumenical Council. Not long afterward, he set the date of the reopening of the Council for Sunday, September 29, 1963—much sooner than had been expected by even the most optimistic, since all preparations had been brought to a standstill during the three-week interregnum. Finally, the first meeting of the Council's all-important Coordinating Commission since Pope John's death was held on July 3rd, showing clearly that Pope Paul VI meant business.

In his speech, Pope Paul affirmed that he had no desire to interfere in the internal affairs of governments, and his subsequent replies to congratulatory telegrams from Premier Khrushchev and from President Zawadzki of Poland, indicated his intention of continuing the discussions that were started by Pope John with some of the Iron Curtain countries. These were not the only politic straws in the wind. The same afternoon, he left the Vatican—itself a significant feature on the first day after his election. He was on an errand of mercy, but this particular errand had overtones. Before the conclave met, it had been reported that the government of Spain was unhappy with Cardinal Montini. In 1962, urged on by the students of Milan, the cardinal had cabled Generalissimo Franco begging him to remit the death sentence of a young Spaniard, and Franco had coldly replied that the sentence was imprisonment, not death. (The Montini cable was called a "blunder" by some, though it was difficult to see how a plea for mercy, even when it was mistaken in detail, could be so regarded.) Thus it was interesting that the first visit of the new pope's reign took him to the Spanish College, near the Piazza Navona, to call on the ill and aged Cardinal Enrique Pla y Deniel, archbishop of Toledo. As Pope Paul arrived to see the cardinal, he was warmly greeted by the Spanish students, seminarians, faculty, and other personnel, who had gathered in the courtyard to pay him homage and to acknowledge that Spain, even as the rest of the world, had a new pope. The following day Pope Paul appeared at the window of his papal library to introduce to the cheering crowd Cardinal Suenens who, at Pope John's behest, had presented a copy of his encyclical *Pacem in Terris* to Secretary-General U Thant, of the United Nations. And three days later, in reply to two Protestant ministers who had sent him wishes for the success of his pontificate, Pope Paul wrote, by hand, of his desire to continue friendly relations with non-Catholics. On June 29th, he again left the Vatican, this time for the Roman church of St. Charles Borromeo to celebrate mass according to the Ambrosian rite for a delegation of pilgrims from his own city of Milan, led by the mayor. They presented him with the new triple tiara that was used to crown him at the coronation ceremony—a tall, rather tapered, and Gothic-looking crown, fashioned according to a design that the new pope had approved himself. Finally, he announced the resumption of the custom of daily audiences *di tabella* (" by schedule") with heads of the various congregations and offices of the Curia.

The election of Cardinal Montini was welcomed by members of the press, if only because he was the man about whom they had the most information. It did not take the public long to learn that the new pope was sixty-five; that he was born in Concesio, a suburb of Brescia, in northern Italy, of a family belonging to the professional class (his father had edited the local daily, *Il Cittadino,* for twenty-five years, and had served three terms in the Italian Parliament before the era of Fascism); that he had first undertaken his studies for the priesthood privately (as Pius XII had), and then in the Brescian seminary; and that he had been ordained a priest on May 29, 1920. During that summer, young Don Giambattista Montini served as a parish curate, and in the fall he went to Rome for graduate work at the Gregorian University. (He also studied literature at this time at the University of Rome.) Recommended to Pope Pius XI by Cardinal (then Monsignor) Pizzardo, who also sponsored his entrance into the papal foreign-service school for diplomatic training, Don Montini was sent to Warsaw as a minor offical in the Holy See's nunciature. His health failed after several months there, however, and he was brought back to Rome, where he was given duties in the Secretariat of State. In 1930, when Cardinal Pacelli became Pius XI's Secretary of State, he singled out Monsignor Montini for special training. From the start, Montini had interested himself in Catholic youth organizations, particularly on the university level; as a keen follower of the political theories of the anti-Fascist priest Luigi Sturzo, whose principal protégé was Alcide de Gasperi, Italy's great postwar premier and founder of the Christian Democratic Party, he had fostered political-training programs for Catholic students. This had brought him into contact with such early anti-Fascists as Dr. Luigi Gedda and Vittorino Veronese, future presidents of Italy's Catholic Action movement, and also into conflict with the Fascist organizers, who singled him out as a "dangerous" cleric.

During the first ten years of his Vatican apprenticeship, he was spiritual adviser to the *Federazione Universitarii Cattolici Italiani,* known as FUCI, whose intellectual pursuits he was able to stimulate by his ability to discuss the writings of Bergson, Spengler, and Mann, as well as modern theological writers and early church fathers. It was during this period that he acquired a preference for the *castelli* or little mountain towns south of Rome in the Alban Hills. (The night before the conclave started, he had stayed with Professor Bonomelli, custodian of the papal summer residence, Castel Gandolfo, and told him that one of his fondest wishes was to revisit these picturesque spots he had come to know so well as a young Vatican official.) While serving in the Vatican Secretariat of State, Monsignor Montini made many American friends whose practical mentality, and minimal interest in intramural intrigues, appealed to him. The late Monsignor Walter Carroll of Pittsburgh, who served as a *minutante,* or minor aide, for American affairs, and slow-speaking but efficient Monsignor Joseph McGeough of New York, with whom in 1950 he made the first of his two visits to the United States, were two of his best friends. He was associated in the early years with Monsignor Francis J. Spellman of Boston, and learned to collaborate with him closely later when, as archbishop of New York, Cardinal Spellman turned out to be one of Pope Pius XII's closest personal friends. Monsignor Montini took a keen interest in the National Catholic Welfare Conference, or NCWC, the organization of the United States bishops. Founded in 1919, this was one of the first effective groupings of bishops on a national scale that was not regarded by the Curia as a threatened revival of anti-Romanism (as with the Gallicanism of the bishops of France before the French Revolution, and the Josephism in Austria prior to World War I). The late Monsignor Howard Carroll, as secretary of the NCWC in Washington, brought promising American clerics to the attention of Monsignor Montini through his brother Walter in the Vatican. All these contacts proved extremely helpful during World War II, when the Vatican was called upon to set up in cooperation with the International Red Cross an organization for the exchange of war-prisoner information.

During the war years Monsignor Montini had become a key figure in the Secretariat of State, and it was assumed that either he or Monsignor Domenico Tardini would succeed the aging Cardinal Maglione as Secretary, on his death in 1944. However, Pope Pius XII decided to function as his own Secretary of State, and named his two chief aides as Under-Secretaries of State. Monsignor Tardini, who was somewhat senior, was entrusted with Extraordinary Affairs, or dealings with secular governments and their diplomats accredited to the Holy See; Monsignor Montini was put in charge of Ordinary Affairs, or dealings with bishops and the internal affairs of the Church. The outlooks of the two men were almost antithetical, and conflict was inevitable. Tardini, the older man, enjoyed the support of such powerful and ultra-conservative figures as Cardinals Canali and Pizzardo, and Monsignor Ottaviani of the Holy Office. Montini's policy, generally speaking, was in favor of a gradual withdrawal of the Church from the political forum in the postwar era. He had supported the worker-priest movement in France, considering it more spiritually than (as it turned out to be) politically oriented, and had encouraged the leaders of Italian Catholic Action in their attempt to find a means of influencing the leftist parties, particularly by approaching such groups as the Nenni Socialists. His final objective was to dissociate Catholic Action from the Christian Democratic Party, as Pope John later succeeded in doing with his ordinances spelled out by the Synod of Rome, convened in 1959. Monsignor Montini had also encouraged the Holy See's relations with UNESCO, in which he was joined by Archbishop Angelo Roncalli, who was then apostolic nuncio to France. They were both overruled by the Canali-Tardini-Ottaviani forces. A final source of disagreement lay in Montini's insistence that representatives of the Holy See, and Catholics generally, should cooperate with organizations throughout the world working for international peace. In July, 1953, writing to the 40th *Semaine Sociale de France,* he deplored the fact that so many Christians still failed to heed the warnings of the Holy See in this grave period of international relations, just as they had been slow to follow papal encyclicals on the equally important question of social justice; he was saddened, he said, by the narrow nationalism and strange inertia of some Catholics, in view of the repeated appeals of the Holy Father for relations with non-Catholic agencies working on the social aspects of international affairs.

In 1953, Pope Pius XII convened what was to be the final consistory of his reign, and on this occasion two things of historic importance occurred— he made Angelo Roncalli a cardinal, and he revealed that both Monsignor Montini and Monsignor Tardini had declined to accept this supreme papal honor. Pope Pius attributed these refusals to the high virtue and humility of both men, and this was true enough, but Vatican observers felt there was more to it than that. A pasquinade soon became current: "When Tardini would not, Montini could not." The internal crisis within the Secretariat was not long in coming to a head. In 1954, at a time when Pius XII was ill, a section of Catholic Action found itself in the position of having helped beat the Christian Democrats in a series of local elections, and it was at this point that the Tardini faction succeeded in convincing the pope that Montini must go. On August 31st of that year, the day after the death of Cardinal Schuster, archbishop of Milan, Montini was chosen as his successor. He was given the news of his new post by Pius XII himself, in an hour-long telephone call, although official announcement of the appointment was not made until November 3rd.

In the postwar period, the city of Milan had become a strong communist center, used by the party as a model for the other great population centers of Italy. Montini's appointment was therefore a challenge to him, particularly since the final years of Cardinal Schuster's twenty-five-year reign had not kept pace with the social problems resulting from Milan's phenomenal postwar industrial and commercial expansion. It was not difficult for the Tardini faction to convince Pius XII that in removing Montini from the Curia he was giving him a task worthy of his great talents. When Montini left Rome for Milan, it was noted that ninety cases of books were shipped after him. In Milan, however, he acted not as a bookish intellectual but as "the workers' archbishop," and he became a familiar sight in the city, approaching workers with a sad smile and an outstretched hand, despite their hoots and jeers; in the end, they usually shook his hand. He visited the communist districts of the city, went down into mines, and toured factories, always carrying a portable kit for saying mass, which he set up and used wherever he went. He preached a message of love to "the unhappy ones who gather behind Marx," and told them that "Jesus still loves you strongly, immensely, divinely," and that the Church works to satisfy "the profound need for a new and worthwhile life that is hidden in your souls." When Pius died, late in 1958, it was said that at the ensuing conclave several voters crossed out the word "cardinal" printed on the ballots and wrote Montini's name in the blank space that followed. Pope John XXIII called his first consistory immediately after his election, in order to bolster up the depleted college of cardinals. Not only was the archbishop of Milan the first prelate he raised to the purple, but Pope John thereafter went out of his way to show the new cardinal special consideration. In 1960, he sent Montini to the United States, where he received an honorary degree from Notre Dame, along with President Eisenhower and the late Dr. Tom Dooley. He afterward went on a mission to South America, and in 1962 he made a visit to Africa, to report to Pope John on the problems that the Church faced on that continent.

When Pope John convened the Council in 1962, Montini was the only cardinal from outside Rome who was invited to stay in the papal apartments during the eight weeks of the First Session, and he was said to have had a hand in the remarkable opening speech that Pope John addressed to the Council. In the Council itself, he spoke twice, and in the debate on "The Church" it was with extraordinary effect. Speaking in support of Cardinal Suenens' statement, he said that the Church was not so much a society founded by Christ as it was Christ himself using us as instruments to bring salvation to all mankind. He said that it was up to the Fathers of the Council to define the collegial nature of the episcopate, to give a truly ecumenical outlook to the Church, and to insist that each bishop was "the image of the Father and the image of Christ." The less we insisted on the rights of the Church, he said, the more chance we had of being heard, especially in those parts of the world suspicious of the Church as a colonial-minded institution. Then in a letter to the archdiocese of Milan, sent from Rome, he significantly laid the blame for the Council's failure to make greater progress on those members of the Curia who had prevented cooperation between the various commissions during the period preceding its opening. Although *L'Osservatore Romano* published excerpts from the late pope's diary before the conclave met, it was concealed from everyone until well after the conclave that the diary expressed Pope John's hope that Cardinal Montini would be his successor.

A reminder of Pope Paul's ecumenical hopes was contained in the special blessing he imparted to non-Catholics during an audience he granted a group of pilgrims from Philadelphia on June 25, 1963: "We wish our thoughts also to go to those of our brethren who are not Catholics. On them and on their dear ones we invoke the abundance of heavenly grace." The most widely quoted incident of President Kennedy's visit to Pope Paul on July 3rd, was the latter's reference to the fight against racial segregation in the United States, but many who quoted it failed to connect Pope Paul's words and the gift that Pope John XXIII had earmarked for the President when he thought that he would live to greet him in person. The gift was an autographed copy of the encyclical *Pacem in Terris,* and President Kennedy was visibly moved when Cardinal Cushing presented it to him.

TOWARD THE SECOND SESSION

The new pope's choice of the name of the Apostle of the Gentiles seemed to most observers a clear indication not only of his intention to carry on the Johannine legacy but of his desire to dedicate himself, in a special way, to the Church's ecumenical mission toward "those who bear the name of Christian" as well as the non-baptized.

On the morning of Sunday, August 18th, Pope Paul motored from his *villeggiatura* at Castel Gandolfo in the Alban Hills to the ancient Greek monastery of St. Nilus, at the foot of Monte Cavo, some five miles distant. There he celebrated mass for a community of Basilian monks who had revitalized the atmosphere and traditions of the Eastern Church, preserved on that spot for close to a thousand years. The pope took the occasion to comment on a major theme of the Council—the unity of Christians. "I long to make mine the wish that spontaneously and generously welled up in the hearts of my predecessors, especially John XXIII," he said. "Come, let the barriers that separate us fall! Let us explain the points of doctrine that are not common to us but are still subjects of controversy; let us seek to render our creed a joint one and a solid one. . . . We wish neither to absorb nor to detract from the great flowering of Eastern Churches but wish it to be engrafted on the tree of the unity of Christ." He also said that his respect for the Orthodox Churches was motivated by "the same feeling of brotherhood that recently authorized a bishop of the Catholic Church to go to Moscow in honor of the eightieth birthday of Aleksei, the patriarch of Moscow." He added, "We did this with the intention of paying homage, of showing that there were no motives of rivalry . . . or any desire to perpetuate discords and disagreements that now seem completely anachronistic." Referring to the day's Gospel story of Christ healing the deaf-and-dumb man, Pope Paul said, "We are all a little dumb, we are all a little deaf. May the Lord open our senses to understand the voices of history."

During the Council's First Session, in the debate on the nature of the Church, it became clear that the Council Fathers favored the view that not only were all men called to be members but vast numbers of people, even if they did not accept the external bonds of Catholic unity, nevertheless belonged to the Church as long as they were baptized and acted in accord with the dictates of conscience. Though this view was an abomination to fundamentalist Catholic theologians, the *American Ecclesiastical Review*—long regarded as the mouthpiece of Catholic theological intransigence in the United States—ran an article in 1963 by the young Dominican Father Colman E. O'Neill, who taught at Lateran University, that certainly amazed a number of its readers. Father O'Neill said:

Those who define Church membership in purely juridical terms are forced to the conclusion that [the baptized non-Catholic] cannot be a member . . . since the matter has been settled by *Mystici corporis* (Pius XII's encyclical) and *Suprema haec sacra* (the Holy Office letter). St. Thomas Aquinas, on the contrary, without the slightest hesitation, says that such a person is a member; and the Council of Trent says exactly the same thing. . . . Monsignor Fenton [formerly of Catholic University] considers that all non-Catholics are positively excluded from any kind of membership. In the case of baptized non-Catholics in good faith, at least, as we have seen, this is not so.

Catholics who had been misled to believe the false notion that the Church never changed—it is the Truth that never changes—found this development in Catholic theology unsettling. On the other hand, Catholics who were shocked when political-sounding labels like "progressive" and "conservative" were applied to individual Council Fathers had been reassured about the validity of these terms by a Council Father himself—Bishop Ernest J. Primeau (Manchester, New Hampshire), who wrote in *America:*

I agree with the general use of the words "conservative" and "liberal" to express the extreme positions taken by the Fathers of the Council. There was a real cleavage, not just a question of semantics. And these labels serve to express the difference quite well. As a matter of fact, this difference of opinion, since it was not of faith or morals, should cause no scandal. . . . Very few men are conservative or liberal on every question.

That final sentence certainly did not apply to the editors of the Italian rightist magazine *Il Borghese,* who were conservative on all questions, especially those concerning Vatican Council II. They thoroughly disapproved of Pope John's policies and blamed him for the size of the communist vote in the Italian election. At the First Session, according to them, it was "almost as if the Church had been transformed into a degenerate democratic assembly." In their view, the "holy liberty" that Pope John allowed the Council Fathers in the debates was a mistake. It would not be repeated in the Second Session, *Il Borghese* felt, because the Curia, "with its humane recourse to logic, good sense, and the light of reason," had regained complete control of the situation during the intersession. *Il Borghese* predicted that the Council would quickly conclude its business in the Second Session "with feet firmly on the ground," acting as the "purely consultative organ of the Supreme Pontiff." By "Supreme Pontiff," the editors meant, of course, not the pope alone but the pope as represented by their party in the Curia.

However, Pope Paul's actions and utterances indicated to anyone who studied them closely that he was in every sense the heir and continuator of Pope John's pastoral policies, wiht a special character of his own. He announced on September 15, 1963 the creation of a steering commission of four cardinals with an "executive mandate" to direct the work of this session, and three of its members—Cardinals Suenens, Döpfner, and Lercaro—were known to be progressives. Nor could the fourth member, Cardinal Agagianian, a representative of the Curia who bridged the gap between the Church of Rome and the Eastern Church (he was for many years the Armenian Patriarch), be fully classed as a traditionalist. These four cardinals were also members of the important ten-member Coördinating Commission, the body that got proposals to the floor and coördinated the work of the various commissions responsible for the Council's agenda. Pope Paul's dissatisfaction with the procedural confusions at the First Session was made clear even while it was being held. In his final weekly letter to the faithful of his archdiocese, just before the close of the First Session, he emphasized the primary importance of the schema "On the Church," which he described as "the foundation of the entire council." It was therefore not surprising when the Vatican announced that the first item on the agenda for the Second Session, after the ceremonial and organizational business of the opening days, would be further debate on *De Ecclesia.*

One of the most interesting and controversial topics in this schema was the relationship of the bishops to the pope and to each other. The very act

148

of calling the Council dramatized this subject, because it made the Fathers more fully aware that they were bishops. It was no small gesture on the part of Pope Paul to announce that the Fathers could wear the *mozzetta* at the Council. (This elbow-length cape, an emblem of episcopal jurisdiction, was never worn outside a bishop's own diocese.) To allow its use in Rome was regarded as a symbolic and highly significant act on the pope's part. It was as if he were saying to the Fathers, "I am the bishop of Rome, just as you are the bishop of your diocese."

The general desire to give concrete form to the collegiality of the bishops was seen in a proposal to revitalize the ancient office of patriarch, as an intermediary stage between the pope and the rest of the episcopate. The Dutch canonist Piet Fransen, S.J., proposed the grouping of the whole Church into patriarchates along regional or continental lines. It was known that the colorful and outspoken Melchite Patriarch Maximos IV Saigh, had long nurtured the hope of one day seeing the Eastern patriarchates enjoy their rightful and historical place in the Church, preceding the cardinalate. (The cardinals, historically the successors of the ancient Roman parish clergy and canonically forming part of the diocese of Rome, were subject to the pope in his office as patriarch of Rome.) For this reason, His Beatitude, following the precedent of the former Melchite patriarchs, had three times refused a cardinal's hat (offered twice by Pius XII and once by John XXIII); however, Patriarchs Tappouni and Agagianian both accepted, thus breaking the solidarity of the Eastern patriarchs (Alexandria, Antioch and Jerusalem) in their claim to be the equals of the pope as patriarch of the West (though not in his primatial authority over the whole Church or primacy). It represented no little compromise therefore when Maximos IV was finally persuaded, along with his eastern colleagues, to accept "associate membership" in the Roman Congregation for the Oriental Churches of which hitherto only cardinals had been members. With the experience of the First Session behind him, and the prospects for change brighter, he undoubtedly felt that he could be more effective in achieving the goals of guarding against Latinization and reforming the Code of Canon Law for the Oriental Churches by having one foot inside the door rather than by remaining entirely outside.

Although it was publicly known that the First Session had exceeded the hopes of the progressives by revealing that they had an articulate majority among the bishops, it was less well known that the shortcomings of that gathering were subjected to a searching examination during the intersession by those responsible for guiding the Council's work. A highly interesting and authoritative critique—made on the level of the Coördinating Commission, and thus close to the top—pointed out that the chief stumbing block was the rules under which the Council operated. The report said—in tactful terms, of course—that these rules were demonstrably contrived to assure domination of the proceedings at all stages by the Curial party. The critique also said that the rules failed to profit from the experience of other parliaments or international assemblies in expediting the flow of business, and were inadequate for guiding a deliberative assembly of over two thousand bishops. They failed to define clearly the functions of the Council presidents, with the result that the supreme direction of affairs had to be improvised and was virtually lodged in the Secretariat for Extraordinary Affairs, a subordinate committee not intended to have this role. Perhaps the worst defect was the organization and excessive number of the conciliar commissions. The commissions ought to have been both fewer in number and better coordinated, with responsibilities corresponding to the matters likely to come before the Council, not merely slavishly reflecting the divisions of the Curia. Moreover, the cardinals presiding over them had powers that were too vast and arbitrary—again a reflection of the Curia. Not enough use had been made, said the critique, of the Council experts or *periti* who not infrequently found themselves virtually excluded from any participation in the work. Finally, there were complaints about the system of voting, both in committee and on the floor. Any Curialist tempted to conclude that because Pope John had promulgated these rules he, for one, considered them infallible, should have remembered what he told a group of Pakistani bishops: "Nobody around here knows how to run a Council, and the reason is simple—none of us has ever been to one before!"

Though there were hopeful signs during the intersession period of a full-scale liberalization of the Church's policy, the "hard-core" Curia group and their collaborators continued to manifest their obstructionism, particularly in the commissions working on the Council schemata. For example, the bishops and *periti* on the Liturgical Commission during the late summer had to fight, word by word, to force the president and secretary of that body to make the document accord with the mind of the vast majority of the Council Fathers as expressed in their speeches during the First Session and in their voting on the first chapter of the schema. An obvious tactic of the cardinal president was to do all the talking at the meetings, until the day one exasperated Negro bishop, in impeccable French, told him off before the whole group, asking whether he had been brought all the way from his diocese in Africa to listen to cardinalatial lectures. In the joint meetings of the Theological Commission and other commissions, veiled hints of retribution against *periti* with advanced views were occasionally uttered by representatives of the Holy Office. In the gatherings of the commission dealing with the schema on the hierarchy, there was so much pandemonium, with everyone talking at cross purposes, that it enabled Bishop Carli of Segni to emerge as secretary of a commission that put together the worst schema reported on the Council floor. (It was not, in fact, the most retrograde of *all* the schemata, however. This distinction belonged to the schema dealing with marriage, which opened with a chapter devoted to "impediments" and continued with solely canonical considerations, the subject of love being mentioned almost accidentally in an appendix. To judge from this schema, Pope John's call for a pastoral Council, and Pope Paul's repetition of this theme, had never been uttered.)

These and similar facts revealed the unyielding temper of the "remnant of Israel," as the thirty or so members of this curial group came to be called. Their conviction that, in the end, they would win caused great concern on the progressive side. Behind the scenes Curial agents pursued their witch hunt tactics in France, Germany, Spain, and even the United States, where several bishops were encouraged by the apostolic delegate to aid him in ferreting out "dangerous" theologians and journalists. Pressures were also put on official representatives of the Catholic press in America to improve the public image and whitewash the reputation of Cardinal Ottaviani, who now began to grant interviews. Commenting on the widely circulated story that he had tried to silence Karl Rahner, the celebrated Austrian theologian who served as a Council *peritus* during the First Session of the Council, Cardinal Ottaviani said:

This is completely false. This whole matter was completely unknown to me until I heard others speak of it. Neither I nor anyone else in the Holy Office, either directly or indirectly, suggested that Father Rahner should leave Rome. Quite the contrary. Twice I invited Father Rahner to address the members of the Preparatory Commission on Theology.

However, Father Rahner in an interview in the *Catholic Reporter* (Kansas City) had this to say:

It is generally known that I had difficulties with the Holy Office, whose chairman is Cardinal Ottaviani, in Rome before and at the beginning of the Council. These difficulties were based for the most part on efforts to subject my future published works to a special Roman censorship.

THE REFORM OF THE ROMAN CURIA

As a preamble to the Second Session, the pope scheduled an audience for 10 A.M. on September 21, 1963. To the surprise of some, who had forgotten the pope's reputation for punctuality, he entered the doorway of the Hall of Benedictions—an enormous room over the portico of St. Peter's basilica—on the dot of ten, and, a slim figure in white, walked the length of the room, which was already crowded with dozens of car-

151

dinals, scores of prelates, and hundreds of clerical and lay officials of the Curia and workers at the Vatican. As he stood near his throne on the dais, a few latecomers of high rank, who had obviously set out for their destination at the usual Roman pace for such occasions, had to trudge to their places toward the front of the hall while the Holy Father waited patiently to begin. Still standing, he told his audience that because the formal talk he had prepared for them might prove to be long, he was declaring the rest of the day a holiday. The crowd broke into pleased applause. He added that in view of the increased cost of living in Rome (rents, for example, had gone up thirty per cent that summer) he was also giving each of them a raise. Louder applause and happy murmurs. The pope then sat down and began a historic discourse. Though it was somewhat overshadowed by his address at the opening of the Council, eight days later, its importance was evident. That he intended it to be heard by the world, and not only by the Roman Curia, was clear from the fact that he could have arranged an off-the-record reception and not permitted the release of his text. It was obvious that he wanted everyone, especially the twenty-three hundred Council Fathers (many of whom were coverging on Rome from various continents at that moment), to hear and understand his words. He used phrases of great tact, courtesy, and praise, yet at the same time he clearly expressed every theme of reform that had been raised at the First Session of the Council by spokesmen for the progressive viewpoint. Speaking as one who knew his audience well, he reminded them that he himself had served for thirty years in the ranks of the Curia. He had called this meeting at the beginning of his reign, he told them, in order to greet those present and to express to them his veneration, gratitude, and encouragement. Another reason for the reception, he said, was "the very beautiful and serious moment being lived by the whole Church"—namely, Vatican Council II. He thought that the Curia should take careful stock of this great event—not that it had failed to understand the enormous importance of the Council during the First Session. "On the contrary," said the Holy Father, "the Council's extraordinary and complex dimensions were discerned more fully by the Curia than by any other sector of the Church or public opinion, even to the point of at times allowing a certain stupor and apprehension to show." When he spoke of the necessity for accord between the pope and the Curia, he seemed to be putting some of its members politely on notice: "We are certain that no hesitation regarding the principal wishes of the pope will ever come from the Curia, and that the Curia will never be suspected of any differences of judgment or feeling with regard to the judgments and feelings of the pope." To make his message perfectly clear, he referred to himself at this point as "the pope who today has made the legacy of John XXIII his own, and has also made it a program for the entire Church." He then spoke of the Curia's critics, and said it was understandable that a body whose present form went back to 1588, and whose most recent reorganization was in 1908, "should have grown ponderous with venerable old age, shown by the disparity between its practices and the needs and usages of modern times." He added that the Curia needed "to be simplified and decentralized, and to adapt itself to new functions," and, after referring to Pope John's word *"aggiornamento,"* he concluded simply, "Various reforms are therefore necessary." He then made one of the most significant statements in the address, insinuating that episcopal collegiality would be one of the chief themes of the session—and indicating that the de-Italianization of the Curia was inevitable:

> We will say more: If the Ecumenical Council wishes to see some representatives of the episcopacy, particularly bishops heading dioceses, associated . . . with [the pope] in the study and responsibility of ecclesiastical government, it will not be the Roman Curia that will oppose it.

Toward the close of his talk, he uttered a fervent message: "People everywhere are watching Catholic Rome, the Roman pontificate, the Roman Curia. The duty of being authentically Christian is especially binding here. We would not remind you of this duty if we did not remind ourself of it every day. Everything in Rome teaches the letter and the spirit—the way we think, study, speak, feel, act, pray, serve, love." He ended with the prayer that "this old and ever new Roman Curia" might shine like a light in the Church of God. He had carried his audience with him completely, and after he concluded, the applause was so great and prolonged that he had to intone the words of the papal blessing to stop it. All over Rome, in the days that followed, certain members of the Curia went around expressing their joy at the talk and their gratitude that the Pope had defended them and shown such appreciation of their work. It apparently did not cross their minds that, as Michael Novak later wrote in *Commonweal,* "the talk was a two-edged sword." *Il Tempo* an ultra-conservative paper, gave its readers what was probably the most peculiarly one-sided report of the talk. Its headline read, "POPE ANNOUNCES RAISE FOR ALL VATICAN WORKERS," and under this was quoted the Pope's praise of the Curia. There was not a word about reform.

The Council's opening ceremony, on Sunday, September 29, 1963, was impressive, if less formal than the rites at the First Session. Instead of marching in procession through St. Peter's Square, the bishops strolled casually, with mitres in hand, to their seats in the nave of the basilica. Though pope Paul, preceded by the Swiss Guard and the College of Cardinals, was borne on the *sedia gestatoria* from the bronze doors of the papal palace to St. Peter's, he dismounted inside the basilica. In place of the papal triple tiara, he wore a mitre like the other bishops, and instead of giving the bishops the customary papal blessing, he contented himself with greeting his colleagues in the episcopate with waves of the hand as he walked down the central aisle to the Confession of St. Peter, where his throne was placed. After the solemn pontifical mass, the pope made his profession of faith and received to the homage of the cardinals. Then the Council Fathers professed their faith, viva voce, and Pope Paul began his opening address.

While unusually long—an hour and four minutes—it was a magnificent discourse, reasserting the purpose of the Council as inaugurated by Pope John XXIII and indicating the concrete steps by which *aggiornamento* would proceed. Pope Paul's voice was somewhat hoarse, but his enunciation was clear and his diction precise, and the Council Fathers, the observer-delegates from non-Roman religious communions, the lay auditors, and the invited guests all knew that they were participating in one of the great moments in church history. Pope Paul expressed the joy he felt at the regathering of the Fathers, who, by the time the Council finally concluded its business, "with one voice alone will give their message to the whole world." He explained that he had first intended to send the bishops the customary encyclical letter of a new pope; instead, he said, "let this address be a prelude not only to the Council but to our pontificate."

He announced four points as the Council's principal aims. First, the Church must impart to herself and to the world a new awareness of her inner nature. Despite great progress in theology since Vatican Council I, the Church still did not have a clear notion of herself that was likely to impress the modern world. This definition did not need to take the form of a dogma, he said, but could be made as an explicit and authoritative declaration. Second, there must be a renewal and reform of the Church— "not by turning upside down the present way of life or breaking with what is essential and worthy in her tradition" but, rather, "by stripping it of what is unworthy or defective." Then, as Pope Paul discussed the third principal aim of the Council—the unity of all Christians—an impressive and moving incident occurred. He turned around to face the tribune on his left, where the observer-delegates from other Christian communions were seated. He said that their presence at the Council stirred great hope in his heart, as well as a feeling of sadness at their separation. "If we are to blame in any way for that separation," he said to them, "we humbly beg God's forgiveness, and ask pardon, too, of our brethren who feel themselves to have been injured by us." This unprecedented and historic utterance no doubt shocked some of the Fathers who had insisted that the Church was without stain or blemish, but for the majority of the pope's listeners it was a great moment. Before taking up the final theme—the dialogue between the Church and the world today—Pope Paul saw fit to point out the vacant benches of those bishops who were suffering under restraint and in prison for their faith. "We must be realists," he said, "and not hide the savagery that reaches into this Council from many areas. . . . In certain countries, religious liberty, like other fundamental rights of man, is being crushed by principles and methods of political, racial, and anti-religious intolerance. The heart grieves that there are still so many acts of injustice against goodness." He said that "while the light of the science of nature is increasing, darkness is spreading over the science of God" through the destruction of intellectual and moral integrity. "Progress is perfecting, in a wondrous way, every kind of instrument that man uses, but his heart is declining toward emptiness, sadness, and despair," he said, and concluded, "The Church today stands ready to aid the oppressed, the poor, and the suffering. Let the world realize that the Church looks on it with profound understanding and sincere admiration, with the frank desire not to conquer but to serve, not to despise but to appreciate, not to condemn but to comfort and save." The Pauline Council had begun.

THE DEBATE ON 'THE CHURCH'

As the bishops gathered in the great conciliar hall of St. Peter's for the first business session of the second phase of the Vatican Council II, on Monday morning September 30th at 9 A.M., they were unusually talkative, exchanging greetings and congratulations as new arrivals, both bishops appointed during the intersession and about 75 apostolic prefects sitting for the first time, were attempting with difficulty to find their proper seats. The first person to be heard over the microphone was one of the council undersecretaries, Archbishop Villot, requesting the Fathers to make the responses to the mass in unison, slowly and distinctly. As a thoughtful touch of the new pope, the first conciliar mass was to be celebrated in the Ambrosian rite by His Excellency the archbishop of Milan, Giovanni Colombo, the successor of Montini on the throne of St. Ambrose. The voices of Archbishop Colombo and of the pope were so remarkably alike that it was not difficult for the Fathers to imagine that they were listening to the mass of the Holy Father himself.

According to the pre-announced agenda, the first item of business was to be the schema *De Ecclesia* on the nature of the Church. The text before the Fathers represented a completely new version of the schema originally submitted for consideration by the Theological Commission during the final days of the First Session which had come in for heavy criticism as a wholly inadequate expression of the Council's mind on this all-important crucial theme. In fact, it would be more accurate to speak of the fusion of

155

various drafts. Chapters I and II, for which the Theological Commission was exclusively responsible, were based largely on a draft by the Louvain theologian G. Philips in which key portions of the original schema had been incorporated. Other drafts which influenced the final version were one, largely scriptural in inspiration, by Karl Rahner, S.J.; another less comprehensive in nature which also furnished some of the ideas which would be incorporated in Schema 17; and finally a French draft based largely on a study by Fathers G. Thils and J. Daniélou published in *Etudes et Documents* (January 15, 1963). Chapters III and IV were worked out by mixed committees of the Commission for the Apostolate of the Laity and the Commission for Religious Orders. Under the circumstances it was not surprising that one of the objections raised against the new version (by Cardinal Gracias) was that it betrayed such a patchwork origin and was lacking in uniformity. However, there were many virtues which helped to compensate for the defects. The schema, in four chapters, ran to 78 printed pages, most of which were devoted to footnotes, so that the actual text was not very long.

Before the Second Session the Coordinating Commission had decided to recommend that the section on the People of God be removed from Chapter III and brought forward as a new Chapter II, thus giving the whole schema greater cohesion and logic. This was intended to emphasize the idea of the basic equality of all members of the Church before distinctions were made according to office or charisma. Since so many of the speakers had seconded this recommendation, it was almost certain that the final text would reflect the proposed change.

In fact, it was truly surprising that a text as "liberal" as the present one could have come out of the Theological Commission in view of the known orientation of its chairman and vice-chairman, Cardinals Ottaviani and Browne. As the debate progressed, both these cardinals had very little to say except with regard to one or two key points, the collegiality of the bishops and the revival of the diaconate, preferring to refrain, publicly at least, from all comment on the schema as a whole. According to unconfirmed reports the elaboration of the present text was achieved only after a prolonged struggle within the Theological Commission itself, with the chairmen ultimately unsuccessful in their attempt to impose a more conservative document on the progressive-minded majority.

Before the discussions began on *De Ecclesia,* Secetary General Archbishop Felici mounted the rostrum and made a series of important announcements. He drew the attention of the Fathers first of all to the changes that had been made in the conciliar Ordo or Rules of Procedure, pointing out what Articles had been changed and commenting on each one briefly. The purpose of the changes was twofold, he said: to facilitate the work of the Council, and to protect the rights of those Fathers who found themselves in a minority as the result of a vote. The law of every Council must be a moral unanimity: this meant that everything which tended to divide the Council into a majority and a minority representing two opposing tendencies should be avoided.

The rules regarding the interventions were then read first in Latin by Archbishop Felici and afterward by the five undersecretaries in their respective languages. The Fathers were requested specifically to observe the provisions of Article 57 of the Ordo which required: 1) that the complete text of a speech, duly signed, must be submitted to the Secretariat at the conclusion of every speech; 2) that the Fathers who had the same observations to make on a given subject should arrange to have one or more speak on their behalf; 3) that the Fathers should avoid repeating what others had said, if need be by withdrawing their names from the list of speakers. Those who spoke on behalf of others should attach a list of the names of those on whose behalf they were speaking. Signatures were not necessary. Moreover, in accordance with Art. 33, the speakers must submit to the Secretariat three days beforehand a summary, or preferably, the full text of what they intended to say.* The summary should be more than a mere outline; it should contain, briefly, the principal arguments to be presented. During the speeches a two minute warning signal would be sounded near the microphone where the bishop was speaking, indicating that eight minutes had elapsed and only two remained in which to conclude.

The secretary general then announced that His Holiness had laid down the following rules with regard to Council secrecy: the obligation of secrecy applied in full force to the contents of the schemata and to the discussions and conclusions reached in sessions of the Council commissions. But with reference to the discussions in the council hall during the General Congregations, His Holiness recommended that a maximum moderation and prudence be observed at all times and in all places. As Henri Fesquet remarked in *Le Monde:*† "The secrecy of the council *tombe en quénouille*—is shattered."

The Fathers were also told on the opening day that there would be no further appointments of Council experts since the number of those appointed was more than adequate to meet the needs of the Council. As a matter of fact, several additional appointments were actually made, for various special reasons, but not on a large scale.

It was then announced that following an initial discussion of the schema *De Ecclesia* in general, a vote would be taken in accordance with Art. 31

* The intention was to allow the moderators a better opportunity for guiding the Council by eliminating needless repetitions, but the Council Secretariat, in effect, eluded their control, remaining subject directly to the Secretary of State, and this measure was rendered nugatory in practice.

† *Le Monde,* October 2, 1963.

by a simple placet or non placet to determine whether the text was acceptable as a basis for discussion in detail. Cardinal Agagianian, moderator for the day, then introduced the discussion by expressing a word of greeting on behalf of the Council presidents to all, especially the apostolic prefects who were sitting for the first time, the lay auditors, and the non-Catholic observers. He invited the Fathers to resume their deliberations under Pope Paul VI and to be inspired by what he had said in his opening address.

As president of the Theological Commission which had prepared the draft, Cardinal Ottaviani opened the debate reading the text of a speech distributed to the Fathers along with the official *relatio* of Cardinal Browne. Ottaviani said briefly that the deposit of faith must not only be guarded, it must also be presented to all (*Non solum depositum fidei servare oportet, sed omnibus proponere*), referring to a dual responsibility of the Church which it was difficult or wrong to separate. The cardinal observed, somewhat laconically perhaps though in a perfectly amiable tone, that the First Session had shown that the Council must speak in a way that could be understood by all, Catholics and non-Catholics. The schema might not be perfect, but it was impossible to satisfy everybody.

The vicepresident of the Theological Commission, Cardinal Browne, then took the floor and read his official "report" explaining briefly the plan and content of the schema. He mentioned that 372 amendments had been proposed at the First Session and afterward, with which the commission had had to deal: 1 on the title, 9 on the preamble, 165 on Chapter I and 206 on Chapter II.

Cardinal Frings of Cologne spoke first in the name of the sixty-five German and Scandinavian Fathers. He began with the significant words *"Valde placet,"* thus indicating that the schema was basically satisfactory to him. This was no small tribute to the work of the commission—in view of the critical attitude of the speaker—and meant that the schema had indeed undergone fundamental changes since the last session. Cardinal Frings approved the schema's pastoral and ecumenical spirit, its avoidance of a juridical and apologetic tone which would not have been fitting for a Council, its reliance on Scripture and tradition, and its treatment of non-Christians. However he stated that the question of who was and who was not a member of the Church could not be decided in this schema. And he had a number of criticisms. He questioned whether the scriptural quotations were always the best or the most concrete. There was much more about the infallibility of the pope than about the teaching office of the bishops. He wished that the Church's relationship to the Virgin Mary and the saints had been set out more clearly. Finally he expressed his thanks to Paul VI who in his opening address, "courageously, not as a tactic but because it is the truth," had acknowledged the faults of the Catholic Church in the separation of the Churches and had humbly asked pardon for its share of the responsibility.

The archbishop of Morcillo (Spain) thought that the schema was good but that it would not be very meaningful to non-Christians. There was nothing in the chapter on the hierarchy about patriarchs—a notable omission. The statements about equality in the Church needed clarification. Priests and deacons should be considered separately from the section on bishops. There was a needless juridical tone at times and too much emphasis on the papal primacy. All these points were raised by other speakers as well.

The Italian prelate of the Order of Malta, Archbishop Ferrero di Cavallerleone asked that the schema on the Virgin Mary be attached to *De Ecclesia*. It was not possible to speak of the Church without speaking of Mary, he said.

Archbishop Florit (Florence) praised the text for its clear, positive, biblical and ecumenical approach, especially for what it said about the laity and the college of bishops. But there were some defects. The title might better be *"De Ecclesia Christi."* Treating the Church as a Mystery created a psychological problem for the faithful who were inclined to think of the mysterious as something unknowable. The theology of the college of bishops should also be better explained, as well as the nature of an ecumenical council. He wished also that the schema *De Revelatione* could be discussed concurrently with the present schema so that the problem of revelation might be considered in another context. The text sometimes gave the impression of being more of a theological treatise than a conciliar constitution.

Bishop Gargitter (Bressanone, Italy) speaking last on Monday, also praised the schema, but said that the notion of the People of God ought to be treated before that of the hierarchy and could be developed without detriment to the place of the hierarchy. The Church was born from the side of Christ on the cross and the schema ought to express more clearly therefore that the Church and its members were sharers in Christ's passion.

The debate continued Tuesday on the schema as a whole, the first speaker being the cardinal archbishop of Santiago de Chile, who delivered his address in the name of 44 Latin American bishops. The schema was good, he thought, but the suggestion of the Coordinating Commission that the chapter on the People of God should come before that on the hierarchy ought to be followed and the same categories ought to be used in both, i.e. the text should speak of the Sacerdotal, Regal and Prophetic People of God. The notion of *"communio,"* or the unity of all the faithful in Christ, ought also to be developed. There was not enough insistence on the eschatological aspect of a Church continuing to develop or unfold. He agreed with the suggestion of Cardinal Frings that the connection of the Church with the saints in heaven should be spelled out. Then, turning to the subject of the schema on Mary, he acknowledged: "In Latin American countries devotion to Our Lady is sometimes too far removed from the proper devotional life of the Church," a statement reminiscent of John XXIII's warning to the Roman clergy against a tendency "to cultivate certain excessive devotional practices, even with respect to devotion to the Madonna." If proposed in a separate treatise, the theology of Mary would be difficult to relate to the whole doctrine of Christian salvation. Therefore he recommended that the schema on Mary should be incorporated in the present schema on the Church.

Speaking in the name of numerous bishops from Africa and Madagascar, Cardinal Rugambwa said that he found the schema generally acceptable, however it did not bring out clearly enough the connection between the Mission of the Church and the Mission of Christ, namely with respect to the evangelization of the world, or, in other words, to the dynamic missionary role of the Church everywhere. The Church, he said, everywhere and always, was sent to all non-Christians, not merely to those "in foreign missions." This universal mission should be brought out. "Mission is needed everywhere, therefore the Church is everywhere missionary." The relation between this idea of mission and the People of God should be expressed clearly.

The exarch for the Ukrainians in Canada, Archbishop Hermaniuk, observed: "The schema pleases me because of its scriptural emphasis, its use of Oriental theology, its insistence on collegiality, and its ecumenical spirit. But the collegiality of the bishops is not explained clearly enough. It seems to be mentioned as something accidental, whereas the government of the Church ought at all times to be collegial." Echoing a thought contained in the pope's opening address which would be taken up by quite a few speakers later, he was the first to suggest on the floor the need for some kind of an episcopal senate to advise the pope. "This government could take the form of a large college, a kind of episcopal council beside the pope, which would include the patriarchs, the cardinals who are residential bishops or archbishops, and delegates from episcopal conferences or missionary areas." There was no true collegiality apart from the pope of course. The way the terms "college and its head" or "body with its head" were used gave the impression that the pope was separate from the episcopal college, which was not true. Instead of such frequent references to "Roman Pontiff," more ecumenical-sounding expressions such as "Pastor of the universal Church" should be used. He proposed the use of the term "Supreme Pontiff" rather than "Roman Pontiff" to show that the pope's role as the successor of Peter was more important than that of bishop of Rome.

Speaking in the name of the French bishops, Archbishop Garrone of Toulouse said that the schema was acceptable as a whole, however a number of points needed clarification: 1) the schema on Mary should be incorporated in *De Ecclesia* in order to preserve a better theological balance—an idea supported by numerous subsequent speakers; 2) the expression Kingdom of God should be added to the list of biblical images by which the Church was defined; this would help explain its eschatological, dynamic and missionary dimensions; 3) the notion of an episcopal college should be spelled out more fully with reference to Scripture which had much to say about the unity of the episcopal body; 4) a grave defect was the absence of any treatment of tradition. Unless this concept were spelled out in connection with and in relation to the Church, there would be difficulty in carrying on the dialogue with the separated brethren. Archbishop Vuccino, on Friday, also urged the claims of tradition to be considered in *De Ecclesia,* "because of the intimate relation between the Word of God and baptism. The Word must be proclaimed before baptism is received," he said. Revelation, Scripture and tradition ought to be treated in one schema.

Bishop Elchinger (coadjutor of Strasbourg) offered a number of observations which were in the main similar to those of Archbishop Garrone. He too felt that the schema on the Church should include a chapter on Mary. The prerogatives of Mary, that is, her singular place in the People of God existed only with respect to Christ and the Church.

The Bishop of Cuernavaca (Mexico) agreed with Cardinals Silva Henriquez and Frings with regard to the latter point. It was desirable to demarcate the boundaries of Marian devotion to correct certain tendencies in popular devotion, and in order to explain the matter better to non-Catholics who sometimes had wrong notions about the Church because of these excesses. "Devotion to Mary and the saints, especially in our countries, at times obscures devotion to Christ."

By contrast, the cardinal archbishop of Tarragona, speaking on Thursday, was to sound the only dissenting note on this theme among the Council's early speakers. In the name of 56 Spanish bishops, he put in a strong plea for keeping Mary separate from *De Ecclesia,* "because the mystery of Mary is greater than the mystery of the Church. There is danger that she would be seen in a merely passive role as representing the Church, as the Church's eldest daughter, and not as the mother of the Church by her vivifying influence." However, if the Marian schema was to be added, he asked that it be made Chapter II and should in content be as profound and extensive as the subject deserved.

The debate on the schema as a whole was brought to a close on Tuesday with several warning notes by Italian bishops whose remarks about "difficult terminology" revealed that they were not abreast of recent theological thinking, while the Belgian Bishop Guffens was interrupted by the moderator for wandering from the subject and sat down in confusion without delivering the rest of his talk.

The Council was then asked to vote on the following proposal:

"Does this schema please you in general as a basis for pursuing the discussion chapter by chapter?"

The Secretary General shortly afterward announced the results:

2301 votes in all
2231 favorable votes (placet)
  43 unfavorable votes (non placet)
   3 votes proposing amendments (iuxta modum)
  24 invalid votes.

The votes proposing amendments were counted as invalid because there were only two choices allowed: *placet* or *non placet*.

While the voting was taking place the Secretary General announced that the Coordinating Commission had decided that the following schemata were to be discussed at the present session in this order, "time permitting":

De Ecclesia;
De beata Virgine Maria, Matre Ecclesiae;
De Episcopis et regimine dioecesium;
De Apostolatu laicorum;
De Oecumenismo.

THE CHURCH AS A MYSTERY

In the remaining time on Tuesday, discussion was begun of Chapter 1, the Church as a Mystery, by Cardinal Ruffini, archbishop of Palermo. In general the cardinal praised the text but said that it was too repetitious and its language too inexact in places. He offered a large number of amendments, criticizing especially the inappropriateness of certain biblical quotations and remarking apropos of the statement that "the Church is a sacrament": "For a long time the term sacrament has been reserved to the seven sacraments; because its use with reference to the Church is obscure today and needs long explanations, it is contrary to the pastoral orientation of the Council. This term was often used heretically by George Tyrrell, apostate priest and leader of the Modernists." His

162

principal point however was that a distinction should be made between the foundation of the Church on Peter, and its foundation on the apostles. The statement that "Christ founded the Church on both Peter and the Apostles together" had no biblical testimony, he said, and could lead to error. "Only to Peter did Christ say: *Tu es Petrus.* In Ephesians 2:20 Paul only wishes to say that the apostles were the first to adhere to Christ, the cornerstone of the Church, after the manner of a foundation wall upon which the faithful are *superaedificati.*" There should be a distinction between charisms in the Church and the functions of the hierarchical government of the Church. He criticized also what the schema had to say about the Church as both a divine and a human society, as the Mystical Body and as a visible society, for Pius XII had said in *Mystici Corporis* that the Mystical Body and the Church were one and the same reality and there was danger of introducing a dualist conception, whereas the two notions should be kept strictly together.

At noon on Tuesday Pope Paul received some 400 journalists in the Hall of the Consistory, along with the members of the Council Press Commission. After congratulating newspaper editors, radio broadcasters and others who had assigned to Rome "so many reporters" to cover the Council, he said (in French):

> It is largely your task to see to it that the entire world, alert and waiting, gets the information it needs in order to understand the progress of this great assembly. . . . Rest assured in any case that the ones responsible for the organization of the Council will do their best to satisfy your desires. . . .

Although the pope admitted that the Fathers' opinions might be colored by their origins and backgrounds, he still insisted that the discussions in the Council were not characterized by *parti-pris.* This was generally true, but observers noted that some of the Fathers still seemed confused about the real significance of the *"balzo in avanti"*—Pope John's phrase for the leap forward into modernity that the Council had inspired—though they seemed to accept it for the most part with a spirit of humility and a sense of humor. One French prelate was overhead to say in Bar Jonah: "To be a good Council Father, you need the patience of Job and the wisdom of Solomon, and it also helps if you have a cast-iron bottom, *alors!"* The bishops were obliged to sit each morning through two and a half hours of Latin oratory, delivered in such dissimilar accents as lilting Italian, nasal French, guttural German, broguish Celtic, and rasping American. Most of the Council Fathers sat there silently deploring the lack of a simultaneous-translation system and straining to make something of the speech whenever an interesting speaker took the microphone. There was no difficulty for anyone with an ear for Latin when Archbishop Felici, the secretary general of the

Council, had the floor; his clear, loud, and agreeable voice lingered consciously on the vowels, and he commanded a flow of Latin that enabled him, by an emphasis or a turn of phrase, to indulge in much appreciated pleasantries. The Council's lay auditors were assigned an interpreter, Monsignor Achille Glorieux, but the one American auditor— James J. Norris, assistant to the executive director of the (American run) Catholic Relief Services—had no need for translations. He was a personal friend of Pope Paul, who was heard to say to him on his arrival, "Well, Jim, we have made you a Council Father." As far back as 1946, Norris worked with the then Monsignor Montini, in the Vatican Secretariat of State, setting up the International Catholic Migration Committee. Though the Council auditors could not speak in the debates in St. Peter's, they were given copies of all the Council documents and were asked for technical advice by the commission in charge of drawing up the schema on the apostolate of the laity.

On the sidelines, one of the greatest single differences between the First Session and the Second was unquestionably the change in press relations. The daily press bulletins were prepared each morning by the Press Office under the direction of Monsignor Fausto Vallainc. Various language press conferences began to shape up during the first few days under the general auspices of the Press Commission presided over by Archbishop Martin O'Connor. Archbishop Pangrazio was the member of this Committee responsible for the Italian Press; Archbishop Stourm for the Fress press; Bishop Wittler for the German press; Bishop Cirarda for the Spanish press; Bishop Zuroweste for the English-language press.* Each day, as at the First Session, a briefing took place in the rooms of the Press Office immediately after the daily session on the content of the speeches. Father Edward Heston, of the Holy Cross Order, briefed the American and English journalists; Father F. B. Haubtmann of *La Croix* briefed the French journalists; Monsignor G. Fittkau the German journalists; Father F. Farusi, S.J., the Italian journalists; and Father C. Calderón the Spanish journalists.† The American bishops, and the Americans only, also decided to have a discussion or panel meeting each afternoon to provide a fuller briefing, with members of the hierarchy and other persons being invited to address the journalists on special topics. During the Second Session this was under the chairmanship of the Paulist Father

---

* Nine other episcopal members were also responsible for areas, as follows: J. Rezende Costa, for the Portuguese press: H. Thiandoum, for Africa; O. McCann, for the missionary press; E. D'Souza, for the Far East; J. Khoury, for the Oriental Churches: G. De Vet, for the Dutch press; H. Bednorz, for the Slavic press; M. McGrath, for the Latin-American press; and H. Routhier, for the Canadian press.

† Other Press Office members briefing the press were: Fr. P. Almeida, S.J., the Portuguese press; Fr. S. Wesoly, the Polish Press.

John Sheerin, editor of the *Catholic World*. The panel consisted of Father Francis J. Connell, CSSR, Father Gustave Weigel, S.J., Father Frederick McManus, Monsignor George Higgins, Father Bernard Häring, CSSR, Father Robert Trisco, and Father F. McCool, S.J., as the more or less permanent members. Those on the panel, of course, had all attended the morning's congregation and could speak from their personal knowledge of what had taken place. After a few days, the principle newspapers reporting the daily sessions in depth, *Il Quotidiano, La Croix, L'Avvenire d'Italia, Le Monde, Le Figaro,* in particular, began to identify the speakers consistently, and the official press bulletins also began the practice of devoting a paragraph to a speech, thus making it easier to identify what each Father had said, though the bulletins refrained from affixing names to the paragraphs in order to escape responsibility for the digests. The English bulletin was not merely a translation of the Italian (the first out), but an independent summary based on the notes of Father Heston and other experts. The French, Spanish and German bulletins were more like the Italian, with differences here and there.

The moderator presiding on Wednesday of the first week was Cardinal Döpfner.

Before the business of the day was taken up, Archbishop Villot, a council under-secretary, read in French a message from the lay auditors to the Council:

> Conscious of the historical event which has taken place as a result of the decision of the Holy Father to invite qualified lay auditors to take part as observers in the Council sessions, these auditors consider it a duty to express to the Council their emotion, joy and profound gratitude of the laity whom they have the honor to represent and to fulfill this responsibility by attentively following the work of the Council and its decisions, and redoubling their prayers for its success.

As Henri Fesquet noted, this message gave rise to various comments of a somewhat cynical nature. Some said, for example: "This colorless ecclesiastical language hardly befits laymen. It employs the very type of sentimentalized terminology which the laity complain about in pastoral letters. Are the laity to attend the Council as the mere mouthpieces of the clergy?" Whatever truth there was in remarks of this kind, he went on to say, the Fathers applauded this statement with marked reserve and they could hardly be blamed for this.

The discussion continued on the Introduction and Chapter I.

Speaking in the name of 153 Brazilian bishops (but mentioning the names of those who offered specific amendments) Cardinal de Barros Câmara said that it should be explicitly stated in the Introduction that dogmatic definitions were to be found only where the words of the text indicated that the Council intended to define truths of faith. The reason was in order to avoid abuses and distortion of what the Council had meant. In contrast to this prudent reserve, caution appeared to be thrown to the winds on Friday by the Spanish Bishop García Martinez who claimed that enough light had been thrown on the question of whether infallibility extended to virtually revealed truths (necessarily connected doctrine) and dogmatic facts, "for a solemn definition to be made on this point" and thus "complete the work of Vatican Council I." A majority of theologians would probably not have agreed.

The archbishop of Bombay, Cardinal Gracias, spoke next and said that the Introduction should be shorter and give a brief history of salvation, indicating that Christ's redemption was for all men. "Why say that the language of the Council should be adapted to modern times? Let us use this language instead of saying that we should use it." Greater clarity and order were desirable in Chapter I. The religious and spiritual side of the Church should be brought out more clearly; it should not be considered as a "state within a state," as some Catholics maintained who "want to be more Catholic than the pope." The Church should be presented as ministering to and serving the world, as Pope Paul VI pointed out in his opening address. The Church grew in the world only to save and enrich it morally and spiritually. This idea should be developed especially with reference to the missionary aspect of the Church. The cardinal quoted Cardinal Newman to the effect that since Catholics were a minority they should attempt to prevail not by numbers but by their example and zeal. He observed apropos of the unity of Christians, that this was less important than union with God and quoted the English aphorism, in English, "Too many cooks spoil the soup," changing the last word so that it would be better understood.

The intervention of Cardinal Alfrink (Holland) on Wednesday made a deep impression, particularly on the non-Catholic observer delegates. He criticized the expression in the schema "Peter and the Apostles" for implying that Peter was not an apostle. It would be better to substitute some other phrase such as "Peter and the *other* Apostles." "No one," he added, "wishes to deny or lessen the primacy of Peter, but it is necessary to restore the pope to his place in the apostolic college. The Church has twelve foundations. Peter is the rock." Peter's place in the college and his primacy should be dealt with simultaneously for they are inseparable. Christ's words "Whatever you shall bind on earth . . ." (Mt. 18:18) were said to *all* the apostles. And the apocalyptic vision of the New Jerusalem "The wall of the city having as a foundation the twelve, and in them the names of the twelve apostles" (Apoc. 21:14) was not merely eschatological. In Scripture, apocalyptic imagery was taken from what was already realized in time. A further indication of this truth was the liturgical practice of having twelve crosses representing the apostles in consecrated churches. "That all the apostles together constitute the foundation does not detract from Peter's singular place among them," he said, thus throwing down the exegetical gauntlet to Cardinal Ruffini.

The first American speaker was the bishop of Manchester, New Hampshire. Introduced by the moderator as an English bishop, he brought laughter when he began by saying that the bishop of Manchester, England, happened to be one of the "separated brethren." Bishop Primeau felt that certain statements in the schema were ambiguous regarding membership or incorporation in the Church. It was necessary to bear in mind certain distinctions, he said, "incorporation in the Church, incorporation in God, incorporation on earth, in purgatory, in heaven," and so forth. The Council should define the relationship between the Catholic Church and other Christian communities. This question—so important for ecumenism—came down to asking what the ecclesial reality was of those communities that were non-Catholic. "The Council would make a giant step forward if it acknowledged the Protestant claim to be 'Churches'." Admittedly this was a question that was still under serious study. He also touched on the theme of the relations between Church and state.—In a press interview later the same day, Bishop Primeau enlarged on the latter idea, observing that there was nothing in the present draft on the subject.

I myself think that the Council should say something on the matter. I do not think the Council should go into particulars, nor into the particular relationships that exist between the Church and state. But some general principles should be laid down.

He said that such matters as the freedom to carry out the Church's mission would be an example of what might be covered by the Council. He acknowledged that such a statement might be more useful for America than for some other countries.

In our country the Protestant intelligentsia are always asking for a definite statement on Church and state. In our pluralistic societies we have some kind of basic principles. . . . We have not come here just to rubberstamp the status-quo; there are knots to be cut.

The same theme was enlarged upon by the abbot of Downside, Dom Christopher Butler. It was not sufficient for the schema to confine itself to the relationship between the Church and non-Catholic Christians *individually,* the question must be faced of whether there was any relationship between the Church and those communities as such. "These communities, in so far as they follow the counsels of Christ, have supernatural qualities, although as supernatural societies they are incomplete." Since there was a distinction between the Kingdom of Christ and the Kingdom of God, the Church must be identified as the Kingdom of Christ. The Kingdom of God had apocalyptic as well as eschatological significance. "This distinction will also help ecumenical relations," he commented.

The concern of a rather large number of speakers with what may be called the ecumenical implications of the schema on the Church indicated that there was a kind of general consensus on this point, which might be summed up by saying that what most desired was a thoroughly biblical definition of the Church based on such scriptural images as the People of God or Kingdom of God, one that would be meaningful to Protestants, Orthodox and even non-Christians, and as free as possible, therefore, from the traditional post-biblical terminology—largely of a juridical inspiration—which had characterized Catholic speculation on the nature of the Church in recent centuries. As Cardinal Bea pointed out, it was futile to think that any impression could be made on non-Catholics by employing the sterile terminology of past centuries already compromised by divisions and misunderstandings. What was needed was a return to the Bible or apostolic age, some common ground on which Christians could be expected to agree particularly in the light of recent biblical research. In the opinion of many speakers, while the present schema was on the right road, it had not yet fully attained this goal.

CARDINAL LERCARO ON CHURCH MEMBERSHIP

One of the most important speeches on this theme, delivered by Cardinal Lercaro on Thursday of the first week, set the tone for the debate, and was confidently believed by many observers to reflect the views of Pope Paul himself. All of the speeches of Cardinal Lercaro merited and received ample attention in this convention. They were also reproduced almost verbatim in the Bolognese newspaper *L'Avvenire d'Italia,* an organ faithfully reflecting the critical left-of-center policies, ecclesiastical and political, of the cardinal himself, thus assuring his views wide publicity.

Cardinal Lercaro's speech was divided into three parts. In the first part, after a few preliminary remarks praising the work of the Theological Commission, he listed three corrections which ought to be made to eliminate any possible misunderstanding over words constantly recurring such as "Church," "society," "Mystical Body," which seemed to be used in different senses. The text said that the Church as a visible society and the Church as the Mystical Body were identical (text: *non duae res sunt, sed una tantum*). Cardinal Ruffini had said on Tuesday that the visible

Church and Mystical Body could not be distinguished (*nullatenus distinguuntur*) and were "coextensive." Cardinal Lercaro held that this was true in one sense, but not in another. He therefore seconded the proposed amendment suggested by Cardinal Alfrink clarifying these distinctions, "lest unfounded conclusions be drawn, as happened after *Mystici Corporis*—a reference to the controversy after publication of Pius XII's famous encyclical on the Mystical Body in 1943.

His second correction related to membership in the Church. The cardinal emphasized that belonging to the Church through baptism was not an ecumenical "novelty" invented in order to please the separated brethren, but a traditional theological truth. Baptism made a person a member of the Church. Neither schism, heresy, nor apostasy could completely break his bond. "All the baptized belong to the Church (the Oriental Code expressly says so) regardless of the schisms or apostasies that may occur afterward." Like Cardinal Bea on numerous occasions, including his intervention later the same morning, Lercaro insisted that the proper way to speak of membership or incorporation in the Church was of complete or incomplete membership. Therefore in section 8 of Chapter I where a definition was given of *fideles Catholici* or full members—as those were called who recognized the Church's perfect structure and all the means of sanctification, that is, those who were united to Christ by belonging to the visible society which was governed by the pope and the bishops, by the bonds of faith, the sacraments, discipline and ecclesiastical communion—the introductory adverbs *reapse et simpliciter loquendo,* which many Fathers considered too restrictive, should be changed to *plene et complete*—fully and completely. "This is suggested not only or principally for ecumenical reasons as a kind of condescension toward the separated brethren; but primarily because the doctrine according to which baptism validly received incorporates once and for all in the Church as a visible society has always been Catholic doctrine." His third correction was that the relation between the Church and the eucharist be brought out more clearly, the latter being not merely a sign of unity but a dynamic entity.

Lercaro's second important point was to the effect that the dynamic nature of the definition of the Church should be brought out more clearly. Scripture was fond of calling the Church a new people, a new creation (*novum genus, nova creatio*). These ideas should be stressed, "since recapitulation in Christ is not just a psychological or ethical assimilation or merely a religious consecration." The Church was a new presence in the world; its witness, service, preaching were not just a history of the Church but *are* the Church. A new creation meant a new birth and the pains of childbirth. "The Church is the womb in which this cosmic rebirth takes place. Hence its dynamic nature, its essential existence not only or principally as a structure but as a *dynamis,* a dynamic force, whose significance and nature should be spelled out in *De Ecclesia."* He did not think, in this connection, that the proposals by Cardinals Rugambwa or de Barros Câmara, Bishop Ancel or others "could be suspected of being an attempt to introduce into a dogmatic constitution a kind of phenomenology of the situation and concrete activity of the Church in our times"—referring to objections by conservative theologians to what those prelates had urged. Their proposals were not concerned merely with external attributes but with the very "essence of the Church." The mystery of the Church could not be explained adequately by reference merely to principles governing its activity, mention must be made also of principles governing its existence or nature. "According to the Gospel, the Church's present mode of existence is that of a *martyrion*—a witness of the truth of the Gospel to all nations, and a *diakonia*—a service, which should cause it always to be humble and the servant of all." The Church was sent primarily to the lowly, the humble and the poor, and did not expect anything in return. It was sent also to all nations, all races, all civilizations, and ought never to consider itself permanently tied to any one.

His third observation related to the revision of the text. So many fine things had been said in the Council that a complete revision was obviously necessary. "The Theological Commission is probably not equal to this task. It would be a good idea to ask those Fathers who have spoken well on this subject to assist it in its labors. This would merely be an application of Art. 65 which allows the Fathers to be heard in the commissions. It would be a good idea to invite Cardinals Silva Henriquez, Gracias, Rugambwa, Bishop Guano and Bishop Ancel to confer with each other and get in touch with the Theological Commission so that the new definition of the Church will correspond more fully to the aspirations of the men of our time." It was doubtful whether the cardinal expected that this indirect public rebuke to Cardinal Ottaviani who had refused on the whole to solicit the cooperation of other commissions or encourage participation by experts in the work of his Theological Commission, would have much effect but he seemed to feel obliged to make the statement anyway for the record.

Following Cardinal Lercaro's lead, the idea of poverty received particular stress on Friday (the Feast of St. Francis of Assisi) at the hands of Cardinal Gerlier, archbishop of Lyons, who quoted from the moving appeal of Cardinal Lercaro toward the end of the previous year's session as well as words of Pope John XXIII and Pope Paul VI, to the effect that the poor and those who suffered were particularly close to the Church. He endorsed the proposal of 13 East African bishops that the Introduction should say something about this place of the poor in the

Church. The schema did not develop sufficiently what he called the theology of the poor, namely that they made present in the Church the mystery of Christ by living his poverty and his passion among us. Christ identified himself with them and what was done for them was done for him. Later the same day Bishop Himmer (Tournai, Belgium) stressed the idea of service to the poor, if the Church wished to reveal its true face to the poor. "We shall be judged with regard to the charity we have shown to the poor, because of the presence of Christ in them."

A number of speakers also followed Lercaro in taking up the subject of membership in the Church, finding the expressions in the schema inadequate or misleading. For Bishop Van Velsen (Kroonstad, South Africa) the schema was not sufficiently positive in its approach to the separated brethren: when dealing with Protestants it failed to mention the Bible and baptism which they had in common with Catholics, and when dealing with the Orthodox it failed to mention their valid orders and eucharist. The words *reapse et simpliciter* had obviously been added for the sake of clarity, but he found that theologians were uncertain what they meant exactly—he himself disclaimed any pretension to technical theological knowledge. Archbishop Heenan (Westminster), speaking in the name of the English and Welsh hierarchies, said that the "duty of the Church and of Christians towards the separated brethren" not only consisted in praying and reforming oneself, as the schema stated, but involved a truly evangelical attitude. "Every Catholic must be an apostle. His apostolate is performed by prayer, example and preaching." Expounding the true doctrine to those separated from Catholic unity was also an obligation.

A rather remarkable intervention along this line was that of Archbishop Baldassarri (Ravenna, Italy) on Friday. He recalled the words of Paul VI in his opening address and insisted that it was necessary to acknowledge faults. "It is necessary to say these things so that the ecumenical dialogue may be started in an atmosphere of mutual pardon." Emphasis should be placed on baptism as the door of the Church. It was regrettable that the schema did not come out clearly enough on this score. Instead, speaking of the "separated brethren," almost fearfully (*timorose*), it referred to them as "those who are adorned with the name of Christian (*qui christiano nomine decorantur*)." They were much more than "adorned," they actually shared baptism in common with us. Ravenna felt particularly close to the East because of its history and traditions. Therefore its archbishop hoped that the schema might put more stress on "the common faith in the Trinity, the sacred deposit of Scripture, and the venerable traditions of the Fathers of the Church" which we shared. "Why not say these consoling things in the text?"

There were a number of criticisms also of the final Paragraph 10 "On bringing non-Christians to the Church" (*De non-Christianis ad Ecclesiam adducendis*). Finally, Bishop Pildáin y Zapiáin (the Canary Islands) raised the delicate question of fallen-away Catholics. While the schema had much to say about non-Catholics and non-Christians, it failed to broach this important subject. "Both Pope Pius XII and Pope John XXIII" had expressed grave concern over the problem of masses of baptized Catholics who had virtually withdrawn from the Church. "It is a new phenomenon of our day and has been called the scandal of the century." He proposed the addition of a new paragraph treating of it. Since most fallen-away Catholics were found among the poor and the laboring classes, he gave strong approval to an amendment proposed by 13 bishops of East-Central Africa that a paragraph be added to the Introduction expressing this concern.

Many speakers concentrated their remarks on Paragraphs 5 and 6, "On the Church as the Mystical Body of Christ" and "Concerning other images of the Church." Some found the images mentioned adequate, others wanted new ideas introduced. Bishop Romero Menjibar (Jaén, Spain) wanted the notion of the Church as the Kingdom of God—occurring often in the Gospels—mentioned and used as a basis for explaining the eschatological, missionary, and social aspects of the Church. According to Auxiliary Bishop Ancel of Lyons "a new paragraph dealing with the Church as the Kingdom of God should be drafted and inserted in the schema immediately after the fourth paragraph. This image reveals the Church as a society both visible and spiritual, and it explains the essence of renewal through charity, the growth of the Church and its universal mission to the whole world, as well as its eschatological goal." Other speakers suggested images such as the "Spouse of Christ" or "Family of God." The bishop of Calahorra (Spain) noted that the image of the Mystical Body conveyed little meaning with regard to the Church as a visible society. He also criticized the ambiguous use of the word *ecclesia*. Sometimes it meant the "congregation of those who have been saved," and sometimes more strictly the society which Christ had founded. In view of the "militancy" of the Church in the present world, according to Bishop Franič (Split, Yugoslavia), such images as Kingdom of God and City set on a Mountain had much to recommend them, not in a provocative sense of course, but in the sense exemplified by Christ who submitted even to the cross. "We must struggle with spiritual, not worldly arms." The Church as the "Family of God" commended itself particularly to the Brazilian Archbishop de Proença Sigaud and the bishop of Dalat, Vietnam, Nguyen-van Hien. The former maintained that the Church was the "Family of God" not in a metaphorical sense, but properly speaking: "God is Father, Christ is the first-born brother, Mary is mother, and all members are brothers through baptism." The Vietnamese prelate was of the opinion that this easily graspable idea emphasizing the unity of the Church could be appreciated especially in Asia where the family had remained a sacred thing. "Here in the council," he said, "we are accustomed to refer to ourselves not as members of the Mystical Body but as brothers in Christ—*carissimi fratres* not *carissima membra*." His remark brought smiles to the faces of his hearers. The following speaker, Bishop Volk (Mainz, Germany), also brought smiles when he turned to the observer delegates and addressed them as *carissimi observatores* while stressing the point that the schema should contain a clearer distinction between the Church as an efficacious sign of redemption and the Kingdom of God as the consummation of redemption.

Several speakers, including Bishop Jelmini (Lugano), Archbishop Martin (Rouen), and the bishop of Majorca, regretted the fact that almost nothing was said in the text about the eucharist and its relationship to the Church. A more fundamental objection was raised by Bishop Jenny (auxiliary of Cambrai) with regard to the lack of a proper Christological orientation.

Two important interventions emphasized the importance of an even more pronounced biblical approach and of the theology of the Word, relatively new ideas in recent Catholic theology. The first by Cardinal Ritter, archbishop of St. Louis—the second American to speak at the session—said that the Introduction rightly described the Church as a sacrament of union between all men and between men and God. But by concentrating on the static aspect of the Church, the schema was silent about those things which constituted the Church's causality in relation to this union. In Paragraph 7 there should be a treatment of the salvific ministry of the Church, which should include consideration of the efficacy of the Word, together with a treatment of the sacraments. "Preaching and teaching are almost synonymous with the Church, but there is little about this in the schema." "The theology of the Word has been left in the shadows, although the Word is always living, illuminating and operating in the Church," he said. There must be a renewed emphasis on preaching. Let no one say: "This is a pastoral subject." It was primarily theological. The Word and the sacraments were elements of the Church.

The first speech by the president of the Secretariat for Promoting Christian Unity, Cardinal Bea, at this session, also was significant. Pope John, he said, had declared that the Council should express the meaning of Christian life by drawing on the primary sources of the faith. Thus a proper use should be made of Scripture and tradition in the text of the schema. The latter was not lacking in scriptural quotations, but, as Cardinal Ruffini pointed out, these were not always well chosen. Among examples, he cited 1 Tim. 3:15 *columna et firmamentum veritatis*— column and foundation of truth—which referred, he said, not to Peter and the apostles as the text had it, but to the teachings of the Church. Ephesians 2:20–22 would have been better here.* The schema was defective also in its use of Tradition and the documents of the magisterium. There was too much quotation from later sources. Whenever possible sources prior to the Reformation and before the schism in the eleventh century should be used, because there was more chance that these would be understood by the separated breathren. Even references to Vatican Council I and the Council of Trent should be cited with due regard for the present situation. For example, in discussing the prerogatives of the pope in convoking and confirming an ecumenical council, only canon 227 of the Code was cited in the text, but this was not accepted as binding by the separated Eastern Churches. Unless there was careful attention to this ecumenical aspect in all quotations from the Bible and tradition, the schema would fall short of its goal which was to promote the restoration of unity.

Cardinal Richaud (Bordeaux) also felt that many more quotations from Ephesians should be included in the Introduction, "because this represented the earliest theology of the Church."

Apart from the speakers already mentioned, the Italian contribution to the debate of the first week was not notable. Bishop Carli (Segni), the spokesman for the conservative wing of the Italian hierarchy, contented himself with seconding Cardinal Ruffini as to the dangers that might arise from a misunderstanding of the phrase "Peter and the apostles" which was used so often in the text. He made a strong appeal for the foundation of the Church on Peter alone, and quoted a number of scriptural references and Vatican Council I purporting to show that Peter was "the one foundation of unity both for the apostles and for all believers." He concluded with the customary warning: "We must avoid the danger of seeing the primacy of the pope only according to his position as the head of the episcopal college." The same thought seemed to be echoed by Bishop Compagnone (Anagni), while Archbishop D'Avack (Camerino) felt that the treatment of the place of the faithful in the Church was a step back from the doctrine expounded in *Mystici Corporis!* Finally, Bishop Pocci, speaking on behalf of Cardinal Micara, vicar of Rome, who was ill, voiced concern over "certain widespread errors about the Mystical Body and the Church's relationship to non-Catholics." Failure to condemn these errors might scandalize the faithful. The conservative cardinal vicar of Rome was obviously not in sympathy with the thinking which had produced *De Ecclesia.* He also felt there was need for condemning those who denied the existence of hell.

---

* "You are built upon the foundation of the Apostles and prophets, Jesus Christ himself being the chief corner stone. In Him the whole structure is closely fitted together and grows into a temple holy in the Lord."

Winding up the debate on Chapter I, Cardinal Browne (Curia) said that all the suggested amendments would be taken into account by his commission. Speaking as a Father, he proposed that the word *sacramentum* in the Introduction with reference to the Church, should be understood in the sense of *sacramentum amoris Christi erga totum genus humanum*—sacrament of the love of Christ for the whole human race, thus replying to Cardinal Ruffini who had questioned the suitability of the term in its present context.

On Thursday of the first week, at the close of the morning's discussions, the Secretary General, Archbishop Felici, had announced that no pamphlets or booklets were to be distributed to the Fathers without the permission of the Council presidents. On Friday at the beginning of the deliberations, he qualified this statement to mean that such permission was necessary only within the confines of the council hall. The remarks had been misinterpreted or magnified in certain organs as an official ban on certain books about the Council which the Vicariat of Rome had attempted to have withdrawn from sale in Rome.* It referred actually to mimeographed sheets and booklets with which the Fathers were constantly being bombarded in order to influence their voting. During the First Session there had been a flurry of such, notably certain notorious pamphlets by Monsignor Spadafora and Monsignor Romeo on the biblical question accusing the Biblical Institute of heresy. Later, during the present session, Father Balič would attempt to invade the council precincts in this way—in spite of the official ban—with his pamphlet on the Marian schema.

THE ISSUE OF COLLEGIALITY

Discussion of Chapter II of the schema on the Church, entitled "The Hierarchical Constitution and especially the Episcopate" began on Friday of the first week and continued for one and a half weeks. The principal topics around which the debate revolved were the controversial proposal in Paragraph 15 to revive the diaconate, and the relationship of the bishops to the pope as head of the episcopal college, or the idea of episcopal collegiality as such, whether the bishops constituted a "college" or "corporate body" in any sense other than a merely metaphorical one.

The debate on this Chapter was the longest, and in some respects the most repetitious and boring, during the entire Second Session, lasting eight and a half mornings or a full week and a half. But it was likewise, unquestionably, one of the most important, owing to the key issue of

* Works by X. Rynne, R. B. Kaiser, Teilhard de Chardin, H. de Lubac.

collegiality, rightly considered as the touchstone of a structural renewal of the Church, just as the liturgical innovations and schema were to be the guarantee of a liturgical or spiritual renewal. The debate on collegiality was in fact the primary *raison d'être* for the Second Session and constituted the core of the new vision of herself which the Church must acquire, according to Pope Paul in his opening address. It was partly in order to prepare the ground for definitive action that such protracted debate was allowed—there must be no accusation that enough time had not been allowed for a thorough discussion—and partly also, no doubt, because of indecision on the part of the council presidency, perhaps of the pope himself.

The debate tended to revolve around a number of key themes most of which were enunciated on the very first day: the idea of collegiality as such and whether the episcopate constituted a college or corporate body; the relationship of such a college, if it existed, to the papal primacy; the question of whether there should be an episcopal "senate" to advise the pope, a topic that would be aired more fully later on when the schema on Bishops would be taken up; the sacramentality of the episcopal office; the position of priests with respect to bishops; the functions of a hierarchy, the oriental patriarchs, and a number of subsidiary questions. Most speakers of course spoke on a variety of themes, but in general a summarization of their views pro or con with respect to these main themes will give the reader an adequate idea of the tenor of the debate on this chapter.

Perhaps the least controversial theme was the issue of the sacramental character of the episcopate. Paragraph 14 took a positive attitude and declared the episcopate the "highest degree of the sacrament of order." If adopted, this would put an end to a question that had been debated since the Middle Ages, namely whether episcopal consecration involved the conferring of a sacramental grace, or merely conferring on one who already had the fullness of the sacrament of order, greater jurisdiction or authority. The majority of theologians had long taught the former opinion, which was confirmed by Pius XII in his constitution *Sacramentum ordinis*. Left open in the present text was the question of whether episcopal consecration also admitted to the episcopal college, or how and when a bishop became a member of the college. The answer to both questions was apparently settled by the queries of October 30. There was almost unanimous agreement then that the episcopate was sacramental, with only 107 bishops voting against the view that membership was acquired through consecration. Archbishop Guerry explained the importance of the whole question on the first day of debate (October 4th), maintaining that the schema did not bring out clearly enough its importance.

The very opposite point of view was represented by the next speaker,

Archbishop García y García de Castro (Granada, Spain). Many still held the opinion, he said, that the episcopate was not a sacrament and was differentiated from the priesthood merely in the jurisdictional sphere. Priests after all could be the extraordinary ministers of the sacrament of order. This would be difficult to explain if the episcopate were regarded as the fullness of the sacrament. Accordingly much of the language in Paragraph 14 must be changed.

Archbishop Florit was favorable to the idea of sacramentality, but felt that the language of the schema needed improvement. Bishop Doumith (Lebanon) wanted it made clear that not only the grace but also the power of the episcopate came from episcopal consecration (October 9th). In the opinion of Archbishop Urtasun (Avignon) the question was quite mature for definition, being evident from liturgical as well as theological tradition. A practical reason would be that it would show that the bishop was united to his clergy not only juridically but sacramentally. A clear statement that episcopal consecration was the source of the threefold power of bishops mentioned in Paragraphs 19, 20, and 21 was desired by Bishop Cirarda (auxiliary of Seville, Spain) while Bishop Henriquez Jimenez (Venezuela) explained that bishops could exercise jurisdiction as soon as they were nominated and before consecration, because they were then acting vicariously, on the authority of the pope, whereas after consecration they acted in their own right, though of course subject to the pope, with his "explicit or tacit canonical mission." He criticized existing canon law which made it seem that the bishops were merely the delegates or vicars of the Roman Pontiff, and questioned the practice of having certain national episcopal conferences presided over by representatives of the Holy See or their decisions submitted to Rome for approval.

The vast majority of speakers preferred to concentrate on the much more tangible and explosive issue of episcopal collegiality as such. A negative note was struck at the outset by Cardinal Ruffini, who nevertheless found Chapter II satisfactory as a whole. The expressions "People of God" and "Mystical Body" should not be used separately as if they were two different things, as the text seemed to imply. The cardinal defended his interpretation of Eph. 2:20,* which Cardinal Alfrink had seemed to criticize. "Apostles" in this passage did not refer strictly to the Twelve, but rather to men gifted with the charism of the apostolate, just as the prophets were gifted with the charism of prophecy. Therefore *fundamentum* in the passage should be taken in a wide sense as "preachers of the Gospel." Others besides the apostles had the charism of the apostolate. He said: "I still have not been convinced that Christ constituted the apostles as a college," or that the episcopal college succeeded the

* See p. 174 for text.

apostolic college, for, with the exception of the Council of Jerusalem, the apostles did not act in a collegial manner. On a purely practical plane, of course, it was possible for the bishops to act as a college, with the pope's permission. In speaking of the relations between priests and bishops, the concept of obedience must not be left out. The Greek word *diakonia* was too vague to describe the office of a bishop. Finally, in speaking of the infallibility of the bishops united to the pope, mention should be made of the fact that the pope could speak infallibly without recourse to the bishops.

Very few speeches disputed the *fact* of collegiality, that is, that the bishops formed a body or order in the Church's hierarchy and that they could and did act, occasionally, in a corporate manner. But the question was whether this "corporateness" or "collegiality" was of divine origin, part of the fundamental organization of the Church, or merely of human or ecclesiastical origin. Cardinal Siri seems to have taken a view somewhat mid-way between the skepticism or negation of Cardinal Ruffini and the divine-right view. "There can be no doubt," he said, "that all bishops, acting with the Roman Pontiff, constitute a true college. The practice of ecumenical councils clearly proves this." He approved of what the schema said about collegiality and regarded it as "an effective contribution to the feeling of solidarity, mutual union, charity and reciprocal assistance, particularly among bishops themselves." But he was concerned that the notion of collegiality must not be considered apart from the primacy of the pope. "There can be no genuine collegiality among the bishops except in union with the Roman Pontiff. In other words, without Peter there can be no college of bishops. Peter does not bring the college into existence, but the college draws its completion and perfection from Peter." The door seemed to be left open, though perhaps not enthusiastically, to divine origin. The same uneasy positiveness was found in a later speech (October 15th). "It is easy to prove that the apostles made up one body and received a collective mission. But it is quite another thing to prove that the bishops of the Church constitute a college. One of the most convincing proofs is the practice of Councils in the history of the Church. . . . Wherever there is a Council there is a college. . . ." But this doctrine must be harmonized with the papal primacy. He objected to the expression "undivided subject of full and supreme authority" as ambiguous. "Wrongly understood it could imply that the bishops might sometimes force the hand of the pope, but this would contradict the teaching of Vatican I."

The interventions of Cardinals König of Vienna and Meyer of Chicago (October 7th) were strongly positive. The former maintained that what the schema had to say about collegiality in Chapter II was "not new teaching" but was found in tradition, oriental theology, the theological manuals, and the practice of ecumenical councils. It was held moreover even by those Fathers at Vatican Council I who upheld papal infallibility, and while there was some fear at that time that the doctrine constituted a threat to the papal primacy, this was no longer the case today. The teaching "was approved unanimously by the Theological Commission" and was a response to the hope expressed by Pope Paul in his opening address that the episcopate and its functions should be "examined more deeply." For the cardinal of Chicago there was no question that Christ entrusted his Church to the college of twelve apostles, for this was the clear testimony of the New Testament. He then cited a number of passages proving the permanence and continuity of the collegial authority handed on to the apostles, and the early Church's interpretation of Christ's actions in this sense. The idea of collegiality was of course juridical, but the New Testament was not a code of law and therefore did not offer a juridical explanation of the facts recounted in its pages.* In his speech on October 11th, Archbishop Gouyon (coadjutor of Rennes) also stressed the evidence from early church history supporting the collegial nature of the episcopal office, the practice of writing letters to other churches, the holding of local synods, the collegial nature of the consecration of bishops, and so on. The custom of having three co-consecrators was not purely formal. It was the expression of the fact that the new bishop was entering the college of bishops. "There has never been any exception to this rule in any liturgies, not even by the Roman Pontiff."

In contrast to these positive assertions of collegiality there were not lacking dissenting voices which questioned the validity of the concept and were critical of the language of the schema. The archbishop of Diamantina in Brazil, de Proença Sigaud (October 9th), speaking in the name of "many" bishops, went so far as to characterize the teaching that the apostles constituted a college *iure divino* a "new doctrine." This would mean that the government of the Church was not monarchical but collegiate. The traditional teaching of the Church was otherwise, according to the archbishop. Bishops were not responsible for the whole Church but only for a portion of it which they had in their charge, except on the rare occasions when they were called together by the Roman Pontiff. "Care should be taken to avoid setting up anything resembling a World Parliament of bishops governing the Church conjointly with the Roman

---

* He thus seemed to spike in advance the opinion of Archbishop Dino Staffa, Secretary of the Congregation of Seminaries and Universities, who in a mimeographed paper spread among the council members in St. Peter's—and therefore against the explicit prohibition of the Secretary General—claimed that the term "college" meant "a group of equals with one given primacy of position," and suggested that if the concept were applied to the bishops it would destroy the primacy of the pope. This was a purely juridical consideration, and quite foreign to conciliar thought. But the tactic was typical of certain Curial officials.

179

Pontiff." For Bishop Mansilla Reoyo (Burgos, Spain) the term "collegiality" was ambiguous. "Tradition does not provide us with apodeictic arguments for the collegiality of the bishops in the strict juridical sense." (October 10th) The intricate historical questions involved in the transmission of power from the apostolic college to the episcopal college seemed to impress Archbishop Van den Hurk (Indonesia), who felt that this was something which could not be settled by a Council, though he was otherwise favorable to the sacramentality of episcopal consecration and the restoration of the diaconate. Cardinal Quiroga y Palacios (Santiago de Compostela, Spain) likewise had his doubts about the exact meaning of such a term as "college of bishops." It was not clear, he thought, whether Christ had constituted the bishops as a juridical moral person or whether the idea of collegiality merely designated the totality of the bishops. That collegiality was of divine law "does not yet seem to have been conclusively proved."

A negative approach was manifested also by Archbishop Slipyi of the Ukrainian Church who, under normal circumstances, might have been expected to be enthusiastically for the notion of collegiality. He was quite categorical: "Strictly speaking, the bishops do not constitute a college." His explanation was that colleges belonged to the juridical order, whereas the links that bound the bishops together were of a sacramental character. The bishops were no more of a college than the human family. While he balked at the word, there were traces in his speech that he partly accepted the idea by recognizing that bishops, through consecration, acquired a "direction toward the whole Church." In this his first speech on the council floor since his dramatic liberation from Soviet captivity earlier in the year, he somewhat startled his supporters by asserting roundly toward the end: "Our own faithful of the East and the Orthodox would be greatly strengthened if our principal metropolitan see of Kiev were raised to patriarchal rank." This wish seems to have been gratified, in part at least, by his later elevation to the rank of "Great Archbishop," a title not hitherto conferred by the Holy See but found in the East, the virtual equivalent of primate or patriarch.

Archbishop Nicodemo (Bari) agreed with Cardinal Quiroga y Palacios that "stronger arguments must be adduced to prove the divine institution of the doctrine of collegiality." Bishop Flores Martín (Barbastro, Spain) concurred and suggested that since it was difficult to prove the divine origin of collegiality, perhaps the Fathers would consider whether there were sufficient reasons for defining it as a matter of ecclesiastical law (October 11th). If collegiality were of divine law, he surmised "the pope would be obliged to set up a permanent council of bishops, which is certainly not true." Speaking later, Archbishop Lefebvre, Superior General of the Order of the Holy Spirit, while accepting the idea of a college of bishops as broadly demonstrable both from Scripture and tradition, warned against any diminution of the supreme jurisdiction of the pope which he felt would be involved in the suggestion of a "senate" of bishops. The only convincing proof for episcopal collegiality, according to Bishop Enciso Viana (Majorca, Spain) "came from the fact of ecumenical councils in the Church." Bishops have certainly acted collegiately, but the idea of collegiality was not a necessary one in the Church. In fact it would weaken the pope's authority.

This last argument was the principal weapon of the objectors. Most speakers, however, dealing with the problem of the relationship of a collegial episcopate to the papacy, came to a positive conclusion and maintained that there was no danger to either from a frank acknowledgment of the claims of both and stressed the intimate, inseparable connection between them. On Monday October 7th, Patriarch Maximos IV Saigh (Melkite patriarch of Antioch) delivered what might be called the keynote speech on this particular issue, laying the cards squarely on the table as was his custom (and speaking in French as was his habit). It was reported that he had encountered difficulties in getting his name on the roster of speakers until it had been arranged by the Secretariat that a mentor should "translate" his speech into Latin in strict compliance with the rules. This was in the early days of the Session. Later on such punctiliousness was not considered necessary. He first observed that the definition of the papal primacy by Vatican Council I had been exaggerated through abusive interpretations and that it had thus become an obstacle to reunion. The primacy itself, clear enough according to the Bible and tradition, was not at issue, but the misinterpretation and abuses of it in practice were. Since the Council proposed to prepare the way for union, it should not be satisfied merely to repeat Vatican Council I but should clarify and complete the doctrine on the primacy by acknowledging the unquestioned rights of the episcopate.

Light was also thrown on the oriental position toward collegiality and the papal primacy by the Melkite patriarchal vicar for Egypt, Archbishop Zoghby (October 16th), who criticized the language of the schema for its emphasis on Western theology and developments. The doctrine of the primacy, he said, which the Eastern Church did not deny, had gone through so many changes and suffered so much elaboration since the separation that it could not be recognized by the Orthodox. Unless this Western emphasis were modified, dialogue with the Orthodox would be made difficult. There was too much emphasis on the dependence of the bishops on the pope. Whenever mention was made of the authority of the bishops, attention was always called to their subordination to the pope, which suggested that papal authority was nothing except some kind of limitation on the power of the bishops. The purpose of the primacy—a wonderful gift to the Church—was not to destroy or limit the bishops, but to safeguard and protect their authority. "The greatest gift conferred on Peter was his membership in the apostolic college." Patriarch Meouchi (Maronite) said substantially the same thing the day before, coming out foursquare on behalf of the divine institution of the apostolic and episcopal colleges, stressing the role of the Roman Pontiff as head of the college exercising his authority *with* the bishops, and approving the language of the schema with respect to an "undivided subject of supreme authority."

There was a lack of agreement among modern exegetes, according to Bishop Charue (Namur, Belgium) as to the meaning of Ephesians 2:20, though the early Fathers were almost unanimous in understanding it as referring to the apostles of the New Testament: "You are built upon the foundation of the apostles and prophets with Christ Jesus himself as the chief cornerstone." Nevertheless that Epistle presented the Church as founded on the gospel preached by the apostles, he maintained, and so from the whole context of the Epistle the apostles were to be considered as the foundation of the Church (October 8th). The scriptural arguments on behalf of collegiality were further marshalled by Cardinal Liénart (Lille) in his intervention on October 9th. He concluded by observing that the twin authorities in the Church, that of pope and bishops, were intended to collaborate not collide with each other in the common service. The "supreme service" exercised by the pope preserved unity; while the service of the bishops dispersed throughout the world yet inseparably united to the pope, manifested the catholicity of the Church. Concurring with the Belgian and French speakers, Archbishop Weber of Strasbourg (October 9th) noted that the term *"dodeka"*—"twelve"—was already used in a technical sense in 1 Cor. 15, where it was found in a passage taken from the early oral tradition of the Church.

Cardinal de Barros Câmara (Brazil) was in favor of speaking out "fearlessly" on the issue of collegiality and saw no conflict with the primacy because of the intimate union between bishops and pope. The subject of papal infallibility also claimed attention. Two Fathers, Archbishop Descuffi (Smyrna, Turkey) and Archbishop Shehan (Baltimore, Maryland) both speaking on the same day (October 10th), dealt with the theme at length in unusually frank terms. Both viewed the dogma, or rather its misinterpretation, as an obstacle to dialogue and suggested concrete ways in which to get around the difficulty. The former suggested a new paragraph entitled *De Magisterio Ecclesiae* (the teaching authority of the Church), explaining the infallibility of Church and pope and clarifying the language of the definition reached at Vatican Council I, particularly the phrases *ex sese* and *non ex consensu Ecclesiae*. After the former he wished to add: *scilicet, ex speciali assistentia divina;* and to replace *consensu* by *assensu*. The text as it now stood could imply—though the interpretation would be false—that the pope was infallible by himself, or even in opposition to the Church, or conversely that the Church, infallible when taken as a whole, could be in opposition to the pope's infallibility. "The two infallibilities should not be opposed, but composed." Archbishop Shehan asked for the inclusion in Paragraph 19 of a statement such as: "Such definition is never to be understood as against the consent of the Church. For since we believe the pope to be infallible through divine assistance, by that very fact we believe that the assent of the Church will never be lacking to his definition, because it cannot happen that the body of the bishops will be separated from its head, and because the universal Church cannot fail."

Speaking on Monday of the third week (October 14th), Cardinal Frings (Cologne) elaborated on an expression by Cardinal Meyer the previous week and said that while collegiality did not appear in ancient tradition as a strictly determined juridical concept, it was nevertheless just as clear as the doctrine about the primacy. There was ample evidence in antiquity of the practice of collegiality and this practice at times assumed juridical forms, for example, the sending of so-called *litterae communicatoriae* (letters of communion). Not all truths of the faith were equally clear from the beginning, and he cited as examples the assumption of Mary, the papal primacy, and papal infallibility. Since collegiality belonged to the essential structure of the Church, it was up to the Council, he maintained, to put this in the proper light.

The opposition, as we have said, concentrated on the dangers of the idea of collegiality, dangers to the papacy, to the unity of the Church, the risk of disobedience, and of subjection of the Church to the civil authorities, and was voiced for the most part by Spanish prelates or by Italians close to the Curia. According to the Latin patriarch of Jerusalem, Alberto Gori, the remedy against these evils was "to retain the traditional practice of all activity being centered in and guided by the Roman Pontiff." If too great a process of decentralization were fostered, difficulties would be encountered in reforming abuses in local Churches. "If bishops throw off the yoke of the tempering authority of the Pope, then priests and laity in the diocese will be encouraged to do likewise." There should be insistence on the authority of the pope and of his legates. With regard to the latter point, he thought that papal legates should be present at all episcopal conferences. The same fears were expressed in a speech on the floor by the energetic secretary of the Roman Congregation for Seminaries, Archbishop Dino Staffa, who did not content himself with this formal statement of his views but like certain other council members, saw to it that his ideas were amply aired in the press and distributed abroad.* He objected to the phrase "undivided subject," preferring what he chose to call "the doctrine set forth by many theologians at the time of the First Vatican Council," namely "the doctrine that full and supreme power is vested solely in the pope, independently of consultation with others." The archbishop was misinformed or a bad historian. That Council decreed no such thing, as was made clear by Bishop Gasser, secretary of the Theological Deputation which had drawn up the infallibility decree, in a report to the council on July 11, 1870, and by Bishop Fessler, council secretary, in a famous exposition of the decree approved by Pius IX. On the archbishop's behalf it could be said that he was merely expressing a widely held—though erroneous—opinion that adoption of the doctrine of collegiality would mean "replacing the monarchical structure of the Church with an aristocracy." The irony was that the Church never had been a monarchy in the strict sense of the term—merely seemed to be such owing to historical circumstances—and it was only justice, many thought, as well as high time, that its government be returned to something more nearly approaching its original divinely appointed constitution.

Bishop Temiño Saiz (Spain) flatly denied that collegiality was "divinely instituted." For the assessor of the Holy Office, Archbishop Parente (October 14th), it was true that "bishops are true teachers and judges for the universal Church, but always dependently on the pope." The preeminent position of Peter must be safeguarded at all costs. Bishops never surpass, much less equal Peter, the foundation. Peter was made by Christ the unique foundation of the Church; the other apostles were associated with Peter as subordinates, "as deeper parts of its walls, but not as its foundation." The archbishop appeared to leave the door open on the question of whether collegiality was an apostolic *datum* but indicated that he was not favorable to the idea of any meaningful episcopal coresponsibility with the pope in the government of the universal Church —the real crux of the matter. Bishops received both the power of order and power of jurisdiction—distinctions introduced later by canon lawyers he said—at their consecration as a sharing in the "single, undivided power" conferred by Christ on his Church. "The pope does not create the jurisdiction of the bishop; rather he makes it possible for a bishop to exercise it." But it was "inconceivable" that any bishop should exercise it "independently."

Some speakers felt that the language of the schema was not sufficiently explicit about collegiality. Bishop Sauvage (Annecy), for example, criticized the last words of Paragraph 13 for implying that the successors of Peter and the successors of the apostles had no relationship to each other. Others that it was too explicit because the question of collegiality by

* See footnote, p. 179.

divine law was not sufficiently mature for definition (Archbishop García de Sierra y Mendez).

Although the rules provided that no speaker should be applauded, there were occasions when the Fathers took the law into their own hands. One such was after the ringing speech by the young new auxiliary of Bologna, Bishop Giuseppe Bettazzi, winding up a rather repetitious and long congregation on Friday, October 11th. It was his "maiden speech." Mixing audacity with humor in masterly proportions, he declared: "Although I am young and Italian, I intend to speak about collegiality. There is no doubt that by his consecration a bishop becomes a member of the episcopal college which succeeds to the apostolic college, and that this college has a universal jurisdiction over the whole Church. This view is neither Gallican nor anti-Roman. Since the time of the Council of Florence the popes have said as much, and even a number of theologians regarded as being among the most intransigent, such as the great inquisitor Torquemada, are in agreement on this point. Moreover this universal jurisdiction is of divine right, while a bishop's power over his own diocese is only of positive law. For if a bishop's power over his own diocese were of divine right, how could bishops pass from one diocese to another without giving the impression of committing adultery?"—he observed, referring to the ancient doctrine that bishops were "wedded" to their sees. "The power of universal jurisdiction is both in Peter and in the college of bishops. It is impossible to separate these two aspects of the same universal jurisdiction. This brings us to the heart of the debate. Vatican Council I was not against this way of expressing things, it simply refused to solve the problem and said so. Scripture, tradition and the liturgy all take this for granted. Those who doubt that the bishops have a part with the pope in governing the whole Church are the innovators." In conclusion he cited the collect for the feast of St. Mathias: "O God, who has associated blessed Matthias with the college of your apostles" (*qui beatum Matthiam Apostolorum tuorum collegia sociasti . . .).*" *Quid melius?*—was any further proof needed?

The issue could not have been put more succinctly. Cardinal Lercaro, moderator for the day whose auxiliary Bettazzi was, allowed a smile to creep across his face, as the majority of the Fathers, roused from their slumbers, clapped loudly. Some interpreted the speech as a sign that Cardinal Siri's influence over the Italian episcopate (as president of the Italian Episcopal Conference) was waning. If so, the conservative bloc among the Italian bishops lost no time in disavowing Bettazzi's "betrayal" of the cause. On Monday, Bishop Carli (Segni), generally regarded as the spokesman on the floor for this bloc, delivered a point by point refutation of what the young bishop had said, denying that the word *collegium* was appropriate either for the apostles or the bishops and preferring the use of some such vague expression as "episcopal body" or "episcopal communion," contesting the pertinence of his references to Torquemada or Bellarmine, and maintaining that what Vatican Council I had decided on this point was clearer than the present text. (It had always been something of a mystery as to just how the Secretary General Archbishop Felici drew up the lists of daily speakers. Theoretically all names had to be handed in well in advance but when there was need for the conservative bloc to reply on the floor to some intervention which they considered particularly dangerous or outrageous, it was noted that they had little difficulty in sandwiching in their speakers at the last minute.)

A subsidiary problem, crucial to the debate, was that of apostolic succession. Nobody denied the fact that the bishops succeeded the apostles, but the question was how, in what way, with what powers, corporately or individually, with all or only some of their authority? Paragraph 13 skirted these questions, while asserting the fact. Cardinal Ruffini, as we have seen, doubted that the succession was corporate or collegial. For Archbishop Veuillot (coadjutor of Paris) the language of the schema did not express with sufficient clarity that the notion of apostolic succession was a scriptural *datum*. Archbishop Jaeger (Paderborn) pointed out that not all the powers of the apostles were transmitted to their successors, namely their extraordinary personal prerogatives. It was essential to express this doctrine more clearly because of its ecumenical repercussions. The text hinted at the distinction—a commonplace in Catholic theology—but did not spell out the details. Protestant theology, in general, recognized a sharper distinction than Catholic theology between the apostolic period or period of the founding of the Church and the subsequent "period of the Church," different norms being applicable to each. It was important therefore to state what the Catholic position was.

Several speakers, following the lead of Archbishop Hermaniuk* and acting on the advice of the pope himself in his talk to the Curia on September 21st, broached the subject of concrete ways in which collegiality could be made effective and greater collaboration between the bishops and the pope assured. According to Bishop de Smedt (Bruges), collegiality had always existed in the Church but there was need today, more than ever, for it to be emphasized that the role of Peter in confirming the brethren and serving as a center of unity was much greater and could only be carried out with the help of others. "We who are farther away, desire the same ease of access to Peter as the Italian bishops." This could be realized by some form of internationalization of the Curia. The following speaker, Bishop Zazinovic (Yugoslavia), while cool to the principle of collegiality said that "it would be advisable to set

* See p. 160.

up a permanent episcopal commission with representatives of all nations, with regular meetings, and with authority to decree changes even in the prevailing practices of the Roman Curia." He cited Pope Leo the Great's relations with the Council of Chalcedon (451 A.D.) as an example of the way in which relations between the episcopal college and the pope should be governed.

A similar stand was taken by the master general of the Dominican Order, Father Fernandez. While stressing the subordinate role of the college of bishops with respect to the Pope, if it were deemed advisable to set up some kind of an episcopal advisory commission, this would have only the power given it by the pope. The symbolical as well as practical value of such a body was stressed by the coadjutor bishop of Portsmouth, Bishop Holland, speaking in the name of the English and Welsh hierarchies. He suggested some organ chosen from members nominated by the various episcopal conferences, as a "sort of continuation of the spirit which inspires this council." Christ founded the Church on Peter and the apostles. Such a body was needed to give concrete expression to the Church being ruled by the pope with the episcopal college. "As the saying goes in legal circles, it is not sufficient that justice be done but it is necessary to show that justice has been done."

The main emphasis of the chapter was on the episcopate—as the title indicated—the other ranks in the hierarchy being dealt with only cursorily and *en passant* as it were. In the intention of the framers the role of the priesthood, primarily a pastoral question, would be dealt with in the separate schema, "On the care of souls" (*De Cura animarum*), which was to be debated later. However this was not a sufficient justification, in the opinion of some speakers, for the relative downgrading of the priesthood which the present text seemed to imply. Bishop Beck (of Salford, England), for example, remarked on the lack of a clear definition of the Christian priesthood as such. The text should offer a summary of the doctrine of the New Testament on the priesthood and its place in the Church. The presentation should stress the oneness of the Catholic priesthood with that of Christ and point out that no other priesthood and no other sacrifice beyond those of Christ were required. There would be difficulty later on in dealing with the question of the "priesthood of the laity" unless the whole concept were clarified in its constitutive elements.

Archbishop Conway (Armagh, Ireland) was of the opinion that the subject merited a separate chapter. The text devoted 9 pages to the episcopate and 7 pages to the laity, but priests had only one-half a page and then were considered primarily in relation to the episcopate. With the world shortage of vocations, the Council should exalt rather than minimize the glory of the priesthood. "The First Vatican Council," he said, "is said to have left the bishops in the shade because of its desire to exalt the papacy. It might be said of the Second Vatican Council, because of its emphasis on the episcopate, that it has left the priesthood in the shade." Archbishop Hurley (Durban, South Africa) favored dividing Chapter II into three parts, devoted to the episcopate, priesthood, and diaconate. The priesthood was treated too casually. As a matter of fact, he said, the bishop often had no contacts with his people except through the priest. The priest was the hands and feet, the ears, eyes, and very voice of the bishop. More emphasis was needed on the idea of the local Church, not only as an administrative center, but in its theological significance, according to Bishop Schick (auxiliary of Fulda). This would lead to consideration of the parish and a better delineation of the role of the priest. "The universal Church and the local Church are two essential poles of the one Church," he observed, reflecting an idea dear to the Orthodox. Bishop Renard (Versailles) drew attention to the ancient teaching that priests constituted, together with and under the bishop, a *presbyterium:* they were not only the bishop's ministers, but also his senate, his counsel. The priesthood was a ministry of the Word as well as of the mass. The bishop should appear as the father of his priests. A short introduction to Chapter II was needed, according to Bishop Boillon (Verdun, France) on Christ the Priest, explaining the office of bishop in the light of a participation in His roles as Prophet, Ruler and Mediator.

One or two speakers also commented on the idea of the Church of the Poor, a subject brought up earlier by Cardinal Lercaro. Cardinal de Arriba y Castro (Spain) maintained that it needed clarification. Insistence on the concern of the Church for the poor should not be interpreted to mean that the Church intended to do nothing to improve the lot of the poor. There was a serious obligation on the part of the Church to help improve the over-all economic situation. The task of improving the lot of the poor should not be left to the Marxists. Fulfilment of this duty could be greatly helped by the establishment in Rome of a central office, or Roman Congregation, to coordinate study of social problems and assist in promoting social justice everywhere in the world (October 8th).

A MARRIED DIACONATE

Although not crucial from the theological point of view, the suggestion for a "restored diaconate" contained in Paragraph 15 (Priests and Deacons) consumed a considerable amount of time and was of course seized upon by the press as a godsend rescuing the debate from boredom.

The first to speak on this controversial theme was the cardinal of New

York, Francis Spellman, in his "maiden speech" on the floor at the Second Session (October 4th). In his opinion, Chapter II was "very well composed" except for Paragraph 15. The proposal to resurrect the diaconate as a permanent degree of the hierarchy was a disciplinary matter, he felt, which should not be included in a dogmatic constitution. "God exercises his Providence over the Church according to present conditions" the cardinal concluded. "It must be decided whether it is better to by-pass the divine will and have fewer priests along with permanent deacons, or more priests without them."—It was obvious that neither the cardinal nor his advisers had sympathy for the pastoral-theological side of the question developed by modern theologians such as Karl Rahner. Other speakers would point out that the alternatives were not quite as stark as the cardinal of New York had suggested.—In a press interview later the same day at the Grand Hotel, Cardinal Spellman repeated the substance of what he had said on the floor. "The reason I am against it," he said, "is that it is unnecessary." When it was pointed out that many bishops in Latin America and other areas felt differently, he commented tersely: "Let them say so."

Cardinal Bacci (Curia) likewise criticized Paragraph 15 and thought that the proposal for a married diaconate, to which it would open the door, was dangerous. Times had changed and old ideas were not always the best, he said. New seminaries would be needed because married deacons and celibate priests could not be educated in the same institutions. The number of priestly vocations would be sure to decline even further, for youth was always prone to choose the easier way. The *finestrella* (little window) opened would soon become a *finestra* (full-scale window).

The inclusion of the proposal was defended by Cardinals Döpfner and Suenens, both Council moderators, in two important speeches on October 7th and October 8th. The former insisted that the measure was in accordance with the Council of Trent which decreed that the functions of the diaconate should not be exercised except by those invested with the order, whereas in present-day practice these functions were very often performed by priests. The present text merely laid the dogmatic foundations for a possible change in the Church's discipline, he was careful to point out, it did not impose any change. It made it possible for its restoration in those areas where it was felt that there was a particular need for this step, owing to the shortage of priests. Nothing could be done, in any case, without the approval of the Holy See, as the wording of the decree indicated. Cardinal Suenens stated the crux of the matter as follows: "The purpose of this restoration would be to attribute greater prominence to the diaconate in the hierarchy of the Church, while at the same time making it possible for vast segments of the faithful to enjoy in

189

greater abundance the gifts which flow from the supernatural riches of the Church." It was not merely a question of ordaining laymen for tasks that laymen could do quite as well as laymen. "The work entrusted to such deacons would proceed from the order they received." The new arrangement was intended, of course, for places where a stable diaconate was necessary for the growth of the Church. As examples, he cited small communities segregated from others, or large communities where it was difficult to experience the Church as a family. In concluding, he asked that this question be put to a vote at the end of the discussion on Chapter II.

It was mainly bishops in predominantly missionary areas who were eager for the change, but even here there were differences of opinion. Not all of the African or Asian bishops were enthusiastic. Cardinal Landázuri-Ricketts, speaking in the name of the Peruvian Episcopal Conference and of 58 other South American bishops on October 8th, voiced the largely favorable reaction of that area to the proposal. He stressed the practical advantages, especially for the wide areas typical of South America where there were so few priests in proportion to the numbers of the faithful and there was no prospect, in the immediate future, of improving the situation. While admitting the strength of arguments in favor of retaining celibacy, he thought that the contrary arguments were more "weighty" and a married diaconate could be justified.

The two Yugoslav bishops, Seper and Franič, took opposite points of view. The latter, speaking for the 16 Latin bishops of the country, declared that a married diaconate would be harmful to a celibate priesthood. He maintained that the Orthodox, while allowing a married clergy below the rank of bishop, esteemed celibacy and had difficulties with those in a married state which were not to be overlooked. Italian speakers were divided too, some being in favor, others against, but they appeared united on the possibility of the dangers to celibacy if the proposal went through. Many of the speakers in their opposition gave the impression that they were dealing with a subject that was somehow "tabu," as one Oriental bishop put it, and their strictures on a married clergy, he said, cast doubt on whether such a clergy was capable of leading an exemplary life.

Discussion of the possibility of a married diaconate gave the European press of course a golden opportunity for speculating on one of its favorite topics, clerical difficulties over celibacy, with emphasis on possible relaxation of the norms for priests. Some of the comments were restrained and factual, but others gave free rein to the imagination. The reports continued throughout the Second Session. The French bishops, in particular, were said to be contemplating the recommendation of a change in the existing legislation. To put an end to these rumors they were finally impelled to issue a communiqué from Rome denying that there was any basis for such *informations fantaisistes,* and pointing out that in spite of hardships in individual cases, "the Latin Church had no intention of giving up a law which, even though of ecclesiastical origin, was based on the Gospel and inspired by the complete gift of the priest to Christ and the Church." They noted also that no Father had suggested any such change in the existing legislation on the floor of the Council. Nevertheless behind the scenes, and outside the confines of the council hall strictly speaking, it appeared that the subject was being given a certain amount of serious attention among the experts. A document drawn up by a prominent religious in Rome commenting favorably on the possibility of a relaxation of the existing rule was circulated (*Le Monde,* November 27, 1963). A certain amount of pontifical pique over the fact that these persistent rumors of change seemed to be aired under French auspices may have occasioned the pope's velvet-gloved warning to the French episcopate when receiving them in audience on November 18, 1963: ". . . Continue to watch with the greatest care over these doctrines and these currents of thought . . . thus any deviation will be prevented, and any intervention by higher authority intended to clarify the matters will be rendered unnecessary." Others interpreted the papal remarks as a veiled warning on the subject of collegiality. Reports circulated in Rome that the pope had been critical of the French Church at his meeting with the French bishops. To put an end to speculation, the French Catholic newspaper *La Croix* published the text of his remarks on December 31, 1963. While full of praise for France and especially for French efforts in the intellectual and pastoral fields, the speech nevertheless contained the above rather mysterious words capable of a variety of interpretations.*

THE PEOPLE OF GOD

Chapter III of the schema on the Church, which the Council took up on Wednesday, October 16th, and debated for one and a half weeks (as long as the debate on Chapter II), was divided into six paragraphs. It was entitled "Concerning the People of God and particularly concerning the Laity." Earlier, as we have said, the Coordinating Commission had recommended removing the paragraph or section on the "People of God" and bringing it forward as a separate, new Chapter II, immediately after Chapter I on the Mystery of the Church. The suggestion, attributed to Cardinal Suenens, was printed and proposed to the Fathers in a separate booklet containing the written *Emendationes* to the text of the revised schema submitted by the bishops. If the suggestion were adopted by the Council, the new arrangement of the chapters would be:

* Robert Rouquette, S.J., in *Etudes,* February 1964, p. 241.

Cardinal Ruffini began the debate with a frontal attack on the new theology of the laity on which the chapter was based. The clergy today were more than ever in need of the assistance of the laity, but this did not authorize us to speak of a "mission of the laity." The text said that the laity have a mission directly from Christ, whereas, as a matter of fact, their mission came to them only through the hierarchy. "They do not share in the mission conferred by Christ on the Apostles," he said bluntly. Laity and clergy seemed to be on the same level according to the schema with respect to the task of spreading the gospel, but this was simply not true. Unless the vague and ambiguous terminology in the text was cleared up, bishops and pastors might encounter difficulties when disagreements arose between clergy and laity. It was dangerous to speak of the "rights" of the laity without defining their limits. It was wrong to refer to the episcopal office as a "service" (*servitium*): this tended to reduce respect for authority. And he objected finally to the implication that charisms, or special gifts, were common in the Church, whereas, today, as a matter of fact, they were very rare.

As president of the conciliar Commission for the Apostolate of the Laity which had helped prepare the text, Cardinal Cento, who spoke next, praised it and thanked those directly responsible for their work. It would serve as a good statement of principle. Like many of the following speakers, he approved of the proposed division of the material suggested by the Coordinating Commission.

A point frequently attacked by conservative-minded prelates were the statements in the schema about the "universal priesthood" or "priesthood of the faithful," which, in their mind, seemed to imply a whittling away of the traditional distinction between a hierarchical priesthood and the rest of the faithful. Bishop Rastouil (France) praised what the schema had to say about the distinction between the universal priesthood of all Christians and the ministerial or hierarchical priesthood. It had always been Catholic teaching, of course, that there was only one priesthood, that of Christ, and each Christian, in different ways, shared in it. "Christ," he said, "communicates his unique priesthood to the Church through baptism, confirmation, and orders, in order to continue his work of redemption." Thus it was true to say that the basic nature of the Church was priestly. He went on to say that while priests were aware of their dignity, the laity were ignorant of the power conferred on them through the characters of baptism and confirmation. At this point he was interrupted by the moderator for wandering from the subject.

To Cardinal Bacci (Curia), on the other hand, what the schema had to say on this point was ambiguous and objectionable. To speak of the laity as sharing in a "universal priesthood" without further qualification might seem to imply that they shared in the hierarchical or sacramental priesthood of the ordained priest. The layman offered only "spiritual sacrifices," not the body of Christ, the priesthood of the laity was of a generic kind, with the word being understood in a metaphorical, not a literal sense.

It was all very well, said Bishop Elchinger (Strasbourg), to emphasize the communal importance of such ideas as the Mystical Body, the People of God, the family of believers, the universal communion of the sons of God through baptism and the sacraments, but experience proved that such ideas were usually understood juridically and abstractly by the faithful. The problem was to get rid of the prevailing deep-rooted sense of individualism and make the feeling for a Catholic community a reality and daily experience. Too many Christians approached the sacraments in a purely personal sense, for their own satisfaction, without any awareness of the corporate nature of their membership in the Mystical Body. The Council must do something about reviving a communal sense in place of the present rampant individualism.

The historical as well as the theological importance of the chapter were stressed by Bishop Wright (Pittsburgh). He felt that, while there was room for improvement, the text expressed very well the basic ideas on the apostolate of the laity. "The faithful have been waiting for four hundred years for a positive conciliar statement on the place, dignity and vocation of the layman." He said that the laity knew that their priesthood differed from the ministerial priesthood of the clergy, but that they wanted the hierarchy, in a formal conciliar statement, to put an end to the false notion that the Church was only "clerical." The traditional negative attitude toward the layman—he was *not* a cleric, *not* a religious—must be replaced by a more positive approach.

Almost all the speakers dealt with this question of the proper definition of the layman, from one angle or another. Paragraph 26, dealing with the relations between the laity and the hierarchy, was a frequent target of comment.

The charge that the granting of more freedom to the laity would endanger the hierarchy's freedom of action or authority was answered by Bishop Hengsbach (Essen, Germany), who said that there was more danger in not recognizing their responsibility, for without their help the hierarchy could not fulfill its obligations today and if it ignored them it would be frustrating the Holy Spirit who was given to all for the growth of the Church. "We should not forget that at the first Pentecost, the Holy Spirit descended on apostles and laity alike."

The African Cardinal Rugambwa asked for a better definition of the layman, not in juridical terms, but showing how he participated in the mysteries of the life of Christ. This participation reached its peak when he shared in offering the sacrifice of Christ. The basic doctrine on the apostolate of the laity should be more clearly expressed in Paragraph 25 and then incorporated in the theological manuals and canon law. Speaking in the name of some of the Fathers, he asked for an increase in the number of lay auditors at the Council so that they would be better representative of different areas and professions.

Bishop Picachy (India) found the treatment of the dignity of the laity acceptable, but not the part dealing with the relations between laity and hierarchy. The text put undue emphasis on the sole obligation of obedience and did not stress the fact that the clergy *wanted* their collaboration. He recalled the words of St. Augustine to the effect that while bishops and pastors were shepherds in charge of sheep, in the sight of the Divine Good Shepherd, they too were sheep along with their people.

The very opposite was urged by the Italian Archbishop Melendro (China, expelled), who said that the text should emphasize more clearly the need for obedience and the fact that all authority acted in the name of God. The Council had a *munus* (a duty) to point out certain unspecified "errors" which were said to be rampant in the Church today. He appealed to what Cardinal Micara had said earlier and to Pope Paul in support of this thesis.

The passage in the Exhortation at the end of the chapter urging the laity not be "ashamed of the Gospel" (*Ne erubescant Evangelium*) was hardly appropriate for them, opined Archbishop Golland-Trindade (Brazil). The words were applicable primarily to the clergy and religious. Bishop McGrath (Panama City) also criticized the unrealistic and negative approach to the layman. The laity were not "little acolytes," at the base of a clerical pyramid, subject to everyone. Echoing Bishop Wright, he said that it was out-of-date to present the apostolate of the laity today as something under the thumb of the hierarchy or as "clerical." The Church today appeared too often to be dominated by an "escapist philosophy" and wholly preoccupied by the supernatural. The task of every Christian was to take part in the great work of bringing to perfection the work of creation by getting rid of inequities and eliminating poverty.

A more positive approach was also called for by Bishop Ménager (France), who said that the lay auditors had found the text disappointingly "negative, clerical and juridical." They had opened the eyes of the Commission for the Apostolate of the Laity when shown the text. The differences between the liberty of the laity and the authority of the hierarchy must be spelled out much more clearly, stated Bishop Primeau (Manchester, New Hampshire), or "there was danger that laymen would lose interest in the mission of the Church" and eventually fall away. He was afraid that Paragraph 26 on the relations between the laity and the hierarchy would do more harm than good for it stressed obedience, when what was needed was an emphasis on lay initiative, freedom and responsibility. The impression would be gained that the whole function of the layman was to *credere, orare, oboedire, solvere* (believe, pray, obey, pay). It was important, particularly, for the clergy to encourage lay "intellectuals" whose work was so necessary to the Church and acknowledge their right to freedom of investigation. He concluded with "We should put these principles into practice by giving our lay auditors an opportunity to be heard in the Council."

The distinction in the text between clergy and laity was still too sharp in the opinion of Archbishop Seper (Yugoslavia). When ordained to the hierarchy the clergy did not lose their place as part of the People of God. Thus it was not correct to say that Christian activity in the world was *primarily* the responsibility of the laity, as though the clergy had only a supplementary responsibility in this field. The apostolate of the laity did not involve merely a carrying out of plans conceived by the hierarchy, the layman's part also extended to planning.

Finally, to promote a greater "dialogue" between the hierarchy and the laity, Bishop Ruotolo (Italy) suggested the creation of a new Congregation for the Laity in Rome to be staffed by laymen as well as clergy.

The great ecumenical importance of this chapter of the schema was pointed out by Archbishop Jaeger (Paderborn, Germany), particularly the idea that the entire Christian people was called upon to carry on the work of Christ and was bound by the obligation to preach the gospel. The oneness of the new People of God should be stressed, because St. Paul said that, with Christ, they were nailed to the cross. More attention should be paid to the eucharist as the principle of unity within the People of God. He mentioned the early Church and its literal interpretation of the meaning of *communio.* The distinction between the ministerial and universal priesthoods as being one of "essence" and not of "degree," which some speakers had drawn, was not adequate or in accordance with the real facts. Theology taught that they both had certain similar and dissimilar elements: they were similar in both being a "consecration in the Holy Spirit"; dissimilar in that "consecration as a minister" was a setting aside for special tasks of one who was already "consecrated in the Holy Spirit." The hierarchical priesthood was a setting aside or further consecration within the ranks of "universal priests."

The sharing of the laity in the eucharistic sacrifice as the "peak" of his priestly activity was also mentioned by Bishop de Smedt (Bruges), a member of the Secretariat for Promoting Christian Unity. He said that the text should bring out more clearly the relationship between the apostolate of the laity and the threefold functions of Christ as Priest, Prophet and King, in the exercise of a priestly office: their lives should be religious and offered to God, with the eucharist as the apex; a prophetic office: a truly Christian life bore witness to Christ and His Church; a kingly office: concrete human life, both individual and social, was to be ordered according to God's will and informed by charity.

Rising to speak on Monday, October 21, 1963 for the first time since his brief remarks opening the discussion on the schema, Cardinal Ottaviani exercised the unwritten prerogative of his order to speak on whatever topic he chose, regardless of conciliar rules, and reverted to the discussion of Chapter II which the Council had left behind some days before.—It is worth noting here that none of the moderators thought fit to call him to account for this flagrant flouting of the rules, nor of course did the Secretary General Archbishop Felici pose any objection when his speech was submitted in advance, if indeed it was.—The cardinal of the Holy Office seemed to speak without benefit of manuscript, though he may have merely been unable to read because of failing eyesight—in any case his command of Latin was so prodigious that he could speak extemporaneously in that language, to great effect, if he so wished. He began by an attack on three of the *periti* or council experts (unnamed but assumed to be Rahner, Ratzinger and Martelet) whom he accused of soliciting various groups of bishops in favor of a married diaconate. He said that the *periti* should stick to their lasts: it was the business of the bishops to do the conciliar thinking and the experts ought not to be lobbying or offering suggestions unasked. Despite his charge, the cardinal's manner was pleasant. When a later speaker (Archibishop Kozlowiecki) rose and pointedly addressed the cardinals, bishops, observers and "beloved *periti*," the cardinal acknowledged this rebuke with a large gracious smile. His proposal for resurrecting the office of acolyte—a minor order in the early Church and now only one of the stepping-stones to the higher orders of deacon, priest and bishop (present-day altar-boys are not real acolytes)—seemed to be untimely and unrealistic, being motivated, in part at least, by the age-long concern felt at the Holy Office that any breach in the wall of celibacy would start an avalanche of requests for dispensations from sources close to home which could not be controlled. His remarks about the *periti* were also unseasonable, for he had scarcely delivered them, when one of his spokesmen, Father Carlo Balič, a (Yugoslav Franciscan) specialist in Mariology and consultor of the Holy Office, began distributing a pamphlet to the Fathers in the council hall—in contravention of Archbishop Felici's repeated warning —printed by the same Vatican Press which printed the official schemata and booklets distributed to the Council members. As an ironical note, it was pointed out by *Le Monde* (November 1, 1963) that the above-mentioned memorandum of the *periti* favoring a restoration of the diaconate did not mention a "married" diaconate at all. Either Ottaviani had forgotten or—because of his bad eyesight—was unable to read what his advisers had presumably written.

While praising the general lines of the chapter, Cardinal Meyer (Chicago) found that the text was not realistic enough about certain facts of life: men continued to be sinners and even after their entrance into the Church they were weak and liable to lapses into sin. Hence the appropriate petition in the Our Father: "Forgive us our sins . . ." Christian life had a double aspect: the heavenly and the terrestrial. This idea was conveyed in liturgical texts and in countless other ways, in particular by the prayer *Adsumus* which the Fathers recited every day before beginning their labors. Consequently there should be a paragraph proclaiming that the Church was the home for the weak and struggling, "before we describe the Church as being without stain or wrinkle." Jesus said: "I have not come to summon the just, but sinners."

The prophetic role of the laity was stressed by Bishop Larraín Errázuriz (Chile). He also felt, with Cardinal Meyer, that a clear distinction was not always made between the stainlessness of the Church and the failings of its members. Historically speaking, the People of God had not always fulfilled their ministry. Renewal in the Church was always necessary.

Speaking for the more than 40 Spanish and 30 other bishops, as well as some auditors, Bishop Gonzalez Moralejo (Spain) criticized the chapter for not dealing sufficiently with the problem of the presentation of Catholic thought on the subject of the apostolate of the laity in terms that would be intelligible to modern man or in accordance with present-day thinking, as John XXIII and Paul VI had asked. The language was unnecessarily technical and theological; the order in which the material was presented was not logical, proceeding from the less known to the better known; and certain important subjects relating to the Church such as the continuation of Christ's work, its entirely spiritual mission, its call to self-denial and charity, and the weakness of its human members, were not touched upon at all. He proposed that these defects be rectified and that a catechism adapted to the modern world be issued by the Council.

In an important speech on Tuesday, October 22nd, one of the moderators, Cardinal Suenens, replied to Cardinal Ruffini's criticism that the schema made too much of the subject of charisms (*charismata*), by saying that in his opinion it touched rather lightly on the subject. Charisms *do* exist in the Church today and recognition of the fact was needed if a balanced view of the Church were to be arrived at. On a more practical level, he urged that the number of lay auditors should be increased and that women should be invited to join their ranks, for "Unless I am mistaken," he said, "women make up one half of the world's population."

The cardinal's reference to the attendance of women at the Council, of course, immediately evoked a number of ironical comments in the press. The cynical right-wing *Il Borghese,* in an article entitled *"Il Feminismo di Sua Eminenza"* conjured up all sorts of supposed horrors that would result from taking the proposal seriously, from a resurrection of the scabrous days of "Popess Joan" and "furtive Boccaccio-esque encounters" to the dire prospect of an "Aristophanian Parliament of Women." It cited the editor of *The Tablet* (London) to the effect that "I had hoped in the near future to be included among the lay auditors at the Council, but it appears now that my wife will beat me to it," as a result of the intervention of "the paladin of ecclesiastical neo-feminism."*

The third intervention at this Session by Cardinal Siri of Genoa proved to be in a more conservative vein than his two previous efforts. He saw no valid reason—unlike the vast majority of speakers—for moving the section on the People of God to an earlier position in the schema. The term "added nothing to the general notion of the Church" and had nothing to do with any important aspect of the constitution of the Church. He also took exception to what he called "the sweeping conclusions" expressed on the floor about the implications of the universal priesthood of the faithful. The treatment in the chapter should be more restrained, because while it was necessary to stimulate the piety and zeal of the faithful, this must be done with a proper sense of proportion. As regards charisms, he said that while nobody denied that they could occur as manifestations of the Holy Spirit, the important thing was that they were to be subject to the teaching authority of the Church. There was "no room for a Church within the Church," or a Church full of "illusions."

Dissatisfaction with the organization of this chapter was stated in blunt terms by Bishop Muldoon who observed: "It is becoming increasingly clear that the contents of this chapter are not worthy of an ecumenical council. As it stands the chapter is a shapeless mass of ideas." He singled out as its "original sin" the lack of a basic theological principle which could serve to unify and organize the whole. He proposed as a new title "Concerning the Dignity and Vocation of Christ's Faithful" and said that the chapter should clearly determine the dogmatic foundation of the supernatural dignity of the faithful, namely their incorporation in the Mystical Body of Christ and their "co-incorporation" among themselves. With this as a basis, the rest would follow.

Bishop Hakim (Israel) endorsed the proposal of Cardinal Suenens that

* *Il Borghese,* October 31, 1963.

the place of women in the apostolate of the laity should be exalted—notice being taken, for example, of the great work they were doing in Catholic Action. A conciliar definition of their dignity was needed because in many countries their position was still insufficiently respected.

The subject of discrimination was brought up in another connection by Bishop Tracy (Baton Rouge, Louisiana), who criticized Paragraph 23 on the equality and inequality of the members of the Church of Christ. A statement ruling out any discrimination on account of race was sorely needed, he said, for it was impossible to reconcile racial discrimination with belief that God created all men equal in rights and dignity, as Christianity taught. Such a statement would also make clearer what St. Paul meant when he said that there could be no distinction between Jew and Greek among Christians. It would help bishops to instruct their faithful with regard to the question of racial prejudice, and reassure those who had been humiliated by racial discrimination. It would also provide a good basis for future treatment by the Council of the subject of racial equality in greater detail.

Opinions differed among the Fathers as to whether there should or should not be included in the present chapter some treatment of the ideal relationship between Church and State. The use of the word "unfortunate" to describe the separation of Church and State rankled with the American and quite a few other bishops, who saw nothing "unfortunate" about a pluralistic solution which has increasingly come to be recognized as decidedly preferable and more logical under present-day circumstances, quite apart from the fact that many held it to be better grounded theologically than the old "Constantinian" view of Church-State relations which has dominated thought especially in the Latin-tradition countries of southern Europe. Bishop Klepacz, speaking for the Polish bishops, stated that the delicate matter could not be dismissed in a few words, especially ill-chosen ones, because too much was at stake, as the experience of the Church with totalitarian states, in Poland, for example, showed. "Separation, rightly understood," he observed, "could benefit both Church and state; it gives the Church an independence that is invaluable." Corcordats were not always the blessing that the Vatican imagined them to be: they often rendered the Church subject to the state especially in financial matters. The word *infaustae* must go, and the whole topic should be treated either at greater length here or in Schema 17.

Archbishop Shehan (Baltimore), speaking in the name of the American hierarchy and voicing the latter's concern (expressed at their annual conference just held in Rome), concurred in the judgment of Bishop Klepacz. The treatment of the problem of Church-State in the schema was entirely inadequate. It pertained primarily not to the laity but to the whole Church. He stated the view of the American bishops that the section should be completely redone or the subject dropped altogether. Speaking then on his own behalf, he took exception to what the chapter had to say about "the world." His final remarks were interrupted by the moderator, who asked him to wait while a question about the voting was clarified, but the archbishop did not resume his talk.

The term "separation" was not univocal but analogous, noted Bishop Boillon (France), because it admitted of various interpretations under different circumstances. The Council should wait before taking up the whole question of Church-State relations until the declaration on religious liberty to be presented by the Secretariat for Christian Unity had reached the floor and been considered. This would provide the basis for a fraternal discussion in the Council. The same sentiments were voiced by the Mexican bishop of Cuernavaca, Mendez Arceo. The separation of Church and State could no longer be considered as a tolerated "hypothesis" because in some countries with constitutional regimes it was positively approved according to the supreme juridical norm in question, the common good of a particular Church or nation.

Many of the Fathers expressed concern about the schema's apparent lack of relevance to "the world," to practical questions facing laymen who lived in the world, as well as to its inadequate treatment of a widespread feeling on their part that they had no responsibility for, or share in, an apostolate at all. The promotion of lay organizations and associations of all kinds seemed to Bishop Hannan (auxiliary of Washington, D.C.) a good way to cause the laity to have a greater awareness of their role in the Church. They must be urged to realize that in activities of this kind, whether business, social and civic, they were being true witnesses to the faith and fulfilling the obligations of their apostolate. The clergy, especially bishops, must provide for closer contacts with the laity in this regard. Canon 1520 of the Code referred to lay advice, but only in temporal matters. The initiative must be taken by bishops to establish organs for consultation with the laity.

Bishop Bednorz (Poland) wanted the schema to mention more specifically that one of the most basic practical forms of the lay apostolate was the work done by parents in educating their children and instilling in them the principles of the faith, a thought echoed by Bishop Philbin of Ireland.

The master general of the Dominicans, Father Fernandez, concurred in what Bishop Hannan had said earlier about lay associations. Catholic charitable organizations certainly merited praise, but Catholic organizational activity was still far short of what it should be in many areas, for example that of communications. The lay apostolate could help advance the Kingdom of God through organizations aimed at a juster distribution of wealth, at developing new ways of exercising charity, or other works such as missionary schools. It might be helpful to set up an International Central Commission to coordinate efforts along these lines.

THE CHRISTIAN VOCATION TO HOLINESS

On Sunday, October 13, 1963, Pope Paul seized the occasion of the first beatification of his pontificate to show his appreciation for Americans and his respect for the American way. Assisting at the afternoon ceremonies in St. Peter's honoring the new *beatus* (the pope traditionally did not take part in the solemn mass in the morning during which the proclamation of beatification was made public, the degree declaring this having been signed several days before or even weeks earlier), the Holy Father praised the virtues of American Catholicism as demonstrated by the new blessed John Nepomucene Neumann, an immigrant from Bohemia, who arrived in New York penniless in 1838, worked as a missionary in northern New York before joining the Redemptorist Order, became a naturalized citizen, succeeded the bluff and beloved Irish Francis Patrick Kenrick as Bishop of Philadelphia 1852, and died, in true pioneer fashion, on Vine Street in the center of the city with his shoes on at the age of 49 in January 1860. Referring to a book entitled "Sanctity in America," written by Cardinal Cicognani when apostolic delegate in Washington, D.C., Pope Paul seemed to go out of his way to exorcise once and for all the ghost of pseudo-heresy known as "Americanism" in theology text-books, which was concocted, before the turn of the century, by a French theologian, the Abbé Félix Klein, who thought that the American way stressed the active instead of the passive virtues. Pope Leo XIII in a letter to the American hierarchy in 1908, known as *Oceano longinquo,* warned against such activism hinting that it stemmed from a theological misapprehension, and historians of the Church in the United States had been divided ever since on whether such a tendency really existed, the *sanior pars* holding that there was not sufficient theological depth in the United States at the time to generate a heresy. The following week at a similar ceremony honoring the Passionist missionary, Father Dominic Barbieri, who had received John Henry Newman, the future cardinal, into the Catholic Church in 1846, Pope Paul took occasion to praise the contribution of the English to the well-being of Christianity down through the centuries. In a third beatification on Sunday, November 3, 1963, he stressed the apostolate for youth, particularly youth of the working classes, that had brought Don Leonardo Murialdo, another late nineteenth-century priest, to the honors of the altar as a *beatus*. A fourth and a fifth beatification, of Vincenzo Romano and Nunzio Sulprizio, followed on November 17th and December 1st, respectively. With the exception of the first candidate, this spate of Italian beatifications could not but strike some observers as a rather strange commentary on the subject which the Fathers took up during the remaining week of October, namely Chapter IV on "The Vocation to Sanctity in the Church," implying as it did—whether deliberately or not was beside the point—that heroic sanctity was predominately an Italian monopoly. Students of the scene were also reminded that it was not infrequently the habit of the Curia to reply to attacks on the Church occasioned by a particular scandal by making some move in the beatification-canonization process of a priest or religious relative to the area where the attack had occurred, and wondered what could have occasioned such a concentration of effort, apart from the fact that the illness and death of John XXIII had no doubt held up some cases.

Chapter IV was divided into nine paragraphs. Two thirds of the text related to Religious Orders, although the subject was clearly one that concerned the whole Church. As in the case of Chapter III, there was a widespread feeling that much that was said here duplicated, and in some respects, perhaps even conflicted with special schemata devoted to the subject which were to be taken up later. There was also the impression that the text had been rather hastily drawn up and that ideas had been lumped together here which did not seem to belong either to the chapter on the Mystery of the Church or the chapter on the People of God. Although only three days were devoted to this final chapter of *De Ecclesia,* the extreme repetitiousness of the rather long roster of speakers coming at the end of an already long drawn-out exhausting debate, coupled with the feeling that the topic of sanctity hardly merited conciliar discussion, helped swell the rising tide of dissatisfaction with the course of the Session which began to manifest itself during the last two weeks of October. As one American bishop expressed it, after listening to speakers dwell on the importance of sanctity in the life of the Church for the hundred and first time, he was frankly bored by the whole subject.

A number of speakers pointed out the vagueness of the text with regard to a definition of holiness and its failure to present the idea within a scriptural context. The idea of sanctity was viewed too much from an ethical point of view and not enough as a grace, a gift of God, or from a Christocentric point of view. Holiness, after all, was essentially a sharing in the holiness of Christ. Sanctity was never perfect on earth, as Bishop Schoemaker (Indonesia) pointed out, but consisted in a continuing effort to respond to the divine invitation. This was important *pastorally,* because Christians who were conscious of their faults would not hold that they had achieved any state of consummated perfection, as the schema said. It was important *ecumenically,* because Christians of the Reformation found it difficult to understand sanctity apart from the general

202

objective sanctity of the People of God. Instead of speaking of "acquiring a state of perfection," it would be better to speak of a "state of imitating Christ according to the evangelical counsels." This would eliminate the implication that the religious life represented a perfection achieved, whereas it only denoted a greater effort at striving toward perfection.

Cardinal Léger welcomed the stress of the text on the holiness of the laity but said that it could be improved. For too long, he maintained, monastic sanctity had been regarded as the only real sanctity in the Church, the ideal being unattainable for the secular clergy and the laity. However, it was necessary to go even further and bring out the sanctity involved in leading a married life, in family activity, and in other activities of the layman. The cardinal expressed it as his opinion that no true lay spirituality would be developed until laymen entered the intellectual life of the Church in greater numbers. Laymen should be allowed to obtain theological degrees and to teach in seminaries. He, too, pointed out that too much stress on such terms as "those in a state of perfection" tended to blur the central theme of the chapter, which was the vocation of all to sanctity.

Both Cardinals Urbani and Cento regretted the failure of the text to bring out more clearly the idea of the communion of saints and the connection between sanctity on earth and the saints in heaven. According to the former: "We cannot live out our own vocation to holiness without reference to those in heaven who offer their merits and continual intercession for our sanctification." The veneration of the saints, he maintained, was not an obstacle to Christocentric worship, because the saints were not persons separated from Christ but intimately united to him. As president of the conciliar Commission for the Apostolate of the Laity, Cardinal Cento formally requested that more attention be paid to encouraging the canonization processes of laymen. He cited the French writer Daniel-Rops to the effect that the health of the Church could be measured by the number of her saints. The following day Bishop Emanuel (Germany) seconded the cardinal's remarks about the canonization of laymen.

Cardinal Ruffini was critical, as usual, about a number of details. Since the schema was dogmatic, it should treat of sanctity from a dogmatic point of view: holiness was not only a vocation, it was also present as one of the main marks or notes of the Church, through the latter's union with Christ, her means of sanctification, and the holiness of her members. The traditional distinction between the degrees of sanctity should also be brought out more clearly: ordinary or common sanctity, and heroic or extraordinary sanctity. He objected particularly to the sentence in the Introduction: "In the mystery of the Church . . . all are called to holiness" as inflated, and said that it made the Church sound like the Archangel Gabriel announcing something new. The term *mysterium,* used five times in this chapter, was too obscure and tended to imply that we knew nothing about the nature of the Church, but this was not true. Though as an object of faith the Church was a mystery, we knew considerable about its nature since it had visible elements in the social and juridical orders. Such expressions as the "Church of charity" which Pope Paul VI had used in his opening address—were dangerous, according to Cardinal Ruffini, as implying a separation between a visible and an invisible Church, or the distinction between a Church of charity and a juridical Church.

The severest criticism of this chapter was that by Cardinal Bea. The text did not distinguish sufficiently between the holiness of a Church on earth, in a state of pilgimage, and that of the Church in heaven or at the end of time. The former was dynamically holy but never perfectly so, the latter perfectly holy. It was not realistic to speak only of a Church of saints, the Church also consisted of sinners while here on earth. If the Church were simply holy, there would have been no cause for the Protestant Reformation. In support of his second major criticism, he cited a number of texts showing how inadequately the chapter treated its subject-matter from the viewpoint of Scripture, and declared that this treatment was "unworthy of the Council." The passage containing Paul's programmatic declaration of Christian holiness, for example: "This is the will of God, your sanctification," was omitted altogether. But this and other texts gave a whole New Testament teaching on sanctity. Since some of these texts also spoke of man's capacity to do good in a moral sense, their inclusion would be a response to those who thought that man himself was so corrupted that he was incapable of good and had to rely on a purely "extrinsic" justification. Since they were also frequently quoted by the Fathers of the Church, mention of them could serve as a bridge for a dialogue with non-Catholics on this particular point.

Apart from these negative criticisms of general import, quite a few of the speakers commented favorably on the insistence of the chapter that *all* Christians were summoned to holiness, not merely certain classes or groups. There was *one* divine commandment applicable to all, but there were different means or ways of achieving the goal. Also welcomed was the emphasis on the ecclesiological and eschatological aspects of a life pursued according to the evangelical counsels, rather than solely upon the ascetical aspects. As Cardinal Döpfner pointed out, it was the ancient tradition of the Church that the religious life was to be led for the entire People of God. The religious were not to lead a life for themselves, but were called along with other groups to form a united Christian people.

The German Benedictine Abbot Reetz repeated the suggestion that the expression "state of perfection," in use since the time of Thomas Aquinas in the 13th century, should be dropped because of its ambiguity. The vocation to sanctity applied to all, though not all were summoned to use the same means or follow the same path. Misconceptions on this point had prompted Nietzsche to write that no one was as proud as a monk. The better term was "religious," since this had been used in a technical sense ever since the 6th century. Finally, some speakers were of the opinion that the general treatment of sanctity should be transferred to the chapter on the People of God, and the present chapter reserved exclusively for those in the religious state.

POPE PAUL AT LATERAN UNIVERSITY

On Thursday, October 31, 1963, Pope Paul took part in ceremonies celebrating the opening of the academic year at Lateran University. Present was a distinguished gathering of some thirty cardinals, the rectors of Roman universities, and a quorum of interested prelates. In the absence of Cardinal Micara, Grand Chancellor of the university, who was ill, the pope was perfervidly welcomed by the Rector Magnificus, who made resounding references to the Holy Father's earlier association with the Lateran, both as a student (1922–23) and a professor (1930–37). In actual fact, during those years the then Monsignor Montini had lectured on the history of Vatican diplomacy primarily for the students of the College of Ecclesiastical Nobles which prepared for careers in the Vatican's diplomatic service and had delivered conferences on moral and doctrinal topics to members of the Federation of Italian Catholic University Students (FUCI), as the pope made plain when he recalled "the brief years in which we first as student, then as teacher, attended the *Apollinare* from which this university was born" and said, with a gracious smile, that he "was not tempted to vanity—since we lack the genius and time to give a glorious account of our twofold attendance." The principal speaker for the occasion was the Stigmatine professor Father Cornelio Fabro, considered one of the ablest Italian clerical philosophers. His hour-long speech was a grandiose defense of thomistic philosophy replete with learned assertions about its competency to handle the existentialist problems of the hour and plentiful references to German philosophers from Hegel and Kant to Feuerbach, Jaspers and Heidegger.

Throughout the pope's talk his tone was calm and affable, his manner of delivery positive. Though warmly praising the speaker, he made no mention of Thomas Aquinas or thomism, despite Roman sensibilities on this score. More ominous were the hopes he expressed for the future of the Lateran. "We are convinced of the beneficent role of this Pontifical University of the Lateran . . . and of the stimulus which its presence affords to all those who have at heart Catholic culture and the training of students, both clerical and lay, who show an aptitude for scientific research, for teaching, and for those tasks which require a specific higher ecclesiastical and academic indoctrination." Then lowering his voice but retaining his affable tone, he said: "Our hopes are all the more justified in that, on the one hand, they expect that a smoothly functioning organization, a seriousness of purpose, and a persistent effort toward improvement will spur on all, both teachers and students alike, to impart to this university the virtues and merits commensurate with the excellence of its name; and, on the other hand, that its contribution in the concert of great and celebrated Roman institutes of higher ecclesiastical learning will be that of sincere recognition, fraternal collaboration, loyal emulation, mutual reverence and amicable concord, *non mai d'una gelosa concorrenza, o d'una fastidiosa polemica, non mai!*—never jealous or irksome polemics, never!" These words were greeted by a tremendous outburst of applause among the students which immediately communicated itself to the rest of the assembly. The Rector Magnificus, Monsignor Piolanti, sat stunned, then quickly recuperating joined in the demonstration. These incisive words at the very end of his talk and especially the repetition of "never" put an end to whatever plans certain clerical minds had been nurturing to absorb all the ecclesiastical institutes of higher learning in Rome, including the Jesuit-run Biblical Institute, information about which came to light soon after Pope John's announcement regarding the summoning of Vatican Council II.* The pope then concluded by saying that Lateran University would in that case have its positive mission to fulfill and "it will then always be favored by our affection and supported by our apostolic blessing."

CRISIS IN THE COUNCIL

It became clear at the midpoint of the Second Session that Vatican Council II was in crisis. Five weeks after convening and five weeks before adjourning, a kind of malaise had spread among the Council Fathers as the debates in St. Peter's droned on. "If things continue to go on like this," one American bishop was heard to say, "we might as well all pack up and go home." Cardinal Cushing returned to Boston not long after the Session began and did not come back.† The single schema, *De Ecclesia* (on the nature of the Church), had taken twenty-three days to debate— half the total debating days allotted for the Session—yet under the

* See p. 34.
† There were repeated notices in the press about the installation of a simultaneous translation service, which the cardinal had offered to pay for, but by the end of the Session nothing was operational.

Council's procedure, a final document was nowhere in sight. The work of revision was far from done: the schema faced amendment in the Theological Commission (whose president was Cardinal Ottaviani); the amendments decided on by the commission must be brought back to the Council and voted on, and there was plainly not time enough at the Session; then new suggestions resulting from the voting would have to be studied and, if acceptable, subsequently incorporated in the schema; finally the individual chapters of the schema would have to be brought back to the Council for final approval. As the debate on the liturgy schema during the First Session clearly demonstrated, the process of revision would take at least another year. At this pace, with sixteen schemata still on the Council's agenda, many prelates were saying that by the time the last document was approved, the Church would be ready for Vatican Council III and a new *aggiornamento*. Why, after the Council opened with such optimism and energy and goodwill, were things moving so slowly? The suspicion grew that the conservative minority was only waiting for the day when more and more bishops, restive and frustrated by the slow and tedious pace, would ask for permission to go home to their own dioceses, where so much important administrative and pastoral work awaited them. As the number of Council Fathers dropped, the authority of the Council as a whole would diminish and that of the Roman minority increase. According to Douglas Woodruff (*The Tablet,* November 2, 1963), the responsibility for the slow pace rested with what could be called the 'Salisbury school of thought' at the Council:

It has been dawning on many Fathers, as October has passed, that there is a very strong body of thought, with Curial cardinals at its head, which has been quietly satisfied at the very slow progress that is being made.

Of the Lord Salisbury, who was Queen Victoria's last Prime Minister, it is related that some of his colleagues proposed to raise a new issue of public interest and concern, to which others objected, saying it would lead to a great deal of speech-making, public controversy and argument, and that at the end nothing would happen. "And is not that," said Lord Salisbury, "precisely what we want?"

This school of thought was not only content with the slow progress, but unfortunately it was—and remained—in an excellent position to see that things moved slowly.

An incident occurred about this time which, while not strictly concerned with the course of the Council, nevertheless serves to illustrate the way in which the minority was prepared to override papal wishes when it suited their purposes. It also lifted the veil, slightly, on the long-known alliance between this minority and Italian political and economic right-wing circles. The incident concerned the pastoral letter which the Italian

207

bishops issued, "from the Council," on the subject of the dangers of communism, dated November 1, 1963. Speculation had been rife in the Italian press for some time as to the nature of the expected document. Some commentators, in anticipation, hailed it as a blow against Pope John's alleged policy of "softness" toward communism which had resulted, so they claimed, in the surprisingly large number of votes polled by the Italian Communists in the last election in the spring (1963). Others were fearful that it might upset the delicate balance between politics and religion in Italy worked out by Pope John and possibly also endanger the prospects for coming to some kind of an understanding with the communist regimes of Eastern Europe in the interests of ameliorating the condition of the Church there. Such a policy had already borne fruit in the release of Archbishop Slipyi from Soviet imprisonment earlier in the year, and the release of Archbishop Beran of Prague during the first few days of the Second Session, and there was continual speculation that something would soon be done about the fate of Cardinal Mindszenty. When finally published, the pastoral letter turned out to be much less sensational than the predictions and bore obvious signs of having been "watered down." To offset this disappointing impression, right-wing elements circulated the story that the document had really been fathered by the pope himself, while archbishop of Milan. Worried by communist gains in the April elections, he was said to have discussed with Cardinal Siri, president of the Italian Episcopal Conference, the possibility of issuing some kind of condemnation, but publication was held up by the death of Pope John. Reflecting on the matter after his own election as pope, and influenced by numerous visitors of course, Pope Paul was said to have decided on a re-orientation of Vatican policy toward a closer "surveillance" of Italian political life, away from the aloofness of his predecessor, and to have commissioned Cardinal Siri to consult with the Italian bishops about the preparation of a suitable text announcing the new policy. According to some versions, a draft was on the pope's desk by October 17th, which he kept for a week and then handed back to Siri, with suggestions for toning down the language, in particular substituting the term "atheistic communism" for the more general "atheistic Marxism," thus avoiding any undue ruffling of feathers in the Socialist camp. The occasion for the publication was said to have been determined by the alarming news—duly conveyed to the pope—that fifty members of the Italian Christian Democratic party were prepared not only to kick over the traces of the party position on an alliance with the Socialists, but to go so far as to ally the Christian Democrats with the Communists in a popular front. Rumors of an imminent resignation of the Italian government tended to confirm speculation of this sort and made it seem plausible.

That there was some kind of a disagreement between the pope and those who had been behind the document emerged when Vatican Radio and the official Vatican newspaper *L'Osservatore Romano* came out with conflicting interpretations of the significance of the pastoral letter. The line of the former was that it amounted to a *dura condannazione* of communism without distinctions. The following day the newspaper appeared with a much more nuanced article, full of all kinds of mitigating phrases and tying it in with other papal pronouncements on social questions (November 3, 1963). It appeared that the pope had intended to have both follow the same line but he had been beaten to the punch by the conservatives who appeared at the radio station first with their own interpretation (cf. *Corriere della Sera,* November 3, 1963). That something went wrong appeared from the unusual vehemence of the editorial comment in *L'Avvenire d'Italia* (a Bolognese paper, generally reflecting the personal views of Cardinal Lercaro) which castigated the conservative Rome daily *Il Tempo* (often the mouthpiece for the Holy Office line) for "specializing in the distortion of ecclesiastical documents and Vatican news" and alternating alarmist interpretations of conciliar decisions with sensational revelations about the imminent statement of the Italian bishops. Specifically with regard to the latter point, it was charged with having "raised a cry of victory in announcing the publication of the bishops' pastoral letter, claiming that it supported their own narrow and politically-motivated views." The *Il Tempo* technique was described by the Bolognese paper as "a clericalism of the laity ignoring the reality of the Church and its mission, putting on the same plane for use in the controversies of the hour, a speech by Lombardi [a communist leader of Nenni's Socialist Party], an intervention by a bishop from Vietnam, Cardinal Mindszenty, a dip in the stock market, a pastoral letter of bishops and a party document."

The prospects for any rapid revision of *De Ecclesia* seemed dim. It was known that the Theological Commission could convene only when summoned by its president, Cardinal Ottaviani, and that he had seen fit to convene it only once a week. It also became known that the bishops' speeches on the Council floor, from which the commission theoretically ought to be obtaining the amendments to the schema, were not being circulated to the commission for twelve days at a time. Finally, as their sense of frustration and anxiety grew, many of the Fathers realized that Cardinal Ottaviani apparently did not regard the daily debates in St. Peter's as having any legislative force whatever. If the Council Fathers had merely an advisory, rather than a legislative, function and the Theological Commission was free to follow or disregard the Fathers' wishes as it saw fit, what guarantee was there that the true will of the Council would be expressed? As the crisis mounted, and the Fathers sought a solution to the deadlock, they found that they faced a real dilemma. The Council had four bodies of authority, excluding the pope, to which they could appeal —the four moderators, the twelve-man presidency, the ten-man Co-ordinating Commission and the six-man Secretariat. Which body took precedence? The rules of the Council did not make this clear.

THE FIVE TEST-VOTES

Though no one outside the Council, and very few inside, were aware of it, the first stage of the crisis broke on October 15th. The man who brought it to a head was Cardinal Suenens, primate of Belgium, who was the moderator that day. He announced that it had been decided to seek a test vote to enable the Council to express its mind on four important points.* He did not spell them out, stating that papers outlining them would be distributed for study the next day, but it was generally accepted that these points would relate to collegiality—the relationship of college of bishops and Pope in the government of the Church—and to the proposed restoration of the diaconate. There had already been many keen exchanges on these topics among the Fathers in the debate on *De Ecclesia*. Oddly enough, the official communiqué for that day made no mention of this unusual announcement. It was, however, noted at the press briefing that afternoon, and it struck most observers as an eminently sensible way to speed up the work of the Council and help the Theological Commission in its work of rewriting the schema. Yet at the Council meeting the next day, the papers promised by Cardinal Suenens were not distributed. Cardinal Agagianian, who was moderator, explained that the four points would not be handed out because the chapter of *De Ecclesia,* closed for discussion the day before, had been reopened at the request of a group of Council Fathers. This delay gave rise to the expression, "mystery points," in news stories, but everyone assumed that the mystery would be cleared up in a matter of days. The rest of that week was quiet. The Council Fathers received complimentary sets of the first Vatican stamps issued in Pope Paul's pontificate; the texts of the amendments to chapter four of the liturgy schema were distributed on October 18th; four days later the amendments for chapter five of this schema, and a monograph on the various forms of the lay apostolate throughout the world, were handed out. It was now seven days since Cardinal Suenens' announcement, and the four points were as much of a mystery as ever. Many of the Council Fathers began to suspect that the delay concealed a real crisis behind the scenes, and they were right.

On the evening of Wednesday, October 23rd, a summit meeting of the

* See p. 190 for an earlier suggestion along this line.

Council authorities—moderators, presidents, coordinators and secretariat —was held in the Vatican. The moderators had announced the proposed test-vote on the four points on their own authority alone, and Cardinal Suenens had made his announcement in St. Peter's without consulting the other bodies. This move had been protested by the presidents as being *ultra vires,* beyond the powers of the moderators. And Secretary General Archbishop Felici had threatened to resign if his authority was undermined, as he thought it was by the moderator's action. This was the essence of the crisis. What took place at the summit meeting? It later developed that there had been two votes, one after the other. On the first vote, the results were 11 to 9 against the right of the moderators to propose a test-vote. Had this result been allowed to stand, the Council might have broken up in confusion. At the second vote, the results were again 11 to 9, but in favor of the moderators. What happened was that the wording of the propositions had been changed, eliminating the suggestion that a *married* diaconate be allowed, which, it was claimed, would have scandalized such areas as Italy, Spain and the United States, and dividing the third proposition in two, making the *divine* origin of collegiality a separate question. These two "sacrifices," it was said, were sufficient to bring about the shifting of two votes, in the moderators' favor. Did the pope have any part in this change? He certainly arbitrated the matter, perhaps suggesting the changes in question.* It was also decided at the summit meeting to hold a vote on whether the separate schema on Mary should be incorporated in *De Ecclesia* or not.

If the Council Fathers expected to find evidence of a crisis at their meeting on Thursday, October 24th, they were disappointed. Instead, Cardinal Döpfner, the day's moderator, announced that two cardinals would discuss the pros and cons of presenting the doctrine on the Virgin Mary as a separate schema, or as part of the schema on the Church. He then told the Fathers that a vote would be taken on this question the following week. The two viewpoints were then argued by Cardinal Santos of Manila and Cardinal König of Vienna, and the texts of their speeches were distributed to the Fathers the following day, Friday. Thursday night Romans were speculating wildly, as only Romans could, about the outcome of the summit meeting. Had there finally been a showdown? What had Pope Paul done, since he alone could now settle the matter? On Friday, *L'Osservatore Romano* carried an item indicating that the moderators had seen the pope. It was also known that a number of bishops, and several delegations of bishops from particular countries, in their anxiety

* According to Abbé René Laurentin, in *Le Figaro,* November 11, 1963. The *Time* account, November 8, 1963, disclosed only half of the story, the Abbé maintained, alleging that there had been only one vote and that Cardinal Suenens had been defeated.

over developments, had gone to see the pope to ask him to intervene. At this low point it was announced that on the coming Monday, instead of a regular Council meeting, Pope Paul had arranged to say a special mass in memory of John XXIII, commemorating his election as pope on October 28, 1958. Cardinal Suenens, it was stated, would give the address. On Sunday night, October 27th, in the papal palace, the pope and Cardinal Suenens dined alone.

Meanwhile this weekend was the occasion for an extraordinary and intensive propaganda barrage on behalf of a separate schema on the Virgin Mary. This seemed to have no direct connection with the procedural deadlock in the Council, or the outcome of the summit meeting, but was the desire of circles closely identified with the Theological Commission and the Curial party, even though the issue at stake here was the manner of presentation rather than doctrine as such. Propaganda for the separate schema was so intensive as to startle many of the bishops. Leaflets were handed to them on the steps of St. Peter's, pamphlets arrived in their mail, and the Italian press joined in the campaign by printing absurd stories of "foreign" bishops wishing to tarnish the glories of Our Lady. Early in the Session Secretary General Felici had uttered strong warnings against distributing pamphlets in the council hall. Yet Father Carlo Balič did not hesitate to use the Vatican Press, as we have seen, to run off a pamphlet soliciting the bishops' votes in favor of a separate schema on Our Lady. This pamphlet looked like an official conciliar document, had the same format and typography (though slightly smaller in dimension), and not only bore the Vatican Press imprint, but Father Balič went so far as to classify it "SUB SECRETO," like an official schema, before it was distributed in St. Peter's. This abuse of a position in the Curia by someone not a Council Father scandalized many of the bishops; they knew the action must have had the sanction of someone higher up. Father Balič's pamphlet was not only an impassioned plea for a separate schema on the Blessed Virgin, but it tried to make the bishops believe that the forthcoming vote was a matter of taking sides "for" or "against" Mary. Altogether, this Roman weekend of "secret" propaganda, campaigning, and Council uncertainty and crisis, was a strange and uneasy one.

On Monday morning, October 28th, St. Peter's was completely filled by 8:30 A.M. and the excitement in the basilica was very great. As Pope Paul walked in, small and slight and almost lost behind the halberds of his guards, the bishops stood up and applauded loudly. As the pope said the introductory prayers before mass, he lost his place and looked embarrassed, and this very human occurrence won him the sympathy of the audience. As the journalist priest, Father Raymond Bosler, wrote in the *Catholic Reporter* of Kansas City:

212

He endeared himself to everyone present when he muffed the prayers at the foot of the altar. It was the sort of thing you would have expected from John, but not from Paul, the perfect diplomat always in complete control of himself. *He* was human, too. And every bishop and priest offering the mass with him was glad he had stumbled over the prayers, for it made the Holy Father seem closer.

After mass, Cardinal Suenens mounted the ambo or pulpit, erected on the side of St. Peter's. He appeared calm, dignified, and very serious as he put on his glasses and took out his manuscript. He looked at Pope Paul on his throne on the papal altar, and then started his speech. He spoke in French, a significant departure from the expected Latin, and he made certain that all could follow him by having arranged for the distribution of advance texts in other languages. His address represented a supreme effort to revive the spirit of Pope John XXIII at the flagging Council. It was a moving talk in itself, but it was also full of overtones of the crisis now facing the Council Fathers, though this was never directly mentioned. Cardinal Suenens reminded his hearers that many of them had regarded Pope John, on his election, as a transitional pope. He had been transitional in only one sense, the Belgian cardinal said; he had opened a new era for the Church and laid the foundation for a transition from this century into the next. Though Pope John had died, he was still present in their midst in the person of Pope Paul, who was continuing John's work, said the cardinal, and who had been given to the Church "to endow the prophetic intuitions of his predecessor with form and substance." For those inclined to fear the spirit of freedom and renewal, he quoted Pope John's words: "We have no reason to be afraid. Fear comes only from a lack of faith." He recalled the Johannine spirit in Paul VI's opening address to the Second Session: "On each line and between the lines, the same breath of the Pentecost was perceptible. We heard the same invitation to openness and dialogue, to doctrinal and pastoral charity, the same insistence on constructive, positive work, the same solicitude to translate the Gospel's eternal message into language modern men can understand." At the conclusion, there was a great round of applause. The Roman ear was attuned to nuance, and it got the message—the cardinal was saying that Pope Paul's Council had begun, and in case anyone had any doubts, the Council was going to continue along the pastoral and ecumenical lines laid down by Pope John. As Cardinal Suenens left the pulpit, Pope Paul stood up. He was smiling broadly. Cardinal Suenens strode with long steps to the papal altar, kissed the pope's ring, and then stood up to be embraced warmly by the slim figure in white. The scene was full of deep feeling and elicited another round of applause that echoed through the basilica. Pope Paul had made his position clear.

At the Council meeting the next morning (Tuesday, October 29th), the

213

nature of the victory was revealed. Secretary General Felici announced that, "by order of Their Eminences, the Cardinal Moderators," a paper containing five (rather than four) points would be distributed for study so that the Fathers could vote on them the following day. Archbishop Felici stressed the fact that the vote would serve to indicate the general mind of the Council on these points, to "assist" the commission in its revision of the text. Despite the possibly qualifying implication of the secretary general's last phrase, it was clear that the moderators were no longer *ultra vires.* An extremely important test in the Council had been won. At this point ballots were distributed in order to settle another question, one that had inspired so much propaganda by the Curial party: should the doctrine on the Virgin Mary be treated in *De Ecclesia* or in a separate schema? A close vote was expected, but no one thought it would be as close as it turned out. Of the 2,193 votes to be cast, a 51% majority would decide the question, since it was a procedural matter. (There were 5 void votes, incidentally, because a few bishops forgot to mark their ballots with the special magnetic pen that made it possible to tabulate the votes quickly in the electronic computer.) When the secretary general announced the results, there was a profound silence. The Fathers had voted 1,074 for a separate schema, and 1,114 for incorporating the doctrine in *De Ecclesia.* Only forty votes separated the two groups. It would be difficult to describe it as a victory for the progressives, since the issue was not a clear-cut one. But one thing was clear: even though they had made such a fuss, and used such extreme measures as faked Council documents, the Curial party had lost by a slim margin.

The following morning (October 30th) the Council voted on the following fateful points (called *propositiones*):

1. Does it please the Fathers to have the schema declare that episcopal consecration is the highest degree of the sacrament of order?
2. Does it please the Fathers to have the schema declare that every bishop, legitimately consecrated in communion with the bishops and the Roman pontiff, who is their head and principle of unity, is a member of the episcopal body (*membrum esse corporis episcoporum*)?
3. Does it please the Fathers to have the schema declare that the body or college of bishops (*corpus seu collegium episcoporum*) succeeds the college of apostles (*collegio Apostolorum*) in the task of preaching the Gospel, sanctifying and shepherding the flock; and that it, together with its head the Roman pontiff and never without this head (whose right of primacy—*ius primatiale*—over all shepherds and faithful remains safe and entire) enjoys a plenary and supreme authority over the universal Church (*plena et suprema potestate in universam ecclesiam pollere*)?
4. Does it please the Fathers to have the schema declare that the said authority belongs to the college of bishops (*collegio episcoporum*) united with it head by divine right (*iure divino*)?

5. Does it please the Fathers to have the schema declare that the opportuneness should be considered of restoring the diaconate as a distinct and permanent grade of the sacred ministry, according to the needs of the Church in the various areas?

Bishop Wright of Pittsburgh called the occasion a "turning-point" in the history of Vatican Council II, and indeed it was. The vote on the first four points was overwhelmingly in favor; that on the fifth point, favorable, with a somewhat reduced majority:

1. Favorable—2,123	Unfavorable—34	Invalid—0
2. Favorable—2,049	Unfavorable—104	Invalid—1
3. Favorable—1,808	Unfavorable—336	Invalid—4
4. Favorable—1,717	Unfavorable—408	Invalid—13
5. Favorable—1,588	Unfavorable—525	Invalid—7

Was the crisis now over? By ordinary standards, there would have been no question about it. But Cardinal Ottaviani was no ordinary man. Losing a battle was not the same as losing a war, and there are some warriors who never admit that they are beaten. In warfare, this can be a most admirable quality, but the ecumenical Council was summoned to increase unity, not to do battle. Nevertheless the votes on the five points in no way guaranteed by themselves that the Council's wishes would necessarily be carried out by the cardinal president of the Theological Commission. The "turning point" vote of October 30th was followed by a four-day holiday of the Council, beginning with the feast of All Saints on November 1st and ending with Italy's Armed Forces Day on November 4th. During this period Pope Paul VI sent a letter to Archbishop Parente, directing that the Theological Commission resume more regular and frequent meetings. At the first such meeting, Cardinal Ottaviani was reported as having stated flatly that the Council's votes on the five points were merely "directive," and would not be considered binding on his commission. It was now apparent that the Council was again headed for an impasse. This impression was strengthened by a report that the president of the Liturgical Commission, Cardinal Larraona (Curia), at a meeting of his body had exclaimed, "Before God, I have not been putting obstacles in the way of this group's work!" To the Roman mind, this could be interpreted only as meaning that he had been chided by the pope for having done just that.

THE DEBATE ON BISHOPS

In this unhappy atmosphere, debate was begun on the second schema to be taken up at the Second Session, on Tuesday, November 5, 1963. The document was entitled "On Bishops and the Government of Dioceses," and it was bound to set off fireworks because its first chapter dealt with the explosive subject of relations between the bishops and the Roman Curia. The schema was not long, consisting of 25 pages of text with notes, and two appendices, the whole not totalling over 38 pages.

In his introductory remarks, Cardinal Marella, president of the commission which presented the schema, was immediately on the defensive, stating that due to excellent modern communications and the outstanding competence of members of the Curia, "it is a fact that the Roman Curia has accurate and precise knowledge of each diocese. The customs, usages, mentality and genius of each place is well appreciated here," he said. This claim was greeted with all but audible derision on the part of the great majority of the Council Fathers, whose dissatisfaction with the Curia was mainly due to its parochial and Italianized outlook. To make matters worse, in his *relatio* about the way the schema had been prepared and description of its contents, Bishop Carli (Segni) all but admitted, by disclosing dates and other information unwittingly, that the final text had been the work of but a few Curial officials in Rome who had not bothered to consult the other members of the commission. The details were disclosed by speakers in the course of the debate. Bishop Gargitter (Bressanone, Italy) charged: "The text as we now have it is certainly not the one drawn up by the Preparatory Commission. It expounds its doctrine in the one-sided light of insistence on the rights and the central organs of the Roman Curia. On the contrary, it should proceed in the light of basic theological principles dealing with the nature of the episcopal office, and should follow through with a practical explanation of the bishops' powers and duties."

Bishop Rupp of Monaco supported this contention. After making an ironical reference to "this shining model of Roman brevity," he continued: "The original text drawn up by the Preparatory Commission was much more complete and better balanced, thanks to the work of Father Felix Cappello, S.J., now deceased. In the meantime the text has undergone several surgical operations. . . . The present text contains few new elements and even when it offers new solutions for problems it almost immediately indicates a loophole through which it will be possible to escape applying the principle indicated." Bishop Correa (Colombia) charged that "fully one half of the members of the Preparatory Commission were not given an opportunity to express their minds on the text of the schema now submitted to the Council." And he said further "that the report read in the name of the commission this morning was not drawn up in conformity with the procedural rules of the Council" and challenged the right of Bishop Carli to act as secretary and *relator* of the commission. On November 13th Bishop Carli answered this accusation, claiming that he had been voted in by a two-thirds majority on a secret

ballot, causing one American bishop to remark that the vote was probably three to two with but five members out of x number present.
Archbishop Leo Binz of St. Paul, a member of this commission, later
referred to the schema as an "unhappy proposal" with "no real introduction, no connecting link, and no conclusion." He explained that five
chapters of the original schema had been deleted after it had been
returned by the Coordinating Commission. He likewise spelled out Bishop
Carli's cryptic remarks in his *relatio* by revealing "that a final version of
the schema was completed in March 1963, but that only the bishops near
Rome and the experts in Rome had been invited to review it." Archbishop Binz indicated that the main difficulty was that the schema
avoided the subject of the collegiality of the bishops, stating that their
relations with the Curia should be in effect strengthened, and that the
internationalization of the Curia could be effected by naming bishops
from various parts of the world as members and consultants of various
Curial congregations. It did grant however that the regional or national
conferences of bishops were useful bodies for coordinating the apostolic
work of the Church.

Cardinals Liénart (Lille), McIntyre (Los Angeles), Gracias (Bombay) and Richaud (Bordeaux) led off the debate on the acceptability of
the schema as a whole as a basis for discussion. The first referred to Pope
Paul's remarks to the Roman Curia calling for representatives of the
episcopate to assist the supreme head of the Church in his care and
responsibility for the government of the Church, and said that now was
the time to respond to the pope's wishes. This could be accomplished by
inserting a new chapter in the schema under discussion on "The relations
between the Pope and the College of Bishops." Cardinal McIntyre
foresaw trouble if episcopal conferences were provided with a firm
juridical basis, as the schema proposed. This could conflict with the
recent debate on the collegiality of bishops and by interposing a new
organ between the pope and the bishops, could "lead to a radical change
in the structure of church government so as to endanger her very unity."
While finding the text weak from certain points of view, the cardinal of
Bombay thought that it could serve as a useful basis for discussion. In
particular he wanted a better definition of what a diocese was and noted
that papal representatives—nuncios and delegates—would be better prepared to deal with the problems of the areas where they were sent, if they
acquired a better knowledge of the languages of the Orient and of the
customs and special traditions obtaining there. Cardinal Richaud criticized the characterization of the faculties of bishops as "concessions" of
the Holy See and thought that the schema would be given greater
coherence and unity if it were based on a clearer expression of episcopal
collegiality and the sacramentality of episcopal consecration. In any

reorganization of the Curia along international lines, it was important to include the heads of sees so that its work would be better coordinated and directed more realistically toward actual conditions. The schema needed complete rewriting. What was wanted, according to Bishop Gargitter, was a spelling out in practice of dogmatic principles enunciated in the schema on the Church. There must be an efficacious decentralization and internationalization of the Curia. The privileged position of certain western nations should be done away with. Bishops could cooperate in assisting the pope to rule the Church in various ways: through commissions of bishops, or through a council of bishops called to Rome for the purpose by the pope.

The extreme juridical tone of the schema was criticized by Bishop de Bazelaire de Ruppierre of France, who complained that there was no trace of the doctrinal lines on the episcopate laid down in the schema on the Church. In accordance with the principle of subsidiarity, there was no reason why bishops today could not freely exercise certain powers which the Holy See formerly reserved to itself. It was not correct to call these powers "concessions" of the Holy See. The schema appeared to fluctuate between two views. In the Introduction it spoke of bishops as true pastors with all the powers necessary for their office; but in paragraph 3 it spoke of granting faculties as a "concession."

Archbishops Garrone and Marty of France and Archbishop Baudoux of Canada were all highly critical of the schema's omission of the basic notion of collegiality. According to the latter, "The approach used in the present text amounts to a downgrading of bishops because it speaks of *granting* faculties to them." He also suggested, as other speakers would later, that the traditional terminology which distinguished between titular and residential bishops was no longer applicable today and a new terminology should be found. Since episcopal consecration incorporated a bishop into the episcopal body (or college) and therefore conferred on him a share in the government of the Church, the traditional distinction was not logical. All bishops were true pastors and responsible for the whole Church.

The debate on Wednesday, still on the acceptability of the schema as a whole, was led off by Cardinal Ruffini who made a number of points. While critical of the text in detail, he thought that it could serve as a basis for discussion. Answering those who had regretted the lack of any reference to the idea of episcopal collegiality, he maintained that this idea had not been sufficiently developed by the debate on the Church. Cardinal Lercaro, he said, had given his assurance that the vote of the bishops on the five points would not prejudice any final conciliar decision. The vote had been merely indicational or directional, and was not definitive. Consequently it would be wrong to base any firm conclusions on it. The treatment of episcopal conferences in the schema was obscure, as Cardinal McIntyre pointed out. It was noted that the cardinal of Palermo's remarks about collegiality and the vote on October 30th were a public statement of what Cardinal Ottaviani had been saying privately, within the confines of the Theological Commission. As such, they were accepted as a challenge by the majority, and the subject became a bone of contention between conservative minority and progressive majority throughout the remainder of the Session.

Cardinal König (Vienna) concurred in the judgment that before speaking of relations between the bishops and the Curia, the text should deal with "bishops with and under the Roman Pontiff collaborating in the government of the universal Church" and that there should be an international college of bishops in Rome assisting the pope. With regard to episcopal conferences, he mentioned the fruitful experiences of the American and German bishops with their respective conferences as an example of how such bodies could function effectively with merely moral, and not juridical, authority. The cardinal of Utrecht brought out that a body of bishops functioning in Rome as advisers to the pope would not be a representative parliament, but a *sign* of episcopal collegiality and an instrument by which the collegial will of the bishops could be made effective. It would serve the same purpose as the episcopal conference on a lower level. If such a body were authorized, he went on, the Curia would then become an executive instrument or branch of the legislative power of the bishops collaborating with the pope.

The principle of subsidiarity was further stressed by Cardinal Bea. It was valid for the Church as well as for other societies. What could be done well enough on a lower level should not be preempted as a privilege or prerogative by a higher level. Special circumstances in the history of the Church had given rise to such intermediate bodies as the patriarchates and the Roman Curia. Nevertheless the rule still held that what bishops could do for themselves, they should be permitted to do without undue interference from on high, unless liberty of action needed to be curtailed for the common good. The establishment of some kind of episcopal body in Rome to help the pope, according to norms laid down by him, would have an ecumenical importance in that it would lay to rest traditional accusations of a lust for power, ecclesiastical imperialism, curialism and over-centralization on the part of Rome. Such charges could only be answered by deeds, not words.

The next speaker, Cardinal Browne, vice president of the Theological Commission, supported Cardinal Ruffini in rejecting the contention that it was a defect of the present schema that it did not take into account the notion of collegiality. "From yesterday's talks," he said, "I suspect that some Fathers think that the word *college* can be taken in a strictly

219

juridical sense, but it seems to me that such a meaning can in no way be admitted." The whole idea needed to be "studied, weighed, and judged" by the Theological Commission, but he gave no indication when this arduous task would be completed. His words "We must await the report of the Theological Commission for a clarification of this basic point before we can take any concrete action" seemed to suggest that the commission had no intention of moving unless it were prodded by higher authority.

Following this casting of doubt on the very basis of the present discussion as expressed in the debate on the Church, Archbishop Veuillot drew the logical conclusion that it would be useless to go on to discuss the details of the present schema and that this should be put off until *De Ecclesia* had been confirmed by the Council. The same thought was echoed by other speakers. Bishop Hodges, in the name of the bishops of the United States, accepted the schema as a basis for discussion, but maintained that it must be correlated with the teaching on the episcopate recently formulated as a result of the debate on the Church. In order to protect popular reverence for the authority of the pope, Bishop Cooray of Ceylon suggested that further debate should be confined to written proposals given to a special commission which would be assigned the task of working out an agreed text that could be voted on in the usual way.

After a number of other speakers had been heard, the moderator for the day, Cardinal Suenens proposed a standing vote on whether the schema was acceptable as a basis for further discussion. The result was 1,610 votes in favor of acceptance, 477 for rejection, with 13 invalid votes. The outcome somewhat surprised observers who had gained the impression from the critical tenor of the remarks that an outright rejection of the schema was possible. But this would have eliminated all debate on a number of important issues connected with the relations between the pope, Curia and bishops, which the majority wanted to air more fully.

The doughty, eighty-five-year-old Patriarch Maximos IV Saigh then took the mcirophone as the morning's last speaker. Speaking in French as usual, he said that whoever put this schema together seemed to think that the Church of God consisted of the pope and the Roman Curia. "This corresponds neither to the nature of the Church," he said, "nor to the needs of the times." He went on to say that the pope was not only the bishop of Rome and patriarch of the West, but supreme pastor of the universal Church, "and it is this final title that absorbs all his other functions." Hence the pope cannot rule the Church merely with an administrative body, the Roman Curia, nor even with a college of cardinals. The latter group, he said, were the successors of the parish priests of Rome and, merely in their office as cardinals, had nothing to do with the universal Church as such. Instead, said the aged speaker, the pope now needed a college of bishops, in which the patriarchs, those cardinals who were bishops of large dioceses around the world, and an elected group of bishops from all regions could serve. This college of bishops, he concluded, "would assist the pope, only at his request, in governing the Church and providing for its needs." As the Council Fathers poured out of St. Peter's, they told one another that the speech of Patriarch Maximos could not fail to have verbal repercussions.

THE FRINGS-OTTAVIANI EXCHANGE

Though the Council meeting on the following day, November 7th, was marked by the important intervention of Cardinal Ritter of St. Louis, speaking for a large number of American bishops, proposing that the chapter be redone in the spirit suggested by the majority of the Fathers, with the title changed to "The relations between the bishops and the apostolic see," instead of the Roman Curia, and though the Armenian Patriarch, Ignace Pierre XVI Batanian, made a vigorous defense of the Curia in an obvious attempt to offset the impression created by the Melkite patriarch, and though Archbishop Florit (Florence), in the name of fifty bishops, called for the establishment of a super-congregation of bishops in Rome that would outrank all existing congregations as a concrete expression of collegiality, while at the same time asserting that "Yesterday . . . some went too far" in praise of the idea, the real fireworks did not occur until the meeting on Friday, November 8th. It began with a mild suggestion by Cardinal de Barros Câmara (Rio de Janeiro) that, in accord with the needs of the Church and the expressed desires of Pope Paul, some action be taken to set up a body, or senate, of bishops in Rome. A speaker then rose who turned this meeting of the Council into a historic one. He was the cultured and drily witty Cardinal Frings of Cologne, a scriptural scholar and a graduate of the Pontifical Biblical Institute. Formerly a mountain-climber but now ailing at 76, the cardinal touched on the heart of the Council's problems. "The vote of October 30th," he said, "is perfectly clear, even though indicative. I am astonished that Cardinal Browne, vice president of the Theological Commission, has put this vote in doubt. The commission has no other function but to execute the wishes of, and obey the directives of, the Council. Furthermore," he added, "we must not confuse administrative roles with legislative ones. This also goes for the Holy Office, whose methods and behavior do not conform at all to the modern era, and are a cause of scandal to the world. No one should be judged and condemned without having been heard, without knowing what he is accused of, and without having the opportunity to repair what he can reasonably be reproached with."

At this point many bishops, though applause was forbidden during the Council debates, clapped loudly and long. He then went on to say that too many prelates were employed in Curial offices, and stated candidly that the episcopacy should not be conferred on anyone as a reward for services. "It is not necessary to be a bishop in order to serve in the Roman Curia, nor even to be a priest," he went on. "Certain tasks of these bureaus can be perfectly carried out by laymen. We have talked a great deal about the laity at this Council; they should be given the places for which they qualify. This reform of the Curia is necessary," he concluded. "Let us put it into effect." There was a sort of stupefied silence when he ended, then the Council Fathers again broke out into sustained applause. The two speakers who followed, Cardinal Lercaro of Bologna, a Council moderator, and Cardinal Rugambwa of Tanganyika, both made an important proposal: that the Council send the pope a petition that he could transform into a separate constitution, creating the new body of bishops to be associated with him in serving the Church. The cardinal archbishop of Bologna spoke from the moderators' table. He noted that the discussion of paragraphs 4 and 5 as to the feasibility of establishing some kind of an episcopal body to advise the pope had so far been too dogmatic in tone, whereas what was needed were arguments or suggestions regarding the opportunities or practical means for establishing organisms capable of fulfilling this role. Certain principles must remain inviolate: "a) the Roman Pontiff enjoys by divine right a supreme jurisdiction over the whole Church; b) also by divine right the supreme pontiff may exercise such jurisdiction without any juridical dependence on the bishops; c) to help him in the government of the Church, the pope may make use of the instruments which he considers the most opportune; d) the episcopal body also has power, together with and under the pope, to teach and govern; e) nothing prevents the pope from using the episcopal body or any organ consisting of his representatives to study the most important problems faced by the Church, however the final judgment always remains that of the pope. In fact the Holy Father is free to follow one method or another of judging the opportuneness of creating new organs to advise him and help him coordinate and decide with regard to the most important matters affecting the Church. This is the role which consistories performed in the Church until the sixteenth century." The cardinal then concluded with these measured words: "However this participation in the government of the Church cannot be effected either by delegating certain bishops representing episcopal conferences, nor by creating a new congregation that will interpose itself between the pope and the existing dicasteries. The problem transcends not only the schema under discussion, but the Council itself, the moment that it touches on the rights of the pope. The expression of a desire is one thing, a decree is something else; therefore the whole question should be stricken from the schema and elaborated later in the form of a *votum* (petition) to be presented to the pope for the renewal of the Curia or for the participation of the bishops in the government of the Church."

Cardinal Rugambwa delivered an equally measured, impressive appeal. But all eyes were on Cardinal Ottaviani, who was to be the next speaker. When he rose, a tremendous hush settled on the gathering.

In a voice shaking with rage and emotion, he said, "I most profoundly protest against the accusations made against the Congregation of the Holy Office. Without any doubt, it is due to lack of knowledge (*nescientia*). I use this word advisedly, so as not to use another which would not be charitable. One commits a great mistake in not realizing that the Holy Office is always assured of the help of the most eminent and the most solid men." He pronounced the next words slowly and emphatically. "In attacking the Holy Office, one attacks the pope himself, because he is its Prefect." As this point, applause was heard from the Italian and Curial group, so carried away that they forgot it was forbidden. "There is much talk," Cardinal Ottaviani went on, "of the divine right of collegiality, as if it had been defined. However, nothing of the sort has been done, and it is the Theological Commission alone that can define it. I respect the moderators, but why did they not ask the Theological Commission to prepare the points put to vote on October 30th? It is the Commission, and it alone, that is competent here, and not the moderators." He then stated that the best theologians had told him no basis could be found in Holy Scripture for collegiality. "I am astonished that the Fathers can speak of collegiality in the juridical sense of the term. When Christ said to Peter: 'Feed my sheep,' He included the other apostles in this group."

Ottaviani was followed by Cardinal Browne. The Dominican cardinal pointed out that the higher officials and consultors of the Roman Congregations were not appointed by the Holy See but were chosen freely and personally by the pope himself. If collegiality were to confer on the bishops the right to participate in the government of the Church, the pope would be obliged to recognize and respect this right and as a consequence would no longer enjoy a true primacy over the whole Church. These propositions seemed to imply a "co-government" of the Church. As formulated, they seemed to be in conflict with the constitution *Pastor aeternus* of Vatican I on the papal primacy and infallibility. If adopted they would mean that it would no longer be Peter who was guiding and feeding the sheep, but the sheep Peter—*sed oves Petrum*. If the collegiality of the bishops should be given a purely juridical interpretation, the authority of the pope would no longer be plenary and supreme. *"Venerabiles Patres, caveamus*—Venerable Fathers, let us be on guard."

These words, too, brought forth applause, emphasizing the division of the Council over this matter. The majority interpreted them, rightly, as a virtual throwing down of the gauntlet to the idea of *aggiornamento* and to the pope himself probably viewing the scene on his closed TV circuit.

Later in the morning, while on the subject of Chapter II of the schema, Cardinal Ruffini took the occasion to attack what Patriarch Maximos IV Saigh had said earlier in the week about an episcopal "Senate" and in criticism of the Roman Curia. Speaking with hardly concealed anger, he said, "I have heard in this gathering a severe and offensive speech against the Roman Curia. I say it is unacceptable! Reparation has happily been made by Patriarch Batanian, my dear friend and colleague. I publicly thank him in the name of Cardinal Siri, president of the episcopal conference of Italian bishops." This last remark seemed to imply that the Roman Curia really was an exclusively Italian affair. In this tense and overwrought atmosphere, the brilliant intervention of Archbishop Eugene D'Souza (India) brought a much needed return to calmness and issues rather than to personalities.

"I hear," he said, "that the thinking of the Council on collegiality is not clear, and that our vote of October 30th can be considered as invalid and illegitimate. It is mockery to speak thus, when 80% of the Fathers have replied in a perfectly clear manner to a series of questions that were no less clear. Further, their answer is in total conformity with the address of Pope Paul VI to the Roman Curia itself. I beg you not to reduce this question of collegiality to nothing but its juridical aspect, for the pastoral care of souls, our *raison d'être,* depends on this collegiality." He then went on to say that the schema they were debating was not pastoral enough, and did not correspond to the intentions of this pope or his predecessor. "It proposes that the bishops be given a few more memberships in the Curial congregations. Is this why 2,200 Council Fathers have been summoned here?" he asked. "The bishops have already resisted the many pressures that have been put upon them. How much more pressure will there be, when they have been scattered to their dioceses?" He then made an important distinction between the Curia and the Council. "The Roman Curia," he said, "does its job in a context quite different from an ecumenical Council. Yet, in every field, today's context is totally different from yesterday's. The administrative problems of today cannot be resolved by the Curia in the same way as in the past." After recalling the scriptural verse, "the letter killeth," Archbishop D'Souza concluded: "Suspicion has been cast on certain authors without saying why, without specifying what part of their writing is to be praised, and what part requires correction. The more we love the pope, the more we believe in his primacy. Why, then, this outcry, as if the Church were in peril?"

That afternoon it was reported that Pope Paul telephoned Cardinal Frings, to express his approval of what he had said on the Council floor. (Among other things the cardinal had said that "the Holy Office is a cause for scandal in the world.") On the same afternoon, the pope also agreed to see Cardinals Ottaviani, Antoniutti and Siri. If the Secretary of the Holy Office came to seek the pope's support, he did not receive it. Cardinal Ottaviani was said to have been so upset by this rebuff that he considered whether he ought not to resign. (This reminded Romans of his similar encounter with Pope John XXIII during the First Session on November 18, 1962, during the debate on "The Sources of Revelation," prepared by his Theological Commission. These debates revealed that Cardinal Ottaviani and his followers, on this subject too, were out of step with the thinking of most of the Council Fathers. That day Ottaviani called on Pope John and complained about the dissension. "Dissension?" Pope John was said to have replied. "Don't you recall that at Trent the dissension became so heated that an Italian bishop tore the beard of a Greek bishop? Nevertheless, the Council of Trent is remembered today as one of the great events in the history of the Church." Ottaviani then said, "If this dissension goes on much longer, the dignity of the Holy Office will be in danger, and I may resign." Pope John calmly replied, "You will stay. There will be no resignations.") One year later, in more heated circumstances, Cardinal Ottaviani was again talking of resigning.* It was reported that Pope Paul was particularly displeased because Cardinal Ottaviani did not confine himself to a defense of the Holy Office, but attacked the person of Cardinal Frings in a regrettable manner by implying ignorance and bad faith. It was also reported that Patriarch Maximos IV Saigh had received apologies from Cardinal Ruffini, for the latter's attack on his person in his speech on the Council floor on this memorable day of November 8th.†

The day was not quite over, however, for a preview showing of Otto Preminger's new film, *The Cardinal,* was scheduled in the evening. The showing had been arranged under the auspices of the Holy Office itself, in that congregation's palace to the left of St. Peter's basilica. Cardinal Ottaviani naturally presided as host on his own grounds. Word of the

* *Il Tempo* (November 15, 1963), published a denial by Cardinal Ottaviani's office that he had been received in audience, had ever thought of resigning, or that his language had been offensive to Cardinal Frings.

† *La Croix* (November 16, 1963) explained that confusion over the audiences was compounded by an error of *L'Osservatore Romano,* which reported Cardinal Frings as having been received on Friday whereas he had been received on Thursday along with the German and Austrian bishops. But not all audiences were, or are, announced! Cardinal Siri was seen leaving the Pope's office on Saturday morning, but his name was not on the official list.

fireworks in St. Peter's only a few hours earlier had already spread all over Rome, and photographers and journalists were everywhere. When the cardinal arrived in person, there was a great flurry of flashbulbs. The film version of Henry Morton Robinson's novel, and the strange occasion of this screening, received a truly Gallic review by Henri Fesquet, who reported on them in *Le Monde,* "From a puerile but readable enough novel, the U.S.A. has made a film that is not only stupid but in dubious taste. Nothing is lacking, not even an *amourette* between the ecclesiastical hero and a young girl with tender eyes. The Council Fathers gave this film the reception it deserved, but many were astonished that their leisure time had been put to such bad use. At the First Session of the Council in the fall of 1962, things had been arranged better by a showing of Bresson's film, *The Trial of Jeanne d'Arc.* It is true that this year, under the circumstances, the showing of such a film at the Holy Office would have had the appearance of a provocation. But between the authentic history of the most famous victim of the Inquisition, and the insipid story of a film that is religious in name only, it should have been possible to find some less questionable distraction for the Council Fathers."

The tension caused by the Frings-Ottaviani exchange on Friday continued to the end of the Session. The question uppermost in men's minds was whether the Holy Father would take cognizance of what was apparently a challenge thrown down by the cardinal of the Holy Office. It was known that the Council moderators had two long audiences with the pope on Saturday and Sunday, November 9th and 10th. Important decisions, including what to do about the present impasse were discussed, but only part of the veil was lifted when it later became evident what steps the Theological Commission was to take Monday and Tuesday. Meanwhile, considerable uncertainty prevailed and questions were raised as to why the pope did not act. The Holy Father however did begin to take off his gloves, in a characteristically velvet-gloved fashion so that most missed the point. In a moving ceremony on Sunday, November 10, 1963, Pope Paul took formal possession of the Lateran basilica, Rome's cathedral, having delayed his ceremonial entrance for five months, in order to emphasize the continuity with the Church of earlier centuries when a new pontiff performed the rite surrounded by as many bishops as could be gathered together. Hence in the course of his discourse Paul stated: "today this basilica, as never before . . . holds almost the entire episcopate of the world present here to receive splendidly and solemnly the latest of her pontiffs, the lowliest and most humble in the line of popes. He has no right to enter as lord and master, other than the irrefutable right of having been canonically elected bishop of Rome." *Il Tempo,* the conservative Rome daily, in one of its habitually slanted interpretations, ignored the first part of the pope's remarks and quoted him as having referred to himself as the "Supreme Pontiff and Master and Lord of the Universal Church"—words which he had not uttered at all. In fact, the pope's speech was the very opposite in tone from a lordly assertion of extreme papalism. It certainly was not an overt defense of Cardinal Ottaviani on Friday, as the paper claimed. There was nothing in it either suggesting that Paul was now emulating "Pope Martin V" in the fifteenth century as another "dominator" of Councils. On the contrary, the pope's speech contained a veiled but definite warning to the Roman people to mend their ways and receive the reforming work of the Council—a theme which *Il Tempo* preferred to pass over in silence (November 11, 1963).

Shortly before this, on Thursday, November 7th, the Vatican newspaper announced that the pope had received in special audience the archbishop of Freiburg in Germany, the editor of the German Catholic publishing house of Herder Verlag, and one of the latter's principal authors, the famous German theologian Father Karl Rahner, S.J., who had been accused by Cardinal Ottaviani some weeks before in a speech on the floor of having solicited bishops on behalf of a married diaconate.* In the course of the audience Pope Paul expressed his deep "appreciation" to Father Rahner for his profound theological knowledge and works, which, along with those of the French Dominican Father Yves Congar, had had such an influence on shaping the course of the Council. Congar was later to be awarded a "masterate of theology" with the full approval of the pope. The "rehabilitation" of both men—who had suffered for years at the hands of the Holy Office because of their supposedly "dangerous" ideas—was Paul's way of replying to the campaign of fear and suspicion which the Holy Office was still waging on all fronts. (An eloquent article by Abbé René Laurentin in *Le Figaro* on December 9, 1963, entitled simply "The Price of Vatican Council II," listed the vexations, bannings and even banishments of which Père Congar had been the victim over the years, from 1935 until the present time. He was now fortunately back teaching and carrying on his studies at Le Saulchoir.)

DISCUSSION OF COLLEGIALITY

The "lull after the storm" wrote Henri Fesquet of the resumption of the debate on "Bishops," on Monday, November 11th. This was only partly true. On the side-lines, all during the week, there was considerable anxious speculation about the problem of religious liberty, for it was known that a statement drawn up by Cardinal Bea's Secretariat for Unity had been submitted to the Theological Commission last June. It was to

* See p. 196.

form Chapter V of the schema on Ecumenism, the next topic to be taken up by the Council, but so far no action had been taken. The Theological Commission had prevented it thus far from being printed, and rumor had it that Cardinal Ottaviani had even refused to discuss the draft. When pressure began to build up in favor of getting it printed, Ottaviani was reported to have failed in a bid to the pope to get the measure tabled. Instead he was told to have his commission meet, discuss the statement, and bring it to a vote. Credit for this decision could be given to Cardinal Spellman who was known to have presented a petition to the Holy Father, signed by the majority of American bishops, urgently requesting that the document on religious liberty be taken up at the Second Session. The distribution to the Fathers on Friday, November 8th, of the text of Chapter IV of the schema on Ecumenism, on the Jews, naturally increased the pressure for a prompt consideration of Chapter V. The atmosphere was tense with expectancy.

Monday and Tuesday, November 11th and 12th, were some kind of a landmark in the history of the Council, for it was then that Cardinal Ottaviani suffered defeat on his own territory. At a meeting of the Theological Commission on Monday, called by the cardinal to consider whether Chapter V on Religious Liberty should be "reported out," Bishop Charue asked Father John Courtney Murray, S.J., an expert on church-state relations, Council *peritus* and consultor of the commission— fortunately present at this session, through the efforts of Cardinal Spellman, after having been "disinvited" to the First Session—to speak on the subject. As the Jesuit weekly *America* (November 30, 1963) described the scene: "The president of the commission, Cardinal Ottaviani, is almost blind. He did not recognize or distinguish the tall figure of Father Murray when he spoke . . . before the commission's members and consultants. Cardinal Ottaviani, one hears, leaned over to his neighbor, Cardinal Léger, to ask who was speaking. The Canadian cardinal, perhaps to spare Father Murray any unwelcome publicity at that point, replied simply: *'peritus quidam'* (One of the experts)." On Tuesday the commission proceeded to a vote. Previously a subcommittee of the commission headed by Cardinal Léger, to which the chapter had been turned over for examination, had, by a vote of 3 to 2, approved the text in principle but recommended its release to the floor unanimously. Cardinal Ottaviani tried to delay the fateful vote on Tuesday by making a great many long-winded explanations and offering a number of wild suggestions, all of which were voted down by the impatient commission members. Finally the members shouted: "Bring the measure to a vote!" When the vote was counted it turned out to be 18 to 5 in favor of reporting the text to the floor, with 1 invalid vote. The five opposing votes were apparently those of Cardinal Ottaviani, Cardinal Browne, Cardinal

Santos, Archbishop Parente and Archbishop Florit, who constituted the small ultra-conservative coterie which had repeatedly held up or frustrated the work of a more progressive majority. The document went at once to the printer and was in the hands of the Fathers when they began discussion of the schema on Ecumenism the following week.

Pursuing the debate on Monday, Cardinal Spellman came out with a rather ambiguous statements on collegiality and the Curia. He declared that there was much misinformation in the press on both these topics. "The theology we all learned in the seminary teaches us that the pope alone has full power over the entire Church. He does not need the help of others. As far as the Roman Curia is concerned it is only an executive organ of the Holy Father. Consequently it is not up to us to try to reform or correct it. We can only offer suggestions and recommendations." He concluded with this warning: "Let us be careful about proposing anything that may be at variance with the decrees of previous councils or papal pronouncements."

Cardinal Confalonieri, Secretary of the Curial Congregation of the Consistory, tried to calm the ruffled waters by posing as a conciliator and observing that the Curia was not all bad. In ten years as bishop of Aquila he had had ample experience of the difficulties bishops encountered in their dealings with the Curia but criticism must be tempered with praise. Reform of the Curia was necessary but the initiative must come from the pope, acting courageously—*"viriliter."* "Let us address our humble requests to him."

This was precisely what the Fathers did. For some days it had been rumored that Cardinal Silva Henriquez of Santiago de Chile would speak on the need for an episcopal senate to advise the pope and would make concrete proposals in response to the wish expressed by the pope himself in his opening talk to the Council on September 29th. But the cardinal never spoke. Instead, it was reliably reported that he submitted to the moderators on Wednesday, November 13th, a document signed by over 500 hundred Latin American, Canadian, African and Indian and other bishops, respectfully requesting the pope to indicate his pleasure about the matter of episcopal advisers. "The Fathers of the Council request that the Supreme Pontiff determine the principles and methods of the aid which the Roman Pontiff himself indicated might be added to himself in the way of greater cooperation of the bishops of the entire world. . . . Just as the Supreme Pastor should according to the command of the Lord confirm his brethren, so by the same token his brethren should know that it behooves them to give to the Supreme Pontiff serious and efficacious support . . ." The document cited the pope's own words about the reform of the Curia on September 21st, particularly the need for a greater decentralization, and expressed the willingness of the bishops to aid in this task in whatever way seemed appropriate. Once in the hands of the moderators however—the fact was never officially announced—this was the last the Council would hear of the petition. The perplexity of not a few of the bishops was only slightly relieved by the pope's vague reference, in his closing talk, to the problem of greater episcopal cooperation in the government of the universal Church.

Following Cardinal Confalonieri on Monday, Cardinal Döpfner, one of the Council moderators speaking on the theme under discussion, the subject of auxiliary and coadjutor bishops, kept alive the tension by replying to Cardinal Ottaviani's contention on Friday that the famous vote of October 30th on the five points of the moderators had been merely indicative and was not binding. Said he, obviously speaking for the other moderators: "Certain interventions in the last few days have implied that an enemy—*inimicus homo*—has sown cockle in the field while the father of the family was sleeping. But this vote was decided on by the moderators, who are in charge of directing the course of the Council according to the rules. After reflecting on the matter for fifteen days, they proposed certain questions based on the language and significance of the schema itself. One cannot therefore say that the moderators have acted furtively—*furtim*—in introducing the word "college" into the questions. This word is found in several places in the text of the schema approved by the Theological Commission and presented by it to the Council. This vote was taken to help clarify the matter for the Fathers. It is purely indicative, to be sure, but what has been indicated is also perfectly clear and cannot lightly be ignored."

Regarding one of the more practical matters under debate, namely whether bishops should retire at a certain age, Archbishop Mingo (Monreale, Sicily), now sixty-two himself, said that it was a *"Dura lex sed necessaria"*—a harsh but necessary law—that bishops should retire at the age of sixty-five, as the schema recommended. On the other hand, Bishop De Vita (Lucknow, India) felt that this requirement was completely unacceptable: "It would be just as outrageous as attempting to change the course of the moon."

Bishop Caillot (coadjutor bishop of Evreux, France) insisted that the practice of naming auxiliary bishops as titular bishops ought to cease. "This custom causes amazement. No one, except the Benedictines, knows where these titular sees are. They are usually nothing but ruins." Coadjutors and auxiliaries should have the title of the see where they are assigned. All auxiliaries should share the episcopal ministry together. Bishops who resigned should become *emeriti* of the see they formerly occupied.

Three American cardinals spoke on Tuesday, November 12th, on the touchy subject of episcopal conferences. The issue under discussion was whether such bodies in future should be able to make decisions juridically binding on the members or merely moral or hortatory decisions. Debate on this theme revealed a rather sharp division between the Fathers. Father Gustave Weigel, S.J., summed up the basic difference when he said at a press conference: The Continental mind holds that you do not have any kind of an agreement unless it is written down and spelled out in law. The Anglo-Saxon mind on the other hand believes that the less law there is the better. As much as possible should be left to the moral sphere.

The three American cardinals curiously represented three tendencies among the Fathers. Cardinal McIntyre (Los Angeles)—whose opinions were seconded the following day by Cardinal Spellman—was definitely not in favor of juridically binding decisions and not enthusiastic about episcopal conferences at all. He said: "Episcopal conferences can be accepted if they are on a voluntary basis but are to be deplored if they assume a strictly juridicial character. The authority given to such a body always tends to take on greater expansion. . . . Wanting to give a national conference juridical character could be interpreted as an attack on the Roman Curia and thus as an indirect attack on the infallibility of the pope." This view was extreme. Few thought that such conferences harbored any threat to papal infallibility. When asked later why the cardinal had seen a danger to infallibility in episcopal conferences, Father Weigel delivered himself of one of his famous bon mots: "We must remember that Cardinal McIntyre probably sees much farther than most of us do, if he can be said to see at all."

A more moderate position was represented by Cardinal Meyer (Chicago), who said that rather rather than run the risk of restricting the freedom of action of the individual bishop, binding force should be accorded only to decisions taken by episcopal conferences concerning matters referred to them by the Holy See. He remarked also that the presidents of such conferences should be elected by secret ballot. This view probably represented that of the majority in the Council.

A third position was voiced by Cardinal Ritter of St. Louis, who came out in favor of juridically binding decisions as proposed in the draft text. The bishop of Lódz, Poland, made an interesting suggestion that the presidents of episcopal conferences should be in charge of relations between church and state in given countries, and not papal nuncios or apostolic delegates. Of more significance was the important intervention by Cardinal Suenens on the need for legislation about enforced retirement for bishops. "To expect bishops to agree to resign voluntarily," he said, "is like brandishing a sword in the water." "Old age creates a hiatus between the bishops and the modern world. One has only to look around at sees governed by aged prelates." Sixty-five was a reasonable age for retirement from every point of view.

In spite of the strong, authoritative statement of Cardinal Döpfner on Monday, Bishop Carli (Segni), the gadfly of the ultra-conservatives, had the presumption to say on the floor on Wednesday: "The votes of October 30th are of doubtful validity since they were taken without a previous official 'report' on both sides of the question and contrary to Article 30 No. 2 of the Rules in that the Fathers were not given enough time for deliberation."

Speaking at the American bishops' Press Panel on Wednesday after his speech on the floor in the morning, on the subject of auxiliary bishops, the chubby-faced, youthful-looking auxiliary bishop of Philadelphia, Gerald McDevitt, displayed a delightful sense of humor when explaining his plea that auxiliaries should be regarded as full-fledged bishops and not be hedged about, as they were at present, by all kinds of restrictions. Said he: "When I was made a bishop I was given a three page description of my titular see somewhere in the south of Tunisia. After reading it I lost any desire ever to visit it. I understand that there is nothing there but a couple of goats and palm trees." Apropos of the subject of enforced retirement for bishops, he remarked that he had done his doctoral in canon law on resignation from ecclesiastical office. Every year he noted that his thesis was still among those listed for sale by Catholic University. When asked how he had dared to speak out on the subject of auxiliaries, being one himself, he replied: "I understand that my salary has already been cut."

In a press interview on Wednesday granted to the Divine Word news service, Cardinal Ottaviani showed that he was conceding nothing, publicly at least, and reiterated everything he had said on the council floor the preceding week, supporting what Bishop Carli had said in the morning of the same day. He came out explicitly against "any episcopal consultative body to advise the pope" as an infringement of the "universal and immediate supreme authority of the pope." All the sheep of Christ must agree to "follow the directions of the pastor appointed by him. There must not be any exception to this rule, not even for bishops," he said, rejecting the idea of any meaningful collegiality of the bishops. He repeated that the five propositions of the moderators voted on by the Council on October 30th were merely an indication of the "thought of the Council Fathers" and that they "had not been formulated as a result of any discussion, but were proposed by the moderators without being submitted to the Theological Commission which was competent in the matter, since they treated of matters touching the dogmatic sphere." His commission, Ottaviani said, would have "rendered the language more precise, eliminating certain equivocal and ambivalent expressions, contained especially in the third proposition on the college of bishops, which governs with the pope." He did not elaborate, but the moderators had already pointed out that the five propositions were suggested by the language of the schema on the Church which the Theological Commission itself had presented to the assembly. Ottaviani concluded with the usual statement that "we must have confidence in the Holy Father who will put into practice all the prudent measures capable of aiding him in the government of the Church" while at the same time openly opposing the will of the pope as expressed by the moderators who were directing the Council according to his wishes.

The following day the archbishop of Utrecht, Cardinal Alfrink, replied to Carli and Ottaviani, by observing that what the Council Fathers wanted was not a juridical definition of "collegiality" but only a declaration of Catholic teaching on the universal authority of all bishops together with the pope, in accordance with the words of the official report of the Theological Commission long in the hands of bishops, that "the bishops gathered with the pope in Council or dispersed through the world (but in communion with him) enjoy supreme authority in the Church." The Moderators were urged to see to it that this doctrine was made clear in some kind of a statement.

The debate on Bishops and Dioceses came to an end on Thursday and Friday amid undertones of contrasting opinions about the relative size of bishoprics and overtones of the still raging controversy between Cardinal Ottaviani and the progressive majority. Bishop Sorrentino (Bova, Italy) urged that the numerous small Italian sees, the boundaries of which had not been changed for over a thousand years, should be consolidated in the interests of greater efficiency. The Lateran Treaty with Italy (1929) had envisaged a redrawing of boundaries, but nothing had been done because of local pride and resistance to change. Bishop Massimiliani (Civiltà Castellana, Italy) on the other hand, put in a strong plea for the small see, noting that "because there were many bishops in Italy, Protestantism could not get a foothold." He might have added that excessive fragmentation was partly responsible for the present indifferentism and anticlericalism. The archbishop of Astorga in Spain, González Martin, brought up the interesting subject of the need for a greater distribution of ecclesiastical wealth. Some parishes were rich while others, in the same diocese, were disgracefully poor and the contrast was very disedifying. More attention should be paid to "the social function of property." Before the close of the debate on the schema, archbishop Zoghby (Melkite patriarchal vicar for Egypt) stressed the importance of synodal government in the Eastern Churches, relating this to the proposal for more episcopal conferences in the West. He said that it was hopeless to attempt any appeal to the separated Orthodox Churches unless respect were shown for this basic principle of church government. The trouble was that all real power had been taken away from the Eastern synods by the Roman

Congregation for the Oriental Churches and that this must be restored. Moreover there was too much fear of nationalism as a bad thing. Some nationalism was good and helpful. The rise of numerous nations in recent years "has proved that national sentiments do not prevent peoples from working together in harmony and on a basis of equality."

CARDINAL LERCARO'S 'REPORT'

Taking cognizance of the unrest among the Council Fathers—it was known that a number of prelates in private audiences had expressed their concern about the confusion caused by the airing of differences over the meaning of the October 30th vote on the floor as well as by the slowness of the debates—Pope Paul summoned another extraordinary meeting of the Council summit for Friday afternoon, November 15th, this time deciding to preside over it himself. The meeting was held in the Hall of Congregations on the third floor of the Vatican Palace. The pope arrived alone at 6:15 P.M. and remained until the end some two hours later. He began the proceedings with the usual prayer *Adsumus* with which all conciliar deliberations begin. The main business at hand was a report (*relatio*) on the work of the Council, delivered by Cardinal Lercaro, one of the moderators. Each of the cardinals and bishops present then offered his comments. According to certain *"indiscrezioni"* which leaked out immediately afterward, there was widespread approval of what the cardinal of Bologna had said. Also discussed, these sources said, were the preparations for a solemn public session at the end of the present Session, the organization of the intersession period, and the prospects for the Third Session. The majority of the Fathers present were in favor of holding the latter in the autumn of 1964, but the pope himself was said to be undecided and unwilling to come to a final decision until he had sounded out more of the Council members.

The text of Cardinal Lercaro's 'report' was distributed to the Fathers on December 2, 1963—in a Latin translation although he delivered it in Italian. Large extracts were printed by the Bolognese paper *L'Avvenire d'Italia* (December 2, 1963). However, coming at the time when it did, this important disclosure was virtually ignored by the world press, yet it contained—and was intended to make public—a whole program of action for the intersession period and beyond. In typical Pauline fashion, the program was revealed, indirectly, in the form of a critique. After a brief review of the Second Session in the form of an appraisal of *De Ecclesia* and *De Episcopis,* a few words about the decision to attach the schema on the Virgin Mary to the former instead of having it as a separate document, and a word about the coming schemata to be debated, *De*

Oecumenismo and *De Apostolatu laicorum*—Cardinal Lercaro made an important observation: he said that the procedure adopted in voting the amendments to the Liturgy schema had revealed the value of what the liturgy commission had done as a norm for the future. This had shown in fact "how confusion and serious delays can occur if a commission—even though there may be valid reasons for so doing—offers a single text on doubtful and controversial matters without any alternative, thus passing judgment itself on important amendments proposed by the Fathers. Therefore the commissions from now on should not presume to resolve *on their own authority* the requests and demands of certain episcopal conferences, but should 'order and evaluate the amendments,' as the Regulations declare, so that the general congregation of the Council may be able to compare, read and decide for itself among the amendments proposed."

He then took up a number of practical points concerned with the debates on the floor, which in the general opinion had seemed to drag on excessively. Many petitions had been received by the moderators to do something about this situation. In general what they had done was to apply the existing rules more rigorously without introducing any essential change and by using their authority more directly. "It was not considered appropriate to alter the Rules at this stage." Most of the bishops approved of the way the moderators had handled the situation. He then put his finger on one of the crucial points. "An acceleration of the work of the Council depends more on quickening the rhythm at which the commissions work, some of which have too many competences and tasks. Acceleration depends also on the commissions' paying more heed to and giving a readier response to the mind of the general congregation, in accordance with their subordinate nature. . . ." Driving home the validity of the five propositions, he said that further acceleration would be achieved if we followed the procedure adopted . . . namely, by having "the moderators pick out certain important questions in each discussion summarizing the gist of the debate and intended to serve as a guide for the commissions, and propose these questions to the assembly for a vote."

Cardinal Lercaro concluded with a number of general observations. The course of the debates had shown that the Fathers were manifesting an increasing sense of catholicity of thought; the whole episcopate was clearly behind the pope, and there was no trace today of any of the separatist movements typical of the past. The present assembly "strongly and sincerely" (*fortiter et sincere*) adhered to what Vatican Council I had decided about the papal primacy and infallibility. The mind of the Church was turned away from narrow factional rivalries toward the great missionary horizon before it, the cardinal concluded. One could say about these remarks of his what was said about Cardinal Bea and Pope John during the First Session: though the voice and words were those of Cardinal Lercaro, the thoughts were clearly those of Pope Paul VI.

THE DEBATE ON ECUMENISM

The last two full weeks of the Second Session, from November 18th to December 2nd, were devoted to a discussion of the schema on Ecumenism, spelling out the Catholic attitude toward the worldwide movement known as "ecumenism" which aimed at the restoration of Christian unity. The document had been prepared by Cardinal Bea's Secretariat for Promoting Christian Unity, technically or theoretically by a mixed commission consisting of representatives of the Secretariat, the Commission for the Oriental Churches, and the Theological Commission, since they were the three bodies sponsoring similar drafts presented, or intended for discussion, at the First Session which the Council had ordered to be combined into one document. Actually, only the draft prepared by the Oriental Churches reached the floor in 1962 and was debated. The revised schema now up for discussion consisted of five chapters.

The debate opened on Monday, November 18th, with Cardinal Agagianian in the chair as moderator. First there was an official presentation of the schema as a whole by Cardinal Cicognani, in the name of the mixed commission, inasmuch as he had been president of the only commission (Oriental Churches) whose draft had already been discussed by the Fathers. His speech was followed by a more detailed exposition of the contents of the new schema by Archbishop Martin (Rouen), a member of the Secretariat, who spoke on Chapters I–III. Archbishop Martin's remarks in appreciation of the work of Cardinal Bea and his Secretariat were warmly applauded by the Council. The following day there was a change of plan. Instead of proceeding with the debate on the first part of the schema, in accordance with customary procedure, it was announced that Cardinal Bea would introduce Chapter IV and Bishop de Smedt Chapter V, at once. This news was greeted with tremendous enthusiasm and applause. In the opinion of some observers there had been nothing quite like the spontaneous response on this occasion. Nothing the Council had discussed so far generated so much warmth of feeling. This was interpreted both as a tribute to the speakers personally (Cardinal Bea in particular for the tireless activity he had displayed during recent years in promoting the cause of unity) and as a general expression of approval for the ideas contained in the document.

A communiqué on the text, released to the press, received widespread approval among Jewish communities throughout the world on the whole.

Speaking on the subject of religious liberty, Bishop de Smedt made a historic statement:

Our schema had already been prepared and had been studied by the Central Commission and by the Commission for Coordination when Pope John, on April 11th of this year, published his last encyclical *Pacem in Terris*. We believe that our text is in complete conformity with his perlucid doctrine, which was received within the Church and outside of the Church with unprecedented praise.

We now submit this text for your consideration. In our historical survey of doctrine, we have shown that, in pontifical documents, along with continuity, we must look for a progressive spelling out of doctrine. It is evident that certain quotations from the popes, because of a difference of words, can be put in opposition to our schema. But I beseech you, venerable Fathers, not to force the text to speak outside of its historical and doctrinal context, not, in other words, to make the fish swim out of water.

Let our document be studied as it stands. It is not a dogmatic treatise, but a pastoral decree directed to men of our time. The whole world is waiting for this decree. The voice of the Church on religious liberty is being waited for in universities, in national and international organizations, in Christian and non-Christian communities, in the papers, and in public opinion—and it is being waited for with urgent expectancy.

We hope that it will be possible to complete the discussion and the approbation of this very brief, but very important, decree before the end of this second session. How fruitful our work would appear to the world if the conciliar Fathers, with the voice of Peter's successor, could announce this liberating doctrine on religious liberty!

Venerable Fathers, we will add our labors to yours. Our Secretariat will study your emendations most attentively and also with the utmost speed. We will work day and night. But our hope is in the Lord. May Jesus Christ assist all of us with His grace. If at the end of this session He asks of us: "Young men, do you have any fish?" seeing the faith and good will of this Council, He might say to their successors what He once said to the apostles: "Cast the net to the right of the boat: and you will find" (Jn. 21:6).

Just as the debate on Bishops had been dominated by its "crisis" (the Frings-Ottaviani exchange and the controversy over the validity of the October 30th vote), so the discussion of Ecumenism came to be pervaded by the nagging uncertainty about the fate of Chapters IV and V at the Second Session. The primary concern was over the last chapter. A large majority, including most of the Americans whose interest in toleration was based in good part on the traditional American stand on separation of Church and state, were eager to have a test-vote on the chapter in principle. The minority, on the other hand, were fearful about the implications of debate on this issue, distrustful of the language employed in the text, and opposed to making any concessions to liberty which, they claimed, could be distorted by the communists and used to undermine the authority of the Church in certain traditionally Catholic areas.

In opening the debate on November 18th, Cardinal Tappouni sounded a warning note that would be repeated by almost all the Eastern prelates. After objecting to the treatment of the Orthodox and Protestants in the same chapter "because the relationship of the two to the Catholic Church is radically different," he said that "to treat of Judaism and religious liberty in this schema was out of place and most inopportune." Ecumenism was concerned with the unity of Christians. It was inappropriate for the Council to take up the matter of relations with non-Christians. The latter should be mentioned only "by accident" and if so, there should be no discrimination by showing more attention to one group than to another. The good intentions of the Fathers would be misunderstood in the Arab press.

Cardinal Ruffini observed that the term "ecumenism" really had quite a different meaning from the one given to it in the text. As employed here it was out of harmony with the authentic meaning of "ecumenical" used with reference to a Council. The word normally meant "universal," but with reference to the schema it had a special meaning pertaining to the apostolate for unity. The term was introduced into theology by Protestants and was used with reference to their conferences intended to promote unity. The term should be clarified so as not to lead to dangerous ambiguities. It would be better to give a simple description of the movement under discussion, referring to it as "The movement called Ecumenism."—The text should speak more specifically about the special bonds uniting us with our separated brethren in the Eastern Churches, who were closer to us than the various Reformed "sects": they had the hierarchy, the seven sacraments, a true eucharistic worship, and devotion to the Virgin Mary. While, apart from baptism and—at least for some—Scripture, there were no other ties with the Protestants. If there was to be discussion of the Jews, who were here given what we might call honorable mention, then the text should also take up those other religions whose members were often less hostile to the Church than the Jews and more open to "conversion" than the Protestants, as many missionaries could testify. And likewise if ecumenism was to be extended to the Jews, "why should there not be mention also of those millions of baptized Christians who follow marxism and daily contribute to the spread of atheism?" Lastly the schema provided no concrete directives for establishing a true and effective dialogue with our separated brethren. "Contacts with the separated brethren should be maintained only by those Catholics who lead a holy life, devote themselves to continual prayer, have a sound knowledge of theology, and have the approval of ecclesiastical authority."

Speaking in the name of "some" American bishops, Cardinal Ritter (St. Louis) declared that the schema was the answer to the need felt for an *aggiornamento* of the Church. The presentation of this text marked the end of the Counter-Reformation, and obliged us to make a thorough examination of conscience. Likewise it put us under obligation to hasten the desirable day of unity by fervent prayer, example and study. "We are happy to hear that Chapter V will deal with religious liberty," he said. Without a declaration of this kind by the Council there could be no mutual discussion and the door would remain closed to any real dialogue with those outside the Church. Such a declaration should not be based on motives of expediency. It should proceed from solid theological principles, namely, 1) the absolute freedom of the act of faith; 2) the inviolability of human conscience; and 3) the incompetence of any civil government to interpret the Gospel of Christ, with consequent independence of the Church from civil authority in the accomplishment of its mission.—In the text greater attention should be paid to the celebration of the eucharist as a symbol of unity and to the importance of the liturgy generally. There should also be a clearer affirmation of the validity of the sacraments and orders of the Eastern Churches. The text should be purged of any expressions offensive to Protestants. There was no valid reason for denying the use of the term "Church" to the religious groups which originated after the 16th century. Like any other living movement, ecumenism was subject to dangers. Excessive intellectualism could make it sterile and it could likewise easily degenerate into indifferentism. This was why we needed a *vademecum* or practical guide which would provide necessary and safe directions.

The cardinal archbishop of Caracas felt that the schema wisely laid stress on the essential foundation of ecumenism, which consisted in interior renewal and holiness of life. Only then would the Church shine and seem attractive to those to whom it might appeal. The splendor of the Church was that of truth, not only of revealed truth, but also of historical truth. It was therefore necessary to recognize, frankly, the responsibility of Catholics for divisions in the Church. It would be desirable if in the spirit of Pope Paul VI's opening speech, the Council would make a declaration acknowledging the faults of Catholics with respect to unity, asking pardon of the separated brethren, and would affirm at the same time that the Catholic Church did not feel the least resentment for whatever it may have had to suffer itself in turn.

The two Spanish cardinals, de Arriba y Castro and Bueno y Monreal, found the schema satisfactory with reservations. *"Placet iuxta modum,"* said the latter. It was clear that both were basically hostile to the modern movement of ecumenism, and skeptical as well as fearful of its possible effects on their Church. Their remarks revealed also that they had not studied the matter very deeply and still regarded as valid the reservations which had caused the Holy See to refuse all cooperation in the twenties and thirties. The former, for example, said that a conciliar decree urging the laity to take part in any dialogue was dangerous and inconsistent with present laws of the Church which forbade the publication or reading of books favoring heresy. He was particularly exercised by the thought that the "less educated faithful" would not be able to make a good showing if they participated in any such conversation. As far as he was concerned, ecumenism meant simply a free rein for "proselytism." The implication was, of course, that while it was all right for the Church to engage in proselytism, the same right could not be claimed by other groups. To make the point clear beyond any doubt, he stated flatly: "It should not be forgotten that only the Catholic Church has the right and duty to evangelize." The schema should be dropped. Cardinal Bueno y Monreal thought that the wording of the text should be more cautious, lest it appear to sanction a kind of "Pan-Christianity" or religious syncretism with all its dangers of indifferentism. Too much praise of things which the Catholic Church shared in common with other groups could obscure the distinctions.

The archbishop of Tokyo, Cardinal Tatsuo Doi, welcomed the schema, but was of the opinion that the missionary aspects of ecumenism required that more attention be paid to those who were non-Christians. The fact should be brought out more clearly that the Church respected truth wherever it was found, among non-Christian religions as well.

Stephanos I Sidarouss, the Coptic patriarch of Alexandria, Egypt, was particularly anxious that the schema avoid giving the impression that it favored any "false irenic approach to unity" by stressing more clearly the doctrinal differences which separated the Catholic Church from others, for example the doctrine of the papal primacy. He found the definition of ecumenism in Paragraph 9 completely unsatisfactory. And he was for dropping all mention of the Jews. If the Council insisted on taking up this touchy subject, "we shall have to face the music" when we, meaning the representatives of Arab Christianity, go home.

The most notable speech of the first day was that by Patriarch Maximos IV Saigh, and all eyes were on him as he rose to state his views. The schema deserved more than mere assent: it was the first to combine doctrinal profundity with a pastoral orientation and it served as an excellent basis for discussion. Among its positive features: it left aside all sterile polemics and false proselytism; it marked the beginning of a dialogue in truth and unity; it breathed the theology of the Church which was traditional in the East. Among its negative aspects, however, must be mentioned, above all, Chapter IV which was completely out of place. Ecumenism was devoted to the reunion of Christians, that is, was a family problem, and time should not be wasted in speaking of non-Christians, unless we were to run the risk of offending the separated brethren. "If we are to discuss the Jews," he said, "then we should likewise take up the question of Moslems, among whom we must live in a minority." This would give us a different viewpoint on the whole problem, because, as an Arab proverb had it, 'The man receiving blows has a different outlook from the man who only counts them.' We should mobilize all our efforts to hasten the advent of perfect unity for the glory of the Most Blessed Trinity and the welfare of the human race. Finally, he hoped that the wish of the recent Panorthodox Conference of Rhodes (September 1963) could be realized: that a permanent dialogue be established between Catholicism and Orthodoxy.

In an important intervention on November 19th, Cardinal Léger of Canada declared: "The present hope for and movement toward unity are not passing impulses, but are inspired by the Gospel and the Holy Spirit. We are fearful when we realize what a burden of history we must overcome. But we must face the task of dialogue with positive and truly Catholic prudence, which not only safeguards but tends toward union." He recalled the words of Pope Paul VI who said recently: "One purpose of the Council is to open every possible way to the unity of Christians." The present schema reflected this kind of prudence and merited approval, in fact it was sorely needed by the bishops as an expression of principle on the local level. The cardinal of Vienna made an important observation about the nature of ecumenism which had perplexed many. "We should avoid any impression that Catholic ecumenism is a closed and perfect system. We are only at the beginning. The dialogue, together with prayer and the Holy Spirit, may lead us to new aspects and a more profound understanding of ecumenism." This remark was offered with special reference to those critics who kept insisting that the idea of ecumenism was "vague" and therefore dangerous. According to the American Jesuit, Father Weigel, the beauty about the ecumenical movement was that it remained something fuzzy and ill-defined; it was desirable to keep it that way and not allow it to become petrified if further progress was to be made.

Bishop Elchinger (coadjutor of Strasbourg, France) described the schema as a "grace" and a "blessing" of God. Its existence was due to the work of many leaders like Cardinal Mercier and theologians like Père Lagrange, who had much to suffer in their day because of the lack of sympathy for their ideas. If progress was to be made, we must recognize frankly the faults of the Church. While the Church was holy, God had entrusted his gifts to sinful men, to vessels of clay. It was important to recognize, for example, that the Reformers did not wish to destroy the unity of the Church. They were anxious to declare certain truths which they believed had become obscured. Secondly, it was wrong to reject as totally erroneous certain assertions which contain a part of the truth. Catholic rejections of Protestantism have been too sweeping and indiscriminate. Thirdly, there was too much of a tendency to consider revelation as something passive, whereas it was something that must always be probed and investigated. It was not sufficient to remain content with Catholic truth. "We must continue to seek the truth which we shall never possess in its entirety." This amounted to saying that the definitions of the faith were always capable of being perfected. Fourthly, we had often made the mistake of confounding unity with uniformity.

For the Armenian Patriarch Pierre XVI Batanian, the schema did not emphasize sufficiently what might be called the "authoritarian" aspects of charity. Charity demanded that truth be in no way compromised. But he found that certain passages seemed to "tone down" a frank statement of Catholic truth on a number of points. For example, the phrase *regiminis fraterna concordia* in paragraph 1 could be understood as referring to a union of many "equal" governments in the Church not under one head, but as arising from human consent and the love of harmony. He would prefer some such expression as *in unitate magisterii et regiminis*. He had often heard the Orthodox say: "You fortunate Catholics. In disputes you have a supreme authority by which you can say *Roma locuta est, causa finita est*." No purpose was served by hiding or toning down the existence of a supreme authority in the Catholic Church. He agreed with his other Eastern colleagues that the Chapter on the Jews should not be included in the schema. The Latin patriarch of Jerusalem, Alberto Gori, also felt strongly that the Chapter on the Jews should be omitted. It was unwise to single out one non-Christian group without mentioning the others.

After this mixed bag of reactions on the first two days of debate, there was some concern in progressive circles that the schema was not going over very well. While a majority of the Council was clearly in its favor, the tenor of the remarks on the floor, amply reported in the world press, could give the impression that things were worse than they really were. Fear that the minority (who were unfortunately virtually in control of the day-to-day operations of the Council) might exploit the situation in an attempt to kill the whole schema on the basis of frequently expressed criticisms of various parts, no doubt prompted the pope and the moderators to agree to a separate debate on Chapters I-III with a deliberately vague promise that the last two chapters would be taken up "later." The first chapters, after all, dealt with the crux of the issue of ecumenism, and attempted to provide the "guide" which all were looking for. The issues of the Jews and religious liberty, while important in themselves, were subsidiary so far as the main argument of Chapters I-III was concerned and could, conceivably, be taken up later in another connection. But the vital question left hanging in mid-air all through these days was, Would this assurance be given? The Jewish question was frankly judged to be of less importance in the mind of most of the Fathers. But the impression was widespread that unless the Church came out strongly in favor of some kind of guarantee of religious liberty and tolerance, the absence of any statement on this subject would make a mockery of whatever the Council chose to declare with regard to ecumenism.

A minor incident at this time served to accentuate the determination of the Curial minority not to be beaten down or overridden. At the end of his remarks on Wednesday, November 20th to the effect that the term "ecumenism" was unacceptable as implying a confusion with "interconfessionalism" and that the text seemed to play down the Roman primacy in favor of a collegial form of church government, Cardinal Bacci, chief Latinist of the Curia, stated that when on October 30th last he had attempted to say that the expression *ius primatiale* in one of the famous Five Propositions was inaccurate and should be replaced by *ius primatus,* he was denied permission to speak by the then moderator. He asked for permission on Wednesday to state this publicly. Later in the meeting that day the moderator Cardinal Agagianian explained that he had been refused permission on October 30th because the moderators considered the expression *ius primatiale* sufficiently clear. Apparently Curia cardinals must not be thwarted in their undeclared right to be heard, no matter how trivial their grammatical quibbling.

The archbishop of Chicago, Cardinal Meyer, voicing the opinion of many American bishops, put his stamp of approval on the schema as a whole. He said that he was particularly pleased that Chapters IV and V formed a part of it, although he recognized that there were differences of opinion on this score. He urged that the whole schema, including these chapters be accepted as a basis for discussion.

Archbishop Heenan of Westminster, speaking for the bishops of England and Wales, accepted the schema "joyfully." He said: "Some consider Catholics in England indifferent to the ecumenical movement; indeed, some of our separated brethren have had to go abroad to engage in dialogue. . . . We do not wish to restrict freedom to attend international ecumenical gatherings. But the Council should recommend that the dialogue be carried on normally within the region of those taking part in it." His speech was clearly a notification that, whatever the sins of the past, in the future the British Catholic hierarchy intended to foster dialogue and the ecumenical movement. "We declare that we are prepared to do anything outside of denying the faith, to obtain the union of Christians. We desire fuller and more frequent dialogues with all Christian denominations." It will be remembered in this connection that it was the opposition of the Catholic hierarchy in England which compelled

Lord Halifax to go over to Belgium to conduct the Malines Conversations with Cardinal Mercier, in the 1920's.

The question of greater latitude in the matter of participation by Catholics in the religious services of non-Catholics, and the admission of the latter to full participation in Catholic services, was raised by Archbishop Weber of Strasbourg. The apostolic prefect of Dahomey, Chopard-Lallier, said that it was difficult for the faithful in Africa to understand why Western missionaries were so careful about avoiding worship with each other.

THE COMMISSIONS ENLARGED

On November 21st two important events took place. It was announced that the Holy Father had decided to increase the membership in the various conciliar commissions with a view to expediting the work of the Council. Each commission was to be increased from 25 to 30 members, except for the Commission for the Oriental Churches and the Secretariat for Unity which had 27 and 18 members, respectively. In both cases the membership would be brought up to 30. Of the 5 new members to be added to all the commissions but these, 4 would be elected by the Council, and 1 would be appointed by the pope. In order to prepare lists of candidates, the presidents of Episcopal Conferences were requested by Archbishop Felici to convoke meetings and decide on the names they wished to vote for. The Council Fathers could vote for any names, but it would be helpful to have joint lists. The names were to be presented by Monday and the voting would take place a week hence (November 28th). The Holy Father, it was announced, would then allow the commissions to elect a second (or additional) vice president and secretary.

The first impression of this announcement was one of pessimism among Council observers. It was felt that by leaving the Curial cardinals in charge of the commissions, the pope would undo whatever good might come out of the elections. It "fell short," in other words, of expectations. However when the results of the voting were announced in record time on November 29th, there was at least a glimmer of hope. Some 59 episcopal conferences had accomplished the feat of agreeing on an "international list" of candidates and practically all of them were elected. Another significant detail: almost all the new members were from Europe, America and Asia, and could be described as progressives. The expectation was, as Father Häring pointed out at a Press Panel meeting, that the new forward-looking vice presidents, with a majority of members behind them, would be able to turn the tide against the conservative leadership. However there were many who were keeping their fingers crossed as to whether the pope's apparent plan to circumvent the conservatives without forcing any resignations would really work.

The same day (November 21st), after further discussion of the Ecumenism schema, the moderators suddenly announced that the Council would proceed to an immediate vote on the acceptance of Chapters I-III of Ecumenism as a basis for discussion. The Secretary General added that the voting on Chapters IV and V would take place *proximis diebus*—in a few days. The voting revealed an overwhelming majority in favor of accepting the text for discussion: 1996 favorable to 86 negative, and was considered a signal victory for the Secretariat for Unity, on the surface at least.

In the speeches that day before the later announcement, praise for the schema continued to alternate with discordant notes calling into question the validity of the notion of ecumenism as such.

After the announcement of a closure, the debate continued on Chapter I of the schema, concerning "The Principles of Catholic Ecumenism."

The harshness of the integralist point of view was brought out clearly by Bishop Carli who said that the schema should state *all* the principles of ecumenism, not just a few. Among the doctrinal principles which should be uncompromisingly spelled out in Chapter I, without any attempt at equivocation, were the "uniqueness of the Roman Catholic Church" which by objective criteria was distinguished from other Churches; the axiom that "outside the Church there is no salvation"; and the grave obligation on everybody to join the Catholic Church as soon as he discovered that it was the "true Church." While the separated communities possessed some of the means of sanctification—which he called the "spoils from Mother Church"—it was these gifts and not the Churches themselves which the Holy Spirit used. And the text should be corrected to remove the impression that the Spirit sanctioned separation and abandoned His unique Spouse. The first paragraph, by stating that "the Church is founded on the apostles and prophets" implied that "the notion of the papal primacy is being obscured!" The *litigiosa vox* of "collegiality" should be omitted because it was not yet proved. It should be stated that the apostles were the "auxiliaries" of Peter, as Vatican Council I declared. The bishop preferred to ignore not only what the moderators themselves had repeatedly asserted, but, more to the point, what the pope himself had just stated in his general audience the day before. Although Pope Paul did not use the word "collegiality," his words left one in no doubt as to what he meant: ". . . an organization, a hierarchy, instituted by Christ Himself, in which the first place is occupied by the apostles, that is, the bishops, and at their head Peter, that is, the pope."

A number of speakers on November 22nd repeated the contention that it was unbalanced for the schema to speak of Jews without dealing with other non-Christian bodies, but that if this was to be attempted a whole new approach would be needed. The schema as it stood was inadequate in this respect.

Bishop Huyghe (France) roundly condemned what he called an erroneous notion of ecumenism put forth by some Catholics, who equated it with "return" pure and simple to the Catholic Church in the sense of a complete "surrender" to its claims. The good lives of Catholics were the best contribution of Catholics to ecumenism, as the schema stated. There was too much of a tendency to sit back and wait for the return of others without making any changes in Catholic procedures or viewpoints. The schema was correct in speaking of reunion as involving an "approach" (*aditus*) or "access" of the others, and not of their "return." The first condition for the success of all ecumenical work was the sincere conversion of *all* Christians, Catholics as well as others. The second condition was common action, for which the schema was to be a kind of directory, suggesting concrete ways.

Archbishop Jaeger (Paderborn, Germany) congratulated the authors of the schema for using "concrete language instead of scholastic definitions." The schema presupposed what had been said in the debate on the Church and at Vatican Council I on the papal primacy, therefore it was not necessary for it to go over all this ground again. Moreover, the schema was not a dogmatic or canonical treatise, and so it would be inappropriate for it to go into these matters. He wanted the eucharist, particularly, to be mentioned as a sign of unity along with the bonds of unity listed in paragraph 1, and for the Holy Spirit to be mentioned as the ultimate, uncreated principle of the Church's unity. Rather than say that our separated Eastern brethren had been "cut off" from the unity of the Catholic Church, Bishop Flusin (France) preferred the text to say that their separation had "broken" or "weakened" the bond of unity. And he wanted a greater distinction between individuals who were personally responsible for schism or heresy and those who were born into groups thus cut off from the Church long ago.

Friday's debate was brought to a conclusion by the intervention of the Chinese Bishop Chang-Tso-huan, who directed the attention of the Fathers once again to the wider aspects of the problem. "As an example for our zeal we can take the ancient Chinese who preached ecumenism many centuries before Confucianism."

THE DEATH OF PRESIDENT KENNEDY

To say that a hushed silence fell over normally bustling Rome when the news broke that President Kennedy had been assassinated (about 7 P.M.

246

Rome time) would be doing less than justice to the feeling of gloom and shock which could have been cut with a knife. Flags were immediately flown at halfmast, including the yellow and white banner of the Holy See to be seen on various buildings throughout the city. Italians of all classes were aware of their loss and showed it. In addition to the sentiments which all felt so profoundly, which Pope Paul expressed from his window on Sunday when he blessed the crowds in St. Peter's Square, his telegrams to Mrs. Jacqueline Kennedy, President Johnson, the President's parents and Cardinal Cushing were all given prominent display in the press. Rome too had its part in mourning the tragic death. Special commemorative services were held at the Episcopal Church of St. Paul on the Via Nazionale and at the Jewish Synagogue. The chief service was a solemn requiem mass celebrated on Monday by Cardinal Spellman, assisted by prelates from the American College, in the cathedral of Rome, San Giovanni in Laterano, and attended by President Segni of Italy and other high dignitaries of the government and diplomatic corps as well as most of the American colony in Rome. Among the 36 cardinals attending were Cardinals Bea, Caggiano, Suenens, Agagianian, Tappouni, Meyer, Ruffini, Landázuri Ricketts, Pizzardo, Ciriaci, McIntyre, Ritter, Lercaro, and Wyszynski. Also present were the non-Catholic observer-delegates to the Council. By special permission of the pope, the mass was celebrated at the papal altar and the proceedings were televised. Representatives of the American armed forces stood guard at the four corners of the catafalque along with four Italian carabinieri all in parade uniform, while four cuirassiers of the presidential guard stood on each side of the transept. The mass over, Cardinal Spellman approached the catafalque and gave the absolution, while all rose and the choir intoned the anthem *Libera me Domine*. The cardinal pronounced the required formula first in Latin, then in English. Afterward he delivered a few brief remarks praising the deceased President, referring to him as "that marvelous and exemplary President" and remarking on the "wave of love for our dear country" which he had evoked. "We have suffered a great loss. May God have mercy on his soul."

All day Sunday and Monday throngs of people kept filing into the American Embassy on Via Veneto to pay their respects and sign the registers, twenty-one of which had to be pressed into service, including the one normally reserved for the diplomatic corps. Beside his signature Archpriest Vitaly Borovoy, the Russian Orthodox observer-delegate from Moscow wrote: "We have prayed for the peaceful repose of the soul of this great Christian who has sacrificed his life for a great truth: the equality of all races and the brotherhood of all peoples under God. May God receive his soul in peace and may his memory endure forever."

There were also numerous spontaneous sentiments, like the following: "To the beloved, great Kennedy." "To Kennedy, missionary of brotherhood among men of peace and freedom." Beneath one expression of harsh feeling toward the assassin, a nun wrote, "Perhaps we should pray for the souls of both men."

Of the many epitaphs on President Kennedy's death published all over the world, one of the most memorable was written by Hannah Arendt in the special Kennedy number of *The New York Review of Books*. "There is a curious and infinitely sad resemblance between the death of the two greatest men we have lost during this year—the one very old, the other in the prime of life. Both the late Pope and the late President died much too soon in view of the work they initiated and left unfinished. The whole world changed and darkened when their voices fell silent. And yet the world will never be as it was before they spoke and acted in it."

THE VOTE ON COMMUNICATIONS MEDIA

On Monday November 25th, the Council was asked to vote on the revised final text of the schema on Communications Media, debated at the First Session. If approved, the text was to be promulgated by the pope as a conciliar decree on December 4th, at the closing ceremony. The rather large number of Iuxta modum votes on this occasion—favorable but with conditions—503 to 1598 in favor (with 1 invalid vote) indicated that a rather large number of the Fathers still had reservations and were not satisfied with the final version. The belief was widespread that the adverse vote would have been even larger, except for the fact that many bishops had not even troubled to read the text much less give it serious consideration. The same had been true of the debate on the floor in 1962. Many thought that the subject merited some attention but was hardly worth the time of an Ecumenical Council. Some felt that it was so unworthy and compromising as to be voted down. To give expression to their view, a mimeographed sheet containing signatures by 24 bishops and 1 head of a religious order, mostly Continental prelates, was distributed to the Fathers as they entered the basilica on Monday to cast their votes. Bishop Reuss (auxiliary of Mainz) was behind the move. As he was entering the basilica, the Secretary General Archbishop Felici discovered what was being done and tried to seize the papers from the priests who were distributing them. Bishop Reuss protested and declared that he was entirely within his rights. Failing to put a stop to the distribution, Archbishop Felici summoned the papal gendarmes and then rushed, in anger, into the basilica and lodged a complaint with Cardinal Tisserant, dean of the

Sacred College and president of the board of Council presidents. In the course of the debate that morning, Cardinal Tisserant denounced the distribution of the sheets as a tactic "unworthy" of the Council. Later on he took the microphone again to state that one of the bishops—whom he did not name—claimed that he had not signed the document. This precipitate action on the part of Cardinal Tisserant caused considerable murmuring among a large number of bishops, who asked themselves why nothing similar had been said during the voting on the Marian schema when Father Balič's pamphlet had been surreptitiously distributed among the Fathers, or when Archbishop Dino Staffa's statement against the collegiality of the bishops had been passed out in the council hall. Later a number of bishops wrote to Cardinal Tisserant protesting his action. Cardinal Tisserant's contention that the schema had already been approved by a two-thirds majority in a preliminary vote as the reason why the request to vote Non placet was irregular, was irrevelant. To some the whole incident was but another sign that the minority were prepared to infringe the Council's freedom of action when it suited their purposes.

Criticism of the final version of the Communications Decree was summed up in a statement issued on November 16th by three American newsmen, John Cogley of *Commonweal*, Robert Kaiser of *Time*, and Michael Novak, correspondent for the Kansas City *Catholic Reporter*, the Boston *Pilot* and other papers. The statement was also countersigned under the words "This statement is worthy of consideration" by four notable theologians: Father John Courtney Murray, S.J., Father Jean Daniélou, S.J., Father Jorge Mejia, S.J., and Father Bernard Häring, C.SS.R. It claimed that the proposed decree was "not an *aggiornamento*, bit a step backward," and said that where the document was "not vague and banal, it reflects a hopelessly abstract view of the relationship of the Church and modern culture. It deals with a press that exists only in textbooks and is unrecognizable to us." They asserted that "it may one day be cited as a classic example of how the Second Vatican Council failed to come to grips with the world around it."

One theory advanced for the pope's action in allowing it to go through was that he decided it would be a good way to get rid of the measure and remove it from the Council's agenda, allowing events and experience to determine whether it should be vigorously applied or not. Since there was no question of its being regarded as infallible—this was expressly made clear on the Council floor—the communications document became, as Father Gustave Weigel, S.J. described it, the "official and authentic doctrine of the Church," it did not or would not become the "irreformable and once-for-all-time doctrine of the Church." The prediction was that it would be enforced loosely, if at all.

THE MYSTERY OF CHAPTERS IV AND V OF ECUMENISM

After the voting, the debate resumed on Chapter I of Ecumenism. Cardinal Léger felt that the doctrine of unity expressed in the schema could be clarified somewhat more. Many Catholics as well as non-Catholics thought that the Church favored an excessively monolithic unity, he said. There had been many signs in recent centuries that this was indeed the case, for example, the insistence on a uniform liturgical worship, or a uniform discipline, and a consequent neglect of legitimate freedom. Variety was still compatible with perfect obedience to the vicar of Christ.

Cardinal Ritter (St. Louis) also called for greater precision in dealing with the concept of unity. The pastoral, doctrinal, and ecumenical aspects of unity should be brought out. Instead of the description of unity in paragraph 1, he suggested that the text should say that unity was not desired for itself but rather because it represented Christ Himself, the achievement of His glory through a recapitulation of all things in Him. If this were done, it would then appear that the Church was a long way from perfection in unity and holiness. From such unity, as the end and basic principle of ecumenism, flowed the need for renewal and for charity toward our separated brothers. In closing, he thanked the Fathers for their expressions of condolence on the occasion of President Kennedy's assassination.

The president of the Secretariat for Promoting Christian Unity which had prepared the schema, Cardinal Bea, rose to say that doubts about the appropriateness of the title as well as the use of the word "ecumenism" would be taken into account. There had been much talk in recent days about the "dangers" of ecumenism. He agreed that there could be such if unity was treated by men who were inspired by goodwill but were not cautious and not acting under the supervision of episcopal authority. The point of the present schema was to provide directives for those who would be authorized to deal with these questions. Directives might come from Rome, but action had to be taken on a local level. The Holy Office instruction 1949 had provided that those who took part in these matters must be well-versed and follow the Church's norms. It would be helpful if regional secretariats could be set up to promote unity in collaboration with the Secretariat in Rome. No false irenicism would result if the movement was conducted along the proper lines. With regard to the language of the schema, he pointed out that it was addressed primarily to Catholics and it was therefore not necessary to spell out everything.

Catholics could be presumed to know their own doctrine. What was necessary was to spell out only so much as was needed. Too often Catholics were ignorant of the riches to be found in the traditions of the separated brethren. Yet popes from Leo XIII to Paul VI had praised the gifts of the Holy Spirit which they possessed. To criticize the schema for acknowledging these gifts, was to criticize the popes. Common prayer *was* permitted by the Holy Office instruction of 1949, he maintained, but of course the faithful must be instructed in what they were doing.

The prospects for conversions might be reduced if the schema were acted on, according to the master general of the Dominican Order, Father Fernandez, but the work of individual conversion and the goal of ecumenism were really two different aspects of the one apostolate of the Church. They were complementary, not incompatible. This difference should be brought out in the text.

While it was true that all elements of divine revelation were important, it was not true that all were equally important. There was a hierarchy of values among revealed mysteries and this must be taken into consideration in evaluating union and divisions. "All dogmas are to be retained, but they are not all of equal importance." Some were concerned with our final end; others with the means toward that end, e.g. the sacraments, the hierarchy, apostolic succession, etc. The schema should mention this important point and stress that we already had unity with the separated brethren in many truths belonging to the first category. Archbishop Pangrazio, who voiced these views, was head of the Italian section of the Council Press Office.

"Our separated brethren have a right to know what kind of a unity we are inviting them to," said Bishop Canesti, auxiliary vicar of Rome. He thought that the schema was vague on this point. While the text said that the separated Churches had a meaning in the mystery of salvation, it should be made clear that this was due to the fact that they retained some of the elements from their pre-Reformation days, but not precisely as separated Churches.

Toward the close of the discussion on Monday, Chapter II entitled "The practical means of pursuing ecumenism" was taken up.

The Spanish Cardinal Bueno y Monreal harped again on what he had said earlier about the dangers of "proselytism." Scandal and confusion were caused by preaching the Gospel differently. Proselytism must not be permitted in those areas, like Spain, where the Gospel had been preached for centuries. Nothing was worse for ecumenism, he maintained, than proselytism among already Christian communities. The schema should bring this point out.

Common prayer was one of the most important elements in helping to achieve the goals of ecumenism and its effects should not be underestimated. We should join with the separated brethren in praying for what Christ prayed and for nothing less than what he prayed, namely visible unity, according to Bishop Darmancier.

A slight dent in the minority position seemed to be registered by the speech of the Italian Archbishop Margiotta (Brindisi), who came out in favor of removing the penalty of excommunication for those who read books on ecumenical matters by non-Catholics. But he stood foursquare in favor of retaining the Index of Forbidden Books as such.

The lack of definite concrete "directives" in the schema was regretted by Bishop Martin (vicar apostolic of New Caledonia) with respect to ways in which the "dialogue" could be carried on. In 1962 Bishop de Smedt had presented norms which he hoped might have been incorporated. "Our separated brethren expect the Roman Church to enter a true dialogue in which all participants come together on an equal footing and all Churches allow discussion of their imperfections and the correction of them." He noted that the Faith and Order meeting of the World Council of Churches in 1963 at Montreal had regretted that the Catholic Church had so far refused this kind of a dialogue. Yet this was the type of discussion they were then having in the Council, within the hearing of the observer delegates whose presence he welcomed. An examination of conscience was needed by all as to whether the visible Church expressed externally in her life the beatitudes of the Gospel, and whether she considered the poor as the image of Christ, who would judge the Church now and at the last day. A practical exercise of charity along this line produced faster results than endless abstract argumentation. The Church was judged by facts, not by words.

An announcement by the Secretary General on Tuesday, November 26th, before the beginning of the deliberations, formalized what Cardinal Ritter had said the day before about the thanks of the American hierarchy for the expressions of condolence by the Fathers on the death of President Kennedy.

Archbishop Manek (Indonesia), in the name of 29 Indonesian bishops, came out forthrightly for a clear designation of Protestant Churches as *Churches,* and a correction of the cautious language of the schema which referred to them regularly as "communities." The dialogue being advocated must take place not only among individuals but among corporate bodies. They were Churches, although the Protestants were perhaps so in a less complete sense than the Orthodox. Bishop Gonzalez Moralejo (Spain) said that the place for the chapter on religious liberty was at the beginning of the schema. These principles must be enunciated first, for without them no ecumenical dialogue was conceivable. The text also did not make clear whether Catholics were to participate in dialogue within the framework of the primarily Protestant ecumenical movement, or whether Protestants were to be invited to discussions with Catholics under strictly Catholic auspices. The text should give clear directives on this point of cooperation.

The most notable intervention that day, from the American point of view, was the speech of the auxiliary of San Antonio, Texas, Stephen Leven. As Bishop Leven explained later at the Press Panel, he had tried unsuccessfully to speak on the floor on at least two previous occasions. His remarks related to Chapter I of Ecumenism but were equally applicable to Chapter II, when he finally succeeded in being heard. He began: "Every day it becomes clearer that we need a dialogue, not only with Protestants but also among us bishops. For there are some Fathers who have already spoken to us frequently . . . as if the only text in the Holy Bible were Matt. 16:18 'Thou art Peter and upon this rock I will build my Church.' " He went on to say that they repeatedly argued against the collegiality of the bishops. "They preach to us and chastise us as if we were against Peter and his successors or as if we desired to steal away the faith of our flocks and to promote indifferentism." Ears naturally began to perk up. He continued: "They speak as if the whole doctrine of the freedom of conscience due every man, so clearly stated in *Pacem in Terris,* were offensive to pious ears." They preferred to blame non-Catholics whom they had never seen for errors rather than instruct the people in their own dioceses. Then in a series of *ad hominem* remarks, he asked: "Why are they so afraid the effects of ecumenism would not be good? . . . Why isn't there an active and functioning Confraternity of Christian Doctrine in their parishes? . . . The prelates who seek a sincere and fruitful dialogue with non-Catholics are not the ones who show disaffection and disloyalty to the Holy Father. It is not our people who miss mass on Sunday, refuse the sacraments and vote the communist ticket. It is not we who make little of the well known and often repeated desire of Popes Paul VI and John XXIII . . ." After getting in these barbs at an undisclosed "they," he concluded on a more harmonious note: "Venerable brethren, let us put an end to the scandal of mutual recrimination. Let us proceed in an orderly way with the examination and study of this providential movement called Ecumenism . . ."

Some of the American prelates were delighted that these things had at last been said. Others turned red in the face at the thought that they should be said at a time when the whole world was mourning the death of President Kennedy. Yet they might have asked themselves whether it were not better to speak out, or run the risk of not saying anything at all, for time was running out. The more realistic, however, were worried by a much more serious problem. As the days wore on and the debate on the first three chapters of Ecumenism seemed to be unduly protracted, the worry grew that the Session might close, after all, without any definite action being taken on the remaining two chapters, Chapter V in particular, in which the American bishops were greatly interested.

Much that was said on the four last days of debate was clearly repetitious. Had the moderators or pope so desired, the discussion of the first three chapters could easily have been concluded on Friday, or even Thursday, and this would have allowed enough time for a vote in principle on the remaining "Mystery Chapters." The prolongation of the debate through Monday December 2nd was obviously arranged to tide things over until the closing ceremonies had been reached. Earlier, it had been announced that December 3rd would be devoted to another commemoration of the centenary of the Council of Trent, and December 4th, of course, had been marked for the final ceremony.

On Wednesday, November 27th, Patriarch Maximos IV declared that he was opposed to a uniform code of canon law for the whole Church. It would be "deplorable" because it would almost automatically assure Latin domination without sufficient attention being paid to the special characteristics of the Eastern Churches. It would be time wasted, from the ecumenical point of view, for the Orthodox would never consider reunion with Rome if they thought that the most that they could hope for was to be obliged to accept Latin discipline. The Latin Church had set up her hierarchy everywhere, as a result of the missions. The Eastern Churches should have their share in this world-wide activity, but on a basis that respected their autonomous rights. Problems in the Near East where there were faithful of different rites could be worked out amicably. Respect for diversity, not uniformity, should be the goal.

Bishop Collin (Digne, France) called for special treatment for the Anglican Communion, because it was in a special category vis-à-vis the Orthodox and Protestants. The same idea was echoed by Archbishop Gouyon and later by Bishop Green. Bishop Dwyer (Leeds, England) stressed the validity of what Bishop Leven had said about those who lived in the midst of non-Catholics having, in some respects, a better right to speak out on the subject of ecumenism than those bishops whose dioceses were wholly Catholic.

At the close of the First Session Cardinal Lercaro had made an impassioned plea for the Church to become once again the "Church of the Poor." Many Fathers, at the end of the Second Session, regretted that this problem, to be dealt with in Schema 17, had still not been taken up in the concrete, although it was noted that 27 interventions referred to the theme of poverty in one connection or another. Cardinal Gerlier was one of the first to do so on October 4th when he said: "The poor are the sign of the presence of Christ in the Church. We shall be judged by our attitude toward them." One of the last to speak on this theme was Cardinal Gracias, who on November 25th asked that the Council take up Schema

17 at the beginning of the Third Session, and remarked that the Eucharistic Congress at Bombay in November 1964 would also take up this subject as one of its principal themes.

Each week during the Second Session a group of bishops and experts from all countries met together under the presidency of Cardinal Gerlier (archbishop of Lyons) and Bishop Himmer (Tournai) to study the doctrinal, social and pastoral aspects of the problem of underdevelopment and poverty. On Thursday November 28th, Cardinal Lercaro transmitted to the pope a "petition" drawn up by the group and signed by Cardinal Gerlier, which formally asked that Schema 17 be taken up at the beginning of the Third Session and that the Congress at Bombay consider the theme too. The following day Cardinal Lercaro announced that Paul VI had agreed that Schema 17 should be discussed during the Third Session, after discussion of *De Ecclesia,* which it was preferable not to interrupt. He promised that it would receive a thorough discussion after theologians and experts had worked out its terms.

On Friday, November 29th, the last day of debate but one, there was a prompt announcement of the results of the election of new commission members the day before and joy was felt over the fact that the progressives had won this round, but the news did little to offset the gloom over the imminent prospect, now regarded as a virtual certainty, that nothing would be done to retrieve the situation so far as Chapters IV and V of Ecumenism were concerned. The grim fact had to be faced that the Session would end without any vote or possibly any mention of the matter at all. Bishop Helmsing (Kansas City–St. Joseph) spoke out in the morning on behalf of calling the Protestant Churches "Churches" instead of resorting to the vague "communities" when referring to them. It was only common decency, he said, to refer to people the way they wanted to be addressed. Since the word "church" had various meanings, there was no reason why it could not be applied to those bodies which preferred to call themselves "Churches," leaving the others to be addressed as "communities" or in whatever way they pleased. A frank use of the term would go a long way toward promoting fraternal feelings. As a kind of afterthought, at the end of his talk, he interpolated the suggestion that a vote on Chapters IV and V be taken at once, that very morning. Though applause followed, he was not answered by the moderators.

At the Press Panel that afternoon there were many pointed questions as to why the American bishops had not done anything concrete about getting a vote on Chapter V. Why, it was suggested, when the American bishops had seen how effectively others had lobbied for what they wanted, had they not done likewise on an issue that directly concerned them? There was no satisfactory answer, except that the American bishops had not wanted to seem to bring pressure to bear if there was any chance of a vote in the normal course of events. It is doubtful, in the light of subsequent events that even if they had lobbied, they could have changed matters. The pope, it seems, had already decided to postpone a vote and this decision was irrevocable. Word to this effect was given to the American bishops over the weekend.

On Saturday, November 30th, Oscar Cullmann, the renowned Protestant theologian and an observer delegate, gave a lecture on "The history of salvation in the New Testament." The circumstances surrounding the holding of this talk were worth recalling. It was expected that large numbers would attend and application was made to the Gregorian University, the Angelicum, and the Biblical Institute, all of which had halls large enough to accommodate the crowds, but to no avail. One after the other had to turn down the professor's request. Finally, Archbishop Weber of Strasbourg—the home-town of Cullmann—placed the hall of the French church in Rome, St. Louis-des-Français, at his disposal. The hall was packed. Monsignor Willebrands of Bea's Secretariat introduced the speaker, extolling "what Catholic theology owed to his work." Rumor had it that Cullmann had been turned down by the Curial Congregation of Seminaries, which was in charge of these institutions, but Archbishop Staffa, secretary of the Congregation, let it be known that no request for permission had reached his desk. It appears that the permission—or lack of it—had been handled higher up. At one of its weekly meetings, the Holy Office had given as its reply to a question, that the professor should be allowed to hold his lecture, not in a Roman university, but in a "Catholic hall." The Holy Office no doubt thought that it was being very liberal in the whole matter. Cullmann was on excellent terms with Pope Paul (who invited him to have lunch with him in the Vatican during the First Session) and could have gone to the pope about it, but, out of modesty, he preferred not to bother him.

Another Protestant observer delegate, Dr. Skysdsgaard, seconded Cullmann's praise for the work of the Council. He maintained that it was simply unbelievable, years ago, that the Roman Church would ever change. Now however, the "Roman Church is in the process of reforming itself." However he was still waiting for a "prophetic voice in St. Peter's to point out the limitations of the Church as an institution." "We all desire unity," he concluded, "but when this unity becomes a reality, no one Church will be victorious. Rather they will all be conquered, so that Christ alone may conquer." He remarked earlier in his speech that it would be a mistake for Catholics to be under the illusion that any number of Protestants looked upon the Roman Catholic Church with "nostalgia" or desired to "return" pure and simple to the bosom of a Church which they still regarded as defective." The Churches must sit down and talk over their differences as "equals" and as "equals" again be reunited. This suggestion was taken up by Bishop Tomášek (Czechoslovakia) on the last day of debate, Monday, December 2nd, when he proposed that representatives of all the major orthodox confessions should sit down at a "round table" with the Catholic Church at which there would be no presidency and discuss differences as equals. This in itself, he said, would constitute a great step toward reunion.

The last day was one of sharp contrasts. Little had been heard of the important opposition, but Cardinal Ruffini more than made up for this by his intervention clearly aimed at influencing the Council in its last moments. He warned against misconceptions about ecumenism "which might arise from unscholarly magazine articles"—referring no doubt to expositions by such Council experts as Gregory Baum, René Laurentin, Jean Daniélou, Yves Congar, Karl Rahner and others who had frequently written on this theme in recent weeks in such reputable organs as *Commonweal, Le Figaro, Le Monde, La Croix, Stimmen der Zeit.* Such misrepresentations "could mislead and confuse priests and the faithful." Instead he offered his own straightlaced, unswervingly conservative definition of "Catholic ecumenism," based on the unshakable conviction that the Roman Catholic Church had nothing to learn and nothing to be sorry for. If mistakes had occurred, they had been due to "disobedient sons," not to the Church herself, which was infallible and indefectible. His whole program was summed up in the terse words: "We strongly hope that our separated brethren will again embrace the Catholic Church of Rome." Dialogue was useful, but only to "bring back" the erring to the one true fold.

It was sobering perhaps for the Fathers to hear once again the voice of Roman *intransigenza,* lest anyone might have been lulled into a false sense of security by the many positive things said about ecumenism in the last few days. The next speaker, Bishop Green (Port Elizabeth, South Africa) raised the question of Anglicanism and specifically of Anglican orders, with which the schema had not come to grips. He said that it was impossible to discuss reunion with Anglicans without coming up against the decision of Leo XIII condemning Anglican orders (1896). In justice to history and the cause of ecumenism, the whole question surrounding Anglican orders should again be examined. Scholars and theologians today were not sure that the decision of Leo XIII was the right one. It was an administrative decision, conditioned by the times, but new facts and a hopeful situation seemed to call for a review of the whole matter. The Council should also address itself to the practical question of the difficult position of married Anglican priests who sought admission to the Catholic Church.

Bishop Muldoon (Australia), in a fit of Irish pugnaciousness, took exception to the short paragraph which sought to explain the origin of the various Protestant communities. He said that as it stood, it would be sure to offend the Anglicans. It was better to say nothing about the subject at all. If it were to stand, many would criticize the Council for not having understood the heart and spirit of Protestantism. "We deceive ourselves if we think that all our separated brethren are in good faith. Many are like eagles hovering over the Church looking for what they can distort." Finally he declared that he was tired of all the breast-beating he had heard. "Some have said that all bishops should get down on their knees and confess their sins and those of their predecessors for the division of Christendom, and they cite the words of Pope Paul. But the Pope said '*If* we are in any way to blame for that separation . . .' *Salva reverentia,* we are tired of the exaggerated importuning of the Fathers. If any feel guilty, let them go to a good confessor but spare the rest of us!"

This forthright statement, intended more as a momentary expression of feeling, no doubt, than as a firm conviction, was answered later by the Abbot of Downside, Dom Butler, a trained historian as well as a theologian, who observed that the Roman Church had had a share in responsibility for the separation and suggested that a paragraph be added deploring the "sins committed by Catholics or the separated brethren, which have caused or which even now continue to prolong the evil of separation." He said that "history teaches that the public confession of sins by members of the Church is the first step toward spiritual emulation." The Anglicans deserved a special mention because of their widespread following throughout the world, their patristic tradition, the active part they have always played in the ecumenical movement, and lastly because they did not consider themselves simply as Protestants but as a bridge between Protestantism and Catholicism.

The surprise of the morning was the intervention of Bishop Tomášek (Czechoslovakia) referred to above. It was useless, he said, to attempt to reach decisions without consulting the other side. A bold step would bring us a good way toward the final goal. The Moscow Patriarchate had stated, he noted, that "the way of Christian love can lead to dogmatic dialogue and thus to the desired reunion. The time is fast becoming ripe for action." The bishop could not have known about Pope Paul's projected pilgrimage to the Holy Land. He was certainly right in reminding his listeners that "What could not have been even attempted in the past centuries can now be carried out in a short space of time."*

The Ukrainian Archbishop Hermaniuk (Winnepeg, Canada) likewise called for "practical steps" to organize mixed theological commissions, on the diocesan level, under the general direction of the Secretariat for Unity in Rome, to further the work of ecumenical dialogue—a thought echoed

* Bishop Tomášek later received a commendation from Patriarch Aleksei of Moscow.

by Cardinal Bea its head on a number of occasions—and urged that full rights be restored to the patriarchs and that synodal rule or government by permanent synods be restored to the Eastern Churches. Strange as these suggestions may have sounded only a year before it was now not improbable that the "impossible" might come to pass. This was some gage of how far Rome had travelled on the road toward a truer appreciation of the ultimate goal of ecumenism.—As Pope Paul put it in his closing address—"To call to the one, holy Church of Christ the separated brethren."

At the conclusion of the debate Cardinal Bea summed up the impressions of the Fathers with regard to the schema on Ecumenism. He said that the suggestions would all be carefully considered in working out a revised text to be voted on at the next session. Some of the proposals would be incorporated in an "Ecumenical Directory" which would be prepared for the guidance of bishops and all interested persons, for experience had shown that furtherance of the ecumenical movement was a primary responsibility of pastors and must be cultivated on the local level, with assistance from Rome. It was regretted by many that there had not been time to discuss the controversial Chapters IV and V of the schema dealing with the Jews and Religious Liberty, but the ancient saying applied: "What is put off is not put away"—*Quod defertur non aufertur.* He repeated these words twice as if to leave no doubt in minds about the intention of the Council leaders to bring the matter up again and quiet rumors which had been circulating for some days that the conservative minority had succeeded in "burying" the dangerous document on religious liberty. The cardinal also repeated the words "There was not time"—with the same end in view. However he observed that the delay, while regrettable, could be put to good use in that it would give the Fathers time to reflect on important issues and come back with more concrete proposals the next session. Suggestions with regard to these last chapters were to be sent in to the Secretariat not later than the middle of February 1964. Unfortunately, because the aged cardinal was slow in speaking, he was cut off before he had time to deliver the last few sentences of his discourse. The moderators apparently thought that he had concluded when he merely paused.

It was announced in the last general congregation on Monday that further consideration of a proposed message from the bishops to priests would be put off indefinitely. A text had been distributed to the Fathers the previous Friday with the request that they propose amendments after considering it over the weekend. Apparently the amendments were so numerous and serious that it became evident to the council leaders that promulgation of the text in its present form would not be possible. More than 200 suggestions had boiled down to 60 major amendments, thus

259

making it impossible to proceed with the document as it was. The original draft was due, it was said, to Bishop Renard of Versailles.

The meeting closed with a few remarks by Bishop Hengsbach about the schema on the Apostolate of the Laity which could not be discussed because of lack of time.

A solemn or public session of the Council on Tuesday, December 3rd, was devoted to commemorating the closing of the Fourth Centenary of the Council of Trent (other celebrations having commemorated the same event earlier in the year). The address that day by Cardinal Urbani was remarkable only for its "prudence." It carefully avoided saying anything that might offend the Protestant observer-delegates present in the Council hall (some of whom had absented themselves) or otherwise retard the prospects for the ecumenical movement. The success of Urbani in straddling a difficult fence could be measured by the lack of any interest in his talk by the Rome conservative daily *Il Tempo,* which preferred to focus its headlines on another incident of the day which occurred after the morning session. The headline "Request for a schema against Marxism at the close of the second session of the Council" made great play of a petition originating among certain Brazilian prelates that the Third Session of the Council take up consideration of a separate schema condemning the "errors of Marxism, socialism and communism, in their philosophical, sociological and economic aspects." The petition was said to have been signed by "more than 200 bishops." It was reported to have been handed to the Secretary of State Cardinal Cicognani the previous Tuesday. At the same time there was also issued a pamphlet on "The liberty of the Church in the Communist State" by a certain Dr. Correa de Oliveira, described as a university professor in Brazil. The pamphlet maintained that "it is contrary to Catholic principles to assert that the Church can exist and enjoy indispensable liberty in a communist state." A feeble, last-minute maneuvre to draw the attention of the world away from the fundamental issues before the Council at this Session, and indirectly a repudiation of the policy of John XXIII laid down in *Pacem in Terris?* The *New York Times* professed to find an anxiety among the Italian bishops, headlining its story on December 2, 1963: "Italian Bishops Resisting a Vote." The account attempted to explain, without adducing any evidence, that the "Italian bishops" had blocked discussion of Chapter V of Ecumenism on religious liberty because an avowal of its principles would be tantamount to an avowal of "atheistic communism."

CLOSE OF THE SECOND SESSION

On Wednesday December 4th the Second Session came to what some observers regarded as a rather inglorious end. The entrance of Pope Paul into the basilica of St. Peter's for the final solemn ceremonies was dismaying to those who witnessed the scene. Preceded as usual by the full panoply of the papal household and liveried guards, the Eastern patriarchs, minus of course the doughty Melkite patriarch of Antioch who entered the basilica in advance as a protest against Vatican protocol (which still ignored the claim to precedence implicit in the pope's act earlier in the Session, when he ordered the patriarchs seated at a special table, directly opposite, and therefore by implication at least, on the same level with the cardinals), and the college of cardinals robed in white copes and mitres, a fifth of whom seemed to be pitifully aged figures hardly able to hobble along, the pope himself appeared carried high on the *sedia gestatoria.* He seemed acutely conscious of the tawdriness of all this faded splendor and perhaps even sorry that he had not decided to make a more appropriate entrance by walking the length of the nave on foot. As he passed down the central nave, the pope scarcely looked to right or to left to acknowledge the fitful applause from the episcopal benches. Everything suddenly seemed to have a worn-out look about it, the vestments, the uniforms, the damask-draped tribunes.

By way of counteracting this impression, once he descended from the *sedia,* the pope seemed to come alive, graciously turning to the non-Catholic observers and greeting them with his customarily graceful gestures, and acknowledging the applause that came from the tribunes of the diplomatic corps, the special guests and the vast throng of people crowded in the transepts and the apse. As the pope unassumingly mounted the steps leading to his throne over the Confession of St. Peter, Cardinal Tisserant, the eighty year old dean of the Sacred College, began the prayers at the foot of the altar in his precise but rapidly enunciated Latin which was answered by the whole congregation with equal precision and dispatch. It was noted that, in his eagerness to proceed with the mass, the cardinal had not waited for the pope to be properly seated. A certain discontent seemed to be reflected in the rapidity with which the prelates recited in unison the words of the Gloria, Credo, Sanctus and Agnus Dei. Immediately after the mass, the Secretary General, Archbishop Felici, mounted the rostrum and instead of his usual peremptory *Exeant omnes*—the daily signal for unauthorized participants to leave the hall at the beginning of each daily congregation—he announced that only prelates were to occupy the seats in the bishops' tribunes, thereby dislodging a number of redfaced episcopal secretaries who had preempted the seats of bishops who were not present.

Turning to the business at hand, the secretary in his customary felicitous Latin announced that, in accordance with Pope Paul's leave, the reading of the 37-page text of the Liturgy Constitution and the 13-page Communications Decree which was to precede the solemn voting of these

261

measures by the Council and the pope's solemn promulgation, would be abbreviated, much to the relief of the Council Fathers, most of whom had come prepared for a long session. He carefully reminded the Fathers to use the magnetic pencils for marking the IBM ballots in order to eliminate invalid votes, and stated that they had a choice between Placet and Non placet, thus eliminating the troublesome Iuxta modum or conditional vote which had caused considerable delay in the Council's proceedings. In an earlier announcement Felici had once humorously remarked that the *modi* proposed by the Fathers were the reason why the commissions were having trouble producing an amended text, and Bishop Rupp (Monaco) had asked in the course of one of his interventions whether the modern equivalent of Iuxta modum might not be *à la mode?*

The actual ceremony of the promulgation began with the solemn chanting of the Creed by the assembled bishops, after which a strange voice—quickly identified as that of Cardinal Ottaviani assisting Pope Paul as the senior cardinal in the order of deacons, cried out *Orate*— Pray. Thereupon Pope Paul knelt at the faldstool and recited the conciliar prayer *Adsumus Domine Sancte Spiritus*—We are here present, Lord Holy Spirit, at the end of which the same voice rang out *Erigite*—All stand. After the pope had intoned the *Veni Creator Spiritus,* the secretary general began the truncated reading of the text of the Liturgy Constitution and the ballots were collected. Some ten minutes later Archbishop Felici approached the pope with the results and announced an overwhelming majority of 2,147 favorable to 4 opposed. Thereupon the Holy Father rose together with the bishops and pronounced the solemn formula making this an official document of the Church. Contrary to the formula found in the Ordo which ascribed to the pope alone the right to "declare, decree and approve," the pope said: ". . . We approve (this Constitution) together with the Fathers . . ." (*Approbamus una cum patribus*), thus acknowledging the reality of the collegial government of the Church still under fire by the minority. The previous week it had been made clear that this promulgation would be disciplinary not doctrinal in character, and as a consequence would not involve the Church's infallibility. The same procedure was followed for the Communications Decree, but this time the vote reflected the uneasiness created by a campaign on the part of certain progressive circles to have this schema rejected as being unworthy of being declared a conciliar document. Apparently resentment lingered over the arbitrary action on the part of the secretary and Council president, for the final result was 1,969 favorable to 164 against. Again Pope Paul promulgated the document. The apostolic protonotaries then solemnly swore, in accordance with custom, to register—*Conficiemus*— the Latin document faithfully, and the pope launched into his address formally closing the Second Session.

A carefully worded, closely reasoned summation of the Council's achievements and of the tasks still ahead, Pope Paul's talk stressed the spiritual rather than the literal successes of the session. He insisted that the conciliar colloquy had given the bishops an unprecedented knowledge of each other and thereby enabled them to experience literally the significance of St. Paul's words which described the Church so aptly. He then quoted Ephesians 2:19-20: "You are no longer strangers and newcomers, but rather fellow citizens of the saints and members of the household of God, built upon the foundations laid by the apostles and the prophets, where the very cornerstone is Christ Jesus." What was remarkable about the pope's citation of this particular text was the fact that its use in the schema on Ecumenism had been challenged on the floor two weeks earlier by Cardinal Ruffini, who maintained that in employing this Pauline citation as a definition of the Church, "founded on the apostles and prophets with Christ as the cornerstone," doubt was being cast upon the Petrine foundation based on Matthew 18:16 where Christ addressed Peter: "Thou art . . . Church." Paul thus indirectly was chiding the cardinal of Palermo—a scriptural scholar of the old school—for his dated unecumenical exegesis.

Making a Pauline contribution, the pope revealed his thoughts with regard to the way the "revolution" in the Church was going to be carried out in the practical sphere by turning his attention to canon law, the instrument by which the Church was governed on a day to day basis. Here he noted that ecclesiastical law was not a static entity but an organic concept that developed, "extending its growth in two directions." On the one hand it should enhance the dignity of each person and office in the Church affording them greater power for development, and on the other hand it should strengthen the intrinsic demands of love, harmony and mutual respect within the community of the faithful that was guaranteed by "the unifying quality of hierarchical government." These carefully chosen and somewhat mysterious words seemed to echo the new concept of the church law that Pope John had so frequently hinted at: the abandonment of the harsh menacing and condemnatory aspects which the Code of Canon Law had inherited from ancient Roman law, and a reintroduction of the liberating and encouraging aspects of Gospel law enunciated by Christ and preached as an *agape* or law of charity in the early Church. It was this direction that Pope Paul seemed intent on giving to a new codification—the recently published Oriental Code—which had been criticized at the Council as an attempt to Latinize their Churches. Later in his speech he stated explicitly that new codes were to be drawn up "both for the Latin Church and for the Eastern Churches," thus officially promising a revision of the debatable Oriental Code.

Sensitive to the criticism that the Council had appeared to be dragging its feet and lacked proper coordination, he admitted that the discussions had been "arduous and intricate" and referred to the work of the Council as "laborious," but these defects had to be borne in order to assure perfect "freedom of expression." The divergent views expressed on the council floor, far from being a source of perplexity or anxiety (as the ultra-conservatives keep repeating), were "proof of the depth of the subjects investigated" and a sign of this "freedom." It is reported that earlier, when pressed by reform-minded bishops to intervene and end the deadlock over procedure, he had replied that he would do so only as a last resort in order not to give any side grounds for claiming that it had been muzzled by papal action.

He rejoiced that the Liturgy Constitution now made it possible "to simplify our liturgical rites" and "render them more intelligible to the people and accommodated to the language they speak." But he coupled this with an admonition: "To attain these ends it is necessary that no attempt should be made to introduce into the official prayer of the Church private changes or singular rites." The decentralization envisaged by this document must be carried out in an orderly way with the bishops in national or regional groups deciding how and how much of the change was to be introduced when the new law went into effect on the first Sunday in Lent (February 16, 1964). Meanwhile, there was to be a *vacatio legis,* Archbishop Felici announced, during which no innovations were to be permitted: This warning on jumping the gun was repeated in a boxed notice on page 1 of *L'Osservatore Romano* the following day, causing one local theologian to remark: "Since they seem to take for granted in the Vatican that *L'Osservatore* is primarily an Italian paper, they evidently fear that the local clergy are finally feeling the revolutionary urge. They know that such a warning is useless for the Germans and many of the French who are already far advanced in the use of the vernacular, and needless for the Irish and Americans who will not move before Rome cracks the whip!"

Some observers discerned a veiled reference to the now famous propositions voted on October 30th and an indication of papal support for the position taken by the moderators in the words: "As you all know the Council has addressed itself to many questions whose solutions are in part virtually formulated in authoritative decisions which will be published in time after the work on the topics to which they belong is completed." With this precise paternal admonition, he outlined the procedure for those conciliar commissions which had seemingly gone at their work in too slow or too unskilled a fashion:

"It is fitting . . . that the competent commissions on whose work we place so much hope, will prepare for the future conciliar meetings, in accordance with the mind of the Fathers, *as expressed especially in the general congregations* (our italics), proposals profoundly studied, accurately formulated, suitably condensed and abbreviated, so that the discussions, while remaining always free, may be rendered easier and more brief." In effect he was saying that the commissions were intended to serve the Council, not vice versa. Though the pope went on to say, "We hope that the Third Session in the autumn of next year will bring (the discussions) to completion," he later declared that he had set no time limit for the Council.

It was noted with interest that the pope studiously avoided any mention of the word "collegiality," but the substance of the doctrine was clearly contained in his reference to the Council's aim to set forth "the powers of the episcopate, indicating how they should be used, individually and *corporately,* so as worthily to manifest the eminence of the episcopate in the Church of God, which is not an institution independent of, or separated from, or still less, antagonistic to, the supreme pontificate of Peter, but with Peter and under him it strives for the common good and the supreme goal of the Church." "We are sure," he added, "that on a subject of such importance the Council will have much to say that will bring consolation and light."

After mentioning briefly that he was in accord with what the Council had decided regarding the place of the schema on the Virgin Mary (applause)—namely to incorporate it as a chapter in the schema on the Church, he promised that the remaining questions proposed for consideration but not yet discussed in the Council "would be subjected to a thorough and deeper re-examination" so that it would not be difficult for the next session to "obtain a judgment of the Council on certain fundamental propositions"—once more seeming to sanction the procedure adopted by the moderators. Details not requiring conciliar action would be left to post-conciliar commissions composed of bishops, experts, members of religious orders, and cardinals. "Experience will suggest to us how, without prejudice to the prerogatives of the Roman pontiff defined by Vatican Council I, the earnest and cordial collaboration of the bishops can more effectively promote the good of the universal Church." These last words were a reminder that at the proper time he would announce what form a proposed episcopal "senate" was to take.

Commentators were in agreement that this carefully worded, balanced, moderate-in-tone speech, completely lacking the enthusiasm which had marked his opening speech on September 29th, reflected the mood of the pope and of the Council itself. He was anxious to draw up a faithful balance sheet, to say what required to be said, but not to indicate any enthusiasm for a session which, as Henri Fesquet wrote: "had more debits than credits."

265

THE HOLY LAND PILGRIMAGE

The pope's historic announcement that he intended to make a trip to the Holy Land was probably one of the best-kept secrets in recent years. It was a remarkable performance at a court notorious for its *indiscrezioni*. Nobody outside the immediate circle concerned had any word about what was coming until eleven o'clock, shortly before the pope began his talk, when word was leaked to a few of the experts. But to the majority of hearers and the vast world outside, the news came as a breath-taking disclosure of incalculable significance. Nobody was prepared for it. And some time elapsed before the significance could be seen in its proper light as there was nothing except the bare fact of the announcement to go on. The Vatican could disclose no further information because nothing had as yet been settled. The details remained to be worked out. As a matter of fact, it was not until shortly before the pope departed from Rome that the final protocol of his meetings with the Orthodox leaders was worked out, signed and sealed.

With the advantage of hindsight it is now possible to see that the main practical purpose of the pilgrimage was to provide an occasion for a suitable encounter with Orthodox and other Eastern religious leaders, specifically with Patriarch Athenagoras I of Constantinople, *primus inter pares* of the Orthodox patriarchs. But there was only the barest allusion to this in the pope's original statement: ". . . to summon to this one holy Church our separated brethren . . ." This was all that he could say for the present in that regard, but the immediately preceding phrases of the announcement must not be left out of account, fraught as they were with meaning. Although somewhat obscurely expressed, the pope's thought seems to have been that his pilgrimage was to be an expression of "prayer, penance and renewal" and that it was his intention "to offer to Christ His Church" in the same spirit, i.e., as a properly humble and renewed Church, to which the separated brethren would be summoned. He was careful to avoid the use of the word "return," or to imply that the Orthodox were being asked to restore unity with an "unrenewed" Church.

In spite of repeated attempts in the press and by various interested groups to make political hay out of the pilgrimage, it was clear in the light of the pope's repeated statements, notably in his Christmas Message (December 23, 1963), in his address to the diplomatic corps (December 28th), and in numerous statements which he made while in the Holy Land, that the sole purpose of the trip was religious and spiritual. It was not intended to serve any political purpose, except indirectly by aiding the cause of world peace and mutual understanding. It was no small accomplishment to emerge from the political maelstrom of the Near East virtually unscathed ideologically-speaking.

Regardless of other factors which may have entered into the picture at the time, there could be little doubt, in the light of subsequent events, that one of the primary reasons why Pope Paul did not want a detailed debate on the floor of the Council on Chapter IV on the Jewish problem, was that he thought too heated a discussion of the matter in Rome might prejudice the success of his Holy Land pilgrimage, which had already been decided upon. The small lifting of the veil during the opening days of the debate following November 18th was enough to convince him of that. The Arab Christians were unanimously opposed to the chapter as a part of the schema though not necessarily to the contents being treated in some other connection. And there could be no doubt that sentiment among the bishops at large was lukewarm, at best. While many were in favor of the principles involved, it was doubtful whether a majority could be mustered for approval of it as Chapter IV of Ecumenism, and the unpalatable prospect therefore loomed of seeing the chapter defeated, if a test-vote were held. The intial mistake may well have been to present it as Chapter IV in the first place, but as spokesmen for the Secretariat for Promoting Christian Unity rather freely avowed this was done as much from tactical as from logical considerations. Under the circumstances, there was little that the pope could do except defer consideration. What specifically irked observers at the time was that he saw fit to give no assurance that it would be taken up again as part of the agenda at the Third Session. In view of the tactics of the minority, it seemed dangerous *not* to make some public statement.

The plan for a meeting with Athenagoras I seems to have matured over a period of time and therefore could not have been a sudden last minute inspiration on the pope's part to rescue the Council from "gloom." Two important steps in the formulation of the plan were a letter from the pope to Athenagoras, dated September 29, 1963, replying to an earlier letter from the patriarch congratulating him on his election as pope, and another letter from the patriarch to the pope, dated November 22, 1963, replying to the pope's letter of September 20th.

The receipt of the letter from Athenagoras during the last week of November apparently precipitated the final decision to go to Palestine and rendered impracticable any further debate on the Jewish question. In early November, the pope's personal secretary Don Pasquale Macchi and Monsignor J. P. Martin, of the Secretariat of State, made a trip to the Near East, in the strictest secrecy, in order to prepare the ground for a possible pilgrimage. It was revealed later that they had visited Jordan and Israel. Diplomatic "soundings" were also made through the representatives of the Arab states and Israel accredited to the Quirinal, who visited the Secretariat of State in a series of audiences in October and November. It is unlikely that the subject of the pilgrimage was directly broached on these occasions, the Vatican officials probably being more interested in determining the general background and atmosphere in which a trip might take place, and the diplomats themselves more interested in possible reactions to the discussion of the Jewish document.

Once the papal intention to go on pilgrimage to Palestine had been announced, Patriarch Athenagoras lost no time in approving the idea and suggesting a meeting of religious heads in Jerusalem to discuss reunion (December 6th). The intention seems to have been to clear the way for a meeting between the pope and patriarch, since a broader gathering could hardly have been arranged on such short notice. Father Duprey, one of the high officials in Bea's Secretariat, was dispatched to Constantinople to "explain the nature of the Holy Father's pilgrimage" and no doubt give assurances that a meeting with Athenagoras in Jerusalem would be welcome. The official nature of the announcements made in Istanbul and Rome (December 10th and 12th) on this occasion, tended to confirm the view that a meeting was being seriously considered. Further confirmation came from the Greek Orthodox Patriarch of Antioch on December 18th, and in the Christmas message of the Patriarch Athenagoras read on December 25th. The latter had sounded out the other Orthodox religious leaders and won their approval to a meeting between himself and Pope Paul. Only the Greek Church, under the leadership of Archbishop Chrysostomos of Athens, remained resolutely opposed in principle, though some of the Greek hierarchy were favorable and supported the step of the Ecumenical Patriarch. The final details of the historical meeting were regulated in the most minute particulars by a formal protocol signed on the occasion of a visit to the Vatican on December 28th by the official emissary of the patriarch and Holy Synod of Constantinople, Metropolitan Athenagoras of Thyateira, Orthodox archbishop of Great Britain.

The first encounter of the pope with an Orthodox Patriarch took place Saturday evening, the day of his arrival after the grueling experience of the Via Dolorosa and mass celebrated under unbelievably crowded conditions in the church of the Holy Sepulchre. Patriarch Benedict of Jerusalem called on the pope at the Apostolic Delegation where he was staying, and Pope Paul then returned the visit at the villa which was the residence of Benedict. The meetings went very well. It is known that Patriarch Benedict had expressed reservations beforehand about the appropriateness of the proposed encounter, but the fact that Pope Paul agreed to receive him first and then to return the visit and graciously took note of the special part which Benedict had played in promoting a better feeling between the various communities in Jerusalem pleased him and helped to cut the ice. It was essential to create the proper atmosphere for the meeting with Athenagoras on the morrow. The same evening after receiving Benedict, the pope also received the Armenian patriarch of Jerusalem, Derderian, who presented a special delegation of bishops sent by the Armenian catholicus of Cilicia, Koren I, to greet the pope.

Sunday was spent visiting the sites in Israel. On leaving the Israeli authorities at the Mandelbaum Gate, before returning to the Old City of Jersualem, the pope unexpectedly said a few words in defense of the memory of Pius XII and his concern for the Jews, with obvious reference to Hochhuth's controversial play. Back at the Apostolic Delegation, he received Patriarch Athenagoras at 9:30 P.M. Everything took place according to strict protocol. The patriarch and metropolitans accompanying him were received at the gate by the three cardinals accompanying the pope, Tisserant, Cicognani and Testa, while the pope waited to greet his guest at the door. After putting their arms about each other and exchanging the kiss of peace, the pope led the patriarch inside for a private talk. This was supposed to last only five minutes but actually lasted twenty. The various suites were then presented. The patriarch read his address in Greek: "Most holy brother in Christ. . . . The Christian world has lived for centuries in the night of separation. Its eyes are tired of gazing into darkness. May this meeting be the dawn of a bright and blessed day, in which future generations, communicating from the same chalice of the sacred body and precious blood of the Lord, will praise and glorify, in charity, peace and humility, the one Lord and Savior of the world." A French translation of the speech was then handed to the pope and read by the patriarch's secretary, Monsignor Simeon Amaryllios. The pope was greatly moved by the patriarch's words. Though protocol decreed that his own speech be reserved for the return visit tomorrow, he did remark: "I may say now that your words are the source of many fruitful thoughts."

He then handed to the patriarch the gifts which he had brought for him from Rome, a gold chalice and a gold medal commemorating the pilgrimage. After some hesitation as to what would constitute a proper gift, the pope had finally decided on the chalice with reference to the hoped-for restoration of fraternal communion between the two Churches. He could not have known that the patriarch would mention the chalice in his speech! Handing the chalice to him, he said: "You have alluded to the chalice in your talk. The chalice is the living root of our fraternal love. Allow me to offer this to you as a symbol of fraternal love."

After the pope had distributed medals to the members of the patriarch's suite, the gathering recited the "Our Father" in unison, in Greek and Latin. Pope Paul then took the patriarch by the arm and led him toward the door. The patriarch said, in French: *"Oui, la main dans la main pour toujours."* He was accompanied to the gate by the three cardinals who bade him farewell. Upon leaving he remarked to one of the newsmen present: "I ardently hope that Pope Paul VI and I will one day mix water and wine in this chalice!" The pope himself was so greatly moved by the meeting that he mentioned it the following day in his talk at Bethlehem, although this was not part of his original text.

The second encounter between pope and patriarch took place the next morning, Monday, January 6th, the last day of the pilgrimage, after Pope Paul returned from Bethlehem and before he was scheduled to depart for Rome. But first a word with regard to the speech at Bethlehem, carefully prepared in advance, perhaps the most important statement during the entire pilgrimage. The original text was delivered in French. It opened with a symbolic "confession of the Church of Rome" offered to Christ at the site of His nativity in the manner of Peter's confession of Christ's divinity or the offerings of the Magi:

This confession is that of the Church of Rome, the church which was Peter's and which was founded on him as a rock. For this reason, Lord, it is Your Church and lives still in virtue of its unbroken connection with Your fountainhead. Be with Your Church, defend it, purify it, give it strength and life, O Christ of the Church of Rome.

These words were promptly misunderstood by the less perceptive, both in the East and the West. Wasn't it shocking that the pope appeared to be claiming Christ for the Church of Rome, how could this possibly be interpreted in an ecumenical sense, etc.? His intention was quite different as the context showed. The Roman Catholic Church made once again its confession of faith in the divinity of Christ and therefore belonged to Christ, who was asked to "defend, purify and strengthen" His Church— the last few words referred to the Petrine sayings quoted immediately before: "Lord, to whom shall we go . . .", "Lord, Thou knowest all things, Thou knowest that we love Thee" (John 6:69 and 21:17). The implication clearly was: Are the other Churches prepared to make the same confession of faith? The words were an indirect challenge to "the others" to do likewise.

A still more significant remark followed. After addressing a few words to Catholics in full communion with the Holy See and noting that the success of the Council and its ultimate goal of imparting "new attitudes of mind, new aims, new standards of conduct" to the Church required the joyful cooperation of all, "concerted effort in which every section of the Church must play its part," he went on to address those "our Christian brothers who are not in perfect communion with us" and to state that

It is clear to everyone that the problem of unity cannot be put on one side. Today the will of Christ is pressing upon us and obliging us to do all that we can, with love and wisdom, to bring to all Christians the supreme blessing and honor of a united Church.

Then came the carefully weighed words:

Even on this very special occasion we must say that such a result is not to be obtained at the expense of the truths of faith. We cannot be false to Christ's heritage: it is not ours, but His; we are no more than stewards, teachers and interpreters. Yet we declare once again that we are ready to consider every reasonable possibility by which mutual understanding, respect and charity may be fostered so as to smooth the way to a future—and please God, not too distant—meeting with our Christian brothers still separated from us.

The door of the fold is open. We wait, all of us, with sincere hearts, our desire is strong and patient. There is room for all. Our affection goes in advance of the step to be taken; it can be taken with honor and mutual joy. We shall not call for gestures which are not the fruit of free conviction, the effect of the spirit of the Lord, who breathes when and where He wills. We shall wait for the happy hour to come.

For the present, we ask for our separated brethren only that which we set before ourselves as our objective, namely that every step toward reunion and interchange of views should be inspired by love of Christ and the Church. We shall take pains to keep alive the desire for understanding and union and we shall put our trust in prayer which, even though it is not yet united prayer, rises up nevertheless simultaneously from ourselves and from Christians separated from us like two parallel columns which meet on high to form an arch in the God of unity.

The speech closed with a "word to the world" regarding the aspirations of humanity.

The pope arrived for his second meeting with Athenagoras at the residence of Patriarch Benedict of Jerusalem, about 9 A.M., and was greeted at the entrance according to the same protocol as was observed the day before, by Metropolitan Athenagoras and Archbishop Iakovos of the Orthodox Church of North America, in the name of the patriarch. All then gathered in the reception room which was so very small it could barely contain those who were present. The fragile glass doors had scarcely been closed when the pope launched into his Latin address: *"Vehementer nos commovet . . ."* He was greatly moved by the occasion, but appeared in complete control of himself, his gray-green eyes riveted on his text, unmindful of the crowded scene around him. By contrast the patriarch appeared pale and could scarcely contain his feelings. He kept his hand on his heart and looked neither to right nor to left at those nearest him. When Paul VI recalled the figure of Pope John XXIII and the patriarch's words with respect to him: " . . . there was a man sent by God . . ." the patriarch smiled and from then on seemed in

271

complete control of his emotions. After the speech had been read, the text was handed to the patriarch. There was no translation. The patriarch then offered the pope his gift, which had been decided on by a special committee set up by the Holy Synod of Constantinople. The decision was in favor of a pectoral chain—called *encolpion* in the Greek Church—worn by bishops, which was symbolic of their apostolic succession and government of the Church. The significance of the occasion was that Patriarch Athenagoras considered Pope Paul in some sort a bishop of the Eastern Church.

Pope Paul had no advance word on what the nature of the gift to him would be. His eyes lit up when he saw what it was. At once, without hesitating for a moment, he removed his Latin papal stole and put the chain on over his head, with the assistance of the patriarch, then put the stole on over it. Other similar chains were then given to the three cardinals accompanying the pope, and to Monsignor Willebrands and Father Duprey, officials of the Secretariat for Promoting Christian Unity, the patriarch gave the Cross of St. Andrew, an Orthodox order awarded for special services on behalf of the Orthodox Church, in recognition of the regard in which they were held.

After the presents had been distributed, the pope said in French: "Now we are going to read the Gospel of St. John, chapter 17, the prayer of Christ for unity." As Monsignor Willebrands held up the small New Testament volume with the Greek and Latin texts facing each other, the pope began with a verse in Latin and was followed by the patriarch with the next verse in Greek. The pope was so overcome by emotion that he lost his place at least three times. The patriarch appeared more in control of himself. The final words of verse 21: "Let them be one so that the world may believe" were enunciated by the pope with particular emphasis. After the reading pope and patriarch recited the "Our Father" in unison, as on the previous day, along with the rest of the gathering. Patriarch Athenagoras at first hesitated to go beyond the words with which the Latin version customarily ends, but the pope insisted, and they all said together the concluding phrase, which the Orthodox say along with Protestants: "For thine is the kingdom, the power, and the glory forever. Amen."

Pope Paul then proposed that they both bless those present. Athenagoras declined and asked the pope to offer his blessing. "Let us bless them together," said the pope. When the pope began with the usual formula: "*Sit nomen Domini benedictum*—Blessed be the name of the Lord," Athenagoras said nothing, but when it came time for the actual blessing, he raised his hand high and in a majestic sweep gave his blessing along with that of the pope. Many were moved to tears by the historical symbolism of the occasion.

A third chance encounter between pope and patriarch took place on the street later the same morning, as the pope was returning from a visit in Jerusalem. The two stood for about ten minutes in private conversation. After receiving Archbishop A. C. MacInnes, Anglican archbishop of Jerusalem and emissary of Archbishop Ramsey of Canterbury, as well as Provost Malsch, the Lutheran representative, Pope Paul left Jerusalem at 12:30 for Amman. His plane touched down at Ciampino near Rome at 6:13 P.M. The return to the Vatican along the historic Appian Way and through the heart of the city was a veritable Roman triumph, the likes of which Rome had seldom seen.

It was impossible for anyone viewing the facts dispassionately to come to any other conclusion than that this carefully planned, carefully contrived meeting—with all the attendant publicity, some of it in questionable taste, no doubt—remained a keystone in the papal view that the aims of ecumenism could only be furthered by concrete steps, by the right persons at the appropriate time, of course. It was one thing for the Fathers in the Council to discuss theoretically the advantages or disadvantages of a program for unity in the short time allotted for this topic, it would be something else again for them to vote in the Third Session on principles of action when they had the example of what the head of the Church had now done to guide them. As some of the bishops pointed out: "Deeds count, not words." In the light of the Palestine experience, it seems safe to conclude that the pope and his advisers, particularly Cardinals Bea and Lercaro, were determined to make a reality of what "intercommunion" already existed, through baptism, the same reverence for the Bible, the sharing of the same sacraments, etc., in the hope that by going as far as one could "in charity"—and the suggestion had already been aired, as we have seen, for a fuller sacramental communion between Orthodox and Catholics, *as of now*—and the hope voiced for a greater "openness" toward cooperation with Protestants along similiar lines, that "full ecclesiastical communion" could be established eventually on the basis of shared common experiences. In other words, for the present, there would be no ringing of church bells or chanting of *Te Deums* as at the Council of Florence in the fifteenth century, when reunion was effected temporarily between East and West, but a slow process of "reconstruction" would be inaugurated leading ultimately to the desired result, perhaps without any fanfare at all, at some future date.

GLOOM AT CLOSE OF SECOND SESSION

At the close of the Second Session a gloomy atmosphere prevailed among many observers and was shared by some of the bishops, in varying degrees. It seemed that something of this gloom was even reflected in the pope's final talk. The accomplishments of the session had been distressingly small, in spite of the tremendous effort expended. Observers also concluded correctly that the fault lay with the relatively small minority who were in a position to hold up the work of the Council and were likely to continue to do so unless they were dislodged in some dramatic move. This "doom and gloom" attitude was reflected particularly in an article in *Time* (December 6, 1963), entitled "What went wrong?" which concluded that the pope was "more a prisoner of the Curia than John ever was. . . ." As an intellectual he was not a man of action and so could not be expected to cope with the opposition of the minority effectively. The implication was that he had given in to them and things looked exceedingly bad for the Church and Council. There were many modifications of the pessimistic line. Some darkly hinted that the Italian and Spanish bishops had brought pressure to bear on the pope to drop Chapter V. "In the context of Italian politics many purely religious and ecclesiastical matters take on political overtones. In the right-view Italian press a criticism of the Roman Curia in the Council and the suggestion that it be placed under an international apostolic council with the pope are interpreted as a political gesture in favor of the left. Why? Because it seems that in Italy the Roman Curia has become the symbol of the anticommunist bloc seeking to prevent a further opening to the left" (Gregory Baum, O.S.A., writing in *Commonweal,* December 27, 1963). Others stated more bluntly that the change which allegedly came over the pope sometime after the weekend of November 8th—at the time when the issue of the validity of the October 30th vote on collegiality was being so hotly debated in the Council—was due to concern for the financial assets of the Vatican in Italy—the fear that is, that a further drift toward the left by the Church would give added strength to the communist vote which had already reached alarming proportions in the spring election. Such an argument was scarcely plausible if one looked at the facts. And it was difficult to imagine Pope Paul being influenced by such considerations in any case. The truth of the matter was that the Holy See had much larger financial assets outside Italy than inside, the largest asset being its virtually unlimited credit with American and European financial circles through the local hierarchies. Concern for the Italian economy might cause nightmares to Cardinal Siri, but it was hardly likely that the pope would be taken in by such parochial considerations. Father Edward Duff, S.J., in a syndicated article dated December 12, 1963, entitled "Pope upsets theories of Council pessimists," correctly assessed the situation— after he had himself helped to contribute to the gloom in several preceding articles. Nor could there be any doubt, after the events in Palestine, that Pope Paul remained determined to carry through his purposes which were still those of Pope John XXIII and the majority of the Council, but of course in his own way and in his own time. Elaborate attempts to explain a fundamental change in his thinking as the result of various conflicting interests or fears failed to hold together. His speeches, statements, actions all showed a remarkable consistency. The same elements were present *after* the alleged "debâcle" of November as before. There was no need to assume a "counter-revolution."

The thesis of gloom was certainly not shared by his intimate advisers, Cardinals Suenens, König, and Lercaro; nor was it shared by Frings, Ritter or Feltin who left Rome with the fullest confidence that the cause they represented would prevail whatever might be the delays or the ottavianesque difficulties still to be overcome. These were the men who were actually closest to the Holy Father in his thinking as Cardinal Montini, and with whom now, evidently, he shared an insight into the problem of implementing the reform from the lofty, timeless perspective that he had to adopt as pope.

An indication of this manner of thinking was given by Cardinal Suenens in a lecture delivered at the Canadian college, on Sunday, December 1st, attended by most of the Canadian bishops as well as the students and priests belonging to the Canadian colony in Rome. Admitting that the three schemata handled during the Second Session were not as full a work-load as they had hoped to accomplish during the ten weeks of conciliar debate, the Belgian cardinal discussed the causes for the slow pace, while insisting strongly on the unquestionable value of the achievement represented by the thorough treatment given the nature of the Church, the general, if contested, acceptance of the idea of the collegiality of the bishops, and the positive approach towards ecumenism manifested in the majority of discourses during the final two weeks. He indicated that he had opposed any idea of a vote on chapters four and five of the latter schema—the problem of the Jews and of religious liberty—without a thorough discussion of these issues. Hence he did not share the disappointment of the more impatient progressives who felt that the Council had been check-mated by the filibustering tactics of the opposition. Questioned as to the possibility of introducing a truly parliamentary procedure into the Council's debates, he observed that many of the prelates were very sensitive about their freedom to speak, particularly those from Africa and behind the Iron Curtain; and while admitting that the present procedure neither permitted a direct dialogue nor prevented a certain manipulation on the part of a small group who still wielded great influence through two or three well-placed individuals in the secretary general's entourage, he did not see much to be gained from a tighter control of the speakers by the moderators, other than an insistence that the individual interventions should be directed to theological issues and principles, while criticism of the conciliar texts should be confined to written communications given to the respective conciliar commissions. He observed that despite provision made in the revised rules for the Council, very few of the Fathers had availed themselves of the right to sit in on the meetings of the commissions preparing texts for the Council's consideration.

Suenens spoke further about two important matters that both he and the pope were determined should be affected by the Council: the seminary training of the clergy, and the collegial function of the bishops' office. With regard to the former point, he said that he had conducted a thorough investigation of seminary legislation beginning with Trent and traced its effectiveness over the last four hundred years. Then he had called in ten lay experts to have them analyze present procedures in his own diocesan seminary, and finally polled all the living alumni of that institution. It amazed him to find that Trent's original suggestion that seminary training should be divided into periods based on six months of scholastic training and six months of practical application, seemed to be the formula indicated for modern training. As to collegiality, he alleged it was the pope's mind that this was now a fact, and it was merely a matter of time and the working out of a proper formula, before such an apostolic college was established. Finally he expressed great satisfaction with the reorganization of the conciliar commissions effected by the Council's election of new members, and the selection of a second vice-president and secretary which had followed immediately.* But he was adamant in asserting that there would be no purge or reprisals for attitudes adopted on either side of the debate, since this would be totally in opposition to the spirit of liberty and charity which it had been Pope John's and now Pope Paul's insistence, was the only possible atmosphere for a Council of the followers of Christ.

There was no sign, moreover, that the pope had given in on the important issue of collegiality. The vague reference to the topic in his closing speech: "at a time, and in a manner that will seem most opportune to us" merely meant that plans would be consummated at the appropriate, Pauline time. In Paul's mind, the collegial government of the Church was an actuality though he had not had time to determine just how or when he would "summon from the episcopate of the whole world and from the religious orders, competent and distinguished brothers . . . who together with the members of the Sacred College [of cardinals] will assist and counsel us." That this was more than a notional

---

* Asked by one of the bishops in the audience if this meant that the presidents of the commissions were to be seated behind the new vice-presidents as the group of Council presidents were behind the moderators in the Council itself, he acknowledged the indiscretion of the query, and shrugged it off with a smile.

acceptance of the idea of collegiality was certified by a sudden visit he made to the Lateran Palace to inspect the work of reconstruction. Originally the plans formulated under Pope John had called for the transfer to the Vatican of the archeological museum housed in the Lateran, and the location of the vicariate (or administrative offices for the diocese of Rome) in the new building. But Paul had cancelled these plans, and he now determined that the new edifice should contain a suite of rooms for himself and offices and quarters for the bishops whom he would summon to Rome for consultation on the Church's world-wide problems. In visiting the site, the pope had been accompanied by two engineers from Milan, and the radical modifications they had suggested with regard both to the specifications and the costs of the new construction led to a rumor that Cardinal Traglia would be sacked as pro-vicar in effective charge of running the diocese of Rome for the pope. But such a change was not in keeping with Pope Paul's manner of handling problems.

As regards the faculties returned to the bishops by the pope in his Motu Proprio *Pastorale Munus,* communicated to the Fathers on December 3, 1963, in carefully chosen words, the pope declared that these faculties belonged to the bishops by reason of their office, and said that this declaration was a positive result of the Council's debate. Here of course he was cutting across a Curial fixation, for the official document bore the title *Concessio facultatum* and in the résumé published in *L'Osservatore Romano,* the author said the pope had "conceded" these powers to the bishops. But this was merely another minor indication of the fact that the Old Guard who were still at work could not bring themselves to believe that a revolution was actually in progress. It was this type of act, of course, that gave some justification to the feeling of the critics that nothing had been actually achieved by the Council. What they could not understand was that Pope Paul had his own reasons for not insisting, all down the line, that his viewpoint be scrupulously respected by the Curial officials, the most obvious being the fact that he had set his own pace for a thorough reform of the Curia, which he was determined should be brought about by an immediate collaboration between himself and the bishops. Evidently he did not want to anticipate this reformation (or possibly prejudice its direction or thoroughness) by interfering in individual and trifling matters.

It was a reflection on the strange vagaries of group psychology that a large portion of the pope's audience, both within and outside the Council, should have considered the pope's closing discourse and the disclosure of his positive plans for the future as somehow inadequate, or even favoring the reactionary tendencies of the intransigents. Not a few of the Fathers and critics felt that somehow or other Pope Paul had let them down. In actual fact, however, a comparison of this talk with Pope John's closing discourse at the end of the First Session indicated that the Pauline phase of conciliar thought was not only a positive development in a direct line with John's designs, but was at once more specific and more hopeful. What the critics wanted was for all practical purposes a daily or weekly declaration of revolutionary principles and a series of de capitations or dismissals that would justify progressively enlarged headlines. John's jovial exterior, magnified almost out of proportion, had taken on the lineaments of a myth in the minds of many of the commentators. Hence they could not see that the tremendously complicated project upon which the Church was now embarked in implementing a vast inner renewal, in making an effective effort to bring about the reconstitution of Christian unity, and in approaching the modern and religiously disaffected world, could admit of only one truly revolutionary upheaval, and that this had been experienced in the convocation of the Council. Thereafter, the Church had to settle down to the painful slow labor, first of convincing its own leaders and people of the necessity and feasibility of this startling project, and then of persuading those outside its immediate control to collaborate in the vast spiritual renewal projected on a world scale by the Council. It was part of Paul's genius, as it had been John's gift, to realize that such a revolution could only be affected by the apparently inadequate day to day debate and small-scale but progressive decisions on the part of both the Council and the pope. If, for example, the actuality of episcopal co-operation in the governance of the Church were to be realized through collegial cooperation, the pope could not be making immediate, Church-shaking decisions on his own, for this would be but a continuation of authoritarian papal rule, the very methods implicitly criticized by the Council.

Mystery surrounded the release of the Motu Proprio on January 27th, putting part of the Liturgy Constitution into effect—at least the mystery of how one who was as well acquainted with Curial procedures as Paul VI could still tolerate men in positions of power around him, who obviously had no intention of carrying out his desires to the letter. The readiest explanation seemed to be that in this matter he probably decided to let the people concerned hang themselves. What happened seemed clear enough. The text of the document was prepared by the Congregation of Rites under the guidance of Cardinal Lercaro and Father Antonelli. Evidently the first draft did not meet with full papal approval, although in an article published in the December 6th edition of *L'Osservatore Romano* Father Antonelli had admitted the full implications of the liturgical reform projected by the Constitution. In any case, the document was at least five days late in coming out, and during the interval it was known that Father Antonelli exhibited considerable irritation. When published, the text of the Motu Proprio was castigated as a betrayal of the conciliar

Constitution. The text was a terrible disappointment in that it not only said nothing about the changes contemplated for the celebration of mass, but it contained a phrase that contradicted the Liturgy Constitution itself. Where the latter had authorized regional groups of bishops to select and approve vernacular texts of the liturgy, the Motu Proprio specified that these translations had to be submitted to the Holy See for acceptance. The very next day Cardinal Larraona, prefect of the Congregation of Rites, let it be known in no uncertain terms that he was not the author of the restriction. "Everyone is blaming me," he confided to a group of associates, "for they know that I was opposed to the original liturgical schema. But once the Constitution was promulgated by the Holy Father and the Council, I accepted it wholeheartedly. That phrase was not in the document when it left my hands." He indicated further that while the document lay on the pope's desk several members of the Holy Office had had access to the Holy Father's presence. What was even stranger, the next evening, *L'Osservatore Romano* carried an article of explanation signed s.m. (for the Benedictine liturgist, Dom Salvatore Marsili), which said flatly that "The Motu Proprio does not grant very much, particularly for the impatient." This conclusion was preceded by a series of reflections that were bold indeed. The good Benedictine reminded his readers that the Constitution on the Liturgy was not a code of rubrics, but called for a "reformation of mind and mentality in ceremonial matters," and declared that it was based on "new theological perspectives." He said it was useless to look for merely external conformity to the new rules, but that a whole mental attitude had to be developed that would constitute the basis for a reorganization of liturgical prayer. He acknowledged that difficulties would arise over the granting of discretionary power to individuals and bishops. The new commission would have rough going in its attempt to keep the needs of the whole world in mind while at the same time working out norms that would be suitable for individual areas. He felt many would be disappointed that the bishops had not been authorized at once to continue with experiments already started in these matters on a local level; presumably, the bishops might have been granted authority to begin at once with simplification by dropping the last Gospel, transposing the blessing to before the *Ite missa est,* and abolishing once and for all the prayers said after mass. But he saw some hope in that the Motu Proprio did not say that the bishops "could not ask for special faculties in particular cases."

The utter frankness of this commentary led observers to believe that it was an "inspired" article; that the author had been asked to write it by someone close to the Holy Father. Whether this was the case or not, a reaction was immediately evident on the part of certain members of the Curia, particularly the secretary general of the Council, Archbishop

Felici, who seemed to take any apparent criticism of things connected with the Council as a personal affront. Father Marsili suddenly found himself literally on the road to banishment. However, as had happened in the case of the Dominican Father Spiazza before the Council, and to Father Bugnini, who was not made secretary of the conciliar Liturgical Commission when Cardinal Larraona succeeded as president, Marsili was rescued: he had the good fortune to run into Cardinal Lercaro in Milan. On learning of his plight, the latter immediately returned him to Rome and had him restored to his former functions.

In early January 1964, on the strength of the Constitution, the German, French and Belgian bishops had authorized vernacular versions of the liturgy, and they immediately protested vehemently to the Holy Father about the Motu Proprio. After considerable infighting between Curial officials, a final version of the document was worked out and printed in the official *Acta Apostolicae Sedis*. The new version not only omitted the offending phrase by stating that only the *acta* or final decisions of the bishops should be submitted to the Holy See, but it removed from the text other phrases which had been introduced insisting on the fact that it was the pope who had been granting privileges rather than the Council's Constitution that had authorized the liturgical reforms.

When the membership of the new Liturgical Commission appointed to oversee the carrying out of the provisions of the Constitution was announced, with Cardinal Lercaro as president and Father Bugnini as secretary, and cardinals and bishops as members who were generally known to be in favor of liturgical renewal, most liturgists were satisfied. The list contained one enigma, however—the name of Archbishop Felici. The only conclusion appeared to be the rather uncharitable thought that the vanity and striving for power of the secretary general were all too apparent.

In retrospect one could say that two movements interfered with the efficiency of the Second Session and threatened to bring the Council to disaster. Both were engineered by the intransigent Curialist party. One was the time-wasting involved in the daily round of certain sacrosanct ritual acts dear to the Italian ecclesiastical mind, and particularly the devotion of whole meetings to the commemoration of events or anniversaries, for example, the centenary of the Council of Trent on December 3rd, which could and should have been handled differently in view of the tight schedule.* The other was the more important dangerous chal-

---

* Abbé René Laurentin listed specifically the recitation of the *De Profundis* whenever a council member died, whereas a simple mention of the name, or names, in the *memento* of the mass would have been sufficient; the Italian luxuriance of prayers accompanying the Angelus; and the enthronement of the Gospel, which could just as well have taken place during the daily mass instead of in a special ceremony afterward. *Bilan de la deuxième session,* Seuil, Paris, 1964, p. 205.

lenge to the authority not only of the moderators, but of the Council itself, implicit in the questioning of the validity of the famous five propositions voted on October 30, 1963. Once the majority had expressed its mind, any effort by a minority to question the Council's decision could only be disruptive. From the behavior of Cardinals Ottaviani, Browne and Ruffini, and the continued irritating assertions of Bishop Carli, it almost seemed as if they—aided by the secretary general —were intent on accomplishing just that. The suspicion was also strong that this group received the backing of the Secretary of State, Cardinal Cocognani, who, since his return from the United States seemed to have been overinfluenced by the fear-inspired approach of his old colleagues (e.g. Browne's *"Patres, caveamus"*). The secretary general seemed to be working directly under the Secretary of State, receiving apparently full support from that quarter in the numerous questionable maneuvers in which he was engaged—one obvious area being his control over the list of speakers; another, the conservative-favoring slant of his announcements and his tactics in closing his eyes to illicit propaganda moves of the conservatives while pouncing on those attempted by the progressives. These human aspects of the conciliar procedure needed to be taken into account, for they had a bearing on the course of the Session and almost compromised its success. A comparison with similar procedures and tactics at the Council of Trent would be instructive.

Furthermore, it was known that the board of presidents was not happy in being supplanted by the four moderators. Cardinal Tisserant, in particular, felt that not only was his dignity being challenged, but that the Four had not functioned with the efficiency of his own unwieldy group of ten during the First Session. It was noticeable that on the first two days of debate, the moderators, Cardinals Agagianian and Lercaro, had interrupted speakers when they wandered from the topic or went beyond their allotted time, but, on instructions from the Holy Father who was overconscious of not wishing to interfere with the freedom of the speakers, this policy was not pursued again until close to the very end. It has been suggested that this was the result of a lack of confidence in their position on the part of the moderators, but this was hardly likely. In fact, however, they discovered that their mandate was not clear: when challenged on minor matters, as they were by Cardinal Bacci, for example, they quickly asserted their leadership and control; but when opposed by Archbishop Felici or Cardinal Ottaviani, they found themselves without the backing of the presidents or the Secretary of State, and eventually had to get the pope's explicit support. As for the pope's failure to intervene in the debates, it could be explained by his unwillingness to interfere on principle, as well as by the large number of issues on which he received petitions from groups of bishops containing from twenty to more than six hundred signatures (e.g. he was invited to pronounce on the validity of the five propositions, to allow the introduction of schemata other than those proposed by the commissions, to solve the problem of what to do about the Virgin Mary, to take a direct hand in getting the chapters on religious liberty and on the Jews to the floor, to sanction a conciliar message to priests which in fact came to nothing, to declare his intention with regard to the episcopal body which was to advise him—this was the petition with over six hundred signatures—to interfere in the affair of the communications decree, to change the formula for promulgating conciliar acts, to authorize the immediate application of the Liturgy Constitution, and to allow a concelebration of all the bishops at the closing ceremony).

All this must have been somewhat disillusioning to one who had made up his mind to pursue a policy that would permit the bishops to enter into their functions as his copartners in the government of the universal Church. One could appreciate his chagrin at finding himself accused of exhibiting a Hamlet-like complex (cf. *Time,* December 6, 1963).

Lacking, in effect, was a concerted effort on the part of the progressive cardinals to answer in kind the power-play assertions and moves made by Cardinals Ottaviani and Ruffini, seconded by Browne, Siri, etc. But from the nature of the problem this seemed to them impossible, without running the risk of disrupting the peace of the assembly. There was question of some disagreement between the moderators themselves, but even though as diverse personalities one need not have expected unanimity from them on all questions, it was certain that they were in full agreement on the general policies for conducting the Council and felt that they had the support of the pope. The rumors regarding disagreement between them were spread mainly by the conservatives, following an old and well-known Roman tactic.

The apprehension felt by a number of the experts and other Council members, as the Second Session came to a close, was based on the not unfounded fear that vengeance would be wreaked on them once the leaders and bishops were out of town. Although several moves were made in this direction, they were on a minor plane and did not go very far. But the possibility of retaliatory action would remain, until a fundamental move was made to reorganize such organs as the Holy Office and the Congregation for Seminaries and Universities, to mention only two of the most important centers. Cardinal Marella was reported to have made this facetious remark about the success of the progressives: "Have no fear, once the talk ceases and the bishops depart, we will change everything back the way it was!"

Nevertheless there were some small signs that the conservatives were perhaps beginning to bend before the wind, convinced as they were that in a "time of troubles" which the Church now seemed to be entering, in their view, with the Holy Spirit remaining somewhat inexplicably aloof, their tactic should be to appear to yield on minor matters regarding externals but to hang on at all costs, until the power of God again manifested itself on their side. Thus the head of the Holy Office, in an interview (March 19, 1964), acknowledged the *aggiornamento* and the collegiality of the bishops to be important facts, something much more sweeping and meaningful than a mere updating of the Church's rules and regulations. But he was still opposed to a married diaconate as opening the door to a married priesthood.

Reports from Rome indicated that Pope Paul's unobtrusive determination that Vatican Council II must speed up work on the remaining schemata had been communicated to the conciliar commissions and had made a great difference in both the tempo and style of their labors. While considerable secrecy surrounded the meetings of the Coordinating Commission under the chairmanship of Cardinal Cicognani in the offices of the Secretariat of State, the fact that one was held on December 28th in the midst of the Christmas festivities, and two more followed in short order (January 15, 1964 and March 10, 1964) evidently impressed the commission chairmen with the seriousness of the pope's intention. In any case, by March 1964, unofficial reports indicated decisive achievements in the commissions dealing with the nature of the Church, with ecumenism, and with the so-called Schema 17, a sort of cover-all document concerned with the Church's attitude toward the modern world. It was a sub-committee of the latter group that seemingly discovered in the principle of a change of venue the secret of breaking the log-jam tactics of the Roman atmosphere. In a meeting at Zurich in mid-January 1964 under the auspices of Bishop Charue, this committee outlined the principles that enabled the secretary to reduce to propositional form the copious material contained in several drafts, the most ambitious of which was a text prepared under the guidance of Cardinal Suenens. An even happier report emanated from the Secretariat for Promoting Christian Unity, which went into almost solitary confinement for two weeks at the end of February 1964 and produced a revision of all five chapters of the schema on Ecumenism that was termed "bolder than the original" by the Paulist Father Stransky.

With regard to the undebated chapters dealing with the Jews and religious liberty (Chapters IV and V), prelates evidently fearful of what they considered to be a "libertarian" attitude bound to destroy the Church's authority, sent Cardinal Bea a substantial number of cautionary recommendations after the Second Session ended. A hurry call from Rome for assistance was spread among the American bishops by the cardinal of St. Louis and the archbishop of Baltimore with gratifying results. The new text was in due course sent to the bishops for study before they reported to Rome for the Third Session, and although, as Archbishop Krol of Philadelphia remarked in a rather unprecedented address to 400 Jewish leaders in his archdiocese, it was not certain that Chapters IV and V would remain in the schema, it was certain that they would be the object of a conciliar vote. This seemed to be confirmed also by Cardinal Ottaviani in an interview. Archbishop Krol admitted that there was opposition to consideration of Chapter IV on the part of prelates from the Near East, who felt that the draft condemning anti-Semitism could not but be construed as a political move by the Arab nations, but he remarked that such opposition was in keeping with the Council's experience thus far, for it was a fact that "no schema was free from such discussion, no schema was spared criticism, and no schema, though accepted, was without its opposing votes." Statements such as this had added weight when it was remembered that Archbishop Krol was one of the six undersecretaries of the Council, a body considered to have been unduly influenced by the dominating personality of the secretary general, Archbishop Felici, during the first two sessions.

Further hints of impending changes seemed to be contained in a speech delivered by Cardinal Tisserant in Paris in January 1964 and, significantly, reprinted by *L'Osservatore Romano*. After praising the work of Paul VI, the cardinal took issue with those who were complaining that the course of reforms was too slow, commenting: *"Des transformations ne peuvent se faire qu'avec discernment et dans le calme."* Cognoscenti found confirmation in these remarks that major reforms were really intended.

284

THE THIRD SESSION

The Opening of the Third Session

The Third Session, it could accurately be said, accomplished more work than the two previous sessions of Vatican Council II combined. For one thing, it covered more ground since the Fathers took up fourteen conciliar texts, as compared with five at the First Session and three at the Second. For another, it promulgated three decrees, the most important of which was the Constitution on the Church, with its crucial Chapter III on collegiality. This constitution in Pope Paul's words would probably come to be considered the crowning achievement that "distinguishes this solemn and historic synod in the memory of future ages." The other promulgated decrees were those on Ecumenism and the Eastern Churches. When this record of achievement was compared with that of the First Session (no documents promulgated) and the Second Session (two documents promulgated), the Third Session could justifiably be ranked high in terms of performance.

Why, then, in view of its obvious accomplishments, did the feeling prevail that the Third Session was nevertheless the most disappointing so far? Why was it possible for the world press to describe the bishops attending the closing ceremony as "stony-faced" and "unresponsive"? Why did so many Fathers leave Rome in a state of sadness and bewilderment? Why did the phrase *magno cum dolore*—the opening words of an urgent petition to the pope at a moment of crisis (see page 319)—become a kind of catchword for the whole Session? Why did a Session that began with such promise end in such gloom?

A widespread opinion was that the answer hinged on one thing—the character of Pope Paul. In contrast to the spirit of joyous expectancy that pervaded the world when Pope John XXIII announced the Council and brought its initial session to a successful close, the hopes of men seemed to have been dampened by the more timorous and cautious Pauline spirit.

287

If the character of Pope Paul was called enigmatic and contradictory, it was due to the fact that he had taken apparently conflicting positions on crucial matters at important junctures. For example, in his opening address at the Third Session the pope called upon the bishops to pass the Constitution on the Church and define the collegiality of the bishops, described by him as "the weightiest and most delicate" problem before the Council. Yet in his encyclical, *Ecclesiam suam,* issued shortly before the start of the Session, he warned: "We reserve to ourselves the choice of the proper moment and manner of expressing our judgment, most happy if we can present it in perfect accord with that of the Council Fathers." Observers at the time were struck by the mysterious Olympian tone and icy aloofness that seemed to be evident in this remark, coming at the end of a long passage expressing confidence in the work of the Council. In the same encyclical, speaking of dialogue with the separated brethren, he recommended observance of the wise precept, "Let us stress what we have in common rather than what divides us," but then proceeded to accentuate the differences by stressing the prerogatives of the papacy in uncompromising terms. He incidentally accused the separated brethren of wishing the Catholic Church to be "without the pope," an opinion that many of them regarded as a strange travesty of their real views. The same contrast was noticeable in his remarks opening the Chair of Unity Octave in January, 1965. After commending the movement of prayer on behalf of Christian unity that had been going on for many years, he suddenly warned against "a temptation that sometimes works its way easily into good souls"—namely, a desire to "hide, weaken, change, deny if need be those teachings of the Catholic Church which are not acceptable today by the separated brethren." In analyzing the pope's penchant for qualifying almost every statement he made, *The Economist* (London) pointed out the disconcerting fact that "but" was a key Pauline word, and characterized him as "The Pope of Buts."

Though well intentioned, Paul's methods were unfortunate in that they produced an impression of negativity, as well as a feeling that he was not wholeheartedly in favor of the positive steps taken. At the Third Session, after the doctrine of collegiality had been defined by the Council and overwhelmingly approved, as the pope had asked, the bishops were obliged to accept without discussion a hair-splitting Explanatory Note at his bidding. Another, and regrettable, example of "Yes, but."

No evidence came to light of any fundamental disagreement between the pope and the majority of the bishops over the ultimate goals of the Council, but the Third Session's final week, inevitably dubbed "Black Week" because of the wave of disappointing events climaxing its closing days, furnished abundant proof that there were differences over methods. Aside from the difficulties caused by the pope's apparent contradictions, there was found to be a certain amount of tension arising from the structural instability of the Catholic system, divinely ordained, with bishops *and* pope sharing supreme authority in the Church. Medieval theorists used the argument that a body with two heads would be a monstrosity to exalt the pope's role at the expense of the bishops. Vatican Council II re-established the rights of the episcopal college, without resolving the delicate problem of the balanced relationship between the college and its head. According to Cardinal Alfrink, the close of this session was marked, not by a "collision of the pope with the rest of the college of bishops nor a collision between the pope and the majority of the bishops," but by a "meeting or possibly a collision of two views of the Church"—i.e., the monarchical and the collegial.

Professor H. A. Oberman, of the Harvard Divinity School, used geometric figures to describe what appeared to be a confrontation between these two different conceptions of supreme power in the Church. Figure one was that of two concentric circles around a single point—the inner circle standing for the pope, the outer circle for the pope *with* the bishops. Figure two was an ellipse with two points or centers which did not coincide—one standing for the pope acting alone, the other for the pope acting *with* the bishops. Figure one could be said to portray the ideal of collegiality as envisioned by its most ardent supporters, implying a constant harmony and identification of thought and action between pope and bishops. This was the image of collegiality that the bishops thought they would get in the Constitution on the Church. Figure two reported what they actually received—an image of unresolved, and at times conflicting, dual headship—the image underlined by the Explanatory Note with its concern for asserting, at all costs, the pope's independence of action, which the bishops never questioned.

The final days of the Third Session were also proof that the period of a Johannine honeymoon between pope and bishops was over, and that relations must soon be put on a more stable, business-like basis. A foreboding of tension, foreseen only as a remote possibility earlier, suddenly became a harsh reality even before final approval had been given to collegiality. Apart from the doctrinal innuendos of the Explanatory Note, nothing was probably so irritating to the bishops as the inconsiderate way in which they were presented at the last minute—without any opportunity for debate—with an official papal interpretation of the doctrine they were to vote. The alternative was the risk of killing the all-important document on the Church, and possibly causing a breakup of the Council itself if they voted no. They were again put in a similar position a few days later over the nineteen last-minute changes in the decree of Ecumenism. No wonder, therefore, if they felt humiliated—as one bishop put it later, "We were treated like children"—or that there was a distinct impression that the spirit, if not the letter, of conciliar freedom had somehow been infringed.

Among the more level-headed voices heard in explanation of the events of "Black Week" was that of the Dutch Bishop Bekkers of 's Hertogen-busch, who called for "a Council that will never end" because of the need for enlightening "people from completely Catholic countries [who are] afraid of full religious freedom, ecumenism, and freedom within the Church." The bishop put his finger on a sore point when he deplored "the methods sometimes used by the minority within the Council," and asked for a program to "insure the success of Vatican II," including the reform of the Curia, the establishment of an episcopal Senate, the overhauling of canon law, freedom within the Church, and Catholic respect for "the spirit of veracity and sincerity," in addition to some form of continued existence for the Council itself. Together with the goal of ecumenism, described by Cardinal Heenan in a statement as now "part of the normal outlook of intelligent Christians everywhere," these points remained the ultimate goal of Pope John's *aggiornamento*.

It was no news that the goals not only of the Council, but the whole program of *aggiornamento,* continued to be fiercely opposed by a small, well-knit group known conveniently as "the minority," nor that the campaign they were waging occasionally erupted onto the surface. What the Third Session revealed more clearly than ever before, however, were the lengths to which Pope Paul was willing to go to soothe the feelings and assuage the doubts of this powerfully placed group of resisters who, it was commonly believed, had no intention of accepting what they regarded as virtual apostasy. Their attitude could be summed up by what a professor of moral theology once told his students: "This is the doctrine on marriage which I have always taught; the Church has allowed me to teach it; therefore the Church is committed to this teaching and cannot repudiate it." Persuasion through argument seemed powerless against such rigorism and irrationalism.

While numerically small, as repeated test-votes showed, the minority made up for lack of numbers by astuteness, cohesion, and the influence it could bring to bear through members well-placed in Rome. Far from having abandoned its intransigent attitude, as might be assumed from the apparent collapse of opposition to collegiality (and other measures it could no longer effectively oppose), it merely shifted its tactics. Efforts were next concentrated on preventing any important concessions in the expected papal Motu Proprio on mixed marriages; postponing as long as possible the announced reform of the Curia, and above all the establish-ment of the proposed episcopal Senate; confusing the channels of author-ity in such a way that, when these two great aims became a reality, the Curia would still be left in a position to veto any unwanted measures;

defending to the last ditch the entrenched position of the Congregation of Seminaries; buttonholing bishops in support of Thomism and scholasticism, two time-honored props of the existing system; scuttling the Declaration on Religious Liberty altogether, but if this proved impossible, then watering it down so that it would amount to little more than a reflection of the Curial view on "toleration"; hindering the work of those conciliar commissions on which they were particularly well represented, e.g. the Missions and Religious Orders; holding off as long as possible with any concrete measures designed to further "intercommunion" with other Churches allowed by the decrees on Ecumenism and the Eastern Churches, from fear that once fraternal accord had become a reality the clock could never be turned back. They did not seem to realize that, at this point, no matter how much obstructionism there was, it was no longer possible for the Church to turn back the clock of renewal and reform. It could be impeded, and stalled, and perhaps even stopped momentarily, but a return to preconciliar and pre-Johannine thinking was clearly no longer possible. What was perplexing and alarming was not that the pope should feel he must conciliate the small group of officials whom he daily saw, but that he should be willing to risk making the mistake of Pius IX in 1870, in reverse, by appearing to sacrifice the majority to the minority.

The Third Session opened on September 14, 1964, with Pope Paul being carried into St. Peter's on his portable throne surrounded by the papal court as usual, but a happy Pauline touch was evident as soon as he reached the altar. There, dismounting from his throne, he immediately joined twenty-four waiting prelates, all vested in red, with whom he intended to concelebrate the mass, as if to anticipate, symbolically, the doctrine of episcopal collegiality, not yet proclaimed by the Council. The altar, which stands directly above the tomb or shrine of St. Peter beneath Bernini's splendid canopy, had been enlarged to a rectangular shape, and was decorated with a severely simple white cloth and six low candles. Attended only by his two masters of ceremony, the 80-year-old Archbishop Dante, secretary of the Congregation of Rites, and Monsignor Capoferri, the pope began the prayers at the foot of the altar in a resolute but peculiarly clouded voice. The basilica choir rendered the introductory motet in the plainest Gregorian chant, in striking contrast to the usual pompous polyphony, while the full congregation recited the Gloria, the Credo, the Sanctus and the Agnus Dei in alternate verses. At the offertory, the *orationes super populum,* or special prayers for the people in litany form, were re-introduced after centuries of omission, and during the canon of the mass, all the concelebrating prelates said the prayers out loud including the words of consecration over the bread and wine. Communion was received by the participating concelebrants, each of whom took a piece of one of three large hosts used for the occasion, and a spoonful of wine from the common chalice; then the sacrament was distributed to the people. While sharp liturgical eyes criticized some of the details as not in accord with the most advanced liturgical thinking, the impression on the assembled prelates and the laity was decisive. Only three members of the Curia—Cardinal Tisserant, the dean of the Sacred College of Cardinals; Cardinal Larraona, and Archbishop Felici, secretary general of the Council—were among the concelebrants, the rest being residential bishops, including Cardinal Lercaro (Bologna), Archbishops Krol (Philadelphia) and Shehan (Baltimore), and two heads of religious orders.

Pope Paul's address was a discourse of single purpose. He declared the convocation of the Council a free and spontaneous act on Pope John's part, which he, Paul, had immediately supported. Recognizing that a primary conciliar objective was to complete the Church's teaching on the governing power of the bishops, he said that, with the aid of the Holy Spirit, the Fathers were to "determine the prerogatives of the bishops, describe the relations between our apostolic Roman see and this episcopate, and demonstrate how, in the diverse expressions typical of the east and the west, the idea of the constitution of the Church is still homogeneous. [The Council] should teach both Catholics and our separated brethren the true nature of this hierarchy of which the Holy Spirit has instituted the members as bishops to pasture the Church of God with an indisputable and valid authority."

Paul referred to the need for the papal office to insure the unity guaranteed to the Church by the presence of Christ, and indicated by Christ's selection of Peter as the head of the apostles. He stated that he had no choice but to continue in this function, and that it was not a domination but a service (*diakonia*). In having to place certain restrictions on the exercise of episcopal power, to make doctrinal decisions, and clarify positions, the pope was only acting for the good of the whole Church; actually it was his wish to strengthen the position of the bishops, delegating both authority and faculties to local pastors. Paul had words of encouragement for the religious and the laity who formed the diverse members of Christ's body. He greeted the Catholic lay auditors and the non-Catholic observer-delegates, thanking them for the time and effort which they were devoting to help demonstrate the ecumenical character of the Council, and he expressed his confident hope that in the mystery of Providence, evident in the calling of the Council, the true reconstitution of the full Church of Christ would not be far off. Of exceptional significance were his emotionally charged exhortations at the end of the speech to the various "Churches" still separated from Catholic communion, and his explicit recognition of the ecumenical principle of "pluralism in practice." "Our thoughts go out to the world about us," he concluded, "with its own interests, with its indifference too, perhaps even its hostility."

Conciliar business began the following morning, Tuesday, September 15, 1964, with a series of instructions read, first by Cardinal Tisserant as senior member of the board of Council presidents, then by Cardinal Agagianian as senior of the Council moderators, and finally by Archbishop Felici as secretary general of the Council. Among the modifications in procedure was an explicit acknowledgment that the moderators would henceforth have control of both the lists of speakers and the course of the debates, thus clarifying their authority with respect to that of the secretary general and the board of presidents. Once closure was voted, the signatures of seventy bishops were required to enable a speaker to make a final intervention. All, including the cardinals, would have to hand in summaries of their speeches five days before the topic was due to be discussed.

It was immediately apparent that under pressure from the Coordinating Commission, in accordance with a plan agreed upon during the intersessional period, a positive attempt would be made to accelerate the proceedings, and all three speakers indicated the hope that, despite the work load, this session might prove to be the final one of the Council. Speaking "like an English headmaster"—the phrase was used by Douglas Woodruff writing in the London *Tablet*—Cardinal Tisserant warned the Fathers about observing great prudence in discussing conciliar business outside the Council hall, particularly matters that were still under the secrecy of the commissions. Archbishop Felici read out a set of rules binding on the *periti*—they must only give opinions when requested to do so by conciliar commissions; they must not grant interviews; and they must be circumspect in what they wrote and divulged about conciliar activities. These were considered offensive by most of these hard-working priests and monsignori, particularly when the archbishop added a threat to deprive *periti* of their privileges if they engaged in lobbying or in the distribution of literature intended to influence the thinking of the bishops. Though couched in humorous terms, Archbishop Felici's warning to the bishops to remain in their seats during the voting periods, and his announcement that the two coffee bars would only open at 11 A.M., instead of 10 A.M. as in previous years, caused some audible groans. Questioned the following day as to the secretary general's authority for these restrictions, one of the moderators said that he had overstepped his mandate; but no attempt was made to correct the generally unfavorable impression they had made. Throughout the session it seemed apparent that the secretary general had the interests of the minority at heart.

This attitude was caught by the correspondent of the Italian daily *Il Messaggero,* Carlo Lazoli, who wrote: "These limitations on the *periti* and Fathers can hardly be considered impartial. They doubtless favor the wing of the assembly which is interested in reducing to a minimum the expression of opinion and the problems being discussed."

CHAPTERS VII AND VIII OF 'THE CHURCH'

The actual debate began with a consideration of Chapter VII of the schema on the Church, concerning the eschatological aspects of the Christian vocation. Cardinal Ruffini led off with an attack on the significance of the scriptural passages quoted, and maintained that there was a lack of order in the discussion of the last things of human existence, namely death, judgment, heaven or hell. Purgatory was hardly mentioned, he complained, and the condemnation of those dying in the state of mortal sin was passed over in silence. He was for rejecting the text outright. On the other hand, Cardinal Urbani (Venice) in his only intervention at the Third Session, proclaimed that any major change in the chapter would destroy the harmony of the text which organically embodied the dogmatic, apologetic, pastoral and ecumenical aspects of the subject. Cardinals Santos (Philippines) and Rugambwa (Tanganyika) agreed, but the Latin rite patriarch of Jerusalem, Alberto Gori, called for an express mention of the doctrine on hell, and Archbishop Nicodemo (Bari, Italy) likewise demanded an explicit mention of eternal damnation for unrepentant sinners. It was Archbishop Hermaniuk, the Ukranian metropolitan of Winnipeg, who pointed out that the true significance of the Chapter was to give the Church a sense of expectancy. of vigilance, of preparation for death which was right around the corner for everybody, and of the end of time which stared the modern world in the face. The debate was continued until 12:30 instead of 12 noon, the extra half hour added to the conciliar time allowing four more Fathers to speak each day.

With the opening of the second general congregation on Wednesday, it was obvious that a pattern and rhythm had been established for the session and that the tempo would be fast. A schedule listing the order in which the various documents would come up for debate was announced; it included the Pastoral Office of Bishops, the Declarations on Religious Liberty and the Jews, the schemas on Divine Revelation and the Apostolate of the Laity, the propositions on the Priesthood, the Missions, Seminaries, and Religious Orders, and finally the schema on the Church in the Modern World—Schema 13. Those wishing to speak on the subjects of Religious Liberty and the Jews were told to hand in the summaries of their speeches by Friday. A vote was taken on the schedule for voting the first six chapters of *De Ecclesia,* the amended text of which was now distributed.

In concluding the debate on eschatology, Cardinal Suenens attacked the present system of canonizations in the Church, complaining that under the present Rome-controlled official processes, religious orders accounted for 85 per cent of canonized saints and 13 European countries monopolized 90 per cent. The procedures were too complicated, financially burdensome, and so far, discriminatory to the laity. The last speaker in this debate was Bishop D'Agostino (Vallo di Lucania, Italy) who made a final pitch reminding modern man of the existence of hell.

The debate on the place of Mary in the economy of salvation, which constituted Chapter VIII of *De Ecclesia,* was introduced by Archbishop Roy (Quebec) and immediately found Cardinal Ruffini on his feet with a mild remonstrance calling for a clearer text, making it obvious to non-Catholics that in speaking of Mary's part in man's salvation the Church was in no way detracting from the dignity of Jesus Christ. Thirteen other Fathers spoke, but before the morning's end Bishops Charue (Namur, Belgium) took the microphone to present the *relatio* on Chapter I of the schema *De Ecclesia,* which the Fathers proceeded to vote on (2114 Placet, 11 Non placet, 63 Placet iuxta modum, and 1 null vote). Thursday, Chapter II of *De Ecclesia* concerned with the People of God was voted in four parts during continuation of the debate on Mary. Non Placet votes came only to 30, 12, 48 and 67, but despite reiterated warnings from the secretary general, each round always produced a series of null votes. This continued until the third week when, with unfeigned relief, Archbishop Felici was able to announce that at least one round of voting had taken place without a single invalid vote.

Despite the pleasure felt over the rapid pace at which the Council was proceeding, there was an uneasy feeling that the desire to make the Third Session the final one boded no good. The minority were known to be as resolutely opposed to the aims of the Council as ever, and in urging the authorities to bring the Council to an end with much of its work left unfinished or perhaps only half finished, their ultimate purpose was to allow the Curia to return everything to normal as if there had been no *aggiornamento* at all. The announcement that summaries of the speeches to be made on Religious Liberty and the Jews would have to be submitted in only two days was regarded as particularly outrageous and ominous. This impression was reinforced by the tone of the speeches of the minority when the next item of business was taken up.

THE PASTORAL OFFICE OF BISHOPS

On September 18th the revised schema on the Pastoral Office of Bishops was distributed in the council hall, after Secretary General Felici had announced that the administrative section of his office had provided accident insurance coverage for all the members of the Council. While a number of missionary bishops who drove ancient vehicles were pleased that their dioceses might benefit from their sudden demise on the traffic-snarled streets of Rome, the more cynically-minded bishops remembered the squabble that had accompanied the discussion of this schema when it was presented at the Second Session under the provoking title, "The Relations between the Hierarchy and the Roman Curia." They presumed that Felici's office was taking no chances on any violent reactions this time. The same morning the whole of Chapter II of *De Ecclesia* was submitted to a vote resulting in 1615 Placet, 553 Placet iuxta modum, 19 Non placet and 3 invalid votes, and the secretary general announced that while it had been approved by a substantial majority, the commission would pay careful attention to the *modi* or suggested amendments. This chapter, dealing with the Church as the People of God, was actually the heart of the Council's break-away from a scholastic approach to the theology of the Church. It described the mystery of the Church in biblical terms adapted to the existentialist world in which the Church now found itself.

The *relatio* on the Pastoral Office of Bishops was read by Archbishop Veuillot (coadjutor archbishop of Paris), after Cardinal Marella delivered a brief introduction in which he explained the history of the revision since the last session. The archbishop declared that the principles motivating the present document had been taken from the theological explanation of the episcopal office as contained in Chapter II of the schema on the Church, and the validity of the collegial principle was assumed. Since it dealt with the bishop's office (*munus*), this term was defined as a duty or service or ministry, of teaching, sanctifying and feeding the flock of Christ. A new article had been added asserting the essential freedom of the bishop in the exercise of his office, particularly with respect to the civil authorities in so-called Catholic countries as well as in communist-dominated states, in each of which influence was commonly brought to bear by way of controlling the nomination of bishops and the exercise of their authority.

Cardinal Richard (Bordeaux), while praising the excellent directives given in the document, felt that too many details were left to the decision of post-conciliar commissions and suggested that a number of these be spelled out as already belonging to bishops, such as full freedom in the appointment of pastors, the responsibilities of national conferences of bishops, and jurisdiction in cases of appeals between dioceses. He felt something further should be said about super-parochial or inter-parochial activities in a diocese. Cardinal Browne, followed immediately by Bishop Carli, attacked the basic assumption of the document by challenging the doctrine of collegiality. The bishop claimed that the doctrine was objectionable on "historical, juridical, dogmatic, liturgical and other grounds." He did not hesitate to state unabashedly: "If this text is approved, we expose ourselves to the accusation of using two standards—we will have adopted a policy of extreme caution in dealing with the Virgin Mary, and a policy of broad liberality in our treatment of the bishops."

Bishop Rupp (Monaco) complained that after a show of grandeur in its initial parts, the document backed down to a mumble when it came to discussing diocesan reorganization. While praising its pastoral directives, he felt it failed in not realizing that no diocese was made up of a static or stabilized population; that as migration was characteristic of modern man, some consideration should be given to this aspect of the pastoral problem on both the local, national, and international levels. Bishop Pildáin y Zapiáin (the Canary Islands) expressed his desire for an absolute renunciation of governmental interference in ecclesiastical affairs.

Continuing the discussion of the schema, Cardinal Léger (Montreal) made a distinct contribution to the pastoral atmosphere of the Council by mentioning the specific reasons for the reorganization of the episcopal office in the contemporary world. Bishops must learn to know the mind of modern *homo technicus,* whose attitude toward religion was highly critical, he said. Modern man thought of obedience in different terms from his predecessors. We must adapt our teaching to those who were to receive it, by being humble and not becoming involved in affairs which did not concern us, particularly in the secular field. There must be closer bonds between the bishop and his clergy and between the bishop and the faithful. The schema should say something about the desired simplification of episcopal titles, honors, dress, etc. in a spirit of poverty. His intervention was greeted with applause.

Bishop Compagnone (Anagni, Italy) and Archbishop Rossi (Ribeirão Prêto, Brazil) both spoke about the relations between bishops and religious orders, but from slightly different angles, the latter being of the conviction that all agreements must be carefully written out, so that there would be fewer disputes between religious superiors and bishops. Bishop Staverman (apostolic prefect in Indonesia) brought up the delicate subject of fallen priests and suggested that there ought to be a more reasonable and less rigoristic attitude toward them. The solution need not be the same everywhere. The principle of decentralization could be applied here. For example, some of them should certainly be allowed to marry.

Archbishop Guerry (Cambrai) felt that the usual role of the bishop as "doctor" or teacher was too conventional. The times have changed, he said. While teaching did not cease to be a primary episcopal function, bishops were now also called upon to be abreast of social, economic, demographic and other matters, including war and peace. Pope Pius XII had led the way in promoting this new type of pastoral emphasis. The bishop must at all times reveal the presence of Christ in the world and, to be effective, he must be "up" on all these things. Archbishop Guerry's speech seemed to put into words what was behind many of the other interventions. The remaining speakers dealt with one aspect or another of the problem of adapting the episcopal office to modern times.

On Wednesday, after the debate had been closed, two final speakers were allowed, in the name of at least 70 Fathers. Bishop Greco (Alexandria, Louisiana) spoke on the subject of confraternities, while Bishop Gonzalez Moralejo (auxiliary of Valencia, Spain) was one of the few to bring up the subject of episcopal nominations. He heartily approved of the last-minute changes in the text calling for freedom from control by the state in this matter. However, better criteria could be worked out governing episcopal nominations, including discussion by episcopal conferences and consulting the wishes of the clergy and even the laity.

THE DECLARATION ON RELIGIOUS LIBERTY

The debate on the Declaration on Religious Liberty began Wednesday, September 23rd, with a report by the *relator,* Bishop de Smedt of Bruges, Belgium, who emphasized that the new text had been greatly improved over the original one, presented but not debated at the end of the Second Session, "thanks to the collegial discussions of the Fathers" who had submitted 380 amendments to the Secretariat. Man's fundamental dignity as God's creature, as well as the present development of human society, he said, made a conciliar statement on this theme imperative.

Despite the assurances of Bishop de Smedt that sufficient care had been exercised to ward off the dangers of subjectivism or religious indifferentism in treating this topic, Cardinal Ruffini rose to begin the discussion by claiming that this was by no means so. The declaration should be entitled "On Religious Tolerance," not "Liberty," because those in error had no rights. In his usual disconcerting fashion—a pose which the elderly cardinal thoroughly enjoyed, for after such interventions he could be seen chuckling over the disturbance he knew he had caused—he laid it on the line that as the Catholic Church was the one and only true Church, it should be supported by governments; while no one should be forced to profess a religion, or have his conscience outraged, it was God's will that the Catholic Church should prevail. There was no denying that the cardinal presented the outdated pre-Johannine position with great candor.

The Spanish Cardinal Quiroga y Palacios (Santiago de Compostela) adopted a similar although somewhat milder approach. He denounced the document as favoring liberalism and said that it seemed to be meant primarily for Protestant countries. Its adoption would mean a revolution in the Church, whereas Paul VI had called for a gradual reform. The tide of the debate was quickly turned, however, by an impressive run of speeches from Cardinals Léger, Cushing, Bueno y Monreal, Meyer, Ritter, and Silva Henriquez. It was the first speech on the floor by the Boston cardinal and he was listened to with close attention and some expectancy. In flawless Latin, despite his disclaimers to any knowledge of the language, and in a high-pitched Bostonese accent that made it difficult for his continental hearers to grasp some of his words, though the purport of his message was perfectly clear, he asserted his joy that the Council was finally coming round to safeguard "a decent respect for the opinions of mankind." While not denying that the subject was complicated, he thought that the essence of the matter could be reduced to two principles: summed up by the traditional phrase which the Church was always claiming for herself, *libertas Ecclesiae,* and the principle of freedom for other Churches and for every human person, which she was now claiming also. His summation, including a quotation in English of Lord Acton's famous dictum, "Freedom is the highest political end," and his reference to Pope John's encyclical, *Pacem in Terris,* as the final word on the subject of human freedom, won him a warm round of applause.

Cardinal Cushing made it clear that he approved of the present text only in a general sense, as a basis for further revisions. His remarks were addressed mainly to the idea of religious liberty as such, which he wanted to emphasize in the strongest possible terms. This was also, in the main, the line which other American speakers took. Cardinal Meyer explained that the text was acceptable to the American bishops primarily for three reasons: because men of today expected the Church to come out with a statement on behalf of religious freedom, which the text did; because it made clear that the act of faith must be freely made; and because a document on this subject would facilitate the Church's mission, for it would show that the faith was not to be spread by violence, conquest, or propaganda, but through freedom. A statement was necessary because of its implications for the ecumenical movement.

Cardinal Ritter's discourse caused some mild consternation. After accepting the declaration, in principle, as both pastorally oriented and necessary, he went on to say that the acceptance of the declaration itself did not necessarily mean acceptance of the reasons for it, as stated therein, and that a simple declaration should be worked out merely noting the need for religious liberty without making any attempt to justify it. The moderators, he said, might distinguish between these two points when putting the text to a vote. This seemed to be playing directly into the hands of the minority, who claimed that indiscriminate religious liberty could not be justified on theological grounds, and that the call for this document was purely an American (or Anglo-Saxon) move based on considerations of political expediency. The St. Louis cardinal was taxed with having used the wrong tactics, delivering the type of speech appropriate only for a stalemate when it was time for compromise, not at the beginning when absolutes were laid down. He took the criticism in good grace. The American position was also represented by Archbishop Alter (Cincinnati), speaking in the name of many American bishops. Unless the Church clearly proclaimed the right of religious liberty as an absolute, how could she insist that it be recognized by the totalitarian states?

When Cardinal Ottaviani rose to speak (the last speaker on the first day of the debate), he seemed to be seizing upon Cardinal Ritter's suggestion and it was expected that he would develop the idea, but instead he fell back upon the usual theological clichés. The schema was acceptable in general, but with reservations, one of these being the suppression of the paragraph on proselytism, which he felt might hinder the work of the missions. The Fathers were reminded that the Council was not an "assembly of philosophers." His assertion that governments were entitled to intervene in religious matters was immediately countered by Bishop Čekada (Yugoslavia), who said that a declaration on religious liberty was a necessity in today's world when Marxist regimes were so actively engaged in the business of suppressing religion. "Yesterday it was Nazism, today it is atheistic materialism or communism. Religious freedom is the problem *par excellence.*" The bishop urged that the Council draft a message to the United Nations, insisting on the right of all men to religious liberty.

On the second day of debate, support for the declaration came from Cardinal König (Vienna), who also wanted some mention of the fact that religious freedom was being denied in certain countries. Freedom of worship was not the sum total of religious liberty. The idea meant much more. In some countries where there was suppression of true liberty, believers were reduced to a kind of second-class status and were subject to real discrimination. Public opinion should be alerted about this problem. His speech drew a round of applause.

A number of conservative speakers, taking up the suggestion of Cardinal Ritter, urged that the declaration be confined to a general statement of principles, leaving aside theological considerations about which there was disagreement. Cardinal Browne observed, first of all, that the present text was totally unacceptable to him because it seemed to accord the same rights to a right conscience as to an erroneous conscience. In attempting to interpret Pope John's statement that a man's conscience was the final arbiter of human liberty, he misquoted the pope. Archbishop Parente, who followed, was more cautious. The present text seemed to be an "inextricable forest," a jumble of theology, law, sociology and politics. It should be reduced to a few simple principles about the dignity of man, freedom of conscience, the freedom of the Church to preach the Gospel everywhere and at all times, and finally the duty of the state toward religion.

The minority position having been laid down, by a curious coincidence, or what some American punsters described as a "Felicitous" bit of maneuvering, a line-up of seven conservative speakers now rose to hammer away at the minority thesis, Archbishop Cantero Quadrado, Bishop Abasolo y Lecue, Archbishop Nicodemo, Bishop Lopez Ortiz, Bishop de Castro Mayer, Bishop Canestri, and Archbishop Lefebvre. The criticism of the text by Bishop Canestri (auxiliary of Rome) was particularly harsh and in strange contrast to the spirit of the pope who had appointed him to his Roman post. Fortunately this impression was erased by a series of vigorous interventions by Father Buckley (American Superior of the Marist Fathers), Bishop Primeau (Manchester, New Hampshire), Bishop Nierman (Holland), and Archbishop Dubois (Besançon, France). Father Buckley insisted that the text should state more clearly what it meant by freedom of conscience, while Bishop Primeau got in a blow against the dichotomy that would recognize freedom of conscience, but deny external religious liberty. Both related to the dignity of man, he said, and were inseparable.

At their weekly meeting in the North American College the previous Monday, the American bishops had prepared for this debate carefully. After listening to an address by the well-known Jesuit *peritus* and authority on the subject, Father John Courtney Murray, they had agreed that at least eight of their number would speak on the floor of the Council. The text of the declaration was unanimously accepted by the bishops, in spite of efforts by two conservative theologians, Monsignor George Shea of Darlington Seminary, New Jersey, and Father Francis J. Connell, C.Ss.R., emeritus professor of moral theology at Catholic University in Washington, to present objections.

On the last full day of debate, the Curial Cardinal Roberti suggested a distinction between the idea of *freedom of conscience,* which he repro-

301

bated as a subjective right leading to religious indifferentism, and *freedom of consciences,* which he explained could be a proper expedient in modern society. This canonical fine point failed to impress most of the prelates.

Both Archbishop Garrone (Toulouse, France) and Bishop Colombo (Milan archdiocese) delivered particularly noteworthy speeches, the former on the necessity of showing the continuity between past and present teaching with respect to the Church's attidude toward religious liberty and how this had changed; the latter on the necessity of a more theological approach to the whole problem. Since Bishop Colombo was the pope's private theologian, his words were listened to with a great deal of attention. He declared that in Italy the debate was considered a "turning point" for the Council. "Unless we have this declaration," he said flatly, "there can be no dialogue with men of good will." But the whole problem of the theological foundations of religious liberty must be studied and worked out carefully. A general statement would not suffice. The three foundation of religious liberty must be: 1) the principle that man had a natural right to the search for truth, especially religious truth, which Cardinal Montini had emphasized at the First Session in his Council speech of December 5, 1962; 2) the principle that man had a natural right to follow his conscience; 3) a principle of the supernatural order, namely the liberty and nature of the Christian faith. If these three principles were taken into account, it would not be difficult to work out a satisfactory text on religious liberty. The only possible limits were the rights of others and the common good.

Following this intervention, Cardinal Suenens called for a standing vote on whether to end the debate and the motion was carried overwhelmingly. Since the debate had been closed somewhat early on Friday, a number of American speakers were deprived of the opportunity to be heard. It was necessary to give the floor to Cardinal Bea so that he could introduce the next item on the agenda, the Declaration on the Jews, before departing on Saturday with the relic of the Apostle St. Andrew, which the pope had ordered returned to the Orthodox Church of Greece, 500 years after it had been entrusted for safekeeping to the fifteenth century humanist Pope Pius II by the last Byzantine prince fleeing from the Turks.

Following the close of the debate on Religious Liberty, on Friday, the floor was again given on Monday to four prelates who asked to speak in the name of at least 70 Fathers. Archbishop Heenan (Westminster, England) pointed to the Catholic experience in his country as an example of the benfits that accrued from an uninhibited, frank recognition of the principle of religious liberty. In the 16th century, he noted, England had been subject to violent religious persecution from which Roman Catholics had suffered. Ever since the "Catholic Emancipation Act" of 1828, however, their rights to complete religious freedom had been respected.

Although the Church of England, of which the Queen was the head, was still the Established Church, Catholics were not discriminated against. In fact they received the same support from the state as other religions in regard to education. The principle of religious liberty must be firmly proclaimed, while the right of the state to intervene in religious matters on the grounds of protecting the common good must not be too freely acknowledged, for abuses were possible. All religions should be treated alike so far as the state was concerned. Bishop Wright (Pittsburgh) developed the relationship between religious liberty and the common good, reading a long quotation from Maritain to the effect that the essential concern of the common good was to provide for the development of the human person, and therefore of human freedom. He pointed out the implications of the document with regard to the Church's missionary activity and its efforts to encourage the practice of religion. The only function of the state should be to see that the rights of religion were not infringed.

THE DECLARATION ON THE JEWS

On Monday, September 28th, the Council finally reached the controversial Declaration on the Jews. In his *relatio* the previous Friday, Cardinal Bea had begun by stating that it was "absolutely impossible" to think of abandoning a conciliar statement designed to improve relations with the Jewish people, as certain bishops had suggested, and he was warmly applauded when he urged the Fathers to adopt the present text as the basis for a conciliar pronouncement. The present document had no political overtones, he emphasized, by way of rejecting one of the most frequently heard arguments against it, particularly in Arab countries. Much of his speech was devoted to rejecting the thesis that the Jewish people as such could be accused of the charge of "deicide." His remarks were an open invitation to the Council to restore the original, much stronger, statement contained in the version presented to the Council, but not debated, in December 1963.

The history of the version presented to the Council in September 1964 was interesting. No other conciliar document probably had been subject to so many influences and counterinfluences. When postponement of the debate at the end of the Second Session was announced "because of lack of time," most observers regarded this as a mere pretext. Different reasons were alleged for this move: because the pope was anxious not to compromise the reception he might receive in Jordan and Jerusalem on his intended pilgrimage; because of sharp Arab protests against the document made directly to the Vatican Secretariat of State through

303

diplomatic channels; because of misgivings on theological grounds by some of the pope's advisers, perhaps shared by Pope Paul; because of pressure exercised by the minority in the Council. The decision to postpone consideration was probably taken because of a combination of factors. However, as Cardinal Bea said, "What is put off is not put away." The Secretariat began its work of revision on the basis of the written observations of the Fathers. According to an announcement made in February 1964, the revised text was "much strengthened." In April, unfortunately, at a meeting of the Coordinating Commission, it was decided to order several changes in the document to make it more palatable to the theological minority and the Arab world. The text was broadened to include mention of the Moslems and other non-Christian religions so that it became a statement of the Church's attitude toward, and relationship to, all non-Christians. The most disturbing changes, however, were a watering-down of the passage exonerating the Jewish people of the charge of "deicide" and a certain emphasis on the idea of their "conversion" presented in such a way as to suggest that this was to be the dominant note governing Catholic-Jewish relations.

Word about the changes was leaked from Rome toward the beginning of May and greatly upset Jewish communities throughout the world, particularly in the United States. In an audience granted to the American Jewish Committee, on May 30, 1964, Pope Paul expressed sympathy for the "horrible ordeals" through which the Jewish people had passed, but made no allusion to any changes in the document. Publication of a report by the *New York Times,* on June 10th, to the effect that the document had been "muted," as rumored, produced a communiqué from the Secretariat denying that any essential "watering-down" had taken place and attempting to take the edge off the controversy. Some days later, however, the Coordinating Commission formally approved the revised text and it was distributed to the bishops. In the course of the late summer, several bishops, including Cardinal Ritter (August 24th), acknowledged that the text of the declaration had indeed been changed in the sense of the rumors, but he expressed the hope that when the Fathers re-assembled, they would restore the passages that had been "toned down."

The conservative minority, perhaps feeling the uselessness of further resistance on the floor of the Council, confined their opposition to the token speech of Cardinal Ruffini. Speaking for the Arab world, only Cardinal Tappouni and Archbishop Tawil spoke on the issue, both calling for rejection of the text as offensive to Moslems and dangerous to Christians living in that part of the world. All the other speakers were in favor of restoring what had been taken out. Cardinal Liénart made a strong appeal on behalf of the document as a just and charitable effort on the part of the Church to right the wrongs of centuries toward a people who had laid the foundations of the Christian religion. Cardinal Frings expressed his pleasure over the fact that more extensive treatment had been accorded the Moslems and other non-Christians in the revised document and urged restoration of the passage absolving the Jewish people of the charge of "deicide." Cardinals Lercaro, Léger, Cushing, König, Meyer and Ritter all called for the same thing and emphasized the bonds that existed between Jews and Christians.

As usual, Cardinal Ruffini's intervention amounted to an attempt to throw a monkey-wrench into the works. He praised what the text had to say about the Jews and agreed with Cardinal Bea that the term "deicide" should be abandoned because "no one can kill God," and he referred to the many Jews whom "we" had saved from the Nazis, as proof of the Church's goodwill toward them, but he suggested that the improvement of relations should be on a *quid pro quo* basis: the "deicide" charge should be dropped, but Jews should be exhorted to love Christians. Certain anti-Christian passages should be expunged from the Talmud, and he blamed the alleged Jewish anti-Christian inspiration of European Masonry as the motive-force behind anticlericalism.

The speakers on the following day, including Bishop Satoshi Nagae (Japan), Bishop Elchinger (France), Bishop Leven (San Antonio, Texas), Bishop Stein (Germany), Archbishop Heenan (Westminster, England), Archbishop O'Boyle (Washington), Archbishop Shehan (Baltimore), and Archbishop Descuffi (Turkey), all urged acceptance and restoration of the text to its original form. The latter stressed greater efforts toward a dialogue with the Moslems, because, as he said, they were closer to us than the Jews. He also suggested that the declaration could be a fitting way to defend the memory of Pope Pius XII, which had been slandered because of his alleged failure to act vigorously enough during World War II in defending the Jews against the Nazis. After Archbishop Descuffi had spoken, the moderator, Cardinal Agagianian, called for a vote of closure and the document was sent back to the Secretariat to be revised according to the sense of the debate.

DIVINE REVELATION

Debate on the revised text of the schema on Divine Revelation, the next item to be taken up, was begun on September 30, 1964. It will be remembered that partial consideration of the original document at the First Session resulted in a crisis, causing Pope John to withdraw it from discussion and confide its revision to a mixed commission, consisting of members from the Theological Commission and Cardinal Bea's Secretariat for Unity. The present schema was completely rewritten and now represented a moderate position on many points, more satisfactory to modern biblical scholars and theologians than the older version which reflected the theological views of the minority to a large extent.

In a futile attempt to hold back the wheels of progress, the session's champion of lost causes, Bishop Franic (Yugoslavia) demanded the right to make a summation of the minority position on divine revelation. Revealing once more a pitiful lack of understanding of the momentous mystery involved in the Church's reception, explanation and preservation of the Word of God as handed down by the apostles and disciples of Christ in the Scriptures, this facile, learned, but single-minded theologian appealed to every possible motive from honesty in ecumenism to his notion of traditional inerrancy to get the schema rejected—or at least get his own antiquated concept of the relation between Scripture and tradition accepted—by the Council. What was disturbing was to discover that men of this calibre, well trained in the arts of logic and technical thought, widely read in theological literature and devoted to the constant search for religious truth through study and prayer, had deliberately cut themselves off from the obvious inspiration of the Holy Spirit at the present juncture in the Church's development. Mistaking a stubborn allusion to outmoded formulas and a misconception of the spiritual nature of Christ's teaching as theological consistency, they used every means possible to thwart the mind of the vast majority of the bishops who were giving witness to the mind of the Church as of now; what was worse, they did not hesitate to challenge the directives of two popes, despite the fact that they were vociferous protagonists of papal supremacy.

What the new decree did was to acknowledge that there was no absolute way in which the Scriptures were to be interpreted; that in each age, the Church, under the inspiration of the Spirit and in keeping with the intellectual progress of mankind, could achieve a more meaningful appreciation of the mysteries of divine revelation in relation to the facts of salvation as lived by Christ in His birth, death and resurrection. In the attempt to counteract a divergent reading of the Scriptures by the 16th century reformers, the Fathers at Trent had insisted on the historical accuracy of the content of the sacred books and had attempted to explain the development of doctrine by appealing to tradition as, for all practical purposes, a separate source of divine inspiration. The danger of this method had been recognized by a few scholars at the time but was later completely ignored owing to the polemical development of Catholic teaching during the next 300 years. Only when this matter came to a head at the First Session of the present Council were the entrenched minority in several Roman Congregations, and particularly the Holy Office, forced to so much as concede that a problem existed. Till then they had fiercely suppressed every scholarly effort to take an honest look at the problem and this despite the progressively more liberal documents of Pope Pius XII, beginning with *Divino Afflanto Spiritu* in 1943 and *Humani Generis* in 1951. The debate on this subject became so acute at the First Session that Pope John withdrew the draft from discussion, as we have said. Pope Paul decided to let it go over until the Third Session, meanwhile involving several mixed commissions in its revision. The architect of the new document was Archbishop Florit (Florence), who gave the majority report, explaining the commission's work on the current text and stating unequivocally that the intent of the document was to deal with the essential fact of revelation, its nature, and its relation to the magisterium of the Church. It did not intend to settle any disputed theological points, he maintained, but wanted to encourage the discussion of these matters rather than hamper or cut off speculation.

As usual, Cardinal Ruffini led the debate. He stated that the minority report expressed the constant teaching of the ordinary magisterium of the Church. He maintained that faith must be expressed mainly in intellectual concepts, and this was not done by the present text. It was precisely this point that Cardinals Döpfner and Meyer seized upon by way of lauding the document. "Faith should not be described in such a way as to make it too intellectualistic," said the Chicago prelate, "as this would be contrary to the spirit and general approach of St. Paul," as well as the Scripture authors generally. Here again a fundamental disagreement on the basic approach to theological knowledge became apparent. The small minority continued to indulge in a sort of gnostic notion of their ability, by force of logic and a few philosophical axioms, to decipher not merely the meaning of Scripture but the historical process by which God must have revealed and transmitted revelation, using both Scripture and Tradition as separate and equal transmitters. This thesis had prevailed in scholastic circles since the 17th century as a counter-Protestant apologetic, but like the various attempts to reconcile impossibly irreconcilable historic statements in the Gospel, it had been forced out of business by modern research. The grave error which the arch-conservatives made in this sphere was to consider the Church's doctrine compromised by their theories (which an indulgent magisterium had tolerated, whereas it should have taxed their views with heresy and turned the tables on them).

Cardinals Léger (Montreal) and Landázuri Ricketts (Lima) brought the full weight of modern research to bear on the notion of revelation, which was at the heart of the Christian religion, as well as at the center of the present attempt to reform the Church.

Cardinal Browne defended the position of intransigent theologians, who he maintained had had a decisive role in handing down tradition. Here, as a leading scholastic, he ran head on into the wall of divinely revealed fact. He quarreled with the text of the document which insisted that revelation was contained in *deeds and words* because, said the Irish cardinal, "words are prior as a means of expressing thought." Denying that "tradition grows," he held that "Sacred Scripture is evolved in its expression, but not in its substantial content." Unconsciously the good cardinal revealed the fact that he fundamentally resembled the Platonists, whose concepts of ideas as the fundamental reality were rejected by early patristic theology in favor of the fact of God's existence, His providence in creating the world, and the redemption of all of mankind through the salvific incarnation, death and resurrection of His Son, and the establishment of a Church with its guarantee of guidance by the Holy Spirit—all of which deeds were recorded as historical events in Holy Scripture. The cardinal also showed some irritation with the assertion that man could "experience" the religious value of faith through the witness of the Scripture, again basing his objection on the rigidly rational concept of psychology that led to excesses in connection with the condemnation of Modernism earlier in the present century. The old concept school of theology was still haunted by this spectre.

Archbishop Jaeger (Paderborn, Germany) took pains to meet the objections of Cardinals Ruffini and Browne by suggesting a clearer statement on the relation between divine revelation and the history of salvation. This could be done, he said, by introducing a parallel between the interior action of grace which followed the exterior preaching of God's Word in the Gospel and the activity of the Holy Spirit whose inspirational mission completed the mission of Christ. He quoted St. Thomas's teaching on the gift of wisdom in the *Summa Theologica* as a direct answer to Cardinal Browne's objection regarding the document's description of "the intimate experience of spiritual things" that followed from acceptance of the Gospel message.

Bishop Romero Menjibar (Jaen, Spain) requested a strengthening of the salvational-history approach through an explicit linking of Moses and the Exodus of the Jewish people with the incarnation and the redemption; while Archbishop Shehan (Baltimore) called for a clearer description of the part played by the human mind in receiving, interpreting, and transmitting divine revelation. Entering the problem carefully discussed by the late 2nd century theologian Clement of Alexandria and St. Augustine in the fifth century, he suggested that the passive sense of revelation was necessary to complete the theological and pastoral understanding of the Church's interpretation of God's Word, while Archbishop Vuccino (France) called for more attention to the Eastern approach to this problem, citing St. Athanasius as witness to the fact that revelation and apostolic tradition were identical. "From the beginning, the only source of the Church's preaching was her consciousness, formed by the Spirit independently of all written tradition. When tradition was put down in writing, only the apostolic tradition was expressed, and faith was put in the Scriptures because tradition was evident in them." In conclusion he asserted that the Church's right to call herself apostolic was based essentially on the fact that it possessed the whole apostolic Kerygma, that is, "the written or unwritten tradition is unfailingly preserved and infallibly interpreted in her with the assistance of the Holy Spirit."

Bishop Guano (Livorno, Italy) called for a more courageous assertion of the intimate relation between Scripture and tradition, which embodied all that the Church was, since inseparably they provided an encounter with Christ, and Archbishop Zoungrana (Ougadougou, Africa), said explicitly that "the very person of Jesus Christ is divine revelation"—the truth that conquered the ancient world, and was so much needed for the encounter with the existentially-conscious man of today. Despite the antiquated views of the continual objectors Bishop Compagnone (Anagni) and Archbishop Ferro (Reggio Calabria, Italy), the remaining speakers gave general acceptance to the document and the discussion of the text as a whole was closed after the debate on October 1st.

During the session on Thursday, October 1st the new text of the schema on Ecumenism was distributed and the following day the Fathers were asked to agree on a procedure for voting on this schema by paragraphs, beginning Monday, October 5th. Likewise it was affirmed that when the Council came to discuss the schema on the Lay Apostolate and that on the Church in the Modern World, the pattern of a general debate on the whole of each document followed by a vote of acceptance or rejection would be resorted to, in accordance with the regular procedure. This had not been done following discussion of the schemas on the Pastoral Office of Bishops or Divine Revelation because they had already been debated at earlier sessions.

The debate on Chapters I and II of Divine Revelation which began on Friday, October 2nd revealed a strong and determined majority in favor of the new approach to the Bible achieved by contemporary biblical research and so hotly contested by the Curial minority. The Dutch Bishop Van Dodewaard (Haarlem) was joined by Archbishop Morcillo Gonzales (Madrid), Bishop Rupp (Monaco), and Archbishop Flahiff (Winnipeg, Canada) in supporting the position of Cardinals Léger, Meyer and Landázuri Ricketts, particularly by breaking away from scholastic definitions when describing the tradition and magisterium of the Church as residing in the pope and bishops "built upon the foundation of the prophets and apostles," according to the expression of St. Paul. Archbishop Beras (Santo Domingo) utilized his intervention which seemed to advocate a return to old-fashioned notions of tradition, to advertise the International Marian Congress being organized in his archdiocese early in

1965. He was able to employ this strategem by announcing the theme of the Congress as "Mary in Sacred Scripture," and while most of the prelates, including the moderators, smiled in benevolent toleration at this self-advertisement, it was not difficult to trace the move to the Franciscan mariologist Father Balič (one of Cardinal Ottaviani's men), the organizer of the Congress, who spent the summer of 1964 in the U.S.A. collecting funds and voicing fierce opposition to the progressive theology of the Council. At the same time rumors were spread that Pope Paul was seriously considering making the trip to Santo Domingo.

Toward 11:30 A.M., Bishop Van Dodewaard presented the *relatio* on Chapters III to VI of the schema on Divine Revelation and stated that whereas the original text had called attention to the so-called "sources of revelation" and the "relationship between Scripture and tradition," the new text concentrated on the Sacred Writings themselves and their message. In so doing it was not being derelict in its duty but was actually avoiding a false problem which had needlessly divided the attention not only of the Council but of Christendom. The new emphasis allowed for the validity of several modern theories and provided a reliable guide for understanding the Word of God. The Old Testament (Chapter IV) was presented as the first part of the "history of salvation" rather than merely as the story of the Chosen People; and the value of the witness offered by the Old Testament books was rightly centered not so much on their content as on the inspiration behind them. The section on the New Testament had been enlarged to include consideration of all the books, while the treatment of the historicity of the Gospels had been adapted from the Instruction of the Pontifical Biblical Commission issued on May 16, 1964. Finally, directives had been incorporated regarding Scripture as the source of the spiritual and theological life of the Church, and recommendations had been made for a cooperative effort, with the separated brethren, toward providing adequate vernacular translations, while the responsibilities and rights of Catholic exegetes and theologians were touched upon.

This latter point formed the basis of Cardinal Ruffini's intervention as soon as the new topic was thrown open to discussion under the moderatorship of Cardinal Döpfner. The Sicilian prelate blasted the "new freedom" allowed Scripture scholars and repeated his condemnation that the employment of literary forms in biblical exegesis was tantamount to admitting that the Church had not understood the Scriptures until modern times. In this respect, he was actually repeating his explicit criticism of Pope Pius XII's encyclical *Divino Afflante Spiritu,* on which he had been publicly challenged before the start of the Council.

Cardinal König (Vienna), delivering the last speech of the morning, courageously broached the central point of conflict between the two

310

opposing conciliar sides, stating that in keeping with the results of modern research in science and natural history and particularly in Oriental studies, it must be recognized that there were factual mistakes in both the Old and New Testaments, which in no way interfered with either divine inspiration or inerrancy. "Lest the authority of Scripture suffer, we must say sincerely and without fear that the sacred writer's knowledge of historical matters was limited according to the conditions of his time, and that God moved him to write in keeping with his background and education. In this way we see the complete condescension of the Divine Word, making Himself conform in all things to human conditions, including the limitations of human speech." This admission was apparently scandalous to the older school who felt that every word, in both Testaments, was guaranteed by divine infallibility, to the confusion of John Henry Newman, for one, when after his conversion in 1846, he consulted the Roman theologian Father Perrone and was told that even such a detail as "the dog wagging his tail" in the Book of Tobias had the stamp of divine authenticity about it. As one bishop remarked, Newman could have been spared much trouble had he lived 100 years later. Now the Book of Tobias itself was no longer considered an historical account but rather an inspirational story.

The Council resumed business on Monday, October 5th, as Archbishop Martin (Rouen, France) gave the *relatio* on Chapter I of the schema on Ecumenism, in preparation for the voting that would take place in the course of the morning's congregation.

Cardinal Meyer (Chicago) began the discussion on Chapter III of Divine Revelation with the statement that while the document contained excellent points, it failed to state clearly or properly the nature of divine inspiration. It seemed to consider inspiration confined to "the establishment of logical truths and to forming a series of propositions, leading to the conclusion that its whole value consists in the quality of inerrancy." The proper consideration of inspiration should begin and end with the fact that it is "a personal communication to men of the Word of God which goes beyond merely manifesting concepts to another." The very idea of the Word of God meant that some fact or object was being communicated by a Person speaking and looking for a response or reaction. As in the early Church, the proper manner of describing the Word of God as contained in Scripture required the acknowledgment that it was the heart of God that was revealed, not propositions; that it was not inerrancy that was guaranteed, but rather the means for "educating and impelling to every good work," as St. Paul insisted; finally, the reconciliation of inerrancy and inspiration must take into consideration human deficiencies and limitations as Cardinal König had pointed out. This speech, coming on the first of the day and from the Chicago cardinal,

311

known as a Scripture scholar whose deep thought and calm objectivity had greatly impressed the Council, was listened to with rapt attention and greeted with applause.

It was followed by a similar speech by Cardinal Bea, who remarked that the schema's tone was in keeping with Pope John's desire for positive rather than condemnatory documents. He recommended a number of changes in both style and doctrine. Archbishop Weber (Strasbourg), also a biblical scholar, described the different types of men whom God used to convey his message: Amos, the shepherd, Isaias, the noble, and Paul, formed in the Rabbinical schools. Yet unity of message and continuity of doctrine were guaranteed by the source of divine inspiration. In interpreting the Bible, therefore, many factors must be employed including the context, tradition, the analogy of faith, as well as positive directions of the Church. He said that the recent Instruction of the Biblical Commission was intended to foster, not impede, biblical studies.

Bishop Simons (Indore, India) stressed the fact that "we should distinguish between what God wished to say and what the sacred authors intended," since as was frequently evident, there was a divergence between God's revelation in the Old Testament directed toward the coming Redeemer, and revelation as understood by the Jewish authors in a local setting. A demurrer was offered by Bishop Gasbarri (Italy), who called for a ban on present-day exegesis that seemed intent on emptying the Gospels of all historical meaning. He cited the deliberately vague 1960 *monitum* of the Holy Office on this matter, asserting that it could only be understood as a condemnation of "modern exegetical techniques," for it would be "foolish to think that the Holy Office was merely dreaming." He was immediately contradicted by Bishop Flores Martin (Barbastro, Spain), who insisted that the authors of the scriptural books should be called "true authors" who acted as "living instruments of God" and not as automatons; while Bishop Maloney (Louisville, Kentucky) defended the use of "literary forms," citing Sts. Augustine and Jerome as two early biblical scholars who understood this process.

The debate on Revelation was closed on October 6th, after ten more speakers had had their say, but not before Bishop Carli (Segni, Italy) warned that "the Council will prove a great disappointment if it does not condemn the dangers threatening the Church from the *form-history* interpretation of the Scriptures," manifesting at once his lack of *rapport* with the mind of the pope and the Church, as well as with modern biblical studies, regarding not merely the subject of tradition but the nature of the Bible itself. While Bishop Čekada (Yugoslavia) expressed doubts about certain points, excusing himself as a simple pastor of souls, Abbot Butler (Downside, England) summed up the difficulties on both sides of the argument and attempted to allay the fears of the minority by assuring them that the historicity of divine revelation was not in jeopardy, rather the apologetic approach of previous Catholic biblical scholarship could now be supplemented by a wider and more factual consideration of the biblical witness to God's Word. "We do not want the childish comfort of averting our gaze from the truth, but a truly critical scholarship which will enable us to enter into dialogue with non-Catholic scholars."

The revision of the text proceeded satisfactorily during the remainder of the Third Session, but it was not possible to offer it for a final vote before the close. The schema was therefore held over until the Fourth Session. The revised version was regarded as even more satisfactory than the October version.

COLLEGIALITY APPROVED

At the start of the Third Session, welcoming a group of Fathers from abroad, Pope Paul showed them a letter signed by some fourteen prelates, including cardinals of the Roman Curia and other Italian bishops. This letter asked that he remove the schema *De Ecclesia* from the Council's agenda, since in the minds of its signers it was replete with heresy. It was reported that Pope Paul pointed to one name, halfway down the list of signatures, and said, "This is the man responsible for this document. He unfortunately has neither the courtesy nor courage to acknowledge authorship."* When informed that the "remnant of Israel," as the small clique still opposing the Council's work of *aggiornamento* liked to think of itself, was praying for divine intervention, Pope Paul was reported to have remarked: "But the Holy Spirit has intervened. He inspired Pope John to summon the Council and He has given us the courage to carry out the directives of the divine will."

In a technical sense the doctrine of episcopal collegiality was the very core of Vatican Council II and, as the pope said in his opening address, "will certainly be what distinguishes this solemn and historic synod in the memory of future ages." The doctrine meant that the bishops as successors of the apostles formed a college with the pope as their head and shared with him in the government of the Church. Never denied, this truth had tended to take a back seat, as it were, while emphasis was placed more and more on the pope's authority over the centuries. Even at the time when the papal primacy and infallibility were being defined at

* It was possible that the document referred to by the Pope and another mentioned by Henri Fesquet were one and the same. The members of the Theological Commission each received a copy of a plea to the pope opposing collegiality, signed by two Italian cardinals, one of whom was Cardinal Ruffini. The minority deserved commendation for its audacity and perseverance, if for nothing else. (Cf. *Le Monde*, October 9, 1964.)

Vatican Council I in 1870 it was realized by farsighted theologians and bishops that a corrective was needed, but plans had to be shelved because that Council was prorogued without finishing its business. Since then the conviction, amounting to a groundswell only in the last few years, had grown that the time was ripe for a definition, or at least a formal statement of collegiality. There was some slight plausibility in the charge of the minority that the doctrine was "immature" and not ripe for definition, to the extent that no doctrine, in modern times, or perhaps ever, had progressed in such a short time from a mere mooting of the point among theologians to formal definition—in the space of only a few years at most—but the doctrine was in no sense "new." The Church was merely returning to a more "primitive tradition." And the minority were at fault for not wanting to examine the claims of a thesis which they regarded on *a priori* grounds as being essentially dangerous and unpalatable. The doctrine had important implications with respect to church government in that it tended to promote respect for the ancient and vital principle of local autonomy, as well as the related principle of subsidiarity—that is, whatever could be done equally well by a lesser authority should not be undertaken by a higher authority. Its ecumenical potentialities were also obvious.

This conviction was finally accepted by Archbishop Pietro Parente, assessor of the Holy Office, who startled the Council Fathers with a turn-about that marked a critical moment in the history of Vatican Council II, when on the morning of September 21st he delivered the *relatio* on the amended text of Chapter III, dealing with collegiality. The speech of Archbishop Parente was not without its internal drama.

Before he gave the speech, Cardinal Tisserant announced that several of the *periti* and certain members of the Theological Commission had been accused of holding conferences and distributing literature in favor of collegiality contrary to the conciliar rules. It turned out, however, that the complaint came from Spanish bishops who were being deluged by conservative pamphlets urging them to vote *against* collegiality, and the cardinal president said nothing more of the matter. Then, by a decision of the Coordinating Commission, Bishop Franic (Yugoslavia), also a member of the Theological Commission, was allowed to deliver a kind of "minority report" prior to Archbishop Parente's speech, summing up all the arguments of the minority against the doctrine of collegiality as expressed in the amended text of Chapter III, as well as the position opposing the sacramentality of episcopal consecration and the proposed restoration of a permanent diaconate. When Cardinal König rose next to present the positive, general introduction to the chapter, he made it clear that Bishop Franic's *relatio* was in no sense to be considered a real minority report, since the entire text had been approved by the full commission. It was rather allowed as a final courtesy extended to the minority. His Eminence then outlined the procedure which had been followed in revising the text and turned the rostrum over to Archbishop Parente.

The archbishop began by assuring the Fathers that he was not speaking as an official of the Holy Office but simply as a bishop. The very word *collegium,* he noted, had evoked no little terror (*non parvum terriculum* [sic!]) on the part of some prelates and theologians, who had immediately associated the idea with an attempt to strip the Roman Pontiff of his authentic jurisdiction. However, these fears were groundless and he advised the bishops to accept both the idea of collegiality and the amended text. It was known that Parente taught the doctrine as a professor of dogmatic theology at the Propaganda Fidei Seminary in Rome some years before, but when preparations for the present Council began he let himself be persuaded by zealots of papal supremacy, including the late Cardinal Tardini, Cardinals Ottaviani and Browne, and Archbishop Staffa of the Curia, that collegiality was "inopportune." This group acknowledged that while the theory of collegiality was theologically possible, it should not be admitted at the present time because of dangerous tendencies among many bishops and theologians toward decentralization of authority. In fact, they opposed Pope John's desire to have this doctrine discussed at the Council at all. Despite the fact that during its deliberations in the spring of 1964 the Theological Commission had approved a text on collegiality (April 19, 1964) (and had accepted the wishes of the majority of the Fathers as expressed in the vote of October 30, 1963 and their numerous petitions and suggested amendments), *nondum quies facta est*—peace had not yet been achieved, Archbishop Parente pointed out. The contrast between Parente's and Franic's arguments was decisive. The impassioned Yugoslav prelate gave final voice to the juridical rationalizations that had hamstrung Latin theology during the last 300 years. By applying the axioms and concepts of Roman law, Aristotelian logic, and scholastic metaphysics to the mysteries of religion, they reduced the doctrines of a supernatural faith to a series of logical propositions. To all of this Archbishop Parente bid a sharp and final *vale, valete.* "If there is difficulty in explaining the relation between the sacred powers of the pope and those exercised by the bishops," he said, "this is not to be wondered at (*mirum non est*), since we are not dealing with a human society, but with the Church of Christ," a mystery, "that can only be elucidated by the theological vision of a St. Augustine and the early Church Fathers, who adhered to the teaching of St. Paul concerning the Church as a mystical body, and thus came much closer to expressing the mind of Christ."

Finally, Bishop Henriquez Jimenez (Venezuela) presented the *relatio* on the second half of the document dealing with priests and deacons and covering the main point at issue, namely the restoration of a married diaconate in those parts of the Church where it seemed called for.

Parente's historic discourse, coming from a prelate considered to be one of the leading conservatives during the Council's first two Sessions, finally dissipated the pent-up fears and hesitations of numerous Anglo-Celtic and American bishops. When the voting began, it was not hard to predict the result on this central issue. The voting on Chapter III began on September 21st and continued through eight congregations. Articles 18–29 were not voted on directly, but in the form of 39 propositions based on the essential points contained in them so that the work of revision would be facilitated for the Theological Commission. All the propositions were easily carried. Only those on the diaconate brought forth rather large negative votes, the final proposition, No. 39, on whether the diaconate could be conferred without the obligation to observe celibacy, not being carried at all. The key votes on collegiality resulted in only 328 negative votes at the most; this probably represented the full strength of the minority opposed to collegiality. The opposition was strongest against Proposition No. 8 (episcopal consecration confers full powers), Proposition No. 10 (pope and bishops form college), Proposition No. 11 (entrance to college through episcopal consecration), Proposition No. 13 (episcopal college was subject of full and supreme authority), Proposition No. 14 (power of binding and loosing also given to college of apostles), and Proposition No. 17 (exercise of collegial authority when pope approved or *accepted* collective action). Oddly, the pattern of resistance had some hilarious overtones. Fifty bishops voted against the divine origin of the episcopate (No. 5), 44 voted against the episcopate as a sacrament (No. 6), 156 voted against the proposition that only bishops could confer episcopal consecration (No. 9). When it was announced that 90 bishops had voted against the supreme authority of the pope (No. 12), the Council burst into laughter. Apparently some bishops had been instructed to vote against collegiality and did not know how to behave, voting simply negative throughout! Those voting Non placet on these propositions were, by their own theology, at least material heretics. As one French bishop remarked, "So determined are the opposition, they are willing to risk heresy to prove their point!"

To make it possible for those who might be opposed to the provisions restoring a permanent diaconate (but were in favor of the part on collegiality) to vote favorably on Chapter III as a whole, the moderators decided to divide the chapter into two sections and allow separate votes on Articles 18–23 and Articles 24–29. Normally all chapters were voted as a unit at this stage. The minority in the person of Bishop Carli immediately challenged the decision of the moderators, who, in reply, at once called for a standing vote; their decision was overwhelmingly upheld. The large number of Placet iuxta modum votes cast on September 30, 1964 on the two parts of Chapter III included some by the majority who wanted further changes made.

THE OCTOBER CRISIS

During the first three weeks of the Third Session, a wave of concern swept through the basilica corridors almost every time that Archbishop Felici rose to make announcements. His penchant for framing almost every statement in such a way as to favor the conservative minority was galling to the majority of prelates, and even some conservatively-inclined bishops began to suspect his motives. For example his repetition of the formula on how to vote Non placet when explaining the proposition on the married diaconate, and his frequent interpolations about submitting *modi* when describing the propositions on collegiality, were regarded as going far beyond the call of duty. It was clear that the minority had a spokesman in an important position who could steer the Council to their advantage.

Having been outmaneuvered and outvoted on collegiality, the same minority now concentrated its efforts on sidetracking or hampering the revision of the Declarations on Religious Liberty and the Jews, with a view to preventing a final vote if possible and eventually burying both. In their next move, they overreached themselves. Their maneuver gave rise to the phrase, *magno cum dolore,* with which historians would characterize the Third Session. The background of their move was this: Council rules provided that texts presented for discussion by a commission ordinarily remained within the competence of that commission right through until final promulgation. Nevertheless, at a meeting of the conservatively-dominated Coordinating Commission on Wednesday, October 7th, under the presidency of Secretary of State Cardinal Cicognani, the channel through whom most of the minority intrigues were mounted, it was decided to take action regarding the two Declarations. With regard to the text of the Religious Liberty document, the suggestion had previously been made, apparently in the presence of the pope, that it should be given to a new mixed commission charged with responsibility for working out a theological basis. Accordingly, Secretary General Felici, armed only with the authority of Cicognani, and without the knowledge of other members of the Coordinating Commission, including the council moderators, it seems, proceeded to draft two letters to Cardinal Bea. In his letter regarding the Jewish Declaration, Felici appealed to a decision of the Coordinating Commission that this document be turned over to a subcommittee of the Theological Commission for incorporation in the

317

schema on the Church. In the letter on Religious Liberty, on the other hand, the secretary general referred to "a desire of the Holy Father that the text be reconsidered and reworked" by a new special mixed commission and then proceeded to appoint the new commission himself including, along with Bishop Colombo (the pope's theological adviser), a number of prelates noted for their opposition to the very idea of religious liberty (Cardinal Browne, Archbishop Lefebvre, Father Fernandez, O.P.). Word of the latter names caused the greatest concern, and this ultimately led to the discovery of the whole "plot." News circulated that the decision to minimize the text on the Jews had been communicated to the five Eastern patriarchs at a meeting in the office of Cardinal Cicognani, on Thursday or Friday, October 8th or 9th, at which they were informed that, because of "political and diplomatic" complications, it had been decided to divide the Jewish Declaration into three parts, incorporating the different sections in *De Ecclesia,* Schema 13 and *De Oecumenismo.*

On Friday evening, October 9th, and during the next morning indignant phone calls from Bea's Secretariat informed the stunned bishops and *periti* of the letters and warned them that a slick move was afoot to defy the authority of the bishops and tamper with the rules of the Council. Under those rules only the four moderators or the pope could reassign conciliar documents. Since the moderators had taken no action, it became imperative to know the precise degree, if any, to which Pope Paul had been involved in Felici's move. Bea accordingly confronted the archbishop and demanded to know whether the letters had come from the pope. When Felici said, "No, but that is what the pope means," Bea replied: "Well, I cannot accept that as final," and proceeded to appeal directly to the pope, from whom he learned that there had indeed been talk about a mixed commission, but that nothing definite had been decided about names. (Fortunately the Theological Commission was not too keen on having the Jewish Declaration foisted on it, because this would have upset the balance of the text on the Church, the revision of which was proceeding smoothly.)

The majority leaders now understood the importance of mounting a counteroffensive of their own immediately. On Sunday evening, October 11th, a group met in the residence of Cardinal Frings, including Cardinals Alfrink, Roepfner, Koenig, Léger, Lefebvre, Liénart, Landázuri Ricketts, Meyer and Ritter, some fourteen in all.* Though Cardinal

* The letter which resulted was said to have been signed by 17 cardinals: Frings, Alfrink, Döpfner, König, Meyer, Ritter, Léger, Lefebvre, Richaud, Liénart, Silva Henriquez, Landázuri Ricketts, Quintero, Suenens, Rugambwa, probably Lercaro, and a seventeenth cardinal whose name was unknown. Cardinal Tisserant may have had some knowledge of, or something to do with, Archbishop Felici's letters to Cardinal Bea. Cf. *Le Monde,* October 17, 1964.

Suenens had returned in haste from Brussels when he learned what was happening, he could not be present; however, both he and Cardinal Lercaro, who was also unable to attend, gave this group their support. The petition they addressed to Pope Paul was interesting for its firmness of tone and for the fact that it did not hesitate to deplore the "appearance of a violation of the rules of the Council." Starting with the famous phrase, *magno cum dolore,* the letter went as follows:*

Holy Father:
   With great sorrow we have learned that the declaration on religious liberty, although in accord with the desire of the great majority of the Fathers, is to be entrusted to a certain mixed committee . . . three of whom appear to be opposed to the orientation of the Council in this matter.
   This news is for us a source of extreme anxiety and very disquieting. Countless men throughout the world know that this declaration has already been prepared, and they also know the sense in which it has been drafted. In such an important matter, any appearance of a violation of the rules of the Council, and its freedom, would be extremely prejudicial to the whole Church in the light of world opinion.
   Impelled by this anxiety, we ask Your Holiness with great insistence that the declaration be returned to the normal procedure of the Council and dealt with according to the existing rules, so that there may not result from it great evils for the whole People of God. However, if Your Holiness feels that a mixed committee is necessary, in our humble opinion it should be formed from the conciliar commissions, as provided in Article 58, Paragraph 2, of the rules.

The letter, with the seventeen signatures, was taken to the pope by Cardinal Frings, apparently Monday morning.† The pope was said to have been much disturbed by the affair, but it was not made clear whether the letter or the secretary general's maneuver caused the greater distress. Not only was Felici's plan to announce the composition of the mixed committee at the Council the next morning nipped in the bud by this quick action on the cardinals' part, but the final suggestion in their letter was adopted by way of compromise. The pope assured Cardinal Frings (Tuesday) that both the Declarations on the Jews and Religious Liberty would remain under the jurisdiction of Cardinal Bea's Secretariat—the important thing—but that the latter would be "examined" by a committee made up in accordance with the Council's rules. The rules, and an important principle, were thus upheld.

   On October 16th, the pope directed Cardinal Cicognani to write a letter to Cardinal Bea, conveyed to the latter by the same Archbishop Felici, and also a letter to Cardinal Ottaviani, asking them each to ap-

* Text disclosed by *Le Monde,* October 17, 1964, through an indiscretion on the part of one of the cardinal signers.
† Monday, not Sunday, according to the Abbé Laurentin.

point two members of their respective commissions to form a joint mixed commission to consider ways in which the text on Religious Liberty could be improved. The pope then chose five from among these twenty members, adding five names on his own, to form a consultative commission to review the text on Religious Liberty. The name of Archbishop Lefebvre, Superior General of the Holy Ghost Fathers, did not appear on the list; it did contain the names of Cardinal Browne, Bishop Pelletier (Trois-Rivières, Canada), Archbishop Parente, Bishop Colombo, etc.

The two essential differences between the old arrangement and the new were: 1) the Declaration of Religious Liberty would remain under the jurisdiction of the Secretariat for Unity, and the new commission was merely to make suggestions; 2) the list of twenty members which served as a basis for the mixed commission would be drawn up by the presidents of the interested conciliar commissions. In this way the stipulations of Article 58 of the rules were fully respected.

No decision was taken regarding the ultimate fate of the Declaration on the Jews, which was treated as a kind of theological football tossed back and forth behind the scenes, but never actually leaving the jurisdiction of the Secretariat. At the final business meeting of the session, on November 20th, it was presented for a vote as an appendix to *De Ecclesia*. The text on Religious Liberty, on the other hand, was presented as a separate *"Schema* of the Declaration on Religious Liberty."

Another principle, freedom of the press, was grossly violated in connection with these maneuvers, however. News about the cardinals' letter was given to the world in a release by the press officer of the Latin American Documentation Center, on Monday, October 12th (the text was disclosed later in the week by *Le Monde*). Angered by these reports of maneuvers involving himself, Archbishop Felici ordered Archbishop O'Connor, formerly rector of the North American College in Rome and principal architect of the heavily criticized decree on Communications Media issued by the Council in 1963, to investigate the "unlawful publication of conciliar documents" and to prepare a statement for the press. When this statement appeared in *L'Osservatore Romano* (October 23, 1964), the following sentences caused a furor among journalists in Rome: "On the basis of deplorable and unusually one-sided indiscretions, certain press organs have indulged in a series of conclusions without any basis in fact, and referring to non-existent maneuvers aimed at preventing the proper progress of the Council's work. The [Press] Commission condemns this method of providing information, a method in conflict with the truth, involving an injustice toward individuals and organs connected with the Council." Two days later the French journalist, Henri Fesquet, challenged the veracity of this statement in his newspaper *Le Monde*. On the same day, following a press conference by Bishop Wright of Pittsburgh, Fesquet had a lively personal confrontation with Archbishop O'Connor and the latter's press officer, Monsignor Fausto Vallainc. Fesquet stated for all the newsmen to hear, emphasizing his remarks with sweeping gestures, that he considered Archbishop O'Connor's communiqué so "improbable" that he had asked several bishops, members of the Press Commission, whether they concurred in the published statement. Since they had assured him that they had not even seen this communiqué, the inference was that the wording was Archbishop Felici's. While Monsignor Vallainc offered the lame explanation that Archbishop O'Connor had acted on his own "but in the sense of" the whole Press Commission, the American archbishop turned red in the face and said nothing. It was said that Archbishop O'Connor was being considered to head a new Vatican press office after the end of the Council. Later, in *Le Monde,* Fesquet made an impressive statement about the great chasm existing between Truth, the central concern of an ecumenical Council, and the utterances of Curial officials, when their maneuvers were exposed to the press. This contrast was also the theme of an audacious conference given in Rome two weeks earlier by Father Hans Küng, the German theologian. After American journalists protested against the aspersions of the Press Commission on their professional integrity, the Commission issued a second communiqué, denying any such intention but retracting absolutely nothing and incidentally expressing renewed confidence in its president, Archbishop O'Connor, and its secretary, Monsignor Vallainc.

About midway during the Third Session, in the Fourth Week, the question arose whether it would be possible to bring the Council to a close in 1964 or whether a Fourth Session would be necessary. The problem was debated at a meeting of the Coordinating Commission on October 7th. There may also have been some disagreement between members of the Commission and the moderators, or between the moderators themselves, about the proper course to follow. A feeling of euphoria had been generated by the rapid progress made thus far in the debates, and it did not seem unreasonable to suppose that if the commissions buckled down and produced revised texts in time, everything could be wound up by the end of November. But the reasoning was wholly unrealistic. The debate on the Apostolate of the Laity and other documents would soon show how much work remained to be done. The minority did their best to propagate the opinion that the Third Session could be the last, but to no avail. Various meetings of the national hierarchies were held to decide whether to petition for a Fourth Session or not. The English bishops were in favor of doing so, while the Canadian bishops voted to end the Council in 1964. The American bishops were divided: Archbishop Krol argued in favor of seeking an end with the

Third Session, but a majority, under the leadership of Cardinal Meyer, was mustered on behalf of a Fourth Session. Most of the other hierarchies were of the same mind. Cardinal Döpfner, it was said, endeavored to persuade the German bishops to change their minds about a Fourth Session, but without success. It was the rejection of the so-called "Döpfner Plan"—of reducing many of the remaining schemata to a series of propositions, ordered in January 1964 by the Coordinating Commission —that tilted the scales in favor of a prolongation of the Council, and incidentally saved certain highly important documents from oblivion.

DEBATE ON APOSTOLATE OF THE LAITY

Consideration of the schema on the Apostolate of the Laity which the Council took up on Wednesday, October 7th, and debated for five days, marked a turning point in the Council in more than one sense. It was the first time, incredibly, that official attention had been given by the Church to the corporate function of the laity as forming an integral part of the People of God. Canon law defined a layman as one "who is not a cleric," and it was well to remember that the general clericalist Italian attitude toward the layman was *"prega, paga, e zita"* (pray, pay, and shut up). As one bishop pointed out, laymen constituted over 99% of the faithful and it was therefore high time that some consideration was given to them. Cardinal Suenens was in the chair as moderator.

The schema was introduced by Cardinal Cento (as chairman of the conciliar Commission on the Apostolate of the Laity), who apparently assumed that the text he was presenting would be accorded a benevolent treatment and then accepted without much discussion. To his amazement, following the somewhat less sanguine *relatio* by Bishop Hengsbach (Essen, Germany), a member of the commission, one speaker after another rose to condemn it. The document suffered from two fundamental defects: though it was supposed to deal with the laity, practically no layman had been consulted about it until the eleventh hour; and the material was badly arranged. The reason for the latter defect was that while the commission had resisted the order of the Coordinating Commission in January 1964 to reduce the existing schema to a set of propositions, the text was stripped of some of its essential parts: the theological portion was incorporated in *De Ecclesia,* while Schema 13 received the part about lay activity in the modern world. The result was a document that was bound to be a great disappointment to the laity, Bishop De Roo (Victoria, Canada) noted, because it sidestepped any real discussion of their character or the spirit of their vocation.

The lack of theological perspective and general formlessness was the theme of many interventions. Cardinal Ritter, in a blast, noted that it suffered from three basic defects: clericalism, juridicism, and favoritism. By the latter he meant that it tended to favor Catholic Action too much at the expense of other forms of Catholic lay activity, as we shall see. He proposed a new plan: the document should speak first of the importance of the apostolate in the life of the Church and then go on to distinguish various forms, not in accordance with their relations with the hierarchy, as the present text did, but according to their specific ends, finally dealing with holiness and the spirituality of the laity. Bishop László (Eisenstadt, Austria) brought smiles when he declared that he had looked up the word "layman" in an old theological dictionary and found the directive, "see clergy." The schema lacked "punch," said Bishop Leven (auxiliary of San Antonio), pronouncing the word in English because there was no Latin equivalent. The lay apostolate should be inspired by a spirit of dialogue. There could be no dialogue when a bishop spoke to the laity as he did to his doctor or his housekeeper. Every bishop should have a lay "senate" consisting of laymen on whom he could call for advice and to explain to him the desires and wishes of the laity. A dialogue of this kind was really called for today, especially by thinking people. It was a "sign of the times." We must not stifle the charisms by which the Holy Spirit acted through the laity.

The theme that the apostolate must be a dialogue was well brought out by Archbishop Duval (Algiers) who focused his attention not so much on internal relations, as on the impact which the Church could be expected to make on those outside the fold, for example on the Moslems. He said that it was important not to limit the boundaries too much. The Church must not be limited by visible frontiers. There were worthwhile values among other religions and other peoples. Christians could give much, but they could also receive much. Bishop Caillot (Evreux, France) also wanted a more open attitude toward the role of laymen among non-believers, and noted that the ordinary daily life of the layman constituted the foundation on which the Gospel was built. A broadening of the concept of the lay apostolate was the theme likewise of the speeches by Archbishop Veuillot, Bishop McGrath, and Bishop Charbonneau, who agreed that the definition of the apostolate in the schema was too hidebound and conventional.

In this connection, a number of speakers pointed out that the schema did not bring out clearly enough that the real basis for the lay apostolate was the royal priesthood of Christ, in which all shared through baptism and confirmation (De Vito, Lucknow). Bishop Rastouil (Limoges, France) deplored the lack of a developed theology of confirmation in the Church, while Bishop De Roo (Victoria), in the name of 15 Canadian bishops, called for a more theologically-oriented preface stressing the dual vocation of man: to build the world and to build the Church, a point more fully developed in Schema 13. Christian concern for the world was not merely humanitarian in inspiration, but authentically religious. The two principles were inseparable. Archbishop Hurley (Durban, South Africa) did not agree. He thought that it was unwise to attempt to treat theological aspects in the present schema, which should concentrate on more practical matters.

The sections of the original schema on the lay apostolate and the missions had been sent to the Commission on Missions and were incorporated in the schema on Missionary Activity, observed Bishop Lokuang, but since the latter text had been reduced to propositions, almost nothing was left of this theme. It would therefore be appropriate to include a few words, particularly about the heroic action of many of the laity, in certain countries, as witnesses to the faith when the clergy had been hindered or exiled.

Quite a few speakers, following the lead of Cardinal Ritter, taxed the document with betraying a spirit of "clericalism." "Clericalism is the enemy," said Archbishop Kozlowiecki (Lusaka, Northern Rhodesia), "clericalism is the No. 1 enemy in the Church." The schema has been "conceived in the sin of clericalism," according to Bishop Alexander Carter (Sault-Ste-Marie, Canada). By the time the laity had been invited to take part in the work of preparing the schema, in the spring of 1963, it was already too late, he said. The present text amounted virtually to a document in which the clergy were speaking to the clergy. The laity would not be inspired by reading it. It scarcely took note of any associations except those that were clerically approved. The present text was a sort of *summa* of existing clerical lore on the subject, little more. The document should cause the laity to exclaim: *Nostra res agitur!*—"This is what we want to hear!" They would never be inspired to say this about a document dominated by a clericalist outlook, according to Bishop Tenhumberg (auxiliary of Münster, Germany), who spoke in the name of the German and Scandinavian bishops. Bishop De Vet (Breda), in the name of the Dutch bishops, warned against giving the impression that what the Church really wanted was to build a "clericalist" civilization. The role of the layman in the world was too neglected.

Perhaps the most detailed exponent of the anticlericalist approach was Archbishop D'Souza (Bhopal, India). It was high time, he said, to start considering the laity as grown-ups. The principle quoted in the text: "Let nothing be done without the bishop," a quotation from St. Ignatius of Antioch, an early Father of the Church, must not be abused. Doubtless nothing should be done *against* the bishop and due order should be preserved, but there was much that could be done without his immediate cooperation. The People of God were not a totalitarian state. He objected particularly to the totalitarian implications of Catholic Action, as practiced in certain Latin countries, where no other outside activities by the laity were countenanced unless they fitted into this scheme. "We are now going through a period of reform in the Church," said Archbishop D'Souza, "and one of the prime attributes calling for reform is the spirit of clericalism. Laymen must be treated as brothers by the clergy and the latter must no longer attempt to usurp responsibilities which properly belonged to the former. Why could they not represent the Church in international organizations, why could there not be laymen in the Roman Congregations, and why could not laymen even serve in the diplomatic service of the Holy See?" he asked. "The missionary work of the Church will fail," he declared, "unless there is much re-thinking along this line."

A further controversial question claiming a great deal of attention in the debate was the nature and role of Catholic Action (or the organized form of the lay apostolate generally understood by that term). Although the expression had a generalized meaning and was often employed in this sense in papal encyclicals, for example, it was usually taken as referring to certain types of organizations or associations which had been approved by the hierarchy and functioned under their close supervision. The schema attempted to straddle the fence between different meanings of the term and did not succeed very well.

It attempted to describe and define four types of relationship with the hierarchy, ranging from those associations organized by the laity on their own, to those having a "mandate" from the hierarchy, and those finally whose functions were purely pastoral and completely under clerical control (e.g. catechetical, liturgical functions, etc.).

In general, while the term Catholic Action was looked upon with favor in Latin countries (particularly in Italy, Spain and South America, also France), it was regarded with less favor by German Catholics, and with no enthusiasm at all by Catholics in English-speaking countries, as implying too much distasteful, compulsory organization. In Italy it turned out to be little more than a flag-waving, anticlerical-provoking, hierarchically-dominated wing of the conservative hierarchy. The French followed a middle course, retaining the name without the compulsory, political overtones associated with the Italian brand. Papal statements on the subject had not always displayed a proper sense of balance, sometimes tending to confuse the forms of Catholic Action in Latin countries with the ideal form of the lay apostolate.

By attempting to steer a middle course, the schema tended to please neither side. It was not surprising that Archbishop Maccari (former head of Italian Catholic Action) should have noted, with regret, that the text did not bring out the "defensive nature" of Catholic Action and generally disapproved of its loose language. Bishop Ruotolo (Ugento, Italy) expressed the belief that all Christians should be bound in conscience to belong to one of the forms of Catholic Action, while Bishop Soares de Resende (Mozambique) called for the establishment of an institute in Rome to train clergy and laity for work in Catholic Action. "Those who live by the Church should have the sense of the Church," said Bishop D'Agostino (Vallo di Lucania, Italy), parroting a phrase often found in documents of the magisterium on the apostolate of the laity where the word "Church" frequently seemed to mean only "clergy." The bishop recalled an ambiguously worded phrase of Pope Paul VI: "Catholic Action belongs to the constitution of the Church." Cardinal Caggiano (Buenos Aires) also recalled that Pope Paul had referred to Catholic Action as the "royal road" for the apostolate of the laity. He was particularly grateful that the schema seemed to accord its rightful place to Catholic Action, but he was disappointed in not finding any quotations from the encyclicals of Pius XI and Pius XII which defined this form of the apostolate. In many countries, he observed, the clergy and laity had shown themselves faithful to these directives.

The principal intervention on this subject was delivered by Cardinal Suenens on October 9th. While still an auxiliary bishop of Malines-Brussels, the cardinal had proposed certain points for investigation with a view to arriving at a better definition of the term Catholic Action, proposals which had been made at the Second Congress for the Apostolate of the Laity. Pope Pius XII had adopted some of them in his discourses. Cardinal Suenens was dissatisfied particularly with the treatment of Catholic Action in the schema. He said it was not a question of persons, but of doctrine. The definition proposed in the text was too ambiguous and narrow.

The debate continued on Monday (October 12th) with attention still being concentrated on Catholic Action. Cardinal Suenens' suggestion that the notion needed broadening was not favorably received by bishops from countries where it was traditional. France being one of the countries where Catholic Action had proved to be successful, it was not surprising that Cardinal Liénart found this suggestion unacceptable. "I can see no reason for broadening the term," he said, "so that it can be applied to any type of apostolic action whatsoever."

Both Archbishop Nicodemo (Bari, Italy) and the military vicar for Spain, Bishop Alonso Muñoyerro, insisted that greater stress must be placed on the subordination of Catholic Action to the bishop and its complete dependence on the hierarchy, in accordance with repeated papal recommendations. The present text gave too much latitude to local bishops to establish whatever forms they pleased under this title. Greater conformity was needed to avoid confusion. "The schema gravely wounds Catholic Action, which should be saved for the good of the Church," he maintained. Bishop Del Pino (Lerida, Spain) professed himself shocked by allegations on the floor that the text was too "clerical." His solution was to banish all such thoughts by considering that ultimately everybody, including the laity, was subject to the pope and "without the pope there is no apostolate." When he embarked on a diatribe about religious liberty, denouncing it as a "liberty to sin," he was called to order by the moderator, but had difficulty getting back on the track.

Exception was taken to Cardinal Suenens' strictures by Bishop Padin (auxiliary of Rio de Janeiro), who offered the support of the Brazilian episcopate on behalf of Catholic Action, which "had done great things for some countries." It was idle to accuse the movement of having claimed a privileged name. Should the name of the Jesuits or that of the Holy Office be changed simply because we all lived in the society of Jesus or because the Church was *per se* holy? It was pointless to fight over names. The important thing was to respect the freedom of the laity which we had been preaching. He also suggested that the clericalism implied by the use of the word "cooperate" (with reference to the part which the laity were to play in the proposed Secretariat) should be avoided in favor of a direct summons to responsibility.

Archbishop Heenan (Westminster) clearly summed up the position with regard to Catholic Action so far as Anglo-Saxon prelates were concerned. He said simply: "It would be better in certain countries if the expression were not used. I hope that each regional conference will be left free to speak of the apostolate rather than of Catholic Action." His final remarks bore on the subject of the proposed Secretariat about which he had some interesting comments:

This is something which is bound to fail unless the laity is fully consulted. This Secretariat will be unique among the secretariats of the Holy See. It would be a disaster to model it on any of the departments already existing in the Roman Curia. Most of the members of the Secretariat must be chosen from the laity. Let me stress that the faithful take it very badly if decisions over matters in which they are well versed are taken without any word of advice being asked from them. Before setting up the Secretariat it is important, therefore, to enquire from the laity themselves how they think it should be set up and how it ought to be run. Many of our Catholic laity know much more than we do about public affairs . . . The proper thing for us to do is to learn from them. It is obviously necessary for this Secretariat to have the guidance of competent ecclesiastics. But this does not mean that all the business must be conducted by prelates or that laymen would not be capable of presiding at any of its meetings . . . The people to choose for this Secretariat are the men and women who in their own countries have taken a lead in the lay apostolate . . . We do not want to send to Rome only old gentlemen who are loaded down with ecclesiastical honors. We must also choose some of our young men and women who have to earn their daily bread.

It was typical of the schema that it was long on the details of Catholic Action and dependence on the hierarchy, but had almost nothing at all to say about the proposed Secretariat. The ideas of His Grace probably struck practiced Roman hands as either absurd or alarming, boldly suggesting as they did an end to clerical domination in this field.

After the last speaker on Monday, the moderator called for a vote of closure on the debate on the lay apostolate, and the motion was approved by an overwhelming majority. The secretary general then announced that the following day the floor would be taken only by those speakers who wished to speak in the name of at least 70 Fathers, and that the debate would be concluded with a speech by one of the lay auditors.

The lay auditor turned out to be Patrick Keegan, president of the International Catholic Workers' Movement. He spoke in English, the first time that any layman had ever addressed a modern ecumenical council during the course of one of its business sessions, since the addresses of Jean Guitton and Vittorino Veronese in 1963 took place on a special day. The tenor of Keegan's remarks was "unexceptional." The loud applause which greeted him at the end was due, no doubt, more to the rhetorical flourish with which he had delivered his remarks than to what he had said. The effect of his remarks was frankly disappointing to those who had expected greater fire from the first layman to have something to say in public on a subject so much criticized by the clergy; his speech appeared to have been "clericalized."

Bishop Hengsbach wound up the discussion by promising to improve the text, in the name of the commission, on the basis of the many suggestions made. He apologized for the defects, especially as regards the "clerical" treatment of Catholic Action. The schema on the Lay Apostolate should be a sort of pendant to the one on the Church in the modern World which could be expected to give definitive form to many of the basic ideas dealt with only cursorily and tentatively in the present text. He called for time to revise the text and spoke of the need to consult more laymen. His emphasis upon the "time" necessary to complete the work of revision naturally caused all thoughts to turn to the necessity for a Fourth Session and he was warmly applauded on concluding. The schema was not submitted to a vote, the general sentiment in favor of a thorough revision being so obvious.

DEBATE ON PRIESTLY LIFE AND MINISTRY

On Tuesday, October 13th, the Council took up the first of the schemata reduced to a series of propositions earlier in the year, on orders of the

Coordinating Commission, according to the so-called "Döpfner Plan." The assembly was to have taken up Schema 13 on the Church in the Modern World next, but the *relationes* were not ready, the secretary general assured the anxious assembly, so the intervening time would have to be spent in considering several of the Propositions.

The schema *De Clericis,* distributed to the Fathers in May 1963, had been revised on the basis of their suggestions submitted in writing and was given a new title, *De Sacerdotibus,* in January 1964. It was then decided to reduce it to a series of propositions, extracted from the revised text. The propositions along with the text of the revised *De Sacerdotibus* were distributed to the bishops (after their approval in April 1964). The text which the Fathers had before them in October 1964 when the debate began was in two parallel columns. The first contained the propositions distributed in the spring of 1964; the second, a revised and slightly expanded series of propositions, amended on the basis of suggestions sent in meanwhile. The chief change was the introduction of a paragraph on celibacy (inserted in Proposition 2), "at the urgent request of 70 bishops, disturbed by so many confusing voices raised regarding a possible abolition of this law." The original text had contained no mention of this subject because it was meant for both the Eastern and Western Churches which had different disciplines. The wording was now such that it was applicable to both cases:

2. Let priests preserve and sincerely love holy chastity, and let those who, on the recommendation or by the command of the Church, have made a vow of celibacy, trusting in the grace of God, be faithful to their vow with their whole heart and rejoice that they are united with Christ directly in this way and can serve the family of God with greater freedom. Let them remain and progress in this state with strength and rectitude, so that they may become more and more able to serve and may acquire more fully a fatherhood in Christ.

Another passage was added toward the beginning (Proposition 1), at the request of German and Scandinavian bishops, explaining the theology and mission of the priesthood more fully and relating it to what was said in *De Ecclesia*. Other notable changes were the addition of a sentence in Proposition 2 stating that priestly obedience (to bishops) was different from that of religious and the laity, because priests shared in the episcopal mission through the sacrament of orders; they were advised to cultivate an "ascetical spirit in fulfilling their pastoral ministry" and to practice contemplation (Proposition 3); wherever possible they were to establish a common form of life (Proposition 4); they were to show a "solicitude for all churches" and to be ready to undertake work in other dioceses according to need (Proposition 7)—this opened the door to a very considerable change from the traditional incardination of priests in one

329

diocese; and they were warned against appropriating ecclesiastical property for their own personal use or using it for gain, and to avoid all "cupidity and carefully to refrain from engaging in any kind of commercialism" (Proposition 9). The title of the Propositions, now numbering 12, handed to the Fathers in October 1964, was "Concerning the Priestly Life and Ministry," a more apt description. The approach was mainly practical and pastoral.

In his introduction Archbishop Marty (Rheims, France), after giving an outline of the various vicissitudes through which the text had passed, referred to one rather radical change now being recommended, not so far mentioned, namely the abolition of the time-honored system of benefices stemming from the Middle Ages, "lest the Church be accused of feudalism and lest it lead to the setting up of social classes among priests," as of course it had long since done. The old system was to be abolished wherever it was in effect, and replaced by a more equitable salary system. The tone of the debate was, if anything, more critical and censorious than in the case of the preceding schema. The "crisis" through which the Council had just passed undoubtedly helped to whet some appetites for blood. The "blood" in this case was not that of the members of the commission that had drafted the text (who had perhaps done as well as they could and in any case displayed no eagerness to defend their work), but the "higher authority" that had ordered the reduction of the original schema to a series of propositions. The impression was inevitable that priests were being downgraded as compared with bishops. For whatever reason, the members of the present commission as well as those of the other commissions whose texts had been reduced to propositions, had not had the backbone or "nerve" of the Commission on the Apostolate of the Laity, which had earlier in the year refused outright to adopt this procedure.*

Cardinal Meyer set the tone of discussion with a critical appraisal of the aims of the propositions. The purpose, as announced by Archbishop Marty, was to relate the life and ministry of the priest to the conditions and needs of today's world, but this was hardly evident from what followed. There had been full discussion of the apostolate of bishops and also of the apostolate of the laity, and there should also be a full discussion of the apostolate of priests, but the present text did not do justice to the idea. The propositions spoke almost exclusively about the obligations of priests, but had little to say about anything that would encourage them to fulfill their duties. The text was badly organized. It was not clear whether the aim was to lay down norms to be followed now, or norms for a future revision of the Code of Canon Law. Mention of the relations between priests and the laity in the first proposition after the preface was

* Asserted by Monsignor George Higgins at the Bishops' Press Panel.

not appropriate, since priests were first of all men of God before they were men among men. Insufficient attention was paid to the subject of the mass, in Proposition 3, "the greatest work and source of the priestly apostolate." Finally, after criticizing the treatment of the "common fund" mentioned in Proposition 12, the cardinal concluded: "A full schema and a full discussion are desired in order to respond to the pastoral aim of the Council and to the expectations of so many priests." His speech was greeted with a wave of applause.

The present document was declared to be basically satisfactory by the conservative Cardinals Ruffini and Quiroga y Palacios who, however, criticized it on minor points, mostly with regard to the arrangement of the material. This was also the view of Archbishops Rosales (Philippines) and Evangelisti (Meerut, India), though the latter wanted more emphasis on the missionary responsibilities of priests. The former felt that it was a good idea to refer to celibacy and obedience at the beginning, as the text stood, while Archbishop Fares (Catanzaro, Italy) was of the opinion that the passage on celibacy had been badly formulated, implying, by the use of the word "vow," that the Church had decided the controversy over whether celibacy was a matter of "law" or a "vow." He approved of what *L'Osservatore Romano* had recently said about the Church's determination to maintain the obligation of celibacy and disapproved of speculation in the press about the subject.

The notion of the *presbyterium* (or college of priests gathered around the bishop in each diocese which assisted him in the government of his see), a concept going back to the earliest days of the Church, needed to be stressed more, according to the Maronite Archbishop Ayoub (Aleppo) in a constructive speech. The idea did not imply that priests were the "slaves" of the bishop, but rather that they formed a "family" around him and considered one another as "brothers" and "co-workers." The schema smacked too much of paternalism and gave advice and commands to priests as if they were "not yet of age."

The idea of a "priestly senate" was still further explored by Archbishop Baldassarri (Ravenna, Italy). Some mention should be made of the rights of priests to share in church administration, he held. While much had been said about the rights of bishops, almost nothing was said about the *rights of priests,* according to Bishop Garaygordobil (Ecuador), their rights particularly when faced by an arbitrary exercise of authority on the part of bishops. "Pardon me for having to say this," he said, "but we are not yet confirmed in sanctity." Priests should be considered the true collaborators of bishops and not merely the latter's assistants. His proposal that in each diocese there should be set up a *Coetus Presbyterorum* to act as consultors to the bishop and that the bishop should govern in accordance with their advice, was much the same as Archbishop Ayoub's recommendation.

Quite a few of the interventions bore on the theme of priestly holiness. A certain minimalizing of the means to holiness was detected by Bishop Añoveros Ataún (Cadix y Ceuta, Spain), who felt that there was not enough emphasis on the mass, the divine office, and an examination of conscience in this connection. The three Spanish bishops, Mansilla Reoyo (Ciudad Rodrigo), Gonzalez Martin (Astorga), and Castán Lacoma (Siguenza-Guadalajara), all spoke on some aspect of the question of priestly holiness. The first wanted the need for specific ascetic-pastoral courses, annual retreats and the like, spelled out and not left to post-conciliar commissions or not mentioned at all; the second thought that priests should have a certain year, like the third year of a novitiate, for spiritual renewal some years after their ordination, not immediately afterward; the third wanted priestly associations, which had proved successful, given recognition in canon law like lay organizations. In conformity with the rather dour attitude generally taken by the Yugoslav clergy (who seemed to think that the world had not progressed much since the days of Pius X), Bishop Čekada (Skoplje) painted a dark picture of the inroads of "laicism" and "modernism" among some of the clergy, "which increases everyday and is a sign of the times." According to him some priests were degrading the confessional by watering down the seriousness of sins against the Sixth Commandment and downgrading confession generally; by bringing into the sanctuary "boys and girls, singing and dancing"; by trying to abolish ecclesiastical precepts or disregarding the rules for clerical attire. "Imagine such things thirty years ago!" he lamented.

The two questions of the "common life" and support for priests from a common or diocesan fund naturally came in for considerable comment. With regard to the former, the objection was made that there were many vocations to the secular priesthood precisely because individuals wished to preserve their individuality and not be bound by any form of life resembling the monastic. There was a place for both types in the Church and the two forms should not be confused. Several bishops raised the point of exactly what was meant by a "common life"? The question of adequate financial support for the clergy was mainly one of interest to Latin American and certain European countries.

On the subject of poverty, Bishop Komba (Tanganyika) observed that it was not a "fair trick" for the Council to recommend this virtue to priests, when nothing had been said about it in the schema on Bishops. What was good for the latter was also good for the former. Regarding the subject of priestly remuneration (Proposition 9), Bishop Hiltl (auxiliary of Regensburg, Germany) was of the opinion that there could also well be some mention of the need for priests to pay a fair wage to their domestics and some word about the "social security" of the latter. It was not enough to repay the services of housekeepers by holding out the hope of some legacy or bequest in a priest's will, they needed some guarantee for the future, otherwise maids would continually be looking for employment elsewhere.

The section recommending greater flexibility in the transfer of priests from one area to another was welcomed by the South American prelate, Archbishop Rodriquez Ballón (Arequipa, Peru), and he thanked those episcopally sponsored bodies which were working to this end, but he pointed to the need for a more equitable distribution of personnel and for training the latter in the customs of the country where they were going. The impression must be avoided that they were a foreign group in the country. One of the chief difficulties encountered by the some 4,000 American clergy (priests and nuns) working in Latin America had been this problem of "adjusting" to local conditions, without compromising the efficacy of their apostolate. Some progress was being made in Latin America, however, according to Bishop Proaño Villalba (Ecuador), who announced the establishment of a pastoral institute for Latin America formed by CELAM to travel from country to country in that part of the world. Special mention should be made of priestly associations, he said, for these had proved very helpful where they existed. And he insisted "the pope should be asked to stop bestowing merely honorific titles since these are a cause of division and envy" among the clergy. It should be remembered, that for all practical purposes, it would be the priests who would make the decrees of the Council work after they had been enacted.

The most notable intervention of the second day, and the one which helped seal the doom of the schema, was that delivered by the Brazilian Archbishop Gomes dos Santos (Goiania). "The text even in its revised form is a great disappointment to us and to many of the Fathers," he said, speaking in the name of 112 Brazilian and other bishops. "The text is almost an insult to our priests. . . . We praise the good intentions of the editors, but we deplore the result which does not give true consideration to either the secular or religious clergy. It is paternalistic and urges on priests things which we dare not impose on ourselves, e.g. poverty, the common life, clothing, the renunciation of titles and honors. . . ." He asked the moderators not to submit the text to a vote now, but to send it back for revision, with the vote to be postponed until the Fourth Session. His remarks were greeted by two outbursts of applause.

At the beginning of the congregation that day, Archbishop Felici had announced that a vote would be taken on different sections of the schema the following days, Thursday and Friday. At the end of the session, about

333

12:30, however, he withdrew this and announced that the vote had been postponed "because the list of speakers was not yet exhausted." This was because Cardinal Meyer had protested to the moderators against following this procedure when so many of the Fathers were against the schema.

During the first part of the congregation Thursday morning, seven more speakers were more or less insistent that the schema must be rewritten. Cardinal Alfrink stated that while the present text represented an improvement over the previous version, it did not come up to the expectations of priests because it did not describe an image of the priest which the modern world could recognize. The Council should adopt a more forthright attitude toward the "crisis" with regard to priestly celibacy by bringing out more clearly the biblical and traditional background of the subject. "Perhaps some consolation and encouragement could be added," he remarked, "for those priests who see celibacy as a burden" and not a "joy." The present text would be a great disappointment to priests today and must be rewritten to provide consolation, strength and hope. There was applause following his intervention. Bishop Köstner (Gurk, Austria) and Archbishop Sartre (Cameroun) followed him in offering general criticisms and calling for a complete revision. Archbishop Modrego y Casaus (Barcelona), Bishop Gugič (Dubrovnik) and Bishop Flores Martin (Barbastro, Spain), confined their attention to specific points. Bishop Jenny (auxiliary of Cambrai, France) favored neither approval nor rejection, but revision, if possible, before the end of the present session.

At this point (Thursday, October 15th) the moderators called for a standing vote on whether to close debate. The motion was carried by a narrow majority, thus indicating that many of the Fathers still felt that the subject had not been sufficiently exhausted. The only other speaker, Cardinal Lefebvre (Bourges, France), who spoke in the name of at least 70 Fathers, was for revision with more attention being paid to the relationship of priests to the priesthood of the laity, so much emphasized these days. Archbishop Marty then summed up in the name of the commission, stating that the members were at the service of the Council and expressing a desire that the Fathers manifest their wishes by Iuxta modum rather than negative votes, so as to give better guidance to the commission. He also referred expressly to the desire of many Fathers that more emphasis should be placed on the notion of the *presbyterium* (or the close bonds which ought to prevail between bishops and priests). The commission also hoped that the moderators would allow expansion of the propositions into a full-fledged schema again. Any suggestions for the solemn message to priests, which it will still intended to issue, should also be sent in.

Later that day the Coordinating Commission met to consider the question of voting on the propositions, in the likelihood that other texts would elicit the same unfavorable reaction as the present one. The moderators also had their usual audience with the pope. As a result of these consultations it was announced on Friday by Secretary General Felici:

A number of Fathers having asked the moderators to remand to commission after discussion the schemata reduced to propositions, the Coordinating Commission has decided that after a brief discussion in general congregation the Council will vote on the motion as to whether these schemata should be submitted for an immediate vote. If an absolute majority (half the votes plus one) is favorable, the vote will take place at once. If it is unfavorable, the schemata will be sent back to be revised as rapidly as possible.

The decision, while saving face, amounted to a tacit acknowledgment of the contention of most Fathers that the texts under question were far too important to be reduced to mere propositions and should be restored to their original form—though no decision was apparently taken regarding this latter point as yet. The first test of the new procedure came when the propositions on the Priestly Life and Ministry were put to a vote on Monday, October 19th. The result was a large majority in favor of returning the document to commission at once.

DEBATE ON EASTERN CHURCHES

On Thursday, October 15th, the Council took up the second of the schemata reduced to propositions, that on the Eastern Churches (*De Ecclesiis Orientalibus*). There were now 30 Propositions as compared with 54 articles in the text debated in 1963, but the length was approximately the same. However, while the material had been considerably rearranged and the tone and emphasis changed for the better, it was obvious from the ensuing debate that the Latinizing tendencies which had presided over the destiny of this document from the beginning were still in evidence. They were unhappily present also in the final version promulgated on November 21, 1964. Anyone comparing the successive stages through which the document passed on its way from the rough draft first presented to the Fathers in 1962 to the final version would be likely to hail the progress made. But it was never possible to free it entirely from a certain condescending attitude toward the Eastern Churches or do full justice to Eastern conceptions when there were important divergences in outlook between East and West, because of an instinctive inability on the part of some of the framers to adopt an objective approach, to abandon some of the preconceptions inherent in *romanità*. This attitude had been typical of the Cardinal Secretary of State, Amleto Cicognani, in particular, both during the years when he presided over the Congregation for the Oriental Churches and later as president of the corresponding conciliar commission which drafted the texts. He had been supported, of course, by a number of prelates (of both rites), who found it difficult to rid themselves of their prejudices. On the other hand, for many years, a number of prelates and specialists in the oriental field, professors and students at the Oriental Institute and in the various colleges in Rome and elsewhere, had been raising their voices in protest against this outmoded Curial outlook, but they had generally not been listened to, or their ideas had been adopted only in part. The classic example of Roman ineptness in this field was the Code of Canon Law for the Oriental Churches, promulgated under Pius XII. The result of many years of diligent work and painstaking research on the part of experts in eastern canon law and theology (allegedly), it turned out to be nothing more than a pale image of the already outmoded Code of Canon Law for the Latin Church and now awaited drastic revision with a view to eliminating its many Latinisms.

The picture had been complicated by divided loyalties among the Uniats (or those Christians of eastern rite in communion with the Apostolic See). Formerly, these bodies were subject to strong Latinizing pressures, not only from without but in some cases from within their own groups, urging them to conform as much as possible to the Latin pattern of church government and teaching of theology by abandoning their time-honored traditions and customs. Lately, the trend had, on the whole, been the other way, toward carefully preserving and reviving and purifying their authentic traditions and especially their autonomous status within the fold of the Catholic Church. These divided loyalties played a part in the ultimate fate of the document up for consideration. A final factor was the unquestioned lack of interest in it on the part of the majority of the Fathers, except for those who were concerned on an ecumenical basis or as ordinaries for the various groups of Eastern-rite Catholics in their midst.

The propositions were introduced by Cardinal Cicognani, who said that three points in particular had caused difficulty for the members of the commission, and that the majorities reached on these points were far from unanimous. The following were the three points around which much of the debate would revolve:

1. When Eastern Orthodox Christians were converted to Catholicism, they were to retain the same rite in the Catholic Church which they had followed in the Orthodox Church, with provision being made for an appeal to the Holy

See in special cases. (This article was later eliminated from the final text in accordance with a vote.)

2. The presence of a Catholic priest at a marriage between two Eastern Christians was necessary for the liceity, but not the validity, of the marriage, unless a dispensation had been granted (Proposition 18). This provision reversed a ruling of Pius XII in a Motu Proprio of 1949.

3. Eastern-rite Catholics could make use of Orthodox sacraments provided no Catholic priest were available, and the Orthodox could, under certain circumstances, be admitted to receive Catholic sacraments (the so-called *communicatio in sacris*, Propositions 26–29).

Archbishop Bukatko, who followed the cardinal, read the report of the commission. The text before the Fathers had been approved in April 1964, and few changes had been made after that date on the basis of suggestions sent in by the Fathers. Those received recently were printed as an appendix and not incorporated in the text itself.

Cardinal König (Vienna), speaking as ordinary for Eastern Catholics in Austria, led off the debate with three fundamental objections (reiterated by subsequent speakers) reflecting on the inveterate pro-Latin outlook of certain circles in Rome: 1) The non-Catholic Eastern Churches were not honored sufficiently as Churches. 2) The Eastern Churches were practically identified with the Churches united with Rome (Uniats), and relations with the Orthodox were viewed under the guise of conversion to the Roman Catholic Church. 3) There was a discrepancy between the outlook in Chapter III of the decree on Ecumenism and the present text. Its language should be brought into line with the former. The Eastern Churches should be viewed not so much with regard to their "separateness" as to the things they held in "common" with the Roman Catholic Church. Further, he found fault with Propositions 2–4 which regarded only the Eastern Churches as "particular churches," whereas there were also particular Churches in the West. He objected to the use of the term "mixed" when referring to mixed marriages, between Orthodox and Catholics, because it was virtually meaningless in such cases, and he felt strongly that because *communicatio in sacris* meant intercommunion, or at least a beginning along this path, it was necessary to come to some kind of an agreement with the separated Orthodox Churches through conferences. He was dissatisfied also with the description of the patriarchates in the document.

The cardinal was followed by the Coptic patriarch of Alexandria, Stephanos Sidarouss I, who was in general satisfied with the text and hoped that it would receive a large majority. While disapproving the provision that Orthodox converting to Catholicism were to retain their native rite, he was in favor of abolishing the legislation of Pius XII regarding eastern marriages. But the speaker of the morning who caused the most stir was the doughty Melkite patriarch of Antioch Maximos IV Saigh, who spoke last and in French, according to his custom. This was his first speech during the Third Session and he was listened to with rapt attention.

After praising the progress shown in the disciplinary portions of the document, he castigated its doctrinal or ecumenical presuppositions:

> The preamble praises the Catholic Church for having always held the institutions of the Christian East in great esteem. It thereby contrasts or distinguishes between the Catholic Church, which addresses this praise, and the Eastern Church, to whom this praise is addressed. This leads one to believe either that the Catholic Church is identical with the Latin Church, which is not exact, or that the Eastern Churches do not belong essentially to the Catholic Church, which is also equally inexact.

But the portion which came in for his greatest ire and sarcasm was the section dealing with the patriarchal office:

> Of all the chapters of the present schema, the weakest is incontestably that devoted to the patriarchs (nos. 7–11). This chapter as it is presented to us is inadmissible. It cocks a snook at history and in no way prepares for the future. For the institution that is the most venerable of the hierarchy after the Roman primacy, the schema has only succeeded in giving scholastic definitions (which furthermore are incomplete) and Platonic aspirations, most often repeating recent canon-law texts, as if Vatican II had not been summoned to make a certain advance but ought to content itself with the prescribed *status quo* . . .
>
> The supreme authority in the Church is without doubt able to renew or to rejuvenate these forms of the ancient ecclesial communion. But the principle that underlies them should not be passed over in silence if it is wished to offer our Orthodox brothers a preliminary draft of the charter of union . . .
>
> Venerable Fathers, when one talks of the East one ought not to think solely of those who humbly represent it today in the bosom of Roman Catholicism. A place must be kept for what is absent. The circuit of Catholicism must not be confined to a dynamic and conquering Latinity on the one hand, and on the other a fraction of the East, a fraction that is more or less weak, assimilated, and absorbed. The circuit must be left open. Let us make Catholicity loyal to its solemn affirmations, to its definition of Catholic in universality. Let us make it great, not for us humble individuals and communities in fortunate communion with Rome, but so that our Churches of origin may find their home there, when it shall grow, in fact as by right, in the realisation of love, to the dimensions of the universe. *Dixi.*

The speech of this venerable dissenter from *romanità* was so typical, and made the essential points so well, that it deserves to be quoted. Pope Paul rewarded the aged patriarch by naming him first on the list of cardinals elevated in the consistory of February 25, 1965.

Support for the right of a convert to choose whatever rite he pleased (when changing from Orthodoxy to Catholicism) came from Cardinal de Barros Câmara (Rio de Janeiro, Brazil) and Archbishop Gori (the Latin patriarch of Jerusalem). The latter's enthusiasm for free choice in the matter of rite was perhaps explicable in view of his position. As a Latin-rite patriarch in the East, he was regarded as an interloper and Trojan Horse of Latinism by the Orthodox clergy and he could therefore hardly be expected to admit the justice of the other side. Typical of him were his constant appeals to Leo XIII's encyclical *Orientalium Dignitas,* as the last word in the matter. He was answered by Archbishop Tawil (Melkite patriarchal vicar for Damascus), who pointed out that the restoration of the Latin Patriarchate of Jerusalem in the last century evoked many bitter memories. For the good of the whole Church, he said, it was necessary to put an end to "Latinization," meaning the Latin Patriarchate. By contrast the Armenian Patriarch Batanian was all for retaining the reading of the text which prohibited a choice of rite. "Like every law," he said, "the text limits freedom but with good reason: a son of a family coming back to his home town should return to his own family." Most of his talk was taken up with the subject of mixed marriages. A return to the pre-1949 legislation was necessary, he maintained, because the remedies applied by Rome, for example the invalidation (*sanatio*) of a previously invalid marriage, were not working well. The only solution was recognition of all the marriages in question as valid.

The attention of Major Archbishop Slipyi (Ukraine) was focused almost entirely on the, to him, apparently, overriding problem of how to protect the Eastern Churches from the inroads of Latinization. "Everyone is aware of the destructive setbacks which Eastern-rite Christians have suffered in the course of history, but the diminished numbers of Eastern faithful are also due to the imprudence of Latin Catholics who try to convert Eastern Christians to their rite." Let the Council learn a lesson from the friendly meeting between Patriarch Athenagoras I and Pope Paul VI in Jerusalem. "Have mercy on us," he said, facetiously, in conclusion, "because we are Orientals!" In response to the archbishop's appeal in 1963 for recognition of a Ukrainian patriarchate, he must have noted with pleasure the paragraph in the text (No. 10) which stipulated that for all practical purposes "major archbishops" had the status of patriarchs.

Enthusiasm for the patriarchate likewise marked the intervention by the Coptic Archbishop Ghattas (Thebes, Egypt). As the Coptic patriarch his superior had done, he asked whether it was really necessary to have a separate document on the Eastern Churches at all, and why these could not be dealt with in a special section of *De Ecclesia?* "How good it would be if our patriarchs could only return home as members of the Church's senate and with the right to elect the pope!" His wish was to be fulfilled, in part, sooner than he realized (on February 25, 1965, to be exact).

The Fathers were treated to a bit of a lecture by Archbishop Zoghby (Melkite patriarchal vicar for Egypt). He agreed with the theological objections to the schema raised by Cardinal König and Patriarch Maximos IV. His principal contribution was an excursion into the field of history. At the time of the Patriarch Photius, he said, in the ninth century, when the patriarch had been restored to the throne of Constantinople with Roman approval (879), the relationship between the two churches was defined as a sort of coexistence. The primacy of the pope was recognized, as well as his right to preside over ecumenical councils, and the right to appeal to him in matters of controversy, but for all practical purposes East and West respected each other's canonical autonomy, and there was no feeling of separation among the faithful at large. The disputes were regarded as local affairs, between pope and patriarch, or among theologians. It was only gradually, in response to certain events, that the two sides drew apart definitely, and the sense of belonging to the same Church was lost. The present text still reflected the latter-day feeling of alienation in its attitude toward the Eastern Churches. He concluded by referring to the rigorous Cardinal Humbert, the Cardinal Ottaviani of his day, who in 1054, as the emissary of Pope Leo IX, laid a bull of excommunication on the altar of Haghia Sophia in Constantinople, excommunicating the patriach and formally breaking off discussions between the two Churches. "If Cardinal Humbert were here . . ." At this point he was interrupted by the moderator who reminded him that he had gone beyond his time, but he managed to finish, "If Cardinal Humbert were here, many of us would be excommunicated!"

The speeches on Monday by Cardinal Lercaro and Abbot Hoeck, the latter a Benedictine and member of the Commission for the Oriental Churches, were important as pointing to a possible way out of the vexing problems of conflicting jurisdictions, precedence, prestige and differing notions about ecumenism in which the Council found itself as a result of having decided to deal with the Eastern Churches as a separate item on its agenda. Both stressed the necessity of a realistic approach toward the institution of the patriarchate, which must be regarded as an integral part of the structure of the Church, and not something merely applying to the East, as a normal thing, not a mere oddity. Both suggested that a general statement of desires and some practical points should be substituted for the present normative and juridical decree, and that the terms of a directory dealing with matters in greater detail should be worked out by a secretariat or mixed commission which would weigh each aspect carefully. Cardinal Lercaro referred expressly to the Orthodox Church and said: "The hierarchy not yet sitting with us here should be heard before legislation is drawn up, and their consent sought." Abbot Hoeck pointed out that it was impossible for the Orthodox to agree to union with Rome as long as the status of their hierarchy was not regulated vis-à-vis the Curia and the cardinalate. Their patriarchs would never agree to be dependent on the Curia. Cardinal Lercaro seemed to say that the question of the ultimate place of the patriarchs in the hierarchy should be left to a decision of the pope, since it concerned the supreme authority. This was in conformity with his recommendation regarding the "episcopal senate" in the Second Session. Abbot Hoeck, however, was for having the autonomy of the patriarchates proclaimed by the Council. He concluded his remarkably outspoken speech by saying: *"Dixi et salvavi animam meam"*—I have spoken to relieve my conscience.

Archbishop Vuccino (France) was for replacing the term "separated brethren" wherever it occurred by "Orthodox," to avoid all suspicion of favoring Latinization, and also because the Orthodox had been extraordinarily faithful to their traditions. He recalled the words of Athenagoras I to Maximos IV when the latter paid a visit to Constantinople in January 1964: "You were the voice of the East in the Council. You were the voice of our common hopes."

Not all the Eastern prelates shared the above fervor for the patriarchate. Bishop Bidawid, in the name of the Chaldean bishops, stressed that the office of patriarch was not of divine but of human origin, and that there was room for reforming the institution. The Church was a living body. Why not increase the number of patriarchs, just as the number of cardinals was increased? This remark was greeted by applause. The Armenian Bishop Bayan (Alexandria) saw danger in exalting the person of the patriarch at the expense of the patriarchal synod. A return to the past would not inevitably solve all difficulties. The applause which followed the remarks of Bishop Bidawid may also have been due to the fact that he was the last speaker. A number of other prelates spoke earlier, but they added nothing significant to the debate. At this point the moderator, Cardinal Lercaro, called for a standing vote on whether to close debate. The motion was carried overwhelmingly.

The following day, Tuesday, October 20th, three more speakers were allowed to address the assembly in the name of at least 70 Fathers each. Bishop Hakim (Israel) pleaded for acceptance of the schema. "A negative vote would throw out everything, good and bad," he argued. "It is true that the text is not perfect. But what text hitherto presented in Council has been perfect? An Arab proverb states, 'Only God is perfect.' " He was followed by Archbishop Baudoux (St. Boniface, Canada) and Archbishop Athaide (Agra, India). The *relator,* Archbishop Bukatko, then summed up the debate and also put in a plea for acceptance of the text, as a basis for revision. The feeling had been that in view of the highly critical tone of the discussion, the Non placet votes might carry the day, but when the votes were counted they were in favor of an immediate vote on the several parts of the text. The final appeals for acceptance undoubtedly counted for something in swaying the Fathers. In the voting on the individual propositions which followed on October 21st and 22nd, all the proposition were carried, except 2–4, which failed to achieve a majority because of dissatisfaction with the ruling that converts were to have no choice of rite. When the result of this particular vote was known, Archbishop Felici announced: "The text has not been adopted," but he later corrected himself and explained that when Iuxta modum votes amounted to less than a third of the total, the commission was not "obliged" to consider them, but when they came to more, the commission was "morally bound" to take them into consideration. The provision was omitted from the final version of the decree.

DEBATE ON 'THE CHURCH IN THE MODERN WORLD'

Tuesday, October 20, 1964, was a red-letter day in the history of the Council. The Fathers had finally reached the long-awaited, controversial Schema on the Church in the Modern World. This document was more commonly known as "Schema 13," because this was the number it acquired in the list of seventeen schemata to which the seventy original conciliar documents had been reduced. (This designation was unofficial, of course; there was no set numbering of the schemata.)

Schema 13 almost failed to make the floor, however. Rumors spread on October 8th that it would be withdrawn from debate in order to allow the Council to end with the Third Session. The suggestion was discussed at a meeting of the Coordinating Commission the day before, but no decision was reached. It was obvious that there was a certain amount of stalling during this weekend of the *magno cum dolore* "crisis," when there was momentary confusion in the reaches of higher authority. The Council was scheduled to take up the schema after debating the Apostolate of the Laity, but Archbishop Felici suddenly announced that this document would be followed by a brief discussion of several of the propositions, because "the *relationes* for Schema 13 were not yet ready." Needless to say, hardly anybody believed that this was the full story, but in a few days it became apparent that the debate would be held after all. The strong protest to the pope drafted by the cardinals on October 11th may have had something to do with reaching a positive decision on going ahead with Schema 13. It was unthinkable that Pope Paul himself could have seriously entertained the idea of side-tracking the document, since he, as Cardinal Montini, along with Pope John and Cardinal Suenens, had been one of its prime movers from the very start.

A mixed commission, headed by Cardinal Cento and Cardinal Ottaviani, presidents respectively of the Commission for the Apostolate of the Laity and the Theological Commission, had been responsible for preparing the text. The drafting was actually done by a subcommission presided over by Bishop Guano (Livorno, Italy), of which the Redemptorist moral theologian, Father Bernard Häring, was secretary. There were a number of other working subcommissions responsible for different parts of the document. The draft schema before the Fathers was worked out by the subcommission in the early spring of 1964 and received final approval from the Coordinating Commission in June. Probably no other conciliar document had gone through so many stages before reaching its final form. It now consisted of four chapters and five appendices called *Adnexa,* the latter containing in part earlier versions of the schema that had been discarded as formal texts but were retained as explanatory matter (helpful to an understanding of the schema itself). Archbishop Felici, the secretary general, had overconfidently announced on October 1st that the *Adnexa* were "private documents" without any official standing, but he was obliged to retract these words, at the direction of the moderators, and explain that they were "conciliar documents" but would not be debated.

The secretary general announced that there would first be debate on the schema as a whole, after which the Fathers would be asked to vote on whether the document should be accepted for further discussion or sent back to commission. If the vote were favorable for a continued debate, the latter would take place in three stages: the Introduction and Chapter I; Chapters II and III; Chapter IV. Since the final chapter covered so many topics, the discussion of it would proceed by paragraphs.

In an optimistic and enthusiastic tone, the schema was introduced by Cardinal Cento, who appeared quite unabashed by the rough treatment accorded the earlier document he had introduced, on the Apostolate of the Laity. "No other document had aroused so much interest and raised so many hopes," he said. "It was evident that Mother Church had not become senile and was not suffering from hardening of the arteries, but had preserved the youthful freshness of her Founder, Christ." Bishop Guano, who followed, delivered the report of the subcommission and entered into more detail. He stressed in particular the novelty of the schema and its lack of perfection. It was not offered as a final text but as a first draft and should be received as such. The Fathers must not be put off because of the differences in tone and content from other conciliar documents. It was not a definitive or exhaustive statement, but one intended to inaugurate a "dialogue," to discuss some of the burning problems of today and the Church's reaction to them. "The Church cannot remain closed up within herself as in a fortress, intent only on defending her own interests and members. The Church recognizes that she is living in the world, sharing the life of men in order to give them the life of God, existing among men and for men." One of the difficulties encountered in preparing the text was in finding a correct balance between the great principles of the Gospel and an adequate description of present-day conditions to be discussed in the light of these principles. Another was the difficulty of finding the right language. Some people would be put off by the unaccustomed terminology; others would find it still too traditional and ecclesiastical. Another was that people would probably expect too much from the document and Bishop Guano warned against this over-optimism. With regard to the *Adnexa,* he explained that they remained as working documents under the jurisdiction of the subcommission which had prepared them, but they were being submitted to the Fathers now for comment, rather than for debate. The subcommissions would reconsider them at their leisure in the light of the comments in writing, with the decision about their ultimate fate to be made later.

The debate was led off with an impressive barrage from the "big-guns" Cardinals Liénart, Spellman, Lercaro, Léger, Döpfner, Meyer and Silva Henriquez the first day. Cardinal Ruffini managed as usual to interject a discordant note, but he could only rate third place on the list this time. The salvoes continued the following day with volleys from Cardinals Landázuri Ricketts, Suenens and Bea, and a host of smaller shots. The reception was on the whole overwhelmingly favorable. The subcommission was delighted. Cardinal Liénart found the schema good in essentials, but the style was too much that of a sermon: "The text proceeds by way of constant exhortations and seems lacking in humility"; and there was not a sufficiently clear distinction drawn between the supernatural and the natural orders in the Preface and Chapter I. He said the schema moved indiscriminately from one order to the other without making that fact clear at all times.

In his first speech at the Council following an illness that had prevented him from attending the first part of the session, Cardinal Spellman termed the schema "admirable." He said that it came up to the Council's expectations and should not be weakened in any way. It manifested the will of the Church for service and dialogue. A condition of dialogue, however, was a proper sense of obedience, of obedience to ecclesiastical authority. He wanted the document to deal with this subject and show that "true filial obedience is fully consonant with liberty."

The importance of the schema was fully acknowledged by Cardinal Ruffini (Palermo), but he found the treatment of the question raised wholly inadequate. Some statements seemed to smack of "situation ethics" which the Church had already condemned. He was particularly critical of the section on the family. "Some statements are either wrong, or else I don't understand them," he admitted, with refreshing candor. When reminded by the moderator, Cardinal Döpfner, that he was wandering from the subject under discussion (the schema as a whole), he replied that he knew this, but his speech had been prepared before it was known what the order of discussion would be, and he went right on with his talk. "I am not against ecumenism, I believe, but *ne quid nimis!*" he exclaimed. The schema should be completely rewritten and based on the papal social encyclicals of the present century.

A plea for a full discussion of the schema was put in by Cardinal Lercaro, who observed that experience had shown that it was possible to arrive at a satisfactory text only on the basis of a generous airing of views in the Council hall (e.g. the schemata on the Church and Divine Revelation). This was necessary in order to avoid too European or Western an outlook. It was unwise to proceed with too much haste. Even a Fourth Session held in 1965 might not find the text ready for final approval. He warned, too, against expecting too much from the present discussion. The world press had become so wrought up over the question, there was danger of a let-down (applause). The approach of Cardinal Léger was similar to that of Cardinal Liénart: while approving of the schema in general, he felt that the distinction between man's terrestrial and his celestial vocation was not made sufficiently clear; however, the avoidance of sterile condemnations marked progress. Speaking in the name of 83 bishops, Cardinal Döpfner surmised that the text could not be discussed and revised in the remaining five weeks of the Council, and that enough time must be allowed so that it could be perfected, "to make it the real crown of this Council." He regretted that not enough space had been devoted to the problem of modern atheism, especially dialectical materialism.

The same sentiments were shared by Cardinal Meyer (Chicago), whose intervention was more theological. The schema appeared to fear the "contagion" of the world too much: this was because of an insufficient emphasis on the theology of salvation and the bonds which redemption had established between God and man, according to St. Paul. Man's work in the temporal order was part of the transformation which God planned for the world. Every act of his fitted into this divine plan. The compenetration of the Church and the world could be better explained if these points were brought out more fully. Cardinal Silva Henriquez saw the schema as a step in the formulation of a "Christian cosmology" and he was pleased that it showed the need for a dialogue with contemporary humanism, especially atheism, along the lines of Pope Paul's encyclical *Ecclesiam suam*. Modern atheism derived its strength from its emphasis on the temporal order and the Church must be prepared to engage in conversation with it on its own ground.

Several speakers found the language inexact and vague. One of the terms most frequently criticized was "world": sometimes it seemed to be used in a favorable sense and again as something opposed to the Church; the word "Church" was also used ambiguously. These points were brought out by Cardinal Landázuri Ricketts, who felt also that insufficient attention had been paid to the problem of famine in the world today.

While concurring in what his fellow-moderators had said, in a "spirit of fraternal collegiality," Cardinal Suenens made several points of his own. It was not stated explicitly enough that the Church "does not evangelize by civilizing, but civilizes by evangelizing," as Pius X had observed. Further consideration should be given to militant atheism. We must ask ourselves why men were atheists and question our own way of speaking about the faith, otherwise we made the idea of God obscure for them. Some of the material in the *Adnexa* could profitably be introduced into the text, particularly the parts on the international order and conjugal love. Cardinal Bea admitted that when he had first read the schema it had seemed to be superficial, but in a second reading he decided that it dealt with profound and difficult matters after all. But he thought the text could be helped if there were more arguments from the Bible and from the fonts of faith, rather than from mere rational principles. After all it was addressed, primarily, to Christians.

On the third day of the debate the temperature suddenly plunged toward zero and it seemed, momentarily, as if all might be lost owing to a chorus of criticisms. Archbishop Heenan (Westminster, England) was the first speaker of the day. His beginning was innocuous enough, with praise for a commission that had labored so hard, but when he referred to the document as "unworthy of a general Council," and "a set of platitudes," ears began to prick up. He soon launched into the heart of the matter.

I must apeak plainly. This document is going to dash the hopes of everyone who has been waiting for it. Its authors do not seem to realize even to whom the message is directed . . . The whole treatise reads more like a sermon than a Council.

He objected strenuously to the advice given that the Council should read the schema in the light of the *Adnexa* (or supplements). "The fact is that the schema even read with the supplements remains obscure and misleading; read on its own, it could be dangerous and misleading." The Council had been told to debate the schema and pass over the rest without comment, but this would be fatal, because it would leave the mind of the Council to be interpreted by "experts" who helped draw up the documents.

> God forbid that this should happen! I fear specialists when they are left to explain what the bishops meant (*Timeo peritos adnexa ferentes*).

Between sessions of this Council, the Church of God has suffered a great deal from the writings and speeches of some of the specialists. They are few in number but their sound has gone forth to the ends of the earth. These few specialists care nothing for the ordinary teaching authority of the bishops— nor, I regret to say, for that of the pope. It is idle to show them a papal encyclical in which a point of Catholic doctrine is clearly laid down. They will immediately reply that a pope is not infallible when writing an encyclical. It really does not seem worthwhile for the pope to write any more encyclical letters since they can apparently no longer be quoted in support of the faith.

We must protect the authority of the Teaching Church. It is of no avail to talk about a college of bishops if specialists in articles, books and speeches contradict and pour scorn on what a body of bishops teaches. Until now it has not been a doctrine of the Church that the theologians admitted to the Council are infallible. The theories of one or two must not be mistaken for a general agreement among theologians which has, of course, special authority.

Archbishop Heenan went on to say that the commission should perhaps not be too much blamed for the document since they "were in fact denied the help of experts who really knew their subjects." In dealing with problems of social life, it was necessary to consult those who knew and lived in the world. "These scholars often have a childlike trust in the opinions of men in the world. Certainly they are simple as doves, but they are not always wise as serpents." The section on marriage was singled out as a particularly glaring instance of misinformation, in the archbishop's opinion, and of the harm that could be done by leaving too many decisions to the *periti:*

> If you are looking for examples of all this, you need only study the section on matrimony. Everyone knows that doctors all over the world are busily trying to produce a satisfactory contraceptive pill. This special kind of pill is to be a panacea to solve all sexual problems between husbands and wives. Neither the treatise itself nor the supplements hesitate to prophesy that such a pill is just round the corner. Meanwhile, it is said, married couples and they alone must decide what is right and wrong. Everyone must be his own judge. But, the document adds, the couple must act according to the teaching of the Church. But this is precisely what married people want to be told—what *is* now the teaching of the Church? To this question our document gives no reply. For that very reason it could provide an argument from our silence for theologians after the Council who wish to attack sound doctrine.
>
> The document thus blandly addresses husbands and wives: "Some practical solutions have made their appearance and there are more to come." This is no

way for a document of the Church to be composed. When our children ask us for bread, we should not give them a stone.

In conclusion, he strongly urged that the document be given to a new commission, on which specialists of the day and priests with pastoral experience were represented, and suggested that three or four years might be necessary to produce a really satisfactory text.

The majority was obviously stunned by the vehemence and unexpected nature of Archbishop Heenan's attack. The speech, of course, evoked a round of applause for its display of rhetorical skill. Cardinal Ruffini was seen to grasp the hand of the archbishop, who looked somewhat embarrassed and uneasy over support from this quarter. Apparently Heenan had momentarily allowed resentment and irritation to get the better of good judgment. His blanket condemnation of *periti* was widely interpreted as an attack on Father Bernard Häring, who had had much to do with the formulation of the schema and was involved in a controversy with the English hierarchy in the spring of 1964 over the question of birth control. It was not true, of course, that competent experts had not been consulted when the document was drawn up, but it was possible that not enough divergent views had been canvassed, a criticism that could be levelled against most of the other commissions as well. If the archbishop really was irritated, he soon got over his pique. Meeting Father Häring later, he invited him to speak to the English hierarchy at the English College. When someone remarked to the Redemptorist, "You must have suffered this morning during the congregation," he replied: "No, I expected something like that. . . . It is not we who are important, but to work which each one should do humbly in his place." Bishop Wright (Pittsburgh) perhaps summed up the general impression of Heenan's speech at a press conference two days later, when asked for his comment: "It is clear that the archbishop felt very deeply and personally about what he had to say—whatever it was he had to say."

The following day Abbot Reetz, superior of the Beuron Benedictines in Germany, amused the Fathers by replying humorously to Archbishop Heenan. "It is with fear and trepidation," he said, "that I speak to the Fathers, because we heard yesterday that it is useless for the Council to call upon men from religious houses, seminaries and universities. I, a monk and abbot, who hardly knows the world, am now addressing the assembly, speaking with the simplicity of the dove rather than the asperity of a serpent." He went on somewhat ironically: "Perhaps the 40 monks once sent to make *angels* of the *Angli* didn't know very much about the world. But it was a monk who was the first primate of England, St. Augustine of Canterbury; and it was a monk, St. Benedict, whom the pope will proclaim as the Patron of Europe, tomorrow, at Montecassino." This remark was followed by applause, which the moderator stifled by saying, *"Ne fiant plausus."* The monk's flight from the world was not a flight from the Church and the apostolate, Abbot Reetz went on. History proved how much those who were monks had contributed to the Church and to mankind. Father Teilhard de Chardin was currently enjoying a great influence, especially over the young. The beauty of his canticle to matter had been compared to the famous canticle of St. Francis of Assisi. But Father Teilhard did not pay enough attention to the presence of sin in the world. The schema must be praised for avoiding this pitfall. Archbishop Heenan, typically, was delighted by the *riposte* and sent a letter to the abbot, saying *"Touché"* and inviting him to dinner at the English College. (Some time after the close of the session, Abbot Reetz was unfortunately killed in an automobile accident.)

The name of Teilhard de Chardin was also brought up by Archbishop Hurley (Durban, South Africa) in connection with what he called "the central theological problem of the century," the value of the natural order in its relation to man's supernatural end. He approved of Teilhard's splendid vision, "at once religious, scientific, evolutionary and eschatological," and suggested the setting up of a special commission to study this fundamental question, along the lines of the intervention of Cardinal Meyer and in the light of the doctrine of Thomas Aquinas on the presence of God in the world, so that concrete problems could be decided on the basis of this guidance. He added, slyly, "there must still be *some* experts left who could be called upon for this." Bishop Charue (Namur) also came to the support of the *periti:* "The schema is premature; it needs a good incubator. The commission has *excellent* experts; if others are added, the results will be good."

Reference to the name of Teilhard de Chardin naturally suggested the propriety of mentioning the name of John Henry Newman in connection with Schema 13. This was done by Archbishop Shehan (Baltimore), who felt that the document should refer, as did Pope Paul's encyclical *Ecclesiam suam,* to the problem of the Church's progress in its doctrines and institutions. "The Church must advance more and more in the consciousness of its task," the pope had said. Newman in his *Essay on the Development of Doctrine* had made the comment, "A power of development is proof of life."

The schema was praised by Bishop Gonzalez Moralejo (auxiliary of Valencia), Archbishop Roy (Quebec), Archbishop Duval (Algiers), Bishop Stimpfle (Augsburg) and some other prelates, but a few of the Latin-speaking bishops took a fear-laden line. The Bishop of Campos, (Brazil) regretted that there was no mention of the devil, "who nevertheless exists"; and Bishop Barbieri (Cassano, Italy) found that the schema said nothing about "the greatest evil today, the loss of any feeling for

God." The same prelates also found it displeasing that so little was said about the threat of communism (e.g. Archbishop Bolatti of Rosario, Argentina), a judgment in which the exiled archbishop of Nanking, Yü Pin, quite naturally concurred. He called for an entire new chapter on the subject.

The questioning of the authority of the magisterium, which Archbishop Heenan had brought up earlier, was mentioned again by Archbishop Beck (Liverpool, England), who felt some uneasiness over the document's treatment of marriage and its implied downgrading of *Casti connubii*. He thought also that the arrangement of the material could be improved by starting out with more practical and concrete questions, including many topics dealt with in the *Adnexa*.

Toward 11 o'clock on Friday, October 23rd, the moderators decided that debate on the schema had been sufficiently exhausted and called for a standing vote on whether to close off discussion. The assembly being willing, the Fathers were then asked to cast their ballots on whether to continue discussion of the various parts of the schema. The results were overwhelmingly favorable: 1,579 to 296. About 200 bishops were either in the bars or had left the Council hall, not expecting a vote that morning. Bishop Guano could not be located at once to sum up the debate, so that Secretary General Archbishop Felici was obliged to fill in with some remarks about the likelihood of some of the Fathers becoming saints, as had happened to one of the bishops at Vatican Council I, St. Anthony Mary Claret, whose feast day it was. He hoped that the secretary general of the next ecumenical council would be able to announce that some of the present Fathers had been canonized, but he, Pericle Felici, would surely be in purgatory expiating his sins. The rumor spread that the reason Bishop Guano could not be found was that he had been to see the pope; there was naturally considerable interest in his remarks, therefore, when he disclosed that while it would not be possible to bring back the schema to the floor before the end of the present session, it was hoped there would be a vote on certain urgent questions such as poverty, hunger, peace and atheism—but he did not elaborate on this. Bishop Guano reminded the prelates that since a special commission of experts had been appointed by the pope to consider the question of birth control, the schema remained somewhat vague on details because it would be unwise to anticipate the results of this body's recommendations. The Holy Father had reserved to himself a final decision in this matter.*

Earlier, at the beginning of the congregation, Archbishop Felici had confirmed that the Third Session would definitely end on November 21st with a concelebration ceremony by the pope and 24 prelates from

* Commission for the Study of Problems relating to Population, Family and Birth, announced in an allocution on June 23, 1964.

countries having Marian shrines. He also had some warm words of praise for the "hard-working *periti*" and expressed the hope that the commissions would have some documents ready in time so that they could be proclaimed on the final day. He continued: "The next session of the Council will be held"—and then paused, as all ears were strained to catch the all-important words—"when the Holy Father decides." A Fourth Session was inevitable.

There was a noticeable relaxation of tension at the end of the meeting on October 23rd. The mood of the Council seemed to change from pessimism to one of cautious optimism and even excitement over the prospect of achieving the essential goals at the present session.

PROBLEM OF ATHEISM

Keeping up its rapid pace, the Council covered considerable ground in the next two weeks, debating a new section of Schema 13 practically every other day. Some held that the pace was too fast and that justice was not being done to important topics, but there was no alternative under the circumstances. It seemed vital to allow every item on the agenda to come to the floor however briefly, so that the commissions could get on with the work of revising the texts in the light of the interventions, oral and written. Above all it was deemed necessary for the Council to express its wishes with regard to the drafts at least by a preliminary vote. Experience had shown that drafts accepted to be voted on in detail, and amended in accordance with the wishes of the Council (*modi*), were more likely to retain their identity, for the commission was then morally bound to respect the wishes of the assembly in such cases. But the rules of the Council had purposely been made vague by their framers, so that even when texts had been "registered" in this way, they were still liable to behind-the-scenes pressures and drastic alterations in the name of "higher authority." The experience of the first two sessions amply demonstrated this. There could be no certainty of a document's integrity until it had finally been promulgated.

The Preface and Chapter I were debated for part of two mornings (October 23rd and 26th). Most of the speeches dealt with points already brought out in the general discussion. The two themes which claimed most attention were atheism and the relationship between the supernatural and the natural orders (or the Church and the world). The schema had purposely avoided involvement in a detailed explanation and condemnation of the phenomenon of widespread disbelief today, contenting itself with listing the "absence of God" as one of the "signs of the times," in accordance with Pope John's recommendation, following St.

Paul, "to conquer evil by good" and with a view to initiating a dialogue with those behind the Iron Curtain, advice which Pope Paul VI repeated in his encyclical *Ecclesiam suam*. There was no point in stressing differences if a dialogue were to be carried on successfully. What must be brought out were the things that people had in common, their common aspirations and ideals, while at the same time an attempt was made to get at the roots of ideological differences objectively, with a view to reaching some kind of a common understanding. But this rather benign and philosophical approach to the problem of atheism was not to the liking of a certain number of prelates, who spoke out in favor of a more forthright attitude, one, however, which took into account Pope John's distinction between "atheists" and atheistic systems as "historical movements." There were no speeches at this session that could be labelled as sterile calls for condemnation, pure and simple.

Taking a lead from Cardinals Suenens and Döpfner, the auxiliary of Madrid, Bishop Guerra Campos, asked for fuller treatment of atheistic communism. The true character of atheistic communism must be explained in such a way that both the simple-minded and the educated person could understand it. The idealistic humanism to be found in theoretical communism was a very powerful force, and communism had its own eschatology: it preached an earthly paradise, devoted to the development of all man's potentialities. Communism accepted mankind's aspirations and did not enclose itself in skeptical agnosticism; therefore it was possible to initiate a dialogue with it.

The archbishop of Ljubljana (Yugoslavia) called for a more positive development of atheism as one of the "signs of the times." He noted that encyclicals like *Mater et magistra* were too often neglected by Catholics and bishops, whereas in his country they were carefully studied by the communist authorities. "If God has permitted this great apostasy, it is because of the cosmic dimensions of sin, including our own sins, and with a view to our correction and perfect conversion to God," he observed. These notions should be brought out more clearly in the Preface.

This insistence on a fuller treatment of atheism inevitably caused uneasiness among the observer-delegates, both Protestants and Orthodox. Did it mean that the Catholic Church was about to abandon the wise precepts of Pope John? The former feared any relaxation of the spirit of reform and self-criticism; the Russian delegates, in particular, saw a danger to their own position if the Council laid too much stress on this theme, for it had been stipulated as one of the conditions for their attendance that there were to be no stereotyped condemnations of communism at the Council. It is just possible that the tone of the first week's debate on Schema 13 influenced the Russian delegation at the Pan-Orthodox Conference of Rhodes, headed by Metropolitan Nikodim, to change its mind and push for a more cautious approach on the establishment of a dialogue with the Roman Catholic Church, a policy which eventually triumphed.

Several speakers complained about what they called a lack of vision in the first part of the schema. According to the archbishop of Rennes, the Preface lacked a broad cosmic vision of the differences between light and darkness in the world. The language was weak and anemic; the text seemed to have been written by men living in peace, not by those having a part in the world's anxieties. It was poorly devised to arouse much hope. A renewed vision of the world was necessary, according to Bishop Pietraszko (auxiliary of Kraków, Poland), because in some parts of the world man had lost a theological outlook and regarded himself as the absolute master of everything. The reality of the world should be presented more in the light of its creation by God, redemption by Christ, and transformation by the work of man.

Speaking in the name of the bishops of Holland, Bishop De Vet (Breda) found the text lacking in a definition of the world in the modern and Christian sense. The world was presented as something too extraneous to the Church, with good and bad elements. The Preface and first three chapters needed revision to bring out a more concrete vision of the world. Another objection was that the term "Church" sometimes seemed to be something existing outside men, and sometimes was identified too closely with the hierarchy.

A particularly suggestive approach was offered by Bishop Schmitt (Metz, France). The schema seemed to pay too little attention to what was "new" about the modern world. He offered an impressive analysis of the situation today, as he saw it. The world was not merely human society and its institutions, but a whole new complex which had arisen in the last four centuries, marked by technical progress, an enormous broadening of horizons, a stirring of the masses, socialization, contrasting ideologies, constant changes. The danger was that the world had grown without any effective collaboration on the part of the Church and in open hostility to it. The world was claiming its own autonomy. What was the attitude of the Church to this new phenomenon going to be? It should seek to take its place in the world. Too long it had been suspicious of humanism. In order to be missionary, the Church must exist in the mainstream of world progress. It must function in what he called "dynamic solidarity with the world's progress."

The whole vocation of man must be explained synthetically, the archbishop of Burgos, Garcia de Sierra y Mendez, maintained. Chapter I must show how the Church made the problems of the world its own and above all explained its view of man, the only sound view, in the face of many false concepts about man prevalent today. A new plan was proposed by Bishop Romero Menjibar (Jaen, Spain). The schema should open with a presentation of the Church as a community of salvation, made up of men and intended by God to continue the mystery of the incarnation. Then deal with the world's problem, etc. And he wanted more emphasis on the reality of sin.

Worry was expressed by the auxiliary bishop of Münster that the Church might not always recognize the "signs of the times," as had happened in the past. For example, the orders founded by Ignatius of Loyola and other saints, were not officially recognized immediately. To recognize the signs of the times the Church should cultivate a renewed theology of the Holy Spirit, be on the lookout for His presence in the Church, and ecclesiastical authority must adopt a new attitude of observing, judging and acting along more biblical lines, acknowledging charisms. The "signs of the times," according to Archbishop Ziadé (Beirut), could be recognized only by faith, particularly in the light of the resurrection, the greatest sign of them all, which looked toward Christ's Parousia. The resurrection helped us to understand all the other signs. We needed prophets to help us read the signs of the times.

The speech of Cardinal Léger stressed the primacy of the supernatural vocation of man over the temporal order which he wanted made clearer, but the text seemed to imply also that the only danger to the Christian was in despising earthly things and taking refuge in the supernatural. This danger certainly existed, but there were others as well. One of them was the general crisis today over "religious practice," he said, citing the difficulty of prayer as Christians were more and more immersed in worldly affairs. While busy about such matters, they should be strengthened by meditation. The correct proportion between earthly and religious duties should be brought out in the first chapter. There was the problem also of the Christian notion of suffering. Something could be said about this.

The intervention of Bishop De Roo (Victoria, Canada) impressed his hearers by its obvious sincerity and spirit of charity. The temporal responsibilities of man must be insisted on, but he warned against any dichotomy between his supernatural and natural ends. Man's vocation was an immersion and real incarnation in the world, he maintained, with all its tensions, aspirations, and victories. Man was like a vicar of Christ in the midst of the world.

One of the younger Italian bishops, Quadri of Pinerolo, who had himself been a *peritus* the previous session, addressed his remarks to the experts primarily. He declared that there should be a special paragraph on the topic of work. A spirituality of work must be developed, especially with regard to the final end of man and the world. A number of speakers stressed particular points, like that of Quadri. Unless there was some treatment of the immortality of the soul, felt Bishop Schoiswohl (Graz-Sechau, Austria), man's hopes would inevitably gravitate toward earthly things. Because men no longer believed in immortality there was such widespread disbelief today, hence the point should be stressed, but not with outmoded philosophical arguments. Abbot Prou (Solesmes) objected to the theological implications of the statement that "all creatures," both spiritual and corporal, were intrinsically raised to the supernatural order. It was sounder, he thought, to hold that "only a spiritual creature, and on earth only the human soul, can be elevated to the supernatural order." This was intended as an indirect criticism of Teilhard de Chardin and Père de Lubac.

THE CHURCH AND THE WORLD

Debate on Chapters II and III of the schema occupied a day and a half (October 26–27), and involved such widely different topics as Church and State, the renewal of the Church, the guidance of the hierarchy, the spirit of brotherhood and poverty, and participation in international institutions.

The present text of Chapter II seemed to be incomplete, according to Bishop Ancel (Lyons). It did not show how the interest of the Church in temporal matters proceeded from its total mission, which was the evangelization of man. The Church would be failing in its spiritual mission if it neglected or ignored temporal things. Modern man expected the Church to declare what it stood for and why it was interested in temporal matters. People would listen, if the Church avoided any appearance of moralizing or proselytizing.

Cardinal Frings called for greater accuracy in the use of such words as "world," "progress," "salvation." Those who accused the Church of a certain Platonism because of its aloofness from the world were not wrong, but it should be remembered that salvation did not come from the world. The true liberty of the Christian would be safeguarded only if account were taken of the three doctrines of the Creation, the Incarnation, and the Cross and Resurrection.

We must find a new way of presenting the Church to the world, said Archbishop Marty (Rheims). The Church was too western, too hidebound by the past. During the Middle Ages the western world was under the Church; today the modern world extended far beyond the confines of the Church and had its own contours. The Church must be in the world like leaven mixed in flour. This was the only possible way. And we must be careful not to say that the laity were a bridge between the Church and the world, for on the one hand this implied that the Church was not in the world, which was false, and on the other that the laity were outside the Church, which was equally false. The Church must be present *as a body,* clergy and laity.

An intriguing point was raised by the next speaker, Bishop La Ravoire Morrow (India). "How," he asked, "can the men and women of our time understand that God is good if we continue to teach them that those who do not abstain on Fridays go to hell? They do not see any proportion between the Church's precepts and God's commandments. How can eating meat on Friday deserve the same punishment as committing adultery or murder? This causes the moral sense of people to become blunted and ecclesiastical authority to be despised. I do not propose that the Church's precepts be abolished, but they should be simplified. No precept should be imposed lightly under pain of mortal sin. Religion is not fear, but love." The bishop's remark about Friday abstinence was only incidental to his general thesis, but it quite naturally caused a considerable stir outside the confines of the Council hall, resulting for example in such headlines as "CHURCH TO ALLOW MEAT ON FRIDAYS?"

In his usual forthright style, Patriarch Maximos IV rose on October 27th and lambasted some of the more glaring maladjustments of the Church with respect to the modern world. "The Church should take an interest in all the problems of her children," he began. "It must consider them not as servants, but as friends." The important thing was to train the faithful in love of Christ and develop a sense of responsibility. The patriarch received a long round of applause when he had finished.

Wholehearted concurrence in the veiws of Bishop La Ravoire Morrow and Patriarch Maximos IV was voiced by Bishop Mendez Arceo (Cuernavaca, Mexico). Turning to the subject of poverty, Archbishop Golland Trindade (Botucatú, Brazil) put forth a strong plea for the Church "to come down from its thrones and rid itself of its ornaments." He remarked that the secretary general frequently addressed the Fathers as *patres ornatissimi.* This was ture in one sense. But people understood the words in another sense. Catholic bishops were loaded down from head to foot with ornaments, as anyone could see, daily, on the streets of Rome. Bishops looked wealthy, but they were often very poor. The Communists, numbering some seven million in Italy alone, saw this and rejoiced, for it was a symbol of the immense distance they fondly believed existed between bishops and faithful. He pleaded that, with the permission of the pope, the bishops should be allowed to come to their daily congregations dressed in black.*

---

* Pope Paul's inability to come to some meaningful decision (1967) about the simplification of episcopal dress, repeatedly urged both during the Council and afterward, has in a way become symbolic of his whole attitude toward aggiornamento, in the opinion of some.

Bishop Fourrey (Belley, France) also was of the opinion that it was necessary not only to profess a sprit of poverty, but to manifest it by deeds, beginning with religious orders and other collective institutions. He warned against the sin of usury today, particularly on the part of trusts exploiting underdeveloped countries.

Also speaking on the topic of poverty, Cardinal Silva Henriquez (Chile), distinguished between its two meanings: the poverty of the Gospel or spirit of poverty, and misery or suffering. The latter was something that should be eliminated and it could be if Christians of the world would unite to employ the wealth of the world properly. He referred to the suggestion made some time before by the Protestant theologian and observer-delegate, Oscar Cullmann, professor at the Sorbonne, for an annual ecumenical collection to be taken up by each Church and devoted to the poor of another Church and said that he highly approved of it. The Church would do well, said Archbishop Zoghby, to imitate the spirit of poverty by abandoning the pompous titles which it used; for example the phrase *feliciter regnans* applied to the pope, because this smacked too much of temporal rule. We should be animated by the spirit of Pope John XXIII, who said at the end of his life: "I have loved all those whom I have met in the course of my life."

Bishop Himmer (Tournai, Belgium) called for a clearer distinction between the poverty of the Church and the poverty of Christians and wanted the role of poverty in building up the Kingdom of God emphasized. "Poverty is the key to the whole schema," he insisted. All problems, such as those of the family and of hunger, could be solved in a spirit of poverty. On the other hand, Cardinal Caggiano (Buenos Aires) felt that paragraph 17 should not begin with Christ's mandate of evangelical poverty, but with mention of natural justice. The Council should call for justice everywhere, including within the Church, and should urge governments to pass just laws. Emphasis should be placed first on justice, before going on to charity and the spirit of poverty, which helped to build up brotherhood.

The schema treated the relationship between the Church and the scientific world well, according to Bishop Spülbeck (Meissen, Germany). However there was not enough emphasis on the effects of the profane sciences. The Church must accept the legitimate findings of science if it wanted to carry on a dialogue with the world. In certain communist countries the Church appeared to be ignorant of some of the discoveries of science, and this brought religion into disrepute with the atheists. The great influence of the books of Teilhard de Chardin was due to the fact that, as a priest, he tried to understand the language of science. Therefore the communists regarded him as particularly dangerous, lest he should be influential in reconciling the discrepancies between science and religion. A dialogue between the Church and the modern scientific world should be expressly encouraged in paragraph 13. The condemnation of Galileo was wrong, and this should be admitted.

On the other hand Bishop Klepacz (Lódz, Poland) sounded a warning note against the evils resulting from modern "scientism" or the glorification of scientific discovery and research and the resulting apotheosis of man, which had built, one might almost say, a new Tower of Babel and confused man with its false optimism and nihilism. A more optimistic view was voiced by auxiliary Bishop Kuharič (Zagreb, Yugoslavia), who pointed out that the Pontifical Academy of Sciences was evidence of the Church's interest in science and its support for scientific progress and that it denoted no contradiction between science and religion.

A remarkably frank intervention by Bishop Huyghe (Arras) drove home the point that before the Church could expect to carry on a dialogue with those outside its borders, there must be a dialogue within the Church itself. This meant that all members of the Church must be in dialogue with each other. They must learn to listen, to look for the voice of the Holy Spirit. The Holy Spirit was given to the whole community on Pentecost. We should do away with all administrative jealousy or authoritarian practices, anything that inhibited a dialogue between subjects and superiors in the Church. For example, the condemnation of books by the Holy Office without giving the author a hearing was contrary to the dignity of the children of God. "Let us begin by instituting a dialogue of friendship, confidence and liberty within the Church before we approach the world." Bishop Huyghe was warmly applauded for these remarks.

The Index Librorum also came in for some caustic remarks from Bishop Cleven (the auxiliary of Cologne), who said that it created a kind of "Catholic ghetto image" that was the very opposite of the image of trust and freedom that we were trying to create. The Index was particularly obnoxious to the young, he noted. The Church had nothing to fear from science. Science would not bring about salvation, of course, but the Church had a long way to go to catch up because of its generally backward attitude on this score.

The Fathers were amused by the intervention of Italian Bishop Garneri (Susa). Speaking in the name of 84 bishops from different countries, he entertained them with a discourse on the importance of tourism as a typical expression of modern life, hailing it as a useful instrument for the dialogue. Last year, he noted, some sixty million Western Europeans travelled outside their own countries. Taking care of them called for special pastoral efforts and presented opportunities for promoting peace and ecumenism which should not be missed.

CHAPTER IV

On October 28th, Wednesday, the Council embarked on a discussion of what was perhaps the most controversial part of Schema 13, namely Chapter IV. The decision to deal with each one of its paragraphs separately, by causing the speakers to concentrate on one or two points at most, undoubtedly gave the debate more coherence than usual; it also helped to sustain public interest, which could hardly fail to be aroused by such provocative subjects as civil rights, the place of women, marriage, birth control, concentration camps, prostitution, and nuclear bombs, as well as the more sedate topics of cultural progress, economic growth, alleviating poverty, international solidarity and peace.

Expectations were momentarily dampened when the moderator, Cardinal Agagianian, suddenly announced that, because of their delicate nature, "certain points" would not be discussed on the Council floor. This measure was intended to forestall possible misunderstanding outside the Council, he said. Written communications could be submitted by the Fathers as usual and all comments would be carefully weighed and considered by the commission. The statement was interpreted as a move on the part of conservative forces to exercise some kind of a restraining hand on the course of the debate, but since the lists of speakers were already drawn up and the content of the remarkably bold speeches that would be made on the following days must already have been known to the Council authorities, to the moderators in particular, who were among those dealing some of the heaviest blows, Agagianian's remarks must have been meant primarily *pro forma*. They may have been nothing more than an awkwardly-worded reminder to the bishops that the pope had reserved a final decision on the delicate subject of birth control to himself, as everybody knew.

The discussion opened with a fine, carefully balanced *relatio* on Chapter IV as a whole, delivered by Bishop Wright (Pittsburgh), who said that it dealt with certain cardinal questions that he called "the masterknots of fate," peculiar to our times. He concluded by noting that Article 20 had logically been placed at the beginning of the Chapter, "because man holds the position of primacy among earthly creatures" and because every attack upon the right social order was sooner or later directed against the dignity of the person. The fundamental purpose of the section was to "state the principles bearing on the Christian's role in restoring and promoting the personal dignity of man," in view of the many ways in which the dignity of man was being degraded today.

There were two speakers on Chapter IV as a whole. Bishop Gonzalez Martin (Astorga, Spain), who gave up his episcopal palace in order to move into a humbler dwelling, suggested that the text could be improved with a somewhat different perspective and concluded with the call: "Before the Church can hope to be heard by those outside, she must devote herself earnestly to renewing herself within!" The Coptic Archbishop Ghattas (Thebes, Egypt) may have been speaking more or less for the record when he observed that the schema seemed to take too materialistic a view of the nation as such. Although exaggerated nationalism was a disease to be healed, genuine patriotism of Christian inspiration was something to be commended. The recognition of new nations by the Church should not be a question of opportunism but the acknowledgment of a true Christian reality in which men had been freed from the yoke of imperialism.

Consideration of Articles 19 and 20 was begun by Cardinal Ritter. The treatment of human dignity was not entirely satisfactory, he thought. The cardinal wanted more stress on what Christians could do to manifest this dignity by witnessing in their lives to the transcendence of God and assuming their responsibilities. Christians, by shirking their individual and collective responsibilities, were doing real harm to the dignity of the person. The description of human dignity in the schema appeared to be based too much on psychology and technical considerations, in the opinion of Bishop Barrachina Estevan (Orihuela-Alicante, Spain). The rights of man were founded on nature enlightened by the Gospel. In contrast to the man-god, Christianity taught the mystery of the God-man, he said. The mild tone of Chapter IV was good, declared Bishop Schick (Fulda, Germany), but the impression must not be given that the Church was offering men simply another ideology. There must be more emphasis on Scripture and theology. In some twelve pages of text there were only four quotations from the Bible. The Book of Acts could be profitably drawn on, because it was an account of the action of the Holy Spirit in the world. Auxiliary Bishop Béjot of Rheims concurred and wanted dignity expressed more clearly in terms of the Gospel. Men today attributed a great value to life, everything was done in order to save it, to find out all that could be found out about its laws, etc. But the Christian view that man was not an end in himself must be brought to bear to counteract the excessive glorification of mankind as such.

There were crimes against liberty of the human person other than unjust coercion, noted Bishop László (Eisenstadt, Austria). Liberty could be abused through excess as well as by restriction. An example of the former would be the widespread sensuality found today; an example of the latter, the tendency to avoid doing what one should do as a matter of justice. Even more pointed was the observation of Bishop Stimpfle (Augsburg) that the more freedom there was in education, science, and the administration of the Church, the more human freedom would be assured in all walks of life. As a sort of rider, Bishop Barthe (Fréjus-Toulon) added that there was really no such thing as absolute liberty: the freedom of some was an evil for others. Full liberty could only be found in voluntary subjection to the will of God. The bishop felt that Article 20 should contain some criteria for judging the dignity of man today.

RACIAL DISCRIMINATION

Three speeches which aroused the greatest interest on the first day were clarion calls for the Church to take a firm stand on the present-day issue of racial injustice and discrimination. Archbishop Athaide (Agra, India), speaking first, deplored racial segregation, *apartheid,* which existed even in countries that professed to be Christian. It was almost incredible, but such things as slavery and the buying and selling of people still were practiced. The world expected the Council to take a stand on this. "I do not ask that countries be condemned by name, but we must arouse the conscience of the world. A magnificent example has been set in this respect by such people as Gandhi, who went about barefoot attempting to get landowners to share their property with the landless, and President Kennedy, who spoke out on behalf of racial justice. Recently Pope Paul VI received Martin Luther King and praised him for his great work of passive resistance in this regard, following the example of Gandhi." (Applause.) "It is a scandal to see parishes deserted," said Bishop Grutka (Gary, Indiana), "whenever Negro families move in. The Council must proclaim the absolute opposition of the Church to all forms of racial discrimination."

Archbishop O'Boyle (Washington), rising to address the assembly in the name of all the American bishops, called for the insertion of a special paragraph dealing with the problem of discrimination not from the viewpoint of sociology and economics, but on moral and religious grounds. "The statement need not be long, but it should flatly condemn all forms of racial discrimination on the grounds that all men are equal and brethren because they are the sons of God. Our experience in the United States," he added, "suggests that this is one area of social action which calls for close cooperation between Catholics, Protestants, Jews, and all men of good will." His remarks were also greeted with applause.

A number of speakers wanted the rather brief reference to women's rights in the schema spelled out in more detail. The evils of racism, tribalism, and the custom of regarding women as mere chattel in Africa was deplored by Archbishop Malula of Leopoldville (Congo). The pope's recent canonization of the Uganda martyrs had brought great joy to African Christians. Tribalism was merely racism on a minor scale (applause). The most detailed talk on the role of women was delivered by Bishop Coderre (St. John, Quebec, Canada), who insisted that the Council should state that woman had her own God-given personality and therefore a specific and necessary task to perform in society and in the Church. Until now woman had been prevented from fulfilling her true role, but as one of the signs of the times she was being accorded her place more and more. Bishop Coderre spoke in the name of 40 Canadian bishops. There were some three million handicapped children in France alone, nearly a quarter of all French children. The Church should have something to say about this problem, Monsignor de La Chanonie, the bishop of Clermont, ventured to suggest. The verdict passed on Chapter IV by Bishop Bäuerlein (Srijem, Yugoslavia) was *placet iuxta modum.* He got ahead of himself somewhat by pronouncing on the treatment of marriage in Article 21 before that subject was taken up, and insisted that it was an "error" to place so much emphasis on conjugal love as the primary factor in marriage. One sensed that the private opinion of the dour and usually very conservative Yugoslav bishop was not entirely favorable to an increased role for women. On the other hand, the opinion expressed by auxiliary Bishop of Cologne Frotz to the effect that the rise and fall of civilizations could be attributed to the public esteem which women either enjoyed or failed to enjoy, undoubtedly represented something of an oversimplification of history, though a highly attractive theory, it must be admitted. Modern women expected to be treated as the equals of men, the bishop held, but the Church had not yet caught up with the idea. This was something of an understatement.

Bishop Quadri (Pinerolo, Italy) wanted a fuller description of the social teaching of the Church inserted in the text at this point, one avoiding any trace of "feminism" or "anti-feminism," however. He said that the old text had a good passage along this line. The Italian bishop was not the only one to fear the perils of an unrestrained "feminism." There were many feminists in Rome for the Third Session, no doubt there to look after their rights. When Archbishop Roberts, S.J., was asked by one such feminist at a crowded press conference—ostensibly on the twin subjects of contraception and nuclear war—whether he still believed that women should agitate in behalf of their rights, as he had apparently written somewhere in an unguarded moment, the archbishop candidly replied: "I hope that I have not heard the question, but I'm afraid that I have."

362

MARRIAGE AND BIRTH CONTROL

After the close of the Third Session there was a noticeable tendency among certain American prelates to issue statements minimizing or playing down the import of the discussion in the Council on marriage, birth control and similar "delicate" topics. The attempt to scotch the idea that the Church was ever likely to revise its traditional teaching on any essential point, and the effort to placate consciences and keep the lid on the pot by making such statements, was indication enough that people were aroused. In defense of the American bishops, it could be said that their reaction was partly explainable by the rebuff they received at the hands of the pope during the last days of the session; their mortification resulted in an understandable re-emphasis of the "don't rock the boat" line. Appeal was usually made to the pope's statement in June 1964 calling for restraint in the public discussion of delicate subjects,* but neither the indefinite postponement of TV programs on birth control, nor the censoring or banning of articles could disguise the fact that people today, Catholics included, were caught up in a movement of intense concern over the related problems of over-population, birth control methods, the procreation of children, their education and their future in a highly uncertain world. One American bishop was quoted as saying: "In my diocese, I *know* that people do not sit around talking about birth control." Whether people talked about these things or not, they were certainly doing a great deal of thinking and acting. In France, for example, loosely regarded as a "Catholic country," a survey showed that 30 percent of women questioned, mostly young women, had had one or more abortions. More than half the sample were Roman Catholics, and among these nearly one-quarter were practicing Catholics. In another survey, 69 percent of the women questioned had used contraceptive methods at some stage in their lives; the older they were, the higher the percentage of such use; among those 37 years or older there were none who had not used such methods. In the United States these methods were used on a much wider scale, as investigations proved. Both in the United States and France surveys had shown that a large to very large proportion of Roman Catholic women used methods forbidden by the Church. In Italy, where the public advertisement of birth control methods was prohibited by law but not the distribution of contraceptives (because of a regulation laid down by Mussolini), there was ample evidence that the pattern was the same. In the face of overwhelming evidence of the increasing use of these devices by Catholics (as well as by people

* See p. 350.

363

generally), the statement of one American bishop that he was "certain" the conservative position condemning the use of mechanical contraceptives would remain "the true Catholic position," sounded like a prejudgment of the issue.*

Other bishops had been more guarded in their pronouncements, referring to the essential distinction that had to be made between what was fundamental and what could be changed, thus leaving themselves a convenient loophole for escape. That this proved to be the wiser policy since the Council began its public sessions was never more amply demonstrated than by the memorable, all too brief but very much to the point discussion, on Thursday and Friday, October 29–30, 1964, of Article 21 of Schema 13. The fundamental weakness of the conservative position, as was frequently pointed out, was that it did not allow for making this distinction. According to the conservative "all or nothing" school, if the Church had been wrong in permitting a certain type of teaching during the past four hundred years, then the Church had failed, *quod est absurdum.* Therefore, that teaching must be correct. The fallacy here was the naïve equation of the terms: Church of God = Roman Catholic Church = Curia = Lateran University (or any Catholic school teaching the conservative line). Fortunately, the Constitution on the Church and the Decree on Ecumenism passed by the Council would help to dispel misconceptions and make the necessary distinctions.

The discussion on marriage was opened with a *relatio* by Archbishop John F. Dearden (Detroit), in which this sensitive prelate spoke of the "principle of conscious and generous procreation" without mentioning the hackneyed formula, "procreation is the primary purpose of marriage." The treatment in the text was not intended as a full doctrinal statement of the Church's position on marriage, he declared, but was a synthesis presented with a view to stating those things which would help the faithful today to appreciate more fully and deeply the nature and dignity of marriage and family life. Marriage was presented as an institution oriented to God, the specific love of the married, and the procreation of children (in that order). Conjugal love must be understood within the context of a stable, sacramental union. Couples could, "for sufficiently grave reasons," regulate the number of their children, but they were not authorized to use any means for regulating family size: "Nothing can be permitted which is opposed to the natural orientation of the marital act or

---

* The English theologian, Father Charles Davis, pointed out that, while this might very well be the case, doubts had been raised by "eminent churchmen" about the traditional doctrine, and the matter could not be regarded as settled. He was of the opinion that a profound change in the theology of marriage had probably already occurred in the Church and that this would, in time, bear fruit if theological discussion could be kept open. Cf. *The National Catholic Reporter,* February 24, 1965.

which destroys the conjugal act's expressiveness of personal and marital love," he declared, choosing his words carefully. The schema avoided the specific question of the use of progesteron (birth control) pills, because this was not a question that could be decided in the Council hall and because the pope had reserved it to himself.

The discussion revolved around the key questions of the ends of marriage, procreation and conjugal love, and whether birth control was permissible or not. Cardinal Léger (Montreal) was the first of four speakers to challenge accepted notions. He pointed out that many of the faithful today were worried about marital problems and were not satisfied with the answers given them. "Pastors, confessors particularly, are assailed by doubts and uncertainties and, many times, no longer know what they can or should reply to the faithful. Many theologians feel more and more strongly the need to examine more deeply in a new way the fundamental principles concerning marriage." Though there were some who feared all renewal in the theology of marriage, on the grounds that it would lead to acquiescence in popular wishes, the final end of such renewal was actually to "enhance the holiness of marriage by a deeper insight into the plan of God" and to find out what contribution recent biological, psychological and sociological discoveries could make to a solution of marital problems. He continued:

A certain pessimistic and negative attitude regarding human love, attributable neither to Scripture nor to tradition, but to philosophies of past centuries, has prevailed and this has veiled the importance and legitimacy of conjugal love in marriage . . . The authors of the present schema . . . have avoided the difficulty of putting into opposition the primary and secondary ends of marriage. However the schema . . . fails to present conjugal love and mutual help as an end of marriage and does not in any way touch on the problem of the purpose of expressions of love in marriage . . .

It should clearly present human conjugal love . . . as a true end of marriage, as something good in itself, with its own characteristic and its own laws. The schema is too hesitant on this point. There is no point in the schema's avoidance of the term "secondary end" if it does not present love as being at the service of procreation . . . Otherwise the fears which have for so long paralyzed our theology would remain. Conjugal love is good and holy in itself and it should be accepted by Christians without fear . . . In marriage the spouses consider each other not as mere procreators, but as persons loved for their own sakes.

It is not sufficient to establish clearly the doctrine which concerns marriage as a state. Unless the problem of the purpose of the actions themselves is dealt with in its most general principles, the difficulties which occupy spouses and pastors cannot be solved . . . It must also be stated that the intimate union of the spouses also finds a purpose in love. And this end is truly the end of the act itself, lawful in itself, even when it is not ordained to procreation.

365

The inclusion of a statement along this line would be entirely in accordance with the principle recognized by the Church for centuries, that the union of spouses was considered lawful even when procreation was known to be impossible. The important thing was to proclaim clearly the two ends of marriage "as equally holy and good."

While the Fathers were catching their breaths, Cardinal Suenens rose to deliver another salvo. He called first for a conciliar commission to work in close collaboration with the commission appointed by the pope to study marriage problems, and suggested that the names of its members should be known so that they could receive the widest possible information. He then proceeded to lay down some of the guidelines for the work of such a commission. The first task of the commission should be in the area of faith, namely,

to study whether up to now we have given sufficient emphasis to all aspects of the teaching of the Church on marriage. To be sure, it is not a question of modifying or of casting doubt on the truly traditional teaching of the Church. That would be folly! It is a question of knowing whether we have opened our hearts completely to the Holy Spirit in order to understand the divine truth.

The Bible is always the same. But no generation can take pride in having fully perceived the unfathomable riches of Christ. The Holy Spirit has been promised to us to introduce us progressively to the fulness of the truth. Thus the Church has never to repudiate a truth that it once taught, but according as, and in the measure that, she progresses in a deeper study of the Gospel, she can and she must integrate this truth in a richer synthesis, and bring out the fuller fruitfulness of the same principles. In this way, the Church draws from her treasure things new and things old.

This established, it is important to examine whether we have maintained in perfect balance all aspects of the teaching of the Church on marriage. It may be that we have accentuated the Gospel text "increase and multiply" to such a point that we have obscured another text, "and they will be two in one flesh." These two truths are central and both are scriptural; they must illuminate each other in the light of the full truth that is revealed to us in our Lord Jesus Christ. St. Paul in effect has given to Christian marriage, as a prototype, the very love of Christ for his Church. This "two in one" is a mystery of inter-personal communion, gratified and sanctified by the sacrament of marriage. And this union is of such profundity that divorce can never separate two whom God unites as one.

Also, it is for the commission to tell us whether we have excessively stressed the first end, procreation, at the expense of another equally important end, that is growth in conjugal unity. In the same way, it is up to this commission to deal with the immense problem arising from the population explosion and over-population in many areas of the world. For the first time we must proceed with such a study in the light of the faith. It is difficult, but the world, whether consciously or not, waits for the Church to express her thought and to be a "light for the nations."

366

Let no one say that in this way we open the way to moral laxity. The problem confronts us not because the faithful try to satisfy their passions and their egotism, but because thousands of them try with anguish to live in double fidelity, to the doctrine of the Church and to the demands of conjugal and parental love.

He proposed that the second task of the commission be to study whether "classical doctrine, especially that of the manuals," took sufficient account of the new knowledge achieved by modern science, for example, with respect to "the complexity with which the real or the biological interferes with the psychological, the conscious with the subconscious. New possibilities are constantly being discovered in man of his power to direct nature. This gives rise to a deeper understanding of the unity of man. We have made progress since Aristotle (and even since Augustine)," he noted. Studies of this kind would help us to understand better "what is according to nature and what is not."

Then, with special emphasis, he pronounced the following words:

I beg of you, my brother bishops, let us avoid a new "Galileo affair." One is enough for the Church.

It should not be said that the new synthesis called for amounted to giving in to "situation ethics," Suenens went on. The explanation of doctrine, which remained unchangeable in its principles, must take into account contingent factors and changes in the course of history. This was what the popes did in writing *Rerum Novarum, Quadragesimo anno* and *Mater et magistra*. They attempted to express the same principles more precisely in terms more in keeping with new times. In conclusion, he recalled the words of Scripture: "The truth—both natural and supernatural—will set you free."

The speech of Cardinal Suenens was followed by a long round of applause.

Some days later, speaking on another topic, the Belgian cardinal took the unusual step of clarifying his previous remarks on the subject of marriage, "owing to certain reactions of public opinion." It had not been his intention to call into doubt doctrine "authentically and definitively proclaimed by the Church's magisterium" he said, but to suggest a study to formulate a synthesis of "all principles governing this subject"; and as regards discipline, to suggest that the commission's findings would have to be submitted to the pope and judged by his supreme authority. The methods to be followed in these studies and what was done with the research would depend solely on his authority. It was not clear what prompted this clarification: whether an article appearing in a French journal misinterpreting his thought, or some remarks made by fellow bishops in the Council hall, or word from the pope himself. In any case the cardinal could hardly be said to have retracted anything; his purpose may have been merely to dissipate an impression that he was presuming to dictate to the pope.

The next speaker was the 87-year-old Patriarch Maximos IV Saigh, whose intervention was probably the most revolutionary of all—certainly the most outspoken—on this theme. It was directed particularly to the "agonizing and burdensome" problem of birth control:

It is an urgent problem because it lies at the root of a great crisis of the Catholic conscience. There is a question here of a break between the official doctrine of the Church and the contrary practice of the immense majority of Christian couples. The authority of the Church has been called into question on a vast scale. The faithful find themselves forced to live in conflict with the law of the Church, far from the sacraments, in constant anguish, unable to find a viable solution between two contradictory imperatives: conscience and normal married life. . . .

Frankly, can the official positions of the Church in this matter not be reviewed in the light of modern theological, medical, psychological and sociological science? In marriage, the development of personality and its integration into the creative plan of God are all one. Thus, the end of marriage should not be divided into "primary" and "secondary." This consideration opens new perspectives concerning the morality of conjugal behavior considered as a whole.

And are we not entitled to ask if certain positions are not the outcome of outmoded ideas and, perhaps, a bachelor psychosis on the part of those unacquainted with this sector of life? Are we not, perhaps unwillingly, setting up a Manichaean conception of man and the world, in which the work of the flesh, vitiated in itself, is tolerated only in view of children? Is the external biological rectitude of an act the only criterion of morality, independent of family life, of its moral, conjugal and family climate, and of the grave imperatives of prudence which must be the basic rule of all our human activity? . . .

How relieved the Christian conscience felt when Pope Paul announced to the world that the problem of birth control and family morality "is under study, a study as extensive and deep as possible, that is, as serious and honest as the great importance of this problem requires. The Church must proclaim this law of God in the light of the scientific, social and psychological truths which, in recent times, have been the object of study and scholarship." . . .

Let us loyally and effectively put into practice the declaration of Pope Paul opening the Second Session of the Council: "Let the world know this: The Church looks upon the world with profound understanding, with a sincere admiration, with a sincere intention not to subjugate but to serve it, not to despise it but to appreciate it, not to condemn it but to support and save it."

Applause began when the patriarch had finished, but it was at once stifled by the moderator, who gave the floor to the Spanish Bishop Beitia

(Santander). The burden of his talk was that marriage should be presented as a contract. The schema seemed to say that the sacrament of marriage depended on love, but the divine law might require heroic sacrifices when it was impossible, at least temporarily, to reconcile the responsibility of spouses to each other with the desire not to have children. All problems could not be solved. Uneasiness was expressed also by Archbishop Botero Salazar (Medellin, Colombia) over the way in which the schema admitted the difficulty of reconciling the teaching of the Church with practical difficulties without offering any solution. Priests and people wanted practical solutions; it was not enough to leave the question to the experts, much less, to married people to decide for themselves. The question of birth control seemed to be considered mainly from the economic point of view. The Church's position on birth control should be stated much more clearly. Bishop Rusch (Innsbruck) pointed to divorce as the reason why there were so many parentless children, and said that insistence on the indissolubility of marriage would help to ward off this evil.

A petition which 182 professional laymen from various countries had recently sent to the pope and the Council asking that "the teaching of the Church place less emphasis on certain formulations of her doctrine which are largely products of their historical context," and that "a way be opened for new scientific and philosophical discoveries in this field to be integrated with the theology and living thought of the Church," was mentioned by Bishop Staverman (Indonesia). The document stated that the laymen who had signed it were responding to Pope Paul's call in his recent encyclical for a dialogue within the Church.* The bishop cited it in support of his thesis that marriage was continually evolving historically toward a more and more authentic form and that the Church should accept this transformation. Merely to repeat the traditional teaching was not acting in a pastoral spirit. A true pastoral approach involved a continual updating of doctrine.

Earlier Cardinal Ruffini had sounded his usual warning note about the failure of the schema to say anything very much about the true nature of Christian marriage as a sacrament signifying unity and indissolubility, according to St. Paul. The fact that the document was addressed to all men should not be used as an excuse for overlooking this central idea and being obscure about Catholic teaching. Unless this was clearly brought out, how could polygamy, divorce, and sexual excesses be regarded as wrong? As for the affirmation that it was up to couples to decide about the number of children they would have, he found this a "hard, obscure and ambiguous" saying. He cited St. Augustine in reproof of selfish sexuality which was rampant today. To meet the needs of our day it was

* The petition was dated October 17, 1964.

only necessary to quote Pius XI's *Casti connubii* and Pius XII's "Allocu-tion to Midwives." "I hope that the experts who revise the text will follow the teaching of the *magisterium*," he concluded.

The heat generated by the debate on Thursday, as well as word which leaked out that a closure vote was imminent, resulted in a number of last-minute requests to speak on Friday. Cardinal Alfrink came to the support of Cardinals Léger and Suenens. He said that all priests were well aware of the pastoral difficulties involved in advising people about marriage problems and why so many people were leaving the Church. The Church could not of course change the divine law, just because difficulties arose, nor could it condone situation ethics. The Church taught that sacrifice, the Cross, belonged to the essence of Christianity. However the joy of the Resurrection also pertained to its essence, and God did not take pleasure in the difficulties of man.

The next impromptu speaker was Cardinal Ottaviani, whose remarks were mainly by way of introducing the Dominican Cardinal Browne of the Holy Office, principal spokesman for conservative theology. The secretary of the Holy Office spoke with considerable emotion, however. "Excuse me," he said, "if I speak *ex abrupto*. I had not expected to speak until tomorrow. I am not pleased with the statement of the text that married couples can determine the number of children they are to have. This has never been heard of before in the Church. Are we to think that the precept, 'Increase and multiply,' is contradicted by the precept 'They shall be two in one flesh'?" This was obviously a specific reference to the intervention of Cardinal Suenens. Continuing in a more intimate vein, Ottaviani said of himself: "The priest who speaks to you is the eleventh of twelve children, whose father was a laborer in a bakery. I purposely say laborer, not the owner of a bakery. My parents never doubted Providence. Their motto was: 'Look to the birds of the air and the lilies of the field . . .' Cardinal Browne will now speak on the doctrinal question. But I issue a warning to you bishops, you who have proclaimed the infallibility of the pope and of the bishops with the pope: a doubt has been raised with regard to the Church's teaching on marriage. Can the Church possibly have erred for so many centuries?"

The intervention of Cardinal Browne was listened to with marked attention as he set forth the classical scholastic doctrine on the primary and secondary ends of marriage.

I thought that the Council discussion would throw light on the text, but I find now that I must bear witness to the traditional doctrine on marriage which has been called in doubt. The primary end of marriage is procreation and the education of the children. The secondary end is, on the one hand, the mutual aid of the spouses, and on the other a remedy for concupiscence. What about love, you may say? Love forms part of marriage, but we must distinguish between the love of friendship which desires the welfare of another, and the love of concupiscence which seeks what is good for oneself. The kind of love required for the stability of marriage is the conjugal love of friendship. There is an element of sensual pleasure in the marital act which often causes the love of concupiscence to predominate. We must be careful, therefore, in vindicating the rights of conjugal love. Conjugal love is good when the spouses act with due regard for the ends of marriage: the begetting and education of children, fidelity in rendering the debt, and the sacrament which renders married life holy. For the conjugal act to be naturally licit, it suffices that the good of fidelity is present in rendering the debt.

He then cited Leo XIII's *Arcanum,* Pius XI's *Casti connubii,* and Pius XII's "Allocution to Midwives."

Difficult problems remain, particularly with regard to the sterile periods. But this is now being studied by true experts. We can do nothing but await the outcome of their studies. I say nothing with regard to other problems, namely that of the pill, because the *relator* has told us that the pope has reserved this to himself. If the Council should wish to consider this question, it seems to me that this could be done only by a restricted commission which would present its conclusions to us.

Of the eight speakers who followed, four spoke out in support of Cardinals Léger, Suenens and Alfrink—Bishop Reuss (Mainz), Archbishop Urtasun (Avignon), Bishop Nkongolo (Luebo, Congo), and Bishop Fiordelli (Prato, Italy). Two were inclined to favor stricter adherence to the position of Cardinal Browne, Bishop del Campo y de la Bárcena (Calahorra, Spain), and Bishop Hervás y Benet (Ciudad Real, Spain). The two remaining, Bishop Rendeiro (Faro, Portugal) and Archbishop Yago (Abidjan, Ivory Coast) dealt with particular topics, the latter seconding Bishop Malula's condemnation of African tribalism and polygamy in an earlier congregation.

At 11:15 A.M., when many of the Fathers were in the bars, Cardinal Agagianian suddenly called for a standing vote to close the debate on Article 21. More than the usual number of bishops remained seated, but the motion was declared to be carried anyway. The essential points had been made.

Two days after the session ended, Cardinal Ottaviani, in a world-wide television interview, again serenely assured his interrogator that the Church's doctrine on marriage could never change because it was based "on the natural law *and several scriptural texts.*"

The doctrine of the Church was actually based on divine revelation and had little to do with the natural law, as was pointed out in the course of the debate; for it began and ended in a great mystery. St. Paul told husbands: "Love your wives as Christ loves the Church," and Christ Himself repeated the commandment recorded in Genesis, "You shall be two in one flesh," adding the injunction, "What God has joined together, let no man put asunder."

It was precisely here that a fundamental issue was bared in the Council. The forward-looking prelates, representing the vast majority, rejected outright a conception of the Church as a natural society whose teaching authority was represented by a juridically-structured doctrine interlaced with the axioms of Roman law, the antiquated guesses of Stoic anthropology, and the so-called truths of the natural law. The Constitution on the Church said explicitly that the Church as a society was a mystery, distributing sacramental grace and witnessing to the presence of Christ in the world. Hence the Church's teaching on marriage was in need of a drastic overhaul, if it was truly represented by the thinking of such men as Cardinals Ottaviani and Browne.

After the challenges thrown down in the debate on Thursday, one *peritus,* a frequent spokesman for the new theology of marriage, summed up his impressions in the following words: "It was the death of *Casti connubii!*"

The abruptness with which the discussion of marriage was terminated—no doubt motivated in part by fears over the public repercussions that might be expected from too detailed and too prolonged a treatment—became symptomatic of the course of the final three weeks of the session, with new topics for debate, texts to be voted on, para-conciliar activities, and rumors of behind-the-scenes maneuvers succeeding one another at a kaleidoscopic pace. Presiding over all was the iron-willed determination on the part of the Council authorities to get through the agenda by the end of the session at all costs, with just enough time being allowed each item so as to finish by the deadline, provided there were no setbacks. As happened during the Second Session, however, the more relaxed spirit of *romanità* managed to assert itself in particularly galling ways at the last moment. Though time was so precious, it was still thought necessary to devote two full days to the "long weekend" of November 1—no congregations were scheduled for November 2nd and 3rd while it was announced later that one full day—November 13th— would be devoted to liturgical exercises, with Patriarch Maximos IV concelebrating in the presence of the pope. The ultimate intention here, no doubt, was to display some kind of feeling of solidarity with the prelates at the Pan-Orthodox Conference of Rhodes which was then ending, as well as to honor the Melkite patriarch, but the question inevitably arose whether the means were proportionate to the end. The interruption of debate on Article 24 of Schema 13, in order to take up the propositions on Missionary Activity (November 6th, 7th and 9th), by distracting the attention of the Council away from the subject under consideration, also proved to be an irritating and rather pointless move.

THE CHURCH AND CULTURE

During the remaining portion of the morning of October 30th and through the session on November 4th, attention was focused on Article 22 of Schema 13, on promoting culture—with much time out for announcements, reports and voting on texts having nothing to do with the subject under debate. Father Ferreira, apostolic prefect for Portuguese Guinea, the first speaker on this topic, put his finger on one of the weaknesses of the text when he noted that the word *cultura* was used 23 times in the schema but not always in the same sense. The Latin word was quite inadequate to distinguish between "culture," properly speaking, and what we today called "civilization," a much broader concept. Hence the ambiguities of the text.

Several speakers objected to the title of the Article, "The Promotion of Culture." The implications seemed to be much too optimistic, said Archbishop de Provenchères. The poor had not yet benefited from any such promotion. It was wrong to assume that great progress had already taken place, so long as "actual discrimination, ignorance and poverty keep most of mankind from cultural achievement." The text must pay more attention to existing inequities. Everything the Council had to say about the human person, culture, and liberty would be useless as long as men did not have the means necessary for a decent human existence, on an individual, family and social level, observed the Master General of the Dominicans, Father Fernandez. With reference to the "right order of values," he wanted it spelled out that spiritual values took precedence over material values, and in the enumeration of the different aspects of human culture, mention should be made of philosophy and theology. For these were the "high point" of human culture. Bishop Proaño Villalba (Ecuador) pointed out that "in Latin America, more than 80 million people did not know how to read or write, and more than 15 million children failed to attend school. Because of the increasing birthrate, some 250,000 new classrooms should be built each year. There was need for 600,000 new teachers. These facts were a scandal, for society has never been so blessed with means as now."

A theme which kept constantly cropping up was that it was not enough for the Church to declare its regard for culture, it must prove this by deeds. It was not a sign of evangelical poverty, said Cardinal Lercaro, to cling to the cultural forms of the past, such as philosophical and theological systems or ecclesiastical institutions. The Church should speak less triumphalistically of these things, which repelled more men than they attracted. True poverty implied an awareness on the part of the

Church of her own inadequacies, joined with boldness in making the necessary adaptations demanded by a true sense of history and a spirit of humility. The Church should act on contemporary life by way of being a leaven. The Church's claim that she was tied to no culture was more theoretical than factual. And he favored a return to the "ancient custom" favoring the scientific study of theology by laymen.

As a way for the Church to prove its good intentions, decisively, Bishop Elchinger (Strasbourg, France) suggested the rehabilitation of Galileo. Such a decision if taken by the supreme authority in the Church would be a fitting climax to the current fourth centenary of his birth. He said that many people believed that the Catholic Church was fearful and on the defensive with respect to modern culture. The action taken by the Church's magisterium in dealing with modernism still caused suspicion and uneasiness, and some concrete act was needed, therefore, to dispel these misgivings.

Showing a proper respect for other cultural traditions really meant keeping our Western culture from swallowing up the East. It was now an accepted principle of missionary work, said the Chinese Bishop Lokuang (Tainan), to recognize the validity of all cultures and to see that the Church was firmly rooted in those cultures, so that it would not disappear when persecutions arose. But while much had been done to win over the masses, little attention had been paid to reaching the educated. It was sad that after so many years of missionary work in Asia, learned men in all branches of knowledge there knew so little about Christianity. There was danger that Africa might lose its own sense of religious values, commented Archbishop Zoa (Cameroun), while absorbing Western science. There should be cultural and theological institutes to help the Africans achieve a proper synthesis and the text should mention Christ as the norm and measure of such a cultural synthesis.

Bishop Carli (Segni, Italy) commented that the study of law, while regarded by some as "pseudo-charismatic," should nevertheless be mentioned along with other liberal studies. The text seemed to give first place to scientific studies. He also wanted some of the dangers of modern culture pointed out.

ECONOMIC AND SOCIAL LIFE

Judging by the number of bishops who spoke on Article 23, on "Economic and social life,"—debate on which began at 11:45 on Wednesday, November 4th and lasted only until 11:15 the following morning—this important section of the schema was hardly accorded the attention which was its due, but there were a great many written communications making up for this deficiency. The text adopted a stand not likely to endear it to proponents of the laissez-faire school of capitalism or rugged individualism in sociological matters. It marked a return to the economic and social teaching of the Church common to the Church Fathers and the Middle Ages, but which had become progressively obscured ever since the sixteenth century. As the Abbé Laurentin pointed out, the Roman conception of *ius utendi et abutendi* (the right of use and abuse) and the modern conception of capitalism became so dominant in the nineteenth century as to cause the thought of Thomas Aquinas to be virtually ignored. According to Aquinas and the traditional teaching of the Church: 1) God gave the goods of the earth to all men; but 2) for their proper use, they were to be divided among men. The right of private property was therefore neither primary nor absolute, but subject to the first consideration. The poor, accordingly, had a claim on the "common patrimony" which could not be denied.

Leo XIII, in his famous encyclical *Rerum novarum,* or rather the drafters of it, in their attempt to restore a proper social outlook, claimed that "private property" was a divinely decreed right, whereas St. Thomas spoke only of the "common destination" as being decreed by divine right. This misinterpretation of tradition naturally resulted in underestimating the rights of the poor, and over-exaggerating the rights of private property. The return to a sounder tradition took time and was not accomplished without difficulty. Pius XII was the first to refer to the matter in one of his discourses. Further steps were taken by John XXIII in his encyclicals *Mater et magistra* and *Pacem in terris.* The Council's text, by restoring the original conception, of course had no intention of downgrading private property or denying its place or efficacy, but was determined to assert that its rights were subject to a higher law. And Laurentin noted that this reassertion of the claims of the "common destination" willed by God for the benefit of all came just at a time when men were so preoccupied about the problem of the unequal distribution of wealth. The principle could be put in a nutshell, according to the Abbé, by saying that, while a man who stole a piece of bread when he was dying of hunger might be condemned by the state as a criminal, he had a right to do so according to the Church.

Most of the speakers purposely avoided going into any detail when dealing with this section, and concentrated instead on such general principles as the need for pointing out more clearly the evil effects of economic systems which denied moral principles, "whether of free enterprise or collectivism." Like several other Fathers, Cardinal Wyszynski thought that the Council should "praise and approve" all the social encyclicals of the popes, as containing "the authentic teaching of the Church on social questions." But as we have just seen the drafters of the

375

text wisely avoided any such blanket commendation. The tone of Cardinal Wyszynski's speech was rather on the conservative side. He hit out at certain modern "progressive Catholics"—apparently referring specifically to the Pax group of Catholics in Poland who were in favor of close collaboration with the Communist government and who had been his constant critics—"who defame the Church as if it neglected the lot of the workers."

Cardinal Richaud (Bordeaux) nevertheless felt that it was advisable to go into some detail in laying down rules for a dialogue between management and labor, to ensure a smooth functioning of the economy, for example, with regard to avoiding lay-offs and worker-training. Bishop Zambrano Camader (Colombia), a South American prelate, declared that he was not satisfied with the treatment of the distribution of wealth. Many people had abandoned the Church because they believed that it was hopelessly indifferent to their needs. More must be said about the moral issue and the duties of owners. Unless a fuller treatment was given of the inequities of the present system based on the law of supply and demand, the assumption would be that the Council approved of the inequities inherent in this system. A rather detailed analysis, replete with statistics, was offered by Bishop Benitez Avalos (Paraguay) of the economic situation in Latin America and he wanted certain conclusions with regard to it incorporated in Article 23 as a "sign of the times."

The questioning of papal encyclicals by recent speakers and what he fancied to be disrespect being shown for the teaching of the magisterium, so exercised Bishop Alba Palacios (Tehuantepec, Mexico) that he never did come to the point of his speech; he had to be reminded by the moderator that the topic under discussion was Article 23, not Article 21 or 24.

As an earnest of the Church's concern for the poor and for the relief of worldwide poverty, numerous bishops suggested that a special effort be made to focus international attention on the plight of the millions of people still in danger of starvation. James J. Norris, an American lay auditor at the Council, who had been dealing with relief and population problems in all parts of the world for some twenty years, proposed that a recognized expert introduce Article 24, on world solidarity, with a special *relatio*. He suggested as an ideal candidate the well-known author and correspondent of *The Economist* Barbara Ward (known in private life as Lady Jackson). After several weeks of intensive campaigning, which involved the buttonholing of cardinals, bishops, and Vatican officials, Norris seemed well on the way to success, but he was then suddenly informed by Archbishop Felici's office that despite the Council's welcome to women auditors (fifteen of them, including Sister Mary Luke, of Kentucky, head of the Conference of Major Superiors of Women Religious in the United States, and Mlle. Marie-Louise Monnet, sister of Jean Monnet, the father of the Common Market, were attending the session in this capacity), it was felt that it would be "premature" to have a woman address the assembly. Obviously, the thought was still too much for the masculine-oriented, Italian-dominated bureaucracy around the pope. Instead, Norris was told to take on the job himself. Also, he was asked to deliver his report in Latin. He did so, on only six hours' notice. This was a precedent-shattering act in itself, for no layman had yet been entrusted with such an official responsibility.

On Thursday, November 5, 1964, about 11:30, Norris mounted the rostrum and delivered his talk in excellent, clearly enunciated Latin and he was listened to with marked attention until the end. This was the first occasion, one might say, that any layman had succeeded in making a lasting impression on the Fathers:

World poverty will not be wiped out speedily, nor will the problem of development be solved in anything short of several generations. Our Christian peoples must not become weary of well doing.

But the goal will be reached if in each wealthy country there is brought into being a strong, committed, well-informed and courageous group of men of good will who are prepared to see world poverty as one of the great central concerns of our time and press steadily and vocally for the policies in aid, in trade and in the transfer of skills, that will lessen the widening gap between the rich and the poor. . . .

From this Ecumenical Council could come a clarion call for action which would involve the creation of a structure that would devise the kind of institutions, contacts, forms of cooperation and policy, which the Church can adopt, to secure full Catholic participation in the world-wide attack on poverty.

This great gathering of bishops represents every continent and every country on earth. Since world poverty affects all humanity, the great contribution of our universal Church can be a world-encircling manifestation of brotherly love, bringing effectively to bear the social teaching of the Church on the problem which our beloved Holy Father discussed in his Christmas message last year when he said that hunger is the principal problem in the world today:

". . . We make our own the sufferings of the poor. And we hope that this our sympathy may itself become capable of enkindling that new love which, by means of a specially planned economy, will multiply the bread needed to feed the world."

Warm applause greeted Norris when he finished. His suggestion about concerted effort was immediately seconded by Cardinal Frings, who called for the setting up of episcopal committees, on a national and international scale, to promote projects designed to alleviate world poverty. Every year collections should be taken up during "the penitential season," and the money collected from each nation should be distributed through a commission of bishops with the aid of a secretariat responsible for examining the projects proposed and with the help of lay experts. The delegates should meet together at least once a year to review their efforts, and the minutes of these meetings should be forwarded to the Holy See. As a token of the seriousness of their intentions, he suggested that the bishops should give up "their triumphalistic vestments."

The following intervention of Cardinal Alfrink on promoting solidarity among the family of nations was really on Article 25 rather than the article under discussion, however, he was not interrupted. He said that he agreed with the proposals of Cardinal Frings. Then turning to the subject of the Church's attitude toward communism, he laid down that, while atheism and communism must certainly be rejected, the rejection must not be done in such a way as to make it impossible to meet the promoters of those ideologies, "who are seeking the truth with good will," in a spirit of charity. The Church should avoid any new sterile condemnation of communism, as some speakers had demanded. This had already been done often enough and it would be useless to repeat what had been declared once and for all. Instead, the Council should promote a dialogue with all people of good will, including communists. No good could come from closing the doors to a dialogue.

Several other speakers were able to offer a few remarks before the end of the morning. Bishop Rupp (Monaco) felt that the schema should attack not only the evils of famine and injustice, but the very roots of these evils. The text appeared to him to be too prudent, too diplomatic, too "feminine."* In its present form it would not attract the attention of the world. The incompatibility of the unequal distribution of wealth with Christian principles, as enunciated by Thomas Aquinas, especially his principle "in necessity all things are common," was the theme of the intervention of Bishop Pildáin y Zapiáin (Canary Islands). The American Bishop Swanstrom, director of the U.S. Bishops' Relief Program, observed that while the text talked largely about what governments and the laity should do to alleviate poverty, it might also say something about the role which Catholic bishops and priests could play in promoting concerted action. The final speaker on Thursday, Bishop Thangalathil (India), dwelt on the moral and spiritual consequences of the increasing gap between the have- and have-not nations.

Debate on Article 24 was concluded on Monday, November 9th, with interventions by Cardinal Rugambwa, Archbishop Seper (Zagreb), Bishop Begin (Oakland, California), Cardinal Richaud, and Father Mahon, superior general of St. Joseph's Society for Foreign Missions, Mill Hill, U.S.A., who noted that Vatican Council I, convened two years after Karl Marx published the *Communist Manifesto,* had had nothing to

---

* Cf. the Italian proverb: *"Fatti maschi, parole femine."*

say about social justice. Today the proletarian classes had been succeeded by proletarian nations. "We cannot remain silent about social justice. The Church is not a mere spectator of the world's miseries, it is not called on to save disembodied souls but men." He gave wholehearted approval to the Secretariat proposed by James Norris and Cardinal Frings.

NUCLEAR WARFARE

The advent of nuclear weapons was unquestionably *the* most important scientific achievement in recent years and their use and effects had revolutionized traditional concepts of warfare. It remained less clear, however, just what their effects had been on traditional Catholic notions of a "just war." The highly controversial matter was still under debate among Catholic theologians and no consensus of opinion had yet been reached. The drafters of Schema 13 were therefore under a particular disadvantage when they came to deal with Article 25 on peace and war. The debate on this issue revealed a rather neat cleavage between Continental bishops and theologians on the one hand, and some British and most American bishops and theologians on the other. The former, representing nations for the most part without access to the "bomb," were decidedly in favor of banning all nuclear weapons. It was significant that "ban-the-bomb" movements seemed to have much more of an attraction for Europeans than for Americans; the latter, representing nations possessing the bomb, were more guarded in their statements and distinctly unfavorable to any categorical and unconditional condemnations of nuclear warfare so long as the discussion of the "just war" remained up in the air. Without presuming to decide this controverted issue, the text of Article 25 had been drafted in such a way as to give more satisfaction to the Continental school. The opposition between the two schools must not be pressed however. The views of individual speakers were often highly nuanced, but in general this distinction was valid. Since the debate produced no clear-cut consensus of opinion, the framers of the draft would have a difficult task working out a text capable of winning the approval of the assembly at the Fourth Session. They might have to sidetrack the issue altogether.

Decisive as the present text of Article 25 was in its condemnation of all nuclear warfare, it was still not clear enough, in the opinion of Archbishop Roberts, S.J., a frequent spokesman on the subject, mainly because it avoided going into the related moral problem of conscientious objection. In a press conference on October 21, 1964, at the Dutch Documentation Center, he maintained that the use of weapons capable of destroying millions of innocent people posed a new problem, that conscientious objection should be recognized by the Church and people

379

ought not to be forced to fight. He drew attention to the fact that it was countries with English law, or possibly Protestant, tradition behind them which had proved to be sensitive to the importance of this issue, rather than countries with a predominantly Catholic tradition. The principle of conscientious objection had first come to the fore in Britain during World War I and had been recognized by parliament and other legislative bodies following the common law tradition.

A number of speakers, while favorable to Article 25 in general, pointed out that they regarded it as a "retreat" compared with the more explicit condemnation of nuclear warfare found in Pope John's *Pacem in Terris*. Cardinal Feltin of Paris (anticipating the discussion by speaking on October 29th because he had to leave Rome) stated that Catholics, and the hierarchy in particular, should be more active in promoting peace, in preaching and in catechetics, "lest the oft lamented divorce between papal encyclicals and Catholic life continue." Peace should be presented as a true apostolate to be furthered by dialogue and cooperation with non-Christians. He called for the establishment of a special commission of theologians and scientists to study the present state of the question regarding peace and war. Cardinal Alfrink, for his part, noted that the Johannine encyclical "speaks more positively than the schema on the subject of disarmament." It was more specific, in particular, with regard to two important conditions for disarmament, namely reciprocity and simultaneity. The present text must not fail to mention this. As for the so-called ABC weapons (atomic, biological, chemical), the text declared that their effects were greater than could be calculated, but in contrast to the "dirty bomb," scientists had produced a "clean bomb" whose effects could be controlled and calculated, both as to duration and area. The language of the text, as drafted at present, seemed to suggest that nuclear weapons were criminal only because their effects were incalculable, and that they ceased to be so if the effects could be calculated. Therefore if the intention of the Council was to condemn the use of all nuclear weapons indiscriminately, the language should be tightened up. The cardinal questioned whether there should be any mention of a "just or unjust war" in the schema at all. What people expected from the Church was an outright condemnation of *all* war, nuclear warfare specifically. "It is not for us to go into the question of whether a war can be just or not," he said, "but to propose the abolition of war altogether." He quoted the saying of President Kennedy: "Unless we destroy weapons, weapons will destroy us." The primary solicitude of the Church should be to exhort men to peace.

The same thought was echoed by Bishop Ancel (auxiliary of Lyons), who insisted that the primary task of the Church was not to become involved in technical details, but to state moral principles. What the schema only insinuated should be brought out more clearly, namely that the good of the human family required that all nations "must renounce the right to war and armaments," retaining only those arms necessary for internal security, and that an international organization be given the means to supress war.

Another forceful speaker on the Continental side, Bishop Guilhem (Laval, France), the author of a bold letter on nuclear disarmament, added his opinion that since the Church was the "Light of the World," its primary function in this important matter was to stir up public opinion, to get the faithful and all men of good will, generally, involved in the (gradual) movement to abolish the arms race and nuclear weapons in particular. Like Bishop Ancel and Cardinal Alfrink, he felt that the apparent contradiction in the text, between the condemnation of war, especially nuclear war, and the legitimacy of a defensive war, should be eliminated. It was wrong, he maintained, to imply that peace could be maintained by a military balance or through fear of the effects of nuclear weapons. Peace must be based on mutual respect, and a dialogue was therefore necessary to eliminate misunderstandings and differences. Patriarch Maximos IV Saigh was also for issuing a more solemn condemnation of all nuclear, chemical and bacteriological warfare, and for revising the traditional concept of a just war. The intervention of 2,000 bishops from all parts of the world, he said, should be capable of bringing about some change in the course of world history and defending the rights of humanity. The interventions of Bishop Hengsbach (Essen, Germany) and Bishop Hakim (Israel) were along the same line.

The American-British position was represented by auxiliary Bishop Hannan (Washington) and Archbishop Beck (Liverpool). Neither spoke in the names of their respective hierarchies, so that it was somewhat inaccurate to imply that they were voicing an agreed "American-British" consensus. The former said that if the Church was going to appeal to the principles of a just war (in its treatment of the morality of warfare), it should consult theologians who were competent in this field and were familiar with the facts about modern weapons, including nuclear weapons. He objected to the easy assumption that all nuclear weapons were automatically incalculable in their effects, as implied in the text. Cardinal Alfrink had stated that this was not true. The trouble was that the schema "apparently ignores the traditional teaching of the Church on conducting a just war." He concluded with a statement approving the principle that a dialogue was necessary to avert war, but made the following pertinent comment:

Article 25 implies that all nations have been equally negligent in working for international peace. This is cruelly unfair to many nations and statesmen, and particularly to nations now suffering under unjust aggression. The world knows the source of this aggression; it would be ridiculous for the Council to pretend that it does not know. In order to have a dialogue with materialistic atheists, we must enjoy full liberty; slavery would render such a dialogue impossible. Therefore, we should praise those who defend freedom, and especially those who have died for it.

Bishop Hannan called for a complete rewriting of the section.

If the speech of Bishop Hannan succeeded in slightly jolting some of the Fathers, that by Archbishop Beck frankly frightened others. Without mincing words, he declared that while the text condemned the use of any weapon whose effects could not be estimated and controlled, as Pius XII and John XXIII had done, it was nevertheless important to "make clear that this is not a univeral condemnation of the use of nuclear weapons. There may well exist objects which in a just war are legitimate targets of nuclear weapons even of vast force (e.g. an attack against a ballistic or satellite missile in the outer atmosphere). Responsibility for the use of nuclear weapons rests with those who exercise supreme authority in the state, and the Council should express sympathy for those who carry this heavy burden. The government of a country has a grave duty to do all it can to prevent war, but in certain circumstances, it may well be true that peace can be assured only by a 'balance of terror,' i.e. by the threat of the use of nuclear weapons as a deterrent against unjust aggression. Let us not too readily condemn these governments which have succeeded in keeping the peace, however tentative, in the world by the use of such means. Let the Council make clear that it does not demand of governments that they decide on a unilateral abandonment of nuclear weapons because of a possibly proximate danger that these weapons may be used in an immoral way."

The interesting question naturally arose why, if these two speakers really were voicing a representative opinion about Article 25, they were not supported by more bishops?

The debate on Schema 13 closed with some general remarks by Bishop Rigaud (Pamiers, France), in the name of 80 bishops, on international organizations; a regret by Bishop Yáñez Ruiz Tagle (Los Angeles, Chile), in the name of 70 bishops, that nothing special was said in Chapter IV about social justice; a recommendation by Bishop McGrath (Panama), in the name of 70 bishops, that the effectiveness of the document could be improved by expanding the introductory paragraphs to each section of Chapter IV as well as to Chapters I–III and by the inclusion of more emphasis on the application of principles to actual problems; and by an intervention by the Argentinian lay auditor, Professor Juan Vasquez. Bishop Guano summed up by proposing a slightly different plan for the revision. The schema would start out with the "signs of the times"; this would be followed by a fuller treatment of what the Church thought about the world with Chapters I–III probably lumped together, and by an expanded treatment of Chapter IV at the end, enriched by the inclusion of material from the *Adnexa*. He repeated his earlier suggestion that the moderators might decide to put certain points to a vote so that the commission would have better guidance, but no action was taken on this motion at the Third Session.

DEBATE ON MISSIONARY ACTIVITY

The Third Session made history when Pope Paul put in an appearance at one of the working sessions of the Council, and took his place not on his throne but at the head of the Council presidents' table. According to canon law, the pope was the head of the Council, but modern popes had studiously avoided giving the impression that they were interfering in any way with conciliar freedom of discussion by absenting themselves from all purely business sessions. Perhaps the pope wanted to symbolize more clearly the close relationship between pope and Council, in keeping with the spirit of collegiality, than was possible by daily behind-the-scenes contacts and appearances at solemn public sessions. On the other hand, it was suggested that his appearance was intended as symbolic of something other than the spirit of collegiality, namely a desire to impress on the Fathers (in case any were inclined to forget) that the prerogatives of his office must not be overlooked, but this seemed an unlikely way of making the point. The pope was under some pressure, it seems, from various quarters to make a personal appearance, and the idea may not have originated with him at all. The question that had to be decided was *when* he should appear. Debate on Schema 13 was already underway, and while the reception accorded the first two schemata reduced to propositions was not very encouraging, a choice nevertheless had to be made, so it was arranged that he should help introduce the text on Missionary Activity, as the least controversial of the remaining documents. The discussion of Schema 13 had to be interrupted to allow for this. Time was running out and the agenda was already overcrowded. The decisions about the James Norris *relatio* and the appearance of Paul were apparently made suddenly, on the spur of the moment. The pope was also badly advised by Cardinal Agagianian, who misled him about the character of the text on Missions and the reception that it might expect to receive at the hands of the bishops. Instead of turning out to be a wise move, the papal visit proved to be symptomatic of the inauspicious happenings during the final days of the Third Session.

On Friday, November 6, 1964, after hearing a mass celebrated according to the Ethiopian rite from a chair placed in front of the conciliar altar, the pope took his place at the table of Council presidents, sitting in the middle between Cardinals Tisserant and Tappouni, at the place normally occupied by the former, as dean of the Sacred College and ranking cardinal. A minor incident occurred while the pope was being seated, or shortly after he was seated. Archbishop Dante, who as papal master of ceremonies normally hovered near the papal side on all occasions, wanted to remain standing behind his chair at the presidents' table, but this was too much for Cardinal Tisserant who sternly ordered him away—after a similar warning by Archbishop Felici had failed to do the trick. The pope was now in safe hands and there was no need for monitors. In the course of a short speech introducing the missionary text, Pope Paul referred to the importance and seriousness of the missionary problem today, and made the specific recommendation: "We hope that, while you may decide on improvements in some parts, you will approve the present text." Cardinal Agagianian then rose to deliver his *relatio* as president of the conciliar Commission on Missions, referring to Pope Paul, in fulsome terms, as *"qualis et quantus missionarius,"* in view of his announced intention to go to Bombay. His Holiness then got up, gave his blessing, walked slowly toward the side aisle of the basilica, greeting various persons and groups on the way, and finally disappeared from view.

The debate on Missionary Activity occupied two and a half days, Friday and Saturday, November 6th and 7th, and Monday, November 9th. When the pope had left, Bishop Lokuang (of the conciliar commission that had drafted the schema) read the commission's report. He pointed out that the present 13 propositions had been extracted from the seven chapters of the original schema. The discussion of this text was extremely well orchestrated: the African secretariats were called upon to provide their quota of speakers; Cardinal Bea, a friend of the Africans and Asians, was pressed into service to help support the views of the missionary bishops, as well as other leading bishops. Everything was done to make the essential points on the floor. The outcome, as one observer put it, was "a resounding Yes for the missions; a resounding No for the skeleton of a schema" which the bishops were asked to accept. The Propositions were adjudged wholly unsatisfactory as an adequate expression of the Church's views about such an important topic.

Cardinal Léger (Montreal) who led off the debate, put his finger on an essential point. He said that it was hoped that the Council would give a new impetus to the missionary *élan* of the Church by directing attention to this vital part of the apostolate. A new plan was called for. There were encouraging signs that a new approach was possible, because of more general recognition in the Church of the principle of diversity and the necessity of adapting the Church's methods to local conditions; because of the restoration of a permanent diaconate; because of a hoped for dialogue with non-Christian religions, but on this score the text had nothing to say; because of a new awareness on the part of the bishops of their responsibilities toward the universal Church. With regard to the central commission proposed by the schema, the cardinal was in favor of a body within the framework of the Congregation for the Propagation of the Faith, but as a supreme council over all the parts. What was desirable, according to Cardinal Frings, was a kind of "senate" of missionary and other bishops, or "missionary strategy board," fully representative of all areas, to be assisted by experts, both theoretical and practical. He was applauded when he called for the rewriting of the schema and its presentation at the Fourth Session. Applause also greeted the Irish-born Bishop Lamont (Umtali, Southern Rhodesia) when, in the course of a highly rhetorical speech, he quoted Isaiah, characterizing the propositions as so many "bare bones" which needed to be revivified in a worthy schema, one that would set on fire not only the bishops, but also religious superiors and the whole Church with the missionary spirit of Pentecost. The moderator's warning to the speaker to be less rhetorical naturally only caused the Fathers to be more generous with their applause when he finished.

The vision of the present text was too limited, according to Archbishop Zoghby (patriarchal vicar for Egypt), and its outlook too Western. The Eastern Churches were capable of suggesting new approaches to the missions, even though they had not been very active along this line in recent centuries. He referred in particular to the close connection between the missions and the mystery of the Trinity, the mystery of Christ as being "sent" by the Father, and the mystery of the "seed of God's word" being sown in men through the action of the Holy Spirit, according to a "divine pedagogy."

Cardinal Alfrink's reminder was of a more practical nature. He noted that the work of evangelizing the world had scarcely begun. There were two billion men who had not yet received Christ's message, but while the needs were vast, the number of missionaries had been steadily declining for years. New churches flourished, but they were short of priests. After twenty centuries it was shameful to admit these facts, but we must.

The dimensions of the missionary problem were rather well brought out by Cardinal Bea, who cited the words of St. Paul to the effect that missionary activity should be directed to uniting all people with Christ and with each other. It was sometimes said that because of the shortage of priests and the need for missionary work at home, as well as the fact that the hierarchy was now established among nearly all nations, it was no longer vital to support foreign missions, properly speaking. But it must not be forgotten that the *first* obligation of the Church was to bring Christ's message to those who had never heard it. And it was not true, of course, that because the hierarchy had been established in certain areas that there was no longer any need there for outside help. The intervention of Cardinal Suenens also bore on this general point, namely the need for not taking too restricted a view of the laymen's role, as presented in the eighth Proposition. In accordance with their role of helping to consecrate the world, laymen had a place in missionary work, but they should of course be well prepared for the tasks they would be called on to undertake. They could help with catechetical work, cooperate in the parochial apostolate, and further the work of various apostolic organizations.

Quite a few Fathers insisted on the necessity of disassociating missionary work from the implication that it was merely a form of spreading Western culture, or the long arm of Western capitalism, or that any such mercenary goal was intended. Speaking in the name of the bishops of Africa and Madagascar, Archbishop Gantin (Dahomey) said that the old prejudices about the missions as an attempt to dominate were still very much alive. Everything must be done to dissipate this misunderstanding, by promoting a cultural dialogue and the establishment of higher institutes, on a "give and take" basis. Speaking in French, he said: "The Church is supranational. It transcends all regimes."

The Brazilian Father Grotti (prelate nullius of Acre and Purus) delivered a rather fiery intervention against the whole tenor of the propositions, which he characterized as "paternalistic exhortations and generalizations." The *periti* who drew them up should be sent to the field to learn the true meaning of "mission." He reminded his hearers of the saying: "Rome also is a missionary territory!"

Father Grotti was opposed to the establishment of a central commission under, or part of, the Congregation for the Propagation of the Faith. It should be established within the Consistorial Congregation, and missionary churches should cease to be called "missionary"; rather it was better to speak of them as "new churches," and of Propaganda itself as the "Congregation for New Churches."

Bishop Geise (Bogor, Indonesia), speaking in the name of the Indonesian Episcopal Conference, announced that the Conference and many other Fathers would vote Non placet on the propositions and demanded that they be sent back for a thorough revision; while Bishop Riobé, (Orleans, France), a member of the Missionary Commission itself, subscribed to the same thesis. He observed that their commission had been torn for three years between a theological and a juridical view of the missions and that the just requests of so many bishops for a full-fledged schema should be satisfied. Only in this way could justice be done to the many suggestions sent in by the bishops, which "lie sleeping in the files."

Bishop Moors (Roermond, Holland), and Bishop Moynagh (Calabar, Nigeria) spoke in the same sense.

The last speaker was Bishop Sheen auxiliary of New York, who approved the proposal for the formation of a central commission, which would be able to cut corners and satisfy legitimate needs without regard to juridical considerations. He closed with the thought that, while chastity had been the fruit of the Council of Trent, and obedience that of Vatican Council I, poverty ought to be the fruit of Vatican Council II.

In the face of such overwhelming and insistent demands for a drastically revised, ampler schema, Bishop Lokuang lost no time in his final summation in assuring the Fathers that they would be presented with a better schema at the Fourth Session, according to their wishes.

The vote on the motion, "Does it please the Fathers to send the text back to commission?"—framed, it should be noted, in keeping with the critical tone of the debate—produced the desired result. The text on Missionary Activity was ordered sent back to commission (1601 Placets to 311 Non placets). Ordinarily, the question would have asked whether it pleased the Fathers to vote on the propositions at once.

DEBATE ON RELIGIOUS

On November 11th and 12th, the Council took up the next schema to be considered, entitled "On the adaptation and Renewal of the Religious Life." The debate was actually begun the day before, toward the end of the session on November 10th, with a reading of his *relatio* by Bishop McShea (Allentown, Pennsylvania) and one intervention by Cardinal Spellman. The present text of four pages comprising 20 Propositions was extracted from the thirty pages of the full text of the schema on Religious Orders, which, in turn, had been condensed from an original schema of some 100 pages.

The debate revealed two tendencies. Those favoring a wider view of the religious apostolate were clearly for a rejection of the present text, which appeared to them to be too conservative and narrow. Representative speakers among this group were Cardinals Richaud, Döpfner, Suenens, Bea, Bishop Charue, Father Buckley, Father Lalande, and Bishop Huyghe. The opposing group were either in favor of the text or strongly opposed to any drastic alterations in religious life. Representative speakers here were Cardinals Landázuri Ricketts and Ruffini, Father Fernandez, master general of the Dominicans, Father Anastasius, superior general of the Discalced Carmelites, and Archbishop Perantoni (Lanciano, Italy).

The most critical evaluation of the schema came from Cardinal

Döpfner, who said that it was weak not because it had been abbreviated, but because it failed to come to grips with the basic problems of religious renewal, of the accommodation of religious life to modern times, of the preparation of religious for their vocation, and because it took too restricted a view of religious institutes. Too many religious congregations were doing the same work. Women religious, particularly, he said, often found themselves torn between "a quasi-monastic regimen and over-demanding work." As to contemplatives, he was even blunter: "In contemplative communities, there is an institutional narrowness which is psychologically unbearable; hence, of many contemplative vocations few persevere." A longer schema was not necessarily recommended, but one including consideration of the above points.

The address of Cardinal Suenens repeated points that he had frequently made in lectures, and in his controversial book on women religious. He confined himself to this theme, beginning with the words: *"Schema non placet."* It was necessary to cease regarding nuns as children or minors and treat them as adults, and they must have freedom to engage in apostolic work. Theologians must elaborate a "spirituality of the active life for them," so that they could get away from "the traditions and mentality of the cloister." Without abandonment of any of the essentials of the religious life, what the cardinal wanted was that the religious apostolate should be directed more to the work of "evangelization," with more frequent contacts between religious and the laity. The role of the nun should be to help inspire the laity in their apostolate. Apart from this theoretical or doctrinal consideration, he called for drastic reforms in practical matters. Nuns should begin acting as "adults" and display a sense of responsibility by working in cooperation with others. "We should give up the habit of treating nuns as minors, an attitude so typical of the nineteenth century, which was still found in many religious congregations today," he said. "This emphasis on infantilism is matched by another disgraceful trait: the exhibition of maternalism on the part of mother superiors. Let us abandon these customs which perpetuate a feeling of inferiority among women religious. They are based not on consideration for the requirements of the religious life, but on outmoded ideas about society. As for cloistering active orders, this serves for the most part as an obstacle to their effectiveness; it prevents nuns from being the leaven in the loaf which they ought to be." He called for canon lawyers and competent nuns to elaborate rules for a more balanced organization of religious orders; for a change in the system of electing superiors; for general chapters to be more truly representative of the order; and for the abandonment of outmoded forms of garb, anachronistic customs and the like. Everything must be eliminated that helped give nuns an inferiority complex. The text should be rejected and a new one drawn up. The cardinal was seconded by Bishop Moors (Roermond, Holland).

Several speakers, like Cardinal Bea, referred overtly to the "crisis" in the religious life now being experienced. According to the cardinal, it was not sufficient, as the schema did, to urge a renovation primarily in the juridical sphere. This was important, but the most vital element, ways whereby the spiritual outlook of religious could be renewed, were hardly mentioned by the text at all. The first requirement was the accommodation of the nature and scope of the religious life to a modern mentality. The text should point out that the consecration of the religious regarded not only the individual Christ, but the whole Christ, that is, the Church, as pointed out in *De Ecclesia*. Each institute had its own rule and purpose, but all the institutes were related to the Church and were dedicated to the service "of the whole human family." There was too much striving to preserve the spirit of the separate orders, and not enough effort being expended on ways in which to participate in the changing circumstances of the world around them. The religious should be encouraged to take an active part in all the movements, biblical, liturgical, missionary and ecumenical, which were animating the Church at the present time.

Current speculation over the place in the apostolate of the contemplative orders, devoted wholly to prayer, was reflected in the concern shown by a number of speakers that there must be no downgrading of their importance in any plans for a renewal of the religious life. In fact, greater emphasis must be placed on such orders, Cardinal Landázuri Ricketts held. He also observed that one reason why there were so many defections from religious orders today was that the candidates who entered them were more interested in apostolic work than in holiness or submitting to the discipline of the evangelical counsels. More insistence should be placed on religious institutes as "schools of sanctity."

The schema in its reduced form was generally satisfactory to Cardinal Spellman, who felt that it contained the essential points that ought to be made. But he warned about any renewal of religious orders that would impose on religious any kind of apostolate inconsistent with the functions which they normally performed. He was referring to the suggestions often made by Cardinal Suenens. Many superiors of religious orders, Cardinal Spellman said, had spoken to him about their anxieties with regard to this recommendation. Instead of promoting an observance of their rules, it would mean a further departure from them. It was sufficient for religious to do whatever they were normally required to do, for example, teaching, nursing, or leading a purely contemplative life. With regard to the last point, Cardinal Spellman said that he was worried lest the contemplative life might be smothered "by the onrush of activism."

389

Cardinal Ruffini expressed himself as worried about the flat recommendation in the text that religious orders should renew themselves. He felt that this ought to be toned down, as there was danger that it might produce imprudent demands for reform. In any case, nothing should be done toward accommodating or renewing religious life without consulting the Holy See, otherwise changes might be introduced which would make it more difficult for religious to lead a life of perfection. He was also opposed to anything that might draw contemplatives away from their form of life, by way of requiring them to take part in active apostolic works. His recipe for all dangers to the vow of chastity, was to recommend that "religious should be urged to implore the grace of chastity, for the preservation of purity amid so many dangers is a great gift." The cardinal was applauded by the conservative benches when he finished.

It was strange, said Bishop Charue (Namur, Belgium), that nothing was said about the relations between conferences of religious superiors and bishops in Proposition 19, and nothing about the relations between religious and diocesan clergy on the parish level. He also noted, in the name of the Belgian hierarchy, that the warning about observing the norms laid down by the Holy See was a good thing because there had been abuses in such things as the recruitment of novices. Some religious, in their zeal for recruiting students for their schools or in speaking to youths about the life of perfection, had given the impression that it was impossible to reach evangelical perfection outside the monastery or cloister. While regretting the impossibility of submitting a "really good and proper schema," Bishop Sol (Indonesia), in the name of the Indonesian Episcopal Conference, indicated acceptance of the present text as a working basis, however, he made it clear in his remarks that he agreed with what Cardinals Döpfner and Suenens had said by way of its inadequacy.

Disturbed by so much adverse criticism Archbishop Perantoni (Lanciano, Italy), former General of the Franciscans Minor, speaking in the name of 370 Fathers, rose to give his approval to the text. He said that he was alarmed "in the face of the rumors being circulated these days by some who are saying that religious do not want the schema retained." As a member of the conciliar Commission on Religious which had drafted the text, he proceeded to defend his handiwork against the intrigues which he said were being directed against it "even from those in high places."

There followed a number of Fathers speaking in the name of rather large groups: Archbishop Sartre (Cameroun) in the name of 265 Fathers; Bishop Guilly (British Guiana) in the name of 265 Fathers; Father Buckley, superior of the Marist Fathers, in the name of 130 Fathers; Archbishop Athaide, O.F.M. Cap. (Agra, India) in the name of the National Conference of India; Father Lalande, superior general of the

Holy Cross Congregation, in the name of more than 140 Fathers; Bishop Carroll (auxiliary of Sydney, Australia) in the name of 440 Fathers, the most so far; Archbishop Baraniak (Poznan, Poland), in the name of the Polish hierarchy; and Bishop Fiordelli (Prato, Italy), in the name of 82 Fathers. Two other superior generals also spoke, in their own names: Father Hoffer, superior general of the Marianists, and Father Van Kerckhoven, superior general of the Missionaries of the Sacred Heart. Sartre, Guilly, Carroll and Hoffer were favorable to the present text, to which number should be added Bishop Čekada (Skoplje, Yugoslavia), but all the rest, including Bishop Huyghe (Arras, France) were highly critical. Particularly outstanding interventions were delivered by Father Buckley, Bishop Huyghe, and Father Lalande. They pointed out that while the conservatively-oriented Congregation of Religious had been "pushing" for the adaptation of religious orders ever since 1950, nothing important had been done and the present text, which was intended to accomplish this purpose, should be completely rewritten. Touching on the delicate subject of relations between orders and bishops, Father Buckley called for a gesture of friendship toward the diocesan clergy, to be included in the new draft. He went on: "We religious may be worried about the greater authority that bishops want to have over us; but we ought to face up to the fact that some of our habits irritate the diocesan clergy, such as our tendency to talk as if we were the only ones in the state of perfection. The sound spirituality of diocesan priests should be recognized. In fact, religious priests of the active life are closer to diocesan priests than to contemplative religious. The canonical distinction, while necessary, should not be insisted on in practice; for what unites us is more important than what separates us." He declared that Pope John had expressed agreement with these sentiments in a private audience which he had granted him. He called further for the dropping of the distinction between Orders and Congregations. As for the "crisis in obedience" about which religious superiors were always talking, it was his feeling that the crisis was with the superiors, not with the religious under them. The truth was that "today's young people don't swallow archaic formulas like 'the will of the Superior is exactly the same as the will of God.' "

Bishop Huyghe called for the cooperation of mother superiors in drafting a new schema, referring particularly to the mother superior who had been appointed one of the Council's lay auditors, Sister Mary Luke, of the American order of the Sisters of Loretto. The bishop noted that it was unfortunately customary for legislation regarding religious to be drawn up by men only. As a matter of fact, no woman religious had been consulted by the conciliar commission which drew up the present draft, at least to the extent that lay auditors and experts had been consulted on the

391

document on the Apostolate of the Laity. This was declared, expressly, by Sister Mary Luke in an interview at the Bishops' Press Panel. While understandably cautious in her remarks about the conservative nature of the conciliar commission and the likelihood that a better document could be produced by them, she expressed it as her fervent hope and as the desire of many women religious that a new text would: a) modernize theological teaching with regard to the religious life in accordance with the aims and goals of *aggiornamento;* and b) provide for the representation of women religious on ecclesiastical bodies which governed them. It was known that Sister Mary Luke had taken an active part in the work connected with the revision of Schema 13.

Bishop McShea's defense of the text in summing up the debate—his remark that "those who offered suggestions accepted the schema in substance" was hardly in conformity with the facts—played an important part in saving the text, when the question was put to the Fathers whether it was pleasing to proceed to an immediate voting on the several Propositions (1155 Placet to 882 Non placet), for it was an almost invariable rule that when a commission defended its own text, the Fathers were unlikely to reject it outright. A factor in support of retention was unquestionably the massive concerted action on the part of many conservatively-inclined bishops and religious to save the text, which they regarded as at least a satisfactory basis for revision and a safeguard against too much reform. Sensing what the outcome might be, Cardinals Döpfner and Suenens marshalled a massive attack of their own, so that when the individual propositions were put to a vote, Propositions 1–13, representing the weakest portion of the text, were not carried because of the large number of Iuxta modum votes submitted. In this way they forced the commission to give consideration to their demands and come up with a more radically revised text than would otherwise have been the case. In this instance, the majority showed that they had learned something from the tactics of the minority.

DEBATE ON PRIESTLY FORMATION

The short series of propositions entitled "On the Formation of Priests," that is, on priestly training in all its aspects, was taken up on Thursday, November 12th and debated for four days until November 17th, with time out for the ceremony on Friday, November 13th, when the pope laid his tiara on the altar as an offering to the poor. It had originally been a schema totalling sixty pages in 1962; it was now reduced to 22 propositions, comprising four pages.

The text was one of the few sets of propositions that were adjudged favorably. The need for a statement of principles had been fulfilled very well by the conciliar Commission on Seminaries, the author of the document, which had somehow managed to escape from the predominately conservative influence of the Curial Congregation on Seminaries and Universities and keep that influence at arm's length. It was almost inevitable that the bishops would approve of it heartily, for the very first Proposition boldly announced the principle that programs for the training of the clergy were to be adapted to local conditions in accordance with plans drawn up by the local episcopal conferences:

So that the general rules may be adapted to each people and to each rite, episcopal conferences are to prepare a program for the formation of their priests. This program is to be constantly brought up to date and submitted for the approval of the Holy See. Thus universal laws will be adapted to the needs and characteristics of individual peoples and all countries, in such a way that the formation of their priests will harmonize with the spiritual needs of the country.

The net effect of this ruling, if enacted, would be to take much of the initiative in controlling and standardizing the training of priests, in the broadest sense of the term, away from the Congregation of Seminaries in Rome and out of the hands of the conservative prelates there who had dominated this sector of ecclesiastical life for so long. It was understandable that the spokesmen for that body, particularly Archbishop Staffa and Cardinal Bacci, both of the Curia, as well as Cardinal Ruffini, expressed themselves as unhappy with the text.

The text stressed the idea of developing a sense of responsibility, proper freedom, and wider outlook among seminarians. Seminarians must come to know more about the world, they must be better acquainted with the various branches of knowledge, and in particular with the Bible, as modern scriptural exegesis understood it. The schema was declared a "masterpiece" by Cardinal Léger (Montreal), who hoped that it would become a solid foundation for the transformation of seminaries, imbuing them with a new dynamism, as had happened after the Council of Trent. The cardinal of Rio de Janeiro concurred in Cardinal Léger's judgment regarding the effectiveness and success of the schema. The principles laid down were good; further practical measures should be left to the judgment of local bishops and local episcopal conferences. Cardinal Meyer, for his part, welcomed the provision for adjusting programs locally. One of the defects of seminary training had been that too much uniformity was imposed. There were other ways of exercising the priesthood beside those assumed to be normal for the Latin clergy and the schema should make this point, to be consistent with Proposition 1.

The schema was also praised by Bishop Charue (Namur, Belgium) because it recommended principles that were sound, viable and productive, not excessively severe or impractical. Bishop Weber (Strasbourg), with 25 years behind him in the seminary at Paris, also gave his approval to the text. It avoided the tendency to throw over everything that the Council of Trent had decreed, while at the same time undertaking the renewal demanded by the changed times and mentalities of today. He put in a word about seminary rectors and hoped that they would be chosen from priests who were well fitted and trained for the job, and they should form a "college" of their own, conducting the seminary on family lines, under the direction of the bishop.

Cardinal Meyer brought out the important point that a priest should be trained not only to be a mediator between God and men but to be a man *per se*. These were the two principles which should form the basis of seminary training. Connected with the latter point, was the need for training priests to be good Christians, of course. Seminary students should be trained in the ethical field as well as in the purely ecclesiastical sciences.

The point made by Cardinal Meyer was also stressed by Archbishop Colombo (Milan), the brother of the Bishop Colombo who was the pope's theological adviser. He pointed out that unless seminary students received the proper kind of training calculated to develop their personalities, they might turn out to be immature, excessively passive, with too detached a feeling toward human society, which would hinder them in their apostolate. The schema was to be praised for recognizing these dangers and making recommendations to counteract and avert them, particularly by its emphasis on the "Christocentric" formation which every priest should receive, a point frequently mentioned by Pope Paul VI in his discourses and by other advocates of *aggiornamento*.

On a more practical plane, there was considerable discussion, both inside and outside the council hall, on the merits of maintaining a minor seminary in each diocese to prepare boys for the major seminary, or seminary proper. Were such schools duplicating parochial schools really necessary? The cardinal archbishop of Seville tended to minimize their importance in his intervention, claiming that, to some extent, it was true that boys had a "more natural and perfect seminary in their own homes" and that they could overcome the crises of youth with the help of a prudent priest. Minor seminaries were therefore not strictly necessary. Cardinal Döpfner also agreed. While minor seminaries were good, they were not the only way to prepare youth for the seminary and priesthood. He observed that in Germany many candidates for the priesthood came not from the minor seminary, but from those who had already completed their examinations in the public high school for the university and there was an advantage in this, because the candidates were very often more well-rounded, since it was "in the nature of man" to prefer family life. Something should be said about this in the text so that Christian families would become conscious of their responsibility to foster vocations for the priesthood more than they did at present. Cardinal Ruffini, on the other hand, was very definitely of the view that minor seminaries were the *only* way to train students for the priesthood and that where there were none to be found, they should be opened immediately in accordance with the wishes of the Council of Trent, which laid it down that vocations were to be fostered *"inde a teneris annis."* The text should state also that Pontifical or Catholic schools were to be preferred when selecting students for special studies. This, of course, was diametrically opposed to the tendency nowadays for bishops to send their gifted students and priests to study at secular universities, with a view to broadening their training in specialized fields.

An interesting proposal was made by Cardinal Suenens, who called for the establishment of a special commission to study programs for the renewal of seminaries. For a pastoral renovation to be effective, it was not sufficient to publish conciliar texts, since the fruits of the Council's work would depend on the men who put these ideas into practice. The hopes of the Council were closely connected with the formation of priests, therefore it was important to go into this matter thoroughly and make recommendations on the basis of an investigation of local conditions and problems. Opposition to this proposal was at once voiced by Cardinal Bacci (Curia), who termed it wholly unnecessary and "very inopportune," since this was the proper function of the Congregation of Seminaries. If such a commision were established, it would have to be within the framework of the Congregation or directed by it. Apparently, in the thinking of people like Cardinal Bacci, the various organs of the Curia, as they existed at the present time, were eternal. His categorical dismissal of the idea was symptomatic of the outlook and fears of this circle.

If the suggestion of Cardinal Suenens was likely to upset the Congregation of Seminaries and Universities, that made by Archbishop Garrone (Toulouse, France) was calculated to cause dismay, for it was nothing less than an indictment of that citadel of conservatism in the Curia, similar to the indictment of the Holy Office by Cardinal Frings during the Second Session. The archbishop was commenting on Proposition 1, calling for decentralization and an increase in the authority of episcopal conferences over seminaries. This meant, he said, that the duties and rights of the Congregation of Seminaries in Rome would be changed. He suggested that to ensure that this took place, it might be a good idea to lay down certain norms for a renovation of the central body in Rome. His remarks summed up the two chief criticisms most frequently levelled against the Congregation: "It must take more account of the necessities and needs of local countries. To accomplish this it must no longer be behind the times or negative in its approach, but should be organically joined to the Congregation dealing with priests, and it should have as members men from all over the world, so that it would be better acquainted with the conditions of priestly life. Secondly, it should be more open to progress and change in the sciences which pertain to seminary training. Hence, the Congregation should use the experience of men who are true experts in every field of higher learning."

Considerable attention was focused also on the problem of how much time should be devoted to pastoral work, during seminary years. Cardinal Suenens was of the opinion that the whole of the seminary period should be marked and dominated by preparation for pastoral work; others thought that a year should be set aside, others that enough practical experience could be gained during summer vacations, etc. There was no consensus of opinion. Two Fathers brought up the subject of priestly celibacy, Bishop Reuss (Mainz) and Bishop Mendez Arceo (Mexico). Both wanted a more positive presentation of the idea of celibacy, so that it would not be presented to students only as a renunciation, something that had to be agreed to primarily as a step before ordination.

Much attention was given the problem of the correct intellectual formation of the priest. The issue was rather clearly joined between, on the one hand, the advocates of a more open attitude, represented by the text of the propositions, and those who favored strict adherence to the existing scholastic norms, on the other hand. A middle view was represented by Archbishop Hurley (Durban, South Africa), who agreed with Cardinal Suenens that the present manner of teaching philosophy in seminaries should be examined, but he thought that scholasticism, as such, could not be brushed aside. Some of its themes were "very essential for the Catholic mind." Nevertheless he was in favor of having students learn to develop their philosophical ideas in the light of man's growing knowledge and to express their ideas in modern language, so that a dialogue would be possible. One of the resolute defenders of the status quo, Cardinal Ruffini, was shocked that Thomas Aquinas was not mentioned in the section on philosophical studies and was named only "timidly" in connection with theology. Other men need not be ignored just because St. Thomas was given his proper place, he declared.

Cardinal Léger objected to the habit of calling scholastic theology "perennial" (*philosophia perennis*) and wanted the term dropped from Proposition 15 dealing with the curriculum of faculties and universities. He said that use of the adjective seemed to be contrary to the nature of philosophy itself, which should be concerned, according to St. Thomas, not with what authors had said, but with things in themselves. It was not for the Council to propose a particular philosophy but to lay down rules, in accordance with the requirements of faith, for the valid philosophical instruction of the students. It was disadvantageous to seem to impose scholastic philosophy, not only because there was really no such thing as "scholastic philosophy" *tout court,* there were various schools of scholastic philosophy; but also because it was unwise to give the impression that the Church was imposing scholastic philosophy on non-Occidental students, who had valid philosophical traditions of their own which they might prefer. The cardinal was glad that the schema did not "dwell ponderously on the teaching of St. Thomas" in Proposition 16, not, he maintained, because his works were to be avoided, but because it was advisable not to give any impression of exclusiveness. The important thing was to recommend not so much the doctrinal ideas of St. Thomas, as his scientific and spiritual approach which was to use the ideas of his day to illustrate and extol the Gospel.

Such liberalism was anathema to Archbishop Staffa, secretary of the Curial Congregation of Seminaries and Universities, a ruthless spokesman for the official line on Thomism. Speaking in the name of "bishops of both the West and East"—it would be interesting to know who the latter were—Staffa indignantly and categorically rejected the imputation of Cardinal Léger that St. Thomas was not all that the Thomists had claimed him to be. Dialogue with the world of today must be "steeped" in the philosophical and theological sciences, with St. Thomas as the leader. Progress in knowledge could not be made apart from truth. (Apparently, according to Staffa, Aquinas was synonymous with truth.) The teaching of St. Thomas should be preserved in seminaries, in accordance with papal encyclicals. After Staffa, the next most spirited defender of Thomism, the Curial Cardinal Bacci, had his say. He was troubled, he declared, by what he had heard several days before about the dethroning of St. Thomas from his primacy. He did not think that the Fathers wished to belittle St. Thomas, whom popes ever since the 13th century had praised so highly. If anyone dared to do this, he would be placing the Council not only above the pope, but *against* the pope—which no one among the Fathers would surely think of doing. On the other hand, he admitted that philosophy, like everything else progressed and needed perfection. Therefore those who defended the "perennial" or Thomistic philosophy today, did so with the knowledge that other philosophers were also approved by the Church and were not to be neglected. Other philosophers were to be studied, and if they taught anything that was new and more perfect, "if it corresponds to right reason, is to be proposed for the study of seminarians." Proposition 15 should certainly state that the "perennial philosophy" was to be held in the greatest honor by our seminarians, but it should be said that the works of other Doctors were not to be neglected, as long as error was separated from truth, so that philosophical studies would better correspond to the needs and mentality of modern men. The speech of Cardinal Bacci represented a backing down from the rather extreme statements of previous speakers, particularly those of Archbishop Staffa, regarding the exclusive role which Thomism was supposed to play in seminary instruction. However the arrogance of his insinuations did not escape his hearers.

As the last speaker, Bishop Reuss, summed up the general impression that the schema accomplished its purpose of stating general principles and he recommended a vote of Placet, with some *modi*, as a gift from the Council to rectors and students of seminaries. The official *relator*, Bishop Carraro, then summed up. By a vote of 2,076 to 41 the schema was easily accepted for immediate voting. Since the final voting on the several propositions produced no upsets, the text was sent back to commission to be revised in accordance with the wishes of the majority.

After Bishop Carraro had spoken, and before the Council went on to the next topic, on November 17th, the floor was given to one of the parish priests invited to be present at the Third Session, Father Marcos, of Madrid, Spain. Instead of being the conventional bow to the powers that be in gratitude for the privilege of being able to address the assembly, with a few truisms and platitudes thrown in, his speech turned out to be a highly articulate voicing of the desires of parish priests almost everywhere. He called for emphasis on the idea of a diocesan *presbyterium* in the schema on the priesthood, that is the notion that bishops were to govern with the advice of their parish clergy. More specifically, he wanted wider permission to be granted to parish priests to confirm, as clergy of the eastern rites were able to do, and for greater flexibility in the hearing of confessions, at least within the confines of one country.

DEBATE ON CHRISTIAN EDUCATION

On Tuesday, Wednesday and Thursday, November 17–19, the Council took up the very short schema in the form of propositions, entitled "Declaration on Christian Education." The original document had been a full-fledged schema "On Catholic Schools," but the Coordinating Commission had ordered this shortened to a series of propositions along with other texts. When the propositions were distributed to the Fathers, in May 1964, they met with considerable criticism, so in the course of the summer the Commission on Seminaries revised them and changed the name to the present title, as more representative of the contents of the document.

The propositions were introduced by Bishop Daem (Antwerp, Belgium), a member of the commission. Their purpose was to state some of the broad principles governing the subject, not to go into too much detail. Consequently the commission proposed, in the revised Preface, that a post-conciliar commission be set up to study all problems in greater depth.

The debate, punctuated by the many exciting events and interruptions of the final days of the Session, quickly showed that there was a general consensus among the bishops in favor of retaining the present draft as a basis for revision. The text was evidence of the progress that could be made when conciliar commissions paid attention to what the bishops really wanted, instead of attempting to impose on them ideas favored by the Curial faction, as some commissions had done. The main differences which emerged were between the American and Continental bishops. While the former urged immediate acceptance with a minimum of discussion, the latter were more critical in their approval of the text and wanted numerous points to be aired for the benefit of the commission. Cardinal Léger (Montreal) seemed to voice the Continental view when he said: "We should not approve too hastily what will be the *Magna Carta* of Christian Education." By contrast, Archbishop Cody (New Orleans), speaking in the name of most American bishops and as president of the National Catholic Education Association, declared: "The Council cannot refuse to approve the Declaration, because it is closely connected with other schemata already approved. Moreover the failure of the Council to make a pronouncement on Catholic education would deeply offend countless lay Catholics who, often with great sacrifice, support the Church in its education work." Cardinal Ritter, Cardinal Spellman, and Bishop Malone (auxiliary bishop of Youngstown, Ohio), also gave it their wholehearted approval. About the only concrete improvement suggested by the American bishops was the proposal of Cardinal Spellman for an additional paragraph stressing the right of parents to be free to choose the school of their choice for their children and for the state, in due measure, to provide for the support of such schools. Since it was a commonly recognized principle in Europe, and elsewhere in the world, for the state to support private schools—in England, for example, all Catholic children in parochial schools received some kind of support from the government—the suggestion was not likely to meet with any opposition from that quarter, but some questioned whether it was altogether wise and expedient, from the viewpoint of American politics, to inject into the conciliar debate an issue that was still so highly controversial in the United States. Would the original wording of the schema not have sufficed?

Not all comments were so entirely favorable, however. Bishop Elchinger (Strasbourg) noted that the present text had been drawn up, essentially, before account could be taken of the important schemata discussed in the Third Session and that it therefore needed a complete overhauling. In the process of revision he wanted a more ecumenical spirit introduced, more emphasis placed on the spiritual or religious side of teaching as a witnessing to the Christian life, and a clearer delineation of the responsibilities of parents. Archbishop Gouyon (Rennes) found the text deficient in spelling out the specific end of Christian education, namely the development of a deep personal faith. Cardinal Léger found that it said nothing about the coordination of Catholic universities. He proposed that the main function of the Congregation in charge of studies in Rome should be to promote such coordination, by the convocation of scientific congresses and by urging Catholic universities to pay greater attention to urgent problems confronting Catholic doctrinal and scientific life. (His hearers were well aware that the Congregation of Seminaries and Universities had consistently done the very opposite.) The schema should proclaim, prudently but clearly, the freedom of investigation which ought to prevail in all the sacred sciences, particularly in the liturgical, biblical and ecumenical fields.

A rather discouraging view of Catholic education was painted by Bishop Henriquez Jimenez (Caracas, Venezuela), who questioned whether the schema had really come to grips with the basic problem of coping with education on a mass scale. Most Venezuelan children were in public schools. The number of Catholic children was steadily increasing, but there was a great disparity between the number and those who could expect to receive a Catholic education. "Our schools," he said, "are lovely 'enclosed gardens' cultivated with much loving care, but whose fruits for the evangelization of the world seem to grow less with each passing day." The absence of the Church from the public school was a pressing problem. No attempt had been made to train Catholic teachers for such schools. The same anxieties were expressed by Bishop Muñoz-Vega (Quito, Ecuador).

Five bishops from Nigeria, one from Vietnam, and one from Indonesia, developed the idea of the close connection between schools and missionary work. After launching into a discourse on the meaning of the term "Catholic universities," the Master General of the Dominicans, Father Fernandez, was soon treating the Fathers to a sermon on St. Thomas as "the Master to be imitated"—the text spoke of him as "the Master who reconciled faith and reason, both divine and human science" —going on at length about the unique role of Thomism and throwing out such far-fetched statements as, "The authority of St. Thomas is that of the magisterium of the Church," and "It is not sufficient to regard Thomas as a model of study, for his teaching is in itself objectively true for all times. The Master cannot be separated from his teaching," and

400

similar remarks, until he was interrupted by the moderator, who was applauded for delivering the Fathers from this tirade.

The *relator,* Bishop Daem, then summed up. He said that most observations would be incorporated in the text and pleaded for acceptance. He proposed that the post-conciliar commission provided for in the text should draw up a fuller schema which would serve as a basis for action by episcopal conferences. The voting being favorable, the document was sent back to commission to be revised as the *relator* had requested.

THE MARRIAGE 'VOTUM'

At noon, on Thursday, November 19, 1964 (called "Black Thursday" because of the hubbub over the postponement of the vote on Religious Liberty), the Council, after the turmoil had somewhat died down, took up the last of the short texts to be considered, the *votum* or recommendations on the Sacrament of Marriage, so-called, because expressed in the form of a proposal by the Council of points to be considered in a forthcoming revision of the Code of Canon Law. The document had started out as a full treatment of all the sacraments, but had gradually been narrowed down to the present 11 Propositions dealing with the sacrament of marriage from a strictly canonical and practical point of view.

The principal changes proposed by the *votum* were: 1) the suppression of the so-called minor impediments to marriage, e.g. consanguinity, etc.; 2) a less rigid canonical procedure for mixed marriages, in the spirit of the decree on Ecumenism, by distinguishing more clearly between different types of mixed marriages, by doing away with regulations which had the effect of seeming to penalize such marriages (nuptial mass, etc.), by recognizing as valid, though illicit, such marriages celebrated before a non-Catholic minister and by giving the bishop authority to grant dispensations in this matter, and by no longer requiring the non-Catholic partner to make the usual marriage promises (*cautiones*) to bring up any children as Catholics; and 3) a revision of the canonical form for marriage, which normally required the marriage to be celebrated in the presence of a Catholic priest.

There were two main purposes behind the new proposals: to simplify marriage legislation so far as Catholics were concerned; and to remove any basis, to the extent that this was possible and permissible, for the charge of non-Catholics that the Church discriminated against baptized non-Catholics and treated them as second-class Christians by requiring them to participate in ceremonies and agree to promises which violated their consciences.

The text was introduced by Cardinal Aloisi Masella, president of the conciliar Commission on the Discipline of the Sacraments, and by Bishop Schneider (Bamberg, Germany), the official *relator,* who read the report of the commission.

Most of the debate touched on Proposition 5, on Mixed Marriages, which, in translation, read as follows:

5. In order that canon law may show greater respect, and in a more opportune way, for the condition of persons, in accordance with the decrees on religious liberty and ecumenism, it is desirable above all to make a clear distinction between the regulations governing the marriage of a Catholic partner with a baptized non-Catholic, and the marriage of a Catholic partner with an unbaptized person. Consequently the following points are to be observed:

a) In all mixed marriages, when asking for a dispensation from the diriment impediment, the Catholic partner is to be seriously enjoined and must sincerely promise that he or she will see that all children will be baptized and brought up as Catholics, to the extent that he or she can (*in quantum poterit*).

With regard to the promise, which is to be made by the Catholic partner alone, the non-Catholic partner is to be informed about this at a suitable time and his or her consent obtained that he or she is not opposed to it.

The non-Catholic partner must also be informed about the ends and nature of marriage, and neither partner must have any reservations about this matter.

b) Mixed marriages must be contracted according to the canonical form, but if for grave reasons this is impossible, in order that a marriage involving a true matrimonial consent may not be lacking in validity, the ordinary shall have power to dispense from the canonical form.

c) Mixed marriages between two baptized persons shall no longer be celebrated in the sacristy but during mass. Also mixed marriages between a Catholic partner and an unbaptized partner may be celebrated in church during mass.

d) The excommunication required by present canon law against those who have contracted a marriage before a non-Catholic minister is abrogated.

All the speakers were favorable to the idea that existing marriage legislation needed modernization, and most of them approved of the proposals in the text. However, there was less enthusiasm for the latter in the concrete, among the American, Irish, British and Australian prelates than among their European confrères. Cardinal Ritter was the exception. He welcomed the document as a prudent measure, pointing particularly to its recommendations regarding the canonical form, which avoided the extreme of abolishing all requirements and that of maintaining an inflexible attitude toward the status quo. Archbishop Heenan of Westminster, while disagreeing with the text on some matters, praised it as containing many excellent points and thanked the commission for its work, saying that it deserved to be "written in letters of gold." He also added a word of praise for the work of the *periti,* thus compensating for the rather disparaging remarks with regard to them which he made in his speech on October 22nd. The archbishop seemed to have a knack for allowing his enthusiasms to get out of hand, however. He went on to say that he thought mixed marriages in the sacristy were more like interments than marriages. Why should the organ not be played on such occasions? "The chief difficulty about mixed marriages concerns the religious upbringing of the children," he said. "In our country, by far the majority of mixed marriages take place with non-Catholic partners who are only rarely found to be active members of any religious community. For this reason the promises to bring up the children as Catholics rarely caused any difficulty, and so I think it would be better to leave the promises by the partners as the normal rule. When a mixed marriage takes place between a Catholic and a practicing Protestant, special rules could be provided." His assumption that the requirement of written pledges was "in no way against the conscience of a non-Catholic," because "other Christian Churches do not claim to be the one true Church, whereas Catholics do" did not go down at all well with non-Catholic church leaders and resulted in several sharp statements by the Archbishop of Canterbury and other churchmen, who pointed out that it was easy assumptions of this kind on the part of Catholic prelates that were at the root of Catholic-Protestant differences about Catholic marriage legislation, which the *votum* was intended to correct. Archbishop Heenan was also for eliminating the saving clause, "to the extent that he or she can," because it seemed to imply that the Catholic was not bound by the promises if they became hard to fulfill; it was tantamount to the Church's saying: "It is not necessary to put up any fight for your children. For the sake of peace, go ahead and let them abandon the faith." He appeared more liberal as regards ceremony, seeing no objection if the bride and bridegroom wanted to go and receive a blessing in a non-Catholic church after the Catholic marriage.

Cardinal Gilroy proposed that the whole matter of canonical form needed study and that it would be unwise to approve what the schema recommended before this had been done. He was opposed to granting the ordinary the authority to dispense, as called for in 5b. "This cannot be done without danger of scandal or indifferentism." In the name of Cardinal Spellman, who had departed for New York, Bishop Fearns, one of the auxiliary bishops of New York, read the cardinal's speech. He also said that he was speaking in the name of more than 100 American bishops. The intention of improving marriage legislation was declared to be "a cause for joy," but the cardinal warned against proposing changes that might be beneficial for some countries, but would "cause serious spiritual harm to our country," because of the special conditions obtaining in countries with a pluralistic religious society. He demanded time for consultation with pastors before any approval was given to the present recommendations. The vague expression "grave reasons" might have the effect of practically abolishing the form for mixed marriages and eliminating any opportunity for spiritual guidance and gaining assurances that the children would be brought up as Catholics. If there were territories where such dispensations were necessary, application could be made to the Holy See. The text ignored the great accomplishment of the present legislation regarding the education of children; it did not provide for the solution of marriage problems in the foreseeable future; and it dangerously diminished the responsibility of pastors. Archbishop Krol was even more specific, along the same lines. He demanded that the pre-nuptial written promises be preserved, with the ordinary being empowered to make dispensations in the case of non-Catholics "of deep religious convictions and strong church affiliations." With regard to dispensations from the canonical form for mixed marriages, he noted that "experience teaches that when the availability of a dispensation becomes known, the requests for such invitations increase." He also thought that "grave reasons" would be used to satisfy the whims of the partners and that the whole matter would become a scandal to the faithful.

A problem of concern to the French hierarchy because of the large number of nominal Catholics in France, but also found elsewhere, was raised by Bishop Renard (Versailles). It was whether to allow religious marriages in the case of two baptized persons who had no faith any longer, and who merely regarded the ceremony as a desirable formality not as a sacrament. Some bishops and pastors refused to allow such marriages to be celebrated because the partners did not have the proper dispositions; others were more tolerant, recalling the statements of the popes about the natural right of marriage. The norms proposed by the present text did not cover this point. He suggested one solution might be to allow such persons to pronounce their vows before the pastor and witnesses without any religious ceremony.

The debate was ended on Friday, November 20, 1964 because of the lateness of the hour without any summation by the official *relator*. The Council was asked to vote on the following motion, proposed in accordance with an earlier recommendation of Cardinal Döpfner in the course of the debate: "Does it please the Fathers to send the propositions on the sacrament of marriage, together with the observations of the Fathers, to the Supreme Pontiff, so that he may take appropriate action in this regard?" By a vote of 1,592 to 426 the matter was left in the hands of the Holy Father, who was expected to issue a Motu Proprio at a suitable time putting into effect some, at least, of the recommendations without waiting for the final revision of the Code of Canon Law. The outcome was not entirely satisfactory to some of the bishops, especially the Americans, because it closed the door to any further discussion of the matter in the Council. Motu Proprios were not debated; they were accepted and obeyed.

NOVEMBER CRISIS OVER COLLEGIALITY

As the Council entered its next to last week on November 9th, the atmosphere of cautious optimism accompanying the debate on Schema 13 changed perceptibly to one of great uncertainty, if not downright gloom, as the evidence mounted that almost all the texts destined to be proclaimed on the final day, less than two weeks away, were in some kind of trouble. Fortunately Ecumenism was in the hands of the bishops and the voting would take place during the week on the Secretariat's handling of the *modi* to each chapter, the last stage before a final (and largely formal) vote approving the schema as a whole. The prospects were good that this text would go through smoothly. But nothing else seemed to be in such good shape.

It was known that the work of revising the two declarations, on Non-Christians and Religious Liberty, had been completed by the Secretariat, but their present whereabouts was something of a mystery. They were said to be variously in the hands of the Secretariat, of the Theological Commission, about to go to the printer, or held up for unknown reasons. It was learned in the course of the week, however, that at a meeting of the Theological Commission on Monday, November 9th, the Declaration on Religious Liberty had been voted on; of the 28 members present, 12 voted Placet, 6 Non placet, and 9 Placet iuxta modum, and 1 abstention. Since the Iuxta modum votes were considered positive, the declaration was carried and it was sent to the printer on Wednesday. The Declaration on the Jews and Non-Christians was to be sent to the printer on Friday or Saturday, according to word from a member of the Secretariat at the Bishops' Press Panel on Thursday. This reassuring news seemed to mean that both would be distributed and might possibly be voted on during the final week.

The schema on Divine Revelation, it was thought, would probably not be ready in time for final voting and promulgation was therefore out of the question, because so much of the time of the Theological Commission had been taken up with work on the amendments to *De Ecclesia*. But this report turned out to be slightly erroneous. Revelation was distributed to the Fathers shortly before the end of the Session, but there was not time for a vote. Likewise the revised schema on the Pastoral Office of Bishops could hardly be readied, in view of the large number of Iuxta modum votes cast on the first two chapters, all of which had to be examined and considered. The prospects for the propositions on the Oriental Churches were brighter. Final promulgation seemed possible, but the text was not yet ready.

The chief worry was over the fate of the remainder of *De Ecclesia* (Chapters III–VIII), which was being held up because of a mysterious disagreement over Chapter III—the heart of the schema—on collegiality. The difficulty was said to be not so much over the text itself, as over the terms of an interpretation, or explanation, of collegiality which the pope was insisting on.

The voting on the three chapters of Ecumenism took place on November 10th, 11th and 14th. The chapters were all passed with overwhelming majorities. By Saturday it was apparent that there would be at least one document to proclaim on the final day.

The Secretariat's firmness in rejecting most of the proposed amendments deserved to be noted. Since most of these were offered by the opposition, the action of the assembly in approving the Secretariat's work amounted to a defeat for the minority. Of the 217 *modi* proposed on Chapter I, only 13 were accepted by the Secretariat. Of the 59 *modi* proposed on Chapter II, only 5 were accepted. And of the 129 *modi* proposed on Chapter III, only 11 were retained. Those accepted related only to minor points. Had the amendments offered by the minority been accepted, they would have had the effect of modifying the whole tenor of the document. But the minority did not acknowledge defeat, as we shall see.

Would *De Ecclesia* fare as well? Would the Theological Commission prove as firm in rejecting the substantial changes to Chapter III which the minority had proposed and, if they yielded to pressure, would the Council have the courage to reject the Commission's handling of the *modi* and so bury the Constitution on the Church for the Third Session, possibly causing a break-up of the Council itself?

Part of the answer came on Saturday, November 14th, when the Fathers and *periti* were handed a fat booklet containing the *modi* to Chapters III–VIII of *De Ecclesia* together with the Commission's comments on each one. A hasty perusal showed that the text of Chapter III had not been substantially tampered with, though some changes had been introduced and there was now prefixed to Chapter III an Explanatory Note or *Nota Explicativa Praevia,* elucidating certain expressions and defining the sense in which collegiality was to be understood.

The Note was solemnly read in the council on Monday morning, November 16th, by the secretary general, Archbishop Felici, and printed copies of it along with certain other important remarks made by him at the same time (see below) were distributed to the Fathers. In his customary authoritarian vein, the archbishop admonished the Fathers "to

406

study it carefully, because it is sometimes difficult to understand," referring to the highly technical and involved language of the Note. He made it clear that the votes on the following day were to be cast in the light of this authoritative interpretation. On Thursday, November 19th, before the vote on *De Ecclesia* as a whole, he repeated this declaration, insisting that even though the Note was not to be found in the booklet containing the final, amended version of the schema, which the bishops had in their hands, it was nevertheless normative and "formed part of the official acts of the Council." The formal vote on the last day must also be governed by this interpretation.

Who was the author of the Note? By whose authority was it communicated to the Fathers? The Note was presented as if it came from the Theological Commission, but considering the circumstances in which it was made known, the fact that it was signed by Archbishop Felici and not by Cardinal Ottaviani (as would have been the case if it had really been issued under the authority of the Theological Commission), as well as the fact that the secretary general failed to mention in whose name he was acting (he normally always stated whether his announcements were made on behalf of the Council presidents or moderators, if such were the case), it was obvious that the Note had come from the pope himself and was being communicated to the Council on his authority, although the pope did not wish to acknowledge the fact openly, preferring to remain anonymous behind the vague Curial phrase "superior authority." It would have been impossible for the Theological Commission to communicate a normative interpretation of this kind to the assembly, because it was merely one of several organs of the Council and was not "superior" with respect to the others. Moreover the secretary general read the communication to the whole Council, the presidents, moderators and everybody, so that there could hardly be any doubt as to the document's provenance.

Why did Pope Paul prefer to act in this apparently paradoxical way? The reason could only be that he did not wish to appear to be intervening in the course of the Council directly, while at the same time it was made perfectly clear that that was precisely what he was doing. The Note was intended as a final effort on his part to win over the coterie of bishops and experts, belonging to the minority, who had resolutely and ceaselessly opposed the doctrine of collegiality ever since the Second Session. The opposition had crystallized then over the question of whether to put the famous Five propositions proposed by the moderators to a vote. It had been insistently contended by the group, consisting of bishops from Latin countries, southern Italy, Spain, Brazil and Latin America, for the most part, as well as well known Roman theologians such as Father Bertrams, S.J. (Gregorian University) and Curial officials like Archbishop Staffa, secretary of the Congregation of Seminaries, that the motion of the moderators was illegal. When the vote finally was held anyway, on September 30, 1963, they contended that the results, so overwhelmingly favorable to the thesis of collegiality, were both invalid and contrary to sound doctrine. The doctrine of episcopal collegiality was, in their opinion, not only unhistorical but gravely injurious to the rights and prerogatives of the Roman pontiff as defined at Vatican Council I. Archbishop Staffa, in particular, spared no effort in making the objections of the group known to all and sundry through lectures, through booklets (mimeographed copies of a treatise in English denouncing collegiality were distributed to all the American bishops in Rome at the start of the Third Session), through visits (on a visit to the United States in the summer of 1964 he thought that he had won a convert in Cardinal Cushing), and in every other conceivable way.

Despite their repeated questioning of the vote of September 30, 1963, the Theological Commission took the results of the vote into account. Subcommission No. 5 (consisting of Archbishop Parente, Archbishop Florit, Bishop Schroeffer, Bishop Henriquez Jimenez, and Bishop Heuschen, together with a large number of *periti* including Bishop Colombo, Father Rahner, Father Gagnebet, Father Ratzinger, Monsignor Thils, etc.) examined the interventions relating to this point and drew up a revised text of Chapter III that was approved by the Theological Commission as a whole on March 6, 1964. Since doubts were still being raised about the doctrine as expressed in the revised text, the pope undertook to examine Chapter III himself. On May 19, 1964, the secretary general transmitted the pope's suggestions to the Theological Commission in a letter with the request that the Commission again examine Chapter III in their light. Since the text had already been approved nearly unanimously by the Commission, the pope noted, the purpose of his suggestions was merely to eliminate any possible misunderstandings and ambiguities.

The Commission then studied the pope's suggestions and adopted most of them at a meeting on June 5, 1964. From then on Pope Paul spared no efforts to win over the minority to acceptance of the idea of collegiality. His statement, opening the Third Session on September 14, 1964, that the principal task of the Session was to formulate a doctrine of collegiality, was chiefly, though not exclusively, directed at them. The permission granted to Bishop Franič, also a member of the group, representing the minority on the Theological Commission, to present a kind of "minority report" on September 21, 1964, was also part of the pope's strategy, in the hope that an impression could be made on them by allowing the fullest possible expression for their views. So was the idea of having Archbishop Parente, the majority spokesman for collegiality, speak last and recommend acceptance of the doctrine as containing nothing contrary to sound teaching.

The tactics of this small group of opponents at the Third Session were principally two: 1) to prevent at all costs a vote on Chapter III, insisting instead that more time was needed for revision and seeing to it that in the course of the revision the dangerous doctrine of collegiality was watered down to an innocuous statement on which all could agree; 2) when this failed and it became apparent how large a majority favored collegiality as a result of the vote on September 30, 1964, they began to urge a revision of at least certain phrases or passages that would allow greater latitude in accepting or rejecting the doctrine, in spite of the fact that the Council had already decided affirmatively on the question. They claimed that collegiality was a vague notion not yet ready for definition; that it was not solidly based on Scripture, tradition or history; and that dire consequences could be expected to follow if a doctrine were proclaimed that was opposed to Vatican Council I—the Church would have to admit that it had been wrong for centuries, the bishops would not stop until they had completely rejected the authority of the Roman pontiff, and other extravagances of this sort.

The majority committed the mistake of limiting the number of their *modi* to Chapter III, on September 30th, with a view to facilitating the work of the Theological Commission and not holding up the document any longer than was necessary. They agreed to have their suggestions submitted by cardinals, patriarchs and prominent bishops in order to lend them greater weight. Most of their modifications related to removing the excessive emphasis on the papal primacy and eliminating certain ambiguities (for example, the exact status of councils like the Council of Constance that had removed three popes in order to elect a legitimate pope, and the validity of the acts performed by the present Orthodox clergy). They received an assurance that their wishes would be met, at least in principle. The minority, for its part, submitted all the *modi* that they could, each member submitting at least one. (Many of the recommendations overlapped and were therefore counted as a single recommendation.) The result was that the majority seemed to have offered relatively few amendments, whereas the minority loomed disproportionately large because of numbers.

Of the 242 amendments to Chapter III recorded by the Commission, 31 were accepted for inclusion in the text, and of these 10 related to collegiality. Among this group there were none that altered the nature of collegiality in any essential way, but there were some that further strengthened the already heavy emphasis on the pope's primacy. However, while the majority received no satisfaction on its demands for improving the text at all, the minority were awarded, in addition to a few slight alterations in the text, the bonus of the Explanatory Note.

The abstemious and overly cautious attitude of the majority seemed to have proved once again the futility, in Rome, of relying on good dispositions or vague assurances and not taking appropriate massive action at the proper time.

When it became apparent to the minority—through an extraordinary indulgence on the pope's part they were kept abreast of the examination of the *modi* at all stages, to eliminate any possibility of a charge that anything had been done behind their backs—that the Commission would not accept their most important requests, they literally besieged the pope with entreaties that he act on his own authority to see that they received satisfaction. The pope was even said to have recommended to the Theological Commission not to be too strict in its interpretation of the rules and reconsider amendments relating to points already approved by the Council, so that its reason for having rejected the amendments could be stated fully in its report.

The result of so many entreaties was that the pope ordered the Theological Commission to prepare the Explanatory Note. There can be no doubt that this was "requested, willed, revised, reviewed and approved" by the pope himself, as Father G. Caprile, S.J., put it.* It also seems clear that the Theological Commission objected to the suggestion for a Note on principle, because such a document would tend to cast doubt on the integrity of the doctrine expressed in the text rather than throw light on it, but they eventually bowed to pressure. Two mysterious plenary meetings of the Commission toward the first of November, from which all the *periti* were excluded, may have had something to do with the controversy. In any case, Father Caprile's assurance that relations between the pope and the Commission were always conducted on an absolutely serene level, far removed from any bickering or haggling, was not very convincing in the light of the numerous "comings and goings" between the Fourth floor and the Commission that were observed about this time. However that may be, on November 10, 1964, Cardinal Cicognani wrote a letter to Cardinal Ottaviani—was this done only after the Theological Commission had balked at the suggestion of a Note?—informing the head of the Theological Commission that because the pope was obliged to make his own and promulgate the Constitution on the Church, he wanted an Explanatory Note added to it dealing with the meaning and purport of the amendments. The Commission was to work out an explanation in such a way as to relieve the doubts of the minority and achieve a unanimous and sincere acceptance of the schema. He particularly asked the point to be made that the collegiality of the bishops depended on the *consent* of the Roman pontiff for its exercise. Enclosed with the letter was a list of the points still contested by the minority

---

* *L'Osservatore Romano*, February 20, 1965 and *La Civiltà Cattolica*, March 1, 1965.

410

together with a memorandum from Father Bertrams, S.J., on the difficulties in question. The Note was to be drafted in accordance with the written and oral communications of the Fathers and the suggestions offered at different times by the pope himself.

The Note dealt with four points:

1. The term "college" as used in the text, was not to be understood in a strictly juridical sense as implying a body of equals, who delegated their powers to a president (= Roman law meaning of *collegium*). It was used in a looser, Christian, *sui generis* sense and that was why other terms such as "stable body," "body," and "order" were also employed.

2. An important distinction was made between the *powers* which a bishop received by the sacrament of consecration (of teaching, sanctifying and governing) and the *exercise* of these powers, the latter being by its nature a juridical determination. Consecration made a bishop a bishop, but he could exercise authority in the Church only "according to norms approved by the supreme authority" and in accordance with the age-old requirements for "hierarchical communion with the head and members of the Church," as the Constitution stated. The use of the term "hierarchical *communion*," the latter word especially, was an important concession to Eastern theology and also to Western theologians of collegiality. However, the Note added nothing to what the text of the Constitution already stated on this whole point.

3. Some had refused to acknowledge that the episcopal college had "full" authority over the Church. But this would be tantamount to denying the pope's plenitude of power, because the college could not exist without him since he was *always its head*. As the Note put it: "This must be admitted so that the full power of the Roman pontiff will not be placed in contention." The term "college" must always be understood as meaning the bishops *with* the pope, never without him. However, the pope's headship of the college did not preclude acting on his own, without every single act of his being strictly collegial in character, or as the Note put it: "whether personally or collegially."

4. The episcopal college always existed, but it did not always act in a strictly collegial manner. In fact, it acted in such a manner only occasionally or at intervals, and always with the consent of its head, who was not outside but formed part of the episcopal collegial body. If the bishops acted independently of the pope, they would not be acting as a college.

A final paragraph, added at the end, introduced simply by the words *Nota Bene,* declared that it was not the intention of the commission to go into the question of the liceity and validity of the power "which is in fact exercised by the separated Eastern brethren." This was one of the points that the majority wanted clarified. By stating that "hierarchical communion" with the head of the Church was necessary for the validity of episcopal acts, the text of the Constitution left the door open to the contention that Orthodox orders and sacraments might be invalid—a thesis maintained by a few recent Catholic theologians (but this of course would contradict the decree on Ecumenism calling for a limited amount of intercommunion and statements by Pope Paul clearly recognizing the legitimacy of the Orthodox hierarchy and the validity of their sacramental acts). By leaving the door open, the Note failed to remove this embarrassing ambiguity, and in fact drew attention to it.

One of the cardinals belonging to the minority, it seems, had objected to the way in which the September 30th vote on Chapter III had been conducted, by dividing the text into two parts and voting on each part separately. He maintained that this was contrary to the rules in that it served to limit the number of *modi* which could be submitted on the chapter as a whole, thus compelling those who submitted their *modi* to confine them to particular parts. As things turned out, however, the minority came out better on the *modi* than the majority who were so careful. In the name of the moderators and presidents, Archbishop Felici declared that "these difficulties have been most carefully examined by the competent authority and they are certain that the rules of the Council have been followed scrupulously."

A second objection related to doubts raised about the exact theological significance of the Constitution on the Church. The reply of the Theological Commission was that only those matters could be regarded as being formally defined *de fide* (or infallibly in the most solemn way), which were expressly declared to be so defined; all other doctrinal statements were to be "received and embraced by each and all of the faithful as the doctrine of the supreme magisterium of the Church." Since neither the Constitution as a whole nor Chapter III on collegiality were intended as solemn definitions in the ultimate sense of the term, unlike the definition of the papal primacy and infallibility by Vatican Council I in 1870, the present text was intended as a solemn statement but not an infallible pronouncement or *de fide* definition.

After receiving all these assurances and explanations, and weighing their consciences, the Fathers voted on the Commission's handling of the *modi* to Chapters III–VIII of *De Ecclesia* on November 17th and 18th. On the crucial Chapter III there were only 46 Non placets; on the other chapters much fewer. It was apparent then that the minority opposition to collegiality had faded away. Word had been received, before the vote, from the leaders of that group (and from the pope himself, it was said) that the text was now satisfactory when interpreted in the light of the Explanatory Note. When the Constitution on the Church was voted as a whole on Thursday, the opposition had dwindled to 10, and in the final vote on Saturday, November 21st, it was only 5. Some of the opposing votes in these ballots unquestionably came from bishops displeased with the Explanatory Note, but the number was almost negligible even so.*

It may be asked, why the majority gave in so easily if it really thought that the doctrine of collegiality had been seriously compromised by additions to the text and the obscurely worded Note? There was much soul-searching over the weekend as to what course of action to follow. In the end the bishops and experts decided that rather than risk having no Constitution at all, it was better to put up with an imperfect text representing years of hard labor and not really substantially altered in any of its parts.† They found themselves caught in the same dilemma which had confronted the Council before, and would again face it in a day or two, namely whether to reject a series of emendations offered *en bloc* because a few were regarded as unsatisfactory, or approve the lot which was held to be satisfactory as a whole. In voting on Chapter I of the schema on the Pastoral Office of Bishops on November 4th, the bishops had swamped the commission with *modi* because of their displeasure over the way in which collegiality seemed to be downgraded, as compared to its treatment in *De Ecclesia,* and they "rejected" Chapter II of the same schema the following day because of dissatisfaction over other emendations, but the circumstances were different. They were voting then Iuxta modum, at a time when revision was still possible. Here the choice was merely Placet or Non placet and the consequences of rejection were incalculable. What was astounding was not so much the fact that the bishops accepted an imperfect text, as the decision of the authorities to require them to vote *en bloc* on such a large number of controversial emendations, at such a late date. Again this seems to have been but another instance of the wishes of

* If it was true that the doctrine of collegiality was not altered in any essential way either by the Explanatory Note or the last-minute changes in the text, then there was a real capitulation on the part of its opponents. One of them, the Brazilian Archbishop de Proença-Sigaud, in a circular distributed on November 2nd, declared categorically: "Collegiality has no basis either in the Bible, in tradition, or in the history of the Church . . . It would give rise to a lack of discipline in the Church, whether with respect to the bishops and the pope, or priests and bishops . . . We have an example of the lack of obedience that would inevitably follow in the recent letter of the 17 cardinals to the pope regarding the declaration on religious liberty. Bishops would be subjected to episcopal conferences, that is a collective authority, the worst kind there is . . ." In a circular distributed the day of the fateful vote, on November 17th, the same bishop wrote: "The difficulties which we had regarding the doctrine of Chapter III have been dissipated by the Explanatory Note [and the announcements of Archbishop Felici] and the anxiety of our consciences has now been laid to rest . . . The Fathers of our group will vote placet and we suggest that all others do likewise in order to realize a moral unanimity which will greatly please the Holy Father." ICI, December 1, 1964, pp. 11–12.

† In a masterful exposition, Father Charles Davis attempted to explain at the Bishops' Press Panel what the Explanatory Note meant and why it was thought to be theologically acceptable (November 16, 1964).

the majority being rather thoughtlessly sacrificed to the need for conciliating the minority.

The dwindling of the opposition to collegiality from less than 300 to something like half of the 46 votes recorded on November 17 was the tangible reward which the pope reaped for repeated efforts on his part for over a year to reduce the opposition to the vanishing point,* and his much discussed remark on November 21, 1964 declaring that "nothing in traditional doctrine is really changed," was probably intended more as a final gesture to this same minority than as a blanket statement rejecting the notion of doctrinal change as such, for the decrees themselves were evidence that there had been much change.

The question might well be raised, however, whether it was really worth all the trouble to achieve a quasi-unanimity on this point, particularly when the doctrine of collegiality, as finally defined by the Council, was expressly declared to be something less than infallible? And whether the amount of time involved in producing this quasi-unanimity could not have been better spent on expediting the work of the Second and Third Sessions? And finally, whether it was really such a good idea, after all, to achieve quasi-unanimity, if this had to be done at too high a cost, through the promulgation of a needlessly unbalanced disfigured document accompanied by a tortuous, ambiguous, over-subtle explanation of an explanation? In his extreme anxiety to conciliate an unimportant minority, Pope Paul seemed to have forgotten that he might be doing less than justice to the majority.†

What consoled the majority and undoubtedly caused many of them to vote favorably on the Constitution was that, despite a disfiguring over-emphasis on the popes' primacy, introduced to satisfy the qualms of the minority, and some other imperfections, the Constitution on the Church still appeared to safeguard an essential point by repudiating the theory, widely held by Catholic theologians and canonists, that all jurisdiction in the Church came from the pope as from its "source," a doctrine which, if pressed to extremes would make of the bishops merely the pope's vicars and rule out any effective collegiality. This doctrine had been the chief weapon in the arsenal of those who had exalted the authority of the pope in the past at the expense of the collegiality of the bishops. The new text expressly declared that bishops were not "to be regarded as vicars of the Roman pontiffs," and both the Constitution and the Explanatory Note (seemed to) speak only of a regulation of the exercise of episcopal jurisdiction by the pope, not of the pope as being the "source" of that jurisdiction. References were made to the pope as the "visible source and founda-

* The Pope sent a letter to Cardinal Ottaviani on November 13, 1964, thanking him for the part played by the Theological Commission in the preparation of the Constitution on the Church.

† Père R. Rouquette, in *Études,* Jan. 1965, p. 116.

tion of unity and faith and communion," but this was not the same thing as saying that he was the source of episcopal jurisdiction. To put it simply, the bishops possessed through their consecration, all the powers needed for the exercise of their office, but they might not exercise these powers without leave from the pope (= *potestas expedita*). The distinction between episcopal *munera* and *potestates,* which the Note sought to develop (apparently an idea of Father Bertrams'), did not seem to have any real ontological basis, any more than the well known distinction between "order" and "jurisdiction," which Archbishop Parente declared, on the Council floor and later in an article in *L'Osservatore Romano* (December 19, 1964), was not ancient at all, but a distinction introduced "through the excessive influence of law on theology, which gradually caused the power of jurisdiction to be torn from the power of order, and the thesis to be maintained that the former power came to a bishop by means of an extrinsic grant on the part of the pope, whereas the latter power came to him from his consecration." Parente continued: "The Council has now returned to a more primitive conception and asserts that the bishop receives, by his consecration, not only the power of order, but also, at least radically, that of jurisdiction which, however, by its very nature cannot be exercised by any organ in the Church except in communion with the hierarchy and especially with the pope, who is empowered to regulate the functioning of the organ for the good of the Church."

RELIGIOUS LIBERTY AGAIN POSTPONED

On Tuesday of the last week, the long awaited Declaration on Religious Liberty made its appearance and it was announced that there would be a vote Thursday, first a ballot by Placet or Non placet on the individual parts, this to be followed by a ballot on the text as a whole at which time Iuxta modum votes could be cast. The following day Wednesday, the Declaration on Jews and Non-Christians was also handed out, and it was announced that it would be voted on Friday according to the same pattern.

The appearance of these two key texts and the information that they would in fact be voted on before the end of the Session shifted attention away from the uneasiness felt by many with regard to the fate of collegiality.

Consequently, when Archbishop Felici announced toward the very end of the meeting on Wednesday, that the Council presidents and moderators had decided to heed a petition submitted to them requesting more time for consideration of the Declaration on Religious Liberty before voting on

415

it, by allowing a preliminary vote on Thursday (Placet or Non placet) on whether to proceed at once to the balloting already scheduled, there was some consternation, but the news was not altogether alarming because the majority were certain of enough votes to overcome this hurdle. The presidents and moderators had made this decision, Archbishop Felici explained, because the issue raised by the petition was so serious that they wanted the Fathers to decide it for themselves. The petition, which he also read, appealed to Art. 30 par. 2 of the rules which specified that adequate time must be allowed for considering the texts of schemata, and Art. 35 which allowed an "examination" of amended texts before they were voted. The new text of the Declaration on Religious Liberty had been so altered that it was virtually a new document, they claimed, and so should be handled in accordance with these provisions of the rules.* The petition was signed by about 200 prelates.

A word must be said about the revised Declaration on which the Fathers were being asked to vote. In the judgment of competent persons it was not the best of the many forms through which the document had gone since its presentation as one of the chapters of the decree on Ecumenism in November 1963. As revised by the Secretariat after the September 1964 debate, in the light of suggestions made by the mixed commission which the pope ordered to examine it in his letter of October 16th as well as by the Theological Commission, it made important concessions to the minority by noting the existence of a universal desire for religious liberty but without attempting to justify it theologically; by stressing, in an awkward way, the connection between the famous *Syllabus Errorum* of Pio Nono's days and the present text; and by attempting to justify a special claim to religious liberty on the part of the Catholic Church because of its sole possession of the truth. In an informative article in *America* (January 9, 1965), Father John Courtney Murray, S.J., one of the drafters, indicated that he was not unhappy about the fate of the text, and he hoped that, as a result of the delay, a better text might be produced for the Fourth Session. He especially hoped the new text would acknowledge more freely the "infringements of religious liberty by the Church in the past," according to a statement made at Union Theological Seminary (February 2, 1965).

Neither the minority nor the majority, therefore, were satisfied with it. But this was not really the primary issue. The minority were determined, as in the case of collegiality, to prevent the document from coming to a vote at all, if they possibly could, on the grounds that it was dangerous

* Art. 30 par. 2: "The schemata of decrees and canons, as well as all texts to be approved, must be distributed to the Fathers in such a way as to permit them adequate time to consider them, for their judgments and decide on their vote." Art. 35: "The general congregation, after hearing the report of the *relator,* shall examine the parts of every amended text one by one and then approve them or not."

for the Church to acknowledge the existence of religious liberty in any sense except that of bare "toleration." The majority were anxious for a vote, both in order to facilitate the work of further revision by allowing the Fathers to indicate their minds with regard to different points, and also because of the vital ecumenical implications of a vote. By persistently refusing to vote on religious liberty, the Council was creating the impression that it was somehow insincere with regard to the principles it claimed to be advocating in the decree on Ecumenism.

In order to get a vote, the Secretariat for Unity worked out a wording designed to attract as many positive votes as possible (from the opposition) with the idea of restoring the watered-down parts to full strength when the *modi* were considered in revision. To forestall action on the part of the opposition, it was deliberately decided to keep the text under cover until the last possible minute. Unfortunately this little maneuvre failed. The opposition got word of what was being done. At a meeting Monday evening, November 16th, consisting mainly of Italian and Spanish bishops (of the 80 Spanish prelates present only 25 signed, as was later disclosed by one of the Spanish bishops), the petition was drawn up and signed which Archbishop Felici read in the assembly on Wednesday. There were about 200 signatures. One of the leading instigators of this protest, as of other moves by the minority, was the Secretary of the Congregation of Seminaries, Archbishop Staffa.

An air of anxiety and uncertainty hung over the assembly as it resumed its labors on the morning of "Black Thursday." There was not only the disquieting announcement about a preliminary vote on Religious Liberty but, strangely, the lack of any word about when the decree on Ecumenism would be presented for a final vote, necessary before promulgation. Things were obviously not going as smoothly as could be expected, yet time was running out: only one more business day remained. The successful vote approving the Constitution on the Church as a whole brought forth cheers, which served to relieve the tension, but the secretary general's disappointing information about the decree on Ecumenism caused a resurgence of fears (see below). It was about ten minutes past eleven, while the Council was part way through its discussion of the propositions on Christian Education and was beginning to grow restless over when the promised vote on Religious Liberty would take place, that Archbishop Staffa was seen at the secretary general's side. The latter motioned him to Cardinal Tisserant, who as president of the board of Council presidents was sitting at the middle of their table directly behind the four moderators. Staffa and the cardinal exchanged words briefly, after which Tisserant was seen hastily consulting with the other presidents on either side of him. Cardinal Meyer, who was sitting at one end of the table, Cardinal Alfrink and Cardinal Frings, apparently either did not hear what Cardinal Tisserant was saying or did not grasp its meaning. Suddenly Tisserant rose, stopped the proceedings, and announced: "Several Fathers are of the opinion that not enough time has been allowed for an examination of the text on Religious Liberty, which appears to be an essentially new document. Therefore it has seemed best to the Council presidents, in conformity with the rules, not to proceed to a vote as announced. After the *relatio* on the declaration by Bishop de Smedt, there will be no vote. The Fathers can then examine the document at their leisure and send their observations to the Secretariat by January 31, 1965."

His words were at first greeted by a feeble burst of applause from the minority bishops, but this was at once drowned out by a wave of grumbling, protests, and commotion which spread throughout the hall. One would have to go back to one of the earlier church Councils, that of Trent, for example, when an enraged bishop pulled another's beard, to find a precedent for the scene of consternation, outrage, and disarray that took place on this memorable morning. The bishops felt cheated, betrayed, insulted, and humiliated. One bishop, not a progressive, said afterward: "We were treated like children!" By what authority had Cardinal Tisserant made his announcement, the Fathers asked? How can *they*—meaning either the secretariat or the pope—treat the Council in this way! The Council was transformed into a beehive, as bishops swarmed from their places. Two of the four moderators and seven of the ten presidents got up from their seats and joined groups milling around the confession of St. Peter's. Nobody was paying the slightest attention to the remaining speakers on Christian Education when finally a semblance of order was restored and the debate went on. The rest of the morning was completely dominated by the agitation produced by Tisserant's thunderbolt.

Cardinal Meyer, normally a calm and dignified figure, turned in consternation to the colleague sitting next to him to inquire whether the postponement of the vote had been discussed with the other presidents, then got up from his chair and went around to the front to argue and remonstrate with Tisserant. The only reply he got was that the decision had been made and there could be no change.

The occasion was a rude awakening for the majority of the Council Fathers, and especially for the American bishops. Though they should have been on their guard against last-minute moves by the minority, they were too trusting and innocently confident that all would go well. It seemed inconceivable when the authorities had announced a vote that they would reverse what they had decided. In the spring of 1964 Cardinal Cushing had stated that if the Council did not make a pronouncement on religious liberty, the ecumenical movement would collapse. In April Pope

Paul himself, in an address to representatives of the United Nations, had declared: "There is every reason to expect the promulgation of a text on this matter, which will have great consequences." Just before the fatal day, Cardinal Cushing had wired the American bishops to bring home the religious liberty declaration with them. There can hardly be any doubt that the American attitude toward the religious liberty question as a whole was somewhat oversimplified and even naive. As Cardinal Ritter, one of the leading supporters of the declaration, said later: "If anyone was at fault, we were, for being too trustful . . . We had been too sure of a vote—which we would have won by a big majority." The impression was sometimes given that achievement of a vote would mean promulgation of the document.

One report had it afterward that the move on Staffa's part, and possibly also the decision of Tisserant, were not as spontaneous as they seemed. Word about what was being planned is said to have reached the ears of certain American prelates connected with various organs of the Council (Bishop Wright for one), but they neglected to forewarn their colleagues in the hierarchy, so that it came as a complete surprise to the majority. If the Americans were faulty in not being sufficiently vigilant, they made up for this defect by their reaction, which was immediate, violent, spontaneous and, for once, instinctively well organized. When Cardinal Meyer and the other presidents and moderators left their places and pandemonium broke loose on the council floor, the pope, who was watching the scene on his closed circuit TV, telephoned Archbishop Felici and ordered him to come to his apartment at once. With the forceful, restraining figure of the domineering secretary general gone from the hall, the pent-up emotions of the bishops were given free play. Muttering "This man is hopeless," Cardinal Meyer stalked away from Tisserant and joined a group of prelates and *periti* gathering beside the tribune on the left side of the nave. Somebody, either Bishop Francis Reh (recently appointed rector of the American College) or one of the *periti*, said, "Let's not stand here talking—who's got some paper?" With the help of several bishops and other *periti*, the following petition to Pope Paul was written out by hand, in Latin:

Your Holiness:
  With reverence but urgently, very urgently, most urgently [*instanter, instantius, instantissime*], we request that a vote on the declaration on religious liberty be taken before the end of this session of the Council, lest the confidence of the world, both Christian and non-Christian, be lost.

Additional copies, also handwritten, were circulated and signatures collected by bishops who moved up and down the banked tiers of seats. When the canvassing was completed, some 500 signatures had been collected, no small feat considering the limited time in which it had to be done. The congregation was due to end in only a little over an hour.* While the copies were still being handed around, Bishop de Smedt rose to give his *relatio* on Religious Liberty. The Fathers listened to him with almost compulsive attention, applauding vigorously from time to time— one line was punctuated by four outbursts of applause. Then when he had concluded, rhythmic applause rose from the seats, the longest and most sustained applause accorded any speech at the Council, which the moderator was powerless to stop. Some of the bishops stood up in order to clap their hands more freely. Thwarted of a formal vote, the bishops took their revenge by voting in this way, if not for the text of the declaration, then for the principle of religious liberty. The pope must allow a vote; the world would never believe that the declaration had again been postponed because of lack of time.

At the end of the morning's session, Cardinals Meyer and Ritter, joined by Cardinal Léger because of his knowledge of the Vatican layout and experience in dealing with its functionaries, left the Council hall to carry the petition to the pope. On their way up to the papal apartment they were met by Archbishop Felici on his way down. Attendants protested that it would be impossible for them to see the pope, but they insisted and were finally admitted to his presence. He received them kindly and tried to palliate their anger, informing them that, according to a ruling of Cardinal Roberti, the Council's legal expert, Cardinal Tisserant's decision had been made according to the rules. The pope said that it was not his policy to interfere in the Council's actions so he could not, under the circumstances, force a vote as they had requested. He ended by giving them a guarantee—repeated publicly in his address two days later—that the Declaration on Religious Liberty would be the first order of business in the Fourth and final Session in 1965.

Later in the afternoon, the cardinals gathered in the pope's study for a "Little Conclave." This meeting had been arranged the previous day and was therefore not directly concerned with the disturbing events of the morning. The pope wished to see the cardinals and have a few words with them before many of them left Rome. The atmosphere of the gathering was said to have been awkward. Cardinal Roberti gave a report on his study of the reorganization of the Curia, which the pope had ordered a year ago. Cardinal Frings, it seems, brought up the subject of the morning's postponed vote and begged His Holiness, in the name of more than one thousand Fathers, to allow a vote before the end of the session.

* Fr. G. Caprile, S.J., says there were only 441 signatures (*La Civiltà Cattolica*, March 1, 1965), which is probably correct, so far as the document presented to the pope is concerned, but during the afternoon apparently additional signatures were collected totalling well over a thousand.

Cardinal Suenens commented that while the decision to put off the vote may have had a basis in the rules, the psychological effect was deplorable. Two of the American cardinals and one German cardinal were said to have intimated that if any attempt were made to put off the vote on the Declaration on the Jews and Non-Christians scheduled for the final day, they would have no alternative but to absent themselves from the closing session in protest. No doubt they had in mind the action of the sizeable group at Vatican Council I in 1870 that left Rome rather than attend the final public session proclaiming papal infallibility.

The contention of the pope and the minority that Cardinal Tisserant's decision was taken in accordance with the rules, and therefore the pope could do nothing about it without infringing those rules, did not stand up under examination, because the articles to which the minority appealed (Art. 30 par. 2 and Art. 35) were vaguely worded and not conclusive. A decision should have been based on the *procedure* of the Council in submitting texts to a vote rather than upon the ambiguously worded rules. Instead of basing themselves on the letter of the law, the minority would have done better to appeal to the "spirit" of the rules. The Declaration on Religious Liberty had not followed the normal course of other conciliar texts. It was not voted on when the rest of the schema on Ecumenism (of which it had originally formed a chapter) had been voted in 1963. It was presented in September 1964 as an appendix of that schema, but no vote had followed the discussion on the floor, and finally it appeared at the end of the Third Session as a separate *"Schema* of the Declaration on Religious Liberty," being offered for a first vote. However, the Secretariat for Unity acted as if it had gone through the earlier stages through which texts passed and was being presented for a vote as though it had reached the stage before a final vote, whereas in reality it had only reached a midway stage, two places removed from the final vote. The minority should have appealed to the procedure adopted for handling the *propositions* and called for a preliminary vote, as announced, correctly, on Wednesday. This was the procedure followed for the Declaration on the Jews and Non-Christians, and the text on Religious Liberty was exactly parallel. The argument that there was not enough time to consider the text was not convincing, because the interval between Tuesday and Thursday was adequate to allow an opinion to be formed with regard to a preliminary vote. The truth of the matter was that the minority, knowing that it would be hopelessly outvoted in any kind of a vote, appealed to Article 30.2 and counted upon the pope's scrupulosity about allowing the opposition every benefit of a doubt to win their point. It was a gamble, but it worked. The question as to whether Cardinal Tisserant was privy to the minority's plan must be left unanswered.

The pope's decision regarding the petition for a vote submitted by the three cardinals was not known until Friday. There had been hope that he would accede to the wishes of such a large number of Fathers. Therefore the news was all the more shattering when Archbishop Felici gave the floor to Cardinal Tisserant, who rose and read from a piece of paper:

Many Fathers were deeply disappointed by the announcement that the vote on Religious Liberty was to be postponed and petitioned the Holy Father that a vote be taken before the end of this Session. In the name of the Supreme Pontiff, I wish to make the following announcement: The request that voting be delayed was granted because according to the *Ordo* (Rules) of the Council it had to be granted out of respect for the freedom of the Fathers in their desire to examine fully and in accordance with the *Ordo* a document of such great importance. That is why the schema of the Declaration on Religious Liberty will be treated in the next Session and, if possible, before any other matters.

His words were succeeded by a stunned silence for a moment, followed by a light scattering of applause. The Council then went on with its work.

LAST-MINUTE CHANGES IN ECUMENISM

Before the incident of the postponed vote, on Thursday, the Council had also received a jolt over the decree on Ecumenism. Archbishop Felici announced that the printing of the final text was not yet completed. This would be done during the coming night. The Fathers, therefore, would not have a chance to look it over before casting their ballots tomorrow. The reason for the delay was that some last-minute changes "had been made to make the text more clear. These changes have been made on higher authority. You will shortly receive a mimeographed copy of the changes. They could not be printed because there was not enough time. I will now read them to you." He then proceeded to read, from a sheet in his hand, the 19 last-minute changes ordered in the text of *De Oecumenismo* by the pope. The emendations were sent to Cardinal Bea as "suggestions," but in view of the lateness of the hour—it was said that they were communicated the previous evening when it was no longer possible to discuss them in a full meeting of the Secretariat and the final decision as to whether to accept or reject them had to be made by the cardinal with some of his aides—there could be little doubt that the papal suggestions were the equivalent of an "order." To have refused them would have jeopardized the whole decree. There were actually 40 suggestions or emendations proposed by the pope, of which the Secretariat chose to accept 19, and this proved to be acceptable to His Holiness.

Where did the emendations come from? Father Caprile, S.J., an editor of the Jesuit periodical *La Civiltà Cattolica,** seems to have established that some or all of them came from the same minority which opposed the decree on Ecumenism earlier in the session, for by comparing the *modi* rejected by the Secretariat with the 19 emendations, he determined that 8 of them, at least, were identical. In other words, when the opposition failed to persuade the Secretariat to adopt its recommendations, which would have had the effect of substantially altering the nature of the text, they appealed directly to the pope, who endeavored to give these opponents some kind of last-minute satisfaction in the way that he did. It must be said in the pope's favor, if Father Caprile's analysis and deductions are correct, that the most ruinous changes desired by the minority were apparently screened out by the pope and not forwarded to the Secretariat. Those suggested, and the ones accepted, were all of a relatively minor nature, mostly verbal corrections designed to change the emphasis slightly, without altering the fundamental sense. Unfortunately all the pope's suggestions, intended merely to effect "a greater clarity in the text," were minimistic in tendency, toning down or qualifying some more direct statement in the original text. Quite a few of them had to do with the introduction of such qualifying adverbs as *fere, etiam, frequentius, non raro,* etc.† While not altering the text substantially, in the opinion of

AMENDED TEXT AFTER 19 EMENDATIONS	MODI INSPIRING EMENDATIONS
1. quae Ecclesiae *catholicae* concredita est	dicatur quae *uni Ecclesiae* Christi concredita est
2. Afflante Spiritus Sancti *gratia*	dicatur afflante quidem Sancti Spiritus *gratia*
3. totius Ecclesiae *facultatem* habere	vox *officium* expungatur
4. formulae *non raro* potius inter se compleri	inseratur *saepe saepius* in sententiam: variae illae theologicae formulae . . . potius inter se compleri
5. Spiritum Sanctum *invocantes*	verba Spiritu Sancto *movente,* deleantur
6. Deum *inquirunt*	loco *inveniunt,* dicatur quaerunt
7, 8. *genuinam atque integram* substantiam	deleatur verbum *plenam;* loco *plenam* dicatur veram

experts, the fact that they had a definite anti-Protestant slant was gravely offensive to the Protestant observers, who were perhaps more aggrieved by the arbitrary, unconventional way in which they were "foisted" on the assembly at the last minute, than by their theological implications. It was almost incredible that Pope Paul, if he really was aware of the above tendency, or thought at all about the bad impression that they might make on Protestants, would have consciously suggested to the Secretariat that

---

* *La Civiltà Cattolica,* March 1, 1965.
† Fr. Caprile's list of the 8 instances where *modi* seem to correspond to corrections was as follows. The last item counted as two:

these emendations be taken seriously. Why was so much placed in jeopardy for so very little?*

The next morning, Friday, at the opening of the final business day of the session, observers were fascinated by the difference in the officials' behavior. When an emissary of the Curial minority approached Secretary General Felici with a petition requesting a postponement, "for further study," of the vote on Cardinal Bea's Declaration on non-Christian Religions, Felici was seen to draw back as if from something unclean. He quickly motioned the unlucky messenger toward Cardinal Tisserant, who dropped the petition on the presidents' table as if it were a hot potato, and that was that. The Council then proceeded to vote on the latest wording of the text of this declaration, which had gone through many hazardous revisions since it was drawn up in 1962 by the Secretariat for Christian Unity. In order to nullify the allegation made by Arab countries that the document was intended to be political and not religious, Cardinal Bea's new draft, exonerating the Jewish people from the ancient charge of deicide, had been incorporated into a larger context, dealing with other non-Christian religions. The declaration now received the following vote from the Fathers: 1,651 Placet, 242 Placet iuxta modum, and 99 Non placet. This vote represented a vindication of the years of work done by Cardinal Bea and his associates. As the elderly and kindly prelate described the long and tortuous history of the text, whose form now appeared to be finally settled and which would be ready for final voting and promulgation in 1965, he seemed to personify all that was best in the Council—an image of a dedicated prelate who had learned through rebuffs and reverses how to find his way successfully through the mazes of determined and ingenious opposition. At the end, he was warmly applauded.

Final approval of the decree on Ecumenism was another bonus for the Secretariat on Friday. There were only 64 Non placets (reduced to 11 in the formal vote on Saturday), an insignificant number. Some were certainly cast by bishops displeased over the 19 amendments. The Council also gave approval to the schema on the Oriental Churches by a comfortable margin. Characteristically, or perhaps prophetically, the lights in St. Peter's went out momentarily, about an hour before the end of Friday's congregation, owing to a power failure.

* The Vatican presses printing the text of the decree on Ecumenism, Thursday evening, were suddenly stopped about 9 P.M. Several members of Bea's Secretariat made a hasty appearance, after which the printing was resumed. There was apparently some uncertainty whether the decree would be promulgated on Saturday: the title-page did not bear the customary words "For submission at the public session on November 21." Some German bishops, it seems, tried to have the decree held over till the Fourth Session in the hope that it could be purified of its disfigurements.

Pope Paul was carried into the basilica on Saturday morning, November 21st, for the closing public session, through tiers of stony-faced bishops in white mitres and copes. There was little applause. He himself looked glum and tense. The strained feelings between the bishops and their head which the events of the last few days had produced were mirrored in the lack of warmth which pervaded the ceremony. Whereas one might have expected that there would be joy over the final promulgation of the Constitution on the Church and the decree on Ecumenism, both milestones on the road to *aggiornamento,* the applause accompanying their proclamation was somewhat perfunctory and came mostly from the throngs of visitors, monks, nuns and tourists crowded in the transepts. The bishops were restrained in their clapping, or preferred not to manifest any emotion at all.

A final disappointment awaited the bishops and particularly the Protestant observer-delegates. Everyone knew that the pope intended to confer the title of "mother of the Church" on Mary, for he had announced that he would do so at an audience on Wednesday, and intimated earlier in the session that this was his intention. What shocked his theologically perceptive hearers was his response to the highly articulate minority of Italian, Spanish, Indonesian and Polish mariological zealots clamoring for the definition of a new Marian dogma. While the pope was not prepared to go quite this far, his speech—fully half his address was taken up with Marian theology—was an indirect rebuke to the Theological Commission for having refused Mary the title which he now gave her. The Commission, in commenting on the *modi* to Chapter VIII of the Constitution on the Church, dealing with Mary, stated its reasons for not acquiescing in the persistent demand of this group that a new title be added to those traditionally accorded Mary: "The phrase *mater ecclesiae* is sometimes found in ecclesiastical writers, but very rarely, and it cannot be said to be traditional. Moreover, it is generally accompanied by such titles as 'daughter' and 'sister' of the Church. It is evident therefore that it is being used in a comparative sense. From the ecumenical point of view, the title can certainly not be recommended, although it can be admitted theologically. The Commission therefore deemed it sufficient to express the idea in equivalent terms." In effect, this sober, carefully worded, balanced, ecumenically-inspired, collegially-expressed reasoning of the Commission was a rebuke to all who would keep mariology as an unnecessary bone of contention hindering the ecumenical movement. Without denying any essential element of the Church's teaching on Mary, it attempted to recommend this teaching in a persuasive, biblically-inspired way. After the Council had gone to so much trouble to achieve a balanced theological statement of an issue disputed among Catholics themselves, it certainly showed poor judgment to appear to be undercutting that statement and reverse a decision of the Council. The pope's own carefully phrased explanation of the term was, typically, drowned out by the applause from the gallery accompanying the pronouncement. Another case of sacrificing the interests of the whole to the desires of a persistent, well-organized minority, which could count on support in high places.

The first part of the pope's speech was a commentary on *De Ecclesia*. The decrees on Ecumenism and the Oriental Churches were virtually ignored. It was known that he worked on the text of the speech until the last minute, because translations were not ready for newsmen Saturday morning in accordance with custom. His remarks were typically Pauline. Nothing really new was said. There were the same vague references to post-conciliar commissions and the projected reform of the Curia, to which his hearers had grown accustomed, but no details were revealed. The only sign that the unprecedented events of the last few days had made some kind of an impression on him came when he insisted, "We do not fear that our authority will be lessened or hampered while we acknowledge and extol yours; but rather we feel strong because of the tie that draws us together," and when he was careful to explain that "It was of the highest importance that this recognition of the prerogatives of the office of the supreme pontiff should be stated explicitly at this time when the question of episcopal authority in the Church was to be dealt with, in order that this authority would not be in contrast with the power of the pope, but should stand out in full harmony with the vicar of Christ as head of the apostolic body." This last passage, virtually a quotation from the Explanatory Note, was probably the key to his whole attitude.

Noteworthy, perhaps, was his reference to "the *monarchical and hierarchical* character of the Church." The second adjective may possibly have been a mere slip for "collegial," which seemed called for by the context, but it also could have been his intention to stress the lines of authority in this subtle way.

After the ceremonies, the grim-faced pope was carried out of the basilica through the same tiers of stony-faced, unresponsive bishops, whose lack of enthusiasm was the dominant note of the proceedings. The contrast with the closing of the First Session under Pope John could not have been more marked.

AFTERMATH OF THIRD SESSION

Yet the conclusion would be unwarranted that the results of the Third Session were wholly negative. The Constitution on the Church and the Decree on Ecumenism, taken together with the Constitution on the Sacred Liturgy, proclaimed in 1963, represented essential segments of *aggiorna-*

mento, for which Vatican II was summoned, and they must be regarded as the Council's real and substantial achievements so far. They were revolutionary documents that bore the seeds of potentially great consequences. Opinion about the decree on the Oriental Churches was mixed, but then it only purported to be a temporary laying down of norms "in view of the present situation, till such time as the Catholic Church and the separated Eastern Churches come together in complete unity." The reaction of one Orthodox archbishop active in the ecumenical movement was: "It could have been worse." The debate on this document revealed that the Eastern-Rite Catholics in communion with Rome were divided among themselves about a number of important points, so that the final text, a compromise, probably represented the best that could be achieved under the circumstances.

Cardinal Bea lost no time in providing the decree on Ecumenism with an official commentary in the two December issues of the Jesuit periodical, *La Civiltà Cattolica,* which was widely translated into all languages. He stressed particularly the positive, and even revolutionary, implications of the principle that baptism joined all Christians in a communion or kind of unity, with each other, however imperfect, which needed to be deepened and strengthened; and the desirability of putting the principles now defined into practice, in concrete ways, so that the momentum gained would not be lost. Practicing what he preached, the 83-year-old cardinal accepted an invitation to visit the seat of the World Council of Churches in Geneva (February 19, 1965), the citadel of Calvinism, sharing the platform in the Hall of the Reformation with the 84-year-old president emeritus of the Protestant Federation of France, Pastor Marc Boegner. Both spoke of the contrasts as well as the similarities between the Reformed and Catholic traditions and expressed the hope that fraternal cooperation "based on love" would eventually lead to organic unity. The cardinal announced officially that the Vatican had accepted the suggestion to enter into dogmatic discussions with the WCC, proposed at a recent meeting in Africa of that body. An ancillary purpose of the cardinal's visit was to help remove any lingering Protestant malaise over the final days of the Third Session. There were other signs that while the Protestants and Orthodox were undoubtedly dismayed and perplexed by what they witnessed, they were not thrown off balance and had no intention of interrupting contacts so full of promise, because of momentary setbacks and inconsistencies. While operational tactics might have to be changed to suit different conditions, as the Orthodox seemed to have done at Rhodes under prodding from the Russian delegation, the ultimate goal remained the same, Christian reunion. As Dr. Douglas Horton, one of the observer-delegates put it, reunion was "the only hope for a united world," but we must not expect "the millennium to be delivered with the morning milk."

427

He also advised against abandoning "our Catholic friends" because of trouble with the Fourth Floor of the Vatican.

While the conciliar commissions labored to revise their texts in the light of the debates to have them ready for the Fourth Session (expected in the fall of 1965), attention shifted away from the accomplishments of the Council to the character of the man who was pope. Even the most casual observer was aware that something went wrong and that all was not well with the Council. It would have been incorrect to concur in the judgment of the popular Italian weekly, *L'Espresso,* that in spite of Pope Paul's jet-flight pilgrimages, the crowds that greeted him with garlands of flowers, and his contacts with the poor, "he is not a popular pope" after a year and a half in office, yet there could be little doubt that he suffered a rather marked loss of prestige and affection in contrast to his predecessor, particularly in Western Europe and the United States. It could hardly be otherwise, given his highly intellectual, lonely, aloof nature, which did not attempt to evoke deep sympathy. It was said that, as Monsignor Montini, he used to criticize Pope Pius XII for not going out of the Vatican more often and coming into contact with different types of people as a pastor should; yet when he himself appeared the feeling of *rapport* was not quite complete. He seemed incapable of inspiring either the warmth of John XXIII or the awe of Pius XII. Paul was known to be an extremely charitable and kindly person and frequently acted on these impulses, but he had no Monsignor Capovilla to draw attention to these acts, so the world generally knew nothing about them. Like a true intellectual, he was capable of real inspiration—that was the only word for the pilgrimage to Jerusalem and the flight to India—but he failed to reap the fullest rewards from these unprecedented acts because a stiffness of manner and an excessive scrupulosity about questions of protocol and prestige seemed to rob them of much of their spontaneity.

He made all the right gestures, for the right reasons and with utter sincerity, but some aspect was often not quite right. For example, various movements were afoot at the Council to promote more respect for the ideal of poverty, which the Church proclaimed but did little to realize in practice in so far as its outward structure and ceremonies were concerned. The pope's gesture in laying his tiara on the altar of St. Peter's as a symbolic gift to the poor (November 13, 1964) was widely hailed as a significant step in the right direction, yet the feeling persisted that its subsequent presentation to Cardinal Spellman as a gift for the American people was somehow an awkward and unsatisfying way to "dispose" of it. His act naturally raised the question whether the bishops ought not to participate by despoiling themselves of some of their finery and trappings—for example, it was suggested that a basket be passed in St. Peter's to collect the episcopal rings—but all movements along this line were firmly discouraged. Those prelates who in the very First Session called for a simplification of episcopal dress are still waiting for their pleas to be answered. In spite of much heralded reports that the costume of the cardinals would be simplified for the consistory of 1965, no changes were apparent. As for the rites themselves, said to have been worked out by the pope and Cardinal Dante jointly, only the most practiced eye discerned the nuances, for example, the cardinal patriarchs were embraced whereas the other cardinals knelt to kiss the pope's ring when receiving the insignia of their new rank, while the *galero* or large-brimmed hat, symbolic of the cardinalate, was no longer held over their heads but merely dispatched to their residences. His Holiness apparently agreed with an editorial in the London *Times,* which declared that "the British, who . . . are firm believers in pomp and colour on great occasions, expect a little pomp from Rome" and warned against "too much drabness of display."

The pope was a man obviously torn by doubts, tormented by scruples, haunted by thoughts of perfection, and above all dominated by an exaggerated concern—some called it an obsession—about the prestige of his office as pope. His remarks on this score at times displayed an almost messianic fervor, a note missing in the more sedate utterances of his predecessors. His innumerable statements on the subject were made on almost every occasion, from casual week-day audiences or Sunday sermons from the window of his apartment to the most solemn gatherings, in season and out of season. It was as if he were tortured by the thought that the world might forget who the pope really was, at a time when the world has never known better. Since it was part of the strategy of the minority to accuse the majority of disloyalty toward the Holy Father, Paul's constant harping inevitably caused the majority to think that he perhaps did share these misgivings, at least to a certain extent. It was noticed by students of Paul's remarks that while he showed an openmindedness about almost any other subject, on the single theme of the papacy his mind remained strangely closed to analysis. He refused to admit any distinction here between what was essential and what has been added through the centuries, as modern theologians like Karl Rahner and Yves Congar did. Everything must be retained no matter how incongruous, transfigured, modernized, simplified but no peripheral attributes were to be surrendered. This naturally shocked and alienated the Orthodox, who felt that some agreement could possibly be reached on the basis of the role and function of the papacy in the ancient Church, but they had no wish to saddle themselves with the extravagant claims of medieval theorists. A classic example of the Pauline style in this connection appeared in the passage in his encyclical *Ecclesiam suam* in which he said that it pained him to think that the Orthodox regarded the pope's "primacy of honor and jurisdiction" as a stumbling-block to reunion. What pained the Orthodox—this passage in particular—was the thought that the pope should appear to be so naïve as to assume that they ever wanted the Catholic Church "to be without the pope." Paul's whole attitude was somewhat mystifying because it seemed to contradict a sound piece of advice he gave in this same encyclical, namely when dealing with the "separated brethren" not to stress differences, but the "things we have in common."

His approach to the problem of reform was typically Roman. Nothing was ever to be repudiated outright. His fondness for gradualism—also called the policy of two steps forward and one step backward—was what causes nightmares to those who were counting on Paul to carry through a promised reform of the Curia and realize the aspirations of the Council with respect to collegiality by setting up an episcopal "senate."

Pope Paul has been called the Pope of "buts," because he never seems to make a positive statement without qualifying it in some way. This was his greatest difference from John XXIII. This typical failing of the intellectual mind was probably related to another trait of Paul's: he had a horror of a void, he could not bear the thought that minority and majority would remain permanently unreconciled. Appreciating the merits of both sides so well, he found all bitter-end resistance unthinkable and abhorrent. Some formula could surely be worked out that would be capable of reconciling opposites, according to the motto *non vincere, ma convincere*. Observers found it difficult to understand why the pope expended so much time and effort on attempting to persuade a minority to accept compromises to the extent of seeming at times to be almost completely under the thumb of this group of conservative bishops, prelates and theologians, some of whom belonged to his immediate entourage and were therefore in an excellent position to press their views on the pope. The answer appeared to be, partly because he was confident that they could be won over, and partly because he shared certain of their misgivings, particularly with regard to a lack of respect for the papal prerogatives being shown by the majority, but also undoubtedly because of an *esprit de corps* which he shared with many of the minority dating from his own days in the Curia.

That Pope Paul was affected by the wave of adverse criticism that swept the world press following the close of the Third Session was clear from his remarks to journalists on January 24, 1965 when he deplored "a certain low level of tone" reached by the press in reporting the events of the session and accounts which were "sometimes completely fantastic and not corresponding to the truth at all," as well as by an unusually detailed defense of the pope's motives and actions against unjust insinuations by one of the Jesuit editors of *La Civiltà Cattolica* (March 1, 1965), excerpted *in advance* in the February 20, 1965 issue of the official Vatican newspaper, *L'Osservatore Romano*. The somewhat overdrawn portrayal of the pope's lofty motives as an "honest broker" striving only to reconcile opposing factions and offering suggestions with a view merely to "clarifying the meaning" of conciliar texts found here, perhaps reflected, to some extent, Pope Paul's own view of his role. The reader was assured that the pope had acted only to "overcome all difficulties, calming the atmosphere, assuring a genuine support and an almost unanimous approval for the Constitution of the Church."—This admission of the need for the pope's frequent intervention only tends to confirm the story as told above. But the hand of the secretary general was unmistakably evident in the last paragraph of Father Caprile's article. It concluded by assuring us that when the full record was published, the various maneuvers, accusations and plots laid at the door of the secretary general would be found to be without basis. It would then be apparent "how prudently and how wisely he acted to handle situations which otherwise could have proved fatal to the success of the Council."

This deduction becomes a certainty, when we compare Caprile's account with the interview Archbishop Felici gave toward the end of November 1964, shortly after the end of the Third Session (reported in *L'Osservatore Romano,* November 29, 1964), in which he accused newsmen who reported the Council of being "parasites and fungi" growing at the feet of "robust and healthy trees," meaning himself and the conservative bishops. Such voices, he said, "promoting confusion, insubordination and error," had to be tolerated as a "necessary evil" and allowed to grow until the end of the Council, according to the Gospel adage, "Let both grow until the harvest." As an old Irish Vatican hand put it, "The very fact that he acknowledges this criticism in public would be sufficient to have him convicted in an Italian court of law, where the party is guilty until he can prove his innocence." It was typical of the worst type of Curial mind that it never presumed to ask what wrongs were committed that gave rise to such widespread indignation and criticism. To do so would be to violate a cardinal rule of the Curia: never acknowledge faults, at least publicly. It was this arrogance and imperviousness of certain officials, their disdainful and careerist outlook, that brought the whole body into disrepute and focused attention on the pope's plans for the reform of the Curia as the key to his intentions with regard to *aggiornamento* as a whole.

In January 1965, at the pope's order, a letter was sent by Cardinal Cicognani to all the heads of Curial offices reminding them of the widespread criticisms levelled against the Curia, and of the pope's own admissions on this score. They were told to "show docility to the reforms which will be decreed in the future," presumably meaning the near future, though not necessarily before the Fourth Session. They were also advised to refrain from engaging in controversy with the bishops over the work of the Council, because experience had shown that "this kind of indiscretion" in the past had done more harm to the Curia than good. One had only to recall the remark attributed to Monsignor Romeo, a staunch critic of Cardinal Bea and the Biblical Institute, characterizing the Council bishops as "Two thousand good-for-nothings, many of whom in spite of the pectoral crosses around their necks, don't believe in the Blessed Trinity or the Virgin birth." The monsignor indignantly denied the charge in a letter to the Vatican newspaper.* Whether the words were apocryphal or not, they could be taken as typifying an attitude that had been all too common, as the debates on the floor of the Council proved. Diocesan bishops would not have complained about the Curia without cause, nor would Cardinal Cicognani have written his letter at the behest of the pope, unless there was good reason to believe that the proposed reform of the Curia would meet with some rather stiff resistance on the part of those about to be reformed. As a curious example of what was probably in store during the post-conciliar period unless lines of authority were strictly enforced, there was the odd spectacle of two Roman organs issuing wholly contradictory orders in the spring of 1965: the post-conciliar Consilium for Liturgical Renewal authorized the Jesuit Biblical Institute to concelebrate freely, whereas the conservative Congregation of Rites restricted the Jesuit Gregorian University to concelebration one day a year.

The whole course of Vatican Council II to date clearly pointed to the urgent necessity for establishing some form of episcopal group as quickly as possible, in Rome, to collaborate with the pope in the business of governing the Church, in a purely advisory capacity. The "burden of office" to which Pope Paul kept referring might become less burdensome if representatives of the episcopal order were on hand to offer advice and by their participation in papal decisions lend the weight of their presence, experience and prestige toward making those decisions seem less arbitrary, less partisan, more balanced, and more universally welcomed, than they were at present. Tension was probably inevitable between the earthly head of the Church and the rest of the bishops, because of the special divinely-ordered constitution of the Church, with the supreme power being shared by a college consisting of the bishops *with* the pope. History amply demonstrated that this was true in the past. While there could be no assurance of ultimately perfect agreement, human nature being what it was, that "harmony" which, as the Constitution on the Church said, ought to prevail between the two could probably be achieved in no better

* *L'Osservatore Romano*, October 21, 1964.

432

way than by the establishment of a really effective "senate." This was now widely regarded as almost a certainty.

PILGRIMAGE TO INDIA

Pope Paul's decision to travel to India for a "brief and simple visit limited to one stop-over" came as a genuine surprise to the majority of the Council Fathers present in St. Peter's on October 18th, the mid-point of the Third Session. This day was also the occasion of the canonization ceremony of the 22 Uganda martyrs. The pope had confided his decision to visit India to tall, handsome Cardinal Gracias of Bombay in late September, saying, "If it pleases the Lord, I will come to India. And I come." But the pontiff made it clear that he himself would divulge the news on the occasion of the canonization, and that the journey would be confined to a strictly spiritual objective—honoring Christ at the international Eucharistic Congress in Bombay from November 28th to December 6th, and visiting the poor without distinction of caste or creed.

In declaring that the Uganda martyrs had been put to death for their religious beliefs by a tribal chieftain in the village of Namugongo in 1886, the pope also cited the 12 Anglican natives who were martyred at the same time. He also pointed out a crucial distinction between evangelization and colonization:

Whereas evangelization implants the Christian religion as a new vitality that releases the spiritual powers and the latent talents of the local population and so sets people free . . . colonization, based on purely utilitarian and material motives, oppresses the native populace.

Alluding to the fact that this was the second time he had occasion to announce a journey abroad while presiding at a function in St. Peter's (at the Second Session he announced his trip to the Holy Land in January, 1964), Pope Paul admitted that the journey was unusual but was part of the papal apostolic ministry in modern times: "The pope is becoming a pilgrim, you will say. Yes, the pope is a pilgrim, which means a witness, a shepherd, an apostle on the move. . . ."

Reaction to the papal decision was uniformly favorable among the Council Fathers and the world press. Resentment was expressed by two sources—religious fanatics among the Hindus, and Catholic Portugal. The Portuguese Foreign Minister, Alberto Franco Noguiera, recalled India's sequestration of three Portuguese colonial enclaves a few years previously and announced that Pope Paul's visit was a gratuitous offense "committed by Catholicism's chief in relation to a Catholic nation. . . . Henceforth we must maintain the deepest silence, wounded and with dignity." It was curious reasoning that would have deprived the Catholics of India of seeing the Holy Father on a religious occasion, because of a political conflict in which the pope had no part whatsoever.

The pilgrimage to India proved to be successful beyond all expectations, perhaps because Indians were people of deep spiritual motivation. It was an example of Pauline inspiration when the pope, in the prayer which he composed and read to the crowds, quoted from the Upanishads. The people sensed his profound humility and sincerity and called him *"bada guru,"* or "great holy man." Oddly enough, it was a pro-Communist weekly, *Blitz,* that carried the most memorable description of Paul's visit: "We have seen Eisenhower, Khrushchev, Chou, the Shah of Persia and the Queen of England, Nasser, Tito, Sukarno and others ride in glory through our capital during the mighty Nehru epoch but this humble pilgrim of God and Vicar of Christ got a reception that surpassed them all."

THE FOURTH SESSION

Toward the Fourth Session

The crisis in the Council as the Third Session adjourned at the end of 1964 was obviously symptomatic in the Church at large of a much broader crisis, termed variously "crisis of authority," "crisis of obedience," "period of readjustment," or "the Johannine revolution." The word *aggiornamento,* used by John XXIII to describe the goal of the Council, apparently had much deeper implications than he perhaps had intended. As Dom Butler, the Abbot of Downside, put it: "At the beginning of the Vatican Council, no one knew which way the Church would renew herself. But by the end of the Third Session last winter, we realized that it was not going to be a superficial adjustment but a radical one. It meant a fundamental reappraisal of Catholicism. By then this was not only the view of a progressive minority, but it had captured the center of the Council."

To some the revelation of dissension in the higher ranks was seen as nothing less than a calamity to be avoided at all costs. In the eyes of others, it was good for the world to know that the Catholic Church was not the rigid and uniform monolith it had generally been assumed to be, if any progress was to be made in adjusting to today's pluralistic conditions. "Startling opinions are freely being expressed," Cardinal Heenan of Westminster noted, "but this proves what Catholicism has always contended—that liberty exists in the Church."

Another lesson that emerged from the painful postmortems following the Third Session was the realization (resisted at first but gradually becoming a conviction) that the Council could not possibly hope to achieve the ideal goal of uniformly "open," biblically-oriented, updated documents, equally admirable in all respects, for each of the areas on which it had proposed to issue a statement. There would have to be compromises. A certain scaling down of ultimate goals was inevitable.

Beyond this, even before the Fourth Session got underway, a marked disposition was evident both in the commissions revising the texts as well as among the planners, to concentrate on proposals and measures that would expedite matters and bring the Council to as speedy and successful a conclusion as possible.

The record of achievement by the end of the Third Session was not very impressive when compared with the total program which the Council had laid out for itself and still expected to accomplish, despite the weightiness of such completed items as the Constitutions on the Liturgy and on the Church, both of which had consumed so much time. Another perhaps decisive reason for the quickening pace and more businesslike, practical attitude prevailing after the Third Session was the unmistakable desire on the part of Pope Paul (shared unquestionably by the vast majority of the bishops, though not necessarily by those who were most active or by the theologians) to end the Council in a Fourth and final session.

An invariable consequence of any débâcle is always the search for scapegoats. There was no tendency to blame the pope exclusively for what had happened. Rather indignation and ire were visited on his entourage and on conservative members of the Curia who had ready access to his person and used the occasion to urge their claims, knowing how scrupulously he would endeavor to give them satisfaction. By contrast, the majority were negligent about making their wishes known with the same regularity. Cardinal Ritter admitted as much when he observed, apropos of the postponed vote on Religious Liberty, "Our feeling of frustration . . . was heightened by the conviction that we were stalled by the delaying tactics of a very small minority. Indeed subsequent events showed how small a minority is opposed." The majority were equally remiss about mustering their strength to prevent the dilution of the texts on collegiality and ecumenism, which might have been avoided if they had acted in time. The brusqueness of Cardinal Tisserant's announcement postponing the Religious Liberty vote and the suddenness of the last-minute changes in Ecumenism were particularly galling. No effort was made to save appearances by avoiding the impression that the majority had been outmaneuvered. Resentment was directed particularly at Cardinal Cicognani, secretary of state, who saw the pope every day, and Archbishop Felici, secretary general of the Council, who saw him several times a week, both regarded as spokesmen for the Curial point of view. Unfortunately the rules of the Council failed to specify exactly how the pope was to communicate with the Council. His wishes were generally channeled through the conservative Cicognani, but whether as secretary of state or as president of the Coordinating Commission (consisting of the 12 Council presidents and 4 moderators), or the extent to which the pope himself was personally involved, was not always made clear. This vagueness about channels of command tended to perpetuate an impression that there was a regrettable lack of *rapport* between pope and bishops.

But the real difficulty brought to light by the experience of the first three sessions was the inability of the Council to express itself spontaneously and effectively. The speeches on the various issues were really not "debates" in any realistic sense since texts had to be submitted days in advance and orators were rarely allowed to extemporize remarks (as when Cardinal Ottaviani replied to Cardinal Frings' charges against the Holy Office in a short first paragraph added at the last moment) because this was normally forbidden by the rules. The interval between discussion and voting was too long. The only spontaneous method left was applause, which on occasion proved to be very effective, as when Bishop de Smedt gave his *relatio* following the postponement of the vote on Religious Liberty, but this too was normally forbidden by the rules. The experiment of putting a number of propositions or questions to the Fathers in order to ascertain their reactions to a particular problem was not repeated after the Second Session because of the furor raised by the minority. The pope gave in and disallowed an improvement that might have shortened the duration of the proceedings. The minority of course tenaciously clung to the predominance which they had gained and were able to retain in some of the conciliar commissions even after Pope Paul enlarged the membership. By their obstructionism they were rather successful in slowing down the work of the Council. Except when the pope personally exerted himself to expedite matters, as he did in the case of the Theological Commission, it would otherwise have continued to block passage of the crucial Constitution on the Church during the Third Session.

But it would be pointless to deny that Pope Paul VI was subjected to an almost unprecedented amount of criticism since taking office. Censorious judgments not only about his conduct of the Council but about his character and person began to be aired during the Second Session and reached a kind of climax in the indignation following the close of the Third. A new factor was that no pope, since 1870, had been so widely criticized by Catholics themselves. Both those on the left and those on the right were disenchanted by his overly subtle attempt to steer a middle course in treacherous waters. Yet, paradoxically, no pope had taken so much trouble to create a favorable image of the papacy. Though words like "mysterious" and "enigmatic" were frequently used to describe him, the truth of the matter was that Paul had consciously reacted against what he regarded as the excessive aloofness of Pius XII. His first encyclical, *Ecclesiam suam,* was quite informal in tone and revealed more about the personality of its author than such documents normally did. His weekly

439

audiences on Wednesdays were transformed into "fireside chats" in which he replied to a number of questions or problems hypothetically raised by those present. The short talks from the window of his apartment after leading the faithful in the Angelus at noon on Sundays or important feastdays had been even more newsy and chatty: for example, one Sunday in late spring he informed his listeners, ". . . better news came from Santo Domingo last night . . . ," as if to share with the crowds the latest cables received by the Secretariat of State about the Dominican crisis. Peace was almost invariably the theme of these Sunday chats and the tone was generally optimistic or hopeful, but in July 1965 he struck a pessimistic note, saying: "People are going backward rather than forward on the path of civilization and peace. It seems to us that the idea of peace is in danger. . . ."

In his message to the Catholic Press Association meeting in New York, in May 1965, read by the editor of *L'Osservatore Romano,* Raimondo Manzini, the pope declared: "We are not ignorant of the difficulties which you encounter, but we can assure you that we will do all we can to make your task easier," and he referred specifically to the Pontifical Commission for the press headed by "our venerable brother" Archbishop O'Connor. This reassurance was not much of a consolation to the delegates who were fully aware what little the Commission and "our venerable brother" had done to facilitate accurate reporting of the Third Session. The failure of the Vatican, thus far, to establish an effective press office run by professional people (the staff of *L'Osservatore Romano* did what they could to ease the task of journalists covering the Vatican, but the paper itself was in need of a thorough updating) was a serious drawback not only to journalists but a hindrance to the pope's efforts to make himself better understood. Journalists were not likely to forget the extraordinary press conference during the Third Session at which officials of the Council Press Office (also headed by Archbishop O'Connor) denied that any maneuvers had taken place behind the scenes and accused the press of distortions, only to have to back down a few days later and issue an apology of sorts. Nor the conference of the secretary general of the Council, Archbishop Felici, shortly after the end of the Third Session, before the *Circolo di Roma,* in which he referred to the press as a kind of "fungus" that would have to be tolerated until the conciliar record could be published. The pope even implied that the press in reporting the Third Session had concentrated too much on secondary matters. The English theologian, Father Charles Davis, summed the matter up perfectly when he observed: "Journalists have made some wrong comments on the Council (though, considering the difficulties, they have done very well), but they were right to expect the interaction of groups, the clash of personalities, the tension of differing aims and outlooks and the struggle

440

to reach agreement. To deny such factors is to engage in elaborate doublethink."

Pope Paul was of course dismayed by the sharp reactions accompanying the closing days. As we have already noted, in February 1965 Father Caprile, S.J., one of the editors of the Jesuit periodical, *La Civiltà Cattolica,* published a highly informative account of what had happened in which he sought to make clear that the pope was trying to play the role of an "honest broker" reconciling conflicting factions, and had not intended to act brusquely, arbitrarily, or uncharitably. The widespread assumption was that Caprile's article had been inspired by the pope himself or at any rate was based on information which only he or somebody very close to him could have supplied about his motives and actions. Incidentally, it confirmed by and large what journalists had already reported about the drama of those days and sustained their contention that there was a struggle between opposing factions constantly going on behind the scenes centered on the pope himself. It also insinuated, though in highly discreet language so as not to ruffle any feelings, that Tisserant's rejection of the vote on religious liberty could have been announced more diplomatically and the bishops might have received it with less shock if they had been prepared in advance for what was coming.*

In an audience with Canon Pézéril one day the pope remarked: "I read in the newspapers that I cannot make up my mind, am restless, timid, and torn by conflicting advice . . . I may perhaps be slow. But I know what I want. After all, it is my privilege to think about matters first."

On January 25, 1965 the pope announced the names of 27 persons he was elevating to the cardinalate. In addition to expected names like those of Shehan of Baltimore and Heenan of Westminster, there was a certain amount of excitement over the inclusion of figures like the theologian Charles Journet, Monsignor Joseph Cardijn, a venerable priest long associated with the Catholic Youth Movement, and the aged Italian parish priest Giulio Bevilacqua who had been the pope's spiritual mentor. What raised eyebrows, however, was the fact that the list was headed by the octogenarian Patriarch Maximos IV Saigh of Antioch, who had long resisted repeated invitations to join the College of Cardinals but now was leading a movement among the remaining patriarchal heads of Eastern-rite Churches to join that body. The pope's words when announcing this historic step were somewhat laconic and mystifying. He said that it was his intention to give to the Sacred College "an expression of more complete communion and more effective representation of authority, colle-

---

* See *La Civiltà Cattolica,* February 20, 1965 (also printed in OR, February 15, 1965), as well as Père R. Rouquette's comment in *Études,* April 1965, p. 566 ff. According to Caprile, the pope tried incessantly to make the language of Chap. III of *De Ecclesia,* on collegiality, as clear and precise as possible, "but without contradicting or destroying the work already accomplished by the majority . . ."

giality, experience of tradition, cultures and merit," by including particularly the Eastern patriarchs. He went on to remark, "The Roman Church cannot be a closed fold, immobile, self-centered and exclusive, but rather should be the indispensable center of a flock which is gathered together: yes, a single, open, and many-faceted flock of Christ, wonderfully characterized by the complementary nature of its constituent parts, unity and catholicity, authority and brotherhood, an identity of faith in the boundless and vast breadth of charity."

Patriarch Maximos issued a statement later the same day explaining more fully why he had accepted the appointment at long last and indicating that certain conditions had been met: the Eastern patriarchs would enter the College of Cardinals but they would not become members of the Roman clergy like the rest of the cardinals; they would retain their patriarchal sees as titles instead of accepting Roman titular or parish churches. This would help to impart an ecumenical dimension to an ecclesiastical post which the Orthodox had always tended to look down on as a purely Western institution and beneath their dignity. Maximos also implied that other concessions had been made, or would be made, but he did not disclose what they were. Despite the protests of some of his clergy (by Archbishop Zoghby in particular) who felt that his action amounted to a surrender of Eastern claims to autonomy, the aged prelate was duly invested with his new rank in the two consistories on February 22nd and 25th. When the papal decree governing the reorganization of the Sacred College was published (February 20th), it was seen that the Eastern patriarchs were accorded precedence over all other members except the six cardinal-bishops, occupants of sees in the immediate neighborhood of Rome who for centuries had always been cardinals and in some cases had traditional functions to perform. (The cardinal bishop of Ostia, for example, was traditionally Dean of the Sacred College and normally consecrated the pope.) The question was therefore left pending whether these posts would be abolished when the aged incumbents died, or whether they would be integrated and equated with the cardinal-patriarchs in some eventual reorganization. Pope Paul's reference to "collegiality" and the *ex officio* status of the new cardinal patriarchs raised the question whether he was perhaps planning to substitute an enlarged College of Cardinals for the proposed Senate of Bishops. The matter was not entirely cleared up, but several days later in a general audience the pope made clear that in making the recent appointments it had not been his intention to "discount our brothers in the episcopate" who would be called upon to lend their assistance "according to needs and in various ways." In a later private audience he cut short speculation by making it clear that the College of Cardinals would not replace the proposed Senate. The two bodies were destined to fulfill separate and different functions.

When investing the new cardinals in a solemn consistory on February 25th, Pope Paul reminded them that "there is no authority in the Church which is not a service." The Dutch *De Volkskrant* observed that the new cardinals "did not bring the reformation of the Roman Curia any nearer: the dominance of the Italian element was still being maintained, with more than a quarter of the total number of cardinals still being Italians, and 24 out of the 34 Curial cardinals being Italians in the new college as opposed to 20 out of 29 in the old." *De Nieuwe Linie* thought that the College of Cardinals was no longer essential for the Catholic Church as it had once been, but that while a better scheme of Church government could be worked out it was not likely to be introduced at present. It was rumored that Pope Paul had ordered the cardinals to simplify their costume and generally cut down on expensive display (a letter from Cardinal Tisserant bearing on this subject was actually circulated among his colleagues but did not become binding until September 1965).

An important clue to the pope's intentions regarding the Council was the fact that he threw himself into the campaign to make the introduction of the vernacular liturgy a success with unremitting vigor. It was announced that he would celebrate mass in Italian in various Roman parish churches throughout Lent, beginning on March 7th, the day the new regulations were to go into effect throughout the Catholic world. In a general audience on January 31st, he declared flatly that the faithful must change their mental outlook if they believed that mass was nothing but an external rite at which they were expected to be passively present. "One must realize," he said, "that a new process of spiritual education was begun with the Ecumenical Council. This is the Council's great innovation, and we must not hesitate to become first disciples, and then supporters of the school of prayer that is about to begin." Urging the Lenten preachers of Rome, on March 1st, to be careful about explaining the liturgical changes to the people who were being asked to alter the habits of a lifetime, he advised them also to alter their own method of preaching and adopt a less florid, simpler style. "Modern man," he maintained, "is intolerant of every form of awkwardness, exaggeration, affected elegance, pseudo-culture, and worldly substitutes for the Word of God." They should conform to the present-day demand for "plain, simple, essential, brief and intelligible language." On March 17th, in a general audience, he proceeded to analyze the reactions to introduction of the vernacular and called for further efforts to make it successful. Addressing the various groups of pilgrims and faithful present, he said: "If the public character of this meeting did not prevent it, we should like to ask you, as we do at other meetings of a private character, for your impressions regarding this great innovation . . . You understand that this liturgical change cannot take place without your willing and earnest cooperation. We desire this response of yours so much that, as you see, we are making it the theme of our words to you today. . . ." Then, to bring home the fact that he meant business, he added: "Before it was enough to attend mass, today it is necessary to participate. Before some could perhaps doze or chat—today this is impossible, you must listen and pray." In any case all thought must be given up that the Church would ever go back to the old days. In Italy as elsewhere the change-over was effected with the minimum of disturbance. There was a certain amount of grumbling but not much more. The right-wing press attempted to foment a campaign to protest the changes, but this came to nothing. *Il Borghese* invited Italian Catholics to fight as the French had done and an open letter was sent to Cardinal Lercaro, president of the Liturgical *Consilium,* charging him with attempting to foist erroneous conceptions of the liturgy on the Church. More indignation was expressed over the pope's gesture returning the Turkish flag captured by the Christians in the famous sixteenth-century sea battle of Lepanto. *Il Borghese* described this and other conciliatory gestures like the return of the head of St. Andrew to Greece, as a "macabre striptease" that would not stop short even of a denudation of essentials, while the neo-Fascist organ *Il Secolo* lamented that instead of waging war against heretics these days, the Church was eager to start a dialogue with communists who were but one step from power in Italy.

In spite of fears expressed at the time that the pope's proclamation of a new title for Mary, "Mother of the Church," at the close of the Third Session would arouse agitation for more dogmas about Mary, the tendency seemed to be toward greater soberness in Mariology. Pope Paul could certainly claim some of the credit for promoting this new trend. In a speech on February 2nd, the feast of the Presentation, he mentioned the Mariological Congress in Santo Domingo in March and referred to the "Christocentric and Church-centered direction which the Council intends to give to our doctrine and devotion toward our Lady." The same theme was stressed in a farewell audience granted to Father Balič prior to the latter's departure for the Congress. Father Tavard absented himself from the gathering because of objections to the "methods" of the Mariologists. However, the tone of the meeting appears to have been rather moderate and more attention was paid to the ecumenical aspects of Marian theology, in keeping with the investigations of such theologians as De Lubac, Rahner, Congar, Laurentin and the publicly-expressed wishes of Pope Paul. The restraining hand of the pope was evident also in the pages of *L'Osservatore Romano* which no longer printed as many extravagant Marian articles by L. Ciappi and others as formerly.

While progress appeared to be made here as well as in a limited number of other sectors, a series of widely reported Wednesday general audiences from early spring until late summer in which the pope endeavored to unburden his mind, as it were, regarding the worrisome problems with which he was faced, provided few clues about what he intended to do but did throw light on the man psychologically and the troubled state of the Church. The uniform theme running through all these talks was the importance of maintaining internal unity in the Catholic Church while the Council was laying down the norms for its updating or renewal, which he repeatedly declared to be necessary and inevitable. Nothing tortured him more, he disclosed on a number of occasions, than the spectacle of disunion and dissension where charity and harmony ought to reign. A group of pilgrims were told that the pope had need of their prayers and consolation, because every moment he was obliged to "face and struggle with the endless, enormous tasks, responsibilities and duties of his office." The burden at times "approaches a real agony."

Nothing could have been more Pauline in style than his quiet rehabilitation of Galileo Galilei more than three hundred years after the famous astronomer's forced recantation and humiliation by the Holy Inquisition in 1633. The rehabilitation took place at Pisa on June 10, 1965 in such an offhand and casual way that few newspapers reported it, and those that did were not quite sure whether it was a rehabilitation. There could be no question about it, however; it was. Paul VI admonished the crowd of over 100,000, gathered for the eucharistic congress in front of the twelfth-century marble baptistery of the cathedral, to "imitate the faith of Galileo, Dante and Michelangelo." Galileo was born in 1564, the year Michelangelo died, while Dante of course lived much earlier, so the pope went out of his way to mention Galileo first. Did the pope use the occasion merely because he happened to be in Pisa, Galileo's birthplace and the scene of his famous experiments? It was interesting that *L'Osservatore Romano* failed to comment on this historic moment, while covering the eucharistic congress in its usual fulsome manner. However, in view of the bold remark by Cardinal Suenens at the Third Session that "the Church could only afford one Galileo case," Paul's statement could only be considered deliberate.

The pope's action was also foreshadowed by the mysterious release for posthumous publication in 1964 of a full-scale biography of Galileo written some thirty years earlier by the late Monsignor Pio Paschini, the dean of Roman ecclesiastical historians. Publication was delayed so long because the manuscript had originally been impounded, on orders of the Holy Office, despite the acknowledged reliability of the author. The appearance of Paschini's work was hailed as a significant event by the Vatican newspaper, but it of course failed to make any reference to the circumstances surrounding the manuscript's suppression. The English Jesuit historian, James Brodrick, in his interesting monograph, *Galileo: the Man, his Work, his Misfortunes* (1964), referred to the seventeenth-century Pope Urban VIII as "wrong and stupid," and to Galileo as "one of the brightest spirits in human history till, broken in health and terrorized, he even offered to add new chapters to his *Dialogue* in refutation of the Copernican views." The decision of Paul VI to make honorable amends for a long-standing scientific scandal was certainly admirable. If he had announced the rehabilitation with more fan-fare, however, there would not have been the feeling that he was still deferring to the Curial tradition of never admitting an error.

A certain amount of anxiety, or at least concern, about the heavy agenda of the Fourth Session was expressed in his general audience on July 28th. "The number and nature of the themes to be dealt with, their gravity and complexity, as well as the fact that with this session the Council will officially come to an end and its immense follow-up problems . . . all these things fill our spirit with great concern and anxious solicitude. It is easy to imagine the burden they place upon us." The Council was described as "a renovating and decisive movement in the life of the Church," and spiritual vigilance was needed "if we want the Council to realize its purposes." What worried him particularly was a "spirit of disquiet and radical reformism," not in harmony with the spirituality of the Council, "both in the field of doctrine and in that of discipline."

On August 4th he spoke of "strange and confused opinions" that had been reaching him, "causing us to reflect, often in surprise and sorrow, since these opinions come not only from the many who have not the good fortune to possess our faith, but frequently from the best among the People of God, faithful and dear to us, where ordinarily the Church's doctrine is cultivated with fervent study and thought and honored by a fruitfulness of Christian life." These words naturally conjured up the thought that respected figures like Cardinals Suenens or Lercaro, Bishops Ancel or Helder Camara, theologians like Rahner, De Lubac, Philips, or possibly even Bishop Colombo, had been urging on him courses of action that he considered to be too daring for the moment. He went on to castigate "echoes of errors, ancient and modern, already condemned by the Church and excluded from her heritage of truth," as well as "would-be scientific affirmations that call in question principles, laws and traditions to which the Church is solidly bound and which it is not to be supposed that she will ever disclaim." It would probably not be wide of the mark to see here another reference to pressure for modification of the rule of clerical celibacy. "If these confused views and unwise proposals were followed," the pope said, "far from deriving that new virtue and aspect which is the aim of the *aggiornamento* sought by the Second Vatican Council, the Church would end by acquiring the likeness of the world, whereas it is the world that awaits from the Church a ray of light. . . ." It was necessary to have "trust in holy Church and in the Chair of Peter in particular." Only this tribunal (he did not distinguish between Church and papacy but seemed to be thinking more of the latter) could "guarantee to each and all of the People of God the same truths, the same certitude, the same way of speech, that of yesterday, today and tomorrow." Vatican Radio and *L'Osservatore Romano* commented copiously on this new papal definition of *aggiornamento*. An earlier comment of the Vatican organ on his July 28th talk was probably the classic remark of the year: "The pope says exactly what he says, nothing more and nothing less!"

The one impression to be gained from all these talks was that Pope Paul was firmly committed to gradualism as a policy of action and to middle-of-the-road solutions as a goal, in an age calling more and more for radical solutions to radical problems. Yet those who saw him privately were convinced that while his tone might sound edgy at times, he was as calm and collected as ever. He assured Père Antoine Wenger, editor of *La Croix,* for example: "One must not attach too much importance to passing crises or to external repercussions which are only a phenomenal aspect of the Council." For Paul, "the eyes of faith seek to grasp the reality of the Council, which is a mystery defying appearances. The plan of the Holy Spirit is not immediately evident in the various activities which constitute the material element of the Council. But we are convinced that this is a time of grace, an important moment in the time of the Church. It is like a striking of the hour, preceded and followed by silence."

The relative uncertainty that prevailed with regard to the pope's intentions toward the Council was enhanced by his failure to take any effective action to reform the Roman Curia, despite repeated references to the problem—two years after his famous address to the Curia (September 21, 1963). Because the minority were not only hostile to the cause of reform but firmly entrenched in Curial positions from which they would be able to block the work of the Council, reform of that body became, as Hans Küng declared, one of the "touchstones of conciliar success." What was more, not all the pope's references to the subject were very encouraging. In his address to the cardinals on December 24, 1964, for example, it did not sound as though he had any extensive reform in mind when he characterized the Curia as "the indispensable instrument, the well-ordered unity, the exemplary crown around the throne of St. Peter." Hopes were raised when it became known that a letter had been circulated in early January 1965 by Cardinal Cicognani to all heads of Curial offices asking them to accept the projected reforms in good grace and to be careful about becoming involved in controversy with persons who criticized the Curia "because experience shows that such arguments tend to harm the Curia rather than help it." This could be interpreted as a mild reminder that the pope wanted no more belligerent replies like Cardinal Ottaviani's rejoinder to Cardinal Frings on the floor of the Council. It could also be read as a muzzling of such people as Monsignor Romeo, Archbishop Staffa and others who in the early days of the Council had not hesitated to equate attacks on the Curia with attacks on the very structure and foundations of the Church. In any case, since that time the leading spokesmen for the Curia had tended to keep their irritation to themselves and not make a public issue of it, except in the case of Cardinal Ottaviani who still allowed himself an occasional riposte. It was regarded as significant that Cicognani had pointed out "defects that were bound to occur in an organization as ancient as the Curia." Rather extensive information about the details of the projected reform were published by the Italian Catholic weekly *Vita* in its February 5, 1965 issue, but nothing was done to implement them.

It was inevitable that this lack of action should suggest that the minority party around the pope were much more powerful than they perhaps were in reality. The words and actions of certain Curial figures also seemed to be at variance with the policy of moderation and concilia- tion the pope was trying to pursue. In a statement during the summer Cardinal Ottaviani declared himself as flatly opposed to the policy of carrying on a dialogue with communists and atheists which Pope Paul had espoused (in very guarded language of course) in his encyclical *Eccle- siam suam*. (The cardinal was to reverse himself somewhat, in a later interview, and declare that he was enchanted by the word *dialogue:* "Yes, yes . . . dialogue, a beautiful word. I like it.") In the spring the pope had established a new Secretariat for Non-Believers, under Cardinal König of Vienna, to try and find a "basis for accommodation" with communists, atheists and all other non-believers. Ottaviani then added this revelation to our store of knowledge: "Let it never be forgotten that communists hold principles that are diametrically opposed to the Church."

The Coordinating Commission met three times to review the agenda of the Fourth Session before its opening, on September 14th: on December 30, 1964, May 11 and September 13, 1965.* At the May meeting it reviewed and approved the revised texts submitted by the various com- missions which had held formal meetings for this purpose as follows: Jan- uary 25–30, Commission for the Apostolate of the Laity; March 29– April 7, Mixed Commission on Doctrine and the Laity; March 29–April 5, Commission for Missions; March 29–April 6, Commission for Dis-

* On the latter occasion the meeting was unusually prolonged, lasting from 5 P.M. until 1:10 A.M. The question of a new voting procedure was discussed.

cipline of the Clergy and Christian People; April 6–May 4, Commission for Seminaries and Studies and Christain Education; April 27–May 4, Commission for Religious. The Secretariat for Promoting Christian Unity met February 18–March 9 and May 9–15. The pope approved the texts on May 28th, and on June 12th it was announced by the secretary general that five texts were being sent to the bishops for their examination, viz. Religious Liberty, Schema 13, Missions, Priestly Life and Apostolate of the Laity, the first four of which would be debated at the Fourth Session. The bishops already had the text of Divine Revelation (distributed before the end of the Third Session). In a departure from customary procedure, it was announced at the same time that the revised texts of five other documents, viz. Pastoral Office of Bishops, Religious Life, Priestly Formation (Seminaries), Christian Education, and Non-Christians were not being sent to the bishops but would be handed to them after the Session began. The explanation given was that these documents did not have to be discussed, merely voted on, but a possible reason seems to have been that the rest were kept back in order to render less conspicuous the retention of the altered text of Non-Christians, so as to control the controversy over this document and avoid a repetition of the previous year's experience.

On August 28th the pope issued an Apostolic Exhortation to the bishops in which he expressed his hope not only that the proceedings would be "orderly and profitable" but that the "hearts of the bishops would remain open to the delicate, powerful, secret and irresistible influence of the Spirit of Truth," while at the same time informing them that on the afternoon of the opening day, September 14th, the feast of the Exaltation of the Cross, he would lead a penitential procession carrying the relic of the true cross from S. Croce in Gerusalemme to the Lateran Basilica, and calling for a "wave of prayer" for the success of the Council.

The pope's third encyclical, *Mysterium Fidei* on the eucharist, was published the weekend before the Fourth Session opened. Some of his advisers seem to have persuaded him that there was a threat to the integrity of the Catholic faith in the current controversy among Dutch, Belgian and French theologians over eucharistic theology. Publication of the document, intended for early August, was postponed until just before the Council convened so that it would have maximum impact. It certainly did; it infuriated the Dutch. While there was nothing exceptional in its presentation, by insinuating that the faith was threatened from nameless quarters it put the finger on those countries where everybody knew discussion was going on. One Dutch observer in Rome summed up the effect: "It was like using a sledgehammer to crack a nut." The *Corriere della Sera,* considered liberal, made the outrageous editorial comment that "The pope has finally and solemnly declared the inviolability of eucharistic dogma and put an end to all symbolic explanations, pernicious Hegelianism, *pastiches à la* Teilhard de Chardin, and all left-leaning reformist tendencies lurking in the Church." One paper ran a banner headline: POPE CONDEMNS HOLLAND. Cardinal Alfrink lost no time in refuting such libellous charges and defending both the good name of Dutch theologians and the orthodoxy of the Dutch Catholic Church, in a press conference in Rome crowded with journalists. His conference inspired a new headline: "CARDINAL ALFRINK'S OFFENSIVE AGAINST ROMAN CURIA." *De Bazuin,* the monthly periodical of the Dutch Dominican Order, seems to have had the last word. It not only questioned both the tone and content of the encyclical because they created the impression that a grave heresy existed in countries like Holland, where there had been controversy over the eucharist, but went on to ask whether the present document was not proof that this type of papal pronouncement was now out of date. The assumption had always been that encyclical letters were equally valid and intelligible everywhere, but it declared flatly that this was clearly not the case.*

THE FOURTH SESSION OPENS

When the Fourth Session convened on September 14th, there was little to indicate a change of climate. From the moment when he entered the conciliar hall, however, Pope Paul indicated unmistakably his intention to direct the Council's work in his own personal fashion. He walked down the aisle of St. Peter's preceded by the prelates and clergy who were to take part in the opening ceremonies. Gone was the pageantry of red-coated lackeys and aristocratic chamberlains who usually cluttered up papal processions. The mass was concelebrated by the pope with 26 other bishops. The practiced eye of professional liturgists detected certain "Dantesque" departures from the established ritual (so-called because they reflected the personal innovations introduced by Archbishop Enrico Dante, for many years papal master of ceremonies before his "elevation" to the cardinalate). However it was made known that the daily masses opening each day's congregation would conform strictly to the norms laid down in the Constitution on the Liturgy (the masses were at first all in the Latin rite, mainly in order to save time, but the custom was later resumed of

---

* In his somewhat loosely worded *obiter dicta* on the encyclical, Father Gregory Baum, S.A. (*Commonweal,* October 15, 1965) put his finger on a sore point likely to be much more discussed in the future, the extent to which relations between the Holy See and the rest of the Church should be reconsidered in the light of the universally applicable principle of dialogue.

varying the monotony by celebrating mass occasionally according to one of the colorful Eastern rites).

The pope's new emphasis on greater simplicity was evident in this opening mass. Paul preferred to enter on foot, vested in a simple cope instead of the elaborate and unwieldy papal mantle, no longer wearing the tiara but only a mitre, like any other bishop. He carried a pastoral staff in the form of a cross which he was said to have designed himself.* An interesting feature was that the pope chose to enthrone the Gospel himself, instead of delegating this to some other prelate, normally the secretary general on opening and closing days. (Partly in order to save time and partly to enhance the symbolic significance of the ceremony, it was decided at the Fourth Session to combine the enthronement of the Gospel with the procession of the celebrant of the mass each morning, instead of having it follow the mass.) Another novelty was that the "obedience" of the cardinals and bishops which normally took place before the enthronement of the Gospel took place after this rite, another example of Paul's eye for the symbolic. As one commentator noted, the whole opening ceremony seemed more like a "family get-together," the impression happily created by the rite of concelebration.

Instead of dealing with dogmatic and disciplinary questions, as had been expected, Paul's opening address began as a mild discourse on charity, the love that the Council should manifest toward God, toward the Church, and toward humanity. It was all the more effective for being unexpected. The pope carefully refrained from touching on any of the matters before the Council, he said, because he did not want to be accused of compromising the bishops' freedom of discussion. Saving his good news for the last, he first announced that it was his intention to make a personal appeal for peace before the United Nations Assembly in New York in October. This was followed by the warmly applauded disclosure that he intended to establish the long-awaited Synod of Bishops desired by the Council.

The reaction to the pope's talk was generally favorable. It was noted, for example, that the tone and emphasis of his remarks had been much less sharp than in some recent statements, such as his talk a few days earlier in the Catacombs in which he had compared the present persecution of the Church behind the Iron Curtain to the persecution of the early Church by the Roman emperors. Both in his remarks on that occasion and in the address to the Council, however, he insisted that instead of condemning, the Church must be concerned to express only feelings of

---

* For centuries the popes had traditionally not used a crozier; whether in order to mark the difference between themselves and all other bishops or merely because the custom never took hold in Rome, is not clear. In any case, Pope Paul decided to abandon a practice at variance with the spirit of the doctrine of collegiality.

love. The main theme of his address had obviously been chosen in order to provide a link with his predecessor, Pope John XXIII, who was never more guided by charity than when he was inspired to summon the Council. It also furnished a proper theme on which to end the Council. Far from being the routine affair that observers had predicted, Paul's address was actually one of the most significant pronouncements made at the Fourth Session.

THE SYNOD OF BISHOPS

On the following morning, as the Council Fathers were hurrying to their appointed places for the first business meeting of the session, Archbishop Felici's resonant voice suddenly rang out above all the hubbub announcing the arrival of Pope Paul. The pope entered the basilica accompanied merely by two secretaries. After assisting at the daily mass, he took his place at the Council presidents' table in a chair slipped in between those of Cardinals Tisserant and Tappouni. It was made known later that the chair would be left in this position, thus implying that the pope intended to give effect to his desire to take a more active part in the proceedings. Cardinal Marella, president of the Council commission that had prepared the schema on the Pastoral Office of Bishops, immediately delivered a report in which it was announced that the long-promised Synod of Bishops was about to be promulgated. The secretary general, Archbishop Felici, read the document, a papal decree or Motu Proprio entitled *Apostolica Sollicitudo*. As he finished there was a hearty round of applause. When on the previous day the pope had declared his intention to proclaim the Synod "in the near future," almost nobody supposed that it would be done the very next day. After imparting his blessing and with a friendly gesture to the non-Catholic observer delegates, who joined in applauding him, the pope left the council hall by the same side door by which he had arrived.

The title of the document was well chosen, *sollicitudo* (care, concern), being a traditional term used by the popes since at least the fifth century, to describe the collegial relationship between themselves and the rest of the bishops. What the document did was to establish a senate of bishops as papal advisers on a permanent basis, in response to repeated requests from the floor of the Council. Of greatest significance was the provision that the bulk of the membership was to be elected by the national or regional conferences of Catholic bishops throughout the world, for this was a step further in restoring the democratic process of electing bishops that prevailed in the early Church and still preserved in principle in the selection of Eastern-rite bishops. The pope reserved the right to appoint only 15% of the total membership, stipulating that his nominees could be bishops or experts. Ten members were to be elected by the generals of male religious orders located in Rome to represent their vast membership; and a sort of preference was given to the Eastern patriarchs and "major archbishops and metropolitans" who were to be *ex officio* members, counterbalancing the cardinal secretaries of Roman congregations—numbering 14—who were also *ex officio* members. The rest of the membership was to be elected according to a rather complicated system designed to effect some kind of balance between the different parts of the world. Conferences were entitled to elect one member for every 25 bishops, with no country (or region) allowed to have more than 4. Thus the United States, with close to 225 bishops, would have as many synod members as Italy, whose total population was approximately the same as the Catholic population of the United States. Moreover the document expressly recommended that bishops be chosen not because of their prestige or prudence but for their familiarity with a particular problem (*cognitio materiae*) in both its theoretical and practical aspects. The assembly's function would be primarily advisory or consultative, but on occasion it could have a deliberative capacity, in which case the Pope must ratify the decisions. As with ecumenical councils, he alone determined the time and place of meeting, and drew up the agenda.

Thus, in a deftly timed move, Pope Paul had acted to redeem part of his pledge to reorganize the central governmental structure of the Church in accordance with the wishes of the Council. (The other half of the pledge related to the reform of the Roman Curia.)

The Curial view of the new organization was presented by Cardinal Marella in a press conference held a week later. He tried to minimize the importance of the term "Synod" as the designation for the new body, claiming that any other term such as "convention," "assembly," or "meeting" would have served as well; nevertheless the choice of this term appeared to be highly significant and deliberate. "Synod" means the same thing as "council." It would have been impossible for Pope Paul to choose a more traditional and meaningful designation. "Senate" was ruled out, of course, because of its unsatisfactory secular connotations. The cardinal pooh-poohed the suggestion that there could be any conflict between the new Synod and the Roman Curia as "unthinkable," and his observation that the Curia would be only "too happy" to avail itself of the help of the roughly 160 bishops who would constitute the new Synod sounded too good to be true of that hitherto omnipotent organ of para-papal government. Bishops resented the idea of being treated as underlings by Roman functionaries, some of whom were of not very exalted hierarchical rank, as was repeatedly declared during the debate on the Pastoral Office of Bishops at the Second Session. Although there could be no question of the "subordination" of one to the other—the Curia remained, as Cardinal Marella correctly pointed out, the "secretary" of the pope—it seemed clear that the Roman congregations were in for a thorough housecleaning, both in function and personnel, after the Council was over. In the inevitable rivalry between the two, much would depend on the collective or collegial influence which the Synod was able to exert—in the long run this might turn out to be considerable—and the attitude of the pope himself, whether Paul or his successor.

After the pope had left the council hall on Wednesday, the proceedings got under way with short speeches by Cardinal Tisserant, head of the Council presidency, and Cardinal Agagianian, moderator for the day. The former assured the Fathers that they would be allowed all the time necessary to transact the Council's business and that there would be no interference with freedom of speech. Nothing was said about the duration of the Session. It was noted with relief that the secretary general limited himself in his various announcements to what was strictly necessary and refrained from indulging in the intimidating tactics of the opening of the Third Session the year before.

THE DECLARATION ON RELIGIOUS LIBERTY

In accordance with Pope Paul's promise, made during the uproar at the close of the Third Session, the first item of business on the agenda was discussion of the revised text on Religious Liberty. The version of the document (*Textus Prior*) debated at the Third Session (September 23–25, 1964) had been so thoroughly altered in accordance with a plan suggested by the pope's personal theologian, Bishop Carlo Colombo, that when the new version (*Textus emendatus*) came up for a preliminary vote, scheduled for November 19, 1964, the minority protested that it had been so changed as to be no longer a revised text but an essentially new text. Therefore further debate must take place before it could be voted, according to the rules. The Council presidency accepted their petition and the vote was postponed, a decision which Pope Paul refused to reverse. Advantage was taken of the interval between the Third and Fourth Sessions to revise the text still further and it was this latter version (*Textus re-emendatus*) that formed the basis for discussion on September 15, 1965.

As Bishop de Smedt made clear in his *relatio,* the purpose of the present document was not to deal exhaustively with the whole range of problems that could be subsumed under the broad heading of religious liberty, but only one limited aspect of the problem, the question of civil liberty in religious matters, that is, the extent to which individuals or groups should be free from coercion in religious matters.

The text was not divided into chapters but had four distinct parts: an opening section devoted to a Declaration of Principles (a new feature of the *Textus re-emendatus*); this was followed by a section on proofs from reason; a third section came next dealing with the "roots" of the idea in divine revelation and emphasizing that religious liberty could not be proved from Scripture, strictly speaking; and finally a concluding section. Bishop de Smedt declared that a number of Fathers had wanted an introductory statement about the broader issue of Catholic doctrine toward freedom *in* the Church, but the feeling of the Secretariat had been that while the suggestion had merit, it was beyond the scope of the limited objective they had set themselves and was beyond the competence of the Secretariat.

Cardinal Spellman led off with an emphatic endorsement: "The schema is very pleasing and timely." It was essential for the Council to approve it so that all the world would know that the Catholic Church was in favor of religious liberty, a principle that could "give great impetus to ecumenism," whereas failure of the Council to approve it would give rise to doubts about the Church's sincerity. Cardinal Cushing, not to be outdone by Spellman, was more detailed about the reasons why the document should be adopted and majestically swept aside all objections. Religious liberty was "solidly based on Catholic teaching," not on the subjective order as some had said, but on the objective order of truth. The promulgation of such a doctrine was a pastoral necessity today "of the first order for the whole world." There were dictatorial governments today in many places that restricted human liberty especially in religious matters; where men were denied the right to religious liberty, they were very often denied other civil liberties as well. Together with St. Paul and Pope Paul, the Church must proclaim the "Gospel of freedom." He concluded with a ringing, "I am not afraid of the gospel of freedom. There are dangers everywhere but one of the greatest is the denial of liberty. We must preach the whole Gospel and approval of this Declaration would be a beginning."

As might be expected, Cardinal Ritter (St. Louis) was also wholeheartedly in favor of approval. "The schema leaves nothing to be desired except a prompt approbation and promulgation." The eyes of the whole world were turned toward Rome, he said, and neither charity, nor justice, nor fidelity would allow of any delay. But he was also, characteristically, more aware of the shadows on the scene. Approval was a matter of justice, he explained, because "our separated brothers in Christ" have suffered in certain Catholic countries owing to disregard for the principles stated in the Declaration. Fidelity to the work of the Council also required the passage of this document, otherwise the decrees on the Church and on Ecumenism would remain "worthless and deprived of any sense."

Approval was also voiced by the two German cardinals, Frings (Cologne) and Jäger (Paderborn), but in a more nuanced vein. The former felt that the whole section dealing with the reasons from natural law could be omitted, because it was not up to the Council but to theologians and philosophers to adduce arguments based on natural law. He also noted that in Part III Art. 9 there seemed to be a confusion between different concepts of liberty. The freedom we had from Christ and the freedom given us by the State were not one and the same thing. And the remarks made about the doctrine and practice of religious liberty in the history of the Church were out of place and inexact. He also expressed puzzlement about the language and style which were not such as one expected to find in a conciliar document. On the other hand, Cardinal Jäger found the order in which the arguments were presented good and calculated to appeal to non-Christians. Moreover, by distinguishing between religious liberty in the civil order and moral freedom, the schema avoided the complicated question of the erroneous conscience in bad faith because this problem did not exist in the juridical order: the state could not judge consciences and had to presume that all citizens acted in good faith in religious matters—an important point which the minority continually overlooked. More enthusiasm was shown by Cardinal Silva Henriquez (Santiago, Chile), who was particularly pleased by the pastoral implications of the treatment of religious liberty in the text. The new spirit of freedom which it breathed would not open the door to relativism, as some had maintained, but would promote a greater sense of responsibility. It offered a clear-cut statement of Catholic teaching and avoided certain explanations that might raise more questons than they would solve. Care must be taken, however, to see that under the pretext of freedom, no one took advantage of the Declaration to refuse necessary obedience. But we should be more interested in promoting the proper use of liberty than in preventing abuses of liberty.

One of the notable interventions in favor of the document was delivered by Cardinal Heenan two days after the opening of the debate. The cardinal was in good form, wide-ranging, caustic, and slightly inconsistent in the impression he made. The main burden of his talk was the inviolable right of every man to obey his conscience. "This is the whole argument of the Declaration," he asserted. It was absurd to charge that Catholics judged religious liberty and tolerance according to two distinct standards, depending upon whether they were on top or not. It was regrettably true that "in certain places" Protestants had suffered persecution at the hands of Catholics. The ecumenical implications of religious belief were a relatively modern discovery. "Practically nobody ever considered—much less conceded—the right of a man to follow his conscience" in the old days of *cuius regio eius religio*. "It was the custom of both sides to burn heretics," he noted, and said it would be ironical if the Council did not follow the pope's lead when he defended the right of every man to follow the dictates of his conscience and practice his religion freely in his recent talk at the Catacombs. "We must back his example and precept because the world is watching us and will judge the Fourth and final Session of the Council by the way we treat this Declaration." And he reminded the bishops of Cardinal Newman's famous quip when asked about toasting the pope at dinner. "First I would give a toast to conscience—only then would I toast the pope," Newman said. It would also be ironical if Catholics did not set an example by helping to banish religious intolerance and hatred, so that people would once again say as they said in the early Church: "See how these Christians love one another!"

Quite a number of speakers while favorable to the schema and desiring its passage were not content merely with praise but launched into a series of modifications they wanted introduced. The effect of some of their interventions, unfortunately, was to create the impression that the text was being more severely criticized than was the case. Cardinal Urbani (patriarch of Venice) was typical of this group and set the tone, as it were. His favorable, but critical, speech on the first day was regarded as highly significant coming from one whom the pope had recently appointed to the board of bishops in temporary charge of the Italian Episcopal Conference in place of the single chairmanship of Cardinal Siri (*L'Osservatore Romano*, August 20, 1965). Not that the cardinal could claim to speak for the Italian episcopate as such, but he certainly spoke for its *sanior pars*. The text was "substantially satisfactory" because it was both timely and true. The question of religious liberty was "in a sense new, and it cannot be solved merely by the simple recalling of the past teaching of the Church." He thus disposed of the frequent contention of the minority that it was enough to appeal to the teachings of Gregory XVI or Leo XIII. "The documents of past Popes," Cardinal Urbani went on, "from Gregory XVI to John XXIII show that the doctrine has been progressively enriched. The teaching on civil liberty in religious matters is a part of that progress." It is difficult to see how the cardinal could have expressed himself more clearly on one of the underlying issues, namely whether the present teaching on religious liberty was an instance of real doctrinal progress or development. It was significant also that he saw fit to mention Pope John XXIII. The minority generally preferred to limit their appeals to Pius XII, or even Leo XIII, implying that recent popes had somehow swerved from the straight and narrow path of orthodoxy. In order to make it perfectly clear that the document had a limited objective, he suggested that the subtitle be changed to read "Concerning *civil* liberty in religious matters." He also wanted the distinction between the juridical and moral aspects of religious liberty brought out more clearly, as well as the fact that religious truth was the one possessed and taught by the Catholic Church. The wording of the schema was intentionally low-key here so as not to antagonize non-Catholics or non-Christians. (Schema: "Therefore [religious liberty] leaves untouched Catholic doctrine concerning the one true religion and one Church of Christ.")

A number of speakers called for greater precision in the use of language and greater clarity about the limited purpose of the Declaration, such as Bishop Muldoon (auxiliary of Sydney, Australia). Archbishop Kozlowiecki (Lusaka, Zambia) called for a revision of the citations from papal documents in the light of Cardinal Urbani's remarks and wanted greater emphasis on the rights and authority of God to offset misunderstandings about the nature of religious liberty ("the Council needs to speak much more clearly about a right conscience, i.e. a conscience formed objectively according to the will of God"); and Bishop Muñoz Vega (auxiliary of Quito, Ecuador) maintained that there was a real danger of confusion in Latin America between freedom of religion and freedom of conscience and pointed to the impact of Protestant proselytism there. A fundamental objection, not to the idea of religious liberty as such but to the method of presenting it, was raised by Bishop Ancel (auxiliary of Lyons, France), speaking in the name of more than 100 French bishops. He wanted the "ontological foundation of religious liberty" made perfectly clear. "This connection between religious freedom and the obligation to seek after truth, which is nowhere expressed in a positive manner in the text, should be included in Art. 2, the nucleus of the Declaration, which is the only part that will come to the attention of the ordinary man. Such an addition will give assurance that the schema is not favoring the growing indifference and subjectivism of our day." This touched on one of the principal points that had divided the drafters of the proposal: the French generally being in favor of a more theoretical approach to the problem, the Americans and others favoring a more pragmatic line.*

Considerable misgivings were expressed about the paragraph inserted to safeguard the privileged position enjoyed by religious communities in certain countries. Its terms were applicable not only to countries like Spain or Italy with which the Holy See had concordats, but countries like England and Scandinavia where the local Churches were established by law. At the Third Session Cardinal Ottaviani had claimed that the whole concordat system of the Holy See was at stake. Unless the legitimacy of

* Fr. J. C. Murray, S.J., the chief spokesman for the pragmatic approach and principal drafter of the version of the document before the Council, revealed at the Press Panel (September 20th) that he had been in touch with French correspondents during the course of the summer and come to an agreement with them about this particular issue.

the "confessional state" was recognized, at least in those places where such arrangements were already in effect, the floodgates would be opened to laicism and the ultimate triumph of communism. This point of view ignored what was going on in most of the civilized world as well as the trend, in papal diplomacy, to move away gradually from too close an adherence to the concordat system, nevertheless the Secretariat considered it prudent to leave the provision in. Speaking in the name of the Dutch episcopate, Cardinal Alfrink warned the Council against the danger of speaking in too positive a way about the privileged position enjoyed by any religious community and said that it would be more appropriate to use conditional language. Cardinal Rossi (São Paulo, Brazil) seconded this suggestion. Several speakers wanted the provision removed altogether: Archbishop Lourdusamy (Bangalore, India), Archbishop Ziadé (Beirut) and Bishop Doumith (Sarba). The latter in particular noted that the language was equivocal and could open the door to discrimination: "A confessional state among Christians means no more than special honor and privileged status for a particular religion, but in non-Christian areas this idea is used as a means of religious discrimination." Cardinal McCann (Capetown, South Africa) wanted the point made clearer that a privileged status did not mean that any special burdens could be placed on those who did not belong to the religion or confession in question. Not with reference to this point specifically but speaking in general, Bishop Lokuang (Tainan, China) insisted that the text should contain a clear statement that "a Catholic state is better than an indifferent or neutral state" (though it is difficult to see how such a principle could be made applicable in his homeland), while Cardinal Browne (Curia) was even more emphatic: "In a Catholic state, those in authority must safeguard this [Catholic] faith because in it consists the supreme good of all citizens. The spreading of another religion in a Catholic state is a violation of public morality and harms the right that Catholics enjoy not to have their faith endangered."

Another problem with which both those who were for and those who were against the schema attempted to wrestle was that of the proper limits to religious freedom. It was agreed that it was not the proper function of the state to interfere with or determine religious matters, which were beyond its province, but to protect the right to religious liberty and free expression of religious ideas within certain limits. However, the difficulty was how to define those limits and according to what standard. The vague juridical language of the schema was not likely to have much appeal for those who were accustomed to the precise language of theology, but these critics were at a loss to suggest any better alternative. The schema said that the exercise of religion must be allowed and "not prohibited by any coercive intervention of the civil authority, unless it disturbs the public peace, or public morality, or infringes the rights of others. That is, the legal principle is to be observed, that the freedom of man is to be respected as far as possible and is not to be curtailed except when and in so far as necessary."

This meager definition of the "common good" was a frequent target. Archbishop Hallinan reminded the bishops, however, that it was thoroughly in accord with "the recently evolved doctrine of the Church concerning the constitutional state" on which the principle of religious freedom itself rested. Bishop Añoveros Ataun (Cadiz, Spain) held that because the notion of "public order" was so all-embracing, including theological as well as moral and purely juridical elements, the "whole text should be quickly submitted to an appropriate subcommission which could provide a more acceptable schema," particularly as the Secretariat was thought by some of the Fathers to be partial to the separated brethren on whose behalf it had proposed the document for the Council's consideration. This suggestion made on the fourth day of the debate was correctly regarded as a thinly veiled move intended to kill the schema.

There was nothing subtle however about the onslaught directed against the document by those who were its bitterest critics. They could be called the "toleration school," because they were unable to get beyond the thinking of the last century. As Father Murray pointed out, they were not opposed to the institution of religious liberty as such but rather to "the affirmation of progress in doctrine that an affirmation of religious freedom necessarily entails." Their spokesman, Cardinal Siri, put it thus: "The schema affirms religious freedom for all religious communities, and so also for those that deviate from the truth, and even for immoral and sanguinary ones. But God only tolerates and promises to punish such abuses of freedom. We cannot defend what God only tolerates." According to Bishop Gasbarri there was a "true conflict between supporters of this theory of right [expounded in the Declaration] and those who uphold the theory of toleration." He maintained that the question of the rights of an erroneous conscience did enter into the discussion, because "civil law cannot prescind from considering the truth and error without falling into juridical positivism and existential functionalism." The present text would open the door to indifferentism. The only solution was to rely on the "traditional doctrine of the popes" which, in the bishop's estimation, fully supported the theory of toleration. Cardinal Siri was more circumspect in his language regarding this latter point, though he fully agreed with the speaker: "Whether the schema really accords with the teaching on religious freedom found in theological sources and in the popes should be more deeply explored." He was certain, however, that if the doctrine of toleration were changed, "we will be undermining theological and our own authority." The opposition had apparently not taken the trouble to examine the *Pars Altera* appended to the schema which dealt with most of their objections, for they kept repeating that the schema's intention was to separate religious freedom from truth and this would promote indifferentism. Cardinal Ruffini, for example, asserted that while the Declaration of Human Rights adopted by the United Nations in 1948 was commendable because it attempted to preserve civil harmony between various religious groups, "it smacked of agnostic indifferentism," a charge that could equally well be levelled against the present schema. He was particularly worried about the possible effects of the Council's Declaration on the concordat between Italy and the Holy See, insisting that both Pius IX and Pius XII had been equally opposed to separation of Church and state (which was not true historically), and vaunting the fact that Catholics enjoyed certain privileges under the concordat which made the latter vulnerable to communist attack.

With a touch of irony in his voice, Bishop Velasco said that "the glorious minority had been over-ridden by the majority" and disregarded because they had remained constant to the teaching of the Church regarding toleration. "We must demand recognition of minority rights," he said, "not only in words but also in deeds. When there is question of a search for truth, it is not the number or quality of the persons involved that counts but the substance of the matter itself." The majority contended that the minority had not understood the text. If this were so, "after long years of study and experience, what chance was there of its being understood by the vast majority of the faithful?" he asked. The broader issue of "the cloven hoof of freedom within the Church" was what worried Archbishop Nicodemo (Bari). The text must be amended to show clearly that the Church had authority to "determine for the faithful the purpose and limits of liberty in religious matters." Otherwise there was danger the document might be used to claim a false freedom within the Church. Bishop Carli (Segni) fastened on the difficulty of reconciling the notion of religious liberty with some of the evidence from Scripture, claiming that the presentation ignored tradition, "perhaps because it was sensed that the doctrine proposed was contrary to tradition." He too purposely ignored what the text itself said, and what the *relator* and other speakers had repeatedly emphasized, with regard to this point.

Contrary to expectations, most of the Spanish bishops who spoke were heavily in opposition. The progress that seemed to have been registered in this quarter since the last session apparently had turned out to be illusory. The danger of proselytism was their main fear, though they felt also that indifferentism would be the end result. It was a mistake to believe that freedom for non-Catholic proselytism would aid the spread of the Gospel, according to Cardinal de Arriba y Castro (Tarragona). "Only the *private* practice of non-Catholic religions could be free; no religion, however, should be forced upon any man." "With the doctrine of the schema," Archbishop Garcia de Sierra y Mendez (Burgos) maintained, "it is impossible to defend the purity of the faith and the unity of the Church because the door would be open to the spreading of all kinds of error. We cannot, in order to please men, afford to do things that would not please God." He further blamed what he called "the modern itch for all kinds of liberty" and termed the schema "opportunistic" and conducive to "humanism." "Naturalistic humanism" was also one of the faults found in the text by Bishop del Campo y de la Barcena (Calahorra) who claimed that "the argumentation of the schema is based on two socio-religious phenomena: religious pluralism and the constitutions of many modern states. But such civil institutions are not worthy to be made the basis of the doctrinal decisions of a Council." It would be the equivalent of proclaiming to the world that the Catholic Church was only one among many, according to Archbishop Alvim Pereira (Lourenço Marques, Mozambique). The entire schema was felt to suffer from a basic weakness, in the opinion of Cardinal Dante (Curia) because it appeared to be based on the nineteenth-century liberalism of Lamennais and Montalembert. If religious liberty were to be restricted only by considerations based on the common good and public order, it would be open to various interpretations of these concepts. In a communist state, for example, ideas like peace and civil rights would be given a completely different meaning from their usual connotations. Archbishop Morcillo Gonzales (Madrid) and Archbishop Modrego y Casaus (Barcelona) both felt that in places the schema contradicted explicitly or implicitly the teaching of the popes and this point must be cleared up.

This question of whether the doctrine was or was not in conformity with papal teaching exercised many of the Fathers and became a kind of touchstone by which to separate the sheep from the goats. After launching into a tirade to the effect that "the roots of this doctrine are to be found in such eighteenth-century philosophers as Hobbes, Locke, Rousseau and others," Archbishop Lefebvre concluded: "The text contradicts the teaching of Leo XIII as directed against the above-mentioned philosophers." It was clear to Cardinal Ottaviani that the document must be revised in the light of the teaching of the modern popes, but he mentioned only Leo XIII and Pius XII. Both Father John Courtney Murray in an exhaustive lecture treating the whole subject delivered the opening day of the debate, and Cardinal Shehan of Baltimore, speaking in the Council on September 20th, had no difficulty in showing the absurdity of trying to prove anything by appealing to some popes while ignoring others, and the impossibility of making sense of the present as well as other conciliar documents, unless allowance were made for doctrinal development or progress.

After the first few days of debate the tide of criticism seemed to be running so heavily against Religious Liberty that Bishop Maloney (auxiliary of Louisville, Kentucky) was persuaded to voice a strong support for the Declaration on the part of the auditors of the Council and their hopes for its speedy approval and promulgation. Behind the scenes the minority were bending every effort to postpone or prevent a vote altogether, spreading rumors to the effect that since the Council was so hopelessly divided on the issue it would be unwise to have a vote, or there was no need for a vote, depending upon the strategy being pushed at the moment. They were unable to control the imponderables, however. One of these was the strong impression made on the bishops by a number of speakers from behind the Iron Curtain, who stressed the importance of the Declaration in the struggle against communism, a theme broached by Cardinal Heenan. Support for the text by the Polish bishops was voiced by Archbishop Baraniak (Poznan) and Archbishop Wojtyla (Kraków). Cardinal Slipyi, speaking in the name of the Ukrainian Episcopal Conference, stressed the "opportuneness of the doctrine of religious liberty" in view of present-day religious persecutions in communist countries, while Cardinal Wyszynski declared flatly, "A clear Declaration must come from this Council in the name of the teaching Church," in order to assist the Church in its struggle with communist states. The testimony of the newly created and liberated Cardinal Beran (Prague) in favor of approval, was probably the most decisive of all. "From the very moment when freedom of conscience was radically restricted in my country," he said, "I was witness not only to grave dangers to the faith, but also to serious temptations to hypocrisy and other moral vices that the oppression of conscience brought in its wake." Experience taught that oppression of conscience, even when intended for the good of the true faith, was pernicious. "Thus the Church in my country now seems to be making painful expiation for the sins committed in the past against freedom of conscience in the name of the Church." He cited particularly the burning of the Bohemian reformer John Hus in the fifteenth century by the Council of Constance, and the forcible re-Catholicization of the majority of the Bohemian people in the seventeenth century under Habsburg rule. These acts in reality wounded the Church, because the "trauma" hidden in the hearts of the people was a grave impediment to spiritual progress and gave the enemies of the Church plenty of material for agitation. He did not mention, but could have, the wholesale departure from the Catholic Church of over a million Czechs after the dissolution of the Austro-Hungarian Monarchy at the end of the First World War. "History warns us that we must declare the principle of religious liberty and freedom of conscience clearly and without any restrictions."

Another impressive reply to the objectors, based on experience, was delivered by Cardinal Cardijn who spoke in the light of his 60 years among young workers. "This Declaration would arouse great hopes among the younger generation," he declared. "The Church cannot expect religious liberty when she is in a minority unless she practices it when she is in the majority." The charges that it would give rise to indifferentism or amount to a surrender of Catholic teaching regarding the one true Church or contribute to the spead of error were effectively rebutted in forceful speeches by Cardinal Lefebvre (Bourges) and Cardinal Journet, the latter noting that it was the task of the Church nowadays "to fight error with the arms of light rather than the arms of force."

On Tuesday, September 21st, exactly a week after the opening of the Fourth Session, the Council surmounted an important hurdle. At precisely 10:45 on that morning, the presiding moderator, Cardinal Agagianian, called for a standing vote to close debate on the controversial Religious Liberty schema. While sudden, the moderator's decision was not altogether unexpected. In four and a half days of debate 62 speeches had been heard. In the judgment of most observers the decision could have come earlier, the prolongation of the debate being due to the pope's extreme willingness to accommodate the opposition. There was an awkward lapse, for a few minutes, before the *relator* Bishop de Smedt could be found to sum up and assure the Fathers that their suggestions would all be taken into account.* The situation was dramatic because for several days it had been uncertain whether there would actually be a vote or not. The fear was that the document might simply be remanded to committee for amendment, without any preliminary vote guaranteeing that it would not be substantially changed. Opponents of the measure had partially succeeded in creating the impression that it might not win a respectable majority (some reports had it that the Non placets might be as high as 500). It was said that some of them, including several cardinals, had petitioned the pope not to allow any vote and that they wanted the document given to a subcommission for rewriting. This would have meant a signal defeat for the English-speaking bishops in particular, who had to some extent staked the reputation of the Council on passage of the Religious Liberty schema.

It was known that at a joint meeting of the Council leadership (Coordinating Commission, moderators, secretary general on the previous evening, Monday, Sept. 20th), a proposal that the schema be presented to the Fathers for a preliminary vote on its merits, in accordance with the usual Council procedure, had lost—some said by a vote of 16 to 9.†

* Bishop Grotti, speaking the next day in the name of 70 Fathers, adjured the bishops to take careful note of what Bishop de Smedt said and see that he lived up to his promise!

† R. Laurentin, in *Le Figaro* (Sept. 23), said that three proposals were considered by the meeting: 1) to vote according to various formulas; 2) to vote on certain key

Cardinal Spellman, one of the Coordinating Commission members, was said to have emerged from the meeting in anger, and Cardinal Shehan was believed to have gone to see the pope to protest the decision. As night fell it was unknown whether the formula for a vote which Father Murray had been working on earlier in the day would become a dead issue or not. All depended on Pope Paul.

A wave of surprise, therefore, swept over the council hall on Tuesday when, halfway through the morning, the voice of the secretary general, Archbishop Felici, announced over the microphone that, by decision of the moderators,* a special secret vote would be taken immediately on Religious Liberty. He suggested that the bishops take pen in hand and write down the following text, and then in schoolmaster fashion read out in Latin: "Does it please the Fathers that the already amended text on Religious Liberty should be taken as the basis for a definitive declaration, after further amendment in the light of Catholic doctrine on the true religion and amendments proposed by the Fathers in discussion, which will be subsequently approved according to the norms of Council procedure?" The alternatives were Placet or Non placet. He repeated the formula, then reminded the bishops that they were not to confuse this vote with a ballot already in their hands relating to the text on Divine Revelation. After several minutes of confusion, the latter ballot was disposed of and new ballots were distributed for the vote on Religious Liberty. The outcome was 1,997 in favor as against 224 opposed (with 1 null vote). This amounted to a landslide for the progressives and was greeted with a long round of applause.

Word quickly passed that the vote had been forced by the pope himself in a dramatic intervention, not unlike Pope John's action in rescuing the schema on Divine Revelation during the First Session. Observant commentators suddenly remembered that Cardinal Tisserant, the Council's president, Cardinal Agagianian, one of the moderators, and Archbishop Felici, the secretary general, had all arrived in the council hall tardily that morning, toward the close of the council mass. The secret was soon out. They had been summoned to the pope's apartment earlier in the morning and informed that, contrary to the recommendation of the Coordinating Commission, Paul wanted a preliminary vote on Religious Liberty. His decision was final. The pope approved the formula for the vote drawn up by the Secretariat and hastily presented to him, adding the final clause "which will be subsequently approved according to the norms of Council procedure." This meant that the document would remain under the juris-

---

points; 3) to have no vote at all. The latter carried the day by a majority of 6 votes.

* Significantly on this occasion there was no mention of the Council presidents, usually included in such announcements.

diction of the Secretariat and any further changes could not affect its substance.

Some of the 224 Non placet votes were unquestionably cast by bishops who were in doubt as to what the complicated formula meant and ignorant of how it had been arrived at.

The drama thus resolved had incalculable significance. Pope Paul was scheduled to appear before the United Nations Assembly in New York on October 4th, to plead for peace and respect for human dignity. With all the world aware of Pope John's encyclical *Pacem in terris,* whose principal theme was the dignity of man as the foundation of human liberty, the pope and his advisers knew that he could not effectively face that international body with an ambiguous Council vote on such an important issue as the Catholic Church's stand on religious liberty.

THE DEBATE ON SCHEMA 13

The vote on Religious Liberty and Pope Paul's announcement of the Synod acted as a kind of tonic. The bishops felt that the shadow of the pope's nervous and somewhat equivocal attitude had suddenly been banished. It began to seem possible that the Council might finish its work by December.

Schema 13 was an entirely new kind of document for a church council to be concerned with; the time was past when the Church could afford to confine its attention exclusively to itself. Pope John XXIII sensed this. Schema 13, according to Cardinal Suenens who was often credited with inspiring it, was really suggested by Pope John himself and reflected his whole outlook.

The attitude of the Council toward this novel schema was still hesitant at the Third Session, and it was subjected to scathing criticism. Secretary General Felici had tried to maintain that the Appendices (*Adnexa*), which dealt in greater depth with such subjects as human dignity, marriage, culture, economic and social life, were merely "private" and not official Council documents. He had to retract this hastily framed judgment. The substance of the more audacious Appendices was eventually incorporated in the body of the schema, by decision of the Coordinating Commission. This marked an important defeat for the minority.

Pope Paul cut short speculation that Schema 13 would be withdrawn when he remarked, at the end of the Third Session, that it would become the "crown of the Council's work."

Schema 13 had many unique features. Apart from being the third Constitution to be considered by the Council (the other two being the documents on the Liturgy and on the Church), it was the first ever to be addressed "to all mankind." It was the first to be drafted in a modern language, French, because modern thought could only be clearly expressed in a modern language. It was the only conciliar document circulated to the bishops in other modern languages (English, German, Spanish, Italian). Though Archbishop Felici made a great point of emphasizing (in the preface to the English translation, for example) that the Latin version remained the *only* official text, nevertheless the facts spoke for themselves.

The text debated in September 1965 was the fourth draft to be produced (the first having been presented to the Coordinating Commission by Cardinal Suenens in 1963). It was based on the third draft debated at the Third Session from October 20th to November 10th, 1964.

The Schema was also unique in its subject matter in that it was oriented toward man and was intended to lay the foundations for a Christian anthropology, something never assayed before on the conciliar level. It had much to say about the importance of the community, the socialization and progressive nature of society, the meaning of freedom, respect for human dignity, the necessity of banishing all types of discrimination with regard to sex, race, religion, etc. It stressed the importance of scientific research, admitting that the Church had sometimes erred in its attitude toward science in the past. Above all, it stressed the essential goodness of creation and the central role of Christ in this connection. It called the Church the sacrament of unity of all mankind and Jesus Christ, according to the felicitous phrase of Pope Paul VI, "the focal point of the desires of history and civilization."

Mankind was destined to reform the world. Therefore the Church, to use another Pauline expression, must "historicize itself," insert itself in history, in order to promote the renewal of the world for which it exists.

Speaking in the name of Bishop Guano, who was ill, Archbishop Garrone introduced the debate on Tuesday, September 21st, immediately after the vote on Religious Liberty. In his *relatio* he pointed out that the new version was both longer and "quite different" from the previous text, because the commission had worked long and hard to do justice to the wishes of the Fathers, by including some of the material from the former *Adnexa* in the body of the schema, and by suppressing certain chapters and generaly rearranging the whole. The introductory sections (Introduction, Preliminary Statement, Arts. 1–9) were considered of sufficient importance to entrust to a special Subcommission that would report on them separately. The title of "Pastoral Constitution" had been chosen and approved by the Coordinating Commission, Archbishop Garrone explained, because conciliar pronouncements nowadays were either "constitutions" or "decrees," depending upon whether they dealt primarily with matters of faith or practice. Meeting the critics head on, he declared that this designation and the fact that it was addressed to "all mankind" made the schema a document in accordance with "the supreme intention and purpose of the Council, as defined by Pope John XXIII."

The 1964 version came to 27 pages of text and included 24 numbered paragraphs; the 1965 version ran to 80 pages of text and included 106 numbered paragraphs. The 1964 version consisted of an Introduction, 4 Chapters, and a Conclusion; the 1965 version was divided into two Parts, consisting of an Introduction (and Preliminary Statement) and 4 Chapters of Part I, and 5 Chapters of Part II. Chapter IV of the earlier version (dealing with human dignity, marriage, culture, economic and social life, human solidarity, peace) had now been expanded into separate Chapters in the new version (human dignity being transferred to Part I). This will give the reader some idea of the extent of the changes.

The discussion opened with consideration of Schema 13 as a whole. While most of the speakers applauded the work of the commission and expressed their approval of the new text, at least in principle, they raised a number of serious objections regarding its tone, emphasis and style. One criticism was that the schema was still permeated by a spirit of excessive optimism. It should attempt to "avoid all appearance of the optimism characteristic of the nineteenth century," according to Cardinal Jäger (Paderborn). The same defect was also pointed out by Cardinal Döpfner and by Bishop Renard (Versailles). True to form, Cardinal König was incisive in his analysis: the schema must be purged of its weaknesses. Among these he included a tendency, noticeable particularly in the Introduction, to concentrate on "transitory matters" rather than upon the real problems. The text must avoid the impression of attempting to provide a "panacea" for all the world's ills. It was not always clear who was speaking: the "People of God," the "Sacred Synod," or simply "we." On the other hand, Bishop Jordan (Edmonton, Canada) found the schema quite satisfactory in this respect.

The question of whether or not it should be called a "pastoral constitution" was also debated back and forth. Cardinal Silva Henriquez was of the opinion that the word "pastoral" should be eliminated because this was a common trait of all the Council's pronouncements and would not help to clarify the status of its authority. Archbishop Morcillo Gonzales (Madrid) questioned the propriety of calling it a "constitution" because this term was normally reserved for documents that were addressed to the faithful and suggested instead that it be designated a "Declaration on a dialogue with the world of today." The secretary of the *Coetus Internationalis Patrum,* Archbishop de Proença-Sigaud, agreed with Archbishop Morcillo Gonzales but the main burden of his criticism was that the schema was too "phenomenological" and not sufficiently scholastic in its approach. Such a method allowed two propositions to be both true and contradictory at the same time, the archbishop maintained, thus opening the way for nominalism and Marxism. The schema's presentation of the world also smacked too much of Teilhard de Chardin, for his liking. "The Church can be present to the world either as a ferment," he said, "while not being 'of' this world. Or the world can penetrate the Church. In the latter case, which seems to be the view favored by the schema, there is danger that the Church will fall into false paganism, as happened to the promoters of humanism at the time of the Renaissance." On the other hand, the Ukrainian Archbishop Hermaniuk (Winnipeg, Canada) found that the schema "follows too slavishly the scholastic method in discussing such questions as human activity in the world, progress and culture . . ." The two interventions by bishops of the United States on this part of the schema were rather unfortunate in the impressions they created. Cardinal Spellman got off to a good start with wholehearted approval and a warning not to weaken the text, but then weakened his own case by defining "dialogue," which he declared to be its goal, too much in terms of "obedience to Church authority." He then compounded the error with a slap at conscientious objection, a subject not slated to come up until later in the debate. The high mark of irrelevance was attained by Bishop McVinney (Providence, Rhode Island), who in criticizing what the schema had to say about concrete solutions launched into a diatribe about "the general breakdown in authority on all levels both in the Church and in the state . . . There is in the Church today a crisis of obedience, not only among the laity but also in the ranks of the clergy, not excluding priests . . ." He was finally reminded by the moderator that the place for such remarks was later when the schema on Priestly Life and Ministry would be taken up.

One of the chief targets was the style of the Latin into which the document had been "translated" from the original French with which the subcommission members had worked. Some found the language excessively classical in places, and in others almost unintelligible. Cardinal Ruffini: "The Latin leaves much to be desired. Nobody expected it to be Ciceronian but in spots it is hardly even Latin." Cardinal Bea noted that though he had taught in Latin for 50 years, it was sometimes necessary for him to go to the French text to determine what was meant. Various speakers ridiculed such Ciceronianisms as *ludricra certamina* for "sports," *officium conscientiae* for "responsibility," *hominum coniunctio* for "solidarity," *cultus humanus* for "culture." Cardinal Bea asked why not simply use such words as *responsibilitas, solidaritas, cultura,* etc.? Father Tucci, S.J., editor of *La Civiltà Cattolica* and one of the drafters of the text, explained at the Bishops' Press Panel that part of the difficulty was due to the fact that the commission had not been allowed as much time for its work as had been expected in December 1964. Instead of the original deadline of June 1965, the commission had been informed that the text must be ready by Easter. The Introduction and Chapter I were the least satisfactory admittedly but they were also almost wholly new; Part II was in better shape because less radically changed from the 1964 version.

In spite of the fact that a special subcommission had been appointed to look into the matter, there were still complaints that the presentation was too "western" and unrepresentative of Asian and African thought. Archbishop Lourdusamy (coadjutor of Bangalore, India) for example, speaking in the name of 6 Indian bishops, said that the description of "man in the modern world" in the text applied mainly to advanced, industrialized regions and would not be recognized by those who constituted the greater part of humanity living in Africa, Asia and Latin America. Unless there were a change of emphasis here, "the people of India would conclude that the Church is not concerned with her problems." The same point was made by Cardinal Rugambwa with respect to Africa and the "viewpoint of peoples who have recently begun to share world government." Like Cardinal Spellman, Bishop de Castro Mayer (Campos, Brazil) somewhat anticipated matters by launching into a detailed condemnation of communism before this subject was reached in Part I.

Late Thursday morning, September 23rd, after little more than two days of debate, the Fathers were asked whether they wished to terminate the debate on Schema 13 as a whole by a standing vote and were then polled by secret ballot as to "whether it was pleasing, the debate on the schema as a whole having been terminated, to pass on to an examination of each part?" The results were announced the next day: 2,111 Placets to 44 Non placets. However, there was no delay. Bishop McGrath immediately rose on Thursday to give his *relatio* on the Introduction and Part I and the debate continued as if the outcome were already known. Everything proceeded as if the Council had given its preliminary approval to the schema (as it had done in the case of Religious Liberty and other texts at the end of the general discussion). Although this was declared to be a fact by the press, such was not the case, technically speaking. Why was the usual question ("Do you approve the present text as the basis for a definitive text . . . ?") not put to the Fathers? Various theories were put forward. One reason may have been a desire on the part of the Council leadership to cover its tracks in case unforeseen difficulties developed preventing promulgation.*

---

* R. Laurentin suggested: 1) fear of upsetting an apparent unanimity; 2) desire not to humiliate the minority; 3) reluctance to bow to democratic procedures. *Le Figaro*, September 25, 1965.

INTRODUCTION AND PRELIMINARY STATEMENT

There were only eight speakers on the Introduction, Preliminary Statement and Part I in general, despite the fact that much care had been given to this part by a special subcommission, probably because most of the bishops wished to save their fire for the detailed discussion of Part I which was to follow.

Although the document was addressed "to all mankind," Cardinal Cardijn did not feel that the Introduction singled out sufficiently three groups in which he personally had always been particularly interested: youth, the working classes, and the *"tiers monde"*—by which he meant the developing nations. "It would be a great scandal," he maintained, "if the enjoyment of earthly goods were too long confined to the so-called Christian nations." The Church must avoid any semblance of adopting a patronizing attitude toward them and be a strong advocate of sharing the blessings of technical assistance and education and the banishment of egoism and racial discrimination. Although the treatment of Christian anthropology was not intended to be exhaustive but merely suggestive, Bishop Abasolo y Lecue (Vijayapuram, India) expressed astonishment that nothing was said about the immortality of the soul in the section on human dignity.

Cardinal Frings criticized certain ambiguous notions that seemed to permeate the whole schema: he mentioned specifically the concepts of the People of God and "the world." Also at fault, in his opinion, was the whole scope of the schema. He concluded, rather gloomily: "This cannot be effected by the mere change of a word or a sentence but will call for far-reaching revision." Bishop Volk (Mainz) also found the Introduction unclear and unsatisfactory from a theological point of view. One fault was that "sin" was never treated *ex professo* in the text. The emphasis was upon a diagnosis of present ills of society without going into such fundamental questions as sin, sickness, death, and the mystery of grace and sin. "We must not water down the Gospel for the sake of dialogue," he warned. "Therefore, I propose that the description of man in today's world be shortened and that a more theological outlook be adopted that would include his relationship to God, his sinfulness and his redemption." The treatment of the world, sin, and the devil was also considered inadequate by Bishop Marafini (Frosinone, Italy). It was while listening to this bishop's long and detailed analysis of the defects of the schema that one of the experts turned to his companion and said, "A wave of pessimism seems to be spreading over the assembly." After three days of debate, the feeling was that if the text were to be as radically revised as these speakers were suggesting, the Council could not possibly promulgate it by December.

The treatment of "the world" came in for particular criticism from the coadjutor bishop of Strasbourg, Monsignor Elchinger. "We should be speaking not of 'the world today' but rather of 'the Church in the world today.'" The schema had much to say about what the world was expected to do but not enough about what the Church should do. It should be stated more clearly exactly how the Church intended to realize the legitimate desires of mankind. The Church of course could not expect to have all the answers to every question, but it must at least try to point out a solution. Moreover, the world would pay more attention to what the Church said, if the Church sought effectively to eliminate those things "in herself" that were a cause of disbelief. He was referring specifically to the problem of atheism. While noting that it was "no easy task to propose a definition and description that can satisfy everyone everywhere" Bishop Himmer wanted greater attention paid to the dignity of labor and working men, "who constitute the bulk of the world with which we now begin to be in dialogue." He felt that it would be profitable to follow the lead of *Mater et Magistra* and *Pacem in Terris* by saying something more concrete on this score.

Finally, the Preliminary Statement needed a greater biblical emphasis, according to Bishop Charue (Namur) and he too joined the chorus of those complaining about the inconsistency in the use of the term "the world." The drafters should determine the exact sense in which they wanted to use the term and then be consistent with themselves. Ultimately, however, after revision, "the draft should be given enthusiastic approval."

The debate on Part I (which actually covered quite a lot of ground) soon narrowed down to a discussion of one single item, Article 19, which was only about one page long in the text. An unfortunate tendency was evident to judge the whole schema in the light of its treatment of this one point. The paragraph had been drafted in such a way as to avoid any outright or drastic condemnation of atheism, the emphasis being put on what was lacking in atheistic systems. There was no mention of communism as such.

This was too much for certain prelates from Italy, Spain, and those representing certain ethnic groups who accused the drafters of being "soft" on this issue and wanted the Council to speak out with a resounding condemnation of atheism and communism. The other school, undoubtedly representing the majority of the bishops, was willing to go along with the schema's moderate approach but wanted certain improvements.

A curious feature of the debate was that the American contribution was almost nil here. The impression given was that this was an issue of no great concern to the American hierarchy, a contest between European prelates in which African and Asian bishops occasionally joined in. But a factor may have been the desire not to "rock the boat," since there were many vociferous anti-communist groups among the American Catholic Right.

A number of important observations were made regarding the relevancy of Part I to the rest of the schema, the order in which the material was arranged, and the inadequacy of its approach to a Christian anthropology. Patriarch Meouchi noted that there was insufficient emphasis on the doctrine of the resurrection, a central idea in Eastern theology. This historical fact was not merely the end of our redemption, but the beginning of our sanctification and because this fact had been lost sight of, the force of the text was greatly weakened. The same could be said about its emphasis on the role of the Holy Spirit. Archbishop Ziadé concurred: "The people of the Orient are so taken up with the place of Christ's resurrection in their lives that a common greeting, even among ordinary people, is 'Christ is risen,' to which the proper answer is, 'He is risen indeed.' " Meouchi went on to say that if these points were corrected, the schema would be more acceptable and not so "western" in tone. The schema's anthropology should be squarely founded on Scripture and tradition. Archbishop Garrone found the chief fault of the treatment to be the unsatisfactory way in which the doctrine of creation was presented. By reason of this marvelous truth, all things were related to the Creator. Realizing that God could bestow material goods as he saw fit should serve as the basis for a spirituality of poverty. Bishop Schick (auxiliary of Fulda) also wanted a clearer emphasis placed on the doctrine of creation.

Archbishop Darmajuwana, in the name of the Indonesian bishops, voiced the opinion that Chapters III and IV of Part I, on which the whole first section of the schema hinged, were weak. There was no dialogue here, merely a monologue. In the opinion of Bishop Romero Menjibar (Jaen), Chapter IV would better be included in the Introduction. Certain details were taken up without a previous consideration of the role of the Church in the world. People were disturbed by the problem of "demythologization" today. "Many think the Christian concept of God is outdated because it is not based on scientific ideas. Hence it is important for the Church to teach clearly what is substantial in the vision of God and what is attributable to a particular mentality or age." Bishop Corboy (Monze, Zambia) criticized the lack of coordination between the principles enunciated in Part I and the concrete treatment that was supposed to come in Part II, a point frequently mentioned by other speakers such as the Dominican Master General, Father Fernandez, who remarked that in order to "solve the present problems of mankind, theoretical principles are not enough. We must get down to the concrete order, if we wish to bring light and not confusion to these problems."

Cardinal Richaud and Archbishop Guerry both regretted that the document did not have enough to say about the Church's social doctrine, the former suggesting that in Part I and especially in Chapter III of Part I, there should be a reference to Pope John's *Mater et Magistra*. Archbishop Guerry's observation that Part I contained no very specific reference to Pope Paul's Bombay appeal for disarmament in December 1964 seemed more appropriate for Part II than Part I. The attitude of Latin American Spanish-speaking prelates toward the schema was somewhat contradictory. Cardinal Rossi (San Paulo, Brazil) pointed to the particular plight of Latin America and other developing nations and said that it was necessary to bear their problems in mind, though he thought the schema was "very pleasing and worth perfecting." He especially wanted the idea of a "Perpetual *aggiornamento*" somehow incorporated in the text. Cardinal Santos (Manila) took exception to Article 27, which implied "that there are nations in which men are forced against their will to embrace the Catholic faith," as well as the horrendous thought that nations granting unlimited freedom in religious matters to their citizens were more praiseworthy than those that sought to establish some form of control over the manifestations of religion. These remarks should be eliminated, he insisted. Bishop Llopis Ivorra (Coria Cáceres, Spain) agreed, declaring that "religious liberty should not be regarded as an absolute good, but only as a good for those areas where Catholic unity does not exist" (as if the Declaration on Religious Liberty had never been heard of). He felt that "there should be no 'joy' if religious freedom would cause conversion to error." On the other hand, Archbishop Soares de Resende's statement caused something of a sensation in the Portuguese press, particularly his call for the schema "to condemn police state regimes, especially in countries under Soviet domination. Many upright persons, often including priests and bishops, are subjected to so much surveillance merely because they do not belong to the party that their nerves are frayed and their wills subdued. Such violence and harm to the human person should be specifically condemned." (Although the archbishop was referring mainly to Iron Curtain countries, his remarks were interpreted by avant-garde Catholics in Portugal as applicable to the Salazar regime. Only the Catholic newspaper *As Novidades* printed his remarks in full.) Bishop Klepacz (Lódz) pointed out that the Council must be doubly clear about its use of such terms as "progress" and "liberty" because these and other words were abused by the communist authorities and used in propaganda against the Church. He also deplored the "principle of state supremacy," insisting that this was still the root of many evils and deserved more outright condemnation. In this connection he called for mention of the Nuremberg trials and the current trials of ex-Nazis in Germany.

THE CHURCH AND ATHEISM

Discussion of Article 19 was formally launched by Cardinal Seper (Zagreb) who regretted the inadequate treatment of atheism, one of the most serious of present-day problems, because men regard atheism as a mark of true progress and the true humanism. The approach must be not a simple condemnation of atheism or demonstration of the existence of God, but must show how the Church understood atheism and regarded atheists and why faith in God promoted progress, whereas atheism was sterile. "Hence we must admit that Christians who defended the established order and the unchangeableness of social structures too stubbornly, wrongly appealing to God's authority, are partly responsible for modern atheism. We must declare that the notion atheists have of God is false . . ." In fact, God was the true foundation for the promotion of genuine progress.

Cardinal König agreed with Seper that the text failed to distinguish adequately between various forms of atheism, of which the militant was only one type among many. He then briefly went into the historical situation that had resulted in present-day atheism: "Christians have had a large responsibility for the rise and spread of atheism." As for the remedies, Christian cooperation and proper study of the subject were essential: "I propose a theological study of the spread of atheism in the world as well as the axiom 'the soul is naturally Christian' to see how the two principles can be reconciled." Ignorance about atheism among priests and missionaries was a great danger for the Church. As for present policy: "We must anathematize no one, but the Council must speak out in defense of Christians and seek to establish communication with all men of goodwill. Atheistic governments should be invited to promulgate a doctrine of religious liberty founded on the natural law." A practical suggestion for those living in communist countries would be to "show that on the purely civil level religion makes a more effective contribution to the national welfare than does atheism."

The schema was essentially good, according to Patriarch Maximos IV Saigh, "because it is centered on Christ and shows the world a spirit of love." But its treatment of atheism was faulty. "Rather we must denounce the causes of atheistic communism and above all propose a dynamic mystique and a vigorous social morale, showing workers that Christ is the source of their true liberation." He contrasted the positive attitude of

John's *Pacem in Terris* and Paul's *Ecclesiam Suam* with that of the schema which "only deplores and condemns." Many true atheists were really not against the Church; they were seeking, as Pope Paul noted, for a truer presentation of God, an up-to-date religion, and above all a Church in solidarity with the poor. "They are scandalized by a mediocre, selfish Christianity which, relying on riches and arms, defends its own interests. If we had lived and preached the gospel of brotherhood, we would have defeated world atheistic communism." His final paragraph contained a discreet reference to worker priests: "Instead of a banal and repetitive condemnation of atheism, let us send to the working man an increasing number of priests and laymen prepared to take part in their work."

Cardinal Florit, archbishop of Florence, professed to be particularly disturbed by the "practical atheism" adopted by so many people in Italy and elsewhere these days. While not publicly denying Christianity as such, they lived as if God did not exist. There was also widespread conviction that "the Marxist system can be accepted with regard to economics without accepting its atheistic or materialistic doctrine." The schema should clearly state that such a distinction was impossible. "Dialectical materialism is monistic," according to the archbishop; "economic life, materialistically understood, is considered the only reality, there is thus no room for God." Naturally with an eye on the local scene, the Rome daily *Il Tempo* headlined the archbishop's speech: "ARCHBISHOP OF FLORENCE CONDEMNS THOSE WHO WANT TO CARRY ON DIALOGUE."

The views of émigré groups calling for a strong statement condemning communism were perhaps best represented by the auxiliary of Toronto, Bishop Rusnack. Truth and charity demanded that the Council speak out about the perils of atheism, "which stems from a politico-economic system that touches Eastern Catholics very closely." The situation in Czechoslovakia was deplorable. "In one night all the religious communities in Czechoslovakia were suppressed, their members being arrested and herded into concentration camps. Priests were taken out of their parishes . . . To combat this plague, we should add a special Declaration on Communism, in line with the message to all men issued by the Council in 1962. There should be no fear that speaking out will cause reprisals behind the iron curtain. Experience shows that communists will react only to forceful public opinion." According to the Ukrainian Bishop Elko (Pittsburgh), unless the Council came out with an "explicit condemnation of dialectical materialism as one of the false doctrines against the dignity of the human person, the world will accuse us of fear." In the opinion of the Jesuit Bishop Hnilica, resident in Italy, "To say only what the schema says about atheism is the same as saying nothing at all." On the other hand, Archbishop Wojtyla (Kraków) called for moderation, approving in general what the schema now said: "Atheism can be taken up here only with difficulty because the question is so complex." It was clear from the absence of any enthusiasm on the part of prelates from behind the Iron Curtain that the subject would have to be handled with extreme caution. The Russian Orthodox observer-delegates were weighing every word carefully, for to a certain extent their presence at the Council was conditional on an understanding that there would be no outright condemnation that would place them in a difficult position.

A different line was taken by Archbishop Marty, who found the present treatment of atheism too abstract. Atheists should be regarded as true humanists who were striving to build a better world, but who saw belief in God as somehow hampering efforts toward improvement. "A revision of the present text might well serve as a plan of action for the Secretariat for Non-Believers," he told the Council. In fact this Secretariat could take the initiative in preparing a statement on this subject for approval by the Council. "Christians would do well to realize that an open dialogue with atheists can eventually bring about a purification of their own faith. Archbishop Bengsch (Berlin) also called for revision, particularly with regard to the analysis of atheistic ideology, and suggested that while the commission had done its work well, the existing text was too long and verbose. It would be better to leave details to the Synod of Bishops and episcopal conferences.

The maiden speech of the new General of the Jesuits, Father Pedro Arrupe, created something of a sensation in the world press. The burden of his talk was that Christians were not adequately coping with the task of spreading the gospel and meeting the challenge of the non-believing world. The Church faced this world with her immense treasures, but "we have to admit that she has not yet discovered an effective way of sharing her treasures with the men of our time." He then cited some telling statistics which seemed to prove his point: Catholics formed 18 percent of the world population in 1961; today they formed 16 percent, an appreciably smaller proportion on a world scale. Thus after 2,000 years Catholics were only a small part of the world's population, "and how much of that tiny portion can be said to be really Catholic?" Efforts were too largely "frittered away" owing to bad planning and lack of coordination; the tendency was for the Church to look at things from too theoretical a point of view. A case in point was the treatment of atheism in Article 19. The solutions proposed were too intellectual. This was a mistake that had consistently been made by the Church in the past. The Church had the truth and the basic principles, but she did not know how to relate theory to action. Nobody was likely to disagree with this, but eyebrows were raised when he suggested that not only the mentality and cultural environment found in the modern world were nourished "at least in practice" by atheism, but that

the world was like the City of Man in St. Augustine; . . . it not only carries on the struggle against the City of God from outside the walls, but even crosses the ramparts and enters the very territory of the City of God, insidiously influencing the minds of believers (including even religious and priests) with its hidden poison, and producing its natural fruits in the Church: naturalism, distrust, rebellion.

He then went on to state that this godless society operated in an extremely efficient manner, making use of all scientific, technical, social and economic knowledge and means, following "a perfectly mapped-out strategy. It holds almost complete sway in international organizations, in financial circles, in the field of mass communications: the press, cinema, radio and television." His detailed suggestions on fighting modern atheism more effectively sounded rather like a page borrowed from the charter of the controversial activist organization (largely concentrated in Spain) known as *Opus Dei*. It called for social action and the widespread penetration of all social, economic, and political structures in order to spread there the values of a Christian life and thus combat the influence of atheism at its source. In order to make progress quickly, according to Arrupe, 1) it was necessary for specialists to draw up a plan of action sufficiently flexible to be adaptable to local conditions; 2) to present this plan to the pope; 3) for the pope "to assign various fields of labor to everyone"; and 4) to invite "all men who believe in God to this common labor that God may be the Lord of human society." He then suggested three principles that ought to govern this coordination of effort: a scientific spirit, animated by faith; "absolute obedience to the Supreme Pontiff"; and all-embracing charity.

It was not so much that Arrupe was recommending a concrete plan for dealing with atheism as the unfortunate fact that he chose to express himself in military terminology (a tradition with the Jesuit Order, or at least some Jesuits, since their founding by Ignatius Loyola, a former soldier). After all, Pope Paul had entrusted the Jesuits with a special role in the struggle against atheism when he received their general chapter in May 1965 before Arrupe's election, but in the Council Arrupe's militant program hardly seemed compatible with the spirit of Schema 13, addressed as it was "to all mankind." He admitted as much in a press interview later, saying: "There have been some misunderstandings and exaggerations. But I don't want to blame the press for this. . . . My remarks were poorly translated into English. I didn't mean that there was a universal atheistic organization." But when *The Tablet* of London printed the Latin text of two paragraphs of his speech alongside the

English translation, it was apparent that the translation was accurate and faithful.*

The fate that overtook the Father General was typical of the predicament in which many of the clergy found themselves nowadays, particularly those in authority. Trained in a conservative tradition, accustomed to expressing themselves in outmoded terminology, yet sensitive to the problems facing the Church and desirous of furthering the work of the Council, they may at first have failed to make the grade but they persisted. Arrupe granted several interviews, the first General of the Jesuits ever to do so, and not only had a number of "brushes" with the press but—*horribile dictu*—had even been publicly criticized by one of his own provincials.† He seemed to be eminently a man of his times.

The bishop of Cuernavaca made an interesting suggestion that also received wide notice in the press, when he regretted that the schema was silent about psychoanalysis "which is a true science today, even if not fully mature, and which is as important as the revolution in technology. The discoveries of Freud are similar to those of Copernicus and Darwin. The subconscious subject is always active and exerts great influence, and its analysis raises questions about man not dreamed of before." The bishop was criticizing the schema's anthropology along the lines suggested by Cardinal Shehan's approach. He continued: "The Church used to assume a position towards psychoanalysis that recalls the history of Galileo. This was due in part to the anti-Christian dogmatism of some psychoanalysts, but because of her distrustful approach, the Church up until now has had no influence on those engaged in this science. Some Catholics have even formed the myth of a 'Christian' psychoanalysis, whereas true science is neither Christian nor anti-Christian. The Church should enter into dialogue with authentic psychoanalysis and the schema should treat the subject at least briefly."

Mendez Arceo's intervention was headlined by *The New York Times:* "MEXICAN BISHOP ENDORSES FREUD." He was referring to an experiment going on in his own diocese. Father Grégoire Lemercier of Louvain, Belgium, who had established a Benedictine monastery there in 1950, decided to see what the results would be if his monks were allowed to submit to psychoanalysis. So with the permission of his superiors this was done. As a result, the monastery of some 50 monks originally, had been

---

* *The Tablet,* October 30, 1965. In a provocative article in *L'Osservatore Romano,* Benvenuto Matteucci quoted large extracts from Arrupe's speech approvingly, including the unfortunate passages in which he accused international financial circles of being dominated by atheism, implying rather paradoxically that the goal of Marxism was ultimately the same as that of international capitalism.

† The Provincial of the Jesuits in Holland issued a statement deploring the harsh tone of Father Arrupe's remarks about criticism of the Church, as reported by the Spanish newspaper *Ya. La Croix,* Nov. 3, 1965.

reduced to about 20, but Dom Grégoire maintained that these 20, because of the purified nature of their vocation after the experience, were ultimately able to do the work of the original 50! The misfits apparently left voluntarily, some to marry and others to take up various occupations in the world. Father Lemercier distributed a brochure to the bishops in Rome toward the beginning of the Fourth Session outlining the experience of his monastery with psychoanalysis. While it would be somewhat premature to claim with a writer in the Italian weekly *L'Espresso* (whose article was headlined "FREUD EMPTIES THE MONASTERY"), that the opposition of the Church to psychoanalysis was now over, it was true that some headway had been made in recent years in overcoming conservative opposition to the legitimate use of psychoanalysis and other techniques in the handling of vocations.

As René Laurentin pointed out, the Cuernavaca experience was not as dramatic or as unique as was sometimes represented. The scandal was not that some monks had left the monastery because psychoanalysis had been applied to vocations, but that the Church, for so long, had adopted an ostrichlike attitude toward the problem of drop-outs and other similar unpleasant facts of life.*

Bishop Kuharič's wish that the Church should "ask pardon for all the scandals committed throughout the centuries and should then exhort all her members to a life that will be holier and more worthy of the Gospel" (with reference to Article 56 on "The vicissitudes of history") of course brought forth a rejoinder from the Italian Bishop Ruotolo (Ugento) who expressed great misgivings about the language of this article which spoke about the "wrinkles" of the Church in every age and deplored the impression created "in some countries" that the Church was "the friend of the rich and powerful." Such admissions, according to Bishop Ruotolo, "run contrary to the pastoral goal of the Council." Paul VI had reminded the observer delegates that the study of history was "beset with difficulties" and therefore lest the faithful be unduly disturbed, it was better to "look to the future, leaving the past to the judgment of God and of history," in the bishop's opinion. Earlier in the debate, Cardinal Ruffini had also expressed displeasure with the attitude that seemed to be calling for the Church to "get down on her knees" and beg pardon for faults at every turn. On the contrary, the Church could be proud of her contribution to progress and civilization. . . .

Tired of all the pusillanimity, misgivings, cautiousness, warnings and criticism continually being voiced by the schema's opponents, Archbishop D'Souza (Bhopal) asked ironically whether the Council intended to produce a *Reader's Digest* of modern problems, or prepare the Church for

* Two years later (1967) the Doctrinal Congregation was still investigating the Cuernavaca case.

coping with them. If the latter was the case, it was necessary to call a spade a spade and to face certain unpalatable facts. In a fine fury he then proceeded to lash out at the hesitant attitude of so many toward adaptation. "How many men were lost to the Church and regarded it as an enemy of human liberty and dignity between the time when the American and French Revolutions clarified the notion of liberty and the time when these rights were first mentioned in a papal document?" It was not until 43 years after the publication of Karl Marx's fundamental work that Leo XIII's *Rerum Novarum* appeared, and in the meantime there had occurred what Pius XI called the scandal of the nineteenth century—the loss of the working man to the Church. "As if the scandal of Galileo was not enough," he went on, "we have since had the cases of Lamennais, Darwin, Marx, Freud, and more recently Teilhard de Chardin. Their works, not without error, were fighting for the very things that our schema recognizes, and yet their works were indiscriminately condemned." History was the teacher of life, Pope John XXIII had said, and past errors should be avoided. Those things should be removed from the Church that prevented it from obeying the voice of God without hesitation. He then proceeded to enumerate a number of such hindrances regarding ecclesiastical organization: automatic promotions, the administrative or political preoccupations of church leaders, seminary education separated from the world and conducted according to "obsolete scholasticism," abuse of censorship, insufficient lay participation in the life of the Church; regarding doctrine: theological texts stressing the immobility of God so much that the political and social orders seemed to be affected by this immobility too; regarding pastoral life: why was there still so much obsolete pomp connected with clerical life? Unless the Council was able to break away from the interminable chain of monologues in a dead language without open discussion in which they had been engaging, how could any positive results be expected to come from their work?

MARRIAGE AND BIRTH CONTROL

Introducing Part II, Bishop Hengsbach explained that the present text was much longer than the previous draft because many of the points discussed in the former *Adnexa* had been incorporated here. The reason why the two sections had been combined was that general principles tend to become too abstract and vague when treated separately, on the other hand there was danger that if too many details were mentioned the treatment would become unwieldy. Accordingly the commission had tried to strike a proper balance. The first chapter on marriage had been little changed, except that the text now put into clearer light the role of procreation and education as well as the true character of conjugal love. A new chapter had been added on political life, and the final or fifth chapter now combined two previously distinct articles in the former draft. The question of giving proper emphasis to the condemnation of war had been a thorny one for the commission. Some wanted an outright condemnation of modern arms and warfare unconditionally. Others felt that distinctions were in order. The commission had followed a middle of the road course that could be formulated as follows: "Any war action that tends indiscriminately to the destruction of entire cities and their inhabitants or, with still greater reason, to the almost total destruction of regions, is of itself and objectively a crime against God and man himself, which must be firmly and unhesitatingly condemned."

On Wednesday, September 29th, after little more than three days of debate on Part I, the Council moved on to the somewhat more colorful theme of marriage, dealt with in the first chapter of Part II of the schema. The text itself skirted the whole issue of birth control, which the pope had reserved to himself,* stressing the importance of conjugal love as a vital factor in Christian marriage along with the reproductive function. In a significant step forward, it did not repeat the classical contention about primary and secondary ends (found in Pius XI's *Casti connubii* for example), but refused to go into this question, leaving it for discussion among theologians. In itself, of course, this marked an advance over the previous position and one that conservative theologians found very difficult to reconcile with their static view of the non-infallible pronouncements of the teaching Church.

Another advance was the statement that the determination of the number of children must be left to the parents themselves, directly contradicting the assertion of Cardinal Ottaviani at the Third Session that "the freedom granted to couples to determine for themselves the number of their children cannot possibly be approved." On the delicate subject of birth control means or methods, the schema contented itself with the very vague statement, "Great reverence must be shown for the human faculty of begetting children, which is wonderfully superior to all that exists in the lower levels of life, and also for the acts proper to conjugal life, when carried out in accordance with true human dignity," in order not to prejudice the work of the special Papal Commission.

Typical of the conservative theology of marriage were the views of the archbishop of Palermo, Cardinal Ruffini: "The nature and ends of marriage do not stand out in the text with proper clarity. . . . Attention could profitably be paid to the traditional distinction between the primary and the secondary ends of marriage." The schema condemned abortion

* See p. 507, for a discussion of birth control policy in connection with Chapter V of Schema 13.

and infanticide, but it was silent about divorce and passed over in silence the vice of "onanism" in all its many forms. "The statements on the fecundity of marriage are obscure," he noted, "and there is no mention of the pill which has been so impudently termed 'Catholic.' " He commented also, "There are times in marriage when chastity is to be observed. This was a difficult requirement but married persons could always count on divine help. Mutual satisfaction was desirable and necessary through marriage, but it was hard to understand what the text intended when it spoke of 'the full perception of the human person.' "

Representative of the new theology of marriage were the sentiments voiced by Cardinal Léger, who began however with a complaint that the treatment of conjugal love "seems to reduce persons to the rank of simple instruments." But he continued, "The text is better in what it has to say about the importance and lawfulness of conjugal love. Its chief defect is that it does not give a proper explanation of the aim of marriage." It was not enough for the faithful to find the text affirming that the purpose of marriage was procreation and the education of children. "We should declare clearly that marriage is not merely a means of procreation, but likewise a community of life and love. We should distinguish between the species and the individual. The text could also be criticized for its order and style. "We must take care," Léger said, "that our Declaration should not turn out to be a diplomatic compromise between various schools of thought. The frequent use of the hortatory tone should be avoided since this gives the impression that the Council is moralizing."

The Polish Bishop Majdanski insisted that the schema must formulate "a clear doctrine on birth control, because of the confusion so widespread in the world today" on this subject. Archbishop Nicodemo regretted the "ambiguous and dangerous use of expressions" and the tendency of the text to indulge in "subjectivism," even to the point of suggesting that praise for large families was insincere. "The text seems to fall into a contradiction," he declared, "when it praises marital fecundity but on the other hand states that married people are free to determine the number of their children according to subjective criteria." He continued: "What is said in Article 101 about conscientious objection is inopportune in a Council document, because it gives the impression that conscientious objectors give a witness to certain principles which is not found in those who answer the call of duty," wandering somewhat from the subject under discussion. Bishop Volk (Mainz) called for an "explanation of marriage as a state" similar to the explanations of the clerical and religious states.

The debate was clearly bogging down in platitudes and contradictory statements when it was saved from complete dullness by Archbishop Zoghby (Melkite patriarchal vicar for Egypt), who raised the question of what was called in Italy *"il piccolo divorzio,"* the right of the innocent party in cases involving adultery, physical impotence, desertion, etc. to remarry. No such right was recognized under current canon law by the Roman Catholic Church which admitted of no exceptions to the indissolubility of a validly performed, consummated and sacramental marriage (between two baptized persons, whether Catholics, Protestants or other). Italian law, tied to Catholic canon law by reason of the Concordat, admitted of no such thing either. There had been a certain amount of agitation there however in favor of revising the marriage legislation since a great many Italians, particularly of the upper classes (but also among the lower classes) were not practicing Catholics and felt unjustly discriminated against because of laws in which they no longer believed. No wonder therefore that the Melkite archbishop's speech aroused considerable interest in the Italian press, particularly since it came at a time when a Socialist deputy was on the point of introducing once again a bill to permit divorce in Italy for those who wanted it.

According to Zoghby, the problem of divorce "constitutes a more serious problem than that of birth control." "What is to be our stand," he asked, "in cases where a marriage has been contracted with great promise but where an innocent spouse has been abandoned and, according to the traditional teaching, must face life in solitude and continence? Another case of the same type," he went on, "would be that of the permanent insanity of one party. The counsel to live a life of solitude . . . calls for heroic virtue which cannot be imposed indiscriminately." He then asked pertinently: "Could not the Church, without prejudice to her doctrine on the indissolubility of marriage, use her authority on behalf of the innocent party in these cases, as has been the case in the Christian East? This practice was also allowed sometimes in the West." Answering in advance the objections of those who maintained that the doctrine and discipline of the Latin Church had always been uniform on this point, he asked: "Did not the Church get from Christ the power to regulate such cases? The Church should decide on the intrinsic force of the passage in Scripture that has been consistently invoked against this practice. The Council of Trent chose a formula that would not offend the Orientals. . . . This is something that should not be done lightly, of course, because of abuses, nevertheless the problem had to be faced."

The next day the Swiss theologian, Cardinal Journet, rose to repudiate the thought—without mentioning Zoghby—that the Roman Catholic Church was not irrevocably committed to the indissolubility of marriage. "The Catholic Church has always observed and taught the same doctrine revealed by Christ on the indissolubility of sacramental marriage." The passage in Matthew 5:32 where the phrase "except for fornication" occurs, could justify separation in the case of adultery, as modern theologians and canonists hold, but not remarriage. The fact that the practice of divorce was admitted "in some Eastern Churches," according to Journet, was due to the influence of the civil law as expressed in Justinian's Code. Other causes were later introduced. "Thus these Churches found themselves following a human policy rather than the Gospel."

Zoghby had little difficulty in showing, at a press conference and later in another intervention, that Journet was wrong about the Orthodox Churches. In allowing divorce, under certain circumstances, they had not bowed to governmental pressure because they had granted divorce and allowed remarriage long before the time of Justinian and some of the Church Fathers countenanced the practice. He explained later, in a second intervention on the floor, that he had not intended to question the doctrine of the indissolubility of marriage. The Orthodox Churches accepted this doctrine also. But there was, or could be, a parallel between the Orthodox practice of allowing the innocent party to remarry according to their doctrine of "economy" and the western practice of dissolving and allowing remarriage in the so-called Petrine cases.* All Zoghby had really wanted to do was to raise the subject of trying to find some solution for the innocent party other than complete chastity, when this proved impossible. The chief result of his intervention, it seems, was not to suggest that the Roman Catholic Church was about to change its doctrine on marriage, but to set people thinking about ways that could lead to this end. Judging by the comments, he succeeded in this limited purpose.

A useful suggestion was made by Cardinal Suenens: "It is greatly to be desired that scientific research in the domain of sexual life . . . be directed to man himself, in all his complexity, particularly on the sexual and conjugal level. We must have a better understanding of the laws of human fecundity as well as the psychological laws of self-control. . . . The efforts made thus far are insufficient. The few Catholic scientists in this area complain that they are not supported and encouraged. Everyone senses the lack of coordination. Therefore an invitation from the Council for scientific research would be a precious stimulant as well as a proof of our pastoral interest. Our Catholic universities should encourage this research through scholarships. . . ." He was careful to note however that "these suggestions do not imply any judgment on the value of any specific method of birth control. They remain purely in the field of science." In a slightly different context, he thought that "it would help married people, to encourage the practice of renewing their marriage vows, as is done for baptismal and religious vows. A particular day could be set aside. . . ." The Rome daily *Il Messaggero* deliberately misrepresented what the car-

* The Pauline Privilege concerns the dissolution of marriages between two unbaptized persons; the Petrine (i.e. papal) Privilege, the dissolution of marriages between an unbaptized and a baptized person. Both marriages are non-sacramental.

dinal had said, for the sake of the publicity, headlining its story: "MARRIAGE SHOULD BE RENEWABLE" and asking whether he had meant to suggest that the marriage contract itself could be renewed. "This would involve a substantial reform," it went on, "because it would amount to establishing a form of divorce, permissible according to certain fixed norms and in a manner acceptable to the Church." Such a preposterous interpretation naturally brought forth a protest from the cardinal, who telegraphed the paper demanding that they print a rectification.

The speech of Bishop Reuss (auxiliary of Mainz and head of the major seminary there, one of the most advanced in Europe, also member of the Papal Commission on Birth Control)* was listened to with particular attention. Chapter I was praiseworthy because it stressed the importance of conjugal love and refrained from becoming involved in questions before the Papal Birth Control Commission. Although "I had no intention of speaking on these problems, yesterday's discussion forces me to do so. If these problems had been so clearly solved already, as Cardinal Ruffini asserted yesterday, the pope's decision is hard to understand. Cardinal Suenens yesterday made a stirring appeal for further scientific research." The norm for this research and the commission's work must be "the truth, sought with zeal, responsibility before God, and prayer." Love could legitimately be called an end of marriage. "Conjugal love could not be strictly identified with the conjugal act since love extended to the whole married life. . . . Hence the truth of the schema, that marriage is not a mere institution for the procreation of children. It is regrettable that the word 'responsibility' is not used in the text, because the responsibility of the spouses determines the whole of married life. By this responsibility, man responds to God's will." Nevertheless, a number of speakers continued to voice regret that the schema had abandoned the classical distinction between the "primary" and "secondary" ends of marriage, notably Cardinal Browne of the Holy Office and Bishop Alonso Muño-yerro (Spain), the latter noting that the Holy Office had condemned an erroneous opinion regarding the "primary purpose of procreation."

Several speakers expressed a certain amount of perplexity, perhaps irritation, over the fact that Pope Paul was deferring his promised statement on birth control methods and their speeches could be viewed as discreet attempts to prod him into action. Cardinal Heenan observed that while "moral principles remain fixed and certain, we still await guidance from doctors, physiologists, and other experts. . . . Would it not be better to say nothing at all about marriage in this document rather than discuss it while leaving the really big problem without mention?" He described the present text as "rather tame." The cardinal also said that

* More accurately, the Pontifical Commission for the Study of Problems relating to Population, Family and Birth.

great care must be exercised in the language of the text. "The Latin text is least important since we are addressing the modern world." Instead of calling it a Constitution, he was in favor of entitling it "Message from the Council to the world today." The document contained "practically nothing that would help married couples in their intimate problems. The difficulties were sketched, but little more. In the name of the Brazilian bishops, Cardinal Rossi agreed with Cardinal Heenan, that unless a decision with regard to birth control means was soon to be forthcoming from the Holy See on which the Council could base itself, it was better to remain silent and to try and work out a "modus vivendi" for priests and faithful. "Is this not more prudent than running the risk of affirming what might be contradicted tomorrow? . . . The indeterminate and imprecise statements in the schema on this question do not suffice at all."

A notable intervention was that of Cardinal Colombo (Milan), speaking in the name of 32 Italian bishops, who put the seal of his approval on Chapter I which he declared to be both "good in its doctrine and in its pastoral approach" because it "places the foundation of the benefits and aims of marriage in a fully human and personalistic light in order that conjugal life may be declared to be intrinsic and coessential with the procreational end of marriage." However, he regretted an unfortunate impression in that "the schema does not reaffirm strongly enough the doctrine of the Church and by its timid and reticent tone seems to justify the suspicion that something basic has been changed in Catholic doctrine."*

Bishop De Roo (Victoria, Canada), speaking in "the name of 33 bishops and many married couples of Canada," put in a strong plea for what the schema had to say about conjugal love, which however was not strong enough. "Placet iuxta modum," he said. The laity should be encouraged to progress toward a fuller, more ecclesial married life. Therefore the bishop should set aside preoccupations with the pitfalls of married life and insist rather on the positive vision of the riches of human love and the heights it could reach through grace. The laity appreciated the value of the doctrinal elements, but they knew that "conjugal union cannot really be understood unless it is realized that carnal union gives rise to a communion of the whole persons and lives of the partners. The classical view of procreation as the end of marriage must be perfected, for procreation requires that parents be not only the authors of life, but also an unfailing source of love for the whole family. . . . We contradict reality if we consider merely one or another gesture of conjugal love apart from the whole context of daily family life, outside of which they cannot

---

* This intervention must have made a certain impression on Pope Paul, because he intervened before the end of the Council and ordered the commission to amend the text so as to eliminate any such suspicion. See p. 554.

487

have their full meaning. Christian marriage is a vocation to seek perfection as a team. . . . Married couples must never abstain from the daily practice and development of authentic conjugal love. The Council will promote the redemption of all humanity by exalting the positive values of conjugal love." Instead of emphasizing the negative side, the Council should exalt what was positive.*

Cardinals Gracias and Slipyi both regretted the excessively "western" approach to marriage manifested by the schema, as did Archbishop Djajasepoetra who declared: "You Westerners always say that people marry because they love each other. In the Orient we say that people get married and then learn to love each other." In his opinion, however, the present text was far superior to the preceding draft. Slipyi went on in a rambling vein about a subject that was not under discussion at all, namely atheism, and insisted that very few speakers had accurately described the situation as it existed in communist countries. Then turning to the subject of marriage, he made his point that East and West looked at marriage from differing points of view: "This could be the most beautiful of conciliar texts . . ." and on and on until he was finally interrupted by the moderator, Cardinal Suenens, who begged him to conclude. Instead of doing so, Slipyi quoted the cardinal, who thanked him and once again asked him to conclude. But the Ukrainian was not to be daunted and was about to launch into a quotation from Pope John's *Pacem in Terris* when he was finally stopped.

Harking back to a favorite theme of some Latin American prelates, Bishop de Orbegozo y Goicoechea, prelate nullius of Peru, insisted once more that the Council must not abandon the teaching on the primary and secondary ends of marriage, and above all must not become an instrument for spreading the birth control propaganda of "certain countries" in Asia, Africa and Latin America. As for what the text said about leaving the number of children to the decision of parents, he hoped that the Council would be more generous. "Soon those who were once considered heroic will have to hide their children if more than two—unless they want to bear public shame for what many think is an irresponsibility and unrestrained lust."

The debate was finally brought to an end by Bishop Hacault (St.-Boniface, Canada), who seconded Bishop De Roo's call for a more explicit treatment of the subject of conjugal love. History disclosed many different types of marriage, polygamy, concubinage, bigamy, etc., "The Council should not merely condemn these inferior covenants but show that they culminate in the Christian conception of marriage."

* Fr. Schillebeeckx gave a much attended conference in Rome on "the changing concepts of Christian marriage," on September 29, 1965.

THE CHURCH AND CULTURE

When Bishop Hacault had finished speaking on Friday, October 1st, Cardinal Suenens asked the Fathers whether they wished to terminate the discussion of the chapter on marriage? The results of a standing vote being affirmative, the Council then passed to consideration of Chapter II on Culture. Since the vote to close the debate on Chapter I had come somewhat earlier than expected, a number of bishops were unable to deliver their scheduled talks, but before taking up the next item the floor was given to Bishop Schmitt of Metz, who in the name of 70 Fathers, had asked to say a few more words about the introduction to Part II of the schema. His point was the rather interesting observation that not enough had been said about the contribution of the world to the Church. As the dogmatic Constitution *Lumen gentium* declared, grace was given to men even outside the boundaries of the Church. In the interests of solidarity therefore it was only fair for the Church to acknowledge its debt to the world. He listed the movement toward socialization, the dignity of the human person, the interdependence of peoples, the distinction between Church and state, etc., as values contributed by the world to which the Church added her own peculiar slant.

The debate on Chapter II was led off by Arthur Elchinger, coadjutor-bishop of Strasbourg. The principal problem of the section was the way the Church ought to conduct herself toward technical civilization. The text was full of many pious exhortations but few practical solutions were offered, he said. The Church must receive the treasures of her own culture, and at the same time convey them to others. "One reason why the Church has lost its influence in the world is that it is expanding now in regions where it had not been previously established. In countries where it had been established, there is a distrust of the Church and it has therefore lost its influence. The Church has not listened to the world as much as it should." Christians must adjust to the cultural pattern of the region where they happened to live and must be in the vanguard of cultural development there.

Elchinger was followed by two other French bishops, Le Couëdic and Lebrun. The former insisted that the text should state more clearly that things were not ends in themselves but means for man's betterment and should be used properly with a view to achieving a higher spirituality. The latter stressed the importance of sports and their value from a spiritual point of view, suggesting that certain ideas along this line be incorporated in the schema. The Master General of the Dominicans proposed virtually a new plan for this chapter, maintaining that not enough was said about the contribution of the Church to the development of culture.

One of the more notable interventions of the Session was delivered by the newly appointed archbishop of Turin, Michele Pellegrino, until recently a professor of ancient Christian literature in the University of Turin, who spoke on a subject dear to his heart, the right to freedom of research. Chapter II was generally satisfactory, the archbishop held, but he called for an explicit mention of the science of history among those disciplines with which the Church should particularly concern itself: "The importance of historical research is evident from its subject matter, which is man himself. . . . Moreover, historical study is closely connected with the knowledge of the history of salvation. . . . Finally, scholars will welcome such a recognition of their labors, especially those who carry on historical research in the fields (biblical, ecclesiastical, patristic, archeological, etc.) more closely connected with the history of salvation." Commenting on the sentence in Art. 74 which reads, "But, to enable them to carry out their task, the faithful must be allowed the freedom of inquiry and thought which befits a Christian, the freedom also to express their point of view with humility and courage in the fields of their competence," he suggested that after the word "faithful," the words "clerical or lay" should be inserted, to show that this right to freedom of expression applied also to the clergy, and not merely to the laymen mentioned in the previous sentence. As an example of what he meant, he reminded his hearers about certain unsavory aspects of the suppression of the heresy of Modernism earlier in this century, particularly in Italy: "The right and duty of ecclesiastical authority to watch over clerics more closely than over laymen must also be exercised with due reverence for human dignity, which includes freedom of inquiry. We are all grateful to the supreme authority for averting the calamity of Modernism, but who would dare to assert that in that necessary repression the rights and dignity of clerics, whether young priests or bishops or even cardinals, were always duly respected?"

There was inevitably considerable speculation in the corridors as to which cardinals he was referring to in the dark days following Pius X's *Pascendi dominici gregis* (1907), whereas everybody knew about the unfortunate cases of Monsignor Louis Duchesne, and Monsignor Pierre Batiffol, the church historians, and Père F. M. Lagrange, O.P., the biblical scholar, to mention only a few of those who managed to remain within the Church in spite of the storm. But lest any of his hearers should get the idea that he was referring to the distant past, Archbishop Pellegrino went on, "Such things do not belong only to the past. A few years ago I found a religious living in involuntary exile for having expressed opinions which today we read in papal and conciliar documents. This was not a unique case." In a strong pleas for the rights of research, he concluded, "Even in the theological sciences, many things must be subjected to revision with the progress of research, and the sphere of things susceptible of various opinions is much broader than is realized by those who have not experienced the hard and often dangerous work of research. If each one knows that he is permitted to express his opinion with wholesome freedom, he will act with the straightforwardness and sincerity that should shine in the Church; otherwise the abominable plague of dishonesty and hypocrisy can hardly be avoided."* Obviously these were the words of one who knew whereof he spoke.†

The fact that an Italian archbishop, a novice—admittedly a northerner—had dared to be so frank on the floor of the Council about internal matters that quite a few of his colleagues still feel to be too delicate or painful or embarrassing ever to be mentioned publicly, was widely hailed as a sign that progress was being made in updating the Italian Church. Many of the Italian clergy, particularly the higher and more conservative prelates, were curiously under the impression that the Church was still engaged in a life and death struggle with the nineteenth-century Italian *Risorgimento.*

The following speaker, Monsignor Blanchet, rector of the Catholic Institute in Paris, was more critical. He found that there were many "surprising gaps" in Chapter II. The description of modern culture was deficient. Like Pellegrino, he deplored the fact that so little was said about history, "which in a singular way characterizes the modern way of thinking. History is very important because it teaches the change and relativity of things. The study of history has given an impetus to other studies in the Church." He also found the schema weak on the subject of the relations between philosophy and faith. Catholic teachers should stop talking so much about the supposed opposition between science and faith. "Attention was always being called to the fact that the weak must not be scandalized; the Church should begin to think about scandalizing the strong." The text paid insufficient attention to the important matter of environment in the determination of human culture, according to Bishop Padim (secretary general of Catholic Action in Brazil), while Archbishop

---

*See p. 14 and Charles Ledré, *Un siècle sous le tiare* (Paris, 1955), p. 82–84, for mention of the heresy-hunting activities of Monsignor Benigni's *Sodalitium pianum,* called "La Sapinière," which was finally suppressed by Benedict XV shortly before his death in 1921.

† *The Tablet* (October 9, 1965), printed almost the whole of the archbishop's remarks, whereas the daily press bulletin in English gave only a six-line summary. The Italian press bulletin did not think it important enough however to mention that he had referred to cardinals, contenting itself with *"vescovi o gli ecclesiastici."*

Morcillo Gonzáles (Madrid) found Chapter II "unworthy of our Council" because it was ambiguous about the relationship between human culture and Christian humanism. God's "role in the progress of cultures is very great since the benefits of redemption are extended to *all* creatures. He restores these creatures, as well as the human elements, to his glory and man's salvation." He proposed that the whole of Chapter II be revised in the light of revelation and history. (The Italian press bulletin had the archbishop calling for the complete suppression of the whole second part of the schema and handing it over to a special post-conciliar commission.) Bishop Frotz (auxiliary of Cologne) regretted that not enough attention was paid to the separate role of men and women in the evolution of human culture. Both Bishop Spülbeck (Meissen) and Archbishop Veuillot (coadjutor of Paris) dealt with the subject of the dialogue between theology and modern science, the former generally approving "the laudable optimism" of the schema with respect to the field of science, the latter certain that "the text, as it stands, will disappoint scientists." The Church should not merely say that she was not opposed to science, according to Veuillot, but declare that she positively fostered it. The tone of the schema did not answer "the growing anguish of modern science in the face of the smallness and fragility of man confronted by the immense and unfriendly universe and in the face of an ever-increasing number of discoveries whose direction and finality are unknown and disputed." The schema should profess a proper reverence for life and exhort scientists to acknowledge the final goal to which science was called, to tell the glory of God.

Science was also the theme of the final speaker on this chapter, Bishop Bettazzi (auxiliary of Bologna), whose point was somewhat different. He recommended that the Council make its own the attitude of Thomas Aquinas toward the science of his day. "St. Thomas . . . loved both the Scriptures and the world of his time. The principles of Thomas we have from tradition; but his method applied today would be one of seeking for and adhering to the mentality of our time and place." He then went on to note that this "was the inspiration of Pope John XXIII when he invited the faithful to dialogue. John's name should be mentioned in the text. This question also merits the attention of the new Episcopal Synod." Commentators immediately interpreted this as a discreet reference to a proposal for the spontaneous canonization (or rather beatification) of Pope John XXIII by the Council being advocated on the sidelines by the energetic young bishop and supported by such cardinals as Suenens of Belgium, König of Austria, Alfrink of Holland, Liénart of France, and Lercaro of Bologna. Interesting as the suggestion was, nobody was under any illusions that the move would have much success, unless it suddenly received a nod from on high, in view of the usual reserves expressed by spokesmen for the Congregation of Rites about the desirability of departing from normally accepted procedures in these matters.*

THE DISCUSSION OF ECONOMIC
AND SOCIAL LIFE

The debate on Chapter III, Economic and Social Life, was over almost before it began, occupying only part of two successive mornings, October 4th and 5th. The inevitable basis of comparison was recent papal pronouncements in this field, some speakers regretting the fact that the schema was not as explicit, others welcoming its treatments as adequate and satisfactory. The fact that the majority of the bishops had little or nothing to say seemed to indicate that they were in substantial agreement. Actually, so far as a statement of basic principles was concerned, the revised Chapter III was fully as good as, and in some respects surpassed, papal documents on the subject prior to the reign of Pope John XXIII. (In the judgment of experts the final version approved by the Council was fully in accord with the spirit of *Pacem in Terris*. This section of the text underwent relatively little revision during the final weeks of the Council.)

Eight of the 21 speakers were less concerned with criticizing the text than with using the occasion to propose the formal setting up of a Secretariat to promote Roman Catholic, and inter-Christian, awareness of the problems connected with world poverty and help coordinate activity in this area. Said Bishop Swanstrom, the director of Catholic Relief Services: "There is a great gulf between our accepting the Church's teaching and our putting it into practice. Hence I propose concretely that the Church launch a deep and long-term campaign of education, inspiration and moral influence to promote among Christians and all men of good will a live understanding and concern for world poverty and to promote world justice and development in all their facets." Similar proposals were made by Cardinal de Arriba y Castro (Spain), Archbishops Thangalathil and Fernandes (India), Father Mahon, Superior General of the Society of St. Joseph of Mill Hill, and Bishop Echeverria Ruiz (Chile). Bishop Swanstrom's proposal was actually not new.† Various suggestions along this line had been made by different speakers at the Third Session, notably by the American lay auditor active in relief affairs James J. Norris in a speech before the Council on November 5, 1964.‡ The plan now being submitted

---

* Certain Italian papers kept up a kind of campaign constantly referring to this proposal throughout the months of October and November.

† The proposals for a secretariat at the Fourth Session were inspired by a paper drawn up by Mgr. J. Gremillion, Mgr. L. Ligutti, Fr. A. McCormack, and J. Norris. Cardinal Cushing made a similar suggestion in July 1965.

‡ See p. 377.

for formal consideration by the proper authorities called for the establishment of a permanent commission of bishops appointed by the pope and forming part of the Curia, possibly headed by a cardinal as president, that would have the advice of a "strategy-committee composed of highly competent authorities, technicians and well-known leaders in the field of economics, aid and development, both clergy and lay." The Secretariat was not to become involved in administration but would help lay down the "guidelines" for other organizations and bring about a greater public awareness of the need and responsibility for action. Its terms of reference were to be rather broadly defined as relating not only to aid in the largely materialistic sense but to concern for the whole range of problems connected with development and social justice.

(The draft of Schema 13 debated by the Council contained no specific mention of "organs" either here in Chapter III or later in Chapter V where it might have been expected. Auxiliary Archbishop Fernandes of India was unsuccessful in his attempt to insert the word in Chapter III when the Mixed Commission considered this part of the text on October 28th, but "organs" are expressly mentioned in the revised text of Chapter V, paragraph 90 (formerly 94). Pope Paul was known to favor the idea for a Secretariat and had promised to give it his support when those more directly concerned with working out the details had come to some agreement on how it was to function.)

Two conservative prelates who normally could be expected to see eye to eye on most issues took different sides on the subject of the Church's attitude toward private property. Cardinal Siri criticized what Article 81 had to say about the goods of this world being meant for all mankind, especially the words, "Consequently, when man makes use of these goods, he must never regard external possessions as his own but rather as being for common use, intended, that is, not for his own utility alone, but also for the service of others." He held that this was "not exactly what was taught in former papal documents" and wanted the point left out altogether. The cardinal was right in believing that there was a certain discrepancy here, but wrong in thinking that the position taken by the schema did not represent the return to a more ancient and authentic tradition about property, reflected only imperfectly in recent papal statements. The note appended to this passage made clear that the wording was borrowed from Thomas Aquinas, whereas the only papal authority cited was Pius XII's allocution for Pentecost in 1941. The implication was obvious: the encyclicals of Leo XIII and Pius XI could not be cited because their teaching was obscure and confused regarding the common use of property.* Although in advance of their times in many respects, on

* See p. 375.

this particular point their encyclicals were behind the times. (In the final version of the schema, a reference to Leo XIII's *Rerum Novarum* was worked in and various minor adjustments made, for the sake of accommodating the sensibilities of people like Cardinal Siri, but the text was not fundamentally altered on this point.) In strange contrast, the generally very conservative Cardinal Bueno y Monreal (Seville) felt that the chapter was "too much imbued with a mentality of individualistic liberalism and capitalism" and did not "take sufficient note of the mentality of collectivism existing in a large part of the world." He maintained, correctly, that the doctrine of the absolute inviolability of private property was not identical with Catholic teaching on the subject. "The doctrine on access to ownership, control of wealth, and latifundia should be revised so as to include the possible common ownership of land."

Several speakers, Bishops Hengsbach and Parteli and Archbishop Castellano, wanted more attention paid to the special problems facing agricultural societies. Bishop Höffner, Bishop Franic, and Archbishop Garcia de Sierra y Mendez called for rather drastic revision, Franic proposing that Chapter III and most of the schema be referred to the Synod of Bishops, "which can consider matters at greater leisure, and, if the Holy Father approves, act on them with conciliar prerogatives." He suggested that a few principles be enunciated in a Synodal Letter now, with the rest being reserved to the Synod. Bishop Coderre (Canada) was concerned that the chapter was already too dated and hoped that it would be made "more prophetic." In a rambling speech that seemed more intended for consumption in Poland, Cardinal Wyszynski tried to strike a balance between the claims of capitalism and communism and left his hearers in some doubt as to where he stood on the fundamental issues. As might be expected, Cardinal Cardijn spoke on the theme: "Workers of the world, unite!", but in a sense somewhat different from the Communist Manifesto. Finally, Bishop De Vito (India) hoped that the position of the Council on economic and social matters would be expressed in language that the poor could understand, not merely experts and theologians, and that the Council would come out strongly against such practices as genocide, the sterilization of women and the vasectomy of men, "which are morally forced on millions of people." Also on the theme of the "Church of the Poor" (Cardinal de Arriba y Castro found the expression objectionable because ambiguous), the Brazilian Archbishop Golland Trindade, in a written intervention, warned the Council: "Pius XI declared that the great tragedy of the Church in the 19th century was that it lost the working class. Let us be careful not to lose the needy, the miserable, the starving who constitute over half of the world's population today!"

THE CHURCH AND THE POLITICAL COMMUNITY

Briefer still was the discussion of Chapter IV, which consumed only part of one morning, October 5th. There were but four speakers. The only really notable intervention was that of Archbishop Hurley of Durban, who spoke in forthright terms about the need for ridding the Church of outmoded forms of expression and thought in the policial sphere: "We hope that the traditional reference to the Church as a perfect society (a cliché of scholastic thought) will be dropped. The Church is a society only in an analogical sense. Human activity cannot be divided simply into the temporal order and the spiritual order. In the past, the Church has insisted too much on her own rights. In the future, it is hoped that we will speak with equal concern about the rights of man." (The reference to the Church as a "perfect society" had been dropped in the version being debated and was not revived in the final text approved by the Council.) The Polish Archbishop Baraniak (Poznan) attempted to throw light on the thorny question of the extent to which the faithful living in communist countries should cooperate with communist governments, while the Spanish Bishop Beitia talked about the relations between Church and state as if the Declaration on Religious Liberty had never been heard of and insisted that the confessional state, along Spanish lines, was the only ideal solution: "No one would dare to defend the essentially lay character of the state, but there are some who do not like the distinction between thesis and hypothesis and propound a diametrically opposite point of view. The contrary, however, has been inculcated by the magisterium. If we look at papal documents from Leo XIII on, we find that the profession of the true religion is required of the state. . . ."

THE POPE'S VISIT TO THE UN

It was not purely coincidental that Pope Paul's visit to the UN was timed to coincide with the opening of debate on the final chapter of Schema 13, on "The Community of Nations and the Building Up of Peace." The Pontiff's dramatic gesture was of course intended to convince the world of the Holy See's genuine and sincere desire to do everything possible to promote world peace, but it would also inevitably have the effect of subtly committing the Council to the same cause without of course in any way impinging on its freedom of action. To make sure that this point would be clear to everybody, the pope deliberately invited a select group of cardinals representative of the different regions of the world and other Council officials to accompany him on his journey.

Early in the year Monsignor Alberto Giovannetti, the emissary of the Holy See at the United Nations headquarters in New York, had handed to Secretary General U Thant a copy of the pope's disarmament appeal which the pontiff had made at Bombay on the occasion of his visit to India in December 1964. After nine days the secretary general replied in a personal letter to the pope. This correspondence seems to have served as a curtain-raiser for a plan which the pope had been nurturing for some time. From the very beginning of his pontificate Pope Paul had evinced a marked interest in the UN. It was he who sent Monsignor Giovannetti there as an observer not long after his election. Since January 1965, however, it was noticed that his references to the UN became more frequent in proportion as the state of world peace continued to deteriorate. What was not generally known was that the pope had been giving serious consideration to a plan for making a personal appearance before the world body to plead for peace, hoping in this way not only to dramatize his efforts but help bolster the waning prestige of that organization. The Holy See had consistently supported the peace efforts of the UN, just as it had faithfully supported every movement tending toward European unity, the Common Market, for example.

During the summer, in a somewhat unprecedented move considering the good relations normally prevailing between them, at least on the surface, differences between the Holy See and French policy came out into the open when the Vatican weekly journal, *L'Osservatore della Domenica,* boldly declared: "French intransigence is endangering the patient work of nearly ten years towards a united Europe." The article viewed the recent impasse at Brussels and withdrawal of the French representative over the failure to reach a common agricultural policy for the Common Market, as well as "the resulting polemics," as a particularly grave development. Some Vatican authorities were apparently unhappy likewise about that part of General De Gaulle's policy that aimed at including the satellite countries of Eastern Europe in some kind of European union, if this should mean any weakening of existing structures as bulwarks against communism.

The first proposal considered was that the pope would make an appearance before the UN in San Francisco, before the assembly there in June commemorating the 20th anniversary of the UN's foundation. Diplomatic soundings were made. However, it soon developed that this would be impractical for a variety of reasons. The Santo Domingo crisis intervened. An American fundamentalist group threatened to picket Kennedy Airport if the pope set foot in the U.S. In any case there was scarcely time to prepare for such a momentous event. It was decided therefore to send a papal delegation of lesser note to San Francisco headed by Archbishop O'Connor of the Curia and including Professor Halecki of Fordham University as well as Monsignor Giovannetti. Cardinal Bea had first been slated to head the delegation but this had to be abandoned. Archbishop O'Connor read the papal message before the assembly in San Francisco on June 26, 1965. Shortly before this it became known that the pope definitely was planning a visit to the UN later in the year. Monsignor Giovannetti left for Rome on July 7th, after an interview with U Thant, to work out arrangements for the pope's appearance.

Papal diplomacy had recently been able to chalk up a success in the way the apostolic delegate in Santo Domingo, Archbishop Clarizio, facilitated the process of getting both sides to discuss their differences. Unlike some members of the Dominican hierarchy, the Holy See tried to remain strictly neutral in the controversy and thus preserve its effectiveness as a go-between. (Ironically some of the communists known to be operating on the island were said to have entered in clerical garb along with the delegates to the Mariological Congress held there in March, before the outbreak of hostilities.) Despite the formidable difficulties facing such a visit, the fact that Pope Paul was willing seriously to consider the step was proof of his determination to do all in his power to avert a world catastrophe. Perhaps too one motive was his determination not to allow even the suggestion of an impression to arise that he has been in any way negligent in this regard.

Monsignor Giovannetti was enthusiastic about the papal visit from the first. Since there were no precedents for such an occasion, difficulties arose over the protocol of receiving the pope. Was the pope to be received as the head of Vatican City or as the head of the Catholic Church? The Secretary General replied that he intended to receive him as Pope Paul VI, thus brushing aside apparently insoluble dilemmas. There was the question of opposition by members of the Curia, particularly those in the Secretariat of State. It was not so much the old-fashioned view of "It is enough for the Church to speak from Rome and wait for men to come to it," or the belief that it was undignified for the pope to become involved in the political mêlée, as it was concern that there might be unpredictable consequences. In addition there was a struggle between Monsignor Giovannetti and the Chancery of the Archdiocese of New York over control of the visit. Giovannetti and the UN officials were anxious not to allow the political overtones to get out of hand; the Chancery was understandably desirous that the Archdiocese perform the role of host with regard to the religious aspects of the visit, and that was one of the reasons why the outdoor mass was held at Yankee Stadium rather than outside the Archdiocese. President Johnson was eager to meet the pope at Kennedy

International Airport, but this was ruled out as implying that the pope had come to see *him* rather than in response to the UN invitation. The meeting with the president, though desired, had to be kept as informal and last-minute as possible. The pope himself took a personal part in all the planning, insisting on the long route through Harlem considered dangerous both by his entourage and the New York police. He wanted to remain in the open car, but was overruled because of the stiff wind and the fact, not generally known, that he had started out on the trip with a sore throat from which some of the other members of his suite were also suffering. Riding in the bubble-top closed car was therefore a necessary precaution although it meant that thousands along the route were able to get only a fleeting glimpse of his white figure. Typically Pauline also was the desire to underline the journey's ecumenical implications. As he was about to board his plane in Rome he received a farewell message from the personal representatives of Athenagoras I, ecumenical patriarch of Constantinople. In New York he received Archbishop Iakovos, local head of the Greek Orthodox Church, in Cardinal Spellman's residence and conferred with him about the difficulties being faced by Athenagoras under pressure from the Turkish government. Finally, the pope met with the UN representatives of various religious bodies, Protestant, Orthodox, and Jewish, in the church of the Holy Family on East 47th Street. Two small incidents, noted by those present at the cathedral were the pope's gesture of offering Cardinal Spellman needed support, during their walk around St. Patrick's, by holding out his arm; and his pronunciation of the name of New York's patron saint, during his brief remarks inside the cathedral, as "Saint *Pay*trick."

The speech to the UN, broadcast over Italian television, made a deep impression. Walter Lippmann's analysis of the speech was much appreciated and this passage is said to have pleased the pope especially: "No one who heard him attentively, or will read him now, can fail to realize that he was speaking a different language from that which is current and conventional. In fact, the pope, who is without pride and has nothing to fear, was thinking what is unthinkable for so many, and he was saying it out loud. His conception of the secular world is quite different from the conception which underlies public discussion—be it in Peking or in Washington. The crucial difference is that in the pope's address the paramount issue is not the cold war or hostile ideologies. Although religion in general and the Roman Church in particular have been treated as the chief enemies of the communists, the pope said that the pursuit of peace transcends all other duties, and that the paramount crusade of mankind is the crusade against war and for peace. This is a different set of values than are accepted as righteous in the public life of the warring nations. The pope was, of course, intending to make this known, and he reached the climax of his message, so it seemed to me, when he declared that the root of evil in this angry, hostile and quarreling world 'is pride, no matter how legitimate it may seem to be.' . . . We shall have heard the pope's message when we have taken those words to heart."

This message was not only "different" and unconventional for statesmen, but for the generality of American Catholics, particularly those clergymen and others who had been expressing scorn for the UN. The moral ratification of the UN by Pope Paul VI, speaking in person from the rostrum of its Assembly, was unquestionably one of the great moments for Roman Catholicism. As Lippmann also said, "This historic act of ratification marks the progress made under the inspiration of John XXIII—the rejuvenation of the Church. The modernizing Church had brought itself into the main stream of human affairs. It has done this by committing itself to the religious reconciliation of mankind." Oddly enough, to the eyes of old Roman hands, this sentiment was echoed in the normally reserved columns of *L'Osservatore Romano*. Not very long ago it would have been unthinkable for the Vatican newspaper to use the word "reform" without a whole string of qualifiers, but the pope's visit inspired this historic statement: "The trip appears to most people as profoundly connected with the reform of the Church now being carried out by itself. The *aggiornamento* undertaken . . . has aroused a great hope in the hearts of mankind. They are convinced that what has been begun will not go unfinished" (October 16, 1965).

The Fathers were anxiously awaiting the pope's return from New York on Tuesday, October 5th, when word reached the Council floor that his TWA Boeing 707 had touched down at Fumicino at 12:01. Exactly forty-six minutes later, the great bells of St. Peter's tolled as his black Mercedes rolled up to the steps in front of the main door of the basilica in St. Peter's Square. Smiling and jubilant, as if it were the most casual thing in the world for a pope to travel half way round the globe and back in thirty hours, he alighted from the car. Then, with a spring in his step, he quickly mounted the red-carpeted steps to be greeted by the Cardinal presidents and moderators in St. Peter's portico, in a reunion happily devoid of the usual protocol. Briskly walking up the center aisle, as the bishops applauded vigorously from their tiered seats on either side, he took his place at the center of the presidents' table. Aware that the morning's session had already been prolonged in order to receive him, he rose at once to give his address but sat down again when Cardinal Liénart (Lille), standing beside him in the place of the Cardinal Dean, who had accompanied the pope to America, indicated that he wished to say a few words of greeting. The pope patiently heard him out, then delivered his own brief talk in a business-like manner, stepped down from the podium, and with a gesture of greeting to the Protestant and Orthodox observers in their tribune at the left, and a final lifting of his arms, hurriedly left the basilica by the side door. The Council ordered the pope's address to be made part of its official records.

The following day in a general audience Pope Paul explained exactly why he had undertaken such an arduous journey. "There has been much propaganda about peace in recent years, but frequently it has not been very convincing. We felt the need to take up this great theme, to try to get it considered in the light of Christian principles and make everybody more aware of it." Some days before in an interview he had declared, "They asked us to come in connection with the twentieth anniversary of the UN and we said that we would. The pope could hardly reply, 'Thank you very much for asking us, but we don't have the time.'" He felt that with so many heads of state and statesmen present this was an opportunity that could not be missed, so he had determined, like St. Rocco, Italian patron saint of travelers, to put on his cloak and go. "We wanted to do as the Psalmist says: 'You shall speak in the sight of kings and shall not be confounded.'" Then with a characteristic Pauline gesture of humility he added, "But who knows whether even *we* will carry it off well or badly before so many important people." By common consent he had carried off the business extremely well.

THE COMMUNITY OF NATIONS AND PEACE

The Council began to discuss the final and in some ways most crucial chapter of Schema 13 the day the pope returned from New York. The debate lasted for approximately 3 days.

The section claiming the most attention was of course No. 2, on a stable Peace or the Avoidance of War, which went into the related questions of the horror of modern warfare (98), conventional versus atomic weapons (98), war crimes (98), just and unjust wars (98), the so-called "balance of terror" (99), international action for the avoidance of war (particularly the need for a "public authority wielding effective power at the world level") (100), the possession of nuclear arms not in itself illegitimate (100), the fear of the escalation of war (101), the right to conscientious objection (101), and the need for respecting the "rules of humanity" during wartime (101).* The section began with a ringing Declaration condemning all acts of indiscriminate warfare.† Section 1 dealt with progress and the sharing of wealth (92), development pro-

* In the final draft of the schema, Section 2, considerably rearranged, was placed before Section 1 and combined with Section 3, making for a more logical presentation.

† Quoted by Bishop Hengsbach in his *Relatio,* see p. 481. This Declaration was retained in the final version.

grams (93), the principles governing such programs (94), training and coordination of such work (95), population explosion (96), agriculture and land distribution (96), and controlling population growth (97). The latter paragraph was very guarded about public birth control policies, never mentioning the word "birth-control" as such, but instead placed the emphasis on responsible parenthood, education and social improvement, warning against "solutions which completely disregard the moral law and aim at putting a stop to population growth by any available means." It then went on, guardedly, "Where circumstances require it, people are, however, to be informed of the proved findings of scientific progress which present sufficient guarantees from the moral standpoint."*

The majority of the 29 speakers naturally addressed themselves to what might be called the "big issues" in Articles 98–100. About one third also made strong statements on conscientious objection (101); while a somewhat smaller number devoted their attention to Section 1, with a scattering of speakers on various miscellaneous points.

It was fitting that the debate should be led off by Cardinal Alfrink, president of the international Catholic group known as *Pax Christi*. Although the text had been revised in such a way as to emphasize the need for banning all war and to stress the commitment of the Church to this cause, concessions nevertheless had been made to the opposite point of view advocating the "legitimacy," if not the theoretical desirability, of armaments under present world conditions. A crucial passage in Article 100 read:

> Nevertheless, as long as international institutions give no adequate guarantee of peace, *the possession of these armaments,* exclusively as a deterrent for an enemy equipped with the same waapons, cannot be said to be in itself illegitimate.

Alfrink commented that the distinction between the possession and use of modern weapons was correct, but the statement about their possession being not illegitimate, "should be dropped from the text because it could serve as an excuse for any nation that wished to participate in the continued equilibrium of terror. The only remedy was the reduction and abolition of modern arms, as Pius XII and John XXIII had often said and as our text should declare in place of the last two sentences of Article 100" (which noted that one of the primary concerns of rulers should be "to limit the production and stockpiling of armaments"). In other words, not limited production and stockpiling, but total disarmament should be the goal.

---

* This whole paragraph was somewhat expanded in the final version and contained a clearer reference to such approved methods of birth control as the rhythm method.

The Dutch cardinal was supported by Abbot Butler: "No one thinks that the great powers merely *possess* such arms. The fact is that, on both sides of the curtain, there is a system of preparation for the use of these arms—and for their illegitimate use in indiscriminate warfare. It might be said: if we think such preparation is legitimate, we had better say so openly, and not hide behind a reference to the mere possession of arms. But then should we not have to go on to say clearly that not only would it be illegitimate to put such preparations into effect in actual war, but the very intention to use them, even a 'conditional intention,' would be gravely immoral? . . . We should do well to avoid such questions. We should not speak about the possession of nuclear arms, because the question is unrealistic and we should also not speak about the legitimacy of preparations for nuclear war. It is obvious enough that the intention of waging war unjustly is itself unjust." Bishop Wheeler (coadjutor of Middlesborough) concurred in Butler's judgment.

According to Bishop Grant (auxiliary of Northampton), "It is true that the words 'exclusively as a deterrent' could and should be understood, in the sense that all intention to use these arms for the destruction of cities is entirely excluded; but at a cursory glance to the ordinary reader this is by no means clear and most people will understand them as meaning that the retention of these arms destined for the destruction of cities cannot be said of itself to be illegitimate as long as the intention is to use them only for one's own defense and never for the purpose of aggression. . . . In order to take away such ambiguity I propose that the words previously cited should be removed from our text; or at least should be so amended that ambiguity is excluded. For example, by adding, after the word 'illegitimate,' the words, 'excluding all intention of ever using them.' " He also suggested that the wording of the previous paragraph should be amended so that it would appear that the Church was not approving the "balance of terror," merely acknowledging its existence.

Other speakers were more nuanced in their remarks and did not call for the outright dropping of this passage. For example, Archbishop Beck (Liverpool) commented: "It seems clear that a government which possesses nuclear weapons as a deterrent and threatens to use them as such is in a proximate occasion of sin. It may be argued that until our international institutions become effective . . . this proximate occasion of sin is what moralists call a 'necessary occasion' to be accepted as a compromise pending the creation of that balance of trust and discussion which must succeed to the present balance of terror."

The schema practically abandoned the classical distinction between "just" and "unjust" wars in view of the terrible repercussions and potentialities of modern warfare, while at the same time admitting the legitimacy of self-defense:

Consequently it may not be unlawful, when all possibilities of peaceful negotiation have been tried without avail, to use force and coercion against an unjust aggressor in defense of rights that have been unjustly attacked; but it is becoming daily more and more unthinkable that war should be a suitable remedy for the violation of justice.

However, this guarded language was not to the liking of some of the bishops. Cardinal Liénart, for example, said that it was no longer sufficient to talk about the distinction between just and unjust wars, because so much depended on the means whereby war was waged. Pope John XXIII, in *Pacem in terris,* pointed out the way the world should forestall the terrors of war and adjust to the path of peace. The schema contained a contradiction, according to Cardinal Léger, in that it tried to show that wars and arms should be absolutely banned, while at the same time admitting that wars could be lawful under certain circumstances. "In our times, the classical theory of the morality of war is unrealistic and inapplicable." New terms should be found. "The Council should refrain from mentioning 'just' wars and from banning arms in the abstract." Archbishop Martin (Rouen) was even more explicit: "The very notion of war must be banned from our vocabulary and from the field of human activity, because the world is sitting on a volcano that can erupt at any time. We cannot talk in the traditional theological terminology about just and unjust wars because the total war of today is completely different from war as known in previous ages. . . . According to the expression of Pius XII, we must wage war on war, and repeat fervently with Paul VI at the UN the prayer that the world may never again behold the dread spectre of war." The one speaker to put in a plea for the classical distinction, Bishop Castán Lacoma (Siguenza-Guadalajara, Spain), was not able to make much headway against the overwhelming sentiment that the traditional view was out of date.* As Bishop Rusch (Innsbruck) expressed it: "The Council should solemnly declare that all aggressive wars are unjust under today's circumstances."

Not that anybody expected one of the bishops to get up and say that he was actually in favor of war. But about the same degree of shock and surprise, though in a wholly positive sense, was caused by the totally unexpected support from Cardinal Ottaviani for the anti-war thesis. The cardinal began by remarking that in his opinion the schema suffered from a number of defects, one of which was that the "aims of justice and

* The final version speaks about the "right to legitimate defense" and "military action for the *just* defense of the people," but abandons use of the adjective "unjust" e.g. in the above paragraph, which seemed to imply that, under certain circumstances, there could be such a thing as "just aggression."

charity needed to overcome wars" were not sufficiently spelled out, such as civic and religious education, the fostering of a spirit of fraternity, more use of arbitration, more respect for the decisions of such international bodies as the International Court of Justice at the Hague and the United Nations. It was somewhat unusual for most of his audience to hear the aged cardinal speaking in this conciliatory and constructive vein, though not for those of course who knew about his background as a teacher of international law. Interest picked up when he began to enlarge on the meaning of war. War must not be understood too narrowly or conventionally in the sense of military warfare. The concept should be broadened to include such things as armed revolution, guerrilla activities, and subtle acts of sabotage and terrorism such as those used by communists to bring about the subjection of other countries. The schema should contain "a sharp reproof of war waged to impose a particular ideology." He then went on to quote a famous passage from Thomas Aquinas' *Government of Rulers,* to the effect that when people see their own government inviting ruin by an aggressive war, they can and must overthrow that government by just means. The sacred right of rebellion! "War would only be a memory," according to the cardinal, "if the words of Pope Paul spoken at the UN were fixed forever in the hearts of rulers and people alike." In a final burst of fervid oratory, carried away perhaps by the thought that this would be his last appearance, he dared to suggest, "The Council therefore should give its vote to the creation of one world republic composed of all the nations of the world, in which there would no longer be strife among nations, but an entire world living in peace: the peace of Christ in the reign of Christ!" Such eloquence of course was greeted by tremendous applause, said to have been one of the longest at the Council, even from those who on second thought probably had misgivings about some of his points. There could be no doubt that the head of the Holy Office was wholeheartedly against war.

None of the other bishops was prepared to go as far as Ottaviani in support of the one-world idea, but many of them gave their enthusiastic endorsement to the more moderate suggestions in the schema for the establishment of a "public authority wielding effective power at the world level" (100), and for various international bodies "to foster and stimulate cooperation between men" (102) as well as the recommendation that the Church should be actively engaged in this lofty work on all levels, "through her official bodies and through a full and sincere cooperation of all Christians" (102). Cardinal Duval, Bishop Rusch, Bishop Brezanoczy, and Bishop Ancel all spoke in this sense, Rusch in particular calling for a "Peace Council at the Holy See, composed of experts in moral, political and military matters."

The text had rather strong language about the necessity of obedience to competent authorities (101): "When God's law is not evidently violated, the competent authority must be presumed to be in the right, and its instructions must be obeyed." On the other hand, its language was rather weak in recognizing a right to conscientious objection:

Furthermore, under present circumstances, it would seem fitting for legislation to reflect a positive attitude towards those people who, as a witness of Christian meekness, or out of respect for human life or sincere distaste for all use of violence, refuse, in conscience, to do military service or certain actions which, in time of war, lead to barbarous cruelty (101).

However, it was a gain to have this much said. Various suggestions were made for watering down the first statement and strengthening the second. Cardinal Alfrink declared: "The sentence regarding the presumption in favor of competent authority should be omitted, even though true, because it will open the way to abuse, as experience under totalitarian governments has shown. What is said on behalf of conscientious objectors, on the other hand, should be retained, since it is the Church's task to defend the freedom of the human conscience." Cardinal Léger wanted the reference to conscientious objection strengthened, so that the objector's motive would not appear to be mere softness. Dom Butler found objectionable the suggestion, or implication, that objectors were in some way "morally immature." "It would be better to speak simply of objections based on genuinely conscientious grounds (and we might refer to our Declaration on Religious Liberty). Some conscientious objectors may in fact be prophets of a truly Christian morality." According to Bishop Wheeler: "The words describing the conscientious objector are so weak and patronizing as to suggest that he is a milksop. The witness of the conscientious objector is something to be valued and welcomed as a special factor in modern life even by those of us who would not be classed as conscientious objectors. I would like to see these weak descriptions changed to 'as a witness of the Christian vocation to bring about peace.' " Bishop Grant and Archbishop Beck also spoke out in favor of strengthening this passage, the latter in particular expressing the wish "to see stronger emphasis both on what public authority must never do or threaten to do under pain of losing its right to the obedience of its subjects and the rights of conscience of all citizens in certain circumstances. . . . We must ask that the rulers of nations should respect the consciences of those of their subjects who look upon certain forms of war as never justifiable even for defensive purposes. This is not a question of Christian meekness or of nonviolence."

On the other hand, Bishops Castán Lacoma and Carli were plainly nervous about the whole business of conscientious objection, the former remarking, lamely, that since theologians were not in agreement on the subject, it was a matter best left to the civil authority; the latter urging that this passage should be removed from the schema, because it was a topic that should either be dealt with consistently or not at all. Carli's attitude was a reflection of the embarrassment felt by various members of the Italian hierarchy about the efforts currently being made to change Italian thinking and laws on this subject, in conformity with the norms widely accepted elsewhere, particularly in countries of the English-speaking world.*

Several speakers availed themselves of the recommendations in Section 1 about aid programs for underdeveloped countries and the need for international cooperation to raise living standards as part of a long-range plan for avoiding and preventing war, to give further endorsement to the idea for the Secretariat mentioned earlier in connection with the debate on Chapter III. Again, there was no formal recommendation to this effect in the text, probably because it would have seemed inappropriate unless other international organizations were expressly mentioned at the same time. Archbishop McCann, Bishop Wheeler, and Bishop Grant spoke on this point. However, the more interesting speeches related to the demographic problem or population explosion and several unusually forthright statements were made about the urgent need for the Church, and responsible authorities, to begin coping with it, with greater vigor and determination than the relatively timid language of the schema seemed to suggest. Bishop Marling (Jefferson City, Missouri) felt that Articles 96–97 did not face up to the basic problem at all, namely that "capital investment in the poorer nations fails to keep up with the rate of population growth. Experts say that to maintain the standard of living in a country with an annual population growth of 3% (which is typical of Latin America), a 10% increase in investments is required. But this is impossible for poorer countries. It is said that if the agricultural methods used in Holland were applied in India, the latter country could easily feed its multitudes. But to raise India to the standards of Holland would require the annual investment of 12 billion dollars over the next hundred years, even if we pretended that the number of Indian citizens remained constant! As the schema points out, richer nations can give emergency help, but this does not touch the basic question of raising the living standard in the face of a demographic explosion." The bishop went on to ask pointedly, "Is it any wonder that poorer nations turn to what our text calls 'solutions which

---

* Unfortunately, in the final version of Schema 13, the passage referring to conscientious objection was somewhat weakened, apparently in deference to Curial and misguided American sensibilities. Cf. what Cardinal Spellman had to say when opening the debate on Schema 13, p. 469. Ironically, Archbishop Roberts claimed that there was a conspiracy to keep him from speaking on this subject in the Council, on the grounds that he might damage the prospects for approval, so he gave his usual press conference.

take no account of the moral law'? The vast difference between rich and poor nations is the basic problem in our economic order and no solution has yet been proposed which is sufficiently daring to be effective. The Council should openly urge public authorities to investigate scientifically those means of family limitation which would be permitted by the moral law." He suggested too that the Church should participate in international congresses exploring this and related problems, such as the Pan-American Assembly on Population that met in 1964 in Colombia.

Bishop Marling's intervention, while strongly advocating investigation of the potentialities of licit birth control methods as a means of controlling the population explosion, was neutral on the subject of which methods might be allowed. Not so Bishop Gaviola (Philippines), whose talk was a commentary on the evil being done in various parts of the world by those advocating both licit and illicit methods of birth control. According to the bishop, Pope John, in *Mater et Magistra,* had affirmed that the conclusions of the theory of over-population were too uncertain and changeable to serve as a basis for any such drastic action. "Lest the Council's words be used for their own ends by dishonest advocates of birth control who are often motivated by a desire for profit rather than by a real concern for the common good, the Council should clearly proclaim the immutable teaching on birth control and the prevention of natural procreation by illicit means.* The Commission should weigh the scientific theories which dismiss the theory of over-population as in no way probable, at least with respect to the entire habitable world. Admission of this theory can lead even believers to question the wisdom of God in creation or can cast doubt on divine Providence, as if God, who gave man the power to multiply life, were failing to provide the means for preserving life." He went on to remark that investigation had shown that a decrease in population had adverse effects on the economic stability of a country, concluding with the pious exhortation: "Let us not contribute to making the People of God lazy and soft."

If the bishop from the Philippines was opposed to letting down any of the barriers with regard to birth control methods, Bishop Simons (Indore, India), in one of the most outspoken pronouncements on this subject ever made on the floor of the Council, was all for throwing the whole question open to thorough investigation and held out the hope that if the alleged natural law basis for banning the use of artificial contraceptive means was seriously examined, it might not constitute such an obstacle as had been supposed. By a curious irony, the bishop spoke two days after Pope Paul had seemed to many to be reasserting the rigid Catholic position when he

---

* The bishop's specific recommendations should be compared with the final version of this section of the schema, modified in accordance with Pope Paul's wishes and approved by the Council. See p. 554 ff.

told the UN: "You deal here above all with human life; and the life of man is sacred; no one may dare to offend it. Respect for life, even with regard to the great problem of birth, must find here in your assembly its highest affirmation and its most reasoned defense. You must strive to multiply bread so that it suffices for the tables of mankind, and not rather favor an artificial control of birth, which would be irrational, in order to diminish the number of guests at the banquet of life." Some of the delegates found the pope's words somewhat self-contradictory in that the Catholic Church was known to favor the use of the rhythm method of birth control but seemed to be warning the assembly rather categorically against "artificial control of birth." This may not have been his intention, however. There was nothing ambiguous about Bishop Simons' recommendations. In substance he said: "The demographic explosion is an undeniable fact. Hence, there arises a grave obligation to arrest this growth in population. It is wrong to say that the riches of the world have not yet been completely tapped and that they are inexhaustible. The means used to bring about this check in population growth will depend for their moral aspect upon their effects. Laws, even the natural law, are for men, not men for the laws. Thus, the conclusions of many theologians need to be re-thought. The traditional arguments against birth control based on the frustration of nature are not at all convincing. Since the Church does not condemn the complete non-use of sex, why should it condemn partial use? The moralists of previous generations failed to consider the many aspects of the problem. Not even the precepts of the natural law impose an absolute and never changing obligation. The natural law forbids taking human life but it is lawful to kill in self-defense, to wage war, and to inflict capital punishment. Lastly, in the present state of the question, the sense and binding force of the law prohibiting artificial means of birth control are open to doubt and, according to our basic juridical principles, a law on whose meaning grave doubt exists is not binding."

Lending poignancy to the scene as the bishops debated the great issues of war and peace, were 20 lay women from various countries, including Dorothy Day of *The Catholic Worker,* who fasted and prayed in a house on the Via dell'Anima calling upon God to enlighten them in their deliberations. The Fathers were reminded about this by Bishop Boillon (Verdun), who also recalled for their benefit the fact that he was the bishop of a see that had been the scene of the bloodiest single battle of the First World War.

Archbishop Garrone then rose to sum up the debate, promising that the sharp judgments passed on certain parts of the schema would be taken into account in revising it, the Latin style would be corrected, more care exercised in the use of such terms as "the world," the scriptural references would be checked, the optimistic tone of certain parts would be modified, Parts I and II would be better integrated. He refused to promise any drastic revision of the section dealing with atheism, and said that it was the "mind of the commission" not to effect any change in the title "Pastoral Constitution," but this matter would be carefully weighed. In conclusion he made it clear that a "major revision" would be undertaken, as desired by so many of the speakers.

THE REVISION OF SCHEMA 13

As soon as the Council had finished debating sections of the schema and the oral and written interventions were forwarded to them by Archbishop Felici's office, the various subcommissions (of the Mixed Commission) set to work revising the text. In addition to 9 subcommissions* concerned with the actual drafting of the text, there was also a Central Subcommission, under Archbishop Garrone, which coordinated the work of all the others, acting as a sort of clearinghouse and settling various questions about procedure, order, style, quotations, etc. It consisted of the presidents of the various subcommissions plus seven prelates from outside who were supposed to aid in the achievement of a more balanced view. Unfortunately this body was not able to function as effectively as had been hoped, because of the tremendous pressure involved in producing a text that could be voted and promulgated by December 7th. There was also a small offshoot of this Central Subcommission called the "Small Editorial Subcommission" (*Parva S. Commissio Redactoria*), consisting of Monsignor Philips,† *relator* for the Central Subcommission, and the *periti* Hauptman, Moeller, Tucci and Hirschmann, concerned only with stylistic questions that later went over the drafts produced by the subcommissions and gave them final form.

The Mixed Commission was presided over by Cardinals Ottaviani and Cento, the presidents of the two Commissions composing it (Theological and Apostolate of the Laity). The meetings were quite large, consisting of the commission members and as many as 30 or 40 periti and lay auditors (both men and women).

At a meeting of the Central Subcommission, on September 30th,

---

* The 9 working subcommissions were as follows: 1. Signs of the Times, Bishop McGrath president; 2. Human Person, Bishop Wright; 3. Human Activity, Archbishop Garrone; 4. Task of the Church, Bishop Ancel; 5. Marriage and the Family, Archbishop Dearden; 6. Culture, Canon Moeller (replacing Bishop Guano); 7. Economic and Social Life, Bishop Hengsbach; 8. Political Life, Bishop László; 9. Peace and the International Community, Bishop Schröffer.

† Mgr. Philips became ill and had to return to Belgium on October 25th. He was replaced by Canon Heylen.

Monsignor Philips summed up the impression of the debate to date, and announced that the section on atheism would be revised by a special subcommission consisting of Cardinal König's Secretariat for Non-Believers and the respective subcommission of the Mixed Commission. Another meeting of the Central Subcommission was held on October 14th. On October 19th the plenary Mixed Commission was able to begin its formal review of the work of the various subcommissions. Monsignor Philips announced that the Commission would meet twice a day every day (except Sunday) until the end of the month and if necessary on November 2nd, 3rd and 4th. A revised text was to be ready for the Fathers by about November 10th. In order to save time, stylistic questions were to be dealt with in writing only. (Fifteen minutes had once been spent deciding whether one word should be moved to another place in the text.) He then said that it would be better for the *relator* to reply to the various points raised at the end of each section, after everybody had been heard. This was agreed, whereupon Cardinal Browne and Bishop Colombo began the discussion of the Introduction.

The Introduction and Chapter I of Part I occupied the Commission during its meetings on October 19th, 20th, 21st, and 22nd (Paragraphs 18 and 19 on atheism were discussed on October 21st). Chapter II and Chapter III on October 22nd; Chapter IV on October 23rd; and Chapter I of Part II on marriage occupied October 25th. Chapter II was discussed on October 26th and 27th; Chapter III on October 27th and 28th; Chapter IV on October 28th and 29th; and Chapter V on October 29th and 30th. The Editorial Subcommission worked feverishly on November 2nd and 8th–9th (on the latter occasion until 5 A.M. the next morning) to get the revised text into final shape. Part II was distributed to the Fathers on November 12th, Part I on November 13th. Because of the unusual length of the booklets (151 pages all told), it was impossible to follow the usual practice of printing the old and new texts side by side.

THE DEBATE ON MISSIONARY ACTIVITY

The Schema on Missionary Activity (which the Council began to debate on October 7th before the conclusion of the debate on Schema 13, and which occupied four days) was a good example of the type of compromise document for which the Council was obliged to settle in the end. This happened partly because of the lack of time for a thorough reappraisal of the missionary role of the Church in all its aspects, and partly because such a reassessment was blocked by an important Curial office whose effectiveness and relevancy would undoubtedly have been reduced by too drastic a revision. In this case it was the Congregation of Propaganda Fide. No doubt Pope Paul's personal penchant for moderation and middle-of-the-road solutions played its part in helping convince the Council that this was the wiser course under present circumstances. Not that Propaganda Fide should be thought of as dominated by conservative prelates with closed minds who were out of touch with the world and its problems. The struggle here was rather between careerists anxious to maintain control over a highly centralized, bureaucratic and reasonably successful enterprise and those who felt that it was important today for all concerned to have a greater share in the direction of the Church's missionary work, in keeping with the doctrine of collegiality and the renewed emphasis on the Church's awareness of itself as being, by definition, missionary.

As a result of the rather harsh criticism to which the "bare bones" of a missionary schema (in the form of Propositions) had been subjected at the Third Session, its commission went to work and produced a much longer, better balanced, and on the whole reasonably satisfactory draft (considering the terms of reference that nothing must be recommended too upsetting to the existing missionary structure). Taking to heart the charges frequently leveled against the Propositions—that they were lacking in theological perspective, and betrayed a certain unfamiliarity with the problems of modern missiology—the commission consulted a number of theologians and missiologists, such as Yves Congar, O.P., the Jesuits Grasso and Buijs, André Seumois, O.M.I., J. Ratzinger, and Professor Glaznik of the University of Münster. The new version now opened with an excellent first chapter on theological principles beginning with the Trinity (Will of the Father, Mission of the Son, Mission of the Holy Spirit) and going on to the role of the "Church sent by Christ," a definition of "Missionary Activity," a statement of the "Reasons and Necessity of Missionary Activity," and concluding with some observations about the "Eschatological Nature of Missionary Activity." This made it clear that the missions were not merely an activity which the Church promoted occasionally and, as it were, over and above its normal call of duty. On the contrary they belonged to the essence of the Church constituting a goal which the whole Church should at all times be promoting as synonymous with its primary responsibility of spreading the Gospel. When the schema went on to particulars, however, this universalist, all-embracing orientation tended to shift somewhat and the missionary idea became synonymous with a certain type of activity carried on in a definite "territory" under the control of a "Dicastery." The conception of such countries as France, Italy, Germany, Spain, Latin America and even the United States being considered as *pays de mission* just like Africa and Asia, was never completely lost sight of, but the suggestion was not explored. This meant that the schema had little or nothing to say about atheism, de-Christianized urban areas, relations with non-Christian religions, and various sociological problems now widely being discussed within the missionary framework, consideration of which might have been expected in the light of the broadly stated theological principles set forth in Chapter I.*

A welcome feature of the new schema was its recognition of the fact that the missionary idea today was going through a kind of "crisis." As Cardinal Suenens expressed it in an interview, the problem was not only that "the world does not seem prepared to listen to us, but the fact is that we are not prepared to talk to it." The question had been raised, were the missions any longer relevant in the light of increased emphasis on freedom of conscience and a deeper understanding of the religious value and "elements of truth" to be found in all religions? Why disturb people in their beliefs if they could achieve salvation without the Gospel? Perhaps efforts should be directed toward improving their lot socially rather than concentrating on the business of evangelization strictly speaking? Was Catholicism in its modern form really a suitable vehicle for conveying to primitive peoples the meaning of the Gospel, loaded as it was with "western" accretions and compromised by too close an association with European civilization? To these difficulties must be added others of a more practical nature caused by the drying up of vocations (not only in the missionary field), the unwillingness of some countries to admit missionaries, differences between missionary institutes and local bishops over the training and control of personnel, the reluctance of ecclesiastical authorities (particularly Propaganda) to condone methods that departed from the usual ways, the time-consuming burden of fund-raising, to mention only some of the problems. The schema proposed few if any radical solutions because of its somewhat restricted outlook, but at least it had the merit of recognizing that problems existed and of attempting to supply answers.

Chapter II dealt with Missionary Work in general, Chapter III with Missionaries, Chapter IV with Planning Missionary Activity (including a recommendation for the reorganization of Propaganda Fide), and Chapter V with Cooperation in support of the missions.†

Most of the speakers were enthusiastic about the revised schema as a

---

* The commission, to its credit, made no bones about trying to hide its motives. It conscientiously endeavored to insert some wording or phrase that would satisfy everybody; with the result that the final draft approved by the Council was something of a mish-mash. However, whenever there was a question of some suggestion that would have broadened the text unduly, the reason for refusing it would be either, "the commission could not become involved in particulars," or "this is a matter that would have to be reserved to the Holy See."

† In the final version promulgated by the Council, those paragraphs of Chap. II dealing with Particular Churches were made a separate chapter, Chapter III. Otherwise the two drafts were structurally much the same.

whole. Bishop Lamont (Rhodesia), for example, who had characterized it as "bare bones" in 1964, now hailed it as "no longer a naked series of frigid propositions but a solid body of doctrine." In his judgment "missionaries do not want a fine literary document or a text in missiology, but rather something that will make all bishops conscious of their missionary responsibility." One thing the new text certainly did was to stress at every possible turn that support for the missions was essentially a collegial responsibility binding on all the bishops. Famous as an Irish orator of the old school, Bishop Lamont was apt to be carried away by his own rhetoric at times. After delivering himself of the magnificently balanced sentence, "No land is so primitive as to be unfit for the Gospel nor is any so civilized as not to need it," a thought that ranged somewhat beyond the limited horizon of the schema, he concluded with the not altogether felicitous suggestion that there was a parallel between the medieval Crusades and the modern missions when he declared that "Bishops must organize the missions of the Church, as Peter the Hermit had organized the Crusades." Praise for the way in which the document laid the "theological foundations" of the Church's missionary activity was voiced by numerous speakers. Cardinal Frings declared, "In this 'crisis of the missionary conscience' old formulas are not adequate; we need a new basis for our missionary activity, and this is provided by our text." Bishop Velasco (exiled bishop of Hsiamen, China) was one of the few who begged to differ, "wondering" whether the present version represented much of an improvement over the earlier text and claiming that it was "too heavily weighted with the 'new theology.' "

Concerned lest the relatively liberal imprint which the "new theologians" had succeeded in imposing on the document should give rise to the impression that the Catholic Church was receding from its traditional stand regarding the necessity of the Church, Cardinal Journet plunged headlong into this number one theological problem, by declaring that "the plurality of religions remains a fact, but to suppose that it is intended by God would be a great mistake." He then went on to explain that God did not desert the multitudes to whom the Gospel had not yet been preached. God's grace was present to such people and therefore the Church was too, although in a rudimentary, abnormal, precarious way. "These beginnings of the Church demand to be set free from internal and external impediments by the preaching of the Gospel. So missionary activity is not merely a matter of advice but rather of command, not for the *melius esse* but for the *simpliciter esse* of salvation." He called for a strengthening of the passage dealing with the necessity of the Church, to make this point doubly clear. The same thought was echoed by Bishop Geise (Indonesia), speaking in the name of the Indonesian Episcopal Conference, who declared that "as far as those outside the Church are concerned, where there is no preaching of the Gospel or administration of the sacraments, salvation can be found in an initial way, but not in the proper Christian form which it requires in order to attain its own perfection." Bishop Lokuang (Tainan) and Bishop Corboy (Monze, Zambia), the latter speaking in the name of 70 African bishops, joined in supporting Journet's recommendation.

On the other hand, Cardinal König, president of the Secretariat for Non-Believers, shifting the emphasis, declared that he was pleased by the schema's recognition of the religious values to be found in the "great religions" and its recommendation that the work of evangelization should be begun by establishing a "dialogue" with those who belonged to such religions as well as others who remained "strangers to the very knowledge of God." "Since almost all Christians," he said, "live in communities with non-Christians, they should give witness to a truly Christian life. They should look upon non-Christian religions as ways of seeking God. Even if these religions are not *the* way to salvation, they nevertheless lead men toward it. The grace of God is the way to salvation. . . . Even if given outside the Church, it draws men to the Church." Many younger missionaries were disturbed by a rumor at the Bombay Eucharistic Congress, according to Bishop Gay (Basse-Terre, Guadalupe), that the Church would no longer insist so much upon missionary work and that the missionary's main task would henceforth be not to baptize and preach the Gospel, but rather to promote conditions that would help men find Christian values in the non-Christian religions. As the schema made abundantly clear, however, the purpose of dialogue with non-Christians was not merely the discovery of common ground or philosophic contemplation, but the recognition and evaluation of truths that would help people to a better understanding of Christianity.

One point on which there was fairly general agreement was that the schema was inadequate in its approach to the ecumenical problem in the missionary field. Many speakers rose to deplore the "scandal of division among Christians" and to suggest various ways in which this obstacle to the spreading of the Gospel could be overcome, or at least rendered less harmful. Bishop Koppmann, vicar apostolic of Windhoek, noted that there were some 1,200 separate religious sects operating in Western Africa, his missionary territory, making the problem of collaboration one of vital concern. The often-made charge that cooperation would result in fostering indifferentism was ruled out by Bishop Van Cauwelaert (Inongo), who maintained that if prudently moderated "it would make manifest to all the necessity of unity according to the will of Christ." Others who spoke on this theme were Cardinals Frings and Jäger, Father Degrijse, Archbishop Cordeiro (Karachi), and Cardinal de Barros Camara (Rio de Janeiro). The common view was probably expressed by Father

Degrijse (Superior General of the Immaculate Heart of Mary) who suggested various practical ways in which the cooperation of "Christ's disciples" in the missionary field could be obtained, through a more accurate knowledge of each other, the common use of external means such as the radio, television, newspapers, hospitals and schools, more emphasis on united Christian social action, for example against such evils as racism, and even a certain collaboration in the business of evangelization. Not all were equally enthusiastic about opening the doors too widely however. Cardinal de Barros Camara, speaking in the name of 57 Latin American bishops, read a statement said to have been signed by 316 bishops warning against the dangers of proselytism: "(The undersigned) desire that this Council explicitly make it known that it is useful for the progress of real ecumenism to present clearly to the faithful the Catholic doctrine in regard to the proselytism undertaken among Catholics by certain denominations of the separated brethren . . . and that it would be very useful to include standards and norms about this in the ecumenical directory that the Secretariat for Promoting Christian Unity intends to draw up and publish."

Father Arrupe, General of the Jesuits, began by launching into a scathing denunciation of the inadequacies of the whole western approach to the missionary problem, dominated as it was by a romantic and infantile outlook. Missionaries who returned to the West were often appalled by the defects discernible in those who were supposedly responsible for the destinies of missionary work, namely their infantile attitude toward the importance of accurate information; their sentimentalism in distributing funds to favored projects rather than where they were most needed; their sense of superiority, so typical of "Westerners"; their myopia, in thinking of the missions only when they had taken care of the needs of their own dioceses; and finally the "mendicity" which required too much time spent on collecting funds that should be used for preaching the Gospel. He proposed that the text should be amended to provide for a greater flow of information to and from the field and for more cooperation in the selection and training of missionaries. Cardinal Suenens also touched on the matter of better training, recommending that special centers be established in every important missionary area affiliated, if possible, with outstanding universities. As the exiled archbishop of Nanking, Yü-Pin, rather plaintively expressed it: "Christ became man. Why can missionaries today not become Chinamen? China also forms part of mankind."

Though the schema had the advantage of being revised after the Constitution on the Church had been passed, which made clear the significant role the laity were expected to play in the People of God, Cardinal Alfrink and a number of other speakers still felt that the document was too hierarchical in its outlook. Missionary work actually belonged to the whole People of God, whereas the schema still occasionally suggested that only the hierarchy were really involved. Bishop McGrath (Santiago Veraguas, Panama) agreed and called for a strengthening of Chapter V in this sense. Fortunately the Council was able to hear the case for the laity put by one of the lay auditors, M. Eusèbe Adjakpley, a Negro from Togo, who was invited to address the assembly on October 13th, the last day of the debate. The point of his talk was that the missionary situation today was very different from what it had been when missionaries first went out to areas like Africa and Asia to lay the foundations of new Churches. The world today was fast becoming one "in which all men are becoming increasingly aware of their dignity and less willing to tolerate inequality and injustice." Consequently the missions were everywhere. "All groups comprising the Church must be missionaries; all can and must cooperate. The laity desires to place their witness and their skills at the service of the Church's mission to evangelize the world." The implication of his speech was that Africa now had something that it could perhaps teach Europe or America.*

Of immediate concern to quite a few prelates nullius in South America and other bishops throughout the world was the rather limited way in which the term "missionary territory" was defined, whereas, as Bishop Gazza (Brazil) pointed out, there were some 130 ecclesiastical territories in Latin America where missionary activity was being carried on as described in the schema but which were not entitled to the benefits of such territories because they did not fall under the official designation. (In its final revision of the text the commission admitted the justice of this claim to a certain extent and redefined the concept of "missionary territory" in a sense acceptable to these prelates.) A similar proposal that formal recognition should be given to the practice of assigning definite missionary territories to certain dioceses, in the way that such territories were assigned to various missionary religious institutes, was received with more reserve. 120 Fathers, including 7 cardinals, actually submitted a request to the commission along this line, but the reply was that the practice of "commissioning" territories was now on the decline and that in any case there could be no question of approving a custom "not proven by experience," however there was no objection to the establishment of such relations on an informal basis.

It had long been the custom of the Holy See (Propaganda) to assign certain missionary territories to religious institutes (or religious orders) which then assumed the responsibility for providing missionaries and

---

* A new paragraph, No. 21, on Promoting the Apostolate of the Laity, was added to the final text, and minor changes were made in Chapter V, No. 41, on the Missionary Task of the Laity.

supporting the missions established there. However, in the course of time these missions developed into full-fledged Churches, with their own native hierarchies and diocesan organizations like other Churches. The resulting conflict of jurisdictions gave rise to endless bickering and controversy, aggravated by the fact that the missionary societies were themselves going through something of a "crisis" owing to a variety of causes, the shortage of vocations, the difficulty of adjusting to new situations, their inflexibility, rigidity, etc. As Bishop Ntuyahaga (Burundi) explained the situation: "Relations between the ordinaries of new dioceses and the heads of missionary orders are still theoretically ruled by the law according to which areas are entrusted to institutes, but practically this law has become antiquated. From this discrepancy, confusion and unpleasantness have arisen. The schema states that it would be good to enter into agreements to regulate these relations, but nothing further. . . . We ask the Council not merely to recommend particular agreements between ordinaries and generals, but also to lay down detailed norms and guidelines for these agreements. The norms thus worked out by Propaganda should be incorporated in the Code of Canon Law." A number of prelates, particularly Father Quéguiner (Superior General of the Missions Society, Paris) and Cardinal Zoungrana (Upper Volta) suggested various concrete ways in which these difficulties could be overcome. (The final text of the schema represented a compromise, endeavoring to do justice to both sides, without proposing any radical solutions.) Many of the African bishops who spoke on this theme, such as Bishop Sibomana (Rwanda) and Bishop Gahamanyi (Rwanda), were firm in their assertion that control of the local Church must be in the hands of the bishop, but they also paid tribute to the debt of gratitude those Churches owed the institutes, and generally minimized the conflicts.

There were few references to the matter of funds for the missions. Bishop De Reeper (Kenya) declared that when the bishops returned to their homes, they would not be asked what the Council had done about defining the concept of a mission, but rather how much cooperation and support they could expect from the dioceses in Christian lands which supplied the funds and personnel. The schema had largely settled this matter by incorporating in Chapter VI, No. 38 (in the final version) the provision that episcopal conferences were to "decide what definite offering each diocese should be obliged to set aside annually for the work of the missions, in proportion to its own budget; they should [also] consider how to direct and control the ways and means by which the missions receive direct help; they should deal with assisting and if need be, founding, missionary institutes and seminaries for diocesan missionary clergy, and the promoting of closer relations between such institutes and the dioceses." This was done in response to repeated requests made at the

Third Session. A plea for more explicit recognition of the vital work performed by the Pontifical Missionary Societies in various countries collecting funds for the missions was lodged by Bishop Poletti, director of the Pontifical Missionary Societies in Italy.* Finally, to satisfy the persistent demands of those Fathers who at the Third Session had called for a "reorganization" of Propaganda Fide and a greater participation by the episcopate in its work, Chapter IV of the revised schema provided that "all those who take part in missionary work, namely cardinals, patriarchs and bishops of the whole world, regardless of rite, as well as the directors of pontifical institutes and works" should be "members" of this Roman Congregation and should "exercise the supreme government of all missionary work under the authority of the Roman Pontiff."

At the last minute, there was substituted for this rather strongly worded text that seemed to meet the essential objections of the critics of Propaganda, a weaker text (printed at the end of Father Schütte's *relatio*) watering down its effectiveness to a considerable extent. However, either because the bishops were unaware of its existence or failed to assess its importance, there was no appreciable discussion of this point on the floor. Nor were there any significant repercussions when the Council voted to accept the schema as the basis for a final text on October 12th by an overwhelming 2,070 Placets to 15 Non placets. Shortly after this vote, however, it became known that a group of 60 Indian, 11 Divine Word, and 20 African bishops had presented a petition to the Council Secretariat, expressing their "amazement" that the schema had been revised by certain authorities (Propaganda) without consulting the other members of the missionary commission, along lines suggested, it was said, by the Papal Commission for the Reform of the Roman Curia, headed by Cardinal Roberti.† The two most important of the proposed changes were that, instead of being "members" of Propaganda Fide, the delegates were merely to "have an active and decisive role" (*partem actuosam et decisivam*) in that congregation; and instead of exercising "supreme government" (*supremam gubernationem*) over all missionary work, they were to exercise merely "supreme control" (*supremam ordinationem*) of such work. If finally accepted, the modifications would largely leave intact the essential structure and present freedom of action of Propaganda which the critics were trying to alter in a collegial sense. Accordingly the petitioners requested a return to the original text and put forth certain counter proposals of their own: the episcopal delegates forming part of the central organism should be elected by their respective episcopal conferences; they should be summoned to meet at fixed times; and their

---

* Paragraph No. 38 was strengthened in this sense.

† It was said that the petition of the African bishops became lost while being circulated and was never presented to the Secretariat.

term of office should probably be limited in order to avoid the risk of careerism. If the number of delegates turned out to be too large, it could be limited provided their distribution were still representative.*

THE SCHEMA ON PRIESTLY LIFE
AND MINISTRY

At 11:40 Monday morning, October 11th, while the Council was still discussing the schema on Missionary Activity, Cardinal Tisserant stopped the debate and announced that Archbishop Felici would read a letter which he had just received from Pope Paul. The letter said:

We have learned that certain Fathers intend to discuss the law of ecclesiastical celibacy in the Council as it is observed in the Latin Church. Therefore, without infringing in any way on the right of the Fathers to express themselves, we make known to you our personal opinion, which is, that it is not opportune to have a public discussion of this topic, which demands so much prudence and is so important. We not only intend to maintain this ancient, holy and providential law to the extent of our ability, but also to reinforce its observance, calling on all priests of the Latin Church to recognize anew the causes and reasons why this law must be considered most appropriate today, especially today, in helping priests to consecrate all their love completely and generously to Christ in the service of the Church and of souls (*applause*). If any Father wishes to speak about this matter, he may do so in writing by submitting his observations to the Council Presidency which will transmit them to us (*applause*).

For several days the press had been printing sensational reports about the number of requests before the Holy Office from priests desiring to be released from their vow of celibacy. Some said there were as many as 10,000, others more. It was known that several bishops did in fact intend to bring the matter up, especially certain Latin American prelates. Afraid of the consequences of a public debate and knowing that the hierarchy was divided on the question, a number of Latin American Fathers, including Cardinal de Barros Camara, talked to Cardinal Tisserant and begged him to intervene with the Holy Father to prevent a discussion. The result was the pope's letter.

However, the announcement was made too late to prevent the printing of one of the intended interventions, by the Dutch Bishop Koop (Lins, Brazil).† The bishop explained later that he had not intended his speech for publication but had distributed it to some of the bishops and it

---

* See p. 548 for the outcome of this move.
† Printed in the October 12, 1965, issue of *Le Monde,* which was on the newsstands the previous day.

inadvertently got into the hands of the press. Whatever the facts regarding its disclosure, the speech showed that what the bishop wanted, and presumably also the others who intended to speak, was not an abolition of the law of celibacy but a modification of the existing legislation that would permit a married clergy to operate alongside a celibate clergy in areas like Latin America, where the pastoral needs were so immense and the possibility of meeting them with the existing personnel almost nil. According to René Laurentin, the problem of a married clergy for Latin America and other areas, along the lines of the Eastern discipline, had been before the Holy See ever since the days of Pope Pius X, but the Roman authorities had always felt that any concession here would inevitably lead to reconsideration of the status of those living in clerical concubinage in Italy and other countries, estimated variously in the thousands, and this they were not prepared to face.

The pope's letter to Cardinal Tisserant was not read until after the seventh vote on the schema dealing with Priestly Formation (Seminaries) which concerned the question of maintaining the law of celibacy in the Latin Church. The results (1,971 for to 16 against) were then cited as evidence of the overwhelming support among the bishops for celibacy, somewhat too hastily and naïvely it would seem. The bishops were not aware that their vote would be regarded as a test case. If the question had been put to them whether they would approve some relaxation of the existing legislation along the lines suggested by Bishop Koop, the outcome might have shown that the Council was more divided on the issue than was generally supposed. It was not unreasonable to assume that the Council might have divided roughly the same way that it did over the question of a married diaconate.

But it was precisely this nearly fifty-fifty split that Pope Paul was anxious to avoid, the fruitless and embarrassing revelation that the bishops were hopelessly divided on a subject that could not possibly be debated and resolved if the Council were to complete its work on time. Few commentators felt that the pope had acted unwisely or arbitrarily. While there was some regret that more attention had not been paid to the matter earlier when there was still time, it was considered significant that the pope had not closed the door to revision of the existing legislation at a later date, but had merely reserved the question to himself in order to remain the master of a controversial issue.*

Pope Paul's action ruled out any possibility that celibacy would be openly discussed on the floor. Cardinal Ruffini, however, could not resist the temptation to gloat over the fact that the rule of celibacy had been

---

* Cf. Gary McEoin, in the *St. Louis Review* (October 29, 1965): "I believe it was a good decision. . . . Better to consolidate the advances and pray for the success of Vatican III."

saved not only in the Western Church but "in no small part of the Oriental Church" as well, thus implying, rather insultingly, that the whole Eastern Church ought to follow the discipline of the West. Cardinal Bea set the record straight in an important intervention on Saturday, October 16th. "Celibacy is not required by the nature of the priesthood," he said. "The schema makes this clear, but it then goes on to insist on the Latin discipline in a way that is too exclusive. It gives the impression that the married clergy of the East are second-class priests, not fully priests. But they are very deserving. Our Council is an ecumenical council. It must speak to the East also. Therefore the schema should refer to two types of priesthood, the celibate and married. This is of the greatest importance (*summi momenti*) for the East. Each clergy should be trained with a view to its special role."

The day before the discussion of the important schema on Priestly Life and Ministry began, on October 14th, Archbishop Marty, *relator* for the commission, read a detailed report explaining that the document attempted to describe the pastoral mission of the priest and to show how this mission was, or should be, the focal point for his whole life and ministry.

In spite of the archbishop's moderate and conciliatory tone, a large number of the speakers preferred to judge the schema rather severely giving the impression that it would have to be subjected to a drastic revision. However, a closer look at their remarks revealed that many, if not all, were in substantial agreement about the general acceptability of the present text and merely wanted this or that aspect brought out more clearly. There was such wisespread agreement among them, as a matter of fact, that this was probably the most prolix and repetitious of all the debates held in the council hall. Instead of reaching an end with the 43rd speaker after three full days of debate, the Council was obliged to sit through two more mornings of 12 speakers, on October 25th and 26th, with part of another morning being devoted to a speech by Monsignor Thomas Falls, a pastor from Philadelphia. Many of the speakers, obviously, were airing their views for the benefit of the record, because this was the final debate, or in order to impress the clergy back home because of a certain feeling that the Council had tended to concentrate its attention too much on bishops to the exclusion of mere priests.

The critics of the schema tended to fall into two categories: those who felt that it did not emphasize sufficiently the ritual or sacramental role of the priest; and those who wanted more attention paid to practical matters and the role of the priest in today's world. The former was represented for the most part by prelates steeped in the "Latin" tradition such as Archbishop D'Avack, Archbishop Fares, Cardinals Florit, Landázuri Ricketts, Richaud and de Arriba y Castro, Bishops Segedi, Garcia

Lahiguera and Compagnone. Among their various suggestions: the title of the schema should be changed to "Priestly Holiness" (de Arriba y Castro); not enough was said about the individual devotion of priests and in particular their devotion to the Holy Spirit (D'Avack); there was too much emphasis on the ministry of priests and not enough on the development of their spiritual life (Richaud and many others); the schema should say more about the central place which the eucharistic sacrifice should occupy in priestly life (Landázuri Ricketts); more should be said about the grave obligation to priestly poverty (Florit and Zak); in order to promote the spirituality of priests, a group of "holy priests" should be formed in each diocese to give retreats and set an example (Garcia Lahiguera); not enough was said about the role of the priest in administering the sacrament of penance (Fares). Finally, priests were letting slip a golden opportunity of preaching to the faithful at funerals (Segedi)!

A number voiced criticisms of a general nature. Cardinals Tatsuo Doi and Meouchi both found the text too "western," the former noting that it had little to say about the clergy in missionary lands because its remarks were directed almost exclusively to the relations between priests and the Catholic faithful, the latter complaining that it was too juridical and had nothing useful to say about the Eastern clergy, particularly those who were married. In Cardinal Döpfner's opinion, the schema read more like a "spiritual lecture" than a conciliar document. What was needed was a plainer style in keeping with today's mentality. Priests would be annoyed, he said, if they found themselves being called "a precious spiritual crown of their bishops." A religious motive seemed to be attributed to everything, even the most trivial of everyday happenings in a priest's life. The schema unfortunately repeated many things that were known to everybody. Its theological terminology might be suitable for a book of devotional reading but was hardly good enough for a conciliar document. "I propose that the style be improved and that the schema stress more the problems of today's priests."

Quite a few speakers had remarks to make about the way in which the schema dealt with the theology of the priesthood. As Bishop Soares de Resende said, the theology of the priesthood was not yet sufficiently mature for a definitive statement, however it was possible to make certain assertions more confidently. According to Bishop Henriquez Jimenez (auxiliary of Caracas), a firmer theological emphasis would help many priests, especially the younger ones, "resolve the crisis of hope and cheerful acceptance of their state" in which many found themselves. Cardinal Colombo summed up fairly well the point that most speakers were trying to make: "The ministry of the priest should be portrayed in close communion with the mystery of the Church, because thus he would be in close communion with Christ. It can never be sufficiently stressed that the fullness of the priesthood can be achieved only in the mission and mystery of the God-Man. The text should delete any remark that makes it seem impossible for a secular priest to be said to be living in a state of perfection. This is an open question which should not be prejudiced by any conciliar statement."

A leading spokesman for a more activist or pastoral approach to the priesthood was Cardinal Alfrink who found the presentation too sacral: "You would think that the priest never left the sacristy or church." The text should stress the importance of carrying on a dialogue with those Catholics who were such in name only as well as with other Christians and even atheists, as one of the daily duties of priests. Unfortunately almost nothing was said about the attitude of the clergy toward social and economic matters. Article 5 called for priests to have a profound knowledge of the encyclicals of the popes, but nothing, strangely, was said about their knowing the documents and spirit of the Second Vatican Council. Many of the Fathers, Cardinal Alfrink noted, had asked for a treatment of the problems that were causing uncertainty and anxiety in the priesthood today, but these topics were barely mentioned. The doctrinal revision of the text gave the impression that "everything is calm and clear concerning the life and ministry of priests."

Cardinal Suenens charged that while the doctine of the schema was solid enough and an attempt had been made to coordinate the schema with *Lumen Gentium,* the statements were too conceptual or related to an age that was now past. They were too remote from the questions being asked by priests today. Priests today were having a difficult time finding their place in a world that regarded them as alien and in a Church that seemed to regard them as mainly useful for the sacramental ministry only. The schema offered the elements of a solution, but in a somewhat haphazard way. He suggested that more attention should be paid to the relationship of priests to Jesus Christ, the episcopal college, and the laity. According to Cardinal Léger too, the presentation of priestly holiness was too otherworldly and unrealistic. The type of sanctity offered was not one suitable for priests today. The schema should avoid any notion of priestly holiness founded on the opposition between the exterior and the interior life. The difficulties which priests today had to face must indeed be mentioned, but as realities of human life which could and should bring them closer to God. "Christ and his grace were found in the men whom the priest meets every day." Instead of defining the priestly life in terms of the religious vows of obedience, chastity and poverty, more emphasis should be put on such virtues as zeal, apostolic concern for all men, universal love, especially for children, the poor and sinners, and the desire for apostolic work and perseverance in the midst of difficulties, as Monsignor Falls brought out in his final talk on October 27th. On the other hand, Archbishop Santin (Trieste) warned the Fathers against making too many concessions to the laity; he objected in particular to what the schema said about "charisms of the laity" as being liable to false interpretation: "We don't want to increase the number of those who think that they are specially inspired."

The last speech by a conciliar Father, the newly appointed archbishop of Turin, Michele Pellegrino, was a moving plea for a more open attitude on the part of the bishops toward the intellectual life of their priests. It was significant that he spoke in the name of 158 Council Fathers including 12 cardinals.

In our day, in some regions at least, a kind of pragmatism is widespread which almost exclusively esteems external works to the neglect of the importance of studies. Thus it happens that clerics seriously engaged in theological studies are considered to be on a lower level than those engaged in strictly pastoral work or even in temporal administration. Why must professors in seminaries often teach for a very poor salary? Why do not a few ecclesiastical libraries suffer from a lack of necessary funds? Why are assistants lacking in some faculties who, while engaging in scientific work in their own fields, help the professors with their work and instruct the students in methods of critical investigation? Why are so few monographs published? Certainly the Church always suffers from poverty, but even in regions where money is said to be lacking for the promotion of theological studies, we see sumptuous new buildings daily rising up for various uses and immense projects being carried out. No less care should be taken to foster intellectual work. Unfortunately there are depressed areas also as regards intellectual activity in the theological field, and the principal reason for this, in my opinion, is not so much a lack of funds, as an insufficient appreciation of the importance of these studies. In the post-conciliar period there will be two dangers: that of watering-down the norms of the Council which change old customs, and that of passing over everything that is old and of undertaking whatever is new only because it is new. To avoid these pitfalls, priests will need not only humble obedience and a vigorous interior life, but also a clear view of problems and the historical reality within which these problems are to be solved. For this reason the Church needs many clerics to indicate ways of both preserving the essentials of tradition and of accommodating this tradition to our times.

The archbishop was immediately surrounded by well-wishers congratulating and praising him for the forthright remarks with which he had brought the Council's discussions to a close.

The archbishop of Turin was not the only Father to speak out boldly on a number of specific problems relating to the schema. A few days earlier Cardinal Heenan had some rather pointed remarks to make about a generally taboo subject, the question of "fallen" priests: "When a wretched man has made shipwreck of his priestly life, it is not at all uncommon for his closest associates to express no surprise. It is easy to be wise after the event. . . . Every language has some version of the saying: 'A stitch in time saves nine.' Priests unhappily, rarely speak up in time. In this matter they are inclined to behave like schoolboys. At all costs they do not want to be regarded as sneaks or informers. So they remain silent while a brother priest rushes to his ruin." It was therefore important for the schema to say something about a priest's responsibility for his fellow priests. Having got this off his chest, the cardinal then went on to recommend the virtues of golf: "It is by no means a waste of time for priests to play a round of golf together. Priestly company brings a kind of blessing in itself." He deplored the standoffishness of the clergy in certain countries: "In countries where the Church has not lost touch with the working-class, the priest spends a great deal of time with the laity. . . . Where the clergy visit their flocks anti-clericalism does not exist." (He did not say that in Italy the parish clergy were expected to be locked in by nine o'clock in the evening, for fear of "scandal.") He concluded with some facetious remarks about monks who "stay at home to write books and articles about the People of God, while bishops are hard put to it to find enough priests to go out into the missions." Bishop Brzana (auxiliary of Buffalo) also pleaded for a more humane treatment of fallen priests: "I have never heard of a priest being scandalized because of mercy shown to a repentant brother."

Nine or more of the Fathers dealt more or less explicitly with the knotty question of priestly obedience and the proper relations that should obtain between a bishop and his clergy. According to Cardinal Shehan, the schema was not clear about the foundation of these relations. It was essential to adhere to the guidelines laid down by *Lumen Gentium* and for bishops to avoid a false "episcopalism" that made them seem more like overbearing masters than true collaborators in the ministry. The document on the Church specified that the bond which priests and bishops shared in common was the priesthood of Christ. The schema gave the impression of reversing the order by implying that the priest participated in the priesthood of Christ because he partook of the episcopal mission; this should be corrected. Cardinal Quiroga y Palacios was afraid that too much emphasis was being put on the dependence of priests on their bishops and that this might stifle their individual initiative; Bishop Renard called for clarification of what the text meant by describing the bishops as the "perfector" of priests; Bishop Mancini (auxiliary of Porto-Santa Rufina), wanted priests "neither to have complete freedom to undertake rash projects, nor to be reduced to the level of mere record keepers";

Bishop Franic thought that if priests and bishops could be persuaded to lead a common life together this would help to conquer Marxism. "What is deplorable today," said Bishop Charbonneau (Hull, Canada), "is not so much the crisis of submission on the part of the clergy as the crisis of responsibility about which the schema does not speak." This was plainly not the view of Archbishop Connolly (Seattle) for whom the blame was almost entirely on the side of the rebellious clergy: "A crisis of obedience seems to have developed here and there owing to a false notion of freedom and independence, of a new atmosphere generated by this Council. Some priests, pseudo-existentialists, denigrate authority as such; each one wants to be a law unto himself. Even the *aggiornamento* of the Church can make it more difficult for a priest today to obey an order whose wisdom for the apostolate he does not personally see, and in these days of ferment, priests are more apt to have their own opinions on many important matters. Obedience has its ultimate root in the divine will. . . ." Fortunately for the archbishop, the bishops were by then so benumbed by rhetoric that his slur on the Council passed virtually unnoticed.

Pope Paul VI unquestionably had an eye for the symbolic and the timing of important announcements. Shortly before the end of the debate on Priestly Life and Ministry, late Saturday afternoon, October 23rd, the French hierarchy suddenly announced at the conclusion of their meeting in Rome that the Holy See had agreed to a revival of the worker-priest movement that had been so popular in France with the working classes during the period 1943–54. Suppressed by Pius XII in the latter year at the insistence of the Holy Office and other Curial bodies because some of the priests had drifted into communism, members of the French hierarchy had never ceased to hope that the experiment, properly overhauled and with adequate safeguards, could be revived as part of a long-range program to help win back many of the French people to the Church. In many audiences with members of the French hierarchy, Pope Paul lent a sympathetic ear to their plea and finally asked the Holy Office to reconsider its ban, making possible the above announcement.

Among the changes insisted on were that the experiment was to last for three years initially; the priests chosen were not to be called *prêtres-ouvriers* but *prêtres au travail,* a subtle distinction safeguarding their sacerdotal status as apostles among the working class rather than workers pure and simple; and they were to maintain close contact with their ecclesiastical superiors and live in community with other priests instead of on their own.

The schema was accepted as the basis for a final text with a vote of 1,507 Placet, 12 Non placet, and 2 invalid votes.

THE COUNCIL DEPLORES ANTI-SEMITISM

Few Council documents aroused as much controversy, or were followed with such close interest, as the famous Declaration on the Jews later incorporated in a more broadly conceived Declaration on Relations with Non-Christians (including Hindus, Buddhists, Moslems as well as Jews). Although the expanded Declaration was destined to become the *magna carta* of the newly formed Secretariat for Relations with Non-Christian Religions, under Cardinal Marella (announced in the spring of 1965), it was on the Jewish portion that public attention was almost exclusively focused, largely because of the intense interest in it shown by a few Jewish groups, notably the American Jewish Committee. As a result of this campaign, the Council found itself in the rather anomalous position of dealing with a subject that seemed at times to be of greater moment to Jews than to Christians for whom its statement was primarily intended. In essence, the Jewish section tried to do three things: stress the close ties that bound Jews and Christians together; kill the old charge of deicide which intemperate Christians frequently hurled against the entire Jewish people; and finally extinguish once and for all the flames of Christian Anti-Semitism.

The history of the Jewish section had been stormy. It originated as an idea of Pope John XXIII in 1960 after he met and talked to the French historian and scholar, Jules Isaac. In the later spirit of *Pacem in Terris,* John expressed the opinion that since it was high time to mend fences, the subject of Jewish-Christian relations was one fence that needed mending most of all. The Secretariat for Promoting Christian Unity, presided over by Cardinal Bea, was entrusted with the task of drawing up a suitable text in 1961, and in May of the following year a first draft was presented to the Central Commission which was passing on the suitability of texts for discussion in the Council due to open in September. Bowing to pressure from Arab states and conservative forces within the Church, the Commission refused to accept the draft. So nothing was done about the question during the First Session.

In December 1962, after the pope recovered from his illness, he asked Bea to revise the document and gave it his approval. To get around any objections from the Coordinating Commission (which had taken over from the Central Commission), it was decided to annex the document to the schema on Ecumenism as Chapter IV. When Ecumenism came up for discussion in the Second Session in 1963, after Bea's official report had already been distributed and as the cardinal was preparing to introduce the text, it was suddenly announced that because of "lack of time" the discussion would have to be postponed until the next session. Pressure had again been brought to bear by the usual quarters. When the text actually reached the floor of the Council in the Third Session, it had been so altered meanwhile that Archbishop Heenan of Westminster, one of the Secretariat members, declared that it was virtually unrecognizable. Mention of the word deicide had been dropped and other changes made along conservative lines. (The sponsoring of this bastardized text was probably Pope Paul's single greatest mistake and gave rise to more misgivings about his intentions than anything else.*) After two days of debate, it became clear that the previous text would have to be restored.

The May 1965 version represented a compromise with the restored version approved by the Council on November 20, 1964. Though the passage rejecting the charge of deicide had been strengthened, the word itself was omitted. The wording of the previous version, "deplores, indeed condemns" hatred and persecution of Jews, was changed in the new version merely to "deplores" but added the words, "displays of Anti-Semitism directed against Jews." The old version warned Christians not to teach anything that could give rise to hatred and persecution of Jews, the new version less explicitly urged them not to teach "anything inconsistent with the truth of the Gospel and with the spirit of Christ." As one of the experts involved in the drafting of the text put the matter: "If it had not been for the publicity surrounding the previous versions, the present text offered to the Council in 1965 would probably be regarded as excellent."

The contention of the Arab states that the document tended to favor recognition of the state of Israel, or the political aspirations of Zionism, was denied by a clause specifying that the Council had been "moved not by any political considerations, but by the Gospel's spiritual love," and by a series of diplomatic trips to the Near East by members of Bea's staff to assuage these misgivings and obtain suggestions for the text from Arab Christians.

It was a foregone conclusion that the document would win a majority when it was put to a vote on October 14th and 15th, the only question being whether those disappointed over the omission of the word deicide, Bishop Carli's *Coetus Internationalis Patrum* who opposed it on theological grounds, and those who felt that there were still political objections,

---

* The pope's apparently casual remark in the course of a Passion Sunday sermon on April 4, 1965 also caused something of a furor: "That people [the Jews], predestined to receive the Messiah, who had been awaiting him for thousands of years . . . when Christ comes . . . not only does not recognize him, but opposes him, slanders him and finally kills him." A charitable explanation suggested that owing to a "slip" the pope had fallen into the centuries-old habit of attributing the death of Jesus to the whole Jewish people without making the necessary distinctions.

would be able to register enough Non placet votes (two-thirds) to bring about rejection or seriously impair the unanimity with which Council documents were supposed to be approved.* One estimate was that the opponents might be able to muster as many as 500 votes but hardly more. As usual the Fathers were deluged with literature beforehand. Bishop Carli's group urged Non placet votes on most counts (there were 8 votes on various paragraphs of the text and 1 vote on the document as a whole) on the grounds that it favored indifferentism by tending to regard all religions as on the same level, would retard the "conversion of the Gentiles," and would "put an end" to missionary work. The specifically Jewish portion was objectionable because "many Biblical scholars hold that it can be proved from Scripture that the Jewish religion is reprobated and accursed." One of the most violent pamphlets was a four-page affair signed allegedly by 31 so-called "Catholic organizations" which trumpeted: "No Council, no Pope, can condemn Jesus, the Catholic Apostolic and Roman Church, its Popes (naming several from Nicholas I to Leo XIII) and the most illustrious Councils. But the Declaration on the Jews explicitly involves such a condemnation, therefore it should be rejected. . . ." It went on to accuse the Jews of trying to compel the Church to disgrace and disavow itself before the world and described the Declaration as being worthy of "an antipope or a schismatic council." Most of the signatories promptly disavowed any connection with the manifesto, which turned out to be largely a hoax concocted by some crank. Father DePauw, for example, publicly stated in Rome that his Traditionalist Movement in the United States had had nothing to do with it and that their name had been used without authorization. Several French organizations issued similar statements.

So much tension had been generated, however, that the authorities naturally took seriously an anonymous letter received by Cardinal Marella, archpriest of St. Peter's, from a person threatening, half in French and half in German, to blow up the basilica and the whole Council if the Jewish document were voted, and extra police were detailed to guard the building. Except for a resounding crash when some workmen's scaffolding collapsed, the voting proceeded smoothly on October 14th–15th. The results: 1,763 for and 250 against on the motion approving the document as a whole. This ensured that it would be promulgated. Pope Paul lost no time in confirming the Council's action and announced on Monday, October 18th that it would be added to the

---

* Bishop Carli published an important article condemning the theological basis of the Declaration in *Palestra del Clero*, 44 (1965) 185–203 (February 1965) to which Cardinal Bea replied, refuting his contentions point by point, in *La Civiltà Cattolica*, November 6, 1965.

list of four texts already scheduled for solemn voting and promulgation on October 28th.

A minor crisis occurred Friday, October 15th, as the Council was preparing to complete its voting on the document. It had been decided earlier to postpone two final votes to Saturday morning's congregation, when Archbishop Krol, one of the Council's undersecretaries, suddenly remembered that many of the bishops would be absent on a pilgrimage to the Holy Land because of the holiday the following week. It would have been disastrous, and something that could probably never be explained satisfactorily, if a sizeable majority had not been reached because of these absences, so he hurriedly consulted Cardinal Cicognani and the entire voting was completed that day. As things turned out, some 700 bishops were absent the following morning.

World opinion, on the whole, hailed the passage of the Declaration as marking an important turning point in the relations of the Catholic Church with other religions, though regret was freely expressed about its shortcomings.

Few would have concurred in the judgment of one rabbi who was supposed to have said, "If the document is approved in its final form, any real dialogue between Catholics and Jews will be impossible for decades." And those writers and commentators who mistakenly seized on words like "pardon" and "forgive" in expressing their outrage over the Church's "absolving and forgiving" the Jews, were guilty of misplaced indignation, for these words do not occur in the text of the Declaration. The document was addressed not to Jews but to Christians, teaching them that anti-Semitism was wrong. One writer called the Declaration "the most astonishing bureaucratic impertinence of all times."* It was, of course, exactly the opposite—the fruit of Pope John's love of all men, and of his determination to do what Jules Isaac had asked, that is, reverse past Catholic teaching approving of anti-Semitism. To label as an "impertinence" the years of effort on the part of Cardinal Bea and his Secretariat, and the Council's final endorsement of this historic Declaration, was mischievously to misread history. Many of the bishops who wanted a stronger text nevertheless voted for this one for fear that if there were too large a negative vote the document might be withdrawn. The adverse vote on the schema as a whole (250), though disgraceful, was offset by 1,763 affirmative votes. All attempts by either side to force last-minute modifications failed, and thus the document was at long last scheduled for promulgation.

* William Jovanovich, *Stations of Our Life,* 1965, Harcourt, Brace & World, p. 25.

THE PROMULGATIONS ON OCTOBER 28TH

The formal debating of conciliar texts ended technically on October 16th, actually on October 27th, after a number of additional speakers were heard who requested to speak in the name of sizeable groups of bishops. The remaining congregations would be devoted almost exclusively to voting and, as Archbishop Felici put it, "gathering the fruits of their labors," with a number of weekly interruptions during which only the various commissions preparing the texts for final voting and approval would be at work. The first intermission lasted from October 17th to October 24th.

Already the Council could rack up an impressive list of accomplishments. Archbishop Felici was able to announce, in the session on October 15th, that four documents would be promulgated by the pope in a first Public Session on October 28th, namely the texts on the Pastoral Office of Bishops, the Renovation of Religious Life, Seminaries and Christian Education. Three other texts, the Declaration on Religious Liberty and the schemata on Divine Revelation and the Apostolate of the Laity were already sufficiently advanced so that final voting could begin on October 25th, with the possibility of a second Public Session on November 18 at which time some or all of these texts could be proclaimed. This left only 4 texts out of the original 11 before the Council at the beginning of the Fourth Session on September 14th, still to be acted on, namely Schema 13, Missionary Activity, Priestly Life and Ministry, and the Declaration on Relations with Non-Christian Religions. The overwhelming approval accorded the latter in an historic vote on Friday, October 15th, before the close of the debates, ensured that this too would be promulgated on October 28th.

Gone was the mood of uncertainty and pessimism prevailing at the beginning of the Fourth Session. It was now clear that real progress was being made and the end of the Council's work was in sight—barring some upset over a failure to reach agreement on the controversial Schema 13 or renewed efforts on the part of the pope to pacify the minority that might result in a crisis similar to the one that accompanied the close of the Third Session. Both eventualities now tended to be discounted.

The mood of the Council Fathers at this point could be called one of resigned euphoria. They were resigned because of the realization that more acceptable texts could not be achieved under present circumstances and it was better to be grateful for the great progress already accomplished than mourn over unattainable ideals. The important thing, as Cardinal Suenens noted, was not whether *aggiornamento* had been

532

achieved, but whether the groundwork had been laid for future action. "Perhaps we can say," he declared, "that we have not yet reached May but are only in April when night frosts still occur, nevertheless there can be no doubt that spring has come and no question of a return to winter."

When the first fruits were garnered in the Public Session on October 28th, statistical evidence seemed to prove what most observers had been predicting for weeks, that all the conciliar documents were going to be voted through with a minimum of stir.

Texts promulgated	Previous Non Placet votes	Final Non Placet votes
Bishops	14	2
Religious	13	4
Seminaries	15	3
Christian Education	183	35
Non-Christians	250	88

The second and fourth were probably the least successful documents of the lot. That the Decree on Renewal of the Religious Life did not arouse more determined opposition at this late date could be explained by its limited interest and the fact that those who hoped for a more vigorous approach to the problem had lost the battle much earlier. The Commission on Religious, dominated by the ultra-conservative Curial Congregation on Religious under Cardinal Antoniutti, consistently refused to allow women religious, for example, to have any deliberative part in their discussions despite the fact that well over half the number of religious in the Church are women (nuns and sisters). Although there were abundant signs that dissatisfaction with the traditional ordering of religious life in convents and monasteries had now reached the boiling point, the Congregation persistently ignored the real causes of this *malaise* and insisted on regarding all instances of disquiet as rebellion against authority. Antoniutti himself set a fine example of insubordination, continually accosting the pope's ears with complaints about the rebelliousness of nuns while refusing himself to comply with the spirit of the pope's directives. The tragedy was that the Decree would do so little for those, namely the religious themselves, for whom it was primarily intended. While ordering a reform of the religious life, it was clear that in the mind of the drafters this reform was to be largely confined to the tidying up of externals such as the updating of religious garb with a minimum of attention being paid to underlying theological issues. Significantly, the section on obedience was five times longer in the finally approved text. However, the difficulty here was that the process of reform, once unleashed, might be impossible to keep under control.

More encouraging was the situation with regard to the Decree on Priestly Formation (Seminaries) and the Declaration on Christian Education, voted by the Council on October 11–12th and 13th respectively, because the commissions preparing them had managed more or less successfully to escape from the control of the equally conservative Roman Congregation for Seminaries and Universities (nominally governed by the senile Cardinal Pizzardo, actually run by the energetic but hopelessly *intégriste* Archbishop Dino Staffa). Distribution of the second text was delayed by the archbishop's efforts to insert wording that would strongly commend Thomas Aquinas, and scholasticism generally, as a unique model to be followed by the Church, as opposed to the more scientific attitude advocated for example by Cardinal Léger at the Third Session and presently reflected by the text. The archbishop also tried to strengthen paragraphs 13 and 16 of the Decree on Seminaries dealing with philosophical and theological studies in the same sense. Both moves failed completely. The commissions preferred to heed the example of Pope Paul VI who in an important address before the Thomistic Congress on September 10, 1965 just before the opening of the Fourth Session, and again in an audience granted to the Canadian Thomas Aquinas Foundation on October 8th, adopted a sensible approach to the whole problem, referring to Aquinas on the latter occasion as "a sure norm for the teaching of the sacred sciences" but not as a master to be followed exclusively or in a formalistic way.

The most interesting feature about the Decree on Seminaries was the provision in the very first paragraph for greater autonomy: "Since only general laws can be made where there exists a wide variety of nations and regions, a special program of priestly training is to be undertaken by each country or rite. It must be set up by the episcopal conferences, revised from time to time and approved by the Apostolic See." The initiative for reorganizing and modernizing seminaries was thus clearly handed over to the local hierarchy which, to an extent as yet undetermined, were to be freed from excessive control by the Roman Congregation of Seminaries and Universities. Another progressive feature was that students were to be "brought to a fuller understanding of the Churches and ecclesial communities separated from the Apostolic See of Rome, so that they may be able to contribute to the work of re-establishing unity among all Christians according to the prescriptions of this holy synod." Such a ruling would have been unthinkable, had it not been for the Council. There was considerable dissatisfaction with the Declaration on Christian Education on the part of some of those most directly concerned both bishops and priests, as reflected in the rather high number of Non placet votes: 183. One commentator described it as "probably the most inferior document produced by the Council," others preferred to reserve this accolade for the Decree on the Apostolate of the Laity, the Decree on the Religious Life, or the Decree on Communications. The state-aid-to-education clause in particular was a disappointment to many of the American bishops, including Cardinal Spellman, who wanted a clearer statement of the obligation of the state to support religious education, whereas the compromise text was more in accordance with world thinking because conditions varied so from country to country (Par. 6: ". . . the public power, which has the obligation to protect and defend the rights of citizens, must see to it, in its concern for distributive justice, that public subsidies are paid out in such a way that parents are truly free to choose according to their consciences the schools they want for their children"). The obligation of parents to send their children to Catholic schools was somewhat mitigated again owing to different world conditions. The Americans saw this too as a possible threat to their extensive and expensive parochial school system. The principles enunciated by the schema were to be "developed" at greater length by a Post-Conciliar Commission and "applied" by the various episcopal conferences according to varying local conditions. Perhaps another reason why the Americans were dissatisfied was the knowledge of how weak their own episcopal conference traditionally was when it came to carrying out any concerted action. After the high Non placet vote on October 13th there was talk of appealing to the Administrative Tribunal to get a new discussion of the text which had been rather thoroughly revised by the commission, but nothing came of this move.* One tired bishop summed up his thoughts as follows: "Last year I would have voted Non placet because the text is so bad that it deserves to be turned down. But this year we all know that the possibility of getting anything better is nil. The pope wants the Council to end. The bishops are all anxious to go home. Negative votes would only complicate matters. Therefore I voted Placet, even though I have grave misgivings about the value of the present text."

The Decree on the Pastoral Office of Bishops which went through without a ripple when voted on September 29th and 30th, October 1st and 6th was not a revolutionary document in any sense of the word, but its provision calling for the establishment and strengthening of episcopal conferences was bound eventually to alter the traditional pattern of church government. No surprise was caused by the fact that the Declaration on Non-Christian Religions registered a total Non placet vote of 88. There was merely relief that the figure was not higher.

---

* In the booklet distributed before the vote on October 13th, the new material was printed in roman and the old in italics, contrary to the usual practice.

THE REVISION OF DIVINE REVELATION

There could be little doubt that the Constitution on Divine Revelation would be regarded as the most important document promulgated by the Council after the Constitution on the Church. Together with *Lumen Gentium,* it enshrined and consecrated the new biblical approach to theology which had become one of the hallmarks of Vatican II. But this victory was not achieved without a struggle. An original draft entitled "The Sources of Revelation" (*De Fontibus Revelationis*), prepared by the ultra-conservative pre-conciliar Theological Commission, after being subjected to a gruelling debate during the First Session (November 14–21, 1962) on its general merits, was withdrawn by Pope John XXIII when a crucial vote showed that 1,368 of the Fathers, as opposed to 822, were not in favor of going on to a discussion of the individual chapters. Revision of the text was entrusted to a Mixed Commission headed by Cardinal Ottaviani (of the Theological Commission) and Cardinal Bea (of the Secretariat for Promoting Christian Unity). This Mixed Commission produced a more liberal version *De divina revelatione* that was approved by Pope John on April 23, 1963 and debated by the Council at its Third Session, September 30–October 6, 1964. On the basis of the debate a *textus emendatus* was prepared, but this was readied too late to be submitted to the Fathers for a vote before the end of that session. The revised text was therefore voted at the Fourth Session, September 20–22, 1965. The schema was approved with a comfortable margin, however there were a rather large number of Iuxta modum votes for each of the six chapters, indicating that a substantial agreement had not yet been reached on several controversial points. An examination of the *modi* revealed that these points were mainly the three on which concord had been difficult from the very beginning, namely 1) the relation of Scripture to tradition; 2) the question of the inerrancy of the Bible or "truth" of Scripture; and 3) the historical nature of the Gospels. The Council's progressive majority was generally satisfied with the highly skillful and balanced way in which the revised text dealt with these problems, in a sense that would not close any doors but leave the way open to future speculation. The minority, on the other hand, felt that the text was too "liberal," abandoned essential Catholic positions, and opened the way to heresy. The Iuxta modum votes of course were not all offered by the minority. Some of the majority felt that various improvements should be made before the document could be finally promulgated, however it was clear from what followed that the minority were the prime movers in the attempt to change the schema on these three fundamental counts.*

Pope Paul followed the revision of this document with very close attention. Although the Secretariat for Promoting Unity had had nothing to do with the work after the presentation of the first revised draft, the pope was anxious that Cardinal Bea should be associated with its closing stages, probably in order to make clear some kind of continuity with Pope John's Mixed Commission and for the effect that Bea's presence would have in helping the commission to reach agreement on a satisfactory text. (When Father Daniélou declared that the Secretariat had been represented at the final commission discussions, thus implying that the Mixed Commission had in a certain sense been revived, Cardinal Bea publicly denied this, maintaining that he had been present in a personal capacity and had given his views without consulting the members of his Secretariat, however it seems that the pope's view was as stated above.)

The Theological Commission proceeded to examine the *modi* submitted by the Fathers and in a series of plenary meetings, on October 1st, 4th and 6th, decided what attitude to adopt with regard to them, on the basis of the recommendations of the special Subcommission headed by Cardinal Florit charged with preparing the text. Approximately about this time the pope began to be besieged by various Fathers complaining that the Subcommission and the Commission had not paid sufficient attention to their opinions. Accordingly, after consulting a large number of people during the first two weeks of October, Paul had Cardinal Cicognani, Secretary of State, send a letter to the Theological Commission on October 17th (dated the 18th) requesting a reconsideration of the revised text with a view to reaching a better consensus of opinion particularly on the three above mentioned points. It was also his wish that Cardinal Bea should take part in the discussions. The plenary Theological Commission met on the afternoon of Tuesday, October 19th to consider the pope's proposals and vote on a final text. This *textus re-emendatus* was then voted by the Council on October 29th.

It is convenient in what follows to deal separately with the three points raised in the pope's letter, though they were of course mentioned in the same communication.

* Pope Paul obviously authorized Fr. G. Caprile, S.J., to publish a full account of the maneuvering relative to this schema in order to forestall erroneous interpretations of his own actions and set the record straight. Caprile's article, *"Tre emendamenti allo schema sulla Rivelazione,"* was published in *La Civiltà Cattolica,* February 5, 1966. (A similarly revealing article was published by the Jesuit editor in February 1965, throwing light on Paul's actions during the controversial closing days of the Third Session.)

1. Paragraph 9, of Chapter II, dealing with the relation between Scripture and tradition, read in part as follows in the version of the text voted by the Council in September 1965:

... Sacra Scriptura est locutio Dei, quatenus divino afflante Spiritu scripto consignata, sacra autem traditio verbum Dei, a Christo Domino et a Spiritu Sancto apostolis concreditum, successoribus eorum integre transmittit, ut illud, praelucente Spiritu veritatis, praeconio suo fideliter servent, exponant atque diffundant. Quapropter utraque pari pietatis affectu ac reverentia suscipienda et veneranda est.

... Sacred Scripture is the word of God inasmuch as it is consigned to writing under the inspiration of the divine Spirit, while sacred tradition takes the word of God entrusted by Christ the Lord and the Holy Spirit to the apostles, and hands it on to their successors in its full purity, so that led by the light of the Spirit of truth, they may in proclaiming it preserve this word of God faithfully, explain it, and make it more widely known. Therefore both sacred tradition and Sacred Scripture are to be accepted and venerated with the same sense of loyalty and reverence.

In the final version, voted on October 29th and promulgated by the Council December 7th, this read as follows:

... Sacra Scriptura est locutio Dei ... diffundant; *quo fit ut Ecclesia certitudinem suam de omnibus revelatis non per solam* Sacram Scripturam *hauriat.* Quapropter ...

... Sacred Scripture is the word of God ... more widely known; *consequently it is not from Scripture alone that the Church draws her certainty about everything which has been revealed.* Therefore ...

Among the 354 Iuxta modum votes on Chapter II, 111 demanded that the following clause (or a variation of it) be added after *diffundant: "quo fit ut non omnis doctrina catholica ex sola Scriptura directe probari queat"* ("therefore not every Catholic doctrine can be directly proved by Scripture alone"). Three *modi* asked that a similar clause be inserted in the following paragraph 10 (on the relation of Scripture and tradition to the magisterium). The Subcommission revising the text at first agreed to accept this latter suggestion, then changed its mind and opted for the first alternative. However, when the proposed amendments were voted by the plenary Commission on October 1st, 4th and 6th, the full Commission rejected the Subcommission's recommendation for an addition to Par. 9, and also a suggestion for amending Par. 10, after having momentarily accepted the latter. In the course of the heated discussion of these points, one of the experts (Father Tromp?) suggested that since the Commission was so hopelessly divided on the question of how to express the relationship of Scripture to tradition, it would be best to return to the old idea of "two sources" and insert a statement to this effect in Par. 9. This naturally caused the majority in the Commission to freeze in their opposition to any change and matters stood at this point when the pope intervened.

The minority was determined to effect some change in the language of the text that would permit the "constitutive" role of tradition to be brought out more clearly, even if there was no hope of going back to the old view of "two sources" of divine revelation. Pope Paul was not averse to trying to satisfy their desires, provided this could be done without upsetting the delicate balance of the existing text. On September 24th he transmitted to the Commission a text from St. Augustine's *De Baptismo contra Donatistas* (V, 23, 31) which suggested a possible alternative wording, but for some mysterious reason his communication never reached its destination.

Members of the minority were not the only ones to make their views known to the pope. Others assured him that the text as drafted was perfectly acceptable. One cardinal suggested that while the text seemed to be satisfactory as it stood, a way out might be for the Commission to introduce the clause *quo fit . . .* which it had first accepted then rejected, because this still left open the question of whether some truths were to be found in tradition which were not found in Scripture, a point that the text was not intended to settle. Pope Paul kept on consulting various people and had a meeting with the moderators on October 12th. Two days later one of the moderators submitted a written memorandum in which he proposed a solution similar to that of the above cardinal, recommending the insertion of another *modus, "quo fit ut Ecclesia certitudinem suam de omnibus revelatis . . ."* shifting the emphasis from "doctrine" to "certainty regarding doctrine."

This seemed to be the best solution, so on October 17th the pope had Cardinal Cicognani write to the Theological Commission and suggested that the latter should consider 7 possible alternative readings, all approximately with the same meaning, and choose the one that seemed to be the best. Cardinal Bea was asked for his opinion first and chose No. 3, the wording suggested by the moderator. There were 28 members of the Commission present. The first ballot was indecisive because the necessary two-thirds majority was not reached. However the second ballot produced the required majority and this clause was inserted in Par. 9.

2. Par. 11 of Chapter III, dealing with the inspiration of Scripture, read in part as follows, in the version voted by the Council in September 1965:

. . . Cum ergo omne id, quod auctor inspiratus seu hagiographus asserit, retineri debeat assertum a Spiritu Sancto, inde Scripturae libri integri cum omnibus suis partibus *veritatem salutarem* inconcusse et fideliter, integre et sine errore docere profitendi sunt.	. . . Therefore since everything asserted by the inspired author or sacred writer must be held to be asserted by the Holy Spirit, it follows that the books of Scripture completely and in all their parts must be acknowledged as teaching solidly and faithfully, fully and without error *the truth of salvation.*

The final text as amended and promulgated by the Council read:

. . . Cum ergo omne id, quod auctores inspirati seu hagiographi asserunt, retineri debeat assertum a Spiritu Sancto, inde Scripturae libri *veritatem, quam Deus nostrae salutis causa litteris sacris consignari voluit,* firmiter, fideliter et sine errore docere profitendi sunt.

. . . Therefore since everything asserted by the inspired authors or sacred writer must be held to be asserted by the Holy Spirit, it follows that the books of Scripture must be acknowledged as teaching solidly, faithfully and without error *that truth which God wanted put into the sacred writings for the sake of our salvation.*

Of the 324 Iuxta modum votes on Chapter III, about 200 dealt with the expression *veritatem salutarem.* 184 of these wanted to eliminate the word *salutarem;* 76 wanted to substitute other wording because the present language seemed to restrict the inerrancy of Scripture to matters of faith and morals. Others approved of the expression, but wanted it more fully explained in a note, with references to St. Augustine (*De Gen. ad litt.* 2, 9) and papal documents. The Commission had made it clear in its commentary on the revised text that *"salutaris* had been added to cover the *facts* mentioned in Scripture in connection with the history of salvation" and that it was not being used in an unduly restrictive sense, but this did not satisfy the minority.

The various alternative suggestions proposed by the bishops were all rejected both by the Subcommission and by the Plenary Commission, which insisted that "the word *salutaris* did not imply that Scripture was not wholly inspired and the word of God." The proofs of the Commission's *expensio modorum* were sent to the pope on October 14th. But before they reached him, a group of the minority had made known their objections through one of the cardinals, probably the same group that had voted the 184 *modi* mentioned above, asking that the word *salutaris* be deleted and complaining about the way in which the Commission had disregarded the objections of so many Fathers. They were afraid that the Commission was restricting the inerrancy of Scripture merely to supernatural matters affecting faith and morals (ignoring the explanations offered by the Commission), that the text would give dangerous leeway to exegetes, would deal a severe blow to the Church, etc. In the following days other views were made known to the pope, pro and con. Some held that the formula should not be dropped but explained, all the more so since it had been introduced into the text by the Commission after the debate in 1964 and not adequately discussed by all the bishops.

After reflecting on all these various conflicting views, the pope proposed, in the letter of Cardinal Cicognani, that the Theological Commission should "consider whether the expression *veritas salutaris* might be omitted. The perplexity of the Holy Father is greater with regard to this point because it is a question of a doctrine not yet commonly taught in biblical theology, and because it does not seem that the formula has been sufficiently discussed in the aula, and finally in the judgment of competent persons, because this formula is not without the risk of misinterpretation. It seems premature for the Council to pronounce on a problem that is so delicate. The Fathers are perhaps not in a position to judge of its importance or whether it could be misinterpreted. Omitting it would not preclude future study of the question."

The Commission was left free to consider any possible alternative wording. In the meeting on October 19th Cardinal Bea was again asked for his opinion first. He opted for dropping the expression *veritatem salutarem* pointing out that it was liable to misinterpretation and that in any case it had been added to the text after the first revised draft had been prepared by the Mixed Commission.

The voting on the proposition "whether the formula should be omitted or retained" was very sticky. There were three ballots, none of which produced the required two-thirds majority. A dispute then arose over whether the Commission should be guided by canon law or the Rules of the Council in determining what constituted a majority. It was finally decided that the Rules alone were normative. An alternative wording was then sought that would be acceptable to both sides. This was found in the clause *"veritatem, quam Deus nostrae salutis causa litteris sacris con-signari voluit"* suggested by 73 of the Fathers among the *modi*. A fourth ballot succeeded in garnering a two-thirds majority for this wording. At this point, in a last desperate move, the minority again raised the question of what constituted a majority. If the Commission took its stand on canon law, then the first vote had been valid and the phrase would have been rejected. Consideration was given to referring this point to the Administrative Tribunal, but this idea was dropped and the Commission stood by its fourth ballot.

The wording adopted had the advantage of spelling out what was meant by *salutaris* without in the slightest departing from the stand that the Commission had adopted on this point.

3. Par. 19, of Chapter V, dealing with the "Historical Nature of the Gospel," read as follows, in the version voted in September 1965:

. . . Sancta Mater Ecclesia firmiter et constantissime tenuit ac tenet quattuor recensita Evangelia vere tradere quae Iesus, Dei Filius, vitam inter homines degens, ad aeternam eorum salutem reapse et fecit et docuit . . . Auctores autem sacri quattuor Evangelia conscripserunt . . . ita semper *ut vera et sincera* de Iesu nobis communicarent.

. . . Holy Mother the Church has firmly and with absolute constancy held, and continues to hold, that the four Gospels just named, truly hand on what Jesus, the Son of God, while living among men, really did and taught for their eternal salvation . . . The sacred authors wrote the four Gospels . . . in such fashion that they told us *the honest truth* about Jesus.

The final version of the text as amended and promulgated by the Council read:

. . . Sancta Mater Ecclesia firmiter et constantissime tenuit ac tenet quattuor recensita Evangelia, *quorum historicitatem incunctanter affirmat,* fideliter tradere quae Iesus, Dei Filius, vitam inter homines degens, ad aeternam eorum salutem reapse fecit et docuit, usque in diem qua assumptus est . . . Auctores autem sacri quattuor Evangelia conscripserunt . . . ita semper ut vera et sincera de Iesu nobis communicarent.

. . . Holy Mother the Church has firmly and with absolute constancy held, and continues to hold, that the four Gospels just named, *whose historical character the Church unhesitatingly asserts,* faithfully hand on what Jesus, the Son of God, while living among men, really did and taught for their eternal salvation until the day he was taken up into heaven . . . The sacred writers wrote the four Gospels . . . always in such fashion that they told us the honest truth about Jesus.

Among the 313 Iuxta modum votes on Chapter V, the majority had to do with the words *ut sincera et vera,* claiming that this expression did not assert unequivocally the historical character of the Gospels. Various suggestions were put forth designed to remove the alleged ambiguity.

In this case too the Theological Commission rejected all their suggestions, maintaining that the addition of the word "historical," for example, would not solve the problem because of its ambiguous meaning. The use of the word *sincera* was not intended to imply that the Commission thought there was anything "fraudulent" about the Gospels. It was merely intended as a complement to *vera.*

This decision caused the minority to appeal to the pope, who had already come to the conclusion that the Commission must be asked to clarify its use of the word *sincera.* Accordingly, in his letter of October 17th, the Secretary of State asked that the historicity of the Gospels should be better defended by the insertion of the following phrase instead of *sincera et vera: "vera seu historica fide digna."* "It seems," the papal letter went on, "that the former expression does not guarantee the historical nature of the Gospels; therefore, on this point, it is obvious that the Holy Father could not approve a formula that left in doubt the historical nature of these holy books."

Cardinal Bea, again asked at the meeting on October 19th to state his opinion first, said that the wording *vera et sincera* was ambiguous and opted for the papal amendment. Other speakers brought out, however, that the new formula would not accomplish its purpose because the Bultmannian and other Protestant schools understood *fides historica* in a purely subjective sense. Therefore in order to make this point perfectly clear, it would be necessary to retain *vera et sincera* and insert above a clearer explanation of what was meant. The wording eventually chosen and inserted in the text was adopted by a vote of 26 to 2.

It is clear from the pope's letter that his one concern was to find some formula that would enable the largest number of Fathers to agree on a final text, without doing violence to what had already been accepted by the Council, much less compromising any essential position. About his sincerity here there could be no doubt. It is obvious also that he was at great pains not to give the impression that he was in any way trying to "impose" his will on the Commission ("The Holy Father regards it as opportune. . . ." "The Holy Father hopes that the Commission will attach the same importance to his suggestion that it attaches to that of any other father. . . ." "The Commission is invited to reconsider the text because he considers this the clearest and best way for the Commission itself to take into account all the elements useful for the task assigned to it . . .").

It was clear also, from the outcome, that the Commission did not slavishly bow to the papal wishes or accept all of his suggestions at least in the form in which they were communicated to them.

What was disturbing about the pope's (Cicognani's) letter was that the language seemed to go beyond what might have been expected of an impartial arbiter recommending the views of the minority to the favorable consideration of the Commission. To a certain extent it seemed to identify the pope with those opinions. What if the Theological Commission had not had the force of character to "turn" the papal requests to its own advantage?

In the course of these maneuverings one of the Council Fathers (possibly a cardinal) wrote to the pope expressing his alarm at the bad impression being created in certain countries, England or the United States, by these papal interventions, at the last minute, designed to alter texts on which the Council had already agreed with sizeable majorities. In his reply the pope defended his right to work for the improvement of all documents like any Council Father and maintained that his interventions had all been "perfectly regular." He then went on, "Finally, regarding the point you make concerning respect for the Council and observance of the customary procedures, nothing gives us more pleasure than to have these principles recalled that are dear not only to Anglo-Saxons but also to Romans. I can assure you that they have been scrupulously observed throughout the Council."*

In his *relatio*, before the final voting on October 29th, Cardinal Florit disclosed that the Commission had also rejected another move of the minority designed to limit the meaning of doctrinal progress. The *modus* in question wanted the text to speak only of "progress in the understanding of tradition," not of "any objective progress of tradition." But this would have been inconsistent with the Church's teaching according to

* G. Caprile, *La Civiltà Cattolica*, February 5, 1966, p. 231. The above account summarizes Caprile's article.

Florit. There was progress in tradition in the sense in which every living thing changed, while remaining substantially the same. "The clearer perception of both things and words in tradition does not remain extraneous to them but freely becomes one of their proper elements. Thence it follows that the Church is really tending to the fullness of Revealed Truth itself and achieves this to the degree that tradition realizes its internal progress." This was obvious from the fact that the Church did not arrive abruptly at the fullness of truth. She could not express and proclaim all at once the entire deposit of Revelation, "as is proved and always will be proved by the history of dogma."

The Commission's handling of the *modi* was overwhelmingly approved by the Council on October 29th. It was later announced that the schema on Divine Revelation would be voted and promulgated by the Council at its next Public Session on November 18th.

That the minority would stop at nothing to prevent itself from being completely worsted on all major issues became evident when an American professor at the Biblical Institute was carefully scrutinizing the Italian translation of the Constitution on Divine Revelation and discovered that a principal passage has been astutely mistranslated. The translator made the clause *quam Deus nostrae salutis cause litteris sacris consignari* read: "God, the author of our salvation, had desired to confide truth to the sacred books." This could be interpreted to mean that every syllable of the Bible was unerring, as Cardinal Newman had once been assured in Rome was the case by the Jesuit theologian Perrone.

Taxed with this literary trickery, the translator, Monsignor Garofalo, said that he had consulted members of the Subcommission and been assured that this was a good translation, though as any Latinist knew, the use of the word *causa* after a phrase in the genitive case could only mean "for the sake of." Abbot Butler had the final say on the matter. He brought up the question of the translation at a meeting of the Theological Commission and offered four reasons why the translation "God the cause of our salvation" was untenable theologically. Father Tromp observed that his reasons were only probable; whereupon Butler retorted, "I take it then that Father Tromp does not believe in the law of probabilities." Butler's view of course prevailed; but theologians and *periti* were properly warned that such attempts to doctor the texts of conciliar documents must be expected. Vigilance was more than ever the order of the day if the work of the Council was to remain intact.*

* Father Tromp's account of this incident is somewhat different, and does not mention the exchange with Abbot Butler: "On November 20–21 the Secretary (Tromp) met with Mgr. Garofalo and Frs. Betti and Castellino in the hospice of S. Marta to go over the Italian translation of the constitution on Divine Revelation which Mgr. Garofalo had prepared. Three of the revisers had failed to note a mistranslation in paragraph 11 which had the text say that the Scriptures '*insegnano*

THE DISCUSSION OF INDULGENCES

Toward the middle of October it became known that the pope intended to consult the various episcopal conferences about a number of documents that he was thinking of issuing. The presence of so many members of these conferences in Rome was said to have suggested to him the desirability of finding out how the proposed Synod of Bishops might be expected to work, while at the same time the consultation would prove that he was serious about his intention to put teeth into the principle of collegiality. The presidents of the various conferences were requested to poll their members about a proposed reform of the penitential discipline of the Church and meet with him in the Vatican Palace on October 21st to report their findings. After delivering a short discourse the pope departed, turning the meeting over to Cardinal Ciriaci, Prefect of the Congregation of the Council, who presided while Monsignor Palazzini read a report on the draft of a Motu Proprio reforming the discipline governing fasting and abstinence and each of the conference presidents rose to make known the views of their respective bodies. The whole dossier was then turned over to the pope to serve as the basis for a final decree.

A second meeting was tentatively scheduled for November 11th on the subject of a reform of the discipline regarding indulgences.* The document under consideration was a draft or Schema for the Revision of the Discipline regarding Indulgences, prepared by one of the Curial offices, the Tribunal of the Sacred Apostolic Penitentiary which customarily handled all matters relating to the granting of indulgences and had worked up a similar draft during the pre-conciliar stage that had never been used. In the mind of the canonists of the Apostolic Penitentiary, one of the conservative strongholds of the Curia, what was called for was not a thoroughgoing theological review of the whole question of indulgences but a limited overhauling of the existing practices that would leave theological presuppositions untouched. The plan was to issue their document eventually as a papal decree without any reference to the Council. However, when Pope Paul read the document and learned of their plan, it

---

con certezza fedelmente e senza errore la verità che Dio, causa della nostra salvezza, volle fosse consegnata.' A literal translation, but not in accordance with the mind of the Commission. Honni soyt qui mal y pense." From his Report on the work of the Theological Commission.

* There were many rumors about other subjects (mixed marriages, regulations for the Synod of Bishops, birth control, the diaconate, emigration, etc.) the pope was said to be considering laying before the bishops, but he was known to have submitted only these two.

was said, he insisted that the bishops be consulted. Whatever the facts, the meeting scheduled for November 11th was cancelled and the conference presidents were invited to deliver their reports in the council aula when the general congregations resumed on November 9th. The Apostolic Penitentiary tried to exercise some control over the scope of the "debate" by limiting copies of the schema at first to the conference heads, compelling the bishops to give their opinions on the basis of mere summaries. But this move too was ultimately defeated. Information soon spread about the true nature of their proposal.

Cardinal Cento, grand penitentiary, rose to deliver his formal *relatio* on the schema on Tuesday, November 9th. In a series of forthright statements alternating with others of a more timid nature on the following three days, the point was made that the present text was wholly inadequate and superficial and that if the question of reforming indulgences was raised at all it was necessary to go into the theological background thoroughly. Strong speeches in this sense were delivered by Cardinals Maximos IV, Alfrink, König and Döpfner. The latter suggested that since the present text had not been prepared largely by canonists, it was advisable to consult theologians also. A new document should be prepared taking into account recent theological thought and a series of papal directives issued to facilitate the transition from the old to the new discipline. Maximos IV let it be known that Archbishop Felici had asked him to suppress certain passages in his talk, which the patriarch immediately gave to the press. Also suppressed was any indication in the daily press bulletins of what the various speakers had said.

Two days after the Dutch Dominican theologian Father Schillebeeckx delivered a lecture on the encyclical *Mysterium fidei* at the Domus Mariae, a hotel for conventions on the Via Aurelia, as part of a series being sponsored by the Brazilian bishops, Archbishop Felici startled the Fathers by announcing that many requests had been received by the already overworked Secretary General's office whether these lectures were official or had been cleared with the Council authorities, to which he replied with a resounding "OMNINO NEGATIVE"—Absolutely not! The next day in the course of his announcements the archbishop remarked rather cryptically that his office was the object of considerable criticism; but since he was functioning under orders from higher authority, he preferred to remain silent about such calumny, observing piously, "In silence one remains close to God." The Council Fathers were all set for an apology for his attack on the Domus Mariae lectures. No such gesture was forthcoming. Instead the secretary general insisted that the reports on indulgences during the past week had come in for considerable criticism themselves. He reminded the Fathers that the Apostolic Penitentiary had deliberately approached the subject of indulgences from a canonical rather than a theological standpoint because it had been asked to do so by "higher authority." However some of the Fathers had disregarded this fact and raised theological issues anyway, "to which certain exceptions would have to be taken." Consequently there would be no more public reading of reports. The Fathers were invited to submit their comments to the Secretariat in writing.

A second Public Session was held on November 18th at which two more documents were voted and promulgated, the Constitution on Divine Revelation and the Decree on the Apostolate of the Laity. Approval of the latter had been voted

Texts promulgated	*Previous* Non Placet *votes*	*Final* Non Placet *votes*
Divine Revelation	27	6
Apostolate of the Laity	2	2

almost unanimously when the Council voted on the commission's handling of the *modi* on November 10th and there was curiously no change in the final balloting. However, the absence of any appreciable opposition was somewhat deceptive. While the document was intended to foster the apostolate of the laity and presumably represented the thinking of the Church on that subject, it had been compiled without much regard for the views of laymen themselves and remained until the end an essentially clerical text. Nevertheless, with this schema and the important Constitution on the Church, the groundwork had been laid for a more balanced statement in the future. The most important result of Apostolate of the Laity would be the Secretariat which the text called for, provided this were properly staffed and allowed to function in the intended way.

Pope Paul's speech on this occasion was notable not only for the number of his announcements, interesting in themselves, about his intention to facilitate the eventual canonization of his two predecessors, Popes Pius XII and John XXIII, to build a church in Rome in honor of Mary commemorating Vatican II, to proclaim a special jubilee for six months following the end of the Council, and to inaugurate the reform of the Curia by "publishing soon a new statute governing the Holy Office," but even more for the concern which he was beginning to express about the post-conciliar period, the way in which the Council would be received, the significance that would be attributed to the work of *aggiornamento* in the years to come. In a Hortatory Letter issued somewhat earlier (November 6th), he had urged the bishops to prepare for the close of the Council by ordering a triduum of prayers to mark the occasion and suggesting that they take advantage of the enthusiasm generated by the Council's activities, by capitalizing on the excellent press which had been accorded to church affairs during the past four years, to bring home to their faithful the essential message which the Council had been attempting to convey. Any delay in complying with the Council's directives could spell disaster, he maintained. Success was not to be expected from a multiplicity of laws but from a determination to make the Council's decisions effective. The faithful must be prepared to accept the new norms and those who refused to conform must be jolted in their complacency; "those who indulge in too many personal initiatives" must be restrained otherwise harm might come to "the healthy renewal already undertaken." The pope's words were the first indication in many months that he was giving serious attention to the possibility of real resistance to the work of the Council.

THE SCHEMA ON MISSIONARY ACTIVITY

On November 10th and 11th the Council voted on the commission's handling of the *modi* on Missionary Activity. Father Schütte explained the principal changes in his *relatio:* the theology of the missionary idea had been somewhat developed; the definition of "missionary area" had been expanded to include various parts of Latin America that were theoretically Christian, but actually *pays de mission* and therefore ought to be treated as such; the inhabitants of missionary areas were to be regarded henceforth not merely as "objects" but as "subjects" of missionary activity, capable of making a contribution on their own; the role of the laity was brought out more clearly; the problem of the relations between missionary and ecumenical activity was more thoroughly stressed; and the right of ordinaries to control all activities within their jurisdictions was made clear, while religious orders could still be exempt so far as internal matters affecting their institutes and orders were concerned. However, on the important matter of the reorganization of Propaganda Fide, the commission rejected the petition of the Indian bishops and stood by the revision that would have watered this down in the sense desired by Propaganda. It was explained that the suggestion for having the delegates elected by the various episcopal conferences could not be accepted, because this would make Propaganda too large and unwieldy. When the votes were counted, it was seen that all the other amendments proposed by the commission went through smoothly enough, but Chapter V, containing this provision about the reorganization of Propaganda Fide, failed to receive the required two-thirds majority (1,428 Placets, 9 Non placets, 712 Placet iuxta modums). The commission was therefore bound to revise it and would have to make some concessions to the minority.

Before the final vote on this schema on November 30th, Father Schütte again read a long *relatio* explaining what the commission had done about the *modi*. It developed that 461 Fathers had again requested a strengthening of that section of Chapter V dealing with the reorganization of Propaganda Fide along the lines suggested earlier by the Indian bishops: they now asked that the missionary delegates be given a "deliberative vote," that they be elected by the episcopal conferences, and for limited terms of office. The commission granted the first request, but in effect rejected the other two as limiting the "freedom of the pope" unduly. The delegates were to be chosen by the Holy See, "after hearing the episcopal conferences," a vague phrase that could mean anything; and the questions of when they were to meet and how long they should serve were reserved for the decision of the pope. 265 Fathers had requested that the text provide for a closer relationship between Propaganda Fide and those dioceses desiring this for missionary reasons. It was merely proposed that Propaganda would endeavor to work out suitable arrangements with the Roman Congregations in charge of such areas with a view to facilitating missionary work. 74 Fathers wanted all missionary work to depend directly on the new Synod of Bishops. The commission rejected this suggestion on the grounds that the relationship between the Synod and missionary work was already clearly enough brought out in the text. Approximately 100 Fathers demanded that the agreements between local ordinaries and missionary institutes should be expressly approved by the Holy See (Propaganda). The reply was that the Holy See would lay down norms and guidelines, but not require the submission of each agreement. This marked an important step in the direction of decentralization. 58 Fathers asked for the removal of the paragraph relating to ecumenical cooperation. This was rejected on the grounds that the Decree on Ecumenism was now binding on the Church. The final text was overwhelmingly approved in a series of 10 votes all taken the same day November 30th, only Article 29 dealing with the reorganization of Propaganda Fide registering as many as 54 Non placets.

THE FINAL REVISION OF SCHEMA 13

The Council had voted on November 15–17th to accept the Commission's revision of the text on the basis of the oral and written interventions, but a rather large number of *modi* were handed in on each chapter. (The figures of those voting Placet iuxta modum only indicate the persons who voted, not the number of *modi* actually submitted. Father Tromp*

* What follows is based on Father Tromp's official *Relatio* or Report of the Mixed Commission's proceedings from Sept. 14–Dec. 1965, dated Feb. 8, 1966,

pointed out, curiously, that on investigation it was found that not all those who had voted Iuxta modum actually submitted a *modus,* while some of those who had voted Placet handed in a *modus* anyway. The latter *modi* were of course ignored by the subcommissions. Nevertheless the number of *modi* which had to be considered was very high and the subcommissions were able to get through the mountain of work only by pushing themselves to the utmost.) *

The Mixed Commission began its review of the work of the subcommissions on November 22nd, Monday, and continued to meet throughout the week, mornings and evenings. In order to expedite matters, it was agreed on the 23rd that only those *modi* would be considered which the subcommission thought ought to be taken up. The subject of whether the title of Schema 13 should be changed was disposed of in the Commission's meeting on November 27th:

ARCHBISHOP GARRONE (*relator* for the Central Subcommission): "The voting in the aula has indicated that 541 Fathers desire a change, most of them preferring the terms 'Declaration' or 'Letter.' On the other hand it is clear that more than 1,500 do not want any change. The Central Subcommission proposes that a Note be inserted either at the beginning of the schema or the beginning of Part II, stating that Part I is doctrinal and that Part II is concerned with applications."

BISHOP QUADRI: "I see nothing objectionable in the use of the term 'Constitution.' However, the Note should say that Part II is *particularly* (*praesertim*) concerned with applications, because it also discusses principles."

ABBOT BUTLER: "Many want a new title in order to lessen the importance of the document."

ARCHBISHOP GARRONE: "This would certainly be the case if we were to add *praesertim* with reference to Part II."

FATHER ANASTASIUS OF THE HOLY ROSARY: "I suggest that the Note be placed at the beginning of the schema. This would make it clear at once what kind of document it is intended to be."

ARCHBISHOP WOJTYLA: "A Note is definitely necessary. The document is really a 'Constitution' but one that is 'pastoral.' This latter term should be carefully explained. It is much more concerned with life than with doctrine. Moreover, I think that Part I is also very pastoral in places, especially where it discusses the human person. Both parts must be seen in a pastoral light."

---

which will presumably form part of the Council's *Acta.* Father Tromp was Secretary of the Theological Commission. Similar reports were compiled for each of the Commissions.

* The final revision of Schema 13 is described in four sections: Generalities; Communism; Marriage; Nuclear Warfare.

BISHOP ARANGO HENAO: "I think that the question of what the title should be ought to be decided by the Fathers themselves in a special vote."

ABBOT BUTLER: "It is possible that many of the Fathers who did not vote were actually in sympathy with those who wanted a new title."

BISHOP MCGRATH: "I agree with the abbot, because it was not really a proper vote."

ARCHBISHOP GARRONE: "He who remains silent is assumed to agree."

BISHOP CHARUE: "I agree with Archbishop Wojtyla that the document is really a Constitution, but a pastoral one. The title should not be changed unless the matter is put to a special vote in the aula."

FATHER ANASTASIUS OF THE HOLY ROSARY: "I propose that the Fathers be asked to vote on the following proposition: 'Is the handling of the *modi* with regard to the title pleasing?' "

BISHOP POMA: "I think there should be an explanation in the aula of the title and why we are retaining it."

The upshot was that the Commission decided to accept the proposal of the Central Subcommission. Consideration of Chapter V was begun the same day and concluded on Monday, November 29th. Bishop Schröffer, president of the Subcommission, and Father Dubarle as *relator,* led off with some preliminary remarks.

BISHOP SCHRÖFFER: "The revision of the *modi* of this chapter had to be done with particular care because one of the Fathers (Cardinal Heenan) said in the aula that the chapter 'was teeming with errors.' The *modi* were concerned with four points primarily: 1) non-violence; 2) conscientious objection; 3) total warfare; 4) balance of terror. I think the members will agree that the revised text is more nuanced than the original (*minus apodictice sonari*)."

There was a long discussion about the *modi* relating to conscientious objection, lasting a full hour (paragraph 79, formerly 83). The Subcommission produced a new text containing the clauses "frequently led by religious motives" (*frequenter religiosis motivis ducti*) and "led by patriotism" (*amore patriae ducti*). Among the speakers were Canon Moeller, Archbishop Fernandes, Abbot Butler, Cardinal Ottaviani, Father Fernandez O.P., Bishop Charue, Bishop Heuschen, Cardinal Browne, Cardinal Cento and Bishop Henriquez Jimenez. Abbot Butler and Bishop Fernandez-Conde kept making the point that a distinction

---

Text as finally approved by the Council:

Insuper aequum videtur ut leges humaniter provideant pro casu illorum qui ex motivo conscientiae arma adhibere recusant, dum tamen aliam formam communitati hominum serviendi acceptant.

Moreover, it seems right that laws make humane provisions for the case of those who for reasons of conscience refuse to bear arms, provided however, that they agree to serve the human community in some other way.

---

must be made between "right conscience" and a "false conscience." The use of the word *frequenter* was displeasing to many. Bishop Charue suggested *forsan,* Bishop Heuschen *etiam,* and Cardinal Browne *interdum.*

CANON MOELLER: "The phrase *amore patriae ducti* does not seem suitable, because there may be other motives for conscientious objection."

ARCHBISHOP DEARDEN: "I suggest that the matter be put hypothetically: *qui vero amore patriae ducti.*"

CARDINAL BROWNE: "The new text of the subcommission seems to be an improvement, but I question whether this is what we ought to say at this particular point."

A vote was then taken and it was decided by a two-thirds majority not to accept the new text.

BISHOPS GONZALEZ MORALEJO AND HENRIQUEZ JIMENEZ: "I propose that we now amend the old text."

BISHOP CHARUE: "The new text was rejected too hastily, because we now have to deal with the old text which many of those who voted against the new text will find even more displeasing, because harsher."

ABBOT BUTLER: "Nevertheless we are bound by the rules. Perhaps some of those to whom the idea of conscientious objection is objectionable voted for the new text because it seemed to be the less undesirable."

Votes were then taken. Whether the old text should stand? Placet. Whether it should remain where it was? On the second ballot, Placet. Whether it should be modified by the clause "laws should *humanely* provide" (*leges humaniter provident*), as suggested by Bishop Doumith? Placet.

The Mixed Commission concluded its revision of the *modi* on Monday, November 29th, at about 11:15 A.M. The grave doubts whether it would be able to complete its work on time were then dispelled. The text went to the printers and was distributed to the Fathers in two brochures on December 2nd and 3rd, for the final voting on December 4th and 6th.

THE ATTEMPTS TO CONDEMN COMMUNISM

The final three weeks were as filled with maneuvering and surprises as any period in the Council's six years. Except for the voting on texts on days when general congregations were held, the main activity took place in commissions which worked feverishly revising documents so that they would be ready in time for promulgation at the closing Public Session set for December 7th.

Meanwhile, the opposition armed itself for a final skirmish. The attack came on four vital points. The *Coetus Internationalis Patrum,* under the leadership of Bishop Carli (Segni), kept up an incessant campaign throughout the Fourth Session in favor of an outright condemnation of communism, thus showing their contempt for the injunction of Pope John that the Council was not to engage in sterile condemnations. Pope Paul VI also had on numerous occasions made it abundantly clear that he was opposed to this fierce desire for vindictive name-calling. Leaders of the Christian Democratic Party in Italy, on the other hand, pointed out that the absence of such a condemnation would play into the hands of the Italian communists who could claim that, as the Council had not condemned communism explicitly, Italians could continue to vote for the PCI with good conscience. At one point, toward the end, the *Carlifato* managed to enlist the sympathy of a number of Eastern-rite bishops, particularly Ukrainians living outside Iron Curtain countries. When one of the latter circulated a letter appealing for a strong condemnation of communism (characteristically *not* signed by Cardinal Slipyi), he was personally rebuked by the Secretariat of State and told that the Church behind the Iron Curtain was being endangered by such action.

Both the subcommission and the Mixed Commission were required to display a certain amount of skill in dealing with Carli's various moves and petitions. When the revised text of Schema 13 was distributed on November 13th (which the Council was to vote on November 15–17th), it became obvious that the subcommission had not been swayed by Carli's last-minute *modi* submitted on October 9th, or by his petition signed by 450 bishops (out of some 800 circulated) of October 19th, all designed to produce a stronger text on communism, in the sense desired by Carli and his supporters. The most that the subcommission was prepared to concede to their point of view was a footnote in the section on atheism referring to the papal encyclicals that condemned totalitarianism of all types. Although Bishop Carli claimed that some two hundred *modi* had been submitted by him on October 9th, only two were acknowledged and dealt with by the subcommission in its report. The indignation of the Carli group can easily be imagined! It seems that Monsignor Glorieux, secretary of the subcommission, receiving from Archbishop Felici the Carli *modi* submitted at the last minute, hurriedly glanced over them, found that they were all identical and related to a point already disposed of by the subcommission, and therefore failed to submit them for the subcommission's consideration as he undoubtedly should have. The Fathers were again circularized with a new *modus* from Bishop Carli on November 15th, prior to the crucial vote that day on the revised text of Chapter I. The voting on this occasion produced 453 Non placets for Chapter I as a whole, approximately half of which were thought to be inspired by Carli. At the same time the bishop wrote an indignant letter to Cardinal Tisserant (and possibly also to the secretary general) complaining about the subcommission's neglect of his petition of 450 names and the way in which Monsignor Glorieux had cavalierly dismissed his earlier *modi*.

While engaged in the work of revising Schema 13 in the light of the November 15–17th voting, the Mixed Commission, on November 27th, received a letter from Cardinal Tisserant forwarding the complaint of Bishop Carli that the subcommission had not paid any attention to "the *modus* submitted by about 340 Fathers who had asked for the condemnation of communism." The subcommission's reply, according to Father Tromp, was that "this particular request had already been dealt with in the reply to a similar *modus* submitted by 220 Fathers. However, in the printed text of the handling of the *modi* a note would be inserted to the effect that the *modus* of the 340 Fathers had been overlooked through error, although the matter had been sufficiently dealt with elsewhere." The Commission's reply to Tisserant was read by Archbishop Garrone in its meeting on November 29th. Although the responsible officials admitted that the subcommission had technically been at fault in not acknowledging Carli's original *modi*, Father Ralph Wiltgen, director of the Divine Word Press Service, which had been used to air the whole matter of the mix-up, would not be appeased and declared so flatly before the American Bishops' Press Panel on November 23rd.

THE PAPAL MODI ON MARRIAGE

While difficulties were also being encountered by the commissions revising the documents on Missions and Priestly Life, the main attack seemed to be centered on the Declaration on Religious Liberty where a final attempt was made to strip it of its full significance. Despite the addition earlier of a sentence affirming that the Catholic Church was the one true Church which all were obliged to seek and embrace (a truth constantly taught by the Catholic Church), the revised text repudiated the thesis that error had no rights, insisted on human dignity as the basis for men's liberty in accordance with Pope John's formula, and said explicitly that the Catholic Church must assist society in vindicating a man's right to freedom even when he was wrong in his beliefs and assertions. These three truths were anathema to the conservatives and they did their best by way of final *modi* to eviscerate them; to no avail.

Their efforts here, however, proved to be a mere distraction. On Wednesday afternoon, November 24th, a mortar shell was catapulted into the Mixed Commission revising Schema 13. Cardinal Ottaviani was in the chair. The meeting was convened at 4:30 P.M. Before finishing the discussion of the amendments to Part I and going on to the crucial Chapter I of Part II (dealing with marriage and family life), the cardinal reminded the prelates and periti of their oath of secrecy and then asked the secretary, Father Tromp, to read two communications. The first was a message from Archbishop Felici stating that the *expensio modorum* had to be ready for the printers by November 29th. The second was a letter from the Secretary of State requesting the Commission, in the name of 'higher authority,' to make explicit mention in the chapter on marriage of Pius XI's *Casti connubii* and Pius XII's Allocution to Italian Midwives. Attached to the letter were four *modi* which, the secretary observed, "seem to have to be included in the text." The words 'higher authority' of course could only mean the pope.* When the *modi* were read, to the consternation of the subcommission members, there was a look of triumph on the faces of the American Jesuit Father John Ford and the Franciscan Father Ermenegildo Lio, advocates of an intransigent position on the subject of birth control, while Cardinal Browne was alleged to have said, *"Christus ipse locutus est*—Christ Himself has spoken.

The move had been perfectly timed and planned. The four *modi* were to be inserted in the text at specific crucial points with a view to exploding the idea that conjugal love enjoyed equal status with procreation as one of the ends of marriage and reasserting Pius XI's doctrine of *Casti connubii* banning all and every type of artificial contraception unequivocally. At one fell swoop not only would the work of the Council so far be compromised, but the Special Papal Commission entrusted with the whole matter of demographic study and family planning by the pope himself would have been rendered useless. The stunned Mixed Commission would hardly have time to work out a compromise. Consideration of the *modi* was reserved for the following day.

It was quickly surmised that Father Lio himself and the Dominican canonist Father R. Gagnebet were the probable authors of the papal *modi*. The previous spring Lio had been expressly excluded from the Subcommission on Family Life headed by Archbishop Dearden, much to the annoyance of Cardinal Ottaviani; but he had now been brought in as that cardinal's personal theologian along with the clerical members of the Special Papal Commission on birth control. The presence of the American Father Ford at the Mixed Commission meetings was a considerable surprise. As a matter of fact, his activities proved harmful to the

---

* The question of the submission of the *modi* seems to have been decided upon, or at least discussed, at a meeting of the pope, Bishop Colombo, and Father De Riedmatten, secretary of the Special Papal Commission on birth control, earlier the same day, November 24th, according to *Il Messaggero*, Nov. 27, 1965. The object of this meeting according to the paper was "to harmonize, if possible, the doctrine of the conciliar text with the results of the Special Commission's labors."

intransigent cause when it became apparent how obstructionist his views really were. Several of the periti suspected that he had been summoned to Rome at the suggestion of the apostolic delegate to the United States, Archbishop Vagnozzi, who brought him to the Secretariat of State in the hopes that he would be able to convince both the Council and the pope that the Church simply had to re-affirm its old position on marriage and birth control or the integrity of its moral theologians would be called in question. Seemingly the rights and perplexities of millions of wives and husbands faced with an intolerable burden had nothing to do with the matter. While it was perfectly proper to hold them to impossible moral obligations, it was outrageously wrong to ask moral theologians to reconsider their teaching in the light of new facts.*

However, when the Mixed Commission reconvened Thursday morning, it was evident that the attack would be met head-on. After disposing of some preliminary matters relating to Part I, the Commission got down to the business of the *modi* on marriage at 10:05 A.M. The chairman of the subcommission that had drafted the text, Archbishop Dearden, was the first to speak. He was followed by Canon Heylen and Father De Riedmatten as *relatores*. The archbishop began by questioning the authenticity of the papal *modi*. In the ensuing discussion he was backed up to a man by the members of his own subcommission and even by some of the Commission bishops who were critical of the revised text but resented the way in which their body was being "bulldozed" into acceptance of the papal *modi*. As Chapter I had received an absolute majority in the previous voting on November 16th, its text could not be substantially changed according to the Council rules. But the insertion of the papal *modi* would involve such substantial changes. Canon Heylen observed that since the matter of birth control had been withdrawn from discussion in the Council, it would perhaps be a good idea to stress the point by adding a sentence at the end of the introductory paragraph, stating "The Holy Synod leaves other matters . . . to the Special Papal Commission." It was decided to take up this matter after all the *modi* had been considered.

When Canon Heylen raised the question of what to do about the first papal *modus* at 10:45, the Commission immediately became bogged down in a heated, prolonged discussion about the meaning of terms (*artes anticonceptionales, abusus conceptionales*) and the importance to be attached to the papal *modi* as well as the method of dealing with them. The secretary was again obliged to read Cicognani's letter. Bishop Henriquez Jimenez felt that it was perfectly proper for the Mixed

---

* Canon Heylen was reported to have said of Father Ford and other conservative theologians: "They obey the pope when the pope obeys them." Cf. Lois Chevalier, *Ladies Home Journal*, March 1966, p. 89.

Commission to consider the *modi*. Bishop Charue, on the other hand, thought there was some doubt about the jurisdiction of the Mixed Commission because it was a matter that had not been discussed in the Council and was up in the air, so to speak, until the Special Papal Commission had given its reply. The Mixed Commission should be able to discuss the matter freely, without any strings, if it took up the question at all. Father Tromp said that according to Cicognani's letter it was "the wish of the Pope that the Commission should follow the doctrine of the Encyclical *Casti connubii* and the Allocution of Pius XII to Midwives, and therefore there could be no question of freedom with regard to doctrine, but only with regard to formulation."

At this point, Cardinal Léger read a strong statement. He deplored the tenor of the proposed amendments and maintained that, if adopted as they stood, the prestige and reputation of the Holy See might be irreparably damaged. Father Anastasius of the Holy Rosary asked that the text of Cicognani's letter and the accompanying *modi* be distributed to the Commission *periti*. Bishop Colombo and Cardinal Browne thought that it was a matter that concerned only the prelate members. At this point it was said that something like pandemonium broke out and the meeting was adjourned for a coffee-break. Cardinal Léger left at 11:37, apparently to go and see the pope. The Commission's afternoon session was devoted to the subcommission's handling of the *modi* on Chapter I and the first paragraphs of Chapter II on Culture.

Despite Cardinal Ottaviani's reminder about the oath of secrecy binding the Commission members and *periti,* news of the morning's proceedings spread like wildfire throughout Rome and the substance of the story was leaked to the press. The next morning *L'Avvenire d'Italia* ran an account of what had taken place.

Bishop Colombo, the pope's personal theologian, also hurried to the pope's apartments after the morning's meeting on Thursday, to explain the situation to him. Representations were also made to the pontiff by the lay auditors. Both sides were girding for a showdown struggle when Cardinal Ottaviani reconvened the Commission on Friday morning, November 26th.

He began with a rather severe statement deploring the fact that information about the four *modi* had become public knowledge, then declared that the pope had decided that the *periti* were not to be excluded from discussion of the *modi*. However, there could be no question of discussing doctrine, it was merely allowed to discuss the way in which they were to be formulated. The secretary, Father Tromp, then read a second letter from the Secretary of State which specified that 1) the pope considered the *modi* to be of great importance; 2) the method of formulation was not obligatory; 3) certain things could be added, provided the sense was retained; 4) the pope himself would later decide whether the Commission's decisions were acceptable. After the reading of the pope's letter, Cardinal Léger was seen to fold a paper he had in his hand and slump back in his chair. He had made an agreement with the subcommission to speak only if necessary. While some of the Mixed Commission members felt that the second papal letter was even stronger than the first in tying their hands, the majority seized upon point 3 and set to work to deal with the papal *modi—secundum spiritum,* according to their obvious meaning and the rules of the Council.

MODUS I.—The first papal *modus* called for mention of the phrase "contraceptive practices" (*artes anticonceptionales*) in Paragraph 47 (formerly 51) after the words "so-called free love" and an explicit reference to Pius XI's encyclical *Casti connubii* condemning artificial contraception in a footnote. Canon Heylen was the first speaker.

Text as proposed by Commission:

47 (51). (Marriage and the Family Today) . . . Yet the excellence of this institution is not everywhere reflected with equal brilliance, since polygamy, the plague of divorce, so-called free love and other disfigurements have an obscuring effect. In addition, married love is too often profaned by an excessive self-love and worship of pleasure.

Text as finally amended and approved:

47. (Marriage and the Family Today) . . . Yet the excellence of this institution is not everywhere reflected with equal brilliance, since polygamy, the plague of divorce, so-called free love and other disfigurements have an obscuring effect. In addition, married love is too often profaned by excessive self-love, the worship of pleasure, *and illicit practices against human generation* (*illicitis usibus contra generationem*).

CANON HEYLEN: "I wish to make three points: 1) The term 'practices' (*artes*) is not good. I propose instead that we say 'abuses' (*abusus*). 2) The term 'anticonceptional' is not good either. An abortion is not contraceptive, although it is an evil; on the other hand, periodic continence may be called contraceptive, although it is not an evil, as Father De Riedmatten has stated. 3) It would perhaps be better to place the *modus* a little later, after mention of 'self-love and worship of pleasure,' and phrase it as follows: 'and by the perversion of love and the sources of life' (*et perversione amoris fontiumque vitae*)."

In the general discussion that followed, Archbishop Castellano, Cardinal Browne and Father Anastasius of the Holy Rosary agreed with Heylen that the *modus* should be placed later. Cardinal Browne thought that it would be better to say "uses" rather than "abuses." Father

Anastasius suggested the phrase "illicit uses against generation." Bishop Poma preferred "illicit means for preventing conception." Bishop Colombo: "illicit uses against conception." Bishop Doumith observed that a single expression would not do, the word "illicit practices" itself needed explanation.

Cardinal Ottaviani proposed that the question first be settled where the *modus* was to go and it was decided to insert it after the words "worship of pleasure."

CANON HEYLEN: "If we wish to avoid the use of the words 'abuses' and 'anti-conceptional,' practically speaking the choice will have to be between the two phrases 'illicit practices preventing generation' and 'perversion of love and the sources of life.' The subcommission recommends that the Commission adopt the second phrase."

Bishop Charue also thought that these words were better because more in harmony with what was said before. When Canon Heylen and Archbishop Dearden noted that this phrasing was better because "more general," Bishop Colombo remarked: "And therefore weaker." Father Anastasius thought that it was illogical to say that love was profaned by the perversion of love. Bishop McGrath agreed with Bishop Doumith that the Commission must not be too vague and misleading.

When Bishop Henriquez Jimenez proposed: "Let the pope himself decide which wording he prefers," many of the members shouted, "only after we have voted!" Whereupon Cardinal Ottaviani put the matter to a vote and it was decided to adopt the first formula suggested by Canon Heylen, by a vote of 22 to 13, with 2 blank ballots.

ABBOT BUTLER: "We must now decide where the reference to *Casti connubii* is to go in the footnotes. It seems to me that it would be better to place it in the text of Paragraph 47 (51) itself, because that would make it clearer that it had not been added as a result of discussion in the aula (by the extraordinary magisterium) but at the specific request of the pope (by the ordinary magisterium)."

BISHOP FRANIC: "I do not agree at all. There has often been discussion of *Casti connubii* in the Council."

BISHOP COLOMBO: "Nor do I, because the pope makes a text conciliar by his approval and corrections. It is up to the Mixed Commission to decide where it thinks the reference should go. The pope himself will decide whether the Council has acted wisely or not."

CARDINAL BROWNE: "There is no reason why the encyclical should not be cited since it has already been mentioned elsewhere."

CARDINAL OTTAVIANI: "The pope has already decided that the encyclical should be cited. There can be no discussion of this."

BISHOP POMA: "It seems to me that we are confronted by two difficulties here: 1) Paragraph 47 (51) is largely descriptive in nature, whereas the encyclical should be cited at a place where the discussion is more doctrinal; 2) the reference to *Casti connubii* is to a specific point, whereas the language of Paragraph 47 (51) is much more general in nature."

ARCHBISHOP GARRONE: "I suggest that we add, to the two references called for in the papal *modus,* a reference to Pope Paul's Allocution to the Cardinals, of June 1964, in which he said that the doctrine of *Casti connubii* is binding as of now (*fin'ora*)."

The pertinent passage of the pope's allocution was accordingly read.

BISHOP CHARUE: "The pope clearly says that the matter is an object of study and that is why it has not been discussed by the Fathers in the Council."

CARDINAL OTTAVIANI: "The pope also says that it is an object of study for the ordinary magisterium (pope)."

BISHOP CHARUE: "Of course, it is *now.*"

ARCHBISHOP DEARDEN: "I do not see any reason why there cannot be a reference to the Pope's Special Commission in a footnote, but I do not think this would be proper in the text."

The upshot was that the majority of Commission members agreed that *Casti connubii* should be cited at some other point in the schema. There was no consensus as yet about citing Paul's Allocution to the Cardinals.

MODUS II.—The second papal *modus* required the omission of the word *"etiam"* and the introduction of the sentence "Children are the supreme gift of marriage and contribute very substantially to the welfare of their parents" (*Filii sunt praestantissimum matrimonii donum et ad ipsorum parentum bonum maxime conferunt*) in Paragraph 50 (54), which would have had the effect of reasserting procreation as the primary end of marriage.

Text as proposed by Commission:

50 (54). (The Fecundity of Marriage). Marriage and conjugal love are by their nature ordained toward the begetting and educating of children. The God himself who said, "it is not good for man to be alone" and "who made man from the beginning male and female," wishing to share with man a certain special participation in his own creative work, blessed male and female, saying "Increase and multiply." Hence, the true practice of conjugal love and the whole meaning of family life which results from it, also (*etiam*) have this aim: that the couple be ready with stout hearts to cooperate with the love of the Creator and the Savior, who through them will enlarge and enrich his own family day by day.

Text as amended an'l approved by the Council:

50. (The Fecundity of Marriage). Marriage and conjugal love are by their nature ordained toward the begetting and educating of children. *Children are*

really the supreme gift of marriage and contribute very substantially to the welfare of their parents. The God himself who said ". . . and multiply." Hence, *while not making the other purposes of matrimony of less account,* the true practice of conjugal love and the whole meaning of the family life which results from it, have this aim: that the couple . . . day by day.

CANON HEYLEN: "The use of the word *etiam* was not meant to imply that procreation was of a secondary nature compared to conjugal love, but was intended to express the doctrine that procreation was not the only end of marriage. I propose that the word *etiam* be deleted and that the sentence *Filii . . . ad ipsorum parentum bonum maxime conferunt* be placed at the beginning of the paragraph, omitting the first sentence now there "Marriage and conjugal love . . . educating of children."

When Father Anastasius of the Holy Rosary objected to the proposed omission, Canon Heylen and Archbishop Dearden pointed out that a similar phrase occurred earlier in Paragraph 48 (52). Archbishop Castellano also felt that such an omission would not be permissible. Accordingly Canon Heylen suggested that the sentence *Filii . . . ad ipsorum parentum maxime conferunt* be inserted immediately after the first sentence and the particle *vero* used to connect the two [changed to *sane* in the final draft]. The insertion of the clause "while not making the other purposes of matrimony of less account" not only robbed the papal *modus* of its last sting, but made the text much clearer than it was before on this matter of the ends of marriage.

MODUS IV.*—At 11:55 it was decided to omit consideration of Modus III for the time being, and go on to the fourth Modus which called for insertion of the words "but if spouses are to overcome their difficulties, it is altogether necessary for them to practice the virtue of conjugal chastity sincerely" (*sed ad difficultates superandas omnino requiri ut conjuges castitatem coniugalem sincero animo colant*) at the end of the sentence which says that there cannot be a contradiction between the divine laws pertaining to the transmission of life and those pertaining to authentic conjugal love, in Paragraph 51 (55).

CANON HEYLEN: "It seems that the best place for a reference to conjugal chastity would be at the end of Paragraph 49 (53). A second alternative would be to combine Modus III with Modus IV and make the end of the third sub-paragraph of Paragraph 51 (55) read as follows: 'Relying on these principles, sons of the Church, *who must sincerely cultivate the virtue of conjugal chastity,* may not undertake methods of birth control which have been or shall be found blameworthy by the magisterium.' " Archbishop Castellano objected that this reading did not

---

* This was the order in which they were discussed by the Commission.

do justice to the implication in the pope's words, *"ad difficultates superandas."* Bishop Colombo agreed and suggested the wording, "Such a goal cannot be achieved unless the virtue of conjugal chastity is sincerely practiced."

After various alternate proposals had been considered, Archbishop Dearden and Canon Heylen rallied to Colombo's suggestion and this was carried by an almost unanimous vote.

MODUS III.—The third papal *modus* had specified that, in Paragraph 51 (55), at the end of the third sub-paragraph, the words "Relying on these principles, sons of the Church may not undertake methods of birth control which have been or may be found blameworthy by the magisterium" (*improbatae sunt vel improbentur*) were to be inserted, and there should be a reference in a footnote to the two important papal documents on the subject, Pius XI's *Casti connubii* and Pius XII's Allocution to Italian Midwives. The text proposed by the Commission spoke of "methods of birth control considered blameworthy" (*improbandas*) but there were no references to the papal documents.

CANON HEYLEN: "The words are clear enough with regard to the past, but can we bind consciences in the future?"

BISHOP DOUMITH: "The Church must always have the same teaching whether as regards the past, present or future."

BISHOP HENGSBACH: "The words *filiis Ecclesiae* mean that the phrase is intended to have reference only to the faithful."

Bishop Colombo proposed that the present tense *"improbantur"* be substituted for the past and apparent future tenses of the *modus,* and suggested that the words be explained in a footnote with reference to the papal documents. This was agreed.

The secretary, Father Tromp, noted that the form *improbentur* seemed to be a grammatical error for the future *improbabuntur,* required by the context.

A proposal of Bishop Gonzalez Moralejo to insert the words "interpreted with the help of the magisterium" (*ope magisterii explicanda*) after "divine law" was rejected by Archbishop Garrone as implying that the magisterium was confined to interpreting the divine law.

Archbishop Dearden moved that mention be made in the footnote of Paul VI's Allocution to the Cardinals, of June 1964, and this was agreed. He also moved that the note should state that while the Special Papal Commission was at work, the Council did not wish to propose any final solutions. This motion was seconded by Bishops Colombo and Ancel, the latter declaring that the facts required such a statement.

Once again, using an opening, the subcommission had strengthened the schema in an open-door sense.

Text as amended and approved by Council (additions in italics):

51. (Conjugal Love). . . . Hence when there is question of harmonizing conjugal love with the responsible transmission of life, the moral aspect of any procedure does not depend solely on sincere intentions or on an evaluation of motives, but must be determined by objective standards. These, based on the nature of the human person and his acts, preserve the full sense of mutual self-giving and human procreation in the context of true love. *Such a goal cannot be achieved unless the virtue of conjugal love is sincerely practiced. Relying on these principles, sons of the Church may not undertake methods of birth control which are* found blameworthy by the teaching authority of the Church in its unfolding of the divine law.

Footnote 14 appended to this last sentence reads: Cf. Pius XI, encyclical letter Casti Connubii: AAS 22 (1930); Denz-Schoen. 3716–3718; Pius XII, Allocutio Conventui Unionis Italicae inter Obstetrices, October 29, 1951: AAS 43 (1951), pp. 835–854; Paul VI, address to a group of cardinals, June 23, 1964: AAS 56 (1964), pp. 581–589. Certain questions which need further and more careful investigation have been handed over, at the command of the supreme pontiff, to a commission for the study of population, family, and births, in order that, after it fulfills its function, the supreme pontiff may pass judgment. With the doctrine of the magisterium in this state, this holy synod does not intend to propose immediately concrete solutions.

The work of revising the text was completed over the weekend and shown to the pope who gave his approval to the Commission's new version.

It appears that one reason for the ease with which the subcommission finally won its points was the fact that it had suddenly occurred to Bishop Colombo that while he was a theologian, his field was doctrinal and not moral theology and he might be swimming in water over his head. He seems to have conveyed this feeling to the pope, for when Father Ford on Monday morning presented the pope with the arguments of the intransigents, the pope was said to have replied: "You, as a moral theologian, tell me there is only one way to look at this matter. On the other hand, Bishop Reuss is also a moral theologian and he tells me just the opposite. Go to him and argue the matter out. When you two moralists reach an agreement, come back to me with an answer."*

The pope's acceptance of the wording of the commission seemed to indicate that the twice-promised papal statement on birth control was still far from being settled in his mind, and was probably not to be expected in

* Lois R. Chevalier has Cardinal Ottaviani writing to the pope at this point and saying, "I did all possible to have the commission accept the modifications of Your Holiness, but I was always in the minority . . ." *Ladies Home Journal,* March 1966, p. 173.

the near future. Actually, the Special Papal Commission on birth control was scheduled to hold an early spring meeting. It was most unlikely that Pope Paul would jump the gun on so delicate an issue. The judgment as to the means for family limitation, at least in principle, according to the new Pastoral Constitution, was left up to the conscience of a married couple, although for the time being they were to follow the norms laid down by Pius XII in 1958. These were strict directives ruling out artificial means, but the open end achieved in the conciliar document left a final decision as to the licitness of various means up to the study of theologians and scientists, and more pertinently, to the couple concerned.

That crisis had hardly passed when new threats momentarily endangered Chapter III on economic and social life and Chapter IV on political life. Throwing caution to the winds, the *Coetus* sent out copies of *modi* demanding a strictly Non placet vote on the fourth chapter, alleging as reasons that it was shot through with modernism, relativism, evolutionism, and could only lead to abandonment of the doctrine that the Catholic Church was the one true Church. However, little attention was paid to their assertions, for the majority of bishops had by now grown tired of their tirades. About the same time, while the Mixed Commission was rushing to complete work on Chapter V on November 29th, it received a communication from the Franco Government of Spain, forwarded by Archbishop Dell'Acqua of the Secretariat of State, requesting certain changes in Chapters III and IV. The archbishop had not even bothered to translate the communication into Latin. The first *modus* asked that the fundamental right to form labor unions be modified by the clause "according to forms recognized by law"; the second asked that mention of "political parties" be qualified by "where they are lawful." Most of the members were indignant at this last-minute attempt to influence the course of events and rejected the suggestions out of hand. Bishop Gonzalez Moralejo was particularly outraged, claiming that the proposed modifications were injurious to Spain and an insult to the Spanish bishops who had already approved the text.

NUCLEAR WARFARE

Meanwhile, the newly appointed archbishop of New Orleans, Philip Hannan, a former paratroop chaplain, had taken a dim view of Chapter V (on peace and the elimination of war). He thought the statement referring to the have- and have-not nations and particularly the condemnation of the use of nuclear arms was palpably disparaging to the United States. He had said this in a speech on the council floor, toward the close of the Third Session. However his contention had been rejected by the American *periti* and most bishops on the grounds that his point of view would give a handle to communist charges that the U.S., and now the Council, was guilty of war-mongering. Despite these remonstrances, however, Hannan began to agitate for his point toward the close of the final session, even though the subcommission in question had all but eviscerated the text of Schema 13 in an attempt to meet this objection.

The amended text insisted that under modern conditions war was all but unthinkable. Actually it was merely reflecting the minds of Pius XII, John XXIII, and most particularly Pope Paul himself in his address before the UN assembly. The document likewise stated that the possession of nuclear arms could give rise to war. Finally, great care was taken not to give the impression that limited defensive warfare was unlawful. Despite these precautions, the archbishop was seen in earnest conversation with Cardinal Spellman and Archbishop Vagnozzi after the meeting of the Council on Thursday, December 2nd, and was overheard talking about the matter with greater agitation each time. Several friends and acquaintances among the bishops and *periti* tried to assure him that his criticism of the document was unjustified. Brushing their arguments aside, he went ahead with his plans, prepared three *modi,* and had them translated into 6 languages to be distributed to the Council Fathers. To compound the mischief, he persuaded 10 bishops to sign his petition, including Cardinals Spellman and Shehan, Archbishops O'Boyle of Washington and Hurley of Durban, South Africa.

The U.S. *periti* were particularly upset as copies of this letter made the rounds. All during the final session their bishops had been severely criticized by the press and most of the European bishops and theologians for their complete lack of interest in the most important conciliar document—Schema 13—dealing with practical problems; this despite the fact that they had always prided themselves on being such eminently practical churchmen. Only a handful of Americans had raised their voices during the final weeks of debate; and the only American bishops who showed any real interest in what was going on were those on commissions and subcommissions who gave a good accounting of themselves.

When approached about his signature on Hannan's letter, Cardinal Shehan authorized Father McCool to declare before the Bishops' Press Panel (December 4th) that he had withdrawn his name from the letter after reflecting on the matter. Archbishop O'Boyle claimed that he had signed because he felt that he should, out of loyalty to his former auxiliary bishop. Just why Cardinal Spellman allowed his name to be used was not clear. In any case, the move served to confuse a large number of non-American bishops. Hannan's *modi* in themselves were obviously erroneous. Where the document stated that the indiscriminate use of atomic warfare could easily "go beyond the norms of legitimate defense," the *modus* said that the document outlawed defense. Where the text claimed that the possession of nuclear weapons could easily be a quasi-occasion for the outbreak of war, Hannan read it to mean a cause of war, and launched into a tirade about hunger and injustice being the true causes of war, as the document itself declared very clearly. Finally, Hannan urged that if there were insufficient votes against Chapter V to kill it or bring about its revision, all the bishops should vote Non placet on the schema as a whole and thus force Pope Paul to withdraw it entirely. Before the crucial voting on Saturday morning, December 4th, Hannan was seen approaching Archbishop Felici in the company of Vagnozzi, apparently in order to persuade the secretary general to make some announcement about their move; but all that he got from Felici was a waving of his two arms in a gesture that said, "Impossible, absurd!"

At the press panel that afternoon Father McCool rose to answer the first question and stated, as we have said, that Cardinal Shehan had withdrawn his signature from Archbishop Hannan's letter. Unfortunately Chapter V had been voted that morning, although the results were not announced until Monday. The auxiliary bishop of Philadelphia, Gerald McDevitt, then assured the reporters that the majority of American bishops did not agree with Archbishop Hannan's position and his statement was concurred in by the other bishops present as well as the *periti*. Monsignor Higgins, in particular, pointed out the absurdity of the *modi* when compared with what the text actually said.

Over the weekend Bishop Schröffer, the subcommission chairman, and Archbishop Garrone, prepared a point-by-point rebuttal of the Hannan thesis, which was accepted by Cardinal Spellman, who suddenly realized that he had been unfairly used in the matter (the cardinal had been suffering from a cold and the inclemency of the Roman weather and on at least two occasions had been seen to leave the Council hall early, giving rise to false rumors that he had gone to see the pope). The Schröffer rebuttal was gladly endorsed by the bulk of the American bishops, and it was even suggested that mention of it should be made in an announcement before the final vote on Schema 13 as a whole, on Monday morning. After a hurried conference, Cardinal Tisserant telephoned the pope to ask whether the vote should be postponed because of the large vote (483) against Chapter V on Saturday, and received the reply that the voting was to proceed according to the rules.

That morning (Monday) when the papal document proclaiming a special jubilee from January 6th to June 29th, 1966 was read in the aula, reporters pounced on its ridiculously outmoded formulas granting confessors powers to absolve penitents from censures incurred for reading forbidden books, or belonging to the Masonic Order or secret or forbidden societies. The panel canonist Father McManus walked a tightrope trying to explain why such a worthy exhortation asking bishops and faithful to meditate on the implementation of the Council should be larded with medieval formulas.

While the Hannan *modi* helped swell the Non placets on Chapter V to 483 on Saturday, the opposition shrank to 251 votes on Monday when Schema 13 was approved as a whole. It is uncertain just what part the apostolic delegate Archbishop Vagnozzi played in all this, but his actions revived murmuring among the American bishops about meddling in U.S. diocesan affairs.

REFORM OF THE HOLY OFFICE

On Monday, before the voting began, Pope Paul's long-awaited Motu Proprio inaugurating the reform of the Curia was read by Archbishop Felici. As announced earlier by the pope himself, the Supreme Congregation of the Holy Office was given a new designation and statute. The former name, recalling unpleasant memories of the "Holy Inquisition" which it had once been called, was now dropped in favor of the less alarming "Congregation for the Doctrine of the Faith." More important, if it could be made to stick, was the stipulation that the new office was to be more concerned with promoting theological investigation than with heresy hunting. Like the old organization, the new would have the pope as its head and a cardinal as secretary,* and its functions would continue to be both administrative and judicial. The Index of Prohibited Books would remain under its jurisdiction. However, there was an important change both with respect to authors and persons who might be denounced for heterodoxy. Instead of being condemned in silence and very often without being able to offer any defense, such persons were henceforth to have the right to defend themselves according to accepted and published norms and no action was to be taken against anybody without informing the local bishop. In short, the charges raised by Cardinal Frings in his famous speech on the council floor denouncing the Holy Office—an attack bitterly resented by the secretary of that body, Cardinal Ottaviani —were accepted virtually *in toto* and became the basis of the new regulation. The tribunal still retained jurisdiction over marriage cases involving Catholics and non-Catholics, an area in which it had generally functioned more or less commendably. Observers were pleased by the pope's announcement, but much would necessarily depend on whether there were to be any corresponding changes in personnel. There had been strong rumors for several weeks that the pope had Cardinal Ottaviani's resignation on his desk. This was denied by members of the Holy Office

* Called Pro-Secretary, as of February 1966.

567

staff, but when the Vatican paper *L'Osservatore Romano* failed to publish an official denial, old Roman hands saw this as a sign that the rumors were probably true. The cardinal described himself as just "an old *carabiniere*" in an interview granted to Alberto Cavallari.

THE CONCLUDING CEREMONIES

Since both previous sessions of the Council held under Pope Paul VI had ended under a cloud, the common assumption was that the Fourth Session too would probably end badly or at least in a draw. Contrary to expectations, however, Vatican II came to a close on December 7th and 8th in something like a blaze of glory. The chief credit for this happy turn of events belonged to Pope Paul who had an eye for the symbolic and eloquent gesture, as the world now knew. While the Council itself was feverishly locked in battle over the wording of the remaining documents, the pope was carefully planning the strategy of the closing days. Pope John had declared that the twofold purpose of the Council was to be the *aggiornamento* or renewal of the Roman Catholic Church and the promotion of Christian unity. The sixteen decrees promulgated by the Council would be eloquent evidence of the seriousness with which the first purpose had been met. But what about the prospects for Christian reunion?

On Saturday, December 4th, four days before the Council was scheduled to close, Pope Paul took part with the non-Catholic observer delegates and the Council Fathers in an unprecedented interdenominational "Liturgy of the Word" in the historic basilica of St. Paul's Outside the Walls, where Pope John had first announced his intention to summon the Council over six years earlier. The service was unprecedented because it marked the first time that any pope had ever taken part in a similar ceremony. It consisted, appropriately, of prayers, psalms, lessons from Scripture, and hymns, the heritage of one or more of the Catholic, Protestant and Orthodox traditions. The lessons were read respectively in English, French and Greek by the Methodist observer Dr. A. C. Outler, the French Catholic priest Pierre Michalon, and the Orthodox observer and rector of the Orthodox parish church in Rome, Archimandrite Maximos Aghiorgoussis. The hymn "Now thank we all our God" in which all joined in English was written by the seventeenth-century Lutheran composer Johann Crüger.

Two hours before the ceremony several members of the Secretariat for Promoting Christian Unity, the American Paulist Father Stransky and the Jesuit Father Long, raced out to the basilica to check on the final arrangements. They found that the good Benedictine monks had erected a papal throne of magnificent, medieval proportions, and had considerable difficulty in persuading the abbot that such a display of pomp was contrary to the pope's own wishes. Finally a straight-backed only slightly ornamented chair was substituted for the elaborate throne. When the pope arrived he seated himself in it, or stood in front of it, as the service proceeded, with the utmost simplicity. There had been no time to bind the booklet containing the service in buckram with the papal arms, so the pope was handed a simple pamphlet like the rest. He joined in the singing of the hymns and canticles as if this type of service was for him the most natural thing in the world.

In the course of his moving talk the pope declared, "We would like to have you with us always." The departure of the observers would not mean the end of the ecumenical dialogue, which had been so fortunately begun "in silence." The Council had shown that reunion could eventually be achieved, "slowly, gradually, loyally and generously" the pope emphasized. In a passage that particularly impressed his hearers, the pope acknowledged that there had been "failures" on the part of Catholics and others in the past with regard to reunion, but such things were the result of un-Christian influences which every effort would be made to transform into sentiments "worthy of the school of Christ." He was referring specifically to the now outmoded polemical approach to reunion and insistence on matters of prestige. Henceforth the Roman Catholic Church would be guided by the spirit of charity so eloquently proclaimed by St. Paul, he assured them. As a sign he pointed to the fact that the Council had not issued any "anathemas, but only invitations." He concluded his remarks, "May this ray of divine light, beloved brethren, cause us all to recognize the blessed door of truth."

Each of the non-Catholic observers was afterward presented to the pope by Cardinal Bea in the same adjoining Benedictine monastery where Pope John had first announced the Council to the cardinals in January 1959. Each was given a special gift of a bronze bell adorned with the emblems of the four Evangelists and the monogram of Christ. As one of the Protestant observers commented later, "It was one of the most impressive moments of the whole Council." Some of them were moved to tears by the solemnity of the occasion and the place.

The thousand or more bishops present who sat in the nave were greatly edified by this unprecedented gesture on the pope's part. Not so, however, a number of those who did not attend. Professing to be scandalized, a select group of bishops apparently under the guidance of Archbishops Staffa and Vagnozzi (the latter acting as spokesman for a number of easily persuaded American bishops) sent a message to the pope the following morning, Sunday, expressing their amazement at the encouragement he had given to what they had been taught to believe was a *communicatio in sacris* with heretics. As one of them put it, "It may be all right for the pope to do this, but half our people would walk out on us if we tried the same thing," thus betraying their abysmal ignorance of what the Council had decreed. The pope was somewhat shocked himself by their reaction. After communicating his opinion to Archbishop Dell'Acqua, the latter passed the word and telegrams began arriving in droves from the bishops stating how pleased they were.

During the final week of the Council the pope managed to see an extraordinary number of people in private audiences. On Tuesday evening, December 7th, he gave audiences to at least 5 separate groups of people connected with the Council, including the Council auditors, chauffeurs and handymen, and finally, at 7:30, the Council *periti,* in the Sala Clementina. On the latter occasion, while reading a short formal paper in French, the pope suddenly dropped the paper and spoke to his hearers directly from the heart. He was obviously greatly moved as he thanked the *periti* for all that they had done and their courage and long-suffering throughout the Council. He acknowledged frankly that it was their efforts, as well as those of the bishops, that had made the Council such a great success. Urging them to continue to love the Church and preserve it from "capricious innovation or exaggeration in doctrine," he suggested slyly that since they had now learned how to talk to bishops, they should go on doing so in the post-conciliar period. As a souvenir he gave each one a pocket-sized copy of the Latin New Testament.

Earlier, at 6 P.M., he had received the Italian bishops. His talk was an intimate, heart-to-heart sharing of confidences and dealt principally with the attitude they would be expected to adopt after the Council was over. "Now that the Council is finished," the pope asked, "will everything go back as it was before? Appearances and custom say Yes. But the spirit of the Council says No. Some things, many things, will be new for us all. Is it merely a question of external changes? In a sense yes, but we are not thinking of these things right now. It is a question of the way we look at the Church. The period following the Council cannot be one of back-to-normal or the good-old-days. It must be a period of immense labor. We must be convinced that pastoral effectiveness will come not so much from the wisdom and authority of what the Council has decreed, as from the docility and alacrity with which its laws are put into practice."

The personal reaction to this speech of the two Italian cardinals so doggedly opposed to the process of conciliar reform was not known; but the two cardinals in question, Siri of Genoa and Ruffini of Palermo, were seated beside the pope directly on his right and it was obvious from the pope's tone that he expected compliance from them too. Cardinal Siri's domination of the Italian Episcopal Conference had been ended in August, but he retained the support of powerful right-wing elements and wealthy industrialists and could still cause trouble. The attitude of this group was illustrated by an incident involving the indomitable Bishop Carli (Segni). On November 18th, during the promulgation of the document on Divine Revelation, Cardinal Ottaviani's former spokesman was seen squirming with excitement at his seat. After the end of the session, Father Balič, a Holy Office consultor, rushed up to him and said: "Calm yourself, *Eccellenza, non sono definizioni*—these texts are not technically definitions of the faith." He was echoing a statement attributed to Cardinal Siri the week before when after a conference criticizing the work of the Council, he was asked by a priest about the value to be attributed to conciliar decisions and replied: *"Non sono definizioni; non ci obblighino mai*—they are not definitions; they will never bind us." On December 7th, by contrast, Bishop Carli had full control of himself and between the final votes joked with the French bishops about De Gaulle's discomfiture. Whereupon a South African bishop asked him whether he had heard the most recent Carli joke. *"No; ne ditemi,"* said Carli. The story was that after the Council's close Carli was going to immolate himself on the Piazza S. Pietro, like a Buddhist monk, in protest against the Council's work, when some bishops offered to chip in for the gasoline. "Don't bother," Carli had told them. "I can buy Vatican gasoline at a much cheaper price, and maybe it won't burn!'

If it was the Protestants who were primarily moved by the significance of the service in St. Paul's, three days later it was the turn of the Orthodox to be gratified. In the course of the final public session in St. Peter's on Tuesday, December 7th, a joint declaration of the pope and the Orthodox patriarch of Constantinople Athenagoras I was read out in which both Churches removed from memory and "consigned to oblivion" the centuries' old mutual excommunications which had poisoned relations between them and declared that their gesture was to be seen as an "invitation" to the entire Christian world to seek the ultimate unity commanded by Christ when He said, That they may be one. When Metropolitan Meliton of Heliopolis, Patriarch Athenagoras' representative, knelt to kiss the pope's ring after receiving the papal brief formally annulling the papal sentence of excommunication against the eleventh century Patriarch Michael Caerularius, he was graciously raised up by the pope and embraced in a kiss of peace. Turning to go back to his place, the metropolitan was greeted by a thunderous burst of applause as the Council Fathers put the seal of their approval on this act of reconciliation. At the same time the aged Melkite Patriarch Maximos IV of Antioch rose from his place at the patriarchal table and went over to the Orthodox observers to give them all the kiss of peace. A similar ceremony took place simultaneously in the patriarchal cathedral in Istanbul, where Atheganoras I read the above mentioned declaration from his throne in the presence of a papal delegation headed by Cardinal Shehan of Balti-more. As one Protestant observer delegate commented later: "If the Church is able to express its regret for the past with such ease and humility, anything is possible."

The concluding ceremony the following day in the open air in front of the basilica of St. Peter's was something overly pompous and anti-climactic by comparison. After the pope's discourse a slight confusion occurred while he was distributing the sum of $90,000 to cardinals and bishops from needy countries for specific pastoral projects. Cardinals Spellman and Heenan, it seems, were to have flanked him at this moment, but instead they found themselves among the recipients and stood there looking somewhat perplexed. A series of "conciliar messages to the world," read in French, were intended to embrace all categories of the human family whom the Council had tried to reach: rulers, scholars, artists, women, workingmen, the poor and sick, and youth. After the reading of the papal brief closing the Council (it was read by Secretary General Archbishop Felici as his last official act), six bishops represent-ing different parts of the world and supported by the expert voices of the Sistine Choir, chanted the Acclamations or Litany, traditional at ecu-menical councils since the fifth century, for the pope, the soul of Pope John XXIII, the moderators, the bishops, the observer delegates, the heads of governments, the people of God and all men of good will. The pope dismissed the assembly with a final blessing, *"Ite in pace*—Go in peace."

TOWARD VATICAN COUNCIL III

In 1961 the distinguished German theologian Father Hans Küng asked, "Can the Council Fail?" The question was not altogether beside the point. Exhilarating as the announcement of the Council was, the full import of what came to be known as "Pope John's revolution," could only be vaguely discerned then. The preparations for the Council were firmly in the hands of Curial bodies bent on rigidly controlling the papal initiative, while the experiment of the Roman diocesan synod which was intended as a sort of dress rehearsal for the Council itself, was frankly discouraging. The first bombshell was Pope John's opening address in which he made clear that he had no sympathy with those "prophets of doom" who were opposing the Church's renewal and that the Council was to have a pastoral rather than a dogmatic orientation, since it was to confront the world with charity and understanding rather than with definitions and the anathema-tizing of errors. As one theologian commented afterward, "In the light of the pope's remarks, we have to do our work all over again." A second bombshell was dropped when the pope withdrew the pitifully inadequate draft schema on Divine Revelation and entrusted it to a mixed commission more representative of the Council for redrafting, after a crucial vote of no-confidence disclosed that this was the only possible course. The era of *aggiornamento* really dated from that memorable November 21, 1962 which first disclosed the real strength of the progressive majority among the Council Fathers. All at once, as one observer noted, "there was let loose a whole batch of movements that had been simmering in the Church for many years" (the biblical, liturgical, ecumenical, and 'new theology' movements), as well as countless trends and tendencies aimed at bridging the gap between the Church and the world in the moral, scientific, social and economic spheres. All acquired a kind of *droit de cité* from that moment which could not be gainsaid, despite the continuing frowns and threats of the Holy Office.

Four years later, on November 3, 1965, Hans Küng emerged from a 40-minute audience with Pope Paul VI in which he gave the pontiff a positive and on the whole quite optimistic appraisal of the work of the Council. The pope, for his part, was pleased that this most outspoken critic of the Curia was now inclined to view events as a step in the right direction.

There could be no doubt that the Council had brought about a fundamental change, both as regards the Catholic Church's attitude toward itself and its outlook on the world, though there was naturally less agreement about the extent and meaning of the change. As Cardinal Heenan put it, "No one can doubt that a beginning of far-reaching importance has been made and that the Church will never retrace the path it has chosen. . . . People without sealed minds could not fail to recognize the changes. They would be blind." In another article the cardinal spoke of the "depressing" atmosphere at the beginning of the Council and contrasted this with the "uplifting" atmosphere at the end. Cardinal Bea hailed the Council as marking the "end of the Counter-Reformation." Archbishop Pellegrino condemned the "myopia of those who still refuse to admit there is any need for *aggiornamento* or renewal of the Church, so often asserted by Popes John XXIII and Paul VI." The mood of change, or at least a popular version of it, seems to have been captured by two Roman artists, Ettore De Concilis and Rosso Falciano, who felt justified in adorning the walls of a new Roman church dedicated to St. Francis of Assisi in pell-mell fashion with the profiles of Pope John, Castro, Kosygin, Mao Tse-tung, Bertrand Russell, Giorgio La Pira, Togliatti, Sophia Loren, and Jacqueline Kennedy.

It became somewhat commonplace to say of the Council, "Nothing has changed, even though things will never be the same again." Taking the work of the Council as a whole and considering it from a purely superficial point of view, it was not difficult to make out that there had been few radical changes and to put the stress on continuity. Almost every conciliar statement had its counterpart in the theological literature of the recent past (though what the shortsighted failed to point out was that many of these statements occurred in the writings of those formerly considered "heretics"). Though all the documents bore the mark of compromise, when the successive versions of the documents were placed side by side one could really see what tremendous strides had been made.

What the Council had really done was to lay the groundwork for a thorough "reappraisal" of Catholicism, appearances to the contrary notwithstanding. More important than the documents themselves, the Council consecrated a new spirit destined in the course of time to remake the face of Catholicism. More important than the specific provisions of this or that decree, were the truly revolutionary, biblically-oriented principles found scattered throughout the Council's work, which in time would bring about the necessary transformation and lead ultimately to the desired goal of reunion.

For example, in the Pastoral Constitution on the Church in the Modern World, it was said that "The Church guards the heritage of God's word and draws from it moral and religious principles *without always having at hand the solution to particular problems*" (Part I, Chap. III, par. 33). A similar statement occurred in the Declaration on Religious Liberty: "(The Council) searches into the sacred tradition and doctrine of the Church—the treasury out of which the Church continually brings forth new things that are in harmony with the things that are old." At stake was the whole question of doctrinal development, called the No. 1 theological problem of Vatican II, the process by which the Church passed from a less complete to a more complete understanding of the word of God without ever being able to understand fully what it possessed. While not new, this acknowledgment of the limitations of its knowledge was a healthy sign that the Church was turning more and more from the triumphalism and dogmatism of the past to a more plausible explanation of its message in terms which the modern world could understand. The humility which this approach implied was also consistent with the pastoral purpose of the Council and its refusal to characterize any of its pronouncements as infallible statements. This "downgrading" as it were of the whole problem of infallibility (notwithstanding the reaffirmation of papal infallibility in terms identical with those of 1870) marked one of the important steps forward taken by the Council.

The Decree on Ecumenism boldly states: ". . . in Catholic doctrine *there exists a 'hierarchy' of truths,* since they vary in their relation to the fundamental Christian faith" (Chap. II, par. 11). This meant that while no part of Christian revelation was unimportant, some elements were more important than others; for example, the doctrines of the Trinity and the Incarnation were more important than papal infallibility. Together with the correlative principles—"From time to time one tradition has come nearer to a full appreciation of some aspects of a mystery of revelation than the other" (par. 17), and "All who have been justified by faith in baptism are members of Christ's body . . . and are correctly accepted as brothers by the children of the Catholic Church" (par. 3)—these liberating truths not only would constitute the firm basis for a fruitful ecumenical dialogue among Christians, but would imply a new attitude toward itself on the part of the Catholic Church. Henceforth Catholic theology would be less dominated by juridicism and conceptualism than by biblical and historical research, less concerned with what divided than with what unites (everything implied by the French word *ressourcement,* going back to the biblical and patristic sources of the undivided Church). Many parts of the Constitution on the Church, the Constitution on Divine Revelation, the Decree on Ecumenism, and the Declarations on Non-Christians and Religious Liberty, already strongly reflected this new biblical emphasis. Another lesson here was recognition of the fact that a certain amount of pluralism, both in theology and discipline, was not only inevitable but positively desirable, and contributed to a deeper understanding of the Christian message. The kiss of peace exchanged between Pope Paul VI and Patriarch Athenagoras I in Jerusalem, as well as subsequent ecumenical developments, suggested that an eventually reunited Church would emerge from the gradual coalescing of different bodies, namely the present large-scale denominations including the Roman Catholic communion, which would probably be very different from what they now were, while retaining essential continuity with the past and their own individuality. When receiving the non-Catholic observer-delegates in 1962, Pope John quoted the words of the Psalmist: "May God be blessed every day!"* In their final message to the Council, read by Archbishop Felici on December 4, 1965, the observer-delegates enlarged on this theme: "Blessed be God for all that he has given us so far through the Holy Spirit, and for all that he will give us in the future." Oscar Cullmann, the noted Swiss theologian, summed up their thoughts when he declared: "The hopes of Protestants for Vatican II have not only been fulfilled, but the Council's achievements have gone far beyond what was believed possible."

It would be difficult to overemphasize the importance of the new definition of the Church in terms of the biblical concept of the *People of*

---

* In an audience the Methodist observer Bishop Corson once asked Pope John: "How long do you think it will be before Christian unity is realized, perhaps 200 years?" The pope replied: "My dear Bishop Corson, you and I have achieved it already."

God, which found such a magnificent expression in the Constitution on the Church. Suffice it to say that older ecclesiologists accustomed to thinking of membership in the Church in terms of data that could be processed in an IBM machine were bound to feel uncomfortable in the new atmosphere which preferred to look upon the Church as a mystery, in the Pauline sense, and to think of it as embracing not three sharply divided groups (clergy, religious and laity), but as a single large community made up of many smaller communities. Laity, religious and clergy were all equally important as members of Christ's Body, they simply had different functions or callings to perform with respect to the whole. Unfortunately there was not time for a thorough redrafting of all the Council documents, so that they would adequately reflect the renewed theology of the lay apostolate, for example. Even if there had been time, it was not likely that the resistance of conservative theologians could have been overcome. Cardinal Ottaviani, in an interview, declared that he was concerned about "overboldness on the part of the laity" and expressed the opinion that "some of them might overreach themselves and try to dominate the clergy, judging from what they were already saying." But, on the whole, the idea of the Church as a living community and the enhanced role of the laity came through with remarkable clearness and seemed bound to have a great influence on future thinking. While not granted a deliberative vote or any real voice in the proceedings, a number of lay auditors, both men and women, by their presence at the Council, did exercise a considerable influence on the course of events.

The most striking accomplishment of the Council unquestionably was the proclamation of *episcopal collegiality,* the principle that the bishops form a college and govern the Church together with the pope their head. Although every precaution was taken to ensure that the pope's special authority would not suffer any infringement, the fact nevertheless remains that the new doctrine was bound to influence the exercise of that authority *in practice,* particularly if Pope Paul's plans for the reform of the Roman Curia and the establishment of the Synod of Bishops were fully carried out. While the pope would thereby become more responsive to the wishes of the world episcopate, the bishops themselves would become more responsive to the wishes of each other through the institution of episcopal conferences, while the individual bishops in turn were advised by the Council to consult the wishes of their clergy and faithful. Thus collegiality, if carried out to its logical conclusion, could mean that the whole clergy, not merely the higher echelons, would become more responsive to the claims of public opinion, in keeping with the idea of ecclesiastical authority as service, *diakonia,* which Pope Paul was never tired of stressing.

With typical conscientiousness Pope Paul began to worry in public about the way in which the Council would be received even before the end, as we have seen. In an Exhortation issued shortly after the end of the debates, on November 6th, he urged the bishops to be "vigilant" about carrying out its decrees, persuading the faithful to accept them, restraining the unseasonable zeal of some and prodding others into action. The text was given to the press on Saturday. The following day he complained, at the Angelus, that the newspapers had not paid sufficient attention to his exhortation which was, on the contrary, he maintained, of considerable importance! Some idea about the pope's own attitude toward the Council could be gathered from a study of the words he frequently used when referring to it at this time. The favorite word by far was *rinnovamento*—renewal. The Johannine word *aggiornamento*, updating, was apparently not a favorite with him, and the word *riforma* hardly ever was used, probably because these words implied too radical a departure which was not congenial to his way of thinking. To the Italian mind the word *riforma* meant either the reform of a religious order or the Protestant Reformation, the latter meaning of course being enough to ruin it for general use without plenty of qualifying phrases. *Aggiornamento* has the disadvantage of implying "conformity with the world" against which Paul is always warning. On the other hand, *rinnovamento* had an element of spirituality about it which particularly recommended it to a person of Paul's spiritual sensitivity. In fact, he told the various diplomatic missions present for the concluding ceremonies of the Council, in a farewell audience granted on December 7th: "The primary purpose of these great assemblies is always inner renewal of each Catholic and the renewal of the whole social body which the Church is. But there is also an influence on the whole human family. . . ." Later in the same address he spoke of "renewal of life and a new ardor to put into practice the message of the Gospel." Earlier he had stated: "The Church meditates, consults, examines itself; it concentrates its energies, purifies its manner of thinking and acting, proceeds to a 'renewal,' but to a renewal that is primarily interior, which concerns the relations between the Christian and his God." The same thought occurred in his talk to the diplomatic corps (January 8, 1966): "Councils are by definition religious events and concern first of all the internal renewal of the Church's life."

Another favorite word of his to describe the Council was "fervor." In his talk to the Curia on December 23, 1965: "The Council has not inaugurated a period of dogmatic and moral uncertainty. . . . On the contrary, it has sought to initiate a period of greater fervor, greater cohesion, greater faithfulness to the Gospel, greater pastoral charity and a greater ecclesial spirituality." Elsewhere he referred to the Council as inaugurating "a spring season," "a rebirth," and of the Church as having been "reborn."

Like everybody else the pope was not entirely consistent in the use of language and too much importance should not be attributed to his use of this or that term in an informal context. For example, in the above talk to the cardinals on December 23rd, he acknowledged that the Council was an "innovating Council." On the other hand in general audiences the word "innovate" was generally reserved for those who were prepared to go too far in introducing changes in contrast to those, like himself, who preferred to do things gradually and prudently. This was a frequent theme as, for example, in a general audience on October 13, 1965. *Il Tempo* headlined this talk: "SEVERE PAPAL WARNING TO IMPRUDENT INNOVATORS," ignoring the fact that the pope went on to say that there was good in both approaches and they should be regarded as complementary.

Again, exaggerating of course in order to make his point clearer, he contrasted those who wanted to return everything to the way it was before the Council and those who would call everything into doubt. The proper attitude for the faithful now, in the post-conciliar period, was "not to put in doubt and subject to inquiry all that the Council has taught us, but that of putting this into practice, of studying, understanding and applying the lessons of the Council in Christian life" (December 15, 1965, general audience). In a general audience on January 12, 1966, the same point was made even clearer with respect to the maintenance of doctrinal continuity: "It would be wrong to think that the Council represents a break or as some believe, a liberation, from the traditional doctrine of the Church. They also would be wrong who would promote a facile conformity to the mentality of our times in its ephemeral and negative aspects rather than those that are certain and scientific, or would allow each individual to attach whatever value he thinks best to the truths of the faith." The teachings of the Council must not be severed from the doctrinal heritage of the Church, but we must see how they were consistent with it and gave witness to it. When seen in this light, the "novelties of the Council" did not imply that the Church had been unfaithful to its teaching, but made that teaching appear in a clearer light. He went on to explain that this was so even though the Council issued no infallible pronouncements. Its teachings carried the weight of the "ordinary magisterium."

The Fourth Session did see some improvement in the overall picture of the pope's relations with the world press. At least it was something that there were no awkward scenes between Council press officials and the working press similar to those that marred the Third Session. The pope made a personal visit to the large *Sala Stampa* on the Via della Conciliazione, where journalists normally gathered to be briefed and to send their dispatches, shortly before the end of the Council (November 26th) and delivered an address in which he told them: "You have fulfilled a role that we do not hesitate to call providential." He went on to remind his audience about the difficulties of reporting Vatican news because of the need to avoid anything "sensational" and criticized them for trying to dramatize the news of the Council by speaking about it in terms appropriate to "civil society," whereas the life of the Church was "entirely spiritual and interior." He concluded on a friendly note, speaking vaguely about "a fraternal, prudent and sincere exchange" and promising to keep the news flowing to them after the Council.

The wall of secrecy normally surrounding the pope and his immediate advisers was breached, at least partially, during the Fourth Session. Disturbed by the adverse publicity resulting from the Third Session, the pope decided to grant an interview to the journalist Alberto Cavallari, which was printed in the Milanese daily *Corriere della Sera,* the day before the pope's departure for the UN in New York. During the following month the same paper published an unprecedented series of interviews with a good many of the top advisers of the pope, such as Cardinals Ottaviani, Roberti, Bea, Colombo, König, Archbishops Dell'Acqua and Samorè. More to the point perhaps was the pope's decision to allow Father G. Caprile, one of the editors of the Jesuit monthly *La Civiltà Cattolica,* to publish a factual, highly revealing account of the pope's intervention in the handling of the *modi* on Divine Revelation, intended to dissipate the impression that Paul had been acting in violation of the rules of the Council and he had taken sides with the minority against the majority. Pope Paul let it be known, privately, that he did not object to what journalists were saying about him personally, his only concern was that "the truth" be made known. His determination to publish the wartime correspondence of Pius XII, contrary to Vatican rules which precluded publicity until at least a hundred years or more after the death of a pope, seemed to be a step in this direction. Apparently the usual Vatican attitude of disdain and hauteur for the calumnies of Hochhuth was not considered good enough by the present pope. There was reason to believe also that the full official record of the Council would be published as soon as possible and that those parts not suitable for publication would be made available to scholars much earlier than was the case with Vatican I.*

The world has had ample occasion to learn by now that a man of Paul's temperament cannot be judged by his words alone. Words must be linked to actions. Judged by this standard, he appeared to be moving slowly but surely in the direction of implementing the Council's decisions as a "bridge-builder" (to use an expression of the Methodist observer Bishop F. P. Corson). Claiming that Paul was "acting for the solidarity

* Several highly prejudicial accounts of that Council were published and widely circulated before the Vatican moved to allow scholars to dip into the records and produce a more balanced account.

of the future and not for the popularity of the hour." Corson was impatient with those critics who found him "a conservative man, fearful of change, suspicious of liberty, myopic on certain areas of modern life." A Motu Proprio issued January 1, 1966 continued the Council's Coordinating Commission as a Central Commission, presided over by Cardinals Tisserant and Cicognani, to supervise the work of five subordinate Commissions for Bishops, Religious, Missions, Education and the Lay Apostolate, charged with responsibility for drafting the instructions that were to be issued following the promulgation of the respective conciliar decrees, after which, when their work was completed, all these organs were to go out of existence. The same Motu Proprio also provided for the publication of the Council's Acts, entrusting this task to the former Secretary General Archbishop Felici who became secretary general of the new Central Commission, and gave Cardinal Bea's Secretariat for Promoting Christian Unity a permanent status in the Curia. Since the above instructions were to be published by June 29, 1966, the date on which the various conciliar decrees were to go into effect, no attempt was made to bring in new men. The same officials on the former conciliar commissions were simply continued in the new organs, to provide continuity.

It was long contended that nothing would come of the proposed reform of the Roman Curia unless new men were brought in to replace those who found it impossible to accept the Council's new spirit. Pope Paul showed by his decree reforming the Holy Office, published December 6th, two days before the final close of the Council, that he intended to give substance to his often repeated promises to bring about an effective reform. Early in February 1966 he appointed two new men to important posts in two offices: Archbishop Garrone of Toulouse, as permanent head (with the title of Pro-Secretary, the aged Cardinal Pizzardo remaining as Secretary) of the Congregation of Seminaries and Universities, and Canon C. Moeller, of the University of Louvain, to the number three post in the Congregation for the Doctrine of the Faith (Holy Office), as undersecretary. Both promptly issued statements making clear the fact that a new era had arrived in both offices so far as they were concerned. Soon after Moeller's appointment, it became known that new procedures would be followed in the future with regard to the censoring of books and while the Index was not formally abolished immediately, it was clear that a new regime had arrived here too.* The appointment of Garrone was all the more significant because he had been one of the most determined critics of Seminaries and Universities and had called for its thorough overhauling at the Third Session. A curious "incident" shortly before Garrone's appointment may, or may not, have had something to do with the timing of the

* According to a *Notificatio* of the cardinal published in *L'Osservatore Romano* (June 15, 1966), the Index is now regarded as dead.

580

announcement of his appointment. Toward the middle of January the Congregation of Seminaries published a decree requiring the use of Latin as a liturgical language in all seminaries of the Latin rite. Although the language was technically consistent with the Constitution on the Liturgy which provided for extensive use of the vernacular, many seminaries, for example, those in the United States, had already been using English in the liturgy for some time and the new decree seemed to be a backward step. An instruction published several days later made it plain that exceptions could be made depending upon local circumstances. It is doubtful whether the decree would have been drawn up in the same language (it was actually drafted before the end of the Council) if Archbishop Garrone had been the congregation's head at the time. The pope's appointment of Cardinal Ottaviani as head of the new episcopal commission to advise him on birth control (to which the already existing Papal Commission of Experts would become advisory) may have been dismaying to some, but a look at the membership of the new commission should have been enough to dissipate any undue alarm. The names of Cardinals Suenens, Döpfner, Lefebvre and Shehan, and Bishop Reuss, were enough to ensure that no mere rubber-stamping of the past was contemplated, since they were among the strongest critics of the existing legislation regarding birth control in the Council. It was curious that this episcopal commission was actually called for by several Council Fathers during the Third Session, but since the pope had removed the question of birth control from the jurisdiction of the Council, it was not expedient to set it up then. The appointments were still another sign that Pope Paul had every intention of consulting his "brothers" the bishops more frequently in the future in accordance with episcopal collegiality, as he so often proclaimed.

The return of the Roman Church to a spirit of poverty, the elimination of an alien spirit of triumphalism, and the ideal of a continual revitalization expressed in the maxim *"Ecclesia semper reformanda"* all required time. The world was no longer asking whether Pope Paul would emulate his mentor, Pope Pius XII, who once said with respect to liturgical renewal, "I will move so far with the reform that a return will be made impossible." It was now clear that the Council had merely laid the groundwork for more extensive long-range changes than the prophets dreamed of in 1959. But the important thing for the pope and for the Church, if this ideal was to be realized, was to keep doors open. Christ Himself, as we are told in the third chapter of the Book of the Apocalypse, laid down an eternal law: "Behold, I have caused doors to be opened before thee, which no one can shut."

Index